The Management & Maintenance of
Historic Parks, Gardens
& Landscapes

THE ENGLISH HERITAGE HANDBOOK

The Management & Maintenance of

Historic Parks, Gardens & Landscapes

THE ENGLISH HERITAGE HANDBOOK

Edited by John Watkins and Tom Wright

FRANCES LINCOLN

THE MANAGEMENT AND MAINTENANCE OF HISTORIC PARKS,
GARDENS AND LANDSCAPES: THE ENGLISH HERITAGE HANDBOOK

Frances Lincoln Limited
4 Torriano Mews
Torriano Avenue
London NW5 2RZ
www.franceslincoln.com

English Heritage
1 Waterhouse Square
138–142 Holborn
London EC1N 2ST

British Library cataloguing-in-publication data
A catalogue record for this book is available from the British Library

ISBN: 978 0 7112 2439 1

Printed in Singapore

9 8 7 6 5 4 3 2 1

FRONTISPIECE
1. A view of part of the picturesque quarry garden at Belsay in
Northumberland, developed from the late eighteenth century to
the early twentieth century.

Contributing authors

David Avery

Toby Beasley

Rowan Blaik

Maggie Campbell-Culver

Alan Cathersides

Elizabeth Collins

Brian Dix

Brent Elliot

Bill Fone

Fergus Garrett

David Jacques

Liz Neild-Banks

James Price

John Thompson

Jenifer White

Russell Williams

Acknowledgements & picture credits

In addition to the specialist pieces provided by the book's contributors listed on page 5, the development of such a comprehensive book would not have been possible without the generous support of many people. Our particular thanks go to all the owners and staff of the case study gardens who were generous with their time and incredibly helpful in providing us with a unique insight on the management of their sites. We are also very grateful to the many colleagues at English Heritage and other specialists who have reviewed and commented on drafts of the book. The talented James Davies, photographer, and Liz Pepperell, illustrator, took on the challenge of visualising many of the concepts and ideas; their results are both clear and beautiful and a major contribution to the book.

As Editors we are particularly grateful for the assistance of Johanna Okon-Watkins and Shirley Wright for their patience reading scripts and their editorial comments.

We would lastly like to thank the team at Frances Lincoln for enabling us to produce the book we wanted and to Jane Havell for her copy editing and inspired design.

English Heritage staff who provided information or help reviewing and correcting drafts:

Annabel Brown, Alan Cathersides, Chloé Cova, Patricia Driver, John Fidler, Aris Georgiou, Debs Goodenough, Rob Richardson, René Rodgers, Caroline Sier, Jenifer White

For the case studies:
Brodsworth Hall: Dan Booth
Chatsworth: The Dowager Duchess of Devonshire, Simon Seligman, Ian Webster
Down House: Toby Beasley
Great Dixter: the late Christopher Lloyd
Hampton Court Palace: Terry Gough
Levens Hall: Charles Henry (Hal) Bagot, Chris Crowder
Sheffield Botanic Garden: Liz Neild-Banks
Sheffield Park Garden: Sue Medway, Andrew Jesson
Squerryes Court: John and Anthea Warde, Terry Darnton

John Watkins, Tom Wright

We would like to thank the following for kind permission to reproduce pictures. References are to picture numbers.

© Alan Cathersides 80, 86, 132, 133, 136, 137, 235, 314–316, 404, 405
© Crown copyright, NMR 351, 372, 386
© Brian Dix 27–32
© English Heritage 46, 60
English Heritage, NMR 10, 15, 39, 75, 178, 256
© English Heritage, NMR 26, 344, 356, 379, 403
© English Heritage, photo: James Davies 1, 22, 33, 41, 42, 47, 51, 57, 58, 62–68, 77, 81, 85, 87–90, 100, 102–105, 108–110, 112, 114–117, 122–126, 148, 152, 153, 167, 173, 174, 183, 189, 201, 206, 211, 212, 218, 224, 229, 230, 233, 236, 242, 243, 245, 251, 253, 257, 268, 269, 276, 277, 280, 281, 283, 287, 288, 292–296, 300, 301, 306–312, 317, 319–322, 324, 327–330, 332–342, 346, 350, 352–354, 357, 361, 369, 373, 375–378, 383, 384, 393, 395, 396, 401, 402, 407, 323
© English Heritage, illustrator Elizabeth Pepperell 35, 69, 74, 76, 94–99, 111, 113, 118–120, 140, 141, 144–147, 155, 156, 168–170, 172, 179, 194–196, 228, 254, 255, 261–263, 279, 291, 297, 298, 318, 392, 397
© Fergus Garrett 199, 207a–f, 232, 234
© Debs Goodenough 134, 325, 331
© The Great Dixter Charitable Trust 363
© Meg Julien 385, 387–390
© Arthur Pickett 380
© The Royal Collection, Her Majesty Queen Elizabeth II 370
© John Thompson 84, 92
© Mr and Mrs J. St A. Ward 398, 399
© John Watkins 2, 4–6, 8, 9, 11, 12, 16–18, 20, 21, 23, 24, 34, 38, 45, 53–56, 59, 61, 70, 78, 82, 83, 91, 93, 121, 128, 130, 131, 138, 139, 142, 149, 151, 158, 159, 164–166, 171, 175, 176, 180–182, 185, 190, 192, 193, 197, 198, 200, 202–205, 208, 213–215, 217, 219–223, 225, 226, 231, 237, 238, 240, 244, 246, 249, 250, 258–260, 264, 266, 270–272, 278, 284–286, 289, 290, 299, 302–305, 343, 345, 347–349, 355, 358–360, 362, 364–368
© Andy Wimble 406
© Chris Wood 154
© Tom Wright 7, 13, 19, 25, 36, 37, 43, 44, 48–50, 52, 71, 72, 79, 101, 106, 107, 127, 129, 135, 143, 150, 157, 160–163, 177, 184, 186–188, 191, 209, 210, 216, 227, 239, 241, 247, 248, 252, 265, 267, 273–275, 282, 313, 326, 371, 374, 381, 382, 391, 394, 400

Contents

Part One Understanding and planning the
historic landscape and garden   8

1.1   Understanding and analysis: introduction   11

1.2   Historic perspective   13

1.3   The Conservation Management Plan (CMP) process   25

1.4   Managing historic parks and gardens   41

1.5   The legal framework   69

Part Two The living garden landscape   84

2.1   Maintenance and management in practice   87

2.2   Nature conservation   103

2.3   Vegetation maintenance and management   115

2.4   Technical maintenance   225

Part Three Ten case studies   246

3.1   Brodsworth Hall, South Yorkshire   249

3.2   Chatsworth, Derbyshire   253

3.3   Down House, Kent   259

3.4   Great Dixter, East Sussex   265

3.5   Hampton Court Palace, Surrey   271

3.6   Levens Hall, Cumbria   279

3.7   Sheffield Botanic Garden, South Yorkshire   285

3.8   Sheffield Park Garden, East Sussex   291

3.9   Squerryes Court, Kent   297

3.10   Stonehenge, Wiltshire   303

Appendices   306

Plant tables   308

Useful contacts   355

Grant aid & funding bodies   358

References   359

Bibliography   361

Index   364

Part One

Understanding and planning the historic landscape and garden

1.1   Understanding and analysis: introduction   11

1.2   Historic perspective   13
        The seventeenth- and eighteenth-century formal garden   14
        The English landscape garden   15
        Historical revivalism   17
        Victorian planting and after   18
        New landscapes for new purposes   19
        The rise of the gardener   21
        Modernism   21

1.3   The Conservation Management Plan (CMP) process   25
        Restoring historic parks and gardens   25
        The development of CMPs for landscapes   30

1.4   Managing historic parks and gardens   41
        The economics of running a garden   41
        Garden staff and organisation   45
        Opening a garden to paying visitors   56

1.5   The legal framework   69
        Planning and development control   69
        Protection of people   74
        Protection of the natural environment   77

Understanding and analysis: introduction

All historic gardens and landscapes require thoughtful management and maintenance if the concepts of original and subsequent designers are to be retained. Garden planting, left to its own devices, will revert to woodland; annual and herbaceous planting will be swamped by scrub which in turn will be succeeded by pioneer tree species such as ash, sycamore or birch, whose seed is blown in on the wind. Even well-built garden structures – given time, lack of maintenance, ingress of water and possibly vandalism – will rot, crumble, collapse and become little more than humps and bumps in the landscape.

There is a tendency for each generation to sweep away the creations of their parents but to value the creations of their grandparents and great grandparents. In England we have a great heritage of gardens from the Georgian, Regency and Edwardian periods; however, gardens created in the 1950s, 1960s and 1970s are now the ones at greatest risk of being lost – to many, they are no longer in vogue and their planting is out of fashion. Only the greater perspective of time and fresh research will give us a full appreciation of their significance and enable us to identify the best gardens of this important period of post-war garden renaissance. In a time of change, many historic parks and gardens are under pressure of development. This chapter aims to provide readers with the tools to understand, plan and manage their landscape so that historic assets of significance are not lost.

An historical overview charts the evolution of gardens and gardening in England and the development of the horticultural and landscape professions. This is to provide readers unfamiliar with garden history in England with some context in which to place particular sites. The Conservation Management Plan (CMP) process (fully covered in 1.3) is recommended for owners or managers to appreciate the significance of a site prior to developing proposals or business plans. Without this intial analysis, valuable opportunities could be lost; at worst, works might be undertaken that could damage the property or destroy important elements of historic or other significance. If you first identify the baby you will be less likely to throw it out with the bathwater! Once significance and protecting policies are established, details can be drawn up of how the site is to be managed and maintained. This planning process provides a structure for organising information, ideas and proposals into a comprehensive and well-thought-out action plan. Details of each element are provided in following sections, with chapters looking at the economics of running a garden, grant aid and external funding, garden staff and organisation, opening gardens and parks to visitors and, finally, planning and the law.

In the last twenty years, CMPs have been used more widely to provide a considered and consistent approach to many large gardens, parks and landscapes. They are now a prerequisite of many government grants. The first stage in drawing up such plans is to uncover a garden's history, carrying out surveys to appreciate what remains of earlier periods and working out the importance and significance of each stage. In developing future management strategies, judgements have to be made between conserving historic garden layouts and new initiatives, and pragmatic decisions are needed to ensure that future maintenance is sustainable.

2. Opposite: view of Trebah.

The maner of watering with a Pumpe in a tubbe.

3. The first illustration of a garden in an English printed book, *The Gardener's Labyrinth*, a little manual published by Thomas Hill in 1571 under the pseudonym of Didymus Mountaine. Despite its poor quality as an illustration, this vignette has been used over and over again as a basis for designing Elizabethan-style gardens, because so little other evidence exists.

English gardens and landscapes were very poorly documented before the late seventeenth century. No one before Celia Fiennes in the 1680s made a tour of England, recording impressions of gardens; no one published a book on an individual English garden until Isaac de Caus published his designs for Wilton House in the 1640s, and no earlier English books illustrate an actual English garden. Hardly any garden plans were published in an English book until Stephen Blake's *Compleat gardeners practice* of 1664.

Documents and archaeology are our principal sources for English gardening before the late sixteenth century, and they can reveal only a limited amount. The most important landscape feature we owe to the Middle Ages is the deer park: the enclosure of an extent of ground for the raising and hunting of deer. It became the boast of England that it had more acres of deer park than any other country, and the custom for country houses that they should be surrounded by large tracts of intermittently 'treed pasturage'. Windsor Great Park was already partly enclosed by the time of the Domesday Book in 1086; other parks were enclosed in the ensuing centuries, and by the fifteenth century deer parks were widespread.

Royal, monastic and aristocratic gardens were instituted primarily for the provision of food, in which isolated houses had to be self-sufficient; but ornamental uses of a garden could follow closely. Fishponds, an important source of food in pre-Reformation England with its regular days of abstinence from meat, began to be treated as ornamental features in the sixteenth century. Literary descriptions and manuscript illustrations both emphasise the use of gardens for leisure activities in the Middle Ages, and these and surviving accounts show the planting of roses and other flowers for decorative as well as culinary and medicinal purposes. Garden depictions reveal the gardens of the fourteenth to the sixteenth centuries as enclosed square or rectangular areas, usually divided into quadrants by paths, with seats and flower beds. All that survives today tends to be the walls, though these are sometimes of considerable extent – as at Knole, where the fifteenth- and sixteenth-century walled enclosure covers more than 25 acres.

The development of the modern ornamental garden can be traced to the sixteenth century, when the introduction of exotic plants, first from Western Asia via Constantinople, and later from the newly discovered Americas, led to plant collections by wealthy amateurs. John Gerard's *Herball* of 1597 records a flourishing network of people introducing, exchanging and growing new exotics, collecting plants from the English countryside, and looking out for variegated and unusual forms of garden plants. Gerard himself, a barber-surgeon, grew everything from acanthus and hollyhocks to American tomatoes; the physician Hugh Morgan had an internationally known collection of cacti before 1570, and there was a prominent Mediterranean holm-oak at Whitehall by the 1580s. The first European botanic gardens had been established at Pisa and Padua in the 1540s; the first in England was founded at Oxford in 1621.

In most cases, we have little idea of the appearance of the gardens that these enthusiasts grew their collections in, and can only assume that the writings of Thomas Hill and William Lawson provide a general guide to their design (see bibliography). Division into quadrants continued to be the most common layout. Individual quadrants were usually laid out in knots, or complex interlacing patterns, sometimes in the form of mazes. (While today we equate knots with planting schemes, we know that in some cases patterns were laid out with crushed brick or coloured earth, so that they could be seen all year round.) Larger gardens had either central mounts or raised peripheral walks from which the knots could be viewed; these frequently had pergolas, shelters or partitions built of wooden trelliswork (called 'carpenter's work'). Topiary figures were popular, cut in yew and rosemary before the rise of box for edging formal parterres in the late seventeenth century. Almost none of these features remains, though some collegiate gardens retained them into the eighteenth century, and the mount at New College, Oxford, still survives.

Elaborate water-works, grottoes and automata excited interest on the Continent, but these were seldom attempted in England – although joke fountains, which could drench the unsuspecting visitor on command, were perpetrated until their condemnation in the eighteenth century. (One such fountain, a weeping willow in copper tubing, was restored at Chatsworth in the nineteenth century.) But layouts based on Italian models can be traced from the late sixteenth century; some, such as the terraces and balustrades at Haddon Hall and Montacute, survive mainly because they were subsequently neglected.

Francis Bacon, in his famous essay 'Of gardens' published in 1601, listed the elements of his ideal garden, a princely one of thirty acres: formal hedges with niches cut in them for birdcages and decorations in coloured glass; a 'heath' of 'natural wildness' with thickets and areas planted irregularly with shrubs trained as standards; no topiary or knots. The planting of British gardens at this time was being augmented by new introductions from the Ottoman empire – tulips, fritillaries, cyclamens, ranunculus – and from the Americas, all of which attracted collectors.

The seventeenth- and eighteenth-century formal garden

During the seventeenth century, French models came to dominate European garden-making, and England was no exception. The course of garden development in France had centred on the parterre, which differed from the knots of the previous generations in extent, symmetry, repudiation of enclosure and pattern selection. Increasingly laid out as two, rather than four, compartments, the parterre was made to be seen from the windows of the house, its paired compartments forming one inclusive visual pattern. In the hands of André Le Nôtre, the royal gardener of the 1660s, a variety of parterre styles emerged, ranging from simple grass compartments to the parterre de broderie, a pattern of arabesques in box. At Versailles, he created the largest garden of the century, an attempt to bring the entire visible landscape into one composition.

Soon after the Restoration of the English monarchy, Charles II commissioned a French-style garden at Hampton Court. Beginning with the excavation of the Long Water, over the following years the maze and Fountain Garden were added, the latter to be revised by London and Wise as part of a more extensive geometric composition at the end of the century.

The gardens of the late seventeenth century followed Le Nôtre in giving greater emphasis to a single axial development from the house. Attempts to dominate the landscape, exemplified at Versailles, were made in England as well, though on a less imposing scale. Formal avenues, sometimes of immense extent, were planted at Badminton, Wimpole and other estates, while at gardens such as Melbourne and Bramham formal patterns of rides and walks were pierced through parcels of woodland. The first thirty years of the eighteenth century were the major period for such channelled vistas.

By the early years of the eighteenth century, sculpted grass terraces were replacing the earlier more architectural handling of terraces. Castle Howard is the most famous example, but allied to it were Charles Bridgeman's grass amphitheatre at Claremont, and the modelling of geometric ponds within a sweeping lawn at Studley Royal. At Stowe, in the 1710s, Bridgeman created a series of grass terraces as part of a long axial vista, with garden buildings as focal points; temples and other structures in classical styles were increasingly favoured for garden ornament.

The gardens of the early eighteenth century, as depicted in engravings by Kip and Badeslade, multiplied compartments within their parterres, but instead of arranging them into a single unified and symmetrical composition, added them incrementally and frequently without axial alignment (the cascade at Chatsworth, for example, is perpendicular to the visual axis of the garden). The patterns of the compartments also differed from their French models: first, arabesques were abandoned in favour of simpler patterns, and simple grass layouts ('plats') became more popular; by the 1720s, these were succeeded by compartments with irregular layouts. Le Nôtre incorporated areas of irregularity within his compositions, but usually in places where they were isolated from the main view; the plans in Batty Langley's *New principles of gardening* of 1726, however, show spiral, labyrinthine or zigzag designs characterising the major compartments. The previous year, the philosopher Francis Hutcheson had written in *Enquiry into the original of our ideas of beauty and virtue*: 'strict *Regularity*

4. Landscape at Painshill created by Charles Hamilton. Amateurs such as Hamilton and the Hoares at Stourhead emerged in the wake of William Kent. They increased his emphasis on natural scenery by the manipulation of woodland, informal lakes and the vista over the wider landscape offered by the ha-ha.

in laying out of Gardens in *Parterres, Vista's, parallel Walks*, is often neglected to obtain an Imitation of *Nature* even in some of its *Wildnesses*. And we are the more pleas'd with this Imitation, especially when the Scene is large and spacious, than with the more confin'd Exactness of *regular Work*.'

By the early eighteenth century, the first large metropolitan nurseries were being established, and the spread of newly introduced plants into gardens became more organised. Asiatic trees such as the weeping willow entered Europe about this time, but regular arrangements with the American colonies ensured that American trees became the favoured introductions.

The English landscape garden

The 1730s saw the beginnings of a programme of systematic reduction, modification or adaption applied to the formal gardens of previous generations, and in many cases their destruction and replacement by a new, 'natural' style of layout. The transformation was most publicised in the case of Stowe, where Charles Bridgeman's garden of the 1710s began to have its formal features softened, so that only an outline of the grand avenue remained. William Kent was responsible for the remodelling; among his typical changes were the erection of buildings in the form of ruins and the introduction of irregular edges to ponds and lakes.

Horace Walpole later claimed that Kent 'leaped the fence, and saw all nature was a garden', but this is to read a later generation's interests back into his work. The attempt to recreate the gardens of classical Rome, exemplified by Lord Burlington's garden at Chiswick; the rejection of what was regarded as ostentatious artifice, as in the campaign of mockery directed at topiary by Alexander Pope and his circle (who treated it, unhistorically, as a Dutch introduction); and Kent's creation of scenes within the garden by the irregular placing of groups of trees — all these tendencies worked together to create a new atmosphere.

In the 1750s Capability Brown, formerly head gardener at Stowe, began his career as a landscape gardener or 'improver', and for thirty years he dominated English garden-making with the most reductionist style yet seen. His characteristic works, exemplified by Blenheim, Bowood and Petworth Park, consisted of great undulating sweeps of lawn studded with groups of trees, serpentine lakes and woodland belts that encircled or framed the landscape. The use of the ha-ha encouraged the illusion that the landscape garden was continuous with the surrounding countryside, while evidence of productive agriculture and human artifice generally — from kitchen gardens to flower beds — was moved away from the principal views. In the case of Nuneham Courtenay, an entire village was notoriously relocated so as not to impinge on the image of unspoiled nature.

Brown incorporated prominent trees into his compositions, and in many cases preserved existing landscape features. Some of his characteristic flourishes probably originated as replications of traditional elements of scenery: the relationship between open lawn, clumps of trees and framing shelterbelt reproduced, to some extent, the pattern of medieval copses and groves, while serpentine lakes in lowland England owed their existence to the creation of mill-races for water power. But these legacies of the agriculture and industry of the past were not understood as such — they were assumed to be natural features of the countryside and therefore worthy of inclusion in gardens aiming to create an effect of nature.

5. View from the grotto at Stourhead.

6. The ha-ha at Levens Hall, one of the earliest in England, made in the 1690s (an earlier one may have been made at Althorp). The idea was introduced from France, where Le Nôtre had used it to provide narrow glimpses of the surrounding countryside; in England, with the name anglicised from the original 'ah! ah!', it was quickly extended to provide wide views. 7. Inset: the ha-ha at Chilham Castle, Kent.

8, 9. An example from Humphry Repton's 'Red Book' for Sherringham before (left) and after (right). This graphic technique enabled his patrons to understand his proposals easily.

By the end of the eighteenth century, the 'natural' appearance of Brown's landscapes was coming under question. Sir Uvedale Price and Richard Payne Knight were the leading propagandists for the Picturesque movement in gardening, which elevated the imitation of landscape painting to an explicit principle. Arguing that Brown's gardens were too carefully manicured and maintained to look natural, they recommended that the texture of garden planting should resemble that of the unimproved countryside, rugged and visually intricate rather than smooth and monotonously green. None the less, the latter half of the eighteenth century was primarily the age of Brown. Other talented designers, such as William Emes and Richard White and, in his early years, Humphry Repton, worked within the stylistic parameters that he had set.

Historical revivalism

Beginning in the late eighteenth century, the idea gained currency that there were no simple truths in artistic style, that every society had its own distinctive style which was incommensurable with the styles of other societies. Gradually, the styles of the European past, and even more gradually those of the non-European world, were explored by architects and garden designers. In garden history, the first phase came with a regret for the old formal gardens that Brown and his rivals had destroyed; in the 1830s, John Claudius Loudon called for surviving formal gardens to be preserved as national monuments. In the first decade of the nineteenth century, Humphry Repton began to re-introduce various formal features that had been condemned in the previous generation – most notably flower beds within the main view from the windows of the house.

Repton proposed a version of history according to which English gardens had been under the domination of Italian models in the sixteenth and early seventeenth centuries, then successively under French and Dutch models, but that these were essentially variants of Italian. This view of garden history prevailed throughout the nineteenth century, with the result that the majority of the period's new gardens were laid out in an 'Italian' style. The popularity of this style was largely the achievement of Sir Charles Barry, whose country house gardens (most notably Trentham, Harewood and Shrubland Park in the 1840s and 1850s) attracted wide publicity and were proclaimed as models. Barry's Italian gardens were based on surviving Renaissance gardens he had seen on the Grand Tour in Italy, and were characterised by formal terraces with Italianate architectural detailing and geometric parterres. The royal seal of approval was awarded to this style when Prince Albert had an Italianate country house and garden created at Osborne in the 1850s.

Briefly, in the 1850s and 1860s, the Italian style was rivalled by a French style, associated with the landscape gardener William Andrews Nesfield, who revived the parterre de broderie and based his patterns on designs from seventeenth-century literature. Nesfield first achieved fame for his design of the Royal Botanic Gardens, Kew, in the 1840s, and thereafter his country house commissions (Somerleyton, Crewe Hall, Witley Court, Holkham

10. Bedded-out parterre designed for the RHS Garden at Kensington by Nesfield.

and Eaton Hall) attracted increasing esteem. Praised as the greatest garden designer of the age in the early 1860s when he designed the Royal Horticultural Society's short-lived garden in Kensington and oversaw alterations in the Royal Parks, he was to fall precipitately from favour, and by his death in 1881 many of his parterres were already being destroyed.

At the beginning of the 1850s, the opening of Elvaston Castle brought to public attention the first example of a garden subdivided into separate enclosures by walls or hedges. The immediate consequence was the sudden revival of architectural topiary, as at Packwood (sculptural topiary – figures of people, chessmen and the like – followed a generation later). Enclosed gardens had long been dismissed as artless, but in the 1860s and 1870s, under the ill-defined rubric of 'old-fashioned gardens', gardens of enclosure became steadily more popular. This tradition was carried forward into the twentieth century by Hidcote, begun in the Edwardian period, and Sissinghurst, begun in 1930.

Garden history as a serious discipline could be said to have begun in the 1890s with Reginald Blomfield's *Formal Garden in England* (1891) and Alicia Amherst's *History of Gardening in England* (1895). In the wake of these books, attempts at replicating period style became more diverse and more exacting. From replications of medieval illustrations of gardens at Sir Frank Crisp's Friar Park (around 1910), to Elizabethan pastiche at the Shakespeare Garden in Stratford (1920s), to a series of attempts to restore the gardens at Hampton Court to an early eighteenth-century and later a seventeenth-century condition (1920s–1990s), to Sir David Bowes Lyon's sympathetic restoration of the early eighteenth-century garden of rides at St Paul's Walden Bury, the twentieth century was characterised by efforts at understanding the past by reconstructing it. By the middle of the twentieth century, there was a revival of interest in the eighteenth-century landscape garden, signalled by Dorothy Stroud's biography of Capability Brown (1950), the 1940s landscape garden at Lexham Hall, and the invocation of the landscape garden as a model for the grounds of the University of York in the 1960s. The second half of the century saw all these period preferences exercised simultaneously, as first the National Trust and then English Heritage undertook programmes of garden restoration for their diverse properties, and sites as different as Claremont, Stowe, Stourhead, Audley End, Biddulph Grange, Waddesdon Manor and Hestercombe were returned as far as possible to their condition at their respective peaks of fame.

Victorian planting and after

The nineteenth century saw the rise of a gardening press, in the form of quarterly, monthly and eventually weekly magazines that provided wide and deep coverage of developments in horticulture. The first of these was John Claudius Loudon's *Gardener's Magazine* (1826–43), and he used it to popularise his aesthetic ideas. Repton had already, in his plans for the Brighton Pavilion grounds, coined the motto 'Gardens are works of art, not of nature,' and Loudon offered a more radical version: 'Gardens are works of art, and should be seen to be works of art.' Any attempt to deceive the spectator into thinking that a garden was the work of unaided nature was deemed to be in bad taste.

Loudon offered two ways in which a garden could be made to appear a work of art: formal or geometrical design (which, for the nineteenth century, meant historically revivalist design) and exotic planting – the use of plants which were not part of the native flora

and therefore owed their position in the garden to the hand of man. There was already a long tradition of planting exotic trees, especially for timber purposes; a fashion for conifers had grown since the late eighteenth century, as had the cult of the 'American garden', an area devoted to American species of rhododendrons, kalmias and other peat-loving plants. But the numbers of new introductions increased significantly in the nineteenth century; experiments in hardiness were carried out, so that around mid-century a number of former greenhouse plants, such as camellias and rhododendrons, moved outdoors; and parklands around the country were transformed, first by coniferous planting, then by rhododendrons, and finally by the development of woodland gardens at Cragside, Bodnant, Minterne and other estates.

Efforts to make woodland walks more floriferous by sowing annual seeds were being made in the middle years of the century. In 1870 William Robinson published a manual on *The Wild Garden*, with advice for naturalising hardy exotics that would establish themselves without much need for maintenance. The later twentieth century saw a double backlash against this fashion, first by the removal of rhododendrons and other later additions from landscape gardens such as Stourhead, and secondly by legal restrictions on the planting of invasive species.

Loudon had recommended that rock outcrops could be made into works of art by suitable exotic planting, and two opposing traditions of rock-garden construction evolved during the nineteenth century. One tradition, associated with Sir Joseph Paxton at Chatsworth and the firm of James Pulham, who made artificial boulders, was that of picturesquely arranged rocks to which planting was kept subordinate; the other, associated with the

11. An example of Pulham rockwork at Waddesdon Manor.

Backhouse nursery in York and, in the twentieth century, with Reginald Farrer and E. A. Bowles, regarded the rock garden as a place for growing alpine plants, so that soil drainage was more important than visible rock. The great rock garden reached its peak of popularity during the inter-war years.

But it was the flower garden near the house where exotic planting made its greatest impact. Loudon and others campaigned in the 1820s and 1830s for a bolder use of colour, with flower beds arranged as large masses of single colours juxtaposed for contrast. New developments in colour theory were eagerly argued over and experimented with by head gardeners on country estates; new plants were bred by nurserymen and gardeners for dwarf habit and increased flower size, and these new bedding plants began to appear on the market in the 1840s. Pelargoniums, petunias, verbenas and calceolarias – all of South African or South American origin – became for a generation the standard bedding plants for the domestic parterre. The 1870s saw a fashion for carpet bedding, the use of dwarf foliage plants to create complex flat patterns. Meanwhile, the restricted season of summer bedding was

13. Hestercombe, Somerset, designed by Gertrude Jekyll.

12. Victorian period planting at Brodsworth.

being extended by the use of bulbs for spring beds and by chrysanthemums for autumn.

Away from the principal flower beds, similar experimentation was taking place in the planting of herbaceous borders. Following Jane Loudon's *The Ladies' Flower Garden*, published in the 1840s, historical revivalists in the 1860s and 1870s began to promote the herbaceous border as more in keeping with English tradition than summer bedding; such borders, planted with groups known to have been in cultivation in the seventeenth century, formed an important part of the 'old-fashioned' garden. In the 1880s, Gertrude Jekyll emerged as an advocate of colour planning of the herbaceous border, subordinating historical accuracy to aesthetic effect as a basis for planting choice; throughout the first half of the twentieth century the herbaceous border formed a mainstay of English gardens.

New landscapes for new purposes

Significant as the changes were in the ornamental garden, they were rivalled by the transformation of the country house kitchen garden, as improvements in glasshouse construction led to the creation of large glass ranges for tender fruits. The idea of protected cultivation under glass had been familiar since the Elizabethan period, but there are no surviving English glasshouses before the beginning of the eighteenth century, and it was not until the nineteenth that improved construction techniques and falling prices for the structural materials made them widespread, whether for exotic plant collections, domestic conservatories or the many and varied structures used for peaches, melons and cucumbers.

At the other end of the social scale, the cottage garden of the agricultural worker began to receive press attention for the first time – or at least philanthropic proposals for its improvement did. Far more advice was published than accounts of cottages that actually existed, so uncertainty must remain about what most cottage gardens really looked like; but a uniform theme of the advice was the need to avoid bedding and other forms of ornament that required greenhouses, so hardy herbaceous planting was no doubt

14. Cottage garden, Hampshire, from W. Robinson, *The English Flower Garden*, 1898 (sixth edition).

the principal form of plant decoration. (In the twentieth century, 'cottage garden' was to become a stylistic term for the informal arrangement of plants in beds, but this usage may have borne little relation to the cottages of the poor.) For the urban working classes, whose dwellings did not incorporate garden areas, allotments were promoted from the early nineteenth century as a means of allowing them to grow their own food – as well as a way of keeping a sober workforce away from the pubs.

Philanthropic concern manifested itself especially in the question of public open space. A Select Committee of 1833 expressed alarm over the loss of open space in London during the building boom that followed the Napoleonic wars, and called for the creation of new public walks to compensate the population for the amenities they had lost. John Claudius Loudon laid out a small and short-lived park in Gravesend in the 1830s, followed by the Derby Arboretum in 1840; Joseph Paxton laid out Prince's Park, Liverpool, about the same time. Both of these parks initially required payment for entrance; but in 1843 Paxton was hired to create Birkenhead Park, the first municipal park that was free to the public. By the time it opened in 1847, Manchester and Salford had commissioned three parks from Joshua Major, which had been hurried through to completion in 1846.

Over the next eighty years, virtually every town in the kingdom acquired a municipal park for its residents. The first design trend was the development of formality. Paxton, the single most influential figure, moved from the implied axial layout of Birkenhead to the formal terraces of Crystal Palace Park (1852–4), and his use of an axial descent from a viewing terrace was widely copied in the 1860s. A reaction swept in with the next generation, particularly associated with Alexander McKenzie, whose Finsbury and Southwark parks returned to informal layout, and who at Alexandra Park violated Paxtonian expectations by sweeping the carriage drive across the descending axis. (Marine Park, South Shields, combined both the Paxtonian and the McKenziean approaches at different points of its terrace.) The late nineteenth century also saw the introduction of the sports park, subdivided into different areas for specific games, and its devolution into the smaller recreation ground. The Edwardian period saw the arrival on a large scale of golf courses, informal landscapes of grass and trees.

15. The Crystal Palace park in its heyday.

Another genre of landscape design that emerged simultaneously with municipal parks was the cemetery. The same pattern of development took place, with largely informal landscapes incorporating elements of formal design (Kensal Green, Highgate), succeeded by strongly axial and geometric layouts (Brompton) and by a return to informality towards the end of the century.

The rise of the gardener

Parks and cemeteries created new employment possibilities for gardeners, whose options had hitherto been restricted to the country house garden (with a small range of royal or scientific gardens) or to the nursery trade. The rise of the gardener to professional (and, to some degree, social) prominence was based in large part on the growth of a gardening periodical literature, which allowed gardeners the opportunity to publicise their activities and innovations. The meteoric career of Paxton, the first gardener to be knighted, set the standard of aspiration for skilled horticulturists.

In the inter-war era (1920–39) successful happy compromises, blending architectural and 'natural' compositions, were created in gardens such as Hidcote Manor, Sissinghurst and Great Dixter. However, the old order of 'master and men' was never restored, and the status of head gardener declined, despite labour remaining comparatively cheap and plentiful. More equipment and machinery were available to take the effort and manpower out of garden maintenance, and the great increase in private gardens and hobby gardening devalued the status of the professional gardener.

The Second World War and the period following it had a further profound and irreversible impact on the lifestyles of many garden owners, their gardens and the staff that had maintained them. The demise of the country house garden as a major employer and source of training in the mid-twentieth century meant that, for two generations, professional gardeners were restricted to the public parks service. Reorganisation and financial cuts in the 1980s and 1990s saw the end of public park apprenticeship schemes. Young people deterred by the low wages and long training of professional gardening trained instead to become landscapers and garden designers to meet the growing demand for domestic gardens.

A buoyant economy since the 1990s has seen a resurgence of well-maintained private parks and gardens. The sustainability of this 'reflowering' is, however, threatened by an ageing population of experienced gardeners and insufficient young gardeners being recruited to replace them. England's reputation as a country of gardens was built out of the creative relationship between garden owners or managers and the horticultural staff capable of putting ideas into practice. The owners of exemplar gardens, managers and local authorities, realising that they must take responsibility for training, have reintroduced apprenticeship and other schemes and some employers are offering more attractive salaries. However, only time will tell if this best practice starts a trend that will encourage more young people into horticulture to provide a sustainable future for England's historic gardens.

Modernism

The nineteenth-century emphasis on historical revivalism bred a twentieth-century reaction. If every style is related to the society it springs from, then it should follow that the society of the twentieth century should have had its own distinctive style, instead of drawing on those of the past. Christopher Tunnard, in *Gardens in the Modern Landscape* (1938), put forward these ideas as characteristically modern: grass terraces; the use of architectural plants; geometric patterns based on modernist painting; paving and its successor, hard landscaping, and woodland glades. These can all be found in inter-war gardens designed by Percy Cane, Oliver Hill and Tunnard.

After the Second World War, Brenda Colvin, Sylvia Crowe and Geoffrey Jellicoe emerged as major figures, all of whom wrote influential books on garden design, bringing into play concepts of ecology and an emotional reaction to place. Increasingly, however, landscape architects, who had formed a professional institute in 1929, were turning their attention to wider vistas and greater perceived social needs than the private garden. The design of

16. Advertisement for lawn mowers and garden rollers in *The Country Gentleman's Catalogue*, 1894.

17. Modernist landscape at the Commonwealth Institute, designed by Dame Sylvia Crowe.

roads, towns, forests and industrial complexes distracted attention from the ordinary domestic garden, which pursued its way through the stylistic legacy that the modernists rejected. Housing estates developed by practices such as SPAN included communal gardens based on glades, abstract sculptures in the landscape and, particularly associated with John Brookes from the 1960s, the reorganisation of the domestic garden as a 'room outside', with social functions taking priority over horticulture – these were the principal signs of modernism in the post-war garden, until the vogue at the end of the century for abstract decoration in metal and other new materials.

The most significant trend in the modernist garden generally was geometric abstraction: the reduction of the more complex patterns of the past to simple geometrical equivalents, and the assertion of spatial relationships over the style of the elements related. Sir Frederick Gibberd's layout of Harlow New Town (1947–60) is a case in point: the Town Hall and water gardens (now destroyed) were arranged on a series of terraces to form a composition analogous to a country house and its parterres, but with ornamentation reduced to purely rectilinear forms.

The post-war decades saw a widespread move to labour-saving devices in the smaller domestic garden and to mechanisation in both public parks and the larger private gardens. The arrival of synthetic pesticides in the 1940s led to an increasing reliance by both on chemical control; and as nurseries increasingly gave way to, or were absorbed by, garden centres which depended on retailing large quantities of limited ranges of stock, the use of peat-based composts for containerised plants became the norm. The closing decades of the twentieth century saw a reaction against the perceived environmental consequences of these trends, ranging from the encouragement of wildlife in the garden to demands for a choice of native species for planting.

At the end of the twentieth century, the demand for modernism in the garden was renewed by a new generation of pundits, this time with more effective communications media, and fashions for new materials and new forms of abstraction developed. It will not be long before the 'thirty-year' rule makes the gardens of the 1990s eligible for inclusion in *The English Heritage Register of Parks and Gardens of Special Historic Interest in England* – will it be neo-modernism, ecologism, a new twist in revivalism, or something unexpected that will most characterise the gardens of that period?

18. Example of Geoffrey Jellico's work at Sutton Place.

19. Hascome Court, Surrey, by Percy Cane, 1925.

20. A garden or garden area may have many layers of significant development. At Audley End a seventeenth-century parterre was swept away by Capability Brown, to be replaced in the early nineteenth century, then removed again in the mid twentieth century. A decision was taken to restore the early nineteenth-century Gilpin parterre following archaelogical investigation in the late twentieth century.

The Conservation Management Plan (CMP) process

All forms of maintenance or development require planning. Traditional estates with consistent long-standing ownership and staffing were often able to plan their maintenance and management in an informal way due to the long experience of the owners and staff, and their own records. However, in recent years, many have found written plans and the process of creating them helpful in setting down thought processes and analysing competing priorities. Owners and estate managers seeking grant aid or development permissions are required to have a formal record of their proposals in the form of conservation management and business plans. This chapter aims to guide the reader through the increasingly important plan process from conservation to management and maintenance.

RESTORING HISTORIC PARKS AND GARDENS

Historic layers

Most designed landscapes date from several periods. Further layers may have deliberately added to existing designs, swept away some features or simply changed them. Judging which features should be repaired or renewed can only be done in the context of an understanding of the complete park and garden structure and development. A quality management regime and good decision-making depends on sound principles and clear policies. Using the Conservation Management Plan (CMP) approach, it is possible to appraise how these features contribute to the overall design, their intrinsic value as artefacts, the adequacy of evidence for their authentic reinstatement and the practicality of doing so. The CMP is the method of recording original surviving features, the state and condition of all features and of appraising the feasibility of restoring the historic designs.

In the historic environment sector, terms such as repair, restoration and reconstruction have technical uses and should be used correctly. Consistent use and wider adoption of these terms would in part help towards a better understanding of the conservation management needs of historic parks and gardens.

Repair Christopher Brereton defined the purpose of repair as 'restrain(ing) the process of decay without damaging the character of buildings and monuments, altering the features which give them their historic or architectural importance, or unnecessarily disturbing or destroying historic fabric' (*The Repair of Historic Buildings*, 1995). Brereton's principles of repair require:

- avoiding unnecessary damage
- analysing the causes of defects to prevent repetition of problems

21. An example of 'repair' at the Brodsworth Hall Fernery.

- adopting proven techniques
- carrying out repairs with truth and sympathy to materials and appearance
- removing later alterations if they are of no intrinsic value
- restoring lost features important to the design if there is sufficient evidence for accurate replacement
- regular maintenance programmes to ensure repairs are kept to a minimum

With historic assets such as buildings, the approach is therefore usually 'conserve as found'. This is also true for designed landscapes, but with the living elements of parks and gardens the design intentions will need to be interpreted as much as the historical facts, in order to recapture the sensual qualities of the landscape design. Planned and regular quality maintenance and cyclical replacement is essential if original garden fabric is to be retained.

Restoration The Australian Burra Charter for Places of Cultural Significance (see box, page 27) gives useful guidelines: '*Restoration* means returning the existing *fabric* of a *place* to a known earlier state by removing accretions or by reassembling existing components without the introduction of new material'. The replacement of structural planting is regarded as restoration rather than reconstruction, since it involves the reassembling of 'existing components', even though they are new tree and plant specimens. In restoring historic parks and gardens the aim should, as far as possible, be accuracy – if historic records are defective, decisions

DEFINITIONS USED IN THE BURRA CHARTER

1.1 *Place* means site, area, land, landscape, building or other work, group of buildings or other works, and may include components, contents, spaces and views.

1.2 *Cultural significance* means aesthetic, historic, scientific, social or spiritual value for past, present or future generations. Cultural significance is embodied in the *place* itself, its *fabric, setting, use, associations, meanings, records, related places* and *related objects.* Places may have a range of values for different individuals or groups.

1.3 *Fabric* means all the physical material of the *place* including components, fixtures, contents and objects.

1.4 *Conservation* means all the processes of looking after a *place* so as to retain its *cultural significance.*

1.5 *Maintenance* means the continuous protective care of the *fabric* and *setting* of a *place,* and is to be distinguished from repair. Repair involves *restoration* or *reconstruction.*

1.6 *Preservation* means maintaining the *fabric* of a *place* in its existing state and retarding deterioration.

1.7 *Restoration* means returning the existing *fabric* of a *place* to a known earlier state by removing accretions or by reassembling existing components without the introduction of new material.

1.8 *Reconstruction* means returning a *place* to a known earlier state and is distinguished from *restoration* by the introduction of new material into the *fabric.*

1.9 *Adaptation* means modifying a *place* to suit the existing *use* or a proposed use.

1.10 *Use* means the functions of a place, as well as the activities and practices that may occur at the place.

1.11 *Compatible use* means a *use* which respects the *cultural significance* of a *place.* Such a use involves no, or minimal, impact on cultural significance.

1.12 *Setting* means the area around a *place,* which may include the visual catchment.

1.13 *Related place* means a *place* that contributes to the *cultural significance* of another place.

1.14 *Related object* means an object that contributes to the *cultural significance* of a *place* but is not at the place.

1.15 *Associations* mean the special connections that exist between people and a *place.*

1.16 *Meanings* denote what a *place* signifies, indicates, evokes or expresses.

1.17 *Interpretation* means all the ways of presenting the *cultural significance* of a place.

23. At Hatfield, a garden was reconstructed to represent an earlier garden laid out by Tradescant the Elder.

have to be made on how to produce authentic-looking reconstructions. Restoration is sometimes assumed to be about reverting back to a particular period, but is not about living in the past. Restoration schemes inevitably reflect current thinking and tastes – it is possible to identify previous restoration schemes, and indeed they are of historic interest in their own right.

Reconstruction In terms of conservation priorities, re-creation or speculative reconstruction of past historic features, especially where evidence is incomplete, is unlikely to receive support from UK public sector grant aid. Reconstruction can be justified where a missing feature is important to the interpretation of the landscape design as a whole, or for educational purposes. In presenting period gardens, managers should be careful to avoid the impression that the gardens are made of genuine historical fabric. English Heritage's Contemporary Heritage Garden Scheme demonstrated that where there is little or no historic evidence for a garden a new design can be integrated well. Re-created features should if possible be reversible, in case historic information later comes to light. Some features, such as planting schemes, can usually be changed, so the degree of accuracy needed can be more flexible. Other countries have different conservation approaches and give different priorities to issues such as re-creation.

22. Opposite: in restoring the parterre at Osborne, English Heritage used archaeology to determine accurately the Victorian layout of the beds.

THE PRINCIPLES OF REPAIR TO HISTORIC PARKS AND GARDENS
David Jacques, 1992

The following points may be useful as a brief summary of the principles of repair. First, the **general priorities** are stated:

1. Historical survey of surviving features, and analysis with the help of documentary sources, are the essential precursors to any form of treatment of historic parks and gardens, since they define the nature and degree of historical interest of the various parts of the site.

2. A management policy and plan incorporating historical objectives into the overall aims is desirable at every site so that its historic interest may be given adequate weight.

3. The conservation priorities for parks and gardens are (in order); protection of the historic fabric of surviving features, recording of fabric, and repairs to conserve the design.

4. Presentation and visitor facilities at a park or garden are often an important aspect of care, but should be subordinate to conservation.

Then there are guidelines relating to historically important **fabric**:

5. The fabric of important surviving features should be protected for as long as feasible. Maintenance is thus essential to avoid rapid deterioration. Continuity of maintenance is preferable to premature decay followed by reconstruction.

6. The aim of protecting fabric need not extend to ill-advised recent repair, nor works resulting from mere short-sightedness, financial pragmatism or neglect, and eroding a planned ornamental design.

7. Maintenance plans, which specify achievable and sustainable levels of care, are desirable.

8. The fabric of surviving features should be recorded sufficiently for future repairs to be accurate.

After which there are guidelines relating to **repairs**:

9. Once the historic fabric is so decayed that it is dangerous or has failed, the emphasis of treatment shifts to the recovery of the design.

10. A detailed record and substantial survival of fabric are preconditions to repairs that seek to replicate it accurately.

11. Repairing the layout and content resulting from the last significant and deliberate change should normally be the aim of restoration.

12. Replacement of plants and some other forms of fabric will be necessary at intervals, and a restoration strategy should anticipate and harmonise the processes of vegetative change and replacement as far as possible.

13. Conjectural detailing, especially of planting, may have to accompany true repairs in order to recover a design. Research on authentic style, detailing and materials should be a precondition to conjectural detailing.

14. The reasons for, and process of, any repairs or reconstruction should be fully recorded. A graphic or photographic record should be undertaken during and after.

There are **other forms of restoration** that should be distinguished from repair, and to which the following considerations apply:

15. Reconstruction is where a feature that has largely or wholly disappeared is replaced. Often reconstruction involves removal of sound, more recent, fabric, and substitution by invented detail. It can thus be destructive as well as of dubious historical value.

16. Consideration should be given to whether interpretation can satisfy presentation aims, and prove a satisfactory alternative to reconstruction.

17. The preconditions to reconstruction should be that a detailed record of the original is available, and that the work is consistent with the treatment of associated buildings, or allows recovery of the design as a whole.

18. Restoration-in-spirit (i.e. re-creating the general spirit of the layout without attention to accuracy) erodes a site's genuine historical interest; straightforward maintenance and repair is nearly always preferable.

19. New work in an historic style should not attempt to give the impression that it is authentic historic fabric.

20. All new or reconstructed fabric, except that which can be classed as repair, should be designed so that it can be installed and removed with no alteration to historic fabric.

In response to changes in conservation planning, heritage protection and the need to involve the public, in February 2006 English Heritage drafted a new set of general principles for the conservation of the historic environment to foster an integrated and consistent approach to understanding, valuing, caring for and enjoying historic places and the heritage. The historic environment is seen as a resource that should be used sustainably for the benefit of present and future generations, a resource which can only be sustained with a broad social and economic policy framework. The new principles build on the long tradition of conservation policy and, like the Brereton and the Burra Charter principles above, English Heritage's proposed principles are value-based.

Conservation is therefore defined as involving continuing management (including recurrent maintenance such as laying hedges), occasional intervention to prevent loss such as structural repairs to walls, the removal of intrusions and the restoration of lost features to recover or reinforce significance, and action other than physical intervention to make use of places or their presentation. Maintaining authenticity and integrity are key to these conservation policies. Similarly, in planning changes, sustainability and reversibility need to be considered. Sustainable stewardship, particularly of public assets, and publicly funded conservation need to be accountable. CMPs and the CMP process can provide a framework for future decision-making.

24. The Contemporary Heritage Garden at Lincoln Medieval Bishops' Palace, designed by Mark Anthony Walker, is an example of a new garden designed and laid out in a historic setting.

THE DEVELOPMENT OF CMPS FOR LANDSCAPES

From the 1970s the management plan was developed as a tool for understanding the significance of large-scale landscapes, all their attributes – designed landscape; forestry and agriculture interests; vernacular characteristics such as farm buildings, hedges and stiles; public access and recreation – and their management, and for planning their repair and renewal. The 10 sq km Blenheim Park was one of the first to experiment with developing an estate plan and has since prepared more sophisticated plans. The leading government agency, the Countryside Commission, used its grant powers to contribute towards the cost of plans and thereby also to develop thinking and ideas through practical experience. Plans for woodland planting and felling schemes were also well established as a forester's tool. Five-year management objectives and plans of operation for forestry grant schemes have been a requirement for many years; in return, owners gain streamlining for felling consents.

By the 1980s there was growing interest in how to tackle the repair and renewal of historic platning and designed landscapes, and an awareness of the importance of historic authenticity. English Heritage began to develop its *Register of Parks and Gardens of Special Historic Interest* and with it the philosophy of restoration. Plans as a condition of grant offers for repair work were catapulted into the mainstream by the great storm of October 1987. The Government-funded joint English Heritage and Countryside Commission (Task Force Trees) grant programme was set up to help owners repair the many devastated historic parks and gardens. Grants of 75 per cent were offered for restoration plans, which helped towards the costs of commissioning specialists to provide a historical appraisal of each park and garden, and to advise on restoration programmes costed over a five-year period. These schemes involved repair but also took the opportunity to reveal the significance of historic designs.

25. Emmets Garden, Sevenoaks (National Trust), after the 1987 storm.

Countryside Stewardship schemes in the 1990s offered farmers and landowners ten-year management agreements with annual revenue payments and capital grants for enhancement work. Parkland was soon added to the list of options and, as with the storm damage grants, funding was also offered towards the costs of restoration plans. These principles have been continued in the next generation, Environmental Stewardship, funded by the Department for Environment, Food and Rural Affairs (Defra). There are also parallels between site plans and strategic plans such as management plans for designated areas like National Parks and Areas of Outstanding Natural Beauty (AONBs), as well as other appraisals such as Environmental or Heritage Impact Assessments.

The plan-led approach is adopted in the Inland Revenue conditional exemption scheme for inheritance tax. The Countryside and Rights of Way Act 2000 and its Code of Guidance introduces management agreements and schemes that require statements setting out measures for the positive management of land for Sites of Special Scientific Interest (SSSI) status. The national Planning Policy Guidance (PPG 17) for Open Space, Sport and Recreation (issued in 2002) requires Local Planning Authorities (LPAs) to prepare green space strategies as part of their statutory plans. These strategies provide a means of linking individual sites plans and parks with other local authority strategies.

English Heritage and others place high priority on plans, which are seen as a long-term investment helping owners and managers to plan resources and to attract alternative sources of funding. The Heritage Lottery Fund's Public Parks Initiative encouraged local authorities and other public green space managers to adopt the plan approach for these sites too. The Heritage Lottery Fund has helped to develop thinking about long-term plans for maintenance as well as restoration, and to engage new audiences in planning, including park users, local groups and volunteers.

Parallel to plans for historic parks and gardens, the approach has also been adopted for historic buildings, monuments and sites. The Department for Culture, Media and Sport and the Department for Transport, Local Government and the Regions issued a statement in 2001, *The Historic Environment: A Force for Our Future*, which 'strongly recommends' CMPs for large-scale properties such as historic parks and gardens.

The CMP process

For historic parks, gardens and landscapes, these plans divide into two parts. The first is about conservation: an analysis of the site and the development of conservation policies. The second is about management: implementing these policies and devising the work programmes. On its own, the conservation plan provides an understanding of the site and what is significant. But a management plan is needed to plan, deliver and monitor practical conservation action.

The conservation plan process (see box, opposite) begins with understanding the site, and moves logically through an assessment

THE CONSERVATION MANAGEMENT PLAN PROCESS
Adapted from Kate Clark, 2001

CONSERVATION

ASSESSMENT
- Understand the historic park and garden
- Assess significance
- Define issues and constraints
- Set vision and policies

MANAGEMENT

PLANNING
- Management programme including management prescriptions and maintenance checklists
- Option appraisal and feasibility study for new developments, e.g. visitor facilities and garden restoration (if appropriate)
- Business planning

ACTION
- Budgets and work programme: contract specifications, staff work programmes
- Monitoring and review of management plan (including programme of condition surveys)

of significance to understanding how that significance might be vulnerable and thus what policies or guidelines are needed to protect it. The plan must be based on sound research and analysis and, unless new information comes to light, it should stand the test of time. Once it is in place, specific strategies or action plans can be developed. The vision and policies set in the conservation plan should be applicable for its full life span; in contrast, the management plan is adjustable. It is usually impractical to devise detailed repair, restoration or work programmes beyond five years; three years is ideal. So these plans need to be regularly reviewed and updated.

The process of preparing the plan has bearings on the final document and its long-term effectiveness. This process itself can be as important as the final document. Early decisions will need to focus on how the plan will be prepared, who needs to be involved and what skills and equipment are needed – e.g. Geographic Information Systems (GIS) for storing and integrating survey data. The project team will need to include a range of skills and expertise to match the complexity of the site (specialists can be brought in for certain aspects). Depending on the site and the scale of the project, these skills could include:

- Horticulture
- Arboriculture
- Garden design and management
- Garden and architectural history
- Ecology and wildlife conservation
- Forestry and farming
- Archaeology
- Community engagement, and many others

Plans can be commissioned through specialist consultants, and it is good practice to do this through competitive tendering. For many sites, public consultation will be essential, and needs to be carefully planned to ensure that people are properly involved.

The first step is to develop a project brief and to evaluate the range of information needed to develop the plan. A host of information usually exists for most sites, and one role of the plan is to collate this information as a ready reference source, and to identify any gaps.

Understanding through research and analysis
All land has a history. Parks, gardens and all green spaces, however small or insignificant, almost always have documentary and surviving physical evidence. Various archival and published sources exist for researching the history of a park or garden, including *A Bibliography of British Gardens* by Ray Desmond (1988), a guide to published material; *Parks and Gardens. A Researcher's Guide to Sources for Designated Landscapes* by David Lambert, Peter Goodchild and Judith Roberts (2006); the research register of the Garden History Society (www.gardenhistorysociety.org) and, increasingly, the internet. Initial searches could include:

- Estate maps and design plans
- Historic Ordnance Survey maps and parish maps
- Paintings, prints and drawings, photographs
- Estate and personal papers
- Guide books
- Visitors' descriptions

The plan should describe the history of the park and garden and cover the following areas:

- History of ownership
- History of development of the landscape and garden design and layout
- History of land management – agriculture, forestry, horticulture, public park, cemetery, visitor attractions and provisions
- Broader historical context for main phases of the site's development, e.g. fashion, politics, technology

SEARCHES FOR HISTORIC EVIDENCE

Adapted from David Lambert, Peter Goodchild and Judith Roberts,
Parks and Gardens, 2006

PEOPLE
- Owners and occupiers
- Designers (landscape gardeners and architects, architects, amateurs, etc., or, for public parks, the borough engineer or borough surveyor)
- Gardeners, estate managers, stewards, the committees responsible for parks or cemeteries of a local authority
- Visitors

DATES
- Different ownerships and occupancies
- Main periods of activity
- Dates of introduction/construction of individual features
- The opening of the park and the dates of the purchase or donation of additional land

FEATURES
- Entrance points and circulation (gates, paths, drives, etc.)
- Main component areas
- Landforms and earthworks
- Water features
- Planting and plants (see page 36 on researching period planting)
- Buildings, constructions and ornaments
- Archaeological features

MAIN DIVISIONS OF THE SITE
- Principle buildings
- Pleasure grounds
- Parkland
- Other land such as farmland and functional areas, e.g. pitches and play areas in public parks
- Land beyond the site boundary which makes an important contribution to the character of the site or its design. For public parks the surrounding neighbourhood will be an important consideration
- Kitchen garden and other productive garden areas

BOUNDARIES
- Past and present boundaries of the site

The garden and park research work would involve the following steps:

- Working out a programme for the research
- Consulting the main bibliographies and printed sources
- Making contact with the relevant archive centres
- Ordering copies of plans and photographs
- Site visits and field walking
- Study of documentary and published sources from archive searches

- Recording and storing research material
- Planning archaeological surveys needed
- Writing up the research and archaeological findings (including a bibliography of published and unpublished sources; identifying gaps in the historical record, and contributing to the thinking behind the CMP)

Surveys and maps are an important part of the research. Plans will need to include three types of surveys and baseline information:

- Surveys and maps of surviving features (from each historic period) and their condition; field walking and archaeological investigation (see below); ecological surveys (see Chapter 2.2); tree surveys (see example, page 36), topographical survey; hydrological information, etc.
- Gazetteers or inventories of historic park and garden features, buildings and structures, and condition survey. A summary of these features and their relationships should feature in the main document, with the detailed information in an appendix
- Condition surveys of historic and wildlife features and land plus aerial maps to use as baseline information.

Archaeological investigations can be very useful, especially in filling gaps and showing how design ideas were executed. Opportunities for more detailed archaeological investigation such as excavations are often limited by cost but could be carried out on a selective basis. Researched information needs to be corroborated and informed by field walking surveys. These are the main archaeological techniques appropriate for researching gardens and parks:

- Topographical surveys
- Building analysis
- Earthwork recording
- Historical ecology investigation
- Analysis of aerial, satellite and other forms of photographic surveys
- Geophysical survey techniques such as resistivity
- Archaeological excavations
- Archaeological science

The research must be drawn together as a set of surveys, maps, gazetteers or inventories to build a picture of the development of the designed landscape, its survival and current condition. In addition, the plan must contain key site information such as:

- Ownership and occupancy details, including leases, land managed under licence, trusts, acquisitions and sources of funding
- Location and geographical information: Ordnance Survey grid reference, landscape description (including wider landscape setting and character, climate and rainfall, prevailing wind etc., geology and soils, geomorphology, topography and landform, hydrology and hydrography, soil characteristics)

26. Aerial photograph of the Chatsworth estate to show constituent parts: house, service wing, stables, home farm, flower garden, kitchen garden, park, rides, woods and farms.

- Services e.g. water, gas, electricity mains
- Current land use: farming and forestry types, agricultural land classification, other land uses and land management agreements
- Designations, e.g. SSSI, Conservation Area, Scheduled Monument, Listed Building or Registered Landscape

Collecting information for a conservation plan requires specialist knowledge and experience. The surveys prepared will provide valuable baseline information for monitoring future change. Each site is different, requiring its own information and range and level of research. Not all sites will require all the information listed above, and for some sites different data and documentation will be needed.

Developing a statement of significance

All the research and information gathered for the conservation plan described above is analysed to develop an overview of the whole garden and park, its historic context and other interests. From this analysis a statement of significance should provide an evaluation of the quality of the landscape, park and garden. The analysis should include:

- Landscape design analysis including views and vistas; relationship of existing historic park and garden with wider historic estate; 'borrowed' features lying beyond site; local community, and principal house
- Character area assessment based on mapping of each distinct part of the park and garden layout
- Buildings analysis and appraisal of architectural interest
- Appraisal of archaeological interest
- Appraisal of wildlife and habitat interests
- Appraisal of other amenity interests such as public access
- Understanding of the park and garden in the context of its wider landscape setting
- Evaluation of the landscape design in comparison with other similar historic parks and gardens

The final statement of significance should include:

- Overall significance of the site
- How its features and parts contribute to its overall importance, which may be regional, national or international

27. Far left: traces of abandoned gardens often survive as earthworks, as at Collyweston in Northamptonshire where a series of low banks denote the former terraces of an early garden layout.

28. Left: previous avenue planting may be identified by careful analysis of surviving hollows left after the removal of trees or through distinctive vegetation growing above rotted root material.

29. Left: geophysical survey, using non-intrusive techniques to measure former disturbance, can reveal the arrangement of buried paths and flowerbeds where surface evidence has vanished.

30. Inset: archaeological excavation enables us to test how much of the buried archaeology layout survives, as well as providing detail of lost features, such as the Elizabethan fountain at Kenilworth Castle.

31. Far left: depending on its preservation, the historic garden plan may be recoverable through complete or selective excavation, with the sequence of features showing how it has changed.

32. Left: the soils within former planting beds can preserve important botanical and other information, which may indicate previous use and the nature of original gardening practice.

Issues and constraints The conservation plan is a practical tool. Issues and constraints need to be considered as they could impact on the significance of the site. These could include:

- Policy framework for the area, including relevant local planning authority policies

- Other policy documents, such as the UK biodiversity habitat action plan for wood pasture and parkland

- Visitor operations

- Public access and common rights

- Other rights of access and way, etc.

- Field sports, licences and rights

- Management principles such as environmentally sensitive farming and sustainability

- Location and size

- Fragility

- Intactness

- Legal obligations or limitations imposed by designations such as Tree Preservation Orders, grant conditions, etc.

- Protective designations for historic or natural features

- Changes beyond the boundary of the garden and park

- Split ownership

- Security

- Revenue generation

With analysis and evaluation completed and issues and constraints identified, an overall vision, principles and policies for restoration, repair, conservation, management and access can be prepared. The vision sets out what is to be achieved and by when. Policies establish guidelines for determining what is appropriate for the individual site, and provide a framework for making decisions. For a historic site, policies are likely to be needed for:

- Garden and landscape repair and restoration: historic period(s); design interests; extent of restoration; design principles where restoring or reinstating features such as fencing or planting; identifying further survey or research needs; standards for restoration, repair and management work

- Land use: agriculture, forestry, wood pasture and veteran trees, horticulture, sport and recreation

- Sustainability and environmentally friendly management: peat alternatives, recycling, reduced use of herbicides and pesticides, integrated crop management regimes etc.

- Plan-led approach to handling future development proposals and conservation-led procedures for instructing for future work, based on an impact assessment and mitigation table

- Visitor access and enjoyment: publicity and promotion, education initiatives, interpretation and information, visitor facilities, access by public transport, disabled access, public rights of way, permissive public access

- Further research and survey

- Longer-term consultation procedures and, in the case of public parks and green spaces, how the local community might be involved

- Maintenance of the archive and its further development, e.g. a record of the restoration and management work

- Heritage impact assessment for new developments: proposed work will need to be assessed against the significance of feature or fabric affected, potential impact of work, information from the conservation management plan and possible mitigation

- Promotion of supporting policy framework in other strategic guidance, e.g. the local planning authority's statutory development plan

The Management Plan

The essence of managing historic parks and gardens is continuity. The management half of the CMP sets out how to carry out the policies that flow from the statement of significance, by defining and programming work and financial and resource requirements. These could include employment and staff management considerations such as health and safety and skills training. The budget and work programme must be realistic. The management prescriptions and work programme are the flexible parts of the plan, which need to be monitored, adjusted, updated and rolled forward on a regular basis.

As well as addressing management prescriptions for each of the plan policies, it is often helpful to look at the garden and park as a series of land management units and to organise management prescriptions and work programmes by these areas. The management plan would need to include:

- Management prescriptions for each policy

- Management prescriptions for each land management unit within the garden and park, addressing management, maintenance and restoration: types of work, and capital and revenue financing

- Performance specifications for each prescription

The conservation plan should include references and locations of all useful documentary sources, which should be kept and used with the management plan on site.

Detailed programmes should be provided for the first three years and outline proposals for next five, ten and twenty years. These must set realistic timescales for developing projects, fundraising, grant applications and securing of consents.

Business planning is needed to realise and prioritise work programmes. It should include a financial appraisal with spreadsheets showing income and spend, a balance sheet and a cash-flow forecast. Financial planning should include:

- Contingency sums

- Management and staffing structure for implementing the plan

- Risk analysis across all areas of the CMP (technical, market, financial, economic, management and legal) and strategies for managing these risks

RESEARCHING PERIOD PLANTING

RECORDING

- First, record existing plants. Priority should be given to trees, stumps of lost trees and shrubs. Perennial planting will not withstand long periods of neglect so is likely to be most recent.

- Prioritise areas to be recorded. Historical maps and aerial photographs can help to distinguish different garden areas.

- Midsummer is the best time of year because the greatest number of clues are available to aid identification (flower, foliage and fruit)

- Measure trees, and record information under these headings:

   Tree number Give each plant a unique reference number and attach it to the tree with a stainless steel tag and wire. The number can then be matched with a name and other information on a database and plan.

   Grid position, or Global Positioning System (GPS) If possible, plot tree positions on a scale plan. Using an Ordnance Survey plan as a base map, global positioning devices enable the accurate plotting of each tree and shrub. A scale of 1:500 is ideal for tree and shrub collections, and 1:100 for herbaceous plants.

   Botanical name If the plant's genus and species cannot be easily identified, take a photograph and prepare a pressed specimen to assist later identification.

   Girth Girth is the trunk circumference in centimetres measured at 1.3m from the ground, which is helpful in determining age. Mean annual girth growth for most trees with a full crown is 2.5cm, which may increase to 7.5cm for faster-growing trees or be below 2.5cm for those that are smaller or slower-growing. See Forestry Commission Information Note, *Estimating the Age of Large and Veteran Trees in Britain* by John White, November 1988.

Comments

- Native trees should be recorded if they are in a prominent position or if native plants are an important aspect of the layout.

- Record tree stumps, since analysis can reveal the genus and species, and ring counting the age.

Information collected can be used in a variety of ways: to calculate age distribution, grouping by botanical classification or to produce maps showing surviving trees from different periods.

33. The measurement of girth on a mature tree.

ARCHIVAL RESEARCH

This is required to gather evidence of earlier plants and their design; documentary evidence can be particularly helpful:

- Nursery receipts may record important importations

- Garden records

- Propagation books

- Head Gardener's diary

- Private diary or correspondence of owner

- Photographs, drawings and paintings

- Descriptions from garden visitors

34. A Victorian gardener's diary and a contemporary nurseryman's description of the fruit house enabled the accurate restoration of a glasshouse structure, plant collection and maintenance techniques at Audley End.

Once a list of appropriate plants has been drawn up, the next stage is to understand how they were used and where they were planted. Photographs can record the growth and development of plants and how they were maintained. If period planting is to be undertaken it is important that those responsible for maintenance develop a specialist knowledge and understanding of gardening during the relevant period by extensive reading of contemporary horticultural books and periodicals. A number of useful references can be consulted to aid the dating of historic plant varieties and to provide modern equivalents to old plant names. These include:

John Harvey, *Early Gardening Catalogues*, 1972; *Early Nurserymen*, 1974; *The Availability of Hardy Plants in the late 19th Century*, 1988
Henry John Elwes and Augustine Henry, *The Trees of Great Britain and Ireland*, 1906
Maggie Campbell-Culver, *The Origin of Plants*, 2001
W. J. Bean, *Trees and Shrubs Hardy in the British Isles*, 1970
G. Stuart Thomas, *Perennial Garden Plants*, 2004

Design implications and maintenance

The qualities that distinguish a good garden from a dull or uninteresting one are invariably to do with its design. Most of the registered and best-known historic gardens and parks have evolved from a successful design, with gradual extensions or changes that have retained or enhanced character. However, as the case studies show (see Chapter 3), there is a close correlation between the design and character of a garden, and the staff and resources necessary for its proper upkeep and conservation. For example, the complex design of the Privy Garden at Hampton Court or the topiary parterres at Levens Hall dictate intricate, detailed, high standards at all times, and a large team of skilled staff. The more relaxed, naturalistic, less intricate landscape and woodland garden at Sheffield Park Garden in Sussex require fewer staff to understand and maintain its unique character, though they are equally skilled. Thus the prime decision must be to agree what standards and detail of maintenance should be set for a particular historic garden or park, consistent with its character, design, layout and the financial and staff resources available.

A case for maintenance priorities

The CMP is an invaluable tool to sort out priorities. Certain areas or features of a garden may become too much of a burden for owners, even with help, perhaps due to age or dwindling resources. It should be possible to establish priority or high maintenance areas, usually around the house, which receive the highest possible treatment, and then grade down to progressively lower levels of maintenance away from the house, or from functional or pleasure sites to possibly wilder zones, woodlands or copses where upkeep may be more infrequent. Complex features, such as rose gardens, parterres or walled gardens, could be rationalised and grassed.

The planned approach helps difficult decisions like these to be made and can result in satisfactory compromises. The total effect can still be very acceptable, and the owner will have objectives to follow rather than working against impossible odds and adopting 'crisis' management. In cases where a property is of historic importance, decisions like this must be reversible as under different circumstances features could be restored. Where structural planting such as hedges or trees is concerned, removal or change to the layout is another matter; it should only be done after serious consideration, as it can destroy the character and design of a garden.

Plans in context

It is important to keep abreast of new ideas, especially if plans need to meet external standards or funding requirements. Similarly, technical advice and information on matters such as climate change and codes of good farming practice do get updated from time to time.

Where funding is sought for a plan, it is important to ensure that the plan both meets the needs of the site and complies with the grant conditions. Updated advice and requirements will be available from the grant body. Those in charge of complex or costly

MANAGEMENT PLAN EXAMPLE

Divide the garden into separate character areas which are identified on a plan. For each, include the following information:

Description A brief outline of the current situation

Possible design (state period) based on historic references, e.g. documents, plans, photographs

Reconstruction/Restoration objectives What character it is proposed to conserve or create, and future use of area

Project work required Basic outline of works required to achieve objectives above. More detailed research and/or specifications would be required for construction in some areas. It is usual to compile a separate list outlining a 3–5 year programme of project work

Maintenance Maintenance specification. Note that where new planting is established there will be an increased maintenance requirement for 5–10 years, according to density of replanting

References If an area is described or seen in a particular photograph, article or picture

public sector projects will be expected to develop a business plan as well as the CMP; a good CMP will include elements of a business plan approach even for smaller-scale projects.

It can also be important to understand the policy context of individual grant schemes. For example, since the inception of plans there has been growing demand to demonstrate the public benefits of grant schemes, with extra emphasis on public access. A grant application to prepare a plan which did not include public access is now unlikely to attract support. Access plans and audience development plans find new solutions to get people involved with sites and to improve access. Agendas for grant schemes follow government directions; government policy can be tracked through the relevant departments and their websites.

Another role of the CMP is to influence others on the care and management needs of the site. Keeping abreast of local development frameworks and other regional government strategies could enable supportive links to be made between the site and wider policies such as those that help protect views and vistas.

Plans should be regularly updated and reviewed. As work programmes progress, individual projects can be signed off and new ones added on an annual basis. Some projects may slip or be stalled, and the work programme will need to be adjusted accordingly. Every five years, the whole CMP should be reviewed, involving all the team. Sometimes it is useful to appoint an independent assessor to appraise and measure success in implementing the plan, and to advise on problems. As part of this review, there should be a detailed inspection and condition report. Policies and objectives should be checked and updated or revised if needed. New information, for example, could necessitate revision of polices and objectives; wholesale revision of the plan could warrant a wider consultation.

THE EVOLUTION OF A GARDEN FEATURE OVER A FEW HUNDRED YEARS

35a. Late seventeenth century: an avenue of formal pleached limes backed by hedging.

35b. Early eighteenth century: the limes have been left to take on a natural form, and the hedge has grown out under the tree canopy.

35c. Late nineteenth century: further development of the tree canopy shades out the hedging.

35d. Mid twentieth century: trees have been lost from the avenue, and replanted with different species with a different form.

35e. Today: the original design intentions are now lost.

36. A high-maintenance garden: a wide range of vegetation types and a long season of high visual impact require a high labour input.

37. A low-maintenance landscape garden, of a type that developed from the 1970s. Shrubs and ground cover plants drastically reduced maintenance costs.

This chapter looks at the realities that owners have to face in managing historic parks and gardens in terms of money, people and visitors. It also looks at the cost of managing a garden, tax and taxation, grants and additional sources of funding, staff, equipment and volunteers (who are becoming particularly important at many sites). Many gardens and parks are either created for the public or are required to open to visitors to raise additional revenue income, so raise challenges in opening a successful tourist attraction.

THE ECONOMICS OF RUNNING A GARDEN

The successful large English country estate was created around the harmony of management between house, farm, park, woodland and country sports with additional income from rents, business enterprises and/or investments. The division of many of these estates during the twentieth century left many houses and gardens divorced from their funding. Subsequently, many estates opened their doors to visitors with the aim of turning the house and garden from an income consumer into an income generator. The success of such an enterprise lies in the production of a realistic financial appraisal (business plan) with definite financial constraints and defined objectives. Separate budgets for costs, staff time and management need to be calculated, and planned and quality cyclical maintenance and repair planned for.

Even in the case of well-managed places, balancing the books and ensuring long-term wellbeing is dependent upon a number of factors. These are illustrated in the Case Studies (see Section 3), and some are examined more closely here under the following headings:

- Cost
- Tax and taxation
- Grants and sources of funding

Cost

Analysis of garden expenses in some recent studies shows more or less the same result – namely, that labour costs can account for over 70 per cent of total expenditure, a proportion that also applies in general to landscape contracting and maintenance work. The following examples show details of annual expenditure for three gardens in different parts of the country, each employing several gardeners and contractors.

In each of the three examples (box, page 42), labour emerges as the greatest item of expenditure with machinery next (except for example 3, where plants bought in for bedding schemes reduce production costs which otherwise would be shown under glasshouse). The high costs of running a glasshouse in staffing, repairs and heating costs are of particular note. Management costs can be estimated from a proportion of the head gardener's, owner's and/or estate manager/land agent's time.

How to estimate annual maintenance costs According to a survey by the land agents Strutt & Parker in the late 1980s, 25 per cent of small gardens employ one full-time or a part-time gardener, along with considerable input from the family. Here is a quick method of estimating the total costs if the staffing costs are known:

Calculate total wages: average 70 per cent of total costs
Add 10 per cent minimum for overheads, etc.: 80 per cent
Divide by eight and multiply by ten to estimate the total annual costs. Example:

Total wages	£44,403.00
Add 10% overheads	£4,440.30
	£48,843.30
Divide by eight	£6,105.41
Multiply by ten	£61,054.13

Thus £61,054.13 is the estimated annual cost

There is always a need to examine measures that can be taken to reduce costs, especially labour; clearly, in all these figures the input of the owner and his/her family has to be taken into account. Administration time should not be underestimated, especially when properties employ staff or open to the public. Increasing legislation and controls mean that time for paperwork must be costed in to the running costs of the garden (see 'The legal framework', 1.5). As well as the annual cycle of maintenance, longer cycles of renewal should be assessed for shrubberies, avenues, water features and paths.

Seasonal patterns of work Garden maintenance shows peaks of work in spring and early summer and troughs in late autumn and winter; well-managed gardens will be equally busy during these quieter maintenance times undertaking development and cyclic regeneration projects. However, gardens with a high proportion of high-maintenance areas may need to take on extra seasonal labour in the summer to accommodate the additional maintenance demand and staff holidays.

GARDEN MAINTENANCE COSTS

EXAMPLE 1

Annual costs at January 2006 of a small garden on the North Downs with a pleasure ground, kitchen garden, orchard, two meadows and a wood (14 ha/37 acres).

Staff costs: 66 per cent of the total (this would come to 89 per cent if contractors were not used and work carried out 'in house'). Higher capital costs are due to garden set-up and development.

Staff
Total wages (inc. 25% on costs, NI and pension contributions)

1 Head Gardener and 1 Student	£47,074
Volunteers' expenses	£1,007
Protective clothing	£886
Total	£48,967

Contractors
(grass, meadows, hedges)	£19,034

Glasshouse
Services	£840
Maintenance	£244
Repairs	£954
Total	£2,038

Machinery
Repairs/servicing	£302
Fuel	£180
Depreciation	£169
Total	£651

Plants/bedding/bulbs	£2,552
Sundries, tools, fertilisers	£710

Grand total	**£73,972**

EXAMPLE 2

Annual costs at January 2006 of a large ornamental garden in the north-east of England with formal areas, extensive quarry garden, ornamental woodland areas and a small propagation facility.

Staff costs: 74.4 per cent of the total (85 per cent if contractors omitted). Very efficient operation, with Head Gardener doing much of the paperwork at home in free time.

Staff
Total wages (inc. 25% on costs, NI and pension contributions)

1 Head Gardener, 1 Senior Gardener, 1 Gardener and 1 Student	£78,872
Protective Clothing	£1,060
Total	£80,932

Contractors
(grass, meadows)	£13,698

Machinery
Repairs/servicing	£1,060
Fuel	£127
Depreciation	£1,986
Total	£3,173

Plants/bedding/bulbs, sundries, tools, fertilisers	£10,912
Tree and woodland work (ave.)	£1,500

Grand total	**£110,215**

EXAMPLE 3

Annual costs at January 2006 of a very large garden in the south-east with extensive bedding, walled garden, ornamental glasshouses, pleasure gardens and woodland walks.

Staff costs: 58.5 per cent of the total (76.6 per cent if contractors omitted).

Staff
Total wages (inc. 25% on costs, NI and pension contributions)

1 Head Gardener, 1 Deputy Head Gardener, 2 Senior Gardeners, 4 Gardeners	£176,490
Volunteers	£3,710
Protective clothing	£4,028
Total	£184,228

Contractors
(grass, meadows, hedges)	£74,200

Glasshouse
Services, maintenance, repairs	£2,650

Machinery
Repairs/servicing, fuel, depreciation	£9,222

Plants/bedding/bulbs	£20,140
Sundries, tools, fertilisers	£5,194
Labels	£318
Hard landscaping inc. fencing, path maintenance/repair	£8,692
Pest control	£212

Grand total	**£304,856**

Tax and taxation

Income Tax, and Value Added Tax (VAT) are the national transactional taxes to be discussed here, but remember that the property may be subject to local rating or other duties.

Charitable status Many properties are owned and operated by trusts with charitable objectives approved by the Inland Revenue. Charities are not necessarily exempt from all forms of taxation. There is no exemption from VAT or stamp duty, and profits generated from commercial activities are generally taxable in the same way as enterprises without charitable status. However, trades undertaken by a charity which form its primary purpose or which are carried on mainly by its beneficiaries are, within limits, exempt.

The calculation of profits from a charity's trading activities and other taxable income is on the same basis as a non-charitable enterprise. As well as deducting any direct costs solely related to the trade, a charity may also deduct a proportion of its overheads that are attributable to the trade.

Owners of heritage property may establish a charitable trust or set aside assets in a maintenance fund for conservation and management. Beyond the benevolent tax status, houses with charitable status are able to apply for Lottery funding and EU preservation grants. An accountant will be required to advise on the specific benefits and constraints of establishing a charitable trust.

Income Tax and trading Taxes on income include both income tax and corporation tax. Although income is not defined in law, it relates to profits derived from an identifiable source on an annual basis. The rates of tax and reliefs allowed are set annually by the government, depending on public spending requirements.

Commercial (trading) and non-commercial activities are treated differently for income tax purposes where historic parks and gardens are concerned, and the distinction is of considerable importance. If the house and garden is maintained wholly as a private residence, no income tax liabilities arise if there is no income, but relief cannot be claimed for the cost of upkeep.

Commercial ventures If owners are carrying on a trade of showing their house or garden to the public and it is 'managed on a commercial basis and with a view to the realisation of profits', then the profits will be liable to income tax. This phrase, however, has no statutory definition for tax purposes: the facts of each individual case will determine whether the Inland Revenue accepts that a property is being run on a 'commercial' basis.

Liability is based not on the full amount of admission fees and associated sales, but on the profit remaining after deduction of any allowable expenses. Owners will be entitled to claim any expenditure that they can demonstrate was incurred wholly, exclusively and necessarily for the purpose of the trade – i.e. on the upkeep of the house, its contents and garden. For tax purposes, the expenses that may be deducted and the ways in which relief is allowed for any loss differ according to the treatment of the source of income. Categories are discussed below.

Remember that income tax is a tax on income received and not on capital expenditure, which cannot be deducted for income tax purposes (though it may, of course, be relieved by other tax measures; see page 44).

The Inland Revenue may review various circumstances in considering whether the property is managed on a commercial basis, including:

- The extent to which the property is likely to attract visitors, having regard, among other things, to its historic, architectural and horticultural interest
- How much of the property is set aside as a show place
- If by appointment to groups and parties, this would usually have to be a substantial number, but must be compatible with the aim of making a profit from opening
- The amount of definite organisation and infrastructure set up for the attraction and reception of visitors – e.g. adequate advertising and publicity; provision of ticket offices, car parks, refreshments and guides; sale of postcards or guide books

A taxpayer must also demonstrate that opening to the public is done with a view to making a profit and not for substantially altruistic motives, or just to secure tax relief. Evidence may include budgets, cash flow forecasts or business plans demonstrating the objective.

The Inspector of Taxes is required to review the results periodically; just because entitlement to relief has been established in one year, it does not follow that it has been established for all time. Continuation in the face of prolonged losses would make it necessary to consider whether the enterprise was really being run on a commercial basis. Action that would, in general, be regarded as evidence of an attempt to attract more visitors towards profitability might include: substantial investment to provide improved or new visitor facilities, e.g. a new car park or refreshment rooms; a venture into new activities, or maybe major improvement to pathways or restoration of a landscape or garden. Tax advice should always be obtained before incurring substantial cost on the renovation of an old garden.

Receipts from special attractions, events, tea rooms, plant sales, brochures or souvenirs that can be associated with the showing of the property to the public will all be taken into account in determining whether the 'realisation of profits' test is satisfied.

Grants received used wholly or partly to meet expenses attributable to the opening of the property to the public are treated as additional income. Grants that relate to the improvement of access or other capital work should be offset against the capital expenditure to which they relate.

The costs of machinery or plant for maintenance, repair or management of gardens and landscape are not deductible when computing taxable profits, but they may qualify for capital allowances at a percentage of cost when arriving at an adjusted profit or loss.

Non-commercial ventures If a house or garden is not maintained wholly or mainly for making a profit, or if the owner simply collects fees from casual visitors, tax will still be due on profits. Deductions are normally allowed only for any additional expenses incurred as a result of opening – such as extra expenditure on public facilities and safety, making good damage done by the public, and so on. The general costs of running the property, e.g. overheads, repairs and day-to-day expenditure, would not be deductible.

Value Added Tax VAT is an indirect tax on the supply of goods and services based upon turnover, not on income or profits.

When goods or services are sold, VAT is added to the price: this is termed 'output tax'. When goods or services are bought, the purchaser has to pay VAT on the price: this is termed 'input tax'.

A VAT-registered individual deducts input tax due from output tax due and pays the difference, the 'added value', to HM Revenue & Customs. If input tax exceeds output tax, the excess payment is returned.

Taxable turnover is the total value of all business supplies in the UK or Isle of Man that are taxed at either the standard or zero rate.

Exempt supplies are business supplies that have no VAT charged on them. If an owner makes any exempt supplies of goods or services, they may not be able to reclaim all their input tax.

It is individuals and not their businesses that are registered for VAT. The registration covers all parts of their businesses, which may include others apart from that involving the property.

An owner needs to register if, at the end of any month, the total value of taxable supplies (goods and services) made in the past twelve months or less is more than the set VAT threshold (see www.inlandrevenue.gov.uk); or if at any time they expect the value of their taxable supplies to exceed the VAT threshold in the next thirty days alone.

When an owner opens to the public and is registered for VAT, either in respect of the house and garden or for some other business activity, he or she will be required to account for VAT output tax in respect of admission fees, catering and the selling of any goods or services which could be regarded as taxable supplies.

Chargeable admission of the public to historic houses or ancient monuments is always considered as a business activity for VAT purposes. The charge is usually standard-rated; possible exceptions are with admission by programme or where a donation is requested rather than an admission charge levied.

Donations are outside the scope of VAT, but for a payment to be accepted as a donation it would have to be entirely voluntary and the amount entirely at the donor's discretion.

The letting of parks and gardens for events, where no services or facilities are provided, or for use as film locations is exempt from VAT.

Capital taxation Capital Gains Tax arises for individuals and trusts when assets such as land and buildings are disposed of. For more than a hundred years, UK governments have offered fiscal and other measures such as tax reliefs to help preserve the nation's heritage. Tax reliefs recognise the value of heritage property of national importance remaining in private ownership and the desirability of its owners being encouraged to look after it, open it to the public and keep estates intact. Where owners can no longer do this, the tax regime helps ensure that the property goes to an appropriate conservation organisation. Heritage property tax reliefs are managed by the Inland Revenue's Capital Taxes Office.

Inheritance tax is triggered when someone dies or when assets are transferred to a discretionary trust or a company. Tax is payable if the assets are worth more than the current tax threshold (see www.inlandrevenue.gov.uk), so most historic parks and gardens are affected.

Exemption and relief schemes

- Property will be considered for exemption if it qualifies as being of outstanding scenic, historic or scientific interest – categories that include botanical, horticultural, silvicultural, arboricultural, agricultural, archaeological, physiographic and ecological features, including man-made landscapes. Buildings of outstanding historic or architectural interest can also qualify, as well as the amenity land around a building, and associated features and objects. Important historic parks and gardens are likely to qualify, and under more than one category. Existing national designations can offer a useful indication of whether a property may qualify, although assessment is not solely made on the basis of other designations. 'Outstanding' status also acts as a form of designation.

- Exemption from inheritance tax is also available where qualifying heritage assets are transferred into an approved trust fund established for the maintenance of a qualifying heritage building.

- Exemption is only offered with conditions. All applicants are required to make undertakings to maintain, repair and preserve the property and to provide reasonable public access; often specific undertakings relate to an individual property. For historic parks and gardens, it would be standard to require a CMP and this may involve restoration as well as repair and conservation work.

- Businesses, farms and woodlands also qualify for business property reliefs; parkland, and sometimes gardens and farm buildings, can be packaged as part of the agricultural holding. There are no conditions attached to such reliefs; and, for smaller properties with farm businesses, these are often more attractive than conditional exemption from inheritance tax. For large country houses and formal gardens, or sites with significant non-agricultural buildings, where the owners are interested in conservation and public access, the conditional exemption scheme offers more advantages.

- There are also schemes by which the state accepts heritage property in lieu of tax, in the same way as it does works of art.

- Some gifts or bequests of property to charities can be exempt from inheritance tax.

- Gifts to non-profit making conservation bodies may be exempt, so long as there is proven provision for maintenance and public benefit. Under the 'douceur' scheme, eligible heritage property can be sold to a conservation organisation, minimising the capital tax bill. This encourages transfer to protective ownership rather than sale on the open market.

Agencies such as English Heritage act as advisors to the Capital Taxes Office on the eligibility of property for these schemes, suitable organisations for schemes such as acceptance in lieu, the undertakings and ongoing monitoring of the legally binding conditional exemptions and maintenance funds. If undertakings are breached, the Capital Taxes Office will reclaim any taxes due.

The Inland Revenue website provides up-to-date information on taxation: www.inlandrevenue.gov.uk.

Grants and sources of funding

There is a range of sources of funding, both public and private, for the repair or restoration of historic buildings, structures and landscapes. It is worth considering these under three categories:

1. Those focused on the repair and restoration of historic buildings and landscapes

2. Those with a broad range of interests including historic buildings and landscapes

3. Those whose primary role has nothing to do with historic buildings or landscapes, but for which projects may qualify on other grounds

The first category is very competitive and usually over-subscribed. Applicants are usually expected to demonstrate public benefit – e.g. public access or education.

The second category covers a broad scope of interests and is therefore often the most difficult to prepare an application for. It is important to undertake research to ensure that an application to a trust can be properly tailored to meet that trust's current priorities. Many such trusts provide only relatively small grants to ensure that they support a broad range of projects.

The third category aims to fund projects such as those based on urban regeneration, the provision of workspace or community facilities. If the applicant is able to demonstrate that their project will fulfil such primary objectives, restoration of a building or garden can be achieved via such funding.

When to apply for grants? It is important to apply for grant aid prior to starting any work. Each source of funding has its own requirements, conditions and timetables, which must be known before planning a project in any detail. Once a potential funder has been identified, make contact and obtain up-to-date guidance and an application form. Ensure before applying that the project meets the stated criteria of the funding body and that the information they require is readily available. Each application should be tailored to a particular funding body's requirements and should include all of the supporting material requested. Poorly prepared or over-generalised applications are often the first to be disregarded, many charitable trusts having only limited administrative support. It is important to be both honest and realistic. Over-idealistic, poorly thought-out schemes will be found out, and charitable trusts may ask for the return of their funds if a project is unable to meet their conditions. Despite good planning, however, the unexpected can happen, and most grant-aiding bodies are understanding of changes to programme if they are kept informed and advised ahead of time.

The application Most applications will require some form of feasibility study. More complex projects will require a conservation plan, a business plan and a management plan for post-completion. If in doubt, seek guidance from the funding body.

Successful applications Once external funding has been gained, note any conditions that may apply – examples may be timetables for the drawing down of funds; getting prior approval for any change in the project; advertising and promoting the sponsorship in an agreed manner. Failure to follow conditions agreed with a funder may, at best, reduce the likelihood of future funding or, at worst, lead to the funds having to be returned.

A list of funding bodies can be found in the appendices.

GARDEN STAFF AND ORGANISATION

The success of any garden CMP will be determined by the number, the calibre and the organisation of the staff. They are responsible in the main for the gardens of historic sites; larger and much-visited 'heritage' places may also have estate and forestry personnel, property managers and recreational, catering or educational staff (see Case Studies, Part 3). The work covered by garden personnel may be supplemented by outside contractors, especially with regard to major restoration and development projects (see 'Contract laabour', page 53). Key to smooth running and job satisfaction are lines of communication and clear direction and organisation of all the groups involved.

Head gardener or garden manager

Part 1.2 (page 21) traces the gradual rise of the profession of head gardeners, which reached a peak in the Victorian and Edwardian eras when many achieved positions of eminence as senior and highly respected figures, often in total charge of the garden. Group photographs of gardening staff from these periods often show the workers with their tools beside them, while the head gardener wears or carries a bowler hat, a sign of authority and respect. The position of head gardener lost status in the last century, and only recently is this gradually being redressed. The expanding and increasingly active Professional Gardeners Guild (www.ppg.org.uk) is doing much to rebuild the authority and status of all professional gardeners.

Responsibilities and job description Terminology can be confusing. The title of head gardener can be used for a single-handed gardener looking after two acres with close supervision from the owner, or for someone with a team of staff looking after 90 acres of pleasure grounds, borders, lawns, walled garden, glasshouses, plant sales, woods and meadows.

The role and importance of head gardeners cannot be over-emphasised. 'For their conservation, gardens need constant replanning and renewal. They need firm and decisive management, and the criticism of advisors and others who come with a fresh eye and an understanding of the garden's history. But without the skill, dedication and the enthusiasm of head gardeners and their staffs nothing could be achieved. It is upon the calibre, training, and supply of gardeners that the future of our gardens overwhelmingly depends' (John Sales, former Chief Gardens Advisor to the National Trust, Symposium held by the Garden History Society and Ancient Monuments Society, 1984)

The head gardener's role is continuing to evolve, and today requires an increasingly diverse range of complex and technical duties and responsibilities. These may need emphasis and, at times, clarification. A clear and comprehensive job description should be an important part of the terms of employment.

A garden with three or more horticultural staff will require personnel with a range of skills, experience and qualifications. In gardens where horticultural detail and high-quality workmanship

39. Victorian and Edwardian gardens were often maintained by a large experienced staff led by a Head Gardener.

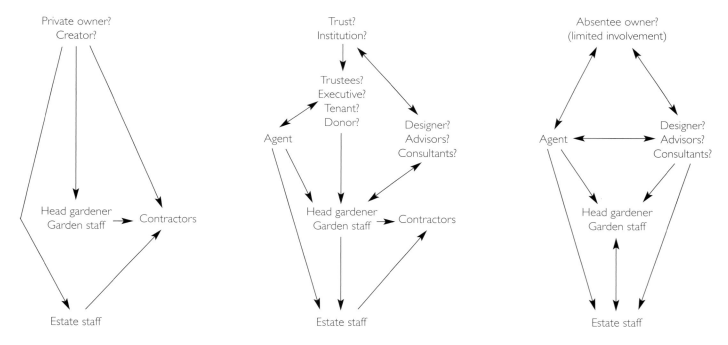

40. The position of the head gardener, and his or her authority in a garden organisation, depends upon the type of place and who owns or runs it. This figure shows three very different situations.

1. Typical of many establishments in the past, with a close and autocratic line of communication from the owner to the head gardener, who in his turn was a supremo for the rest of the staff.

2. Likely situation today, where a trust or organisation has taken over the garden and far more people have a say in how it is run. The head gardener may be somewhere in the middle of the network, with the added input of consultants, other experts and contractors.

3. Also more prevalent today, with new owners or the heirs of a once-committed family not having a really close interest but still wanting the garden to be managed effectively. A head gardener with initiative and confidence may assume considerable authority in some of these situations.

EXAMPLES OF JOB TITLES, GARDEN STAFF ROLES, RESPONSIBILITIES, SKILLS AND QUALIFICATIONS

JOB TITLE	QUALIFICATIONS AND EXPERIENCE	SKILLS	RESPONSIBILITIES
Head Gardener/ Garden Curator/ Garden Manager	M.Hort. (RHS), Degree, Botanic Garden Diploma, HND, or equivalents + 7 years' appropriate experience, including the effective management of a garden	Specialist technical skills and ability. Proven management and policy-making ability. Ability to curate a historic garden and its plant collections. Excellent communicator. Ability to manage and deliver garden projects.	Management, policy, budgeting for large workforce, either in a large or complex garden/estate. High-level quality control and strategic planning and site promotion. Managing contracts, contractors and staff. Curation of garden and its plant collections
Garden Supervisor/ Garden Foreman	NVQ Level 2 + 5 years' appropriate experience, or NVQ Level 3/ND + 4 years' appropriate experience, or HND + 3 years' appropriate experience, or Degree + 3 years' appropriate experience, or Botanic Garden Diploma + 3 years' appropriate experience	Proven specialist technical skills with supervisory and management ability. Ability to manage a small garden with the minimum of supervision or parts of a large garden.	Either has full responsibility for a small or singleton site or is a Deputy to a Garden Curator. Responsible for the day-to-day running of the site and supervision of staff, contractors and volunteers
Gardener (can be graded with level of experience and responsibility)	NVQ Level 2 + 3 years' experience, or ND/NVQ Level 3 + 3 years' experience, or HND + 1 year's experience	Skilled Craft Gardener skills but usually with one or more specialisms as required on site. Ability to maintain defined garden areas with minimum of supervision.	Basic supervision and training of Trainees, Modern Apprentices and Gardeners. Ability to lead small teams of junior staff and volunteers under guidance of line manager
	NVQ Level 2 or equivalent + 1 year's experience. Enthusiasm and aptitude for gardening	Basic horticultural ability including machinery	Supervision of Volunteers and Trainees under guidance by higher management
Graduate Gardener Trainee	Higher-level qualification + 1 year's experience. Enthusiasm and aptitude for gardening	Good technical knowledge but requiring practice to develop skill base	No supervisory responsibility
Undergraduate Gardener Trainee	Work experience as part of college sandwich course. Enthusiasm and aptitude for gardening	Skills development with knowledge of basic gardening tasks and machinery usage	No supervisory responsibility
Modern Apprentice	4 GCSEs at Grade 'C' or above. Enthusiasm for gardening	Skills development	No supervisory responsibility

NVQ: National Vocational Qualification
HND: Higher National Diploma
ND: National Diploma

HEAD GARDENER'S JOB DESCRIPTION

This could include:

- Medium- and long-term strategic planning of the garden, restoration plans, maintenance, interpretation and presentation to the public

- Project research undertaken as part of the garden's curation, development and presentation

- Writing of specifications, preparing contracts and tenders

- Supervision of all garden staff and contractors on site including: day-to-day work programmes and work schedules including standards; site representative for all garden-based contractors and contracts, and project manager for garden-specific contract works outside the remit of a regional landscape manager

- Overseeing and monitoring of all garden staff personnel issues, including appraisals and training requirements

- Control of garden maintenance budget and its spend, either through tender, account, draft order or credit card purchase

- Establishment of the garden's curatorial programmes including plant collection records, plant labelling, national plant collection authorisation and registration; production and management of all garden-based risk assessments, including reviews and modifications and their implementation

- Responsibility for all garden purchases, including plants, tools, machinery, health and safety equipment and associated materials

- Responsibility for the supervision of health and safety in the garden

- Production and maintenance of all paper and computer records

- Development of relationships with interested groups and societies and links with other beneficial organisations, including the running of talks and walks around the garden

- Line management supervision of volunteers

Some or all of these may also involve, or be an important responsibility of, a garden curator or manager. Some sites may require additional items such as estate management.

are important, the head gardener's role needs to be filled with an appropriately experienced and qualified person. In small gardens the owner, with sufficient time and experience, can take on this role; contractors should have appropriate supervision by trained and experienced eyes if high standards are sought. As one year represents a single cycle of horticultural activity, it is important to try and retain experienced staff for a minimum of five years to ensure continuity. Gardens with good staff retention rates often provide a competitive employment package of a pleasant and professional working environment with good pay and conditions. Pensions and health insurance are on offer from some employers.

Owners or managers considering new planting design, major restorations or other new works may need to a employ garden designers or landscape architects; clarification of their roles and responsibilities at an early stage is important as they will require full professional fees. Garden designers' expertise lies in planting design and small-scale landscaping, whereas landscape architects are qualified to design and manage projects of any size. Contact the Landscape Institute to find landscape architects or managers, or the Society of Garden Designers for advice and a list of registered practices. If design work is required, clients should make themselves familiar with a practice's work; satisfied former clients are often happy to show off work and can provide references.

It is worth asking a shortlist of suitable practices to tender for the work, so that a selection can be made on both price and detail. Landscape consultants should be qualified, with a proven track record, be easy to work with and able and willing to deliver what is wanted of them. It is important to clarify who is supervising and agreeing the consultant's work – is it the owner, estate manager or head gardener? Confusion, upset and additional expense can result from lack of clarity.

Some owners, perhaps with less experience or time, may wish to employ a landscape manager, garden advisor or experienced horticulturist to provide strategic advice and guidance to assist in the management of the garden and garden staff or contractors.

Students and trainees

There is a great tradition in England of employing horticultural students in both private and public gardens. Students, trainees or apprentices may be considered by some as unskilled, cheap labour – but they should be seen as an investment in the future. The investment of time, money and expertise can provide a worthwhile return. Even the most conscientious student will need to be shown how to undertake practical tasks and will need time to get up to the speed and proficiency of a professional.

Formerly, students wishing to undertake a further or higher education course were advised, or even required, to undertake a

STAGES FOR THE APPOINTMENT OF A LANDSCAPE CONSULTANT
from The Landscape Institute

PRELIMINARY SERVICES

Work Stage A: Inception

Work Stage B: Feasibility

STANDARD SERVICES

Work Stage C: Outline Proposals

Work Stage D: Sketch Scheme Proposals

Work Stage E: Detailed Proposals

Work Stage F: Production Information

Work Stage G: Bills of Quantities

Work Stage H: Tender Action

Work Stage J: Contract Preparation

Work Stage K: Operations on Site

Work Stage L: Completion

year or two of work experience prior to their course. This tested a potential student's suitability, resulting in more experienced students and lower drop-out rates from courses. Many further and higher courses longer than a year incorporated twelve months of work experience ('sandwich courses'). Regretfully, in line with other professions, pre-college work experience has now largely disappeared, and the work experience 'meat' in the middle of the sandwich course has either vanished or in some cases shrunk to just a few months in the summer. Gardens that take on students or recent graduates for their first work experience should be applauded for playing an important role in providing the contemporary 'journeyman' experience. Advice on qualifications can be found on the Lantra website (www.lantra.co.uk).

More opportunities are opening up for municipal and private gardens to take on apprentices, providing a chance for gardens to train up their own skilled gardeners on site, with the support of a specialist training establishment or local college. Small to medium private gardens, with perhaps an insufficient range of opportunities to train apprentices, could join together to share an apprentice. Advice on taking on students, trainees or apprentices may be sought from local horticultural colleges.

Volunteers

Volunteers are becoming increasingly important in supporting the maintenance of many large gardens. They add value to a garden's activities – by involving the wider community; by providing work experience for those considering horticulture as a career; and by undertaking garden work that otherwise would not be possible within staffing resources. Volunteers should not be considered as replacements for staff, but additions that can add value to the work of the paid team. Successful volunteer schemes provide an opportunity for more junior staff to show off their expertise and gain their first supervisory experience.

Volunteer work Volunteers can assist with routine garden maintenance tasks, site clearing, countryside maintenance, educational and group visits, garden stewarding and (subject to environmental health guidelines) the provision of teas and refreshments where a commercial concern would not be profitable. Volunteer schemes are successful when the volunteer's aspirations and technical and physical capabilities are matched with the garden needs; if this is not the case, either side may become dissatisfied. Volunteers who are looking for social benefits and a little light gardening are well suited to dead-heading, edging and light weeding. Volunteers who may be considering horticulture as a career will be more willing and able to carry out strenuous activity, such as digging, carting compost, landscaping and planting.

It is important to identify volunteers' skills and personal objectives during the recruitment process so that their suitability can be judged and matched to a potential work programme. They could be asked to check a list of the tasks available and mark those they are interested in undertaking, and to explain why they wish to volunteer. For a volunteer scheme to work, both sides need to benefit from the transaction: the volunteer needs to achieve

41. A garden can provide a wide range of opportunities for education for learners of all ages.

personal gain, and the garden should see a benefit over and above the work put in by staff to administer and supervise the scheme. Effective organisation and co-ordination is essential: at Kenwood a volunteer group, called the Heath Hands, have their own co-ordinator, who recruits and organises them to arrive for regular work parties on days agreed in advance with the head gardener. Garden staff then join the large work party, supervising and guiding the work. Eltham Palace has a wide range of volunteers – from pensioners who are keen gardeners who help to keep the rose gardens in prestige order and look after the glasshouses, to career changers and those on government unemployment schemes who assist the staff with almost all of the seasonal garden work. At Down House volunteers help maintain the glasshouse and kitchen garden, have been trained as guides and act as stewards in the glasshouse (see Case Study, page 259).

Great care must be taken with programming the garden's maintenance and volunteer input. At different times of year, certain jobs will dominate the horticultural calendar – weeding in summer, planting in spring and autumn, digging in winter – which sometimes makes it difficult to achieve a balance between the cultural needs of the garden and the morale of the volunteers (and staff!). Good communication should resolves these issues. To retain harmony among staff and volunteer teams, dominant personalities must not be allowed to cherry-pick the best jobs. Prior to joining, volunteers should be made aware of what they are likely to be asked to do, and advised against joining up if they are unwilling to fit in with the organised programme.

EXAMPLE OF A CONCISE MAINTENANCE SCHEDULE

AREA	OPERATIONS	TIME OF YEAR	PRIORITY
Front entrance shrubbery	Remove fallen laburnum and dead conifer. Prune some shrubs	January–early March	High
Holly hedge	Systemic weedkiller to control perennial weeds followed by bark mulch and fertiliser	February	Low
Parkland	Some trimming needed of existing trees and removal of ties/stakes of newly established trees	January–February	Low
Wild garden	Generally in reasonable condition but still a few roses to prune before bulbs emerge	January	Moderate
Tennis courts	Cut holly hedges. Cut Leyland hedges to agreed height. Use new power hedge cutter	January–March	Moderate
Pool garden	Thoroughly clean out and replant pool. Mulch beds with bark fibre	March–April	Moderate

Volunteer recruitment and employer responsibilities Large organisations such as the National Trust and English Heritage advertise for volunteers through promotional literature and magazines. Local and national press are usually keen allies in promoting what is always an interesting human heritage story. Local recruitment can also be bolstered via lectures and talks to local groups and societies and at the end of guided garden tours.

Volunteers are best considered as inexperienced staff when undertaking risk assessments. Even those who are keen experienced amateur gardeners need to be advised of safe ways of working to protect themselves and others. Volunteers can undertake any task in a garden as long as they are qualified, experienced and capable of doing it; where there is any doubt, it is better to be cautious. Some gardens provide specialist training, followed by proficiency tests, to enable volunteers to carry out specific tasks or use specific equipment such as brush-cutters or tractors. Volunteers need to purchase or be provided with appropriate personal protective equipment, such as wet weather clothing, overalls and steel toe-capped boots.

Gardens are sometimes approached by schools requesting work experience for pupils considering gardening as a career. This should be encouraged, but the garden's management should seek advice from the school – garden staff who come into contact with young people may have to have police checks on their suitability. Tasks undertaken by young people should be risk-assessed to prevent accidents. It is important to remember that youngsters are not used to a working environment, and may inadvertently put themselves at risk if not properly guided.

Garden owners must check with their insurers to make sure that they are covered for personal and any other liabilities that may arise from taking on volunteers.

Rewarding volunteers Volunteer work should be recognised and rewarded: this will aid recruitment and bolster morale. At English Heritage, volunteers committing themselves to more than 30 days work a year receive free membership of English Heritage, which comes with a magazine and free entry to over 400 properties. Travel costs and out-of-pocket expenses are reimbursed, and coffee and tea facilities provided. Many gardens organise group visits for volunteers to another property or Christmas parties – these are small but important gestures of thanks to hard-working volunteers.

Determining and establishing staffing levels

Annual maintenance cycles and operations should be carefully scrutinised to enable useful management judgements to be made. Such investigations result in a better understanding of the maintenance operations and may also bring efficiency savings.

Owner-occupiers and single-handed gardeners The simplest method is to draw up a basic list of all the main areas of the garden or grounds to be maintained, then add additional jobs such as replanting, winter pruning and any new works, such as patio laying or rock garden construction. Agree on the standards of upkeep that are realistic and/or acceptable. For each area or task listed, produce an estimate of the time anticipated to get through

WORK STUDY SYSTEM

STAGE I: AREA MEASUREMENT

All areas to be maintained, such as lawns, plant borders, shrub areas, hedges, drives and paths, are measured as carefully as possible using tapes. This sort of work can easily be done by vacation students or school leavers, given adequate instructions and some supervision. The measurements may be of extensive areas of grounds and gardens, and can be related to an existing plan by a coding or colour key system. Below is a working example.

AREA MEASUREMENT BY TYPE OF VEGETATION

Description	Area (sq m)	%age of total area
Annual bedding	175	0.89
Shrubs	790	4.02
Perennials	271	1.38
Mixed borders	1,127	5.74
Ground cover	65	0.33
Rose borders	12	0.06
Close-mown grass	11,169	56.88
Rough grass	4,642	23.64
Hedges (in metres)	616	3.14
Hard areas	770	3.92

STAGE II: WORK MEASUREMENT

Having determined the actual areas to be maintained, it is now necessary to produce average figures for the time taken to carry out all the essential operations involved in their upkeep. These figures can be produced in two ways:

1. Obtain Standard Minute Values (SMVs) from publications such as Spons Landscape and External Work Price Book (published annually). A factor can be built in for stoppages due to breakdown or bad weather or for the time taken to repair equipment or transport it from one site to another. It is important to relate the work being measured to acceptable standards achieved. SMVs can only be used as a rough guide, as the quality of work will depend on the experience and supervision of the staff, and the speed on their capability and motivation. Poor access to garden areas can more than double the SMVs for some jobs, with materials and equipment having to be carted large distances by wheelbarrow rather than tractor. Specialist computer software packages are available for work measurement and for a range of landscape maintenance monitoring and analysis; professional organisations will be able to advise on the relative value of individual products.

2. Simpler but less accurate is to use time sheets to estimate the time involved in most of the major operations. Often, however, smaller but time-consuming tasks such as glasshouse work tend to be lumped under one general heading, so that specific analysis becomes difficult. 'Tidying up' is another lumped figure, or it may be included in the heading 'All other' work. Much depends on how time sheets are filled in and the time staff have to do this.

STAGE III: ESTABLISHING STAFFING LEVELS

Having assessed how much is to be maintained, and how long the various tasks should take per unit area, it is now possible to calculate staffing levels in terms of the number of hours needed to maintain all such areas and components, provided agreed standards of maintenance have been built in to the work measurement exercise.

all the jobs in the draft schedule. Estimate any additional help needed to complete the tasks satisfactorily.

Try out this schedule for one full season. If the estimates prove moderately accurate, this is a reassurance that the staffing level is about right. If, however, the schedule goes badly adrift, perhaps after a second season, with many of the target jobs uncompleted, then several things can be done:

- Accept the inevitable and alter the standards, accepting a lower one if necessary, devise different levels of maintenance or consider additional staffing

- Look closely again at the design of the garden and the methods used to look after modifications to the design and layout; if necessary, undertake a more drastic rationalisation

- Introduce more mechanisation and aids such as mulches, which in combination with a rationalisation of work may bring about really effective results

- Adjust the work programme – for instance, if most of the hedge-cutting and pruning can be done in the winter, this eases the pressure on the peak summer period

Gardens with two or three full-time staff A schedule of maintenance tasks and related work should be drawn up for the full calendar year, involving the head gardener, the employer and clerical staff, if any. It should naturally be based on existing or agreed standards of upkeep.

The box (opposite page, above) gives one example of a maintenance schedule containing a limited amount of information. More precise details could be given, but much depends on who is to use the schedule and the time available to prepare it. All sorts of variations on such a schedule are possible to suit the garden and the type of organisation.

Weekly time sheets should be kept as a matter of routine, since the information gained from them can be extremely useful in many ways. For instance, the actual times taken for most jobs should be shown to help with work schedules and staffing levels, but the integrity and degree of accuracy set down in the time sheets will depend on the attitudes and the consistency of the staff responsible for filling them in.

There should be a column or heading on the time sheet for loss of work due to adverse weather, and a considerable amount of time is bound to be spent in general or miscellaneous duties and tidying up; holidays and sick leave should also be considered.

Gardens, parks and estates employing five or more people It is usually a matter of routine – and indeed a necessity today, certainly for contractors and local authority parks using directly employed labour – for accurate records to be kept of many aspects

ESTIMATES OF AVERAGE ANNUAL LABOUR REQUIREMENTS
From Parker and Wright, *Landscape Techniques*, ed. A. E. Weddle, 1979

Landscape/Garden category	*Approx. hours per year Small areas*	*Approx. hours per year Extensive areas*
1. **Fence lines** Annual weed spray and rotary cut long grass	3h/100m	11/1000m
2. **Hedges** Formal hedge cut four times a year, e.g. privet:		
1.5 m high (approx. 5 ft)	8h/10m	50h/100m
2.5 m high (approx. 8 ft)	13h/10m	95h/100m
Hedge cut once a year, e.g. beech:		
1.5 m high	2h/10m	18h/100m
2.5 m high	4h/10m	30h/100m
3. **Large grass areas** Playing fields, mown up to once a week (24 cuts/year) with five-unit tractor-trailed gang mower (excluding travelling to and from site)	up to 0.5 ha 24h/ha	over 1 ha 14h/ha
Rough grass cut with a tractor mounted flail four times a year	20h/ha	17h/ha
4. **Lawns and grass banks** Large lawns cut up to once a week with a 900mm cylinder mower	11h/100m²	34h/1000m²
As above with cuttings boxed off	13h/100m²	45h/1000m²
Smaller lawns cut up to once a week with a 500mm cylinder mower	14h/100m²	70h/1000m²
As above with cuttings boxed off	17h/100m²	80h/1000m²
Rough grass cut up to once a month with a hand-propelled rotary mower up to 500mm	4h/100m²	25h/1000m²
Steep banks cut with a small rotary mower up to once a month	8h/100m²	50h/1000m²

NOTE The hours shown for the smaller quantities are for isolated amounts and reflect additional time to prepare and put away equipment and tools for small amounts of work.

	Approx. hours per year
5. **Shrub borders** Light digging in winter and mulched	15h/1000m²
Light digging in winter and hand-hoed	33h/100m²
6. **Ground cover** (established) Summer hand-weeding, clip and tidy in winter	8h/100m²
7. **Annual bedding** Spring and autumn replanting with hand-hoeing in summer (excludes provision of plants)	80h/100m²
8. **Amenity woodland** (established; excluding major felling)	up to 50h/ha
Newly planted (or tree screens)	up to 50–100h/ha
9. **Extensive parkland with woodland** Without grazing animals	90h/ha (up to 20 ha/person)
With grazing animals (excluding care of animals)	50h/ha
10. **Road verges** (grass cutting) Rural roads (four cuts per year with tractor-mounted flail)	12h/km of road (mainly summer work up to 80km/person)
Urban roads (twelve cuts per year with pedestrian mower)	75h (up to 15km/person)

of maintenance and management work. Where budgets are critical and economies are being attempted, or where a new manager is taking over responsibility for a garden, a system of work study may prove useful. This sort of exercise, perhaps in simplified form, is worth the consideration of large privately owned establishments.

The calculated staffing level figures (see box, opposite) are used to draw up weekly or monthly schedules of work that allow for agreed standards to be met within the times set. A great deal of useful management information can be extracted and applied from this data – for example, in spreading seasonal workloads. A summer peak is a very decided characteristic of all garden maintenance work, mainly due to vigorous vegetative growth. The size and gradient of the peak depends on the design and character of the garden or site and the diversity of the components contained in it, and also on the effectiveness of the organisation of maintenance staff. There are several ways of easing this summer pressure:

1. *Use part-time staff* at peak times. It is often the case that if there are sufficient staff to cope with the summer workload, there may be too many for the winter months. Try to find winter work, such as woodland felling, thinning or replanting, landscaping and border renovation. Using more casuals from May to September may bring a saving in the payroll as well as help to cope with the summer peak. This would also enable full-time staff to take their holidays at this time of year. Seasonal staff, however, will need training and higher supervision, a management investment that is lost when they leave.

2. *Allow more overtime* by regular staff in peak periods. This is not a solution usually favoured by gardening staff, who have their own lives to lead and may feel the extra money is not worth the loss of their leisure time. Such overtime usually provides at most an average 10 per cent over normal working hours. Staff working excessive hours are less productive, and care should be taken that they do not work beyond what is legally permitted. Some gardens with full-time staff require longer hours in the summer as a condition of employment, with staff paid a monthly salary averaged across the year.

3. *Apply more mechanisation* and labour-saving techniques to the summer tasks.

4. *Mulch beds* in the late winter or early spring (but not in snow or frost). This can save money and many hours of hand-weeding in the late spring and summer.

5. *Concentrate tasks in the winter* to save time. It is very worthwhile approach, even for the single-handed gardener, to do as many jobs as possible in the quieter winter months, such as hedge-cutting, woodland or shrubbery work. In a large and intensive garden, winter troughs in maintenance provide an opportunity to renovate garden areas on a cyclic basis, to prevent perennial and shrub plantings from becoming senescent and avoid the need for major restorations. Gardens on heavy, silty and clay soils will need regular attention to drainage systems, which may also be carried out at this time. Fencing, forestry, repairs

to gates, seats and equipment are all obvious examples of winter tasks.

6. *Evaluate glasshouse use* Glasshouse work for raising annuals, pot plants and young plants is also winter work, but a point should be made here about glasshouse maintenance and the hours involved. When the cost of raising bedding plants and decorative half-hardy plants is considered, it is often cheaper to buy them in from a commercial supplier. On the other hand, owners and managers must realise that propagation and glasshouse work is of great importance to most gardeners and can contribute to job satisfaction, which in turn can contribute to increased productivity. To close down glasshouse units on economy grounds alone may not be justified if the savings achieved are at the expense of staff motivation. This is a delicate area, yet so often in large gardens ranges of once-productive glasshouses are now too expensive to run and maintain; new roles have to be found for them. An efficient compromise would utilise glasshouses to propagate, grow on and overwinter plants that are difficult to grow or obtain, or expensive to buy. This can also add to the character and attraction of the garden.

Contract labour: advantages As a complete or partial alternative to all these labour problems, it is possible to have a garden or part of it maintained by contract using a garden or landscape contractor. Contractors can be used to carry out all work or a proportion of the work on a regular basis, or as ad hoc support during particularly busy periods, or for occasional one-off specialist work.

- No administrative responsibilities connected with staff employment such as wages, NI, PAYE tax, sickness benefit

- No machinery or general equipment supply or maintenance

- The contractor has primary responsibility for the health and safety of his staff, including the preparation of a health and safety policy and of risk assessments. Owners and managers still have a duty of care for anyone on their site, and need to ensure that work practices are sensible, that the site is not unsafe and that working practices do not constitute a hazard.

- No training responsibility, although for sites with particular features of interest a joint approach to staff training is generally in the best interests of all involved.

- Flexibility on staffing levels. Contractors often have a range of work for different clients and are better able to target resources where and when required, such as undertaking landscaping or planting work off-site during a quiet period.

- Flexibility on machinery. Contractors undertaking a wide range of work are often able to maintain a much greater range of machinery than could be justified by a single garden or estate. They are also more likely to be able to keep machines fully employed over several sites and thus minimise their unit costs.

- 'Down time' savings. Contractors are paid on the satisfactory completion of a task, whereas directly employed staff are paid for being at work despite, say, poor weather conditions that prevent a job being completed.

- 'Poor work' savings. Contractors are paid only once, on satisfactory completion of a task. If staff do poor work which needs re-doing, the cost is doubled.
- Peak work management. Contractors may be used alongside or in addition to employed staff to help manage work at peak times, such as grass-cutting and weeding in spring and summer.
- Site start-up. On new sites it is not immediately clear what the maintenance or ideal staffing requirements will be. A contractor has the flexibility to increase or decrease staff as necessary for a year or two until the full management implications are understood. Note that regulations may require that if work is taken 'in house' following such an arrangement the staff used on the contract must be recruited (Transfer of Undertakings [Protection of Employment] Regulations 1981 [TUPE], section 5).
- Specialist work. It is often an advantage to employ specialist contractors to undertaken one-off or irregular work such as tree surgery, drainage, installation of sprinkler systems, semi-mature tree planting, chemical control, etc.

Contract labour: disadvantages These are usually a fault of management rather than the contract system itself.

- 'Contractors have no interest in doing the job properly.' This is certainly the case with a minority of 'cowboys', but the majority of well-established, reputable contractors have a vested interest in doing the job properly – because unless they do there is no payment! Problems with bad workmanship are most likely to occur when the client is not completely clear at the beginning about what is required and when there is insufficient supervision by both the contractor's manager and the client. Lack of proper instruction and supervision is just as likely to result in bad work from directly employed staff.
- 'Contractors have no long-term interest in the site.' This may occasionally be the case but, more often than not, contracts are for a period of 3–5 years (or longer, particularly with maintenance) and the contractor is looking to establish a long-term relationship with the site. Even with one-off jobs, most reputable contractors will always consider the possibility of future work that results from a satisfied client, and the good publicity.
- 'Contractors are never there when you want them.' Again, this may be true if a permanent workforce is not required on the site – for example, if the contractor only undertakes grass-cutting this may be done by a mobile gang who spend one day per week at the site. However, with the exception of genuine emergencies, this is a fault of client management in not understanding what the site requirements are or not properly anticipating work requirements. If contractors are employed to empty litter bins and pick up rubbish every day in a park before it opens at 8 a.m., by the afternoon bins may be overflowing

and the park looking a mess. This is not the fault of the contractors, but of the park manager who has failed to anticipate that every lunchtime the park is full of office-workers eating their lunches. The answer is either to change the schedule so that the job is done immediately after lunch, or have the contractors visit twice a day.

- 'Contractors' staff are not properly trained or paid to do a good job.' Once again, this is the fault of client management, who should specify exactly what standards are required, immediately challenge unsatisfactory work and replace poorly performing contractors.

Choosing a contractor There are a wide range of garden, landscape and grounds maintenance contractors throughout the country ranging in size from single-person operations to large organisations employing hundreds of staff. They vary widely in what work can be undertaken – some stick solely to maintenance, others to landscaping, while many will undertaken a full range of work from initial construction and planting of gardens and landscapes through to regular maintenance. Other firms, usually small or medium-sized, specialise in high-quality horticultural work.

It is always advisable to seek references from satisfied customers. The British Association of Landscape Industries (BALI) maintains a list of members who are expected to maintain certain standards, although these tend to be firms of middle and larger size which may not be suitable for small jobs. Consideration should be given to the size of firms approached, and the amount of work they already undertake. If the work in question is large and wide-ranging it is clearly necessary to engage a firm with the capacity to undertake it within the time scales required, whereas smaller parcels of work may best be dealt with by smaller companies. The use of firms that are based nearby or have a branch close by is advantageous for obvious reasons, but not practicable for every site.

Consider the overall value of the work being tendered in comparison to the amount and spread of work contractors have in your area, particularly for long-term maintenance contracts. If the parcel of work is small and nearby contracts are much larger, they may be given priority over resources – clear guarantees should be sought to prevent this. Additionally, if a contractor is not locally based but is able to offer a competitive price because it has a large contract nearby, it is important to investigate the stability and length of tenure for the larger contract. If the large contract finishes other local contracts may become unviable, and the contractor may pull out or his service levels may drop.

Types of contract If a contractor is asked to undertake a piece of work it is a contract under law, even if it is only verbal. For small, simple jobs and with contractors where good working relationships have been established, this may be a perfectly adequate means of getting work done. Unless unavoidable, work should not proceed on the basis of an estimate, which is not a firm price and could increase; always get a quotation, which is a firm price.

For larger amounts of work, for complicated jobs and always for work involving the expenditure of public funds, agreements must be properly documented. This may be as simple as a quotation from the contractor stating exactly what he will do, when it will be done and how much it will cost, and a letter from the client accepting the quotation and asking the contractor to start. The client may want to invite several contractors to bid for the work; in this case it is usual for a specification to be produced. For very large jobs or long-term maintenance contracts, the procedure is much the same, although the paperwork is likely to be more complicated. For all contracts involving the use of public funds there are rules regulating the way in which tenders are invited, opened and awarded. These vary between organisations but will all be aimed at ensuring that public funds are spent wisely, fairly and transparently.

Specifications, whether for large or small jobs, should be comprehensive and clear. Ensure that the details are exactly what is wanted, and include any particular methods which must or must not be used, any known or potential problems, any restrictions and what timescales are required. It is in no one's interests to produce an unclear specification – it is unfair to contractors who will all tender on a slightly different basis and may be forced to carry out work they had not anticipated; and it is bad for the client, who will not get the work he expected and may have a series of arguments over what work is to be done.

A number of different types of contract may be employed for maintenance work. They are not mutually exclusive and a contract may be a combination of more than one type.

- **Lump sum** A set amount of work is to be carried out and contractors tender a single figure for doing it. This type of contract is very useful for one-off blocks of works which are clearly defined, such as tree surgery, drainage, tree planting, etc.

- **Per occasion** A set amount of work (or several distinct set amounts) is to be carried out and the contractor tenders a figure for each occasion. This type of contract can be used for regular defined blocks of maintenance work such as grass-cutting, hedge-trimming, bed-weeding, etc. Its disadvantage is that the costs will vary depending on the weather conditions of any year (and therefore the amount of times the work is ordered). It also requires a higher level of administration.

- **Performance** A standard is to be maintained for different features and the contractor tenders a figure to maintain that standard for a set period, usually a year. For example, a defined area of fine grass is to be maintained using a cylinder mower with the height of cut set at 15mm, so that the maximum height of the grass does not exceed 25mm, with the cuttings removed on each occasion. Like the 'per occasion' type, this kind of contract can be used for regular defined blocks of maintenance work, such as grass-cutting, hedge-trimming, bed-weeding, etc., with the advantage that the client has a known annual price.

- **Schedule of Rates** Rather than a specification, the contractor is presented with a Schedule of Rates, a list of all the operations likely to be used on the site, often broken down into component parts and defined on a per item or per $100\text{m}/\text{m}^2$ basis. The contractor prices individual items and these prices remain in force for the life of the contract. A Schedule of Rates can be very flexible, allowing a wide range of different operations to be undertaken as and when necessary. Commercially prepared and costed schedules are available.

- **Daywork** Contractors are asked to submit hourly rates for different grades of staff. Staff time can then be ordered as and when required.

Contract periods Most maintenance contracts are for 3–5 years, although 5–10 year contracts are now becoming more common. In theory there is no maximum period for a contract, but the longer the timescale the more important it is to have a contract constructed with enough flexibility to adapt to changing circumstances and with sufficient safety clauses for the client to ensure proper compliance with standards and, *in extremis*, terminate the contract. The advantage of longer contracts is that both client and contractor can establish a long term-working relationship and the stability offered by a longer term encourages the contractor to invest in machinery and staff development.

42. Research has shown that sitting and relaxing is one of the most popular activities for garden visitors.

OPENING A GARDEN TO PAYING VISITORS

Gardens of every scale and complexity are open to visitors – occasionally, seasonally or all year round. Some are low-key attractions, with the plants and the place almost speaking for themselves. Others set out to entertain the visitor in every conceivable way, even including theme-park attractions to keep everyone in the family happy all of the time. Most are somewhere in between.

Owners and managers of historic parks and gardens open their properties for a variety of reasons. Many private gardens and estates are managed and maintained purely for the benefit of a family, relations and friends. Other properties open occasionally for charitable events or as a condition for grant aid received. However, with the increasing costs of managing and maintaining gardens and landscapes more properties are being opened to visitors with the aim of capitalising on visitor income.

This section aims to provide a basic guide for owners and managers considering opening their garden with the aim of generating income, and considers the range of visitor facilities that may be required. The main focus is on the needs of larger sites with regular opening; however, many of the general principles may be of help to properties for occasional events.

Why open? When considering opening to the public, it is important to be clear about the purpose. It could be:

- To open occasionally as part of a voluntary scheme for charity, e.g. the National Gardens Scheme Yellow Book
- To open on a regular basis but in a low-key manner with the intention of visitor income supplementing the cost of garden maintenance
- A professionally managed operation to maximising visitor income to cover maintenance and management costs

With the second or third option, it is important to prepare an accurate business plan so that the costs and potential income can be considered over a period of business operation, and a CMP to evaluate any impact. If bank loans or grants are required to fund the setting up of visitor infrastructure, accurate business planning is a prerequisite so that risk can be assessed. Without careful planning it is all too easy for a property to end up with high costs and high turnover, but little return for the effort put in. When researching and planning opening, it is valuable to learn from local and more distant competition; this will provide a useful guide to the facilities that visitors expect and help establish a competitive pricing structure.

On the duty of care – Occupiers' Liability Act, CROW Act and Health and Safety at Work Act and Regulations – see 1.5, pages 74-5, 82).

Understanding the tourist market The domestic and overseas tourist market has risen dramatically over the last thirty years. This is generally attributed to an increase in leisure time; a generally higher standard of living; the expansion of car ownership, creating wider personal mobility, and an increase in the percentage of the population retired and in good health. Steep rises in visitor figures in the 1970s and 1980s levelled out during the latter 1990s as the tourist market became saturated, with attractions in many areas competing for the same pound. At the same time, competition from major retail outlets has increased following relaxation in Sunday trading regulation. Such a saturated tourist market is highly vulnerable to outside factors. The foot-and-mouth outbreak in 2001 wiped out the rural tourist market, and the 11 September terrorist attacks in the US the same year, and bombs in London in summer 2005, deterred many Americans from sub-

TOURISM FACTS AND FIGURES

- In 2004 over 11.5 million visits were recorded to gardens. While gardens account for 15 per cent of tourist attractions, they receive 20 per cent of visits. The hot summer of 2003 produced a rise in visitor numbers of 6 per cent

- Research undertaken for Heritage Counts 2003 showed that between a quarter and a third of visitors were domestic tourists, with the rest from overseas

- London received the highest proportion of overseas visitors; the North East and East Midlands the lowest

- The South West, a traditional holiday destination, had the highest proportion of domestic visitors

- Gardens are particularly popular with visitors to rural and coastal areas

- The Historic Houses Association has estimated that the full economic contribution made by its members' properties (many of which include gardens) is about £1.2 billion

- On average 39 per cent of total income is from admissions, with the rest made up from catering, retail sales, private hire, fashion and film location hire, events, weddings and corporate hospitality

- In 2004 it was estimated that there was a minimum of 32,054 staff employed in the historic visitor attractions sector, of which historic houses and gardens employed the highest number of full-time permanent staff

- Many sites indicated an increase in the proportion of volunteers in the workforce

sequently flying abroad on holiday. However, tourist figures have shown a healthy recovery, particularly for visits to gardens.

Gardens form an important part of the tourist market, particularly in rural areas where they provide direct employment not only to garden-based staff but to those in retail and catering enterprises.

The 2006 edition of the National Gardens Scheme Yellow Book lists around 3,500 gardens that open annually on its behalf in England and Wales. The Good Gardens Guide lists some 1,400 properties in the UK, and estimates that some 5,000 gardens are open to the public on announced days of the year. These range from small domestic gardens to large private gardens opening for only a few days a year for charity to organisations such as the Royal Horticultural Society, the National Trust and English Heritage, and many privately owned gardens run as tourist attractions open for much of the year. With so many wonderful and varied gardens to choose from, garden visitors have become very well informed and demanding. Growth of interest in gardens and gardening is reflected in a host of popular television programmes, books, magazine and newspaper features; with greater urbanisation it has been suggested that gardens are becoming a spectator occupation, like sport. Behind the scenes or 'meet the gardener' events at properties are increasingly popular. Numerous surveys indicate that gardens are more likely than historic houses to attract repeat visits.

Profile of a garden visitor The majority of garden visitors are white, aged forty plus, and fall into more affluent social groups. With an increasingly saturated tourist market, gardens wishing to maintain and expand their visitor numbers need to attract a wider profile, especially among the young. The ecological sector has been very successful in promoting nature conservation issues and gaining the support of a young audience; useful lessons can be learned for attracting younger visitors to historic houses and gardens.

- Painshill Park, an eighteenth-century landscape garden in Surrey, has a very successful outreach programme for schools that use the gardens as an outside classroom. The gardens can also be booked for children's parties: they dress up in period costume and engage with a broad range of activities using the landscape as a resource for exploration and discovery.

- At Newby Hall gardens in Yorkshire, a children's play area has been developed in the walled garden which separates the excitement and noise of play from the peace and tranquillity found in the rest of the garden.

- At Broadview Gardens at Hadlow College, a Saturday morning gardening club was organised to occupy young children while their parents were doing the shopping, walking around the garden or relaxing, offering children an experience that could develop into a lifetime interest.

- Alnwick Castle gardens in Northumberland recently opened a 'poison garden' to interest children in the dangerous side of plants.

Many groups and communities who have never visited a historic garden – because of difficulties of transport, or fear of the unknown are unaware of the enjoyment and benefits they can offer. The Gateway Project of the Welsh Historic Gardens Trust

43. At Painshill Park, Surrey, an eighteenth-century landscape, primary schools are encouraged to use the gardens as open-air classrooms in which children can discover aspects of the arts and sciences.

44. Enabling disabled access is an important consideration under the Disability Discrimination Act.

has achieved great success in organising and guiding visits for disadvantaged and disabled groups. After a visit, useful information is fed back to the owners or managers.

Most English gardens contain plants and design elements originating from all over the world. Garden owners or managers wishing to encourage a wider range of ethnic groups can follow the example of Osborne, which featured Indian-inspired planting to celebrate the restoration of Queen Victoria's Durbar Wing. Within the framework of a historic garden there are many such opportunities for innovation to encourage a wider spectrum of visitors.

The case studies in the last section of this book highlight the different approaches than can be taken.

Marketing and promotion Whatever reason a garden is open, whether for charity or to provide revenue income, carefully thought-out marketing and promotion is vital if visitors are to find themselves at your door. English Heritage and the National Trust spend a large amount of money promoting their sites in radio, print advertisements and billboards on public transport – this is effective at reaching a wide audience, but beyond the scope of any but the largest organisations. For sites that open regularly, it is worth producing a publicity leaflet and getting it into all tourist leaflet racks at local hotels, guesthouses, pubs, other attractions and tourist information centres.

Free promotion The best promotion is free, via word of mouth by satisfied customers, or features on local or national television,

COOPERATIVE MARKETING

In Cornwall a number of private garden owners undertook cooperative marketing to promote their sites, a highly suitable strategy for a holiday area where tourists are based from one or two days to a few weeks. A joint leaflet was produced, providing details of all the partner gardens; further leaflets and an exhibition at each garden promoted the others, with photographs, contact numbers and opening hours. Tourists were thus guided towards this select list of gardens at a fraction of the normal cost had the owners worked independently.

radio, magazines and newspapers. It is worth holding a familiarisation event to promote a garden to local Tourist Information Centre staff, hoteliers, B & B and guesthouse owners and managers. If they experience an enjoyable and memorable visit, know your garden and what it offers to visitors, they are more likely to recommend it to their guests.

Managing the media The press are always looking for a good story with a good photograph – if it includes children and animals, all the better! Local and national newspapers like pictures that express the current season. Encourage professional photographers to come and take pictures: the more images of a garden in their libraries, the more likely they are to appear in magazines and newspapers. Local newspapers are always interested in local stories, so get to know the local features editors and feed them with seasonal stories about your site – the tallest sunflower competition or the prolific blooming of a tulip tree. Send out press releases to local and specialist national newspapers, and consider holding an annual press day, a useful opportunity to enthuse potential writers. The key to fostering press interest is to provide information and, if possible, photographs they can use. As journalists often work to a tight schedule, any delay or hesitation in providing requested information may result in them going elsewhere.

Television coverage can provide a dramatic impetus for increased visitor numbers, and gardens should prepare themselves to cope with the extra visitors that will arrive following television coverage. A range of opportunities can bring television cameras to a garden – features on national or local gardening programmes;

45, 46. Keeping leaflet racks fully stocked can be time-consuming; distribution agencies will undertake the work, but at a cost. Get advice from your tourist authority on the local tourist market and worthwhile marketing opportunities.

WHY DO PEOPLE VISIT GARDENS?

- a relaxing day out in a pleasant environment to walk and sit

- a safe family visit – somewhere for children to let off steam

- a nice venue for Sunday lunch or afternoon tea

- a dramatic backdrop for outside events

- historic layout and design

- horticultural interest

- inspiration for the garden at home

- outside classroom for educational activities: sciences, history, geography, art and mathematics

- a place to volunteer

- a place to get married (wedding venue)

- a place to scatter ashes

A National Trust survey of members in 2002 showed that:

- 89 per cent valued 'natural beauty and landscape'

- 79 per cent appreciated 'authentic historic surroundings'

- 65 per cent sought peace and tranquillity

IDEAS FOR GENERATING VISITORS

- Seasonal extravaganzas – e.g. snowdrops at Audley End in February, roses at Mottisfont in June, autumn colour at Westonburt in October

- Special events – plant fairs, antique fairs, horticultural demonstrations, walks and talks relating to different aspects of the management of the garden, e.g. containers and their planting, wildflowers, etc.

- Concerts and theatrical performances

- Children's activities – discovery guides, Easter egg hunts

- Plant sales special events – e.g. auctioning excess stock at the end of the season

- Corporate entertaining and wedding packages (including the ceremony and reception) – these can generate valuable income for historic houses and gardens

- Filming and fashion shoots

BROWN SIGNS

Brown Tourist signs on approach roads and motorways serve a double purpose they promote the site and direct visitors to it. The signs are designed and installed in accordance with county council and national standards; the cost varies from hundreds to thousands of pounds depending on the status of the road. Applications for new signs are usually made through the county council, approval is sought from the Highway Agency, and decisions are taken in consultation with the county council and district tourism officers. The criteria for eligibility, which may vary from region to region, are likely to include the following:

- All facilities must be permanently established

- All destinations must be open to visitors, within advertised opening hours, without the need for membership or pre-booking

- All sites must comply with statutory requirements

- All destinations must be publicised in tourist publications or via tourist information centres

- All sites must meet the standards of the English Tourist Board's Visitor Charter

In addition to erecting brown signs, costs are usually involved in the initial application. There is an annual maintenance charge, and full replacement costs will be charged should signs need replacing through wear, damage or theft.

Despite the high cost and bureaucratic procedures of brown signs, many gardens are enthusiastic about their positive benefits. Well-positioned signs can lead visitors from motorways and other major roads towards gardens that are often hidden down rural lanes.

---

the garden as a backdrop for other televised programmes or events, such as BBC's Antiques Road Show or a news item on extreme weather, or even early bud burst! Offering the garden as a backdrop or set for filming or fashion shoots can bring in useful income and attract visitors who have seen the beautiful images. Tim Smitt, mastermind behind the restoration of Heligan and the creation of the Eden Project, has very effectively harnessed the interest of the press: 90 per cent of his publicity appears as free editorial.

Websites Many people now have access to the internet and use it to plan and book their leisure time. An attractive, well-illustrated, informative and easy to find website is an essential promotional tool. It is important to keep it updated and provide seasonal pages to attract repeat visits, attendance at special events and, if appropriate, low season visitors. As a minimum, a website should provide basic information to explain to potential visitors:

- What they will see

- Access for disabled visitors

- When the site is open,

- How much it will cost

- How to get there

- Seasonal events

- Children's activities

- Whether dogs are allowed

A tour of the websites of the Case Study gardens will provide a useful range of ideas for garden website design.

Access standards for disabled visitors Under the Disability Discrimination legislation, all service providers such as garden businesses open to the public are required to make reasonable adjustments to overcome physical barriers to access. Disability spans all physical and mental impairments and short-term conditions as well as long-term problems. An access audit can help identify potential problems and plan necessary improvements. The whole visitor experience needs to be assessed, from planning a visit, arriving and getting around the garden, and comfort aspects. Barriers can include lack of information to plan a visit, to types of paths, steps and ramps, interpretation materials and ease of use, seating and shelter. Often small-scale changes or staff training can help overcome access barriers.

Arriving at the site Thought needs to be given as to how visitors physically get from their cars or public transport stop to the garden, and the impact on their first impressions of the site. For disabled visitors, the best option is usually to provide car parking spaces as close to the main entrance as possible, but this may not be acceptable because of the historic character of the site. Car parking spaces designated for disabled people need to be clearly marked and signposted. The Office of the Deputy Prime Minister publishes the Building Regulations which set out guidance on topics such as the design and layout of car parking.

Easy-to-use information – on-site leaflets, maps, guides and signs, and information for planning visits – helps people enjoy their visit, learn more and establishes a good reputation for the site and its staff. A lack of information or poorly designed information can be a barrier to access and a missed opportunity to encourage more people to visit.

The law Since 1996, under the Disability Discrimination Act 1995, it has been unlawful to treat disabled people less favourably than other people for a reason related to their disability. Since 1999, all service providers, such as gardens, businesses and organisations open to the public, have had to make reasonable adjustments for disabled people such as providing extra help or making changes to the way services are provided. Since October 2004, service providers have also had to make reasonable adjustments to their premises to overcome physical barriers to access. The Disability Discrimination Act 1995 has been amended by the Disability Discrimination Act 2005 to place a duty on all public sector authorities to promote disability equality. The Disability Equality Duty comes into effect in December 2006 and will have a significant impact on the way in which all public services are run and on improving the lives of disabled people. For more information see the Disability Rights Commission website, www.drc.org.uk. See also page 75 in 'The legal framework', 1.5.

Assessing a garden's visitor capacity When opening a property as a commercial attraction, a balance has to be found between public demand, enjoyment, conservation and income. A well-prepared CMP will help guide owners and managers to achieve this balance when setting visitor targets. A garden with too few visitors may not be financially sustainable; one that becomes over-visited may be damaged and appear worn-out or be too crowded to enjoy. Visitors days out may be spoiled, deterring them from making a return visit. It is therefore important to estimate a garden's maximum capacity at peak times and try to stay within these. Once peak capacity has been reached, marketing should be refocused to encourage visitors to come at low-peak times – by holding events during quieter months; promoting spring, autumn and winter seasonal interest, and/or encouraging visitors to come

47. Although many wheelchair users prefer hard surfaced paths, grass paths are accessible in dry weather.

OBSERVED EFFECTS OF INCREASED VISITORS
From recent studies by the National Trust

- Increased wear and tear, especially to grass paths, verges and entrances

- Decreased hours when vital maintenance work can be done that requires closure to the public – e.g. spraying, mowing, hedge-cutting and arboricultural work

- Increased interruptions to staff through questions: it is natural that enthusiastic visitors like to speak directly with the gardeners on site

- Greater plant losses through accidental damage, theft, accumulated effects of sneaking cuttings (called 'finger blight') and some vandalism

- More demand for plant sales and expert advice

- Greater need for interpretation guides, etc.

- Increased time and labour in connection with events, especially beyond normal working hours

THE SISSINGHURST EXPERIENCE

48, 49. The inevitable widening of hedges and narrowing of paths was occurring at a time when visitor numbers were steadily increasing (left, 1969). A programme of cutting hedges to their original size and introducing more paving and gravel surfaces led to easier public access and less wear and tear, but some loss of mystery and secrecy (right, 1987).

In 1991 the annual visitor numbers to Sissinghurst peaked at 190,000. At times this compact garden of domestic-sized 'rooms' became so full that only people could be seen, neither plants nor garden. The grass became worn and bare in places and the edges of beds trodden down, rather than overflowing with vegetation as Vita Sackville-West had planned. In order to manage the overcrowding and reduce annual numbers closer to 175,000, the National Trust carefully controlled marketing, tried to persuade visitors to go at off-peak times, and introduced a timed ticket system that permitted a maximum of 400 people in the garden at any one time. A fixed number of tickets were issued at half-hourly intervals, and once inside visitors were allowed to stay as long as they liked, which was on average 90 minutes. In some seasons, this led to a delay of up to two hours before entry, which in turn resulted in overcrowding in the shop, restaurant, car park and woods. Ten years later, annual visitor numbers had dropped to 135,000, which improved visitor enjoyment and garden conservation, but is in fact too low to sustain the garden.

---

earlier or later in the day. Those responsible for marketing should liaise with the garden team to ensure that there are sufficient 'quiet' times to undertake key maintenance tasks. Large landscapes with fewer 'honey pots of interest' have a much greater capacity for visitors, but surprise peaks in numbers can lead to local road congestion, insufficient parking, and queues to enter the garden, lavatories, shops and catering facilities.

Wear and tear: the wages of success! A key section in any CMP should be the policies and techniques for visitor management where public access is a normal part of a property's operation. Many gardens, while welcoming increased visitors and income, have experienced a noticeable downside in wear and tear and other impacts. Increased maintenance costs from visitor opening and special events should be costed in to the business plan, and the degree of fragility and its impact linked to the CMP.

Most of the finest historic gardens were created by informed amateurs and eccentric enthusiasts for the pleasure of their families and a circle of friends. Apart from the royal palaces and a few of the greater houses, visitor numbers would have been quite small. From the public's point of view, most places would have been strictly private. The intricate designs of Sissinghurst and Hidcote, for example, with narrow paths, secret spaces and intimate corners, were never devised for crowds of visitors. Many gardens in remote rural locations which now open to visitors can present access problems, and local communities may show concern about over-commercialisation.

50. Wear and tear can be sudden and severe, such as this vehicle damage to turf after 2.5cm of rain.

Reducing or preventing wear and tear

- **Restrict the numbers of visitors** The National Trust have been considering trying to assess the 'carrying capacity' of certain intricate gardens such as Sissinghurst, to reduce the pressure and volume of people in the garden at any one time. A timed ticket system is operated during peak periods, and reduced publicity and promotion is also possible, particularly at specific times of the year.

- **Devise a guided route or path system** that makes better use of the less visited parts of a garden, in order to spread the load or pressure more evenly.

51. Metal edging at Osborne House has been used to define the complex scroll patterns of the parterres.

- **Modify the design and layout** if possible, but not so as to detract from the garden's historic or original character. There may be places where grass paths can be converted to paving or gravel over hard core, and widths may be modified, particularly where wheelchair access is requested.

- **Reinforce grass** Some techniques to strengthen grass are considered in the Grass and Turf section, Part 2 (page 81). Raising the height of close-mown turf to 25–30mm can produce a sward more resistant to both drought and wear. Reseeding or turfing with the newer hardwearing 'sports turf' grass mixtures – particularly rye grass strains – is a possibility. Stepping stones or slabs for narrow paths have proved successful, but the incorporation of shredded rubber from old tyres just beneath the grass surface has had variable results.

- **Use metal edges** for important drives and pathways to produce a longer-term and more easily maintained system.

- **Ensure drainage is effective** for all surfaces, especially grass. Wet or soggy places are very vulnerable to wear, and can soon become muddy and impassable. The elaborate and usually efficient drainage patterns installed in many older gardens have become damaged or blocked up over time; they should be restored or renewed wherever possible.

- **Plan and control events** to reduce the risk of damage and wear and tear.

- **Carry out risk assessments** to pathways and repair them as soon as necessary (this also applies to paved surfaces).

Visitor facilities The aim in providing visitor facilities should be sufficient services to make a visit safe and pleasurable while causing minimum impact on the original character of the site. These days visitors to larger gardens expect to find adequate parking, lavatories and refreshments. All three need to be planned for carefully: over-supply will lead to unnecessary expense, and under-supply to lost revenue and potentially dissatisfied visitors.

Once basic visitor welfare has been satisfied, some garden owners or managers will want to assess the desirability of other facilities such as restaurants, shops, information centres with interpretative displays, signage, educational facilities, picnic sites and improved access for the disabled visitor. Planning, listed building and building regulation consents will be required from the local authority for the development of visitor facilities (see 'The legal framework', 1.5).

Provision of safe access roads and parking spaces is a very significant expense when opening a site to the public. Considerable thought needs to go into the siting and design of any new roads and car parks to avoid damaging the aesthetic qualities of a landscape that is intended to be attractive. Cars will cause damage to grassland, particularly on poorly drained soils and in wet conditions (see page 179), but this can be minimised by selecting well-drained sites for parking and by laying trackways over grass to spread compaction along busy access routes. In addition to problems of compaction and rutting, oil or petrol pollution will need to be dealt with and litter removed before stock can return to graze.

When planning permanent access routes and parking, accurate estimates need to be made of the number of parking places required at peak times on average days and at full capacity during special events or bank holidays. Architects can advise on the most appropriate road placement and design to suit the environment, intended use and available budget. The local Highways Authority will need to be consulted if new entrances are created or altered on highways. Permanent parking needs to accommodate average daily use, with overflow parking providing additional capacity. Coach parties must be carefully scheduled to enable vehicle parking and other facilities to cope with large influxes of visitors.

When planning lavatory facilities, the minimum provision should be able to cope with average mid-season visitor numbers; temporary facilities can increase the supply at peak times such as bank holiday weekends or special events. If a new water main and foul drainage are required they should have sufficient capacity for future expansion. Lavatories are needed for each sex, plus baby-changing facilities and adapted lavatories for disabled visitors. Lavatories are high-maintenance: they need cleaning regularly throughout the day, by on-site staff or contractors. On large sites requiring visitors to walk long distances, if there are no lavatory

52. Grassed fields can provide useful temporary parking for sites open a few days a year, or as overflow capacity on high days and holidays (see 'The legal framework', 1.5, on planning regulations, page 69).

53. Kenwood has benefited from excellent caterers for many years, with lunchtime trade in the café attracting many visitors during the week and at weekends.

facilities on the site then this information must be displayed (this is of particular help to the elderly or those with small children).

The average period a visitor spends on site is called 'dwell time'. Its length depends on a site's size, complexity, interest and facilities. A site offering a whole day's visit will need to provide a dwell time of at least four hours. The largest sites, such as Chatsworth and Osborne, can hope to attract visitors for a whole day. They arrive at 10.30 or 11 a.m., have a cup of coffee before visiting the house or garden, then have lunch, walk round the rest of the site, and follow this by tea and a trip to the gift shop and plant centre before leaving. Those on a half-day visit may have coffee, lunch or tea as well as a visit to the shop and plant centre. Excellent catering facilities can make a big difference to the popularity of a site, particularly to local and frequent visitors. Gardens producing fruit and vegetable produce should try to feature this in their café or restaurant, as it is a unique selling point. Gardens without catering facilities are advised to work with nearby tea shops and pubs that offer food, so that refreshment needs are catered for.

The income from out-of-season/winter opening should be balanced against the cost of damage and its impact on essential winter repairs.

Historic crop production Many historic house establishments had considerable areas for food production, such as walled kitchen gardens, glasshouses, trained fruit trees and extensive orchards (see also 'Walled kitchen gardens', page 204). Ancillary or working buildings went with them. Walled gardens were often sited on south or south-west slopes to maximise production, the soil enriched by many years of careful craft and management. Many of these facilities still survive intact or in part, although their original raison d'être has greatly changed or no longer exists; some are derelict or neglected. New uses have to be found, which could be car parking, visitor centres or catering, but more recently a number of restoration projects have been undertaken in order to retain the character of these once-prized 'centres of excellence'

which the public love to see. Some of these are considered in the Case Studies. They are primarily aimed at visitor appeal and education, and the horticultural crops that are an essential part of the operation are for display in the first place. Sales or outlets for surpluses are limited.

Income from such inevitably labour-intensive enterprises will therefore be largely from gate money and not from crop sales. Demand may be greater if the produce is genuinely organic, and there could well be a place for volunteers to help harvest crops or pick fruit. If land is available, extra areas could be used for this to avoid denuding the demonstration crops, and there might also be a case for a 'pick your own' section. However, the plan for the overall property should consider the resources available, especially manpower, for the proper running of walled garden complexes. They will only be part of a much larger layout of gardens and possibly parkland, and standards elsewhere may suffer if too much priority is given to them.

Plant sales There is a steady demand for ornamental plants, when they are offered at a well-located sales area or plant centre at a historic garden. However, a number of important considerations are worth thinking about before a plant sales enterprise is embarked upon.

What is the scale or scope of the operation? This needs careful thought and assessment of the costs and the likely returns. For example, a simple plant stall strategically placed by the garden entrance, offering usually surplus plants not wanted in the garden, may bring in a modest return of a few hundred or possibly a thousand pounds or so, and the labour and effort of supplying and selling is comparatively small. If this is a success, it may lead to a more organised and larger sales area or plant centre, and this is where things may start to go wrong. Questions are:

- What range of plants or nursery stock should be on sale?
- Who will grow or supply them?
- Who will run the centre and ensure quality and standards?
- Where will the sales point be?

If the usually hard-pressed garden staff are mainly responsible, what may have begun as a surplus plant outlet could develop into a nursery production business, which may divert staff from the main responsibility of the upkeep of the gardens. In many ways, therefore, it is preferable to keep the plant sales and the garden maintenance operations separate. Certainly an eye must be kept on the production and running costs of the plant centre. A decline in standards of garden maintenance may reduce visitor numbers, which will impact on garden income.

What range of plants should be available? Most historic gardens are unique, with their own particular character and planting themes, so wherever possible it is sensible to offer notable plants that the visitor has seen growing in the garden itself. These might include special shrubs or old roses, the more unusual cultivars of herbaceous perennials, and other plants that help to determine the character of a garden, which perhaps cannot easily be obtained at a

54. Plant sales at Chelsea Physic Garden. A compact, well-stocked and attractively presented centre, offering quality plants to be seen in the garden itself, is infinitely preferable to a large garden centre-like feature, inadequately stocked and maintained, with little individual personality.

local nursery. Scarcity value could justify a mark-up in price, provided that the quality is good – usually it is most cost-effective to focus on unusual or rare plants that are not commercially available and can be sold at a higher premium. Other stock may supplement the range on offer, but beware of the situation where a unique garden containing many unusual plants has in its plant centre too many everyday plants that can easily be bought at major commercial garden centres.

An alternative is to let the site to a concessionaire to run the plant centre, but there should be control over the style, plant range and stock, and a system to ensure that diseases are not introduced to the garden.

Where should the plant sales area be located? Experience and practice at many heritage sites have shown that plant sales are best located near the car park and other facilities such as the shop or visitor centre, where staff can handle the sales and packaging of the plants. A member of the garden staff should keep an eye on the quality and care of the plants on sale and the replenishment of the stock, and should liaise closely with the shop management. First impressions are important, and good labelling and helpful advice will add to the USP (Unique Selling Point).

Shops Shops selling books, gifts and confectionery can, if imaginatively stocked and managed, prove popular with visitors and earn useful income. When business planning and reviewing the effectiveness of shops, it is important to ensure that the enterprise generates sufficient profit to make the investment in infrastructure, stock and staff worthwhile. Some of the most popular shops carry stock that is unique to the garden, estate or locality – with so much competition about, quality and individuality are most important.

Interpretation Gardens are living works of art and cultural treasure chests, yielding many historical, cultural, social, scientific, artistic and horticultural stories. Good interpretation can help visitors make choices about what they want to see and help them uncover stories that otherwise would be lost. With the growth and development of museums and heritage sites, an extensive interpretation industry has grown up to offer a wide range of interpretative solutions, but there is a cost. Garden owners should beware of being seduced into purchasing unnecessarily complex interpretative systems – they may have a short life span, be expensive to maintain and repair, and remove any sense of exploration or discovery.

All information should be accurate, well laid out, accessible and legible. All site signage and displays should be well maintained, appropriately located and fit for purpose. All interpretative materials should aim to inform, enlighten or assist the visitor, in the place where it is most appropriate. At Belsay Hall, head gardener Adam Stenhouse maintains a seasonal information board, with photographs and a little text to inform visitors of plants of seasonal interest. The messages conveyed on interpretative displays should not be confused by racks of promotional leaflets or by barriers at garden entrances displaying rows of posters upon which the visitor cannot immediately act.

Signage All signage must meet the needs of the visitor as well as the historic, aesthetic and environmental sensitivities of the site. A good rule of thumb is to provide the minimum to be fit for purpose, designed to a house style and laid out in a logical and uniform manner. Too much badly designed signage will confuse the visitor and look ugly.

Directional signs guide the visitor to where they want to be. These are often in the form of fingerposts that may point towards the car park, garden entrance, lavatories, tea room or particular

55. Temporary board giving details of garden works.

56. Interpretation exhibition boards interpret the historic bothy at Audley End.

57. It can be a challenge to find safety signs that are both easily visible and in keeping with a historic setting. This sign incorporates a ring to pull someone in difficulties from the water.

area of the garden. The size and placement of signs will depend on their purpose: signs in the car park should be large and made of reflective material so they can be seen by a driver in the dark; signs for pedestrians will be smaller.

Information signs, such as a welcome board at the entrance, large enough to be read from a car, should give the name of the site or garden, ownership and office address, phone number, times of opening and closing, and entrance fee. This will help visitors plan the essentials of their stay. A further board, designed to be read by those on foot, may repeat the above information and also provide site orientation, a map and a list of main attractions and facilities, including suitability for disabled visitors. Special attractions or events, or seasonal work of interest being carried out in the garden, should be signalled through appropriate signage at the entrance to the property. The use of explicit notices warning visitors of potential hazards will not exonerate owners and managers from negligence claims; however, they have a practical value in that they may prevent injuries in the first place.

58. Interpretation chalk board in the walled garden at Osborne.

Orientation signage is usually in the form of a panel and best placed at the start of the garden tour. It can be in the form of a garden or landscape plan, indicating in graphic form alternative routes that can be followed. Owners or managers may wish to reinforce key site rules at this point – e.g. no dogs, ball games or picnics, etc. Great care should be taken when selecting and placing such signs, as they can easily detract from the site.

59. An orientation plan helps visitors to plan their garden tour.

Understanding the garden Gardens can be appreciated in a variety of ways, and a wide range of tools is available to owners and managers to help visitors interpret the garden.

Leaflets Many National Trust properties sell a folded leaflet with a map of the garden and park showing alternative routes and a list of the main garden features with a brief descriptive text. Many owners find that it is best to charge a small fee for such leaflets – not only does it help to cover production costs, but it discourages visitors from discarding them as litter in the garden!

60. Guide books provide visitors with a valuable souvenir of their visit.

Information panels These are often best used to explain botanical or historical information. The buildings that form part of many eighteenth-century landscapes are ideal covered spaces for exhibition boards to convey the garden's history and art. They provide an opportunity to offer interpretation in phases, rather than overload visitors with information on arrival. At Kenwood, one of the estate cottages is used to house an information centre — information boards, photographs, sketches and artefacts are used to explain the landscape's history and inform visitors of ongoing developments. A well-informed volunteer stationed at the centre is also able to answer many visitors' queries or guide them to where they can find an answer (see Down House Case Study, 3.3).

Audio-visual A short film or slide presentation with a recorded commentary can be useful in explaining complex ideas in an accessible way at the start or end of a visit. A slide presentation was used by Hampton Court to explain the process of the restoration of the Privy Garden. A short film has been made by English Heritage to explain the design and construction of the Contemporary Heritage Garden at Lincoln Medieval Bishops' Palace — for disabled visitors unable to access the garden due to its very steep topography, the film, promoted in the local press, has provided an opportunity to find out more.

Interactive computers Widely used by art galleries to enable students of art to view both historical information and high-quality photographic details of pictures, they could be used in a similar way at gardens with important plant collections. Linked to a plant database, they could show photographs and taxonomic, natural habitat, historical and horticultural information, with the potential of printing out a data sheet for each plant of interest. These could help visitors identify plants they have seen in the garden or locate plants that may be growing there. The major disadvantages of interactive computers are their high set-up and maintenance costs, the requirement of a supervised exhibition space, and the fact that only a few individuals can interact with one computer at a time.

Guidebooks Visitors to gardens rarely use guidebooks in their entirety at the site. They will use a map, perhaps read an introductory piece or look up specific information, but will usually buy a guidebook as a souvenir of their visit to enjoy later.

Garden tour guides The best garden interpretation comes from a well-informed guide who is able to adjust their tour to suit the interests of the visitors. At Down House, volunteers have been briefed so that they can answer visitors' questions in an informed way; trained volunteers may be booked to guide groups. Volunteer guides have been critical in the success of interpreting the complex history of the eighteenth-century landscape at Painshill Park; some have undertaken their own research and become specialists on the history or planting of the garden. Garden staff can be used to give garden tours but this will compete with their main work. However, special 'meet the gardener' or 'connoisseur' events, when visitors can glimpse behind the scenes, are very popular and usually sold out.

Plant labelling This is always a controversial subject among gardeners. Those strongly influenced by large botanic and demonstration gardens like to see each plant with an engraved label showing its botanic name in Latin, its family and common names, country of origin, and accession and collector's number. Others do not wish to see any labels in a garden because they detract from its design; they argue that owners and gardeners know their plants and visitors are always welcome to ask if they want to know a name. One problem with labelling is that it can be expensive to implement and maintain; visitors without pen and paper to hand have been known to take labels away with them or, more infuriatingly, pick up a label and put it back next to a different plant! Shiny aluminium or zinc tags are attractive to some squirrels and jackdaws; if this is the case, another less reflective material is worth using. For gardens with complex or interesting plant collections, it is often necessary to label plants in order to keep track of the collections: this can be achieved with inconspicuously placed zinc or aluminium labels bearing the plant name and accession number, or just the accession number for collection management purposes. At English Heritage gardens, trees are all marked just above eye height with a zinc tag nailed to the bark of the tree, bearing the tree number. The numbered trees are then plotted on a map of the site, which enables individual trees to be easily located by managers, gardeners and tree surgeons wishing to examine them.

61. Left: Many gardens and parks give accession numbers to trees to aid the curation of their collections and to maintain accuracy when monitoring tree safety. 62. Centre: aluminium labels. 63. Right: wooden labels.

64. A visitor centre may have a number of uses, including selling tickets, a plant shop or centre and exhibition or interpretation space.
65. Inset: Audio-tours are used by English Heritage at many of their monument sites: they allow visitors to tour the site at their own pace and hear detailed historical, social and architectural information when they want it. Such tours are less suitable for gardens, however, as they can distract from visual messages. They are no replacement for well-informed staff or volunteers.

METHODS OF DISPLAYING PLANT LABELS

Technique	Pros	Cons
Nailed into stem/trunk	Good for display height (at average height for the able-bodied). Less clutter at base of tree/shrub. Discreet method for tree survey numbering tags	Damages bark and cambium – potential entry point for P+D. Nail will be swallowed up by plant's lateral growth – needs annual checking. Only good with clear stems/trunk
Directly plunged next to plant/in pot	Most discreet method for specimens where labels have to be on display. Most suited to very small plants, potted plants (nursery and display) and rowed crops where space is at a premium	Traditional small rectangular labels are written along the length of the label making the text 90° from the reader's line of sight. Not good for display purposes unless near to paths or potted plants are on staging
Short stand in front of plant	Best method for general herbaceous plants and shrubs where label display is needed. Can be seen from a fair distance. Formal style, used especially in commemorative plantings	Look overbearing for smaller plants, and are lost in dense borders. Easily damaged accidentally by gardeners; plastic ones often broken. Can be lost under fast-growing bushy shrubs
Sunk into media (hidden)	Safe method of marking accessions where label theft and mix-ups are prone. Often useful where high winds remove labels and tip over small pots	Only really viable with potted plants. Labels often lost into the rootball as plant grows. Pots need removing to find the label leading to root disturbance
Tall stand/atop post	Less easily removed by visitors	Can dominate a display
Wired to branch (or protective netting)	Good display height and less damaging than nailing to a stem	Wire will eventually strangle the branch as it grows, therefore needs regular checks and wire replacement
Display board with plant names and details	Fewer labels, more information	Siting the board, high capital cost and maintenance

One of the most significant changes that owners and managers have had to face in the last hundred years has been an increase in legislation relating to employment, health and safety, land management and planning control.

The first part of this chapter concerns land use and the carrying out of development and its regulation through the planning system. Because many of the parks and gardens that concern us are historic or 'heritage' sites, they may be subject also to specific statutory designations such as a scheduled monument or listed building, or they may fall within a conservation area. It is critical to establish whether any such designation of a site exists, to ensure that the correct procedures are followed. Failure to do so can, in some cases, constitute a criminal offence.

The second part concerns legislation covering the protection of people, particularly important for sites open to the public or employing staff.

The final part considers important provisions for the protection of the environment, through legislation such as the Wildlife & Countryside Act 1981 and the Countryside and Rights of Way Act 2000.

Legislation and guidance is constantly evolving to meet a changing society and environment; this chapter merely aims to highlight some of the legal issues that may affect historic parks and gardens. The areas of law referred to are complex, and reference should always be made to the relevant legislation or regulations for full details. This guide should not be used as an alternative to seeking qualified legal or other appropriate professional advice. It has been our aim to give a brief overview of the legislation that those managing historic parks and gardens are likely to encounter. We have provided a greater level of detail for legislation that is likely to impact on day-to-day garden management.

---

1. PLANNING AND DEVELOPMENT CONTROL

Historic parks and gardens are increasingly vulnerable to development pressures. Elegant houses and mature landscapes are attractive to many potential developers. Most historic houses and their associated gardens and parks were built and managed as family homes; even some of today's public parks originated this way. They can be expensive to maintain and complex to manage, as the Case Studies show (section 3). The question of survival often hinges on income generation and this in turn requires a business approach to adapt a family home into a profitable enterprise. Opening properties to the public is now widely practised but this can bring about the pressure for development and for perhaps inappropriate changes.

There is now a much greater awareness of the importance of and the need to conserve historic sites and landscapes, and in this respect organisations such as the Garden History Society and county gardens trusts have been doing good work in advising planning authorities of the existence and possible threats to such places. English Heritage also plays an important role in England, advising on development proposals affecting listed buildings, conservation areas, scheduled monuments and registered parks and gardens. English Heritage is a statutory consultee as well as the Government's advisor on the historic environment.

A park or garden owner wanting to develop property or intensify or change its use needs to establish whether planning permission is required. Development control through the planning system covers a wide range of changes from small-scale developments, such as an extension to a house, to major new developments, such as the building of a hotel or a new visitor attraction. Under the Town and Country Planning Act 1990, permission is required for the carrying out of building, engineering, mining or other operations in, over or under land, or the making of any material change in the use of any buildings or other land.

As well as for new buildings, planning permission is likely to be needed for development within parks and gardens, such as amenity lakes, conversion of farm buildings, provision of holiday accommodation, stables for horses and caravan sites. Extending a garden to include former agricultural land would constitute a material change of use as might an intensification of use, such as a proposal to increase the use of a site by opening up a garden more regularly or for larger groups of people. Permission may also be needed for other park and garden developments such as farm shops, food processing, farm visits, trails, pick your own produce and car parks.

It is important to seek appropriate professional advice at an early stage and to seek clarification from the Local Planning Authority (LPA) when proposals are being considered.

66 Opposite: potential hazards must be identified and managed to prevent harm to the public.

Permitted development

In order to respond to day-to-day maintenance and land management, the planning system provides for a system of General Permitted Development Orders (GPDOs) for carrying out certain minor development without the need to make an application for planning permission. (The Town and Country Planning [General Permitted Development] Order 1995 is the one currently in force.) There are a large number of classes of permitted development but perhaps most relevant are those relating to development within the curtilage of a dwelling house, minor operations, changes of use and temporary buildings and uses. However, the extent and scale of any development and location of new structures under permitted development rights is limited. Examples of development covered by GPDOs include swimming pools, new walls and fences (up to 2m) and security cameras, but permitted development rights generally come with conditions attached, or may not even apply where listed buildings are concerned. Also, such permitted development rights can be withdrawn by the local planning authority by way of Article 4 directions where a house and garden or park is in an Area of Outstanding Natural Beauty (AONB), conservation area or national park.

It is important to note that notwithstanding the grant of planning permission by way of development order or otherwise, other forms of statutory controls continue to apply. Works affecting listed buildings and their curtilages, for example, may be subject to a requirement for listed building consent. It may be that both planning permission and listed building or other statutory consent would be required for some types of development.

The occasional use of open land may be permitted up to a maximum of 28 days in any calendar year. Such permitted development is, however, limited; some activities such as markets and motor racing are restricted to a maximum of 14 days and there are separate rules for caravan sites. Again, however, although such temporary uses may be permitted under the GPDO, other statutory consents may be required depending on what is proposed.

Use Class Orders (UCOs)

Certain changes of use may not amount to development. The Town and Country Planning (Use Classes) Order 1987 specifies a number of classes of use; changes of use within the same use class will not require planning permission. However, a park and garden open to visitors could involve several uses such as shops and retail sales, tea shops and restaurants, leisure facilities, hotels and homes, and the position may not always be clear.

Applications and planning considerations

Where an application for planning permission is required, it must be submitted to the LPA. Those wishing to make an application are recommended to consult the appropriate LPA before submitting a formal application.

A fee will be charged for handling applications, and the applicant will be required to submit appropriate plans and drawings with any application. Historic parks and gardens are inevitably more sensitive cases and special considerations apply. Appropriate

---

FACTORS AFFECTING PLANNING PERMISSION

As well as the historical or achaeological significance of a property, many other factors come into play. Applicants need to think about:

- Neighbours
- Design
- Covenants
- Trees and hedgerows
- Wildlife
- Building regulations
- Rights of way
- Advertisements and signs
- Environmental health
- Licensed sites
- Roads and highways

---

specialist advice should be sought at an early stage. Applicants may be asked to provide information on the possible impact of the proposed development on the historic property and curtilage, and proposals to mitigate such an impact.

For major projects, it may be necessary to submit environmental impact assessments, photomontages and site analyses. Computer modelling is increasingly used to present proposals. The application is open to public inspection and the LPA will advertise this and post notices on site to alert all those with an interest. The LPA will also notify appropriate statutory bodies (including English Heritage in appropriate cases) of the proposed development.

At the end of the consultation period the application will be considered by the LPA. The LPA must have regard to any special designation the planning application site may have, such as a listed building or conservation area. It will also take into account any representations made (see below).

First, regard must be had to the Local Development Framework (formerly Local Plans), which sets out the LPA's policies for local development. The Authority must taken this into consideration when determining applications for planning permission, which in turn must be made in accordance with the Framework unless material considerations indicate otherwise. The Framework should provide guidance as to form types and location of new

---

THE PLANNING PORTAL

This is the UK Government's one-stop shop for planning information and services online, with guides on applying for planning permission.

www.planningportal.gov.uk

development, and may contain policies for the protection of historic parks and gardens. These policies reflect government guidance as set out in planning policy statements (PPSs), which will gradually replace existing planning policy guidance notes (PPGs) on topics such as advertisements, tourism, nature conservation, open space, sport and recreation. There are specific PPGs on the historic environment and archaeology too. Such government guidance will be a material consideration in considering applications for consent. The applicant will then be notified of the decision. If permission is granted, it may be subject to conditions. An applicant has a right of appeal to the Secretary of State within a specified period if a planning application is refused, granted subject to conditions or not decided within the specified period (currently 8 weeks).

In the case of historic parks and gardens, where consent is given there may be conditions specifying requirements such as the restoration of historic features. An outline CMP can be very instrumental in presenting short- and longer-term proposals (see Conservation Management Plans, 1.3).

There are situations where the applicant may also offer to provide additional benefits or 'planning gain', by funding infrastructure that is not necessary in planning terms for the development to proceed. At a historic property, the developer may also offer to undertake non-beneficial work such as the repair of listed buildings or the restoration of the designed landscape as part of an overall development scheme within the site where this is to compensate for what may otherwise be a damaging development. This may be referred to as 'enabling development'. Such benefits or 'obligations' may be secured by way of a legal agreement under Section 106 of the Town and Country Planning Act 1990 or by conditions.

If proposing potentially controversial or novel schemes, the applicant would be wise to seek advice at an early stage, and show a willingness to involve those whose concerns and interests might be affected. Pre-application discussions are important to avoid costly later revisions and delays in considering the applications.

Signs and advertisements

The planning system also seeks to control potential eyesores such as advertisements. These are controlled by regulations made under the Planning Acts, namely the Town and Country Planning

(Control of Advertisement) Regulations 1992. The definition of what constitutes an advertisement is very wide. Consent is required for any advertisement falling within the regulations unless consent is deemed to be given under them and, of course, separate listed building consent may be required if the advertisement is attached to a listed building. Deemed consent is given under the regulations for certain advertisements such as those for fêtes, sales and other temporary events and site boards at building sites, but these are subject to limitations as to size and location. The general rule is that outdoor advertisements must not harm the local amenity and they must be safe. Special considerations apply to advertisements in a conservation area.

As indicated above, the planning regime is complex and it may not always be clear as to what development or activities require planning permission or other statutory consent. Applicants are strongly advised to discuss any proposals with their relevant LPA in advance.

Designations affecting planning

The following special statutory designations are likely to be of most interest to owners and managers of historic parks and gardens. However, it should be noted that the Government has published a document entitled *Heritage Protection: The Way Forward* which proposes a new, single, unified *Register of Historic Sites and Buildings of England*, to be introduced at some stage instead of the various designations relating to historic heritage referred to below. This is with a view to simplifying the designation regulation.

ADVERTISEMENTS

These must:

- Be kept clean and tidy
- Be maintained and safe
- Be removed when required by the local planning authority
- Not be displayed without the consent of the owner of the site
- Not obscure traffic signs or create a traffic hazard

CRITERIA DEVELOPED BY ENGLISH HERITAGE FOR INCLUSION OF SITES ON THE REGISTER

- Sites with a main phase of development before 1750 where at least a proportion of the layout of this date is still evident, even perhaps only as an earthwork
- Sites with a main phase of development laid out between 1750 and 1820 where enough of this landscaping survives to reflect the original design
- Sites with a main phase of development between 1820 and 1880 which is of importance and survives intact or relatively intact
- Sites with a main phase of development between 1880 and 1939 where this is of high importance and survives intact
- Sites with a main phase of development laid out post-war, but more than 30 years ago, where the work is of exceptional importance
- Sites which were influential in the development of taste whether through reputation or references in literature
- Sites which are early or representative examples of a style of layout, or type of site, or the work of a designer (amateur or professional) of national importance
- Sites having an association with significant persons or historical events
- Sites with strong group value

GRADING OF REGISTERED SITES

- **Grade I** (approximately 9 per cent of registered sites) Parks and gardens which by reason of their historic layout, features and architectural ornaments considered together make them of exceptional historic interest when considered in the national context; many are of international importance.

  Such sites will survive as a largely complete or coherent design, or as the result of consecutive designs, or might contain a discrete and distinctive component of exceptionally high significance.

- **Grade II*** (approximately 26 per cent of registered sites) Parks and garden which by reason of their historic layout, features and architectural ornaments considered together make them if not of exceptional historic interest, nevertheless of great historic interest when considered in the national context.

  They include sites that would be Grade I had not their condition deteriorated such as to preclude this status, and also those where the whole, or a particular component, is of high significance. The best surviving examples of the work of major national or local designers often justify a high grade, as do particularly intact examples of early layouts.

- **Grade II** Parks and gardens which by reason of their historic layout, features and architectural ornaments considered together make them of special historic interest when considered in the national context. As with the higher-graded sites, parks and gardens designated Grade II on the register warrant every effort being made to safeguard their historic interest.

  The criteria used in the level of grade depends upon the unique importance of the garden or park in historic terms and the extent to which any subsequent changes have been made (see Case Studies, section 3).

DESIGNATION SYSTEM OUTSIDE ENGLAND

- **Wales** Cadw (Welsh Historic Monuments) has published a Register of Landscapes, Parks and Gardens of Special Historic Interest in Wales which includes other historic landscapes as well as parks and gardens.

- **Scotland** Historic Scotland and Scottish Natural Heritage have produced An Inventory of Gardens and Designated Landscapes

- **Northern Ireland** The Northern Ireland Heritage Gardens Inventory was championed by the Northern Ireland Heritage Gardens Committee and records significant existing and extinct sites.

1. Register of Parks and Gardens of Special Historic Interest in England

Although historic buildings were listed soon after the Second World War, gardens were not included, and the Register was an important step in the move to afford some means of protection for them. In 1983 the newly constituted English Heritage was given the authority to compile 'a register of gardens and other land which appears to be of special historic interest'. In 1988 the first Register was produced for each county in England, totalling 1,085 sites. A grading system similar to that used for houses was followed, indicating their relative importance: Grade I, Grade II* and Grade II.

The Register is periodically reviewed and updated, and by 2004 it comprised over 1,500 sites (cemeteries, public parks and more recent important gardens are being added). This is still quite a small number compared to the 400,000 or more listed buildings. The Register represents known nationally important sites and, as such, only constitutes a small proportion of the many hundreds of historically interesting parks and gardens. There is a growing knowledge and recognition of these other sites, and an increasing number of complementary inventories of sites of local significance.

No additional statutory controls follow from inclusion of a park or garden on the Register, but the effect of any proposed development on it will be a material consideration in determining any planning application. LPAs should seek to protect registered parks and gardens in preparing development plans and determining planning applications (Para 2.24 PPG 15: *Planning and the Historic Environment*). The Garden History Society will be consulted by the LPA in respect of all planning applications affecting registered landscapes and English Heritage will be consulted on Grade I and II* sites.

2. Listed buildings

Principal houses are often the focal points of historic landscapes and, if of historic or architectural interest, it is likely that they will be included on the list maintained by the Secretary of State under section 1 of the Planning (Listed Buildings and Conservation Areas) Act 1990. This has the effect of conferring special protection on them and listed building consent may be required for proposals affecting them. Garden buildings may also be individually listed in their own right for their architectural or historical interest: these may include grottoes, temples and follies; boundary features such as ha-has, walls, grilles and structures, and sculptural features such as terraces, balustrading, urns and statuary. However, even if not listed in their own right, consent for proposals affecting such features may still be required: protection for a listed building extends to include any object or structure fixed to it or within its curtilage (in the latter case provided it has formed part of the land since before July 1948).

In considering whether to grant planning permission for development which affects a listed building or its setting, the LPA must have special regard to the desirability of preserving the building or its setting or any features of special architectural or historic interest which it possesses.

It is a criminal offence to demolish a listed building or to execute works of alteration or extension to it in any manner which would affect its character without first having obtained listed building consent from the LPA and then carried out the works in accordance with that consent.

PPG 15, *Planning and the Historic Environment*, sets out in more detail the role of planning in protecting the historic environment and the criteria to be applied when considering listed building consent applications.

3. Conservation Areas

These are designated by LPAs under the Planning (Listed Buildings and Conservation Areas) Act 1990. Conservation areas are defined by the Act as areas of special architectural or historic interest, the character or appearance of which it is desirable to preserve or enhance. There are now more than 8,000 conservation areas in England. They have been used to protect the setting and vistas of important historic parks and gardens, and many urban conservation areas include historic parks and green spaces.

The LPA may have relevant conservation area policies in its Local Development Framework which should be considered when framing proposals for development. In considering any proposals the LPA must pay special attention to the desirability of preserving or enhancing the character or appearance of a Conservation Area.

Conservation Area status confers control on the demolition of most buildings within it. Conservation Area consent from the LPA will generally be required for demolition of any buildings in a Conservation Area.

PPG 15 states that the general presumption should be in favour of retaining buildings which make a positive contribution to the character or appearance of a conservation area.

It is an offence to carry out works without giving notice unless the works are exempted. Therefore, it is important to check whether any exemptions apply. Further information on designation and planning controls for conservation areas is set out in PPG 15.

4. Scheduled Monuments

Some parks and gardens may contain structures, ruins or buried archaeology considered to be of national importance which are designated Scheduled Monuments (SMs). Some gardens and designed landscapes are also of archaeological importance and classified as SMs in their own right.

The Schedule of Ancient Monuments was first established by the 1882 Ancient Monuments Act (current legislation is the Ancient Monuments and Archaeological Areas Act 1979). The effect of a monument being included on the Schedule is that Scheduled Monuments Consent (SMC) from the Secretary of State is required before undertaking certain work to an SM; in fact, virtually all works to an SM will require SMC. Failure to obtain SMC and carring out work for which an SMC has been refused are offences. The following are also offences:

- Intentionally to destroy or damage a monument knowing it to be scheduled
- To be reckless as to whether a monument might be destroyed or damaged

- To use a metal detector or remove an object found with one without a licence from English Heritage

Early consultation with English Heritage (as adviser to the Secretary of State on these issues) is recommended before considering any works to a scheduled monument. Again, it should be noted that planning permission may be required in addition to an SMC.

Owners and managers of historic parks and gardens may also have to consider the archaeological remains. PPG 16 states that 'care must be taken to ensure that archaeological remains are not needlessly or thoughtlessly destroyed'. Where nationally important archaeological remains and their settings are affected by proposed development there should be a presumption in favour of their physical preservation whether or not they are scheduled. Further information is contained in PPG 16.

5. Sites of Special Scientific Interest (SSSIs)

SSSIs are designated by the English Nature under the Wildlife and Countryside Act 1981 in order to identify and protect important sites of wildlife, ecological and geological interest. English Nature's powers regarding SSSIs have been further expanded by the Countryside and Rights of Way (CROW) Act 2000. Sites have been selected according to rigorous published guidelines and English Nature has a duty to notify the LPA, the Secretary of State and every owner/occupier of the land affected of any sites they consider meet these criteria.

PPG 9, 'Nature Conservation', confirms that development proposals in or likely to affect SSSIs are subject to special scrutiny, and that nature conservation can be a significant material consideration in determining planning applications for such development. In such cases, the LPA is required to consult English Nature before making a decision. The Secretary of State may decide to determine applications affecting SSSIs if they raise issues of more than local importance.

In addition, there is a duty on public bodies to take reasonable steps to further conservation or enhancement of special features in an SSSI (or on land is likely to affect one) in exercising their functions.

While SSSIs and AONBs are designated by national agencies, sites of local importance may be listed at a county level and each will be considered in the planning process.

Tree Preservation Orders (TPOs)

As will be clear from the above, the planning system is concerned about protecting amenity generally, and section 198 of the Town and Country Planning Act 1990 enables an LPA to make a tree preservation order where it is expedient in the interests of amenity to do so. Thus trees which can be enjoyed by the public or have an intrinsic value, such as scarcity, may be protected by such orders. TPOs can be made on individual trees, woodlands or as 'blanket' over a particular area – this could affect individual garden specimen trees, parkland clumps, shelterbelts and woodlands. Consent

TREES IN CONSERVATION AREAS

Six weeks' notice of any work planned for such trees – including all arboriculture work, not only felling – must be given to the local authority, unless the tree falls within a category of exempted case – for example, under the Town and Country Planning (Trees) Regulations 1999, where a tree has a stem diameter less than 75mm at 1.5m above ground level, or less than 100mm at that height and the work is to benefit other trees. Within this six-week period, the local authority may place a Tree Preservation Order (TPO) on the trees affected; if not, the work may be carried out after the six-week period without further reference.

from the local authority is required before carrying out specified works to the trees covered. If permission is refused, the work may not be undertaken and it is an offence to undertake any unauthorised works.

There are certain exemptions, however. If a tree is considered to be dead, dying, dangerous or a legal nuisance, for example, work including felling may be carried out immediately and the local authority notified in retrospect. However, this is clearly a matter of judgement and it is always best to check with the local authority wherever possible. Tree work immediately required as part of a granted planning permission does not require separate TPO consent. No consent under a TPO will be needed for works that are subject to a felling licence; such licences are considered in more detail below.

Fruit trees may be protected by TPOs provided it is in the interests of amenity. However, LPA consent is not required to cut down or carry out work if the tree is cultivated in the course of a business. If it is not cultivated on a commercial basis LPA consent is required to cut it down – but not to prune it, provided such pruning is carried out in accordance with good horticultural practice.

Roads and highways

New parks and garden developments may have traffic implications. Roads and highways are the responsibility of the local highways authority, usually the local council, and the authority needs to be consulted where highways are affected during or after construction work.

2. PROTECTION OF PEOPLE

Occupiers' liability

Under the Occupiers' Liability Act (OLA) 1957, a 'common duty of care' is owed by an occupier to every lawful visitor. This is clearly of relevance to properties open to the public. The duty is defined as 'a duty to take such care as in all the circumstances of the case is reasonable to see that the visitor will be reasonably safe in using the premises for the purposes for which he is invited or permitted by the occupier to be there'.

There are two key issues:

*   The occupier is required only to act reasonably in all circumstances. The courts do realise that there is such a thing as a 'blameless' injury

*   The court will bear in mind the purpose for which someone is invited or permitted to be on the premises, and whether they have deviated from that purpose.

WHAT IS AN 'OBVIOUS' RISK?

In the case of Darby v National Trust (2001), the Court of Appeal considered the application of the OLA 1957 following a claim arising out of the death by drowning of a visitor to Hardwicke Park in Derbyshire. It decided that the Trust did not need to put up signs warning competent swimmers against the risks of swimming in ponds, as the risks were perfectly obvious. Although they would not have affected the Court of Appeal's conclusion, explicit warnings, had they been present, might have prevented the accident in the first place.

That said, occupiers must be prepared for children to be less careful than adults. In situations where an adult might be a trespasser, children are likely to be treated as implied licensees.

In determining whether an occupier has fallen short of the standard required, the court will take account of all relevant circumstances, including whether or not the occupier has warned his visitor of any potential danger. However, this does not offer a great deal of comfort: if a lawful visitor suffers a personal injury, the use of explicit notices does not exonerate occupiers from negligence claims. Accordingly, it is important for owners and managers to consider how best to communicate the risks of potential hazards to visitors.

In contrast, if the only thing damaged is property, it is possible to restrict or exclude liability for negligence by a notice or contractual term, as long as that notice or term is 'reasonable'.

Any person entering any premises in exercise of rights conferred by the CROW Act 2000 (covered in more detail below) is not, for the purposes of the OLA 1957, a visitor of the occupier of the premises. In addition, CROW inserted into the OLA 1984 a provision to the effect that no duty is owed by an occupier of land in respect of a risk resulting from a natural feature of the landscape, or any river, stream, ditch or pond (whether or not a natural feature). Where the danger is created by the occupier – whether intentionally or recklessly – a duty is owed, but in such cases the court will consider that the duty ought not to place an undue burden on the occupier, and will look at the importance of maintaining, among other things, features of historic or traditional interest.

Disabled access

The Disability Discrimination Act 1995 (DDA) aims to end the discrimination which many disabled people face. It covers a wide range of issues, including employment, property rental and purchase, use of public transport and access to goods, facilities and services.

In short, the Act makes it unlawful to treat disabled people less favourably because they are disabled. Service providers are required to consider making reasonable adjustments to the way they deliver their services so that disabled people can use them. This also includes considering making permanent physical adjustments to their premises.

Employers of 15 or more people have a duty to make reasonable adjustment to avoid substantial disadvantage to a specific employee who has a qualifying disability.

Service providers have a duty to make reasonable adjustments to any physical features which make it impossible or unreasonably difficult for disabled people to use the service. This is an anticipatory duty – service providers are required to anticipate the needs of people with disabilities and to accommodate them in a wide variety of ways. The duty is also continuous, so service providers are expected to review changes made and the changing needs of disabled people, at appropriate intervals.

The first step in undertaking these responsibilities is to undertake an 'access audit' which should cover the whole area over which the service is provided and will recommend measures which should be undertaken. The audit should be carried out by someone experienced in assessing access issues, such as those included on the National Register of Access Consultants.

Further information about DDA can be obtained from the Disability Rights Commission at www.disability.gov.uk.

High hedges

Part 8 of the Anti-Social Behaviour Act 2003 deals with the nuisance caused by high hedges and enables local authorities to deal with high hedges having an adverse effect on a neighbour's enjoyment of his property. Intervention by the local authority is seen very much as a matter of last resort and neighbours will be expected to have made every effort to resolve the situation amicably. The provisions only apply to protect domestic properties if an owner or occupier believes that a high hedge (but not its roots) affects the 'reasonable enjoyment of that property' (or a part of it). They may make a complaint to the local authority in whose area the land is situated. See also 2.3, 'Shelter, hedges and screens', pages 153–4.

A 'high hedge' refers to a line of two or more evergreens which rise to a height more than 2m above ground level. 'Evergreen' means an evergreen or semi-evergreen tree or shrub; hedges consisting of deciduous trees and shrubs are not covered by this legislation.

If the authority decide action is necessary, copies of a remedial notice must be sent to the complainant and the every owner and occupier of the neighbouring land. The notice must include a number of matters, such as what initial action must be taken, the period for compliance and what preventative action must be taken in future to stop a recurrence of the adverse effect.

There is a right of appeal for complainants and owners/occupiers. Appeals must be made (in accordance with regulations made by the Secretary of State) within 28 days of the date on which the remedial notice was issued or the date of notification given by the local authority of the decision being appealed.

It is an offence not to comply with the requirements of a notice within the compliance period. The local authority have powers to carry out the work in default after giving at least 7 days' notice of intention to carry out the work to every occupier of the land. The local authority may also recover any reasonable expenses from anyone who is an owner or occupier of the land.

Employment

The employment of staff carries with it the requirement to work within the provisions of extensive employment legislation and appropriate expert advice should be sought. However, it is considered that a couple of areas may be of particular relevance in the context of the management of parks and gardens and some of the main provisions are identified below.

Transfer of Undertakings (Protection of Employment) Regulations (TUPE) TUPE 1981 were introduced into UK law to implement the European Acquired Rights Directive. The objective of this legislation is to ensure that employees' rights are safeguarded in the event of the transfer of a business to a new employer, and to allow them to remain in the employment of the new employer on the same terms and conditions as they were employed under before the transfer. So, for example, managers need to be aware that changing the way services are provided or work is undertaken – e.g. contracting out work, or changing from

---

HEALTH AND SAFETY AT WORK

Employers have a duty to ensure, so far as is reasonably practicable, the health, safety and welfare at work of all their employees. This includes:

- provision and maintenance of plant and systems that are safe and without risk to health

- arrangements for safe use, handling, storage and transport of articles and substances

- provision of information, instruction, supervision and training to ensure health and safety

- provision of a safe place of work, including access and egress

- provision of a safe work environment and adequate welfare arrangements

It also places duties on each employee to:

- take reasonable care for the health and safety of himself and other persons who may be affected by his acts or omissions at work

- co-operate with his employer regarding any statutory safety requirements

using a contractor to directly employed staff – may trigger these provisions.

Health and Safety at Work Act This 1974 legislation imposes duties on employers and their contractors to ensure health, safety and welfare at work not only to employees, but also to neighbours, passers-by and the public at large. It also covers the self-employed. Breach of these duties is a criminal offence, enforced by the Health & Safety Executive (HSE), infringements of which can result in fine and/or imprisonment. The Act provides the legal framework under which a range of safety regulations are made, including the Control of Substances Hazardous to Health (COSHH) Regulations 2002 (see below) and the Personal Protective Equipment at Work Regulations 1992. In addition, the Management of Health and Safety at Work Regulations 1999 make more explicit what employers are required to do to manage health and safety.

No person, whether employer, employee or self-employed, may recklessly interfere with or misuse anything provided in the interests of health and safety. Manufacturers and suppliers must ensure that articles and substances for use at work are safe, as far as reasonably practicable, when properly used; must carry out appropriate testing, and provide information and instruction regarding safe use of the product.

Where the requirement is to take such steps 'so far as is reasonably practicable', the onus is on the duty holder (such as the employer) to prove that everything reasonably practicable has been done. Following approved codes of practice and good industry standards is a good way of showing this.

An employer of five or more employees must have a written health and safety policy statement, and carry out suitable and sufficient risk assessments under the *Management of Health and Safety at Work Regulations* 1999. A risk assessment is an invaluable means of identifying hazards, the potential risks they pose and actions to minimise risks. It may well minimise the chances of accidents occurring which might lead to civil or criminal liability, or both. These documents are likely to be the first demanded by the HSE if they decide to investigate an accident.

Pesticides

Under the Food and Environment Protection Act 1985, pesticides are defined as 'any substance, preparation or organism prepared or used for destroying any pest'. The term therefore encompasses a number of products including (among others) herbicides, fungicides, insecticides and masonry biocides.

The two main areas of legislation of principal significance concerning the use of pesticides are the *Control of Pesticides Regu-*

lations 1986 (introduced under the Food and Environment Protection Act 1985) and the *Control of Substances Hazardous to Health Regulations* 2002 (introduced under the Health and Safety at Work Act 1974). The first aims to protect human beings, creatures and plants, safeguard the environment, ensure safe, effective and humane methods of controlling pests and make pesticide information available to the public. Of the numerous controls introduced by these regulations, five are of particular relevance to gardens using pesticides (as opposed to producing or supplying them):

- Only approved products may be sold, supplied, stored, advertised or used
- Users of pesticides must comply with the Conditions of Approval relating to use
- A recognised Certificate of Competence is required by all contractors and persons born after 31 December 1964 applying pesticides approved for professional agricultural and horticultural use (unless working under the direct supervision of a certificate holder).
- Only those adjuvants authorised by Defra may be used
- 'Tank mixing' may only be carried out using pesticides approved for that purpose and in approved combinations

Pesticides form a very wide and complex subject and reference to the full terms of the requirements are essential for those affected by them. The *UK Pesticide Guide*, a useful reference book revised annually and published by the British Crop Protection Council, gives detailed profiles of the main pesticides used in agriculture, horticulture, forestry and amenity situations. Due to the colour of its cover it is commonly known as the Green Book.

Hazardous substances

The COSHH Regulations 2002 require that the risks associated with the use of any substance hazardous to health at work must be assessed before it is used and the appropriate measures be taken to avoid or minimise that risk. In order of preference these measures should be followed:

- Substitution with a chemical or product less hazardous
- Technical or engineering controls (e.g. the use of controlled handling systems)
- Operational controls (e.g. operators located in cabs fitted with air filtration systems)
- Use of personal protective equipment, which includes protective clothing

To assist with COSHH assessments, manufacturers will supply product safety data sheets. The COSHH Regulations also require that:

- Consideration be given to the necessity of using pesticides at all in a given situation
- Label precautions be used as a minimum
- Safety equipment and clothing is properly maintained and staff are instructed and trained in its use

- Where necessary, exposure of workers is monitored and health checks are carried out
- Adequate records of all operations involving pesticide application must be made and retained for at least 3 years

Again, it is important that those who may be affected by these regulations refer to the full provisions.

3. PROTECTION OF THE NATURAL ENVIRONMENT

Government policies and regulation concerning the countryside emanate from Defra, advised by specialist agencies such as English Nature. It is proposed to merge the current roles of English Nature, parts of the Countryside Agency and the Rural Development Service into a new agency to be known as Natural England, due to be established by late 2006. This new, independent, statutory organisation will be responsible for championing integrated resource management, nature conservation, biodiversity, landscape, access and recreation. The Natural Environment and Rural Communities Bill will update and amend legislation naming English Nature, the Countryside Agency and their predecessor organisations.

Hedgerow regulations

Hedgerow removal, caused by the decline in mixed farming and increasing intensification, has caused environmental concern for a number of years. On 1 June 1997, the Hedgerow Regulations came into force, to protect important hedges from removal. Unless a hedgerow is excluded because of the type of land it borders or because of its length, or unless the works are considered 'minor' under the regulations, any owner wishing to remove all or part of a hedgerow must give the LPA 42 days' notice of their intentions (the 42 days start when the notice is received by the authority). During this period the authority may decide that the hedgerow is important and issue a 'hedgerow retention notice' which prohibits the work from being carried out; if not, the work may proceed.

The importance of hedges is judged on a number of criteria. For example, a hedge may be considered important if it has existed for more than 30 years and satisfies at least one of the criteria contained in the regulations. These include, among other things, the marking of a pre-1850 boundary or the incorporation of an archaeological feature. For practical purposes most hedges, except ornamental garden hedges, are covered by the regulations and notice does need to be given. If a hedge is believed to be less than 30 years old, evidence of the planting date may be required. Failure to give notice constitutes an offence.

Felling licences

The Forestry Commission is the government department responsible for forestry in the UK. Under the Forestry Act 1967 (as amended) it has powers to prevent woodland being destroyed and this is achieved by requiring owners to obtain a felling licence before work is undertaken. Where a felling licence is required, it is the responsibility of all concerned with the felling – owner, agent,

FELLING THAT DOES NOT REQUIRE A LICENCE

- Up to 5 cubic metres per calendar quarter, provided that no more than 2 cubic metres are sold
- Lopping and topping, including tree surgery, pruning and pollarding
- Felling included in a plan approved under the Woodland Grant Scheme before 1 April 1998
- Fruit trees or trees growing in a garden, orchard, churchyard or designated public open space
- Trees with a diameter of 8cm or less at 1.3m from the ground
- Thinnings, with a diameter of 10cm or less at 1.3m from the ground
- Coppice or underwood with a diameter of 15cm or less at 1.3m from the ground
- Felling immediately required as part of a development with planning permission
- Felling necessary to prevent a danger or abate a nuisance
- Felling necessary to prevent the spread of a quarantine pest or disease, and done in accordance with a notice served by the Forestry Commission in compliance with an Act of Parliament

contractor and timber merchant – to ensure that the licence has been issued, and it is an offence to fell without it. See the box (above) for exemptions.

Further details and information on how to apply for a felling licence are available from the Forestry Commission: www.forestry.gov.uk.

Wildlife law

The Wildlife and Countryside Act 1981 (as amended) deals with a wide range of issues, but perhaps the most relevant for historic parks and gardens are the provisions relating to SSSIs and the protection of plants and animals.

Sites of Special Scientific Interest (SSSIs) SSSIs form a series of nationally important sites related to special habitats and important locations of rare or endangered animals and plants, the aim being the conservation of wildlife and geology. Many of the geological sites are standard reference localities for particular rock types or formations.

SITES OF SPECIAL SCIENTIFIC INTEREST

In England in 2004 there were:

- 4,115 SSSIs on public and privately owned land
- They covered over 1 million hectares, or
- 7.6 per cent of the land surface

SSSIs are mapped at MAGIC (the Government agencies' information website), along with a variety of information on statutory and non-statutory designations and grading of sites such as SSSIs, SMs, Registered Landscapes and Special Protection Areas: www.magic.gov.uk.

Under the Wildlife and Countryside Act 1981, Natural England is required to notify every owner or occupier (including planning and water agencies) of each SSSI. These notifications comprise a map of the site's boundary and location and a statement of its special interest features – animals, plants, geological features or landform. It must also list those operations likely to damage the SSSI. There is a requirement to consult Natural England if any such operations are planned; they are officially called 'operations likely to damage' (OLDs) (previously known as PDOs, 'potentially damaging operations') and may not be carried out without consent.

In addition, since January 2001, notifications have included 'Views about Management' that were English Nature's formal advice on the positive management of each SSSI. These will be issued retrospectively for all existing SSSIs. The position regarding notification, consent and any financial assistance is complex; owners, agents or occupiers are strongly advised to consult their local Natural England office. In practice, many beneficial park and garden management practices would comply with Natural England guidelines.

It is an offence knowingly to damage or destroy any of the flora, fauna, or geological or physiographical features on land of special interest, or intentionally or recklessly to disturb any of those fauna. There is a maximum fine of £20,000 (2004) in a magistrate's court (unlimited in a crown court) for causing damage, and the courts may also require restoration where practicable. There are special provisions for specified bodies exercising their functions.

In cases where neglect may lead to a loss of the ecological interest, Natural England may issue a management notice to owners or occupiers of SSSIs. This sets prescriptions for necessary work and there is a requirement to comply. Failure to comply is an offence which carries a maximum fine of £5,000 in a magistrate's court (unlimited in a crown court). Natural England have powers to carry out works in default and then recover the costs from the owners/occupiers.

Natural England may extend the boundaries of an SSSI and increase the described interest and, if necessary, the list of OLDs in the light of new evidence. The Act provides a right of entry on to an SSSI and also on to land that might potentially be of SSSI quality for the purpose of survey.

There is a requirement for owners/occupiers to notify Natural England if the land forming an SSSI (or part of an SSSI) changes hands. Natural England also have designated compulsory purchase powers and powers to make by-laws.

Protected animals are listed in Schedule 5 of the Act. In addition to bats and the reptiles and amphibians covered below, they include red squirrels, a number of rare butterflies, moths and other insects, and some molluscs and spiders. It should be noted, however, that species can be added to or withdrawn from the Schedules to the Act by order, and the level of protection may vary.

The Act prohibits certain methods of killing or taking wild animals, including self-locking snares, bows, crossbows and explosives. It also particularly limits the methods by which certain specific animals may be taken or killed (listed in Schedule 6 and including badgers, bats, dormice, hedgehogs, otters and red squirrels).

The Act prohibits any person from releasing, or allowing to escape, into the wild any wild animal which is not ordinarily, in the wild state, a resident in or a regular visitor to Great Britain or which is included in Schedule 9 (part I), a list of more than 40 species including edible dormice, ruddy duck, mink, several species of pheasant, black rats, grey squirrels, wallabies and terrapins. The relevant sections for land managers are summarised here.

Birds (generally) All wild birds are protected under Section 1 of the Act. It is an offence to:

- Kill, injure or take any wild bird
- Take, damage or destroy the nest of any wild bird while that nest is in use
- Take or destroy an egg of any wild bird

Certain exemptions are listed in the Schedules to the Act.

Birds of prey It is an offence to:

- Kill, take, damage or destroy their nests or eggs without a licence
- Release them into the wild

For many years, birds of prey were taken from the wild, as eggs or chicks. However, this was prohibited by the Act in 1981 and all diurnal raptors in captivity have to be registered with the Wildlife Licensing Section of Defra. The Act has since been amended to include only the species listed in Appendix A. Any falconer keeping unregistered birds of these species, or birds of other species taken from the wild without a licence (unless injured) would be guilty of an offence.

Falconry displays Another relevant conservation issue is the possible disturbance to wild birds of prey caused by captive display animals nearby. Birds of prey are relatively solitary animals, and particularly during the breeding season may be seriously disturbed by the presence of captive birds within their home range, even for short periods. Falconry displays should not be held on sites known to support birds of prey during the breeding season, although falconry displays could be held on these sites at other times of year. There is a growing list of birds of prey that require registration with Defra.

The Act also sets standards for the keeping of captive birds. They remain the responsibility of their owners at all times, including during displays. All captive birds of the species listed in Appendix A should have Defra registration documents, and will usually wear a ring issued by the department.

Badgers are protected under the Protection of Badgers Act 1992. This makes it an offence to kill, injure, capture or cruelly ill-treat a badger, or to interfere with a badger sett by damaging, destroying or obstructing access, causing a dog to enter, or disturbing a badger when it is in occupation.

Under Section 10 of the Protection of Badgers Act, licences can be issued to allow otherwise prohibited actions for a number of specific purposes. For example, Natural England can issue licences to interfere with badger setts for the purpose of the preservation or archaeological investigation of a monument scheduled under the Ancient Monuments and Archaeological Areas Act 1979. This means that where an operation to preserve or investigate a scheduled monument is likely to result in interference or disturbance to a badger sett, a licence application must be made to Natural England's Licensing Section.

For the purpose of preventing serious damage to land, crops or any other form of property, Defra can issue licences. If a badger sett is causing damage to property, including scheduled or non-scheduled monuments, listed buildings or historic gardens, a licence application must be made to Defra's National Wildlife Management Team. Neither of these licences negates the need to obtain, in addition, scheduled monument consent (SMC) before carrying out work on a scheduled monument.

Bats Protection is given to all species of bat because of their special requirements for roosting. It is illegal

- Intentionally to kill, injure or handle any bat
- Intentionally to damage, destroy or obstruct access to any place that a bat uses for shelter or protection, whether or not the bat is present
- To disturb a bat while it is occupying such a place

In this context, 'damage' means make worse for the bat, and so would include such operations as treatment with the toxic chemicals found in wood preservatives. Building, maintenance or remedial operations can be carried out in places used by bats, but only in consultation with Natural England; in some instances a licence may be required. Local planning authorities are obliged under PPS 9 (Biodiversity and Geological Conservation) to take the presence of bats, and other protected species, into account in determining planning applications.

Reptiles and amphibians In Britain there are six native reptiles (snakes and lizards) and six native amphibians (frogs, toads and newts). All native reptiles and amphibians are protected under the 1981 Act, and four species (smooth snake, sand lizard, natterjack toad and great crested newt) are also protected by European Directive. The position varies for different species and is summarised in the table below.

It is an offence to sell, or advertise for sale, any of the species subject to control, and this applies to eggs and young as well as adults. Deliberate killing of snakes has been a problem in the past and persecution of the adder has made this species quite uncommon in some areas. As a result it is an offence intentionally to kill or injure most species. In addition, the smooth snake, sand lizard, natterjack toad and great crested newt may not be caught, handled or disturbed, and this includes damage or disturbance to their habitats. For those wishing to change or develop an area that may provide a habitat for these species, it is advisable to employ a specialist to undertake a survey of the site prior to any work. If these species are identified, a mitigation strategy will need to be agreed with Natural England before work can be undertaken. Discovery of a protected species at a late stage could delay or even prevent the project going ahead.

PROTECTED REPTILES AND AMPHIBIANS

Species	Prohibited to sell or advertise for sale	Prohibited to kill or injure	Prohibited to handle, capture, posses or disturb
Grass snake *Natrix natrix*	✔	✔	
Smooth snake *Coronella austriaca*	✔	✔	✔
Adder or viper *Vipera berus*	✔	✔	
Common or viviparous lizard *Lacerta vivipara*	✔	✔	
Sand lizard *Lacerta agilis*	✔	✔	✔
Slow worm ((a legless lizard) *Anguis fragilis*	✔	✔	
Common toad *Bufo bufo*	✔		
Natterjack toad *Bufo calamita*	✔	✔	✔
Common frog *Rana temporaria*	✔		
Smooth or common newt *Triturus vulgaris*	✔		
Great crested or warty newt *Triturus cristatus*	✔	✔	✔
Palmate newt *Triturus helveticus*	✔		

Note that it is illegal to release, or re-release once captured, non-native species of reptile or amphibian to the wild. This may have implications where non-native species, e.g. terrapins, are found on a site.

Natural England issues licences to take and handle protected species in order to conserve them, for scientific research and for use in education.

Wild plants The provisions relating to plants are rather more straightforward. The Act makes it an offence for anyone intentionally to pick, uproot, destroy, sell or offer for sale any wild plant included in Schedule 8 (60+ species including spring gentian, red helleborine, fen violet and many species of orchid). It also makes it an offence for any person intentionally to uproot any wild plant without the permission of the land owner.

Weeds The Weeds Act 1959 (as amended) applies to five species of native plants that traditionally have been considered potentially poisonous to livestock or rapidly colonising agricultural land at the expense of the preferred crops. These are classed as 'injurious weeds' (see box, below) and Defra can serve notice on the occupier of land where they are a problem to take action to control them. Failure to comply is an offence. The ministry is also empowered to carry out the work by default and recover the cost from the owner.

Alien Species Concern about native plants and habitats led to controls being placed on the spread of some 'alien species'. In controlling them by other than chemical means (i.e. by cutting down or pulling up), the arisings become 'controlled waste' and are subject to the controlled waste regulations: this means they require transport in sealed containers to licensed landfill sites according to the Environmental Protection Act (Duty of Care) Regulations 1991.

Habitats Directive

Council Directive 92/43 EEC on the Conservation of Natural Habitats and of Wild Fauna and Flora was approved by the Council of Ministers in 1992; it is more commonly known as the Habitats Directive. The Conservation (Natural Habitats, etc.) Regulations 1994, known as the Habitats Regulations, transpose the Habitats Directive into UK national law. They introduce rigorous tests for the protection of habitats and species of European importance. The key to the complex assessment process is the application of the precautionary principle, which for the first time is enshrined in wildlife law. Planning policy advice can be found in PPS 9.

The Habitats Directive provides for the creation of a network of protected areas across the European Union which will be known as Natura 2000. Its aim is to maintain or restore the extent and quality of rare habitat types and to ensure that rare species can survive and maintain their populations and natural range on a long-term basis.

This section is a basic introduction to the Habitats Directive and the way it might affect those sites readers are involved with. It is not meant to provide a detailed guide for dealing with work proposed within sites covered by the directive; English Nature's 'Habitats regulations guidance notes' 1–6 should be consulted for more detailed information and any proposed work should be discussed with English Nature local staff at the earliest stage of planning. The guidance notes can be found at www.english-nature.org.uk.

The aims of the directive apply not just to the designated site itself, but also to activities which might have an effect on the site – for example, draining an adjoining (non-designated) site, which might cause the lowering of the water table on the protected site.

The directive has a number of implications:

- It establishes the basis for a framework of protected sites throughout the European Union to be known as Natura 2000

- It introduces a rigorous protection process for designated sites, known as Special Areas for Conservation (SACs)

- It affords the same rigorous protection to sites designated under the earlier Birds Directive, known as Special Protection Areas (SPAs)

INJURIOUS WEEDS

Circium vulgare	Spear thistle
Circium arvense	Creeping or field thistle
Rumex crispus	Curled dock
Rumex obtusifolius	Broad-leaved dock
Senecio jacobaea	Ragwort

ALIEN SPECIES

It is forbidden under section 14(2) of the Weeds Act 1959 to plant or otherwise cause to grow in the wild the plants listed in Schedule 9 (Part II) which includes:

Fallopia japonica (syn. *Polygonum cuspidatum*)	Japanese knotweed
Heracleum mantegazzianum	Giant hogweed

It is forbidden under the Environmental Protection Act 1990 to spread by seed or vegetatively the above two plants plus:

Impatiens glandulifera	Himalayan balsam

OBJECTIVES OF THE HABITATS DIRECTIVE

- The conservation of natural habitats and wild fauna and flora

- To ensure that measures taken shall be designed to maintain or restore the natural habitats and species of wild flora and fauna

- To ensure that measures taken shall take account of economic, social and cultural requirements and regional and local characteristics (this objective is not applied at the time sites are designated)

- It introduces strict protection for individual species
- It encourages the management of landscapes to support Natura 2000
- It introduces monitoring provisions

Natura 2000 sites

The assessment process required by the Habitats Regulations, in transposing the Directive, applies to European sites which can also be termed Natura 2000 sites. European sites are defined by the Habitats Regulations as:

- Special Areas of Conservation (SACs), a status that is only conferred once the sites on the list approved by the European Commission have been designated. At present sites are known as *candidate* Special Areas of Conservation (cSACs). There are currently 210 cSACs in England
- Special Protection Areas (SPAs) designated under the Birds Directive. Sites which have been put forward as apparently meriting classification but which have yet to be classified are known as *potential* Special Protection Areas (pSPAs). There are currently 85 pSPAs in England
- Ramsar sites, designated under the Convention on Wetlands of International Importance Especially as Waterfowl Habitat 1973 (the Ramsar Convention). There are currently 78 Ramsar sites in England
- Sites hosting a priority habitat or species which the European Commission thinks should be on the list submitted by the government

All terrestrial European sites in England will also be SSSIs (but not all SSSIs will be European sites), but they may be aggregates of several existing SSSIs and will often have different names form their SSSI components. As a matter of government policy, cSACs and pSPAs are afforded full protection as soon as they are nominated; Ramsar sites are afforded the same protection at a policy level as those sites which have been designated under the Birds and Habitat Directives.

The object of European site status is to provide sites with stronger safeguards commensurate with their European importance. The 'precautionary principle' for these sites is that 'a competent authority shall only agree to a plan or project having ascertained that it will have no adverse effect on the integrity of the European site' (The Conservation [Natural Habitats, etc.] Regulations 1994, regulations 20 and 48). In dealing with a plan or project affecting a European site, a competent authority needs to demonstrate an audit trail to show due consideration about the effect the plan or project will have on the site.

Plant health regulations

With increasing trade in living plants both within Europe and around the world, legislation is in place to monitor plant movements, control the introduction of exotic plant pathogens and restrict the movement of endangered species.

Defra has responsibility, through its Plant Health & Seeds Inspectorate (PHSI), to prevent the movement of certain notifiable diseases into and within the country. For example, in England and Wales, PHSI requires rhododendrons and viburnums to be visibly free from Ramorum dieback (Sudden Oak Death) at all stages down to retail level, before plant passports can be issued. These are issued by registered nurseries, following inspection by PHSI, for stock shown to be healthy. Requested information, including Defra registration, origin, plant name and quantity in consignment, is given on labels attached to the plants, or on delivery documents, or split between labels and consignment. Phytosanitary Certificates are issued on freedom from notifiable pests and diseases for plant material moving from non-EU to EU countries. Inspections take place in the country exporting the plant material. Diagnostic tests associated with notifiable pests and diseases are also used in plant certification schemes.

Certification schemes are operated in England and Wales by Defra, to provide planting material that is healthy, vigorous and true to type. Material of this nature is multiplied under controlled conditions with official growing season inspections, to ensure continued freedom from pests and diseases. Crops meeting the specified standards are granted an official certificate, providing quality assurance to the buyer – for example, currently all seed potatoes produced in England and Wales must be classified under the Seed Potato Classification Scheme. The Plant Health Propagation Scheme is a voluntary scheme for certain fruit crops, hops, narcissus and bulbous iris.

Defra is also responsible for UK Seed Certification and UK National Listing. Seed Certification ensures that seed is not marketed unless it meets specified standards. UK National Lists include varieties of the main agricultural crops and vegetables: to be added, a variety must be distinct, sufficiently uniform and stable (DUS). Plant Breeders' Rights (PBR) provide legal protection for the investment plant breeders make in developing new varieties, preventing others from propagating material without authority. Currently, ornamentals covered by PBR include chrysanthemums, dahlias, delphiniums, herbaceous perennials, narcissus, roses, seed-propagated ornamentals, trees, shrubs and woody climbers.

The Earth Summit (1992) established Agenda 21 as the blueprint for sustainable development and the importance of biodiversity. In the UK, a national strategy for the conservation of biological diversity has been developed with action plans for species and habitats and, at a local level, biodiversity action plans. In 2004, the UK Government published its response on *Global Strategy for Plant Conservation*. Gardens and plant collections have a role in plant conservation, and the genetics of garden plants are part of our biodiversity resource.

The Convention on International Trade in Endangered Species of Wild Fauna and Flora (CITES) is an international agreement between governments. It aims to ensure that international trade in specimens of wild plants and animals does not threaten their survival. Currently 28,417 species of plant are covered by the three categories of protection. This includes many succulents, cycads, some insectivorous plants and orchids, among others.

The Countryside and Rights of Way (CROW) Act 2000

Many large gardens and designed landscapes are crossed with footpaths and other rights of way. The landlord's statutory duties with respect to public rights of way relate to keeping paths open and safe to use; examples include cutting back overgrown vegetation, maintaining stiles and gates, and the management of livestock. The CROW Act has four main parts, dealing with:

- The right to roam
- Public rights of way
- Nature conservation and wildlife protection
- Areas of outstanding natural beauty

Each section introduces a number of new arrangements and/or changes to existing ones. Some main provisions are detailed below.

The right to roam This part of the Act is intended to give greater freedom for people to explore open countryside. It contains provisions to introduce a statutory right of access for open-air recreation to mountain, moor, heath, down (collectively described as open country) and registered common land. It includes a power to extend the right to coastal land by order. It also enables landowners voluntarily to dedicate irrevocably any land to public access.

These access rights are not unrestricted. There are provisions, for example, which allow landowners to exclude or restrict access for any reason for up to 28 days a year, and to exclude dogs on grouse moors and in small fields during lambing time (subject to certain limitations) without permission. There is also provision for further restrictions or exclusions for reasons of land management, fire prevention and to avoid danger to the public. Natural England (formerly the Countryside Agency) and the National Parks Authority are the bodies which in England can grant these extra restrictions. They may also direct the restriction or exclusion of access on grounds of nature or heritage conservation.

While some land qualified as access land straightaway, most did not qualify until it was shown on conclusive maps issued by the Countryside Agency on 16 August 2005, showing the estimated 4 million acres of 'open countryside' for which public access rights came into force on 31 October 2005. More information is available from the Countryside Agency: www.countryside.gov.uk/access/mapping.

The right to roam is subject to various restrictions set out in the Act. It does not extend to cycling, horseriding or driving a vehicle. Excepted land includes buildings and the land attached to them, e.g. courtyards; land within 20m of a house or building containing livestock; parks and gardens; golf courses, and arable land (land ploughed for growing crops within the past year).

The Act amends the Occupiers' Liability Acts of 1957 and 1984 so as to restrict the occupier's liability towards those exercising the new right of access. The Open Access website provides more information for land managers and on how to manage public access: www.openaccess.gov.uk.

Public rights of way This section contains provisions designed to reform and improve public rights of way. It introduces measures for the strategic review, planning and reporting of improvements to rights of way and the promotion of increased access for people with mobility problems.

Landowners have a new right to apply to a local authority for an order to divert or extinguish a footpath or bridleway, and a right to appeal against refusal. There is also a new provision to divert a footpath or bridleway temporarily where it passes over land where works are likely to cause a danger to users. The Act also provides new powers enabling the diversion or closure of rights of way for crime prevention and school security, and diversion for the protection of SSSIs.

Stronger measures are provided for dealing with obstructions. The existing requirement on landowners to trim back vegetation overhanging a right of way is extended to include vegetation obstructing horseriders. The courts can now order people to remove obstructions from rights of way and fine them up to £5,000 (Level 5 on the standard scale) if they do not comply, then up to £250 (1/20th of Level 5) for each day the obstruction remains.

Individuals can now serve notice on a local authority to secure the removal of an obstruction, and if necessary seek a magistrate's court order requiring the local authority to comply with the notice. The Act also introduces the power for individuals to prosecute for failure to restore a footpath or bridleway after ploughing.

The Act also makes it clear that driving any mechanically propelled vehicle, including quad bikes, on routes recorded on the definitive map as footpaths, bridleways or restricted byways is an offence, unless the driver has lawful authority, e.g. the landowner, or can prove that they have rights or that the route is recorded incorrectly. The Act makes provision for this to be extended at

---

CLASSES OF RIGHTS OF WAY

Existing classes of public rights of way are being changed slightly to help clarify those on which the use of vehicles is prohibited. The four classes will be:

- Footpaths: highways over which there is a public right of way on foot

- Bridleways: highways over which pedestrians, horseriders and bicyclists (who must give way to people on foot or horseback) have public right of way. A bridleway may also carry a public right to drive animals

- Restricted byways: all existing RUPPs (roads used as public paths) will be redesignated as restricted byways which will have rights for walkers, cyclists, horseriders and horse-drawn vehicles. Vehicular rights will not be extinguished and anybody with evidence will be entitled to apply for a byway to be reclassified as a BOAT.

- Byways Open to All Traffic (BOATs): highways over which the public right of way is for vehicles and all other kinds of traffic, but which are used mainly for the purposes for which footpaths and bridleways are used

a later date to add that the driver must also be driving to reach premises as owner, visitor or on business.

Rights of Way, a guide to law and practice, is available from the Ramblers' Association. Advice is also available on the Countryside Agency website: cms.countrysideaccess.gov.uk.

Nature conservation and wildlife protection The CROW Act gives further protection to wildlife and natural features by making provision for the conservation of biological diversity and by improving protection for SSSIs and the enforcement of wildlife legislation.

There is now a general duty on government to have regard to biodiversity and to list the most important species and habitat types for biodiversity conservation, and a specific duty to further their conservation. This duty falls on all government departments and the non-departmental government bodies they sponsor.

Because of the difficulty in proving that defendants went with the objective of causing disturbance to birds listed on Schedule 1 of the Wildlife and Countryside Act 1981, a new offence of 'reckless disturbance' has been created, to make it easier for a prose-cutor to show that a person either took an unacceptable risk or failed to notice an obvious risk and thereby caused disturbance. This offence has also been extended to certain marine species, namely cetaceans and basking sharks, listed on schedule 5 of the Act. Anyone harming endangered wildlife is liable to up to two years' imprisonment and fines of up to £5,000.

Areas of Outstanding Natural Beauty (AONBs) This section aims to allow for the better management and protection of AONBs. It states explicitly that the purpose of designating AONBs is to conserve and enhance the natural beauty of the area, and places a duty on any relevant public body to have regard to this purpose when exercising their functions.

It provides for the creation of conservation boards for individual AONBs, where there is local support. It also requires the preparation and publication of a management plan for every AONB by the appropriate local authorities or by an AONB conservation board where one is established. These management plans must be reviewed at intervals not exceeding five years.

Part Two

The living garden landscape

2.1   Maintenance and management in practice   87
      The plant environment   87
      Soils and plant growth   94

2.2   Nature conservation   103
      The role of gardens and parks   103
      Maintenance and management   112

2.3   Vegetation maintenance and management   115
      Trees   117
      Conifers   129
      Arboreta, pineta, historic features, woodlands   131
      Shrubs   137
      Wall plants and climbers   143
      Roses   146
      Shelter, hedges and screens   149
      Herbaceous perennials   161
      Annuals and biennials   169
      Turf and grassland   175
      Water features   187
      Rock gardens   193
      Ferneries   198
      Parterres, knot gardens, mazes and labyrinths, topiary   199
      Walled kitchen gardens   204
      Conservatories, greenhouses, glasshouses, etc.   210
      Container growing   218

2.4   Technical maintenance   225
      Weed control   225
      Pests and diseases   229
      Machinery   233

Maintenance and management in practice

While recognising that the components of many gardens and parks will comprise structural and non-living features (the hard landscape), it is the living vegetation in all its many forms (the soft landscape) that gives the life, character and personality of many such places. Managing this vegetation in one form or another can often take up a large proportion of the garden staff's time, particularly in the peak growing periods. A range of differing knowledge and skills are needed: depending upon the size and character of the garden or park, these could cover vegetable and fruit growing in kitchen gardens and orchards (many now being restored); the great variety of features of ornamental gardens from short to longer term; and the most dominant and often the longest-term tree components as specimens or in avenues and arboreta and woodlands. These longer-term living components and their management may often be the dominant feature in many historic parks and gardens.

This section is a guide to the environments that control a plant's growth and the animals and native plants that share our gardens, followed by a detailed review of the maintenance and management of vegetation types, garden features and technical maintenance.

THE PLANT ENVIRONMENT

The plant environment is made up of a complex of physical and chemical factors, all of which will influence the way in which plants establish and survive. All plants depend upon five essentials for their healthy growth and reproduction: air, water, light, temperature and nutrients. The first four can be grouped under climate and microclimate, while nutrients are mostly derived from the soil or rooting medium.

The challenge of climate and planting

The gardening profession, botanists and enthusiastic amateurs have always been faced with the difficulties of successfully cultivating new plant arrivals from many parts of the world, whether in outdoor favourable climates or microclimates, or in the protected environments of orangeries, conservatories and glasshouses. The arrival of new plants caused a crescendo of excitement and fascination during the nineteenth and early twentieth centuries, and the gradual accumulation of experience and experimentation with these new introductions led to their eventually being found locations in gardens suited to the habitats where they originated.

The sustained and successful cultivation of garden plants in outdoor sites in the UK depends, in the first place, on the suitability of the climate – this will include the incidence of frosts, rainfall, sunshine hours, exposure to damaging winds and other climatic agencies. Variations in the weather will also determine how well or badly plants will do in any particular season. A hardiness factor may determine the longevity of certain plants, particularly those that are borderline, and this is where a knowledge of microclimates in a garden can be very beneficial in matching a plant to its preferred site.

Over 90 per cent of the UK population now live in towns or suburbs. In this rather shielded environment, it is all too easy to lose contact and first-hand acquaintance with the full realities of climate and weather in the less protected wider landscape. Generations of farmers, gardeners and country landowners in the past built up a keen awareness, knowledge and sensitive appreciation of the weather and its effect on their own localities, and developed shrewd powers of observation and forecasting. This enabled them to take certain courses of action and plan in advance, to prepare for the effects of seasonal weather changes or of likely adverse weather, such as gales, frost or freak storms. There is no doubt that national and regional forecasting has shown remarkable progress in the last few decades, and is becoming increasingly accurate. There are also other sources of information such as weather-watch programmes and weather information on the internet. However, these may not always provide detailed information of local or regional weather changes, which can sometimes be unexpected. There can be distinctive and at times dramatic variations in the British climate, depending upon the locality in which one lives or works.

CLIMATE, MICROCLIMATE AND WEATHER

These terms are often loosely used when talking about 'the weather' as a topical subject, but it is important for the understanding of the plant environment and its management to be precise about what they mean.

- Weather refers to the current meteorological conditions at any one place or location, including short-term fluctuations.

- Climate covers longer-term average weather conditions, and this is often shown as records over a fixed period of time.

- Microclimate refers to the local and often very specific climatic conditions of one site, or areas within that site, ranging from a particular garden and its possible components – such as a shaded wall or sunny border – to a more extensive feature or an entire estate.

---

67. Opposite: skills, care and understanding are essential in the proper maintenance of historic features.

REGIONAL VARIATIONS IN THE PLANT ENVIRONMENT IN ENGLAND AND WALES
Adapted from MAFF Technical Bulletin 35, *The Agricultural Climate of England and Wales*, averages for 1941–70

Region	Latitude	Height above sea level, ave.	No. and period of growing days	Last frost (mean)	Daily sunshine hours, ave.	Monthly rainfall, ave.
Durham, Northumberland, Cumbria	55.6°N	67m (220ft)	237: 4 Apr–27 Nov	Late May	3.75	54.2mm (2.1in)
N. Pennines, upland zones	54.4°N	315m (1,033ft)	189: 25 Apr–31 Oct	Late May	3.25	89mm (3.5in)
Merseyside, Cheshire, Wirral	53.6°N	28m (92ft)	258: 23 Mar–6 Dec	Late April	4.1	69.75mm (2.75in)
Lincolnshire Wolds	53.2°N	42m (138ft)	248: 27 Mar–30 Nov	Early May	4.0	54.2mm (2.1in)
N. Midlands	52.0°N	83m (273ft)	251: 23 Mar–29 Nov	Late April	3.9	55mm (2.2in)
Norfolk	52.6°N	33m (108ft)	248: 26 Mar–29 Nov	Late April	4.2	52mm (2.0in)
Severn Valley, S.W. Midlands	51.6°N	91m (300ft)	263: 19 Mar–7 Dec	Late April	4.0	64.6mm (2.6in)
Surrey, E. Berkshire	51.0°N	107m (351ft)	258: 18 Mar–5 Dec	Late April	4.3	64.6mm (2.6in)
S.E. England	51.2°N	58m (190ft)	266: 18 Mar–11 Dec	Late April	4.5	48.1mm (1.9in)
South Coast	50.8°N	64m (210ft)	268: 19 Mar–12 Dec	Late April	4.5	52.5mm (2.1in)
S.W. England, Devon, Cornwall	50.2°N	83m (272ft)	322: 20 Feb–8 Jan	Early April	4.6	87.25mm (3.4in)

Above: the south-west peninsula of Britain has nearly 100 more growing days a year than the north-east coast – an advantage for growing a wider range of exotic plants, but a distinct disadvantage if there are large areas of grass to mow or weeds to deal with.

Latitude and temperature

Temperature, closely related to both latitude and altitude, is often the major limiting factor to plant growth and the cultivation of ornamental plants in Britain, assuming that other requirements, especially light and water, are favourable. Generally speaking, the plants that can be grown out of doors with reasonable success decrease in range as one travels north and, to a lesser extent, east. Thus if one moves from a garden in Sussex or South Devon to one in Lincolnshire or Northumberland, unless the microclimate is exceptionally favourable, one would expect to have more difficulty in growing and over-wintering plants classed as half-hardy. In this group are those that originate from warm temperate or Mediterranean climates, many of them evergreen. The altitude factor may also be very important in accentuating or modifying extremes of temperature. Temperature and light levels also have a marked effect on the growing season, which can be more precisely defined as the actual number of 'growing days' in the year, i.e. when a plant is actually making growth. This is defined as any day when the mean air temperature does not fall below 6.1°C (43°F), which varies considerably in different parts of the country. This is well illustrated in the box above.

Altitude

Marked variations in regional or local climate and microclimate can result from differences in altitude. For every 300m (1,000ft) above sea level there is an approximate decrease in mean air temperature of 1.7°C (3°F). This is very noticeable in hilly areas, even in the south and south-west where weather conditions on the hilltops can be cooler and breezier than in the valleys. In a sheltered valley one may enjoy nearly two weeks more growing days throughout the year than 150m (500ft) up in the hills, even if the two sites are only a couple of kilometres apart. In wintry conditions, snow can often be seen lying on the hills above 1,000m, while the valleys are free from snow. But this situation can be reversed during times of frost (see radiation frost, below).

Wind and exposure

The British Isles are often windy, due to their location on the western edge of the European land mass and facing the Atlantic ocean, from where much of our weather comes. We have a temperate or maritime, and very changeable, climate, with a prevailing south-westerly wind. This should always be remembered when working within the microclimate of a site, although obstacles or topography may alter it slightly. There are few days in the year when there is little or no wind.

68. A weather station.

The strongest winds are usually around the sea coasts and in hilly and mountainous regions, where the wind force can be up to 30 per cent greater than in more sheltered inland and lowland sites. Planting for shelter, and planting in hilly and maritime areas, are covered in 2.2, 'Shelter Belts and Shelter Planting', page 150.

Frost

In winter and early spring the earth loses more heat at night than it gains during the day. Even the warming effects of sunshine in March and April are largely lost at night, as what heat that has accumulated is lost to the atmosphere by radiation, especially on clear still nights when there is no cloud cover or wind to help reduce heat loss. It is often in late spring that gardeners most dread frosts, which can come sharply and unexpectedly, damaging fruit blossoms, magnolias and wisterias. There are two types of frost, which affect gardens and plants in different ways.

Ground or radiation frost is the most common and widespread, usually occurring in calm, clear conditions when the temperature at ground level falls to 0°C or below. Temperatures fall away rapidly after sundown, and frost forms on the ground and on surfaces that lose heat most rapidly – typically, dry sand and long grass, roofs of houses, and windscreens and roofs of parked cars, which are all good conductors of heat. As they radiate heat their temperature falls, chilling the air in contact with them.

Air frost can also occur when air temperatures fall consistently below 0°C. They may be associated with black frost conditions, which can have damaging effects on some garden plants. Hoar frost is usually seen under more humid conditions when dew deposited at night freezes. This causes a white rime with picturesque effects, especially on cold surfaces (such as car windscreens); it provides some insulation for sensitive plants.

Frost pockets Dense tree belts, hedges and even walls may act as barriers or dams that collect the damaging cold air, whereas gaps and openings (even a door left open) allow the cold air to flow away, reducing the risk of frost.

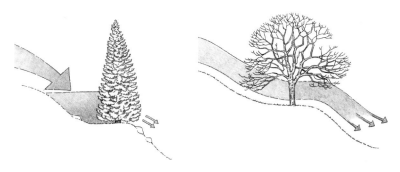

69. Dense planting such as conifers (left) can encourage the pooling of cold air, creating localised frost pockets. Planting that is more permeable (right) avoids this. See also picture 71, page 90.

Nearer to the sea are the tempering effects of the maritime climate, especially in wide estuaries and river mouths. The seas have a buffering effect on air temperature and humidity, as sea temperatures move from seasonal extremes more slowly than air temperatures, cooling the land in summer and moderating minimum temperatures in winter. However, sheltered valleys can still be deep in frost, while neighbouring estuarine and coastal flats remain several degrees above freezing.

'Black' frost This is so called because the usual signs of white or hoar frosts may not be evident, but temperatures may be well below freezing. Often the only evidence, apart from penetrating cold, is ice on ponds and frozen ground surfaces. Black frost is usually associated with high pressure over Scandinavia which can drive very cold east or north-east winds from the Arctic or from Siberia across the UK. Lakes and ponds turn to ice, even the sea in some places. The ground can freeze to a depth of several centimetres. These frosts can be penetrating and, if associated with arctic winds and low humidities, can cause serious damage or death to many susceptible plants. Evergreen woody plants from warmer climates can be desiccated by frozen soil water and low-temperature drying winds. In the severe winters of 1962/3 in the West Midlands and 1985/6 in Kent, a whole range of these plants were killed outright or cut to the ground, including sweet bay (*Laurus*), Cistus, Hebe, Pittosporum, Olearia and many more. Woody plants can be wrapped and protected if in the open, but this will only keep out a certain degree of cold.

Black frost is fortunately much less frequent than radiation frost, but nevertheless it does occur. Our present run of mild winters is perhaps engendering a sense of false security, tempting gardeners to try sub-tropical plants such as bananas, tree ferns and other exotics – there may well be a day of reckoning when this type of arctic winter weather occurs again. The colder winter of 2005/6 was a reminder that global warming trends do not rule out the incidence of cold winters in the future.

Frost protection and safeguards The need for protection against possible frost damage depends on the character and range of plants in the historic garden or park, its aspect and location, and known experience or records of frost incidence, as well as other data such as weather data collected at the site or from the nearest meteorological station.

Radiation frost This is the most likely type to ward against, especially in late spring. The use of walls in gardens has a long tradition, especially for fruit and other less hardy and sun-loving plants. The aspect of the walls is important as a guide to the range of plants that can be grown (see page 91).

Where practicable, a fleece-type temporary covering gives protection in the open – e.g. for fruit bushes or soft fruit (especially strawberries) coming into flower, and when local frost is forecast. These light coverings will need some form of anchorage if there is much air movement.

70. Frost protection of exotic planting at Wisley.

A 'curtain' of plastic or fleece may also be hung on walls where fruits such as peaches, apricots and pears are in flower and the frost looks like being quite sharp. Traditionally, straw mats were used for this purpose. Cold frames that may be bringing on young plants can be covered with an insulating layer.

Ornamental pot plants and exotics, normally over-wintered in glasshouses or orangeries, should not be taken outside until the real risk of a frost has passed. This is usually mid or late May for many regions (the box on page 88 gives a guide for a sites where the last frost is likely to occur). The same timing applies to planting out summer bedding displays or frost-tender plants such as dahlias, and other exotics used in sub-tropical gardening. Local nurseries and garden centres have a strong commercial incentive to offer such plants for sale in April, but it is wise to avoid premature planting out. John Evelyn, in *Kalendarium Hortense* (1664), advised that in the month of May 'observe the Black Mulberry-tree, when it begins to put forth and open the leaves (be it earlier or later), bring your oranges etc., boldly out of the conservatory'. This is an excellent guide, and a worthy indicator of favourable soil temperatures for planting out – and an incentive to grow a black mulberry tree!

Black frost can be devastating, especially when accompanied by freezing winds, and is much more difficult to ward against. Susceptible specimens such as tree ferns, bananas and others can be well wrapped in a thick package of straw, but this is not likely to save most plants if the weather is severe and prolonged. Less hardy evergreen shrubs can be protected with bracken or straw to reduce desiccation from wind frosts, and cold frames will need extra insulation and protection.

Frost damage to ceramic pots and vases (frost proof only to a certain extent) can be reduced by placing them on wooden blocks above the frozen ground. Statuary and fountains may need physical protection and the latter also draining, depending on the

construction material and its porosity. Absorbed water expands and contracts in cracks and porous materials during the freeze–thaw process, which can cause shattering. Specialist conservation advice should be sought to identify the likelihood of frost damage and, if required, physical protection.

Wildlife and livestock suffer from these arctic conditions, too. Animals require extra food, bedding material, shelter and unfrozen water to drink. If possible, try and keep pockets of open water on frozen pools and ponds.

Rainfall

Weather in the UK predominantly comes from the south-west. Moisture gathered by clouds over the Atlantic Ocean is shed as rain over high areas in the west of the country; by the time these clouds reach the eastern coastline their capacity to produce rain is exhausted, making areas on the east cost some of the driest in Europe. The west coast is ideal for moisture-loving ericaceous, Japanese and Chinese woodland plants, while the east is most suited to Mediterranean and Californian plants, adapted to hot dry soils. The variable patterns of rainfall in the UK only cause management and maintenance issues when there is too much rain, leading to flooding or drainage problems, or periods of drought, raising serious questions of irrigation and water conservation.

The occasional local phenomena of 'rain shadows' are mentioned in the box on page 92. The contribution of rain as a factor in soil erosion is discussed in 'Soils and Plant Growth' (pages 94-7).

Snow

Snow occurs when water droplets in clouds or rain reaches close to, but not below, 0°C in temperature. It can be both beneficial and detrimental to plants in the garden. When it forms a blanket across the ground and low-growing plants, it insulates and protects them from later sub-zero air temperatures – this is how alpine plants and

71. Fog in a low-lying valley indicates that the area is susceptible to frost due to the pooling of cold air.

bulbs stay naturally protected from the extremes of cold at high altitudes. But snow can cause physical damage to plants by its sheer weight bearing down on stems and branches. This is a particular problem with flat-topped hedges, especially when they have not been kept in good shape and are wider at the top than at the bottom. The weight of the snow may split the hedge downwards into two. Picturesque 'cloud' hedges (such as at Walmer Castle, Kent) often started because of such snow damage. Horizontally branched mature cedars are also prone to such damage, especially from wet snow.

Most plants require minimal amounts of water during winter, and both they and the soil beneath snow can remain totally dry. Some plants may suffer from this lack of water until the thawing process begins. Sudden thawing can pose the opposite problem: if the equivalent of several days' worth of rainwater thaws in one go it can cause waterlogging of soils and localised flooding in a very short period of time.

Hail

Hailstones are formed when raindrops are carried upwards and downwards in turbulent air currents generated in cumulonimbus or thunderclouds containing super-cooled water. The droplets gradually grow in size and become ice crystals, and this process can continue if there is sufficient turbulence, forming hailstones that will eventually fall to the ground if they are heavier than the updraughts can sustain. Hailstones in Britain can cause damage in gardens and nurseries, and especially in orchards at the time when fruit is at a sensitive stage of development. Lush-leaved plants can have leaves punctured, and glasshouse panes can be smashed.

The microclimate of gardens and garden walls

The box on page 88 shows the broad variations in climate and weather in England and Wales, the figures representing a mean over the period. Further modifications and ameliorating effects of these regional climates can be brought about by exploiting or developing microclimate or small-scale climates in gardens and parks in order to create more favourable habitats.

It is important to understand that all species of plants introduced into cultivation in this country, and usually the cultivars and hybrids derived from them, have evolved over very long periods in their countries of origin, and have certain ecological preferences or habitats. These habitats are determined by such factors as microclimate, altitude, soils and location, with examples ranging from the cool, leafy, temperate woodlands of Japan or North America to the hot, dry, stony slopes of the Mediterranean or west California. It is very helpful, and indeed often essential, to try to match the original microclimate and habitat preferences as closely as possible, with temperature and sunshine often the most critical factors. Garden walls, or the walls of houses and outbuildings, are very effective for exploiting these microclimates; picture 72 shows the relationship between walls and their microclimates and the possibilities of plant selection. This is, of course, generalised, but it does show the potential for a large range of ornamental and also fruiting plants.

City microclimates and heat islands

Large urban conurbations are generally more frost-free in winter months, and have an average warmer climate, than many rural areas. They produce energy through combustion of fuels and a concentration of heated buildings at rates comparable with incoming solar radiation in winter. These heat islands may result in minimum temperatures being 5°–6°C (9°–11°F) higher than in

72. A bird's-eye view of a house and garden in southern England where a fascinating range of microclimates and plant habitats has been created. Walls, hedges and changes of level have all been fully exploited.
A. Some exposure to prevailing south-west winds. Open site full sun. Rather windy. Gentle slope to south.
B. Part shade of apple trees. House protects from north winds.
C. Damp, sheltered habitat.
D. Open lawn. Good protection from planted shelter belt on west/north-west side.
E. Enclosed intimate areas. Sculptured hedges.
F. Very warm terrace area. Dry, full sun. Half-hardy plants here.
G. Warm, fairly protected border, except for south and south-west gales. Important background hedge on north and north-east side.
H. Enclosed kitchen garden areas with gentle slope to south giving good uninterrupted aspect to sunshine. House, buildings and hedges protect from cold north-west and north winds.
I. Enclosed semi-shaded meadow garden areas.
J. Cool, shaded, north walls. Good for ferns.
K. Small, very protected garden. Excellent protection from north with oast houses and farm buildings.
L. Warm, sheltered, sunken garden. Full sunshine for most of the area, but good shaded walls also. Heat reflection from buildings, even in winter.

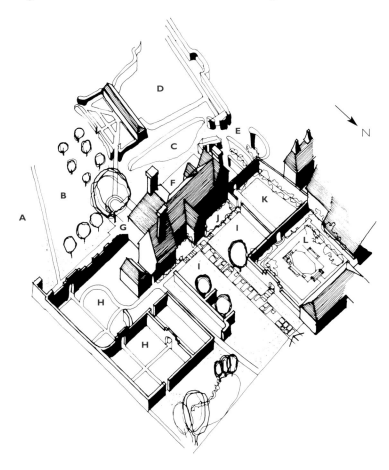

RELATIONSHIP BETWEEN WALL MICROCLIMATE AND PLANT SELECTION

WALL	MICROCLIMATE	PLANT HABITAT EQUIVALENT	PLANT GROUPS
North	Perpetual shade. Cool in summer. Cold or very cold in winter. Good, 'steady' light unless heavily shaded. 'Rain' shadows with high building or projecting eaves. Limited evaporation. Shelter from north winds beneficial.	Woodland or semi-woodland. North facing cliffs or step banks. Asiatic, N. American and European species depending on soil pH, moisture content and organic matter.	Woodland and shade-loving species. **Shrubs:** *Camellia* (pH 5-6), *Garrya, Mahonia, Cotoneaster, Pyracantha*. **Climbers:** *Hydrangea petiolaris*, winter jasmine, honeysuckle, *Parthenocissus* sp., also woodland shade herbaceous sp., ferns, Hosta, hardy cyclamen, bulbs, etc. **Fruit:** morello cherries, gooseberries, currants.
South	Usually the warmest habitat in a garden, given shelter and full sunshine. Favoured mild winter conditions to hot or very warm in summer. Drought or 'sun scorch' can be limiting factors. Exceptionally favourable growing conditions for many sun-loving plants with good soil management.	With good drainage, this offers excellent habitats for plants from the Mediterranean regions, W. United States, S. America, S. Africa, E. Europe and Middle East, parts of China, and Australia and New Zealand.	**Shrubs and woody climbers:** *Ceanothus, Clematis, Campsis, Callistemon, Abutilon, Jasmine, Hoheria, Cestrum, Chimonanthus, Cistus, Cytisus battandieri, Hebe, Leptospermum, Robinia hispida, Passiflora, Wisteria*. **Half-hardy annuals and herbaceous plants:** *Agapanthus, Nerine, Gazania*, etc. **Fruit:** Apples, peaches, pears, plums, apiricots, nectarines.
East	Generally cool but variable with considerable extremes in winter and summer: warm, dry in summer to very cold in winter. Wind frost damage to evergreens in severe E.–N.E. wind conditions: protection needed.	An intermediate type between semi-woodland or open scrub to exposed habitat of direct morning sunshine, especially in late spring or summer. Cool desiccating winds can be a limiting factor in E and NE regions, particularly in spring.	The north wall group, plus many hardy **Shrubs** and **Climbers** which can withstand the occasional very cold wintery conditions. Climbing and rambling roses. Shade from early morning sun for camellias and magnolias. Many herbs and bulbs. **Fruit:** plums and hardy pear varieties.
West	Equable, temperate, throughout year. With shelter, a very favourable microclimate for plants that prefer reasonably warm and mild conditions with none of the extremes of the south or north walls.	Woodland edge species. West-facing cliffs, slopes. Similar to south wall habitat but for plants that prefer indirect sunshine. Shelter from SW gales is important.	**Shrubs and Climbers:** As for south walls, until orientation becomes NW-facing (too cool). Examples: *Magnolia, Azara, Actinidia, Clematis*, honeysuckle, *Akebia*, roses. **Herbaceous perennials:** Very many of these. A range from S to NW habitat. *Euphorbia, Salvia, Lilium, Eremus, Viola*. **Annuals:** *Nicotiana*. **Fruit:** Plums, cherries, apricots, apples.

Note: intermediate aspects – in clockwise order, NE, SE, SW or NW – will usually have a corresponding gradation of planting.

the surrounding countryside, with differences as much as 6°–8°C (11°–14°F) in the early hours of calm, clear nights in large cities, when the heat stored during the day is released. This effect is most marked in calm conditions. The thermal contrasts of a city also depend upon its topographic situation and degree of shelter (picture 73). The effect on minimum temperatures is especially noticeable – e.g. Kew in London has an average of 72 more frost-free days than Wisley in Surrey. Figures for central London are probably even more marked.

In practice, those who own or manage parks and gardens in cities and urban areas know that the range of plants that can be grown – especially the half-hardy or normally tender kinds – is much wider than in more outlying areas. In London spring-flowering shrubs and bulbs may be two or three weeks ahead of gardens in rural (or semi-rural) places in the south-east.

There is a downside to this benefit. Heat islands can mean uncomfortably high temperatures in summer – together with the air pollution this was experienced during the hot summer of 2003.

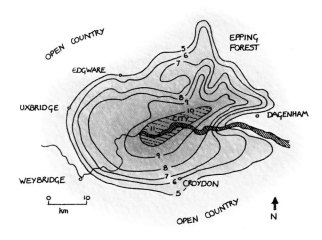

73. Heat island effects in the London area. Large cities have their own microclimates: temperatures can be as much as 5°C warmer in central London than the surrounding countryside, enabling Chelsea Physic Garden to flower and fruit olives and citrus outside. (Diagram after Chandler and Gregory 1976)

Planting for ameliorating urban climates

Related to the climate and microclimates of large towns and cities, and the discomforts of high temperatures and air pollution, are the important and often underrated benefits of planting and green-space vegetation. In historic gardens and parks there is often a legacy of mature trees and shrubberies, as well as other planting, and an increasing awareness of need for their conservation and periodic renewal. In particular, trees – apart from the pleasure they give and their visual and psychological value – can improve air quality and local microclimate. Some of these benefits are illustrated in picture 74 (below).

Other effects

These are probably less important, but all help to determine the characteristics of the plant environment in the city. There is generally slightly more rainfall and more cloud; reduced wind speeds, apart from the turbulence effect of tall buildings; higher pollution and, of course, more noise. Humidity in towns is usually lower,

due to the high evaporation rate and the run-off effects of surface water; in cities it may be as much as 30 per cent lower than in the country. This means that irrigation or augmented water supplies for plants may be necessary, especially those in raised beds, roof decks and containers. Trees, especially thrifty species such as planes, some maples and some conifers such as pines and cedars, have a remarkable ability to survive on the limited water available beneath the hard surface areas of car parks and streets.

In conclusion, therefore, the 90 per cent of the population of Western Europe who live in towns or suburbs mostly enjoy a milder microclimate than those in the countryside, but the atmosphere is not so clean, there may be less sunshine and some localised wind turbulence. All of these factors have implications for maintenance. Noise disturbance can be somewhat minimised by thick planting and screening with large-leaved evergreens.

Global warming and climate change

The lessons from climate history are important in showing that there is nothing new about climate change, and gardeners and farmers have been the first to experience at first hand these ever-changing cycles.

However, there is now growing concern that the undoubted evidence of global warming may in part be due to the steady rise in greenhouse gases in the atmosphere, especially carbon dioxide, as a result of human activity. The warming effect is being closely monitored by many scientists including the UK Meteorological Office's Hadley Centre in Exeter. Their analysis of historical climate data shows that the mean annual temperature for central England increased by about 0.7°C during the 150 years of 1750–1900 and rose to 1.0°C in the twentieth century; it may rise further during this century. These may seem small increases, but they are indicators of the trend. Other dramatic occurrences are the acceleration of the melting of arctic ice and the retreat of glaciers in some alpine areas.

In April 2002, an important workshop was organised by the Royal Horticultural Society, the National Trust and others under the UK Climate Impact Programme. Their report (UKCPO2 Scientific Report, Tyndall Centre, School of Environmental

74. Trees are important in cities to help filter pollution and ameliorate the urban microclimate.

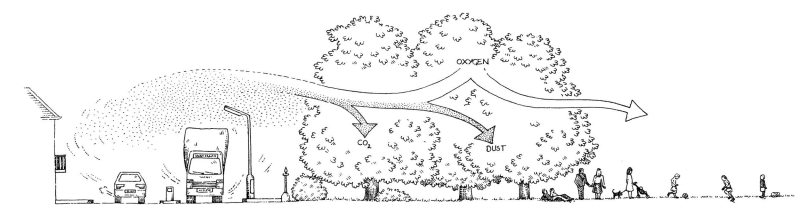

Sciences, University of East Anglia, 2002) acknowledges that the impact on gardens will be difficult to assess on a given time scale, but it presents a number of predictions which, if eventually realised, could have a dramatic effect on the plant and human environment.

75. Skating on the Serpentine, London, in the early 1960s when many large ponds and lakes froze sufficiently to take the weight of skaters.

SOILS AND PLANT GROWTH

'The answer lies in the soil' is a saying well proven over a long period of time, and is as true today as it was when gardens were first created. The aim in this section is to concentrate on those aspects of soils and soil management most likely to be the concern of those who own or manage historic gardens. These are:

- A reminder of the main soil types derived from underlying rock formations, their management and characteristics and typical associated vegetation
- Principles and methods of soil cultivation and management
- Maintaining soil fertility and protecting soils from erosion

Soil – an overview

The soil is a superficial layer that covers parts of the earth's crust, overlying most geological rock formations in varying depths and types. Soil does not cover all of the earth's dry land due to its varying geology, topography, ecology, exposure and climate and is therefore is a valuable commodity, especially in areas with an environment suitable for horticulture, agriculture or forestry.

The soil above the bedrock is made up of several distinct layers. These are known as soil horizons and are often, but not always, built up in visible profiles. They can vary in depth greatly, from just enough to support plants to several hundred metres deep.

- Horizon A, the upper layer, is usually composed of open-structured, fertile soil, often called topsoil. Usually no deeper than 30cm, this is where decaying organic matter (humus) and a whole range of micro-organisms are concentrated. Most plant roots utilise this layer, including deeper-rooting species during their establishment. Depending on local vegetation, this layer may also be covered by an organic, humus-rich litter layer of decaying leaves and plant matter.

- Horizon B, the middle layer, will be generally less fertile, and less active with organisms the deeper you get.
- Horizon C, the deepest layer, is the true subsoil and is nearest to the underlying rock strata.

Soil is the growing medium for most plant life on earth, providing both nutrition for growth and development and acting as a structural support for root anchorage. It also forms an important habitat for various micro-organisms and animals. It has five main components, of which all must be present in differing percentages to make a healthy living soil. These are:

- **Mineral particles** Derived from the weathered bedrock below or otherwise deposited by wind, water or glaciations. The proportions of these different-sized mineral particles (clay, silt, sand and gravel, etc.) dictate the natural soil type and texture
- **Decaying and decayed organic material** From dead plant, fungal and animal remains, and animal excrement
- **Living organisms** Plant structures, fungi, bacteria, micro-organisms and larger animals such as earthworms
- **Air** Present in the porous spaces between larger soil particles
- **Water** Washed down from precipitation and irrigation, a fixed coating on smaller soil particles, and drawn up from the underground water table

Due to landscape changes during the last Ice Age and the subsequent temperate climate, the soil in the UK is very young in geological terms, and still quite inconsistent in its mixture of parent ingredients compared to older, more consistent soils worldwide. Soil characteristics change on both a regional and local scale, often several times in one garden. This, together with our temperate climate, is a contributing factor in the diversity of gardens in the UK and the plant life they support. Because of the requirements that gardening puts on soil, good soil husbandry and some forms of active management may be required.

Soil texture is largely determined by the variable ratio of three size grades of mineral particles – clay, silt and sand – and, to a lesser extent, by organic content.

- Soils high in clay particles are very sticky when wet, solid and brick-like when dry. Their lack of pore spaces means that they are not free-draining, and water is more likely to coat clay particles than be free for plant root uptake. However, clay soils are very fertile.
- Silty soils have a soapy texture and are quite rich in nutrients. They are prone to compaction.
- Sandy soils have a high component of the largest particles; they are gritty or very gritty to the touch, and are light and very free-draining with plenty of pore spaces. Any nutrients in this soil are likely to be washed away (leached).

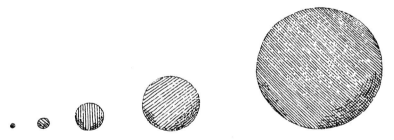

76. The relative size of soil mineral particles, shown in a much exaggerated form. From the left, they are clay, less than 0.002mm; silt, 0.002–0.05mm, and sand 0.05–2.00mm (very fine, medium and coarse). This ratio of particles has the most profound implications on the soil type and its overall characteristics – from colour, temperature, drainage and fertility to the types of plants suitable and their ease of cultivation.

Between these three extremes are the loams, ideal garden soils, in which the particle ratios are roughly equal (the term loam is derived from the Anglo-Saxon lam, signifying 'fat, unctuous, tenacious earth', according to Dr John Lindley in his Theory and Practice of Horticulture, 1840). Loams have the merits of each particle type without the problems of extremes. There are subtly different types, determined by the overall proportions, such as clay loams or sandy loams. Organic matter will also be present in the best loams.

Soil structure defines how soil particles bind together to form larger units or clods; each soil type has its own natural structural characteristics. With careful husbandry, soil structure can be protected and improved; correspondingly, it is prone to excessive damage through bad management and over-cultivation. You can generally improve soil structure through cultivation, but you will not change the overall soil type without replacing the soil almost entirely.

Soil organisms, complex and variable in range, are an essential component of living soils that include many invertebrates, bacteria and an important group – the mycorrhiza. Mycorrhiza are fungi which occur naturally in almost all soils on earth. Most higher plants have symbiotic associations with specific mycorrhiza which develop around the plant's root systems, either as sheaths around the root hairs or actually tapping in to living root cells. There is increasing evidence that mycorrhiza supply mineral nutrients to the host tree – in effect extending the feeding area of the tree – while obtaining various carbohydrates in return. Mycorrhiza can have a role in minimising water stress and increasing tolerance to root attack by pathogens and phytotoxins, both of which can affect a tree's overall health and stability. It seems likely that inorganic fertilisers can disrupt these beneficial connections. Under infertile or poor soil situations, the gradual addition of plant-based organic matter is preferable and should encourage the development of mycorrhiza.

Although certain species of mycorrhiza may be so specific that they are only found on one type of host plant, others act as good all-rounders and form relationships with a wide range of host plants. These generalist mycorrhiza are increasingly becoming available in the form of granular and liquid inoculants which can be incorporated into the soil to improve plant growth on damaged soils or to inoculate otherwise sterilised soils in nurseries. It is too early to say whether this improves long-term plant health and vitality, but extensive research is under way, particularly in commercial horticulture, arboriculture and forestry.

Drainage The ability of soil to retain water is vital for healthy plant growth, but water in the soil is a delicate balancing act – too little and plants cannot sustain life, too much and the roots cannot respire so quickly die (followed by the rest of the plant).

Signs of poor drainage include:
- Visible standing water
- Growth of plants associated with bog conditions, such as rushes and sedges

NATURAL DRAINAGE

This varies widely, depending on a number of factors:

- **Soil texture** Sandy soils drain quickly and freely; heavy clay soils barely drain at all

- **Soil structure** Well-structured soils with plenty of interconnected air spaces and fissures drain freely; compacted or badly structured soils drain badly

- **Sub-soil conditions** In some instances the topsoil and subsoil can be considerably different: a badly drained sandy soil may be caused by an underlying impermeable clay subsoil

- **Water table** This is the level of groundwater in an area, which may be influenced by rivers, rainfall, type of bedrock, etc., and may vary throughout the year

- Ground wet underfoot for a long time after rain or even during dry periods
- Dark grey or blue-blackish discoloration in the soil profile, indicating permanent waterlogging at that level (healthy soils show a uniform brown profile)
- Rust-coloured mottling in the soil profile, indicating periodic waterlogging at that level
- The formation of soil pans (impervious layers)
- Poor soil structure, principally a lack of air spaces
- Poor root growth

The advantages of good drainage are:
- Soil warms up faster in spring, promoting good growth
- Aeration is improved
- Soil structure is improved, hastening the removal of excess water and promoting healthy root growth
- Use of areas can be extended because damage is less likely
- Soil is easier to cultivate after wet periods

For drainage methods, see 'Turf and grassland' (page 175).

Soil cultivation

Some historic gardens have had continuous and consistent soil management over many years or even centuries; others are not so lucky. The regular addition of organic matter, particularly in walled and kitchen gardens, can result in a fair depth of very fertile, manageable soil overlying the main soil type. No matter what the quality of a soil, when it is gardened some form of management or cultivation must take place.

Some cultivation operations can be sufficiently deep to invert or disrupt the various soil horizons, burying fertile topsoil under barren subsoil. This should be avoided at all cost. Where major landscaping works are planned, topsoils should be carefully removed and temporarily stored for future use. If additional topsoil is required, it should meet the standards set out in British Standard 3882:1994, 'Specification for Topsoil', and should be free of weeds and plant pathogens.

Two main types of cultivation are practised. The first and most common, traditional, method is to dig and turn the soil using spades or similar, repeating the task again when needed. The second is the 'organic' method, to dig and turn the soil once only, then maintain it with no further digging.

Traditional cultivation: digging Cultivating the soil by hand is a traditional skill practised by generations of gardeners; the tools and techniques have changed very little over many years. In many situations in historic gardens such digging has value, especially where alternative cultivation techniques would look out of character. In the past, active and regular cultivation through 'proper' digging was regarded as a fitting test for all gardeners.

The tools and methods of cultivation are well known, and single digging and double digging (also known as 'bastard trenching') are common techniques. A spade is the best tool and it covers a number of operations, including turning over and burying ephemeral annual weeds (but not perennial invaders!); incorporating organic matter; breaking up compacted layers; mixing in gravel or grits to heavy soils; and allowing frost to break up clods of such lumpy soils by autumn or winter digging. It is also, of course, good exercise!

Forking over, or light digging, is effective in removing perennial and other weeds in borders, but a dangerous practice if done too deeply among shrubs and many garden plants, as root systems can be easily damaged. The organic approach (see below) is infinitely preferable in these cases.

Digging by hand will often be the only option available in some historic gardens. Although a mechanical cultivator may be light enough for two gardeners to lift safely over hedges in a parterre, for example, where no other access exists they are often not manoeuvrable or safe enough to be used in confined spaces. More details on machinery used in soil cultivations can be found in 2.4, 'Machinery', page 233.

Organic cultivation: no digging and deep bed methods Most soils do not become waterlogged, airless and infertile without traditional cultivation, otherwise how did plants grow before gardeners walked the earth? No digging and the deep bed system are not new principles – one has only to look at the mounds and ridges of ancient raised 'lazy beds' around the UK, where soils too shallow for cultivation were built up using locally sourced organic matter.

Soil cultivation may be required before an organic system is established if the soil structure below is poor to begin with. Afterwards, the system should be viewed as an efficient *minimal* cultivation method, providing the best output from the soil using the minimum input of resources and effort.

The two systems aim to recreate the natural process in which organic matter works its way into the ground, where organisms such as worms drag leaf litter and humus deep into horizon A of the soil. Over time, a deep, fertile, open-structured soil is formed.

'HOW TO DIG'
From *Gardening Illustrated*, 1879, edited by Willam Robinson

'An indifferent man will simply shuffle over the ground, inserting his spade at an angle of 45 degrees and turning the soil over to a depth of about 6 inches, whilst a man who understands how to dig and perform his work properly, will keep a straight and open trench, put his spade in perpendicularly, take thin spits, and turn the soil over thoroughly, breaking it well as he goes on, and do the work generally as it should be done. There is a vast difference between good and bad digging . . . I do not know any single operation in gardening so illustrative of personal character as digging . . . No young gardener who wishes to rise, ought to despise the spade, as its proper use either by himself, or others, has more influence upon his future career than any other tool with which I am acquainted!'

Deep bed system Large amounts organic matter are added to the soil using the conventional method of double digging. The soil is never compacted under foot and it is worked on from set paths. Further cultivation is unnecessary; more organic matter is added when required as a top dressing or a mulch and is allowed to work its own way into the soil by natural processes.

No digging system This is slightly more extreme. Well-rotted organic matter is placed directly on the soil surface and not worked into the soil at all. Planting with hand tools rather than spades is preferred. Seeds are SOWN directly on the soil surface with the organic matter covering around them.

If both these organic methods are sustained correctly, over time a soil will improve in fertility, structure and diversity of organisms. Additional benefits of these minimal digging methods are that the soil structure is not constantly broken down and exposed to the drying atmosphere; any weed seeds in the soil are not brought to the surface to germinate, and tasks can be carried out in weather conditions that would be detrimental to conventional cultivation. For general organic principles see page 100.

Soil fertility and erosion

Soil fertility Plants that are cropped or removed from the soil take away some of the fertility from it, causing gradual chemical degradation. This fertility needs to be replaced for soil to remain fertile in the long term.

Plants vary slightly from species to species regarding what quantity of nutrients they require from the soil. If woody perennials have been *in situ* for years or sometimes decades, they will have been putting the same nutritional demands on the soil for a long time. This can lead to depletion of fertility in certain soils and symptoms of nutrient deficiency in plants. If many biochemical processes require a particular nutrient, a deficiency will cause a whole range of problems.

Fertility should be increased gradually to prevent a sudden bolt of soft growth that will either be killed by frost or attacked by pests. The best option is the addition of small amounts of organic matter on a regular basis. Applying organic matter in excessive amounts can cause nitrates to leach into watercourses, causing environmental damage.

If the area is clear of vegetation, a green manure crop could be an option. Usually part of a crop rotation programme, green manures are annual crops mainly from the *Leguminosae* or *Fabaceae* family which are grown as an annual crop. Some legumes have root nodules containing bacteria that fix free nitrogen from the atmosphere and make it available to the plant. If a green manure crop is turned into the soil at the end of the season, this nitrogen becomes available to subsequent crops. Clover and lupins are commonly used as green manure crops.

Soil additives Very light or very heavy soils can also be gradually improved over time with good husbandry. Sandy soils can be given more structure and made more water-retentive by using plentiful bulky organic matter. Aeration and drainage of heavy clay soils can be improved with the addition of grit, coarse sand or gravel.

Feeding As well as major nutrients, plants also need small amounts of iron, boron, manganese, copper, zinc and molybdenum. These are usually present in soil or loam-based composts, but low or virtually absent in peat-based composts, in which case they must be added – either in fertiliser or in the form of metabolisable ('fritted') trace elements (chlorine, cobalt and nickel). If any nutrients are present in too concentrated a form toxicity can result, so care must be taken not to apply more than is required.

The acidity or alkalinity of soil vitally affects the nutrients that plants can take up. This is measured on a pH scale of 1 to 14: below 7 soil is acid, and above 7 it is alkaline. The ideal for the healthy growth of most plants is pH6.5, slightly acid. Certain plants called 'calcifuges' prefer more acidic conditions (for example, most ericaceous plants) whereas others called 'calcicoles' prefer more alkaline conditions (for example, buddleias). Fertilisers may be bought in organic form (from plant or animal origin) or inorganic form (from a manufactured, non-living, mineral substance). Most organic fertilisers can be used in bulk, such as manures to help to improve soil structure and supply small quantities of major nutrients and trace elements. Alternatively, these can be supplied in concentrated form – for eaxample, dried blood which is quick-acting and constitutes 10–13 per cent nitrogen.

Fertilisers can be grouped according to the way they supply their nutrients:

- Straight fertiliser will supply only one major nutrient, such as ammonium nitrate, which provides only nitrogen.
- Compound or mixture fertilisers will supply two or more nutrients, such as potassium nitrate giving potassium and nitrogen.
- Slow-release fertilisers can be straight or compound, but have the ability to release their nutrients over a long period of time

See also the boxes on pages 98 and 99.

Soil erosion Soil erosion is the physical loss of soil particles, which can take place on any soil type, on gradients and level ground. It is a natural process which over time has helped weather parent rocks into the soil around us; however, now that we have got this soil, we want to hang on to it! It is especially critical on shallower soil.

Soil erosion has a greater effect where vegetation and root cover is minimal or non-existent. Vegetation slows down the wind and protects the soil surface from direct rainfall, while a fibrous root system helps bind the soil particles together.

There are four major causes of soil erosion: wind, water, topography and human activities.

Wind Especially on lighter soil or where the structure is fine, wind will constantly blow particles away. This is especially the case in coastal situations where sandy soils can move around with ease; particles can even be carried from one continent to another. A dry windswept soil is also likely to have less organic content binding its

NUTRIENT CHART
From John Watkins, *The Glasshouse Garden*, 1993

Chemical	Use	Deficiency	Excess
MAJOR NUTRIENTS			
Nitrogen (N)	Required at all times by plants. Component of green chlorophyll	Stunted growth. Foliage pale green, yellow or reddish-yellow. Lack of vigour	Soft fleshy growth. Failure to flower and fruit in some cases
Phosphorus (P)	Important for germination, root production and seed/fruit ripening. Required in smaller amounts than nitrogen	Lower leaves small, dark green with purplish undersides. Plants stunted, with restricted shoot and root growth. Flowering reduced	Yellowing between leaf veins, only a problem with sensitive plants such as Proteas
Potassium (K; potash)	Encourages flowering and helps to produce strong, healthy, disease-resistant growth by thickening cell walls	Decreases in availability in very acid or alkaline composts. Marginal scorching on foliage. Die-back of shoots in severe cases	Potassium prevents uptake of magnesium, inducing deficiency
Calcium (Ca)	Makes up part of cell wall, therefore required at growing tips	Distorted and curled young foliage. Death of leaf margins and tips. Death of shoot tips. Soil acid (low pH)	Makes soil alkaline (high pH). Prevents uptake of iron. Makes phosphates insoluble
Magnesium (Mg)	Forms part of chlorophyll essential for photosynthesis	Caused by high potassium levels. Yellowing between veins in older leaves. Leaf margins curl upwards	Prevents uptake of potassium and calcium
Sulphur (S)	Important in biochemistry for synthesis of proteins and enzymes	Young foliage pale, leaves sometimes rolled downward or with reddish tints	Rarely a problem
MINOR NUTRIENTS			
Iron (Fe)	Essential in the synthesis of chlorophyll	Yellowing between veins in young foliage	Induces manganese deficiency
Molybdenum (Mo)	Important in metabolism of nitrogen	Yellowing of older leaves. Marginal wilting. Distortion of leaves and stems	Leaves turn golden-yellow, sometimes with blue tinge
Boron (B)	Assists movement of materials within the plants	Death of stem and root tips. Young leaves blacken and shrivel	Margins of old leaves yellow followed by scorching
Copper (Cu)	Plays a part in photosynthesis	Scorching of leaf tips extended to margins	Induces iron deficiency and stunting of roots and shoots
Manganese (Mn)	Involved in many aspects of plant metabolism	Yellowing between leaf veins and yellow, water-soaked spots	Induces iron deficiency. Produces cupping and yellowing of leaf margins
Zinc (Zn)	Essential for cell enlargement	Reduced leaf size and internode length producing a stunted plant	As for iron deficiency

COMPONENTS OF COMMON FERTILISER

Fertiliser	Nutrients provided			Other nutrients		Notes
	N	P	K			
Ammonium nitrate	34%	–	–		I	Quick-acting. Used in compost base and liquid feeds
Potassium nitrate	13.8%	–	39%		I	Quick-acting. Used in compost base
Nitrochalk	26%	–	–	Carbonate of lime in varying concentrations	I	Quick-acting
Urea	45%	–	–		O	Slow-release
Hoof and horn	13%	–	–		O	Slow-release
Dried blood	10–13%	–	–		O	Quick-acting
Fish meal	8–10%	2–4%	1.5-2.5%		O	Available in powder or concentrated liquid form
Superphosphate	–	8%	–	Sulphur 11%, Calcium 21%	I	Used as base dressing in borders and compost
Triple superphosphate	–	21%	–		I	Base dressing
Mono ammonium phosphate	11.8%	26%	–		I	Contained in slow-release fertilisers
Bonemeal	1–5%	6.5–14%	–		O	Apply to borders, low in phosphates
Sulphate of potash	–	–	45%		I	Apply as quick-acting source of potash
Seaweed	0.4–0.8%	0.1–0.2%	1–2%		O	Available as powder or liquid
Epsom salts (Magnesium sulphate)	–	–	–	Magnesium 9%	I	Corrects magnesium deficiency
Magnesium limestone	–	–	–	Magnesium and calcium carbonate	I	Supplies lime to help reduce acidity
Ground limestone	–	–	–	Calcium carbonate	I	As for Magnesium limestone
Fritted trace elements	–	–	–	Balanced minor nutrients	I	Slow-release. Only one application required
Chelated trace elements	–	–	–	Balanced minor nutrients	I	Water-soluble form. Immediately available to plants. Used as a foliar or compost application
Chelated iron	–	–	–	Iron	I	Soluble form of iron. Apply as foliar or soil drench

N = Nitrogen, P = Phosphorous, K = Potassium   I = Inorganic, O = Organic

Fertilisers should be marked with the percentage of each that they contain, so that in a compound fertiliser the ratio of nutrients can be calculated:
N:P:K 3:1:1 High in nitrogen: for the start of the growing season, when vigorous growth is required
N:P:K 1:1:1 For later in the season, when balanced growth is needed
N:P:K 1:1:2 For use during the autumn and winter, to help harden up growth and promote flowering

structure together. Wind problems are exacerbated when soils have no vegetation cover.

Water After heavy rain, surface water may not drain into the ground quickly enough especially where it is already saturated, and will run off across the soil surface to the lowest point it can find. This run-off can shift large amounts of soil from the surface, washing it away with the flow into drains, gullies and water bodies. Irrigation that replicates this can also cause damage. Waterlogged soil will have a weakened structure, in which landslips and the uprooting of trees are more likely to occur.

Topography The main soil types each have their own characteristics when it comes to being placed on a gradient. Imagine pure sand poured out of a barrow: it will form a shallower and wider heap than pure clay. This is known as the 'angle of repose'. Each soil type has its own maximum angle at which it can remain before it starts slipping away. If a gradient is too steep for a particular soil, it will start to erode. Again, vegetation cover increases the angle of repose.

Human activities People, animals and vehicles can all erode the soil. The passage of vehicles and pedestrians can cause direct scuffing and damage to the surface, or damage the vegetation that normally protects the soil. Bad soil cultivation techniques, such as over-use of mechanical cultivators, can break down the structure making it prone to erosion. Careful site management and good horticultural practices should minimise this threat.

Combating soil erosion The main factor in controlling the causes of erosion in a garden is vegetation cover. Exposed soil is much more prone to erosion, whereas if it is bound together by the root system of a plant and shielded by vegetation, it is a lot less likely to erode. If vegetation is not an option due to site restrictions, a semi-permeable layer of organic or inorganic mulch or matting will also protect the surface. Windbreaks protect soils from the wind. More information on the use of mulches and windbreaks can be found on pages 149 and 226.

On gradients, where possible, the addition of low-growing vegetation will help stabilise the soil surface. Steeper slopes, prone to landslips, may require physical reinforcements or the use of geo-textile membranes as advised by a structural engineer.

Organic gardening principles

To many, the soil is the heart of the organic movement. It has the natural ability to support the plants we need to survive, so it must be nurtured and protected. Organic gardening principles build from good husbandry practices, but go one step further and exclude the use of non-organic fertilisers, herbicides and pesticides. These substances can upset the natural balance of the soil chemistry and soil organisms, both of which in turn can affect the physical characteristics of the soil. Where plants absorb these substances from the soil and through foliar treatments, they can also be passed in small amounts into the food chain through the crops we eat, and through

ORGANIC CERTIFICATION

This is governed by the Soil Association, which sets the standards which farmers and growers have to meet if they want to market their produce as organic. The Soil Association also helps farmers undergo conversion to organic methods, which takes two years to ensure that any residues of artificial chemicals have degraded and that non-sustainable cultural practices can cease.

the fodder crops of the animals we eat. This has implications not only for public health, but also for wider social and moral issues about how we live our lives alongside nature.

The broader organic movement also takes into account the way we treat animals, the materials we clothe ourselves in and build with, and how sustainable our activities and demands on the natural environment are. Food, whether plant- or animal-based, clothing, building materials and other consumables of certified organic origin are increasingly available.

Organic methods of horticulture are often the traditional methods used in historic parks and gardens well before our reliance on artificial fertilisers, herbicides and pesticides began in the twentieth century. The Henry Doubleday Research Association (HDRA), a registered charity, is Europe's largest membership organisation dedicated to the research and promotion of organic gardening and farming. It has three organic display gardens, and holds a collection of historically important vegetable varieties as seed which its members participate in cultivating and conserving.

Soil structure The main principle of organic soil husbandry is the protection of the soil structure, organisms and fertility. The addition of organic matter (from organic sources) is recommended only for soil actively supporting plant growth, and not in quantities liable to leach nitrates into watercourses. Crop rotation plays a major part in sustainable soil use, allowing the soil to have a break from crops with specific nutrient requirements, and to break the life cycle of soil-borne pests and diseases.

Mulch or vegetation cover is used to prevent drying, erosion and the development of weeds. Soil is cultivated by hand rather than by damaging mechanical cultivators – these are acceptable to improve aeration and drainage, but should otherwise be kept to a minimum. Soil pH should be maintained at an acceptable level for plant growth by the careful choice of organic matter.

Plant health and crop yields Prevention of pests and diseases is the first priority. However, some pest and disease damage should be accepted, along with yields of varying size and quality in the case of certain crops. Plants should be matched to existing conditions, including any requirements for additional water. Putting the right plant in the right place will improve its tolerance to pests and diseases; if it does not work, try other plants instead.

A healthy soil is more likely to support healthy plant growth, especially where horticultural tasks take place at the right time of year – for example, establishing new planting when insect pests are dormant. Good hygiene and monitoring are vital, particularly when importing plants and seed to a site. A crop rotation system helps fertility and reduces pests and diseases. Good plant spacing is required, wide enough to allow ventilation but not too wide to allow growing space for weeds.

Habitats can be created for natural predators and parasites. The use of introduced biological control agents is also acceptable. Particular pests can be scared away from plants or put off by the use of companion planting. Some can be prevented with barriers on boundaries or on individual plants. Structures such as glasshouses, pots and containers can be sterilised with steam.

Lawns can be maintained organically through good cultural control, including seasonal scarifying, aeration and top-dressing; regular mowing at a suitable height, and allowing good light levels to reach the lawn. Whenever conditions allow clippings should be left *in situ*.

Weeds should be suppressed with careful plant spacing and crop rotation wherever possible, and the use of a suitable mulch. Weeding manually by hoeing, pulling and slashing are the preferred options since herbicide cannot be used. Hard surfaces should be maintained so that weeds cannot penetrate them.

Composting and growing media Composting should take place on site, and compost heaps should be topped with a waterproof cover to prevent nutrients leaching from compost piles into watercourses. If additional planting media are needed, they should be peat- and weed-free, and certified organic.

Environmental conservation Habitats for native flora and fauna should be protected and, where possible, created. The use of native species (preferably of local provenience) and wildlife-friendly non-natives should be encouraged. Plant material with a known genetic provenance should be preserved through cultivation and propagation, and biodiversity encouraged in the garden.

77. Compost bays allow storage and processing of green waste and other organic materials.

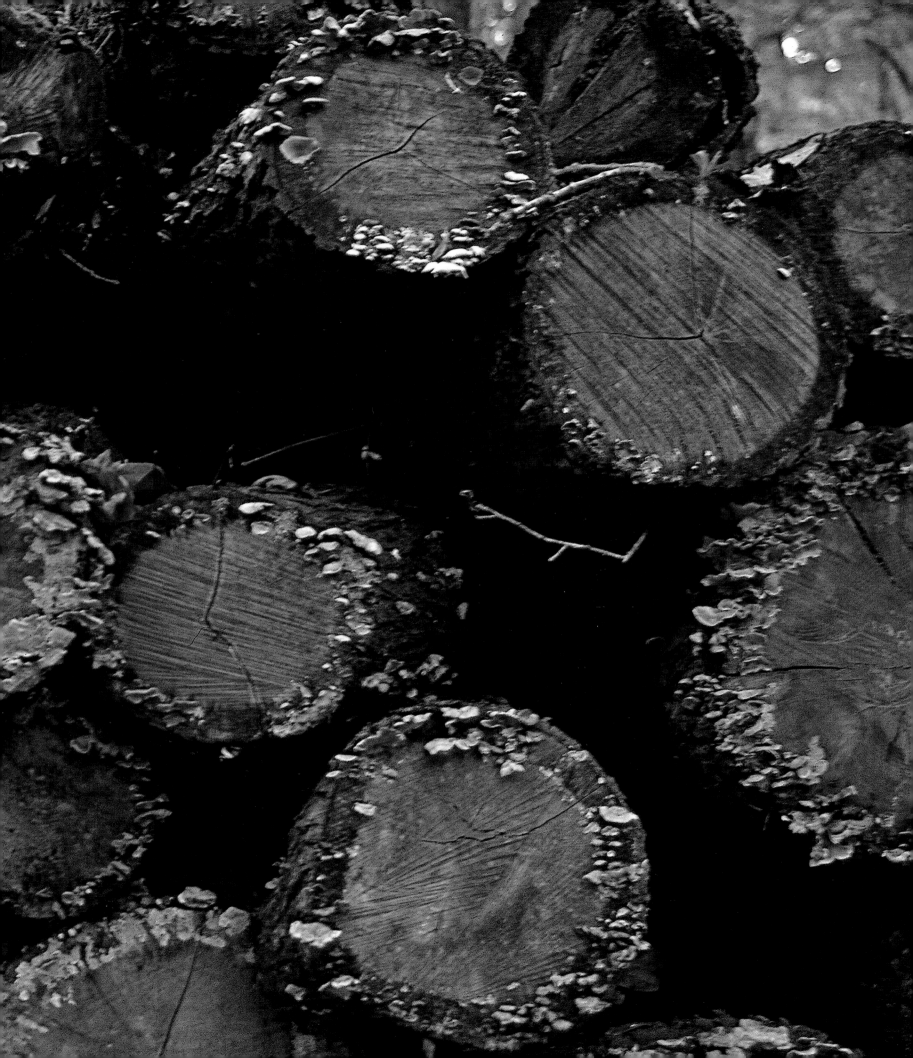

All gardens and parks, irrespective of their age, function or design, support a wide range of 'wild' plants and animals. These range from the microscopic, through colourful butterflies and song birds, to elegant deer and nocturnal creatures such as moths, badgers and bats. They include beneficial sorts such as pollinating insects, aphid-eating predators and earthworms, as well as others that are harmful, such as slugs and rats. They number many thousands of species. Most are benign, and the vast majority go unseen or unnoticed even to the most diligent observer.

In recent years there has been growing recognition of the important role that parks and gardens play in nature conservation (see, for example, Harding and Rose 1986). Nature conservation is essentially about maintaining native fauna and flora, the communities that exist in nature, and the habitats where they occur. It is also, of course, about avoiding extinctions. All of this is frequently summed up in the phrase 'the maintenance of biodiversity'. It is not necessarily about preserving things exactly as they are. Populations of plants and animals are never static: the 'balance of nature' is often very dynamic indeed. Distributions and numbers of organisms are constantly changing, sometimes very dramatically. The familiar house sparrow has declined significantly in the last decade, especially in rural areas. The collared dove did not arrive in Britain until 1955 but is now common in suitable habitats; but the once-common turtle dove has become quite scarce. Similar changes are occurring with quite a few of our familiar plants, birds and insects. The reasons are complex and not always necessarily connected with global warming.

THE ROLE OF GARDENS AND PARKS

Gardens and parks provide a wealth of habitats and support huge numbers of common and widespread species. They can also include some unique habitats and harbour rarities. With a few notable exceptions, however, comparatively little detailed study has been undertaken of what lives in them. Popular books describe and illustrate some of the wild plants and animals to be found in the average garden, but few go into much detail. One exception is an account of the surveys carried out in the gardens of Buckingham Palace. Building on earlier work by experts and enthusiasts of the South London Entomological and Natural History Society, David Bellamy surveyed the native flora of this 49-acre oasis in the heart of London in 1984, and produced a highly readable account including some sound advice for gardeners.

78. Opposite: log piles can be a valuable habitat for many invertebrates and amphibians.

WHAT LIVES IN A GARDEN?

The most comprehensive study to date is that of the modest suburban garden in Leicester belonging to Dr J. Owen (Owen 1991). This very typical quarter-acre plot, with a lawn, vegetables, shrubs, flowers and a tiny pond, offers a remarkable glimpse of what an ordinary garden can support. With the assistance of experts in universities and elsewhere, Dr Owen systematically identified all the animals and plants that lived in, or passed through, over a period of thirty years. The results are truly astonishing – nearly 400 flowering plants, including grasses, and 2,600 species of animal. The latter include, for example, as many as 533 species of ichneumon wasps and over 400 different beetles. Even these extraordinary figures are underestimates: the flies, for example, were only partly recorded, and the abundant soil fauna was largely ignored.

Historic parklands, which have often remained relatively undisturbed and agriculturally unimproved since their enclosure as deer parks in medieval times, are particularly important for nature conservation. One feature that makes these parklands so distinctive and valuable is the occurrence of ancient (veteran) trees and the organisms associated with them. Old trees with dead limbs, cavities, rots, sap runs and other features are vital for the survival of scarce bats, beetles and other invertebrates. Such trees would have been a normal feature of unmanaged forests in former times but are rarely retained in managed woodlands; where they do occur, they are often heavily shaded by crop trees. Deer parks and other ancient parks are the principal places where open-grown, wide-crowned, old – and often decrepit – trees now survive. They represent some of the last vestiges of the system of wood pasture that would have been widespread in medieval times. They have often evolved directly from the wildwood of ancient times and are a dwindling resource. Fortunately, a number of parks in England still support some of these old forest species; several have been notified as SSSIs and at least three are managed as National Nature Reserves.

However, in some cases, the value of such parks has been affected by modern management. Bushes have been cleared, dead and fallen timber removed, grasslands re-seeded, drained and limed or fertilised. Broad-spectrum herbicides may have been applied. The old trees remain, but other habitats that insects and other fauna require to complete their life cycles have been diminished – in particular, sources of nectar for adult insects.

A particular merit of parks and gardens, in terms of nature conservation, is the diversity of different habitats that they contain and the intimate mosaics that they often comprise. Even gardens, although generally tidier, more ornamental and more intensively

79. The Majesty Oak, a magnificent veteran tree at Fredville Park, Kent.

80. Wall growing ferns at Lesnes Abbey.

81. House martin nests.

martins, swallows and swifts; also barn owls and kestrels. Open-fronted sheds and boathouses are particularly attractive to swallows, robins, wrens and pied wagtails. Culverts may be used by bats, or even otters.

Lakes, ponds and watercourses

Wetland of various types is often a component of parks and gardens, which often include lakes, ponds, streams and marshy areas, sometimes of considerable size. These may be natural-looking, with shelving margins and a wide range of native vegetation, including submerged, floating and marginal communities (see 'Water features', page 187). In some parks, the margins may be grazed by cattle or deer. At the other extreme, ponds may be very formal and hard-edged, with perhaps only a limited range of, say, water-lilies or iris cultivars. Whatever the context, some native animals or plants will always be present. These will usually include dragonflies, damsel-flies, may-flies, water-beetles and other insects as well as algae. The latter can sometimes cause problems, but the health of a pond and the clarity of the water usually depend on a balance between various organisms including algae. Garden ponds can be particularly important as breeding sites for frogs, toads or newts. If the latter include great-crested (or warty) newts, there are legal implications (see page 79).

Lakes are used by a wide variety of birds as well as possibly otters and water-voles. Birds usually include various diving and surface-feeding ducks, depending on the depth of the water; dab-chicks, great-crested grebes, coots, moor-hens and herons. Sedge warblers or reed warblers may breed at the margins if suitable reeds or other cover is available. Numerous other birds are associ-

managed than parks, are likely to support a multitude of creatures. The reasons lie in the diversity of habitats and their juxtaposition.

Walls, buildings and other structures

Parks and gardens commonly contain walls, buildings and other artificial structures – including, for example, brick or stone walls, steps and terraces; gazebos and pergolas; boathouses; bridges and culverts; barns and stables; ha-has; pump houses; dams and weirs; and even cottages or other dwellings. At first sight these highly artificial constructions might seem unlikely places for much in the way of wildlife, but they can be particularly important because they offer an abundant and widely spread alternative habitat for species normally confined to natural rockfaces. Walls often support assemblages of specialised plants such as sedums, ivy-leaved toadflax, pellitory of the wall, wall rue and other ferns, naturalised wallflowers or even antirrhinums, as well as a wide variety of mosses, liverworts or lichens.

Holes and crevices in walls may be used by bats or hibernating newts. Weather-proof buildings such as barns, cottages and icehouses may provide suitable sites for bats to breed or over-winter. Some are frequently used as nesting sites for birds including robins, wrens, spotted flycatchers, starlings, house

---

LAKES, PONDS AND BATS

Lakes and ponds are often particularly good feeding sites for bats. At a historic park in the west of England, one of Britain's largest known colonies of the rare greater horseshoe bat breeds in the roof of the mansion. The bats are known to feed on insects over a series of ornamental lakes, as well as taking beetles as they fly over the adjacent cattle-grazed pasture. This site is an SSSI, and on the English Heritage Register of Historic Parks and Gardens.

82. The horse pond at Great Dixter is an example of an attractive informal pond which provides a valuable wildlife habitat.

ated with lakes – for example, swallows, swifts and house-martins will feed there on midges and other flying insects; and swallows may roost in reed beds prior to migrating to their winter quarters. Herons may breed in nearby woodland or on islands. Canada geese can present problems in terms of aggressive behaviour towards other water-birds, excessive messing of margins or grazing of adjacent farm crops (their management is discussed in the Appendices, Table 13).

Dams, bridges and waterfalls add to the diversity of water features and the variety of plant and animal life. Waterfalls favour mosses, liverworts and ferns such as the Hart's-tongue. Bridges are frequently used by bats for roosting; some bridges are important breeding sites for house martins.

Lawns and other grasslands

In deer parks the grassland may be very ancient, but even in designed landscapes, which have experienced massive disturbance and re-shaping of contours, areas of semi-natural grassland frequently exist. Some of those will have been derived by succession from sown grasslands, assisted by seeds coming from less disturbed areas nearby; others will be old grassland which has

83. The formal pond in the sunken garden at Great Dixter does not contain fish and is a valuable amphibian habitat.

84. Grazing is an important part of the annual cycle of many biologically rich meadows.

survived. The nature and composition of these grasslands vary according to local circumstances, depending on soil, geology, climate and aspect as well as on the type of management, intensity of grazing and so on. At one extreme are acidic, heathy, grasslands and, at the other, on chalk or limestone for example, are highly calcareous communities with a rich, diverse flora of lime-tolerant grasses and numerous, often colourful, wildflowers including several species of orchids. The majority of old grassland in parks is likely to fall between those extremes and contain a range of typical grasses (see 'Turf and grassland', page 175).

Unfortunately, many of these old grasslands will have been agriculturally 'improved', either by ploughing and re-seeding or by surface treatments such as the application of fertilisers or herbicides, destroying botanical diversity and its dependent creatures. Any that have escaped such treatment are likely to be important, and may represent some of the last in the district. Their significance lies not only in their value as havens for traditional grassland wildflowers and other plants, but as food sources for a wide range of invertebrates which, in turn, are eaten by bats and birds. Some rare beetles and flies that breed in ancient trees require the nectar from flowers in order to be able to complete their breeding cycle. Dung from cattle and other grazing animals is an important source of insects, such as dung beetles and flies, which are vital food for birds and bats.

At first sight, lawns may seem unlikely places for much in the way of wild nature. However, if neglected or deliberately managed less intensively, the lawn may support a colourful array of wildflowers which, in turn, will feed numerous bees and hoverflies. Even lawns that are neat and well maintained may have some interest. A number of plants can thrive under intensive mowing regimes so long as they are not fertilised, sprayed or mown too closely; this is especially true of old, long-established lawns. Repeated close mowing usually prevents most of these plants from flowering, but they survive by vegetative propagation and can give an old lawn a real sense of longevity and permanence as well as creating a diverse environment for numerous small creatures.

The fruiting bodies of numerous fungi often decorate old lawns. Several species form the well-known 'fairy rings', but there are many others and some are quite rare. Much survey work remains to be done, but as knowledge of fungi develops it is becoming increasingly clear that tightly cut, mossy old lawns, together with some churchyards and the unimproved grasslands in some parklands, are a very important scientific resource. The correct management of such sites is critical (see below and 'Turf and grassland', page 175).

A surprisingly large number of invertebrates occur in lawns and other short grassland. One group of well-known and conspicuous insects are the crane-flies; the larvae of some species

TYPICAL SPECIES FOUND IN OLD GRASSLAND

COMMON TO NEUTRAL OLD GRASSLAND

Crested Dog's-Tail	*Cynosurus cristatus*
Red Fescue	*Festuca rubra*
Sweet Vernal Grass	*Anthoxanthum odoratum*
Meadow Foxtail	*Alopecurus pratensis*
Smooth Meadow-Grass	*Poa pratensis*
Bird's-Foot Trefoil	*Lotus corniculatus*
Clover	*Trifolium* sp.
Yarrow	*Achillea millefolium*
Lady's Bedstraw	*Galium verum*
Pignut	*Conopodium majus*
Sorrel	*Rumex acetosa*
Cuckoo Flower	*Cardamine pratensis*
Oxeye Daisy	*Leucanthemum vulgare*
Germander Speedwell	*Veronica chamaedrys*
Common Vetch	*Vicea sativa*
Bush Vetch	*Vicea sepium*
Tufted Vetch	*Vicea cracca*
Meadow Vetchling	*Lathyrus pratensis*
Field Woodrush	*Luzula campestris*
Ribwort Plantain	*Plantago lanceolata*
Meadow Cranesbill	*Geranium pratense*
Dovesfoot Cranesbill	*Geranium molle*
Cut-leaved Cranesbill	*Geranium dissectum*
Devil's-bit Scabious	*Scabiosa pratensis*
Hay Rattle	*Rhinanthus minor*

COMMON TO ACIDIC GRASSLAND

Sheep's Fescue	*Festuca ovina*
Common Bent	*Agrostis capillaris* (syn. *A. tenuis*)
Purple Moor Grass	*Molinia caerulea*
Mat-Grass	*Nardus stricta*
Sheep's Sorrel	*Rumex acetosella*
Heath Bedstraw	*Galium saxatile*
Lousewort	*Pedicularis sylvatica*
Heath spotted Orchid	*Dactylorhiza maculata*
Lesser Butterfly Orchid	*Platanthera bifolia*

COMMON TO ALKALINE GRASSLAND

Common Spotted Orchid	*Dactylorhiza fuchsia*
Green-winged Orchid	*Orchis morio*
Pyramidal Orchid	*Anacamptis pyramidalis*
Meadow Buttercup	*Ranunculus acris*
Bulbous Buttercup	*Ranunculus bulbosus*
Greater Knapweed	*Centaurea scabiosa*
Cowslip	*Primula veris*
Field Scabious	*Knautia arvensis*
Small Scabious	*Scabiosa columbaria*

COMMON WILDFLOWERS FOUND IN UNSPRAYED AND UNFERTILISED LAWNS

MEDIUM TO LONG GRASS MANAGEMENT

Daisy	*Bellis perennis*
Dandelion	*Taraxacum* sp.
Buttercup	*Ranunculus repens*
Cat's Ear	*Hypochoeris radicata*

SHORT GRASS MANAGEMENT

Field Wood-Rush	*Luzula campestris*
Pignut	*Conopodium majus*
Mouse-Ear Hawkweed	*Hieracium pilosella*
Glaucous Sedge	*Carex flacca*
Thyme-Leaved Speedwell	*Veronica serpyllifolia*
Slender Speedwell	*Veronica filiformis*

WAXCAPS

This large family of toadstools – with thick waxy gills, moist brittle flesh and often brightly coloured caps – are very sensitive indicators of habitat quality. Very old grassland that has not been affected by modern farming methods may have more than 20 species, whereas an improved pasture is unlikely to have any. Really old lawn turf that has not been fertilised or treated with herbicides can be very rich in waxcaps (as well as other fungi). A series of lawns at a Leicestershire mansion built around 1820, which have never been treated with chemicals, are so rich in waxcaps (as well as sedges and other plants) that they have been designated as an SSSI.

85. Wax cap fungi in the lawn at Down House.

86. Meadows are a valuable habitat for many invertebrates.

BUTTERFLIES AND DAY-FLYING MOTHS ASSOCIATED WITH FLOWERY GRASSLAND

		Larvae feed on
Meadow Brown	*Maniola jurtina*	grass
Wall Brown	*Lasiommata megera*	grass
Gatekeeper	*Pyronia tithonus*	grass
Large Skipper	*Ochlodes venatus*	grass
Small Skipper	*Thymelicus action*	grass
Common Blue	*Polyommatus icarus*	trefoils and clovers
Small Copper	*Lycaena phlaeas*	sorrels and docks
Orange-tip	*Anthocaris cardamines*	various crucifers
Green-veined White	*Pieris napi*	various crucifers
Cinnabar	*Tyria jacobaeae*	Ragwort
Burnets	*Zygaena* sp.	mostly low growing legumes
Chimney Sweeper	*Odezia atrata*	pignut and other small umbellifers

(leather-jackets) feed on the roots of lawn grasses. Another insect particularly attracted to short turf is the tawny mining bee, often noticed in early spring when it unplugs its burrows in the lawn and leaves little conical piles of earth surrounding round holes.

Many larger gardens, especially those with orchards, have areas of grass that are cut less often, perhaps only once or twice a year. These are often associated with spring-flowering bulbs such as crocuses, snowdrops and daffodils or sometimes tulips. In other cases they may be managed simply as flowery meadows, relying on spring or summer wildflowers for effect. Such grasslands are likely to be among the most diverse and productive wildlife habitats in any garden. They can contain a very wide range of grasses and wildflowers, including many that were typical of traditionally managed hay meadows, and support a huge range of insects and other invertebrates as well as small mammals, reptiles and amphibians.

Generally speaking, the most diverse flower-rich grasslands will be on the least fertile soils. If a site is very fertile the coarser grasses – such as cock's-foot (*Dactylis glomerata*), false oat-grass (*Arrhenatherum elatius*) and yorkshire fog (*Holcus lanatus*) – are likely to be present and may come to dominate; docks (*Rumex*) and thistles (*Cirsium*) may proliferate.

A variety of colourful butterflies are associated with these flowery grasslands, as well as day-flying moths, especially the various small grass moths. At dusk the males of the ghost moth may sometimes be seen hovering (pendulating) a few feet above the grass, apparently to attract the attention of passing females. Other invertebrates include flies, spiders and beetles; maybe grasshoppers or ants. Dry grasslands with ant hills may attract green woodpeckers to feed. Swallows and house martins will swoop over these areas, picking up vital insect food for their young or to build up reserves in preparation for migration.

Tall grassland is a favoured habitat of frogs, toads and newts, which move about in the sheltered and often humid environment at the bottom, feeding on slugs and other small creatures. Slow worms and grass snakes may also occur. Small mammals such as the field vole, wood mouse and common shrew are usually present, providing food for kestrels or barn owls.

Old trees

All trees are important for nature conservation, but especially the native species such as oak, ash, elm, beech, lime, field maple and so on. Many introduced species and varieties are also valuable,

87. Old trees with suitable roosting cavities are likely to be used by bats, whether in parkland or in gardens and close to habitation.

88. A large, dead, veteran tree will offer both visual interest and wildlife value for some decades.

particularly if they have been in place for a long time. Sycamore, for example, though it can be considered a weed in important semi-natural woodlands, is a valuable source of aphids and other insect food for breeding birds such as titmice and warblers; the bark of old sycamores often supports particularly good communities of lichens. Quite a few caterpillars feed on the leaves of American red oaks, and there are numerous other examples of invertebrates utilising non-native trees and shrubs.

However, the most important trees in terms of nature conservation are native trees, and in general the older they are the better. If they have hollows, rot holes, rots, snags, dead or broken branches, sap runs, fungal fruiting bodies or other features associated with ageing and neglect, they are likely to support a greater variety of both plants and animals. These can include rare lichens and fungi as well as bats, beetles, flies and other invertebrates. Some of these creatures are extremely rare, as they are totally dependent on suitable very old trees. In a few cases a species of beetle, for example, may be known from only one or two individual trees in the whole country – if that tree is felled, or blows down and is cleared away, the species is likely to become extinct.

Several of Britain's bat species roost in holes, splits or hollows in trees; even in roots where they are accessible. Some use trees almost exclusively – the rare Bechstein's bat, for example, is particularly associated with mature wooded sites where it roosts in tree holes, usually in the canopy, mainly in old trees with dead

branches. Another bat particularly associated with parkland, pasture and woodland edges is the Serotine. Daubenton's and Noctule's are mainly found where old trees occur near water. One National Trust estate in Somerset has as many as 14 species of bat roosting in and around old trees and woodland.

Lichens are another special feature of old trees and parks. Many rare species are still found on old trees in ancient deer parks. Even where there have been extensive landscaping and replanting, some old, lichen-encrusted trees often survive. Oliver Gilbert in *Lichens* (2000) gives a fascinating and highly readable account, listing some of the most important parkland sites in England, several of which have international importance for their lichen species and communities.

Fungi associated with old trees are of considerable conservation importance and include rare and threatened species. Only a few are seriously pathogenic – the appearance of bracket fungi may cause alarm but it does not necessarily indicate the imminent death or collapse of the tree. Most species attack heartwood not living sapwood, and by recycling the nutrients they actually feed the tree and prolong its life. These fungi are also important for invertebrates and other creatures that feed on them or complete their life cycles with the fruiting bodies.

Because of the special importance of veteran trees and the parklands in which they occur, some of the best sites are notified as SSSIs. This has important implications for management (see below, page 111 and page 77).

89. The flowers of ragwort, like most *Compositae*, are very attractive to a great many insects, including the cinnabar moth whose caterpillars feed on its leaves. It is thought that cinnabar caterpillars can control or even destroy ragwort, and they have been deliberately introduced to some countries with that intention. They are available from commercial suppliers, but the cost of large-scale use would be considerable, and most observers consider the results disappointing. Ragwort is a serious weed in grazed areas since it is poisonous to livestock.

Scrub, bracken and wild plants

Veteran trees cannot function effectively on their own or in a sterile environment; it is their combination with scrub, old grassland and ponds and lakes that is so vital for long-term conservation. The bushes and brambles that thrive without much help in most parks – often regarded as undesirable scrub – are also very valuable. Birds use them for nesting and roosting, insects and other invertebrates depend on them, and other animals rely on them for cover. The flowers of hawthorn, sallow and brambles are important nectar and pollen sources for butterflies, moths and many beetles. Grassland wildflowers can be vital for the survival of scarce invertebrates that breed in old trees.

Bracken is another common feature of many parks that is often regarded with misgiving. It can certainly get out of hand and, especially on deep or fertile soils, come to dominate large areas at the expense of grassland or heathland. But it does in fact support a quite varied fauna and a rich flora – bluebells, violets and other spring flowers can often thrive if the bracken is not too dominant. Some quite scarce butterflies are particularly associated with bracken communities, particularly if they include violets, primroses, wood anemones or bugle. The high brown fritillary frequents bracken-covered hillsides typical of some deer parks; it is in serious decline and has become quite rare. Other scarce butterflies that favour this type of habitat are the dark green fritillary, pearl-bordered and small pearl-bordered fritillaries. More widespread species include the speckled wood, small copper and gatekeeper.

Two other plants that can be a real nuisance in parklands are ragwort and creeping thistle. Both have their merits – they support a great many insects, especially moths and butterflies – but these are usually outweighed by the problems they cause. Methods of controlling them without destroying other, benign, wildflowers include weed-wiping as well as husbandry techniques (see also page 228).

Other features

Exposed rocks, cliffs and caves offer further opportunities for plants and animals, whether natural or enhanced or even created by a landscape designer. Rocks and cliffs in shade can support mosses, liverworts and ferns; in the open they may have rich communities of lichens. They warm up in the sunshine, attracting insects and spiders. Caves tend to have specialised fauna and flora – most obviously bats, especially when hibernating, which benefit from the low and constant temperatures. Swallows and swifts occasionally nest in caves; dippers, too, if running water is present. Many invertebrates will be present. If cave systems are complex, they will support a very extensive fauna and flora with numerous species especially adapted to life in total darkness.

Walled kitchen gardens, potting sheds, greenhouses, statues, pots and other ornaments all provide homes or feeding places for plants and animals. Peacock and small tortoiseshell butterflies are not the only insects that attempt to hibernate in sheds – the herald moth is perhaps the most frequently noticed of the moths, and lacewings and ladybirds are also familiar denizens. Nesting, roosting and the occurrence of specialised wall plants are common to garden structures. In gardens rather than parks the maintenance may be more intensive but the benefits are likely to be similar.

Flower and shrub borders are very important feeding and breeding areas for a whole range of living things, from insects to birds. Although the majority of border plants may be introductions, many have leaves, buds, stems and roots that are avidly eaten by our native fauna. But it is the flowers that are most attractive, particularly to insects. As well as the butterflies that are so welcome in the flower border, myriads of other insects visit, including hover-flies and other *Diptera* (two-winged flies), hive bees, bumble bees, other bees and wasps and beetles. Spiders, centipedes and other groups abound. Many of these, in turn, are food for robins, flycatchers and other birds; and some are prey for dragonflies such as the southern hawker which patrols most gardens in high summer.

Management considerations

Gardens and parks are extremely significant for nature conservation, particularly if they are old and varied, and if chemical use is carefully minimised. Apart from that proviso, there are few specific measures that a manager need take in order to maintain the wildlife interest.

It is important to understand that the management of historic parks and gardens for their historic, landscape and ecological

90. The great crested newt hibernates under the winter protection provided to shelter these tiles from frost in winter.

interests can often be achieved without the need for one to take priority over another. With a good understanding of the different interests, it is usually possible to establish a management regime beneficial to all and greatly enhance the interest of the park. This reinforces the importance of developing a management plan for a site, since it is an ideal opportunity for all parties to consider the varying interests, many of which will not be contradictory. Where interests do clash, a reasonable compromise can usually be found.

Legal constraints

In terms of nature conservation, two types of legal constraint affect some historic parks and gardens. One is designation, as in SSSI or cSAC (Candidate Special Area of Conservation); the other is species protection.

Designation At the time of writing, as many as 100 of the 1,500 sites in the English Heritage Register are also, wholly or partly, designated as SSSIs. Owners and occupiers will have been notified by Natural England, with a plan, a description of the reasons for notification, and a list of activities that could damage the interest. Early consultation with Natural England about any planned works will usually enable operations to proceed smoothly. A management plan to which all parties have contributed at the drafting stage is often the best way to ensure that all interests within the site are fully understood and catered for.

Species protection Many gardens contain protected plants or animals, with the degree of protection varying from one species to another. Most legitimate maintenance activities are unlikely

to be in conflict with the law – for example, although it is illegal to kill (or sell) frogs or toads, it is not illegal to disturb or move them accidentally. The same applies to most snakes and lizards. 'Unauthorised persons' may not legally kill or uproot the majority of wildflowers on your property, but owners and managers may do so.

Natural England can give advice and, if necessary, recommend surveyors or consultants who can investigate and negotiate the timing of works or other measures that may be needed to comply with the law. If protected species are found after work has started, long and expensive delays can result. See page 77 for more detail, but the most important species are listed below:

Great crested or warty newts are strictly protected against disturbance, capture or killing; even their habitat may not be changed except under licence. If a pond or lake is to be drained, seek advice.

Bats may not be taken, killed or injured, or their roosts interfered with. If it is known or suspected that bats use any site that is going to be repaired, altered or removed, seek advice. As well as buildings, they use trees, walls, culverts and other places.

Birds are protected in various ways. You may not kill or injure a wild bird, damage its nest or take its eggs. So you cannot legally remove the nests of swallows or house martins, even though their droppings may be causing damage or nuisance. Nor may you cut a hedge in such a way as to damage a nest that is in use or being built (ornamental hedges are exempt). Certain birds are given protection against disturbance, such as the barn owl. There are exceptions in the case of listed pest species and game; further information can be obtained from local offices of Natural England or the Royal Society for the Protection of Birds.

91. In some areas, Canada geese have increased to such numbers that they cause problems by their aggression towards other water birds, soiling of waterside grassland, and grazing of farm crops.

MAINTENANCE AND MANAGEMENT

This section concentrates on some of the more significant activities that impinge on wildlife conservation.

Trees

- Retain dead and rotting wood, preferably on the tree itself but, failing that, as close to the tree of origin as possible. Fallen trees are best left lying as they fall. Dead and fallen timber may be cut and piled but it is more effective if left lying, and tends to look more natural. Special considerations apply where the public may have access, both in regard to safety and appearance.

- Retain very old, dying or diseased trees. All such trees are valuable habitats, especially if there are hollows, rot, holes and splits, or sap runs.

- A replacement programme of planting sufficient young trees of the right species, at intervals over a period of time, is essential to replace the older generations.

Shrubs

- Sufficient hawthorn, sallow, blackthorn and other native shrubs should be available to provide nectar sources for adult insects emerging from the old trees and dead wood.

- Other shrubs including buckthorn, hazel and dog roses can provide a variety of benefits including food for caterpillars.

This may simply mean allowing some naturally regenerated shrubs to survive; if this is not happening, they should be included in the planting programme and suitably protected from browsing animals.

Grassland

- Semi-natural grassland in parks should be managed to maintain its diversity and floristic interest.

- Levelling and draining should be avoided.

92. A wood habitat pile is an important environment for invertebrates such as stag head beetles.

- Ploughing and re-seeding are particularly damaging.
- Grazing stock should be suited to the conditions, using hardy breeds and, in some cases, old and rare breeds. The *Breed Profiles Handbook* (ed. Tolhurst and Oates, 2001) is a very useful source of information.

Wild flowers

- Fertilisers and herbicides should be avoided if at all possible.
- Where wild plants such as docks, nettles, ragwort, thistles or bracken have to be controlled it is preferable to use physical methods such as cutting, pulling or bruising.
- If herbicides have to be used they should be applied by weed-wiping. The *Practical Solutions Handbook* (ed. Coleshaw, 2001) gives details of techniques and equipment including specialist weed-wiping and weed-pulling equipment designed specifically for use in parklands and rough terrain.

Wetlands

- Ponds, lakes, watercourses, marshes and all wet ground should be carefully protected from all forms of pollution including fertilisers and pesticides as well as effluent of any kind.
- Livestock may need access to streams and lake margins for drinking. Even if troughs or pumps are available, there is merit in allowing some access to such habitats – the trampling and poaching creates conditions that encourage a greater diversity of plants and animal life, and can outweigh the harm done by some dung and urine getting into the water.

Gardens

- Maximise the structural and habitat diversity by including a wide range of features such as lawns, borders, ponds, waterfalls, bog gardens and built structures such as pergolas and gazebos. In many historic gardens the existing design will often have a wide range of habitats.
- Maximise structural and species diversity in herbaceous borders and shrubberies, with plants and shrubs of various heights, shapes and flowering seasons. Intimately mixed to create mosaics, they will provide feeding and basking opportunities for the greatest variety of insects and other creatures.

- Wherever possible, use plants, shrubs and trees that are particularly attractive to a wide variety of wildlife through their flowers, foliage or fruits and seeds. Do not cut down herbaceous planting until late in the season, to provide a food source and shelter for wildlife for as long as possible.
- Minimise the use of chemical pesticides. Although the majority of commercially available products have been carefully screened and are considered safe when properly applied, they are all poisons and are intended to kill plants or animals. They are bound to have unwanted side effects, either directly or indirectly. It is better to control weeds by physical methods and to control unwanted pests by encouraging birds, amphibians, ladybirds and other predatory creatures.
- Use seeds and plants from native sources, preferably originating in the locality, when sowing or planting native grasses, wildflowers, trees or shrubs, to maintain the genetic integrity of local plant populations. Many commercial seed and plant suppliers include material of foreign origin that often contains strains unsuited to local conditions; fortunately, there are now a number of suppliers offering genuinely native material, often from named sources. Bulbs and other plants taken from the wild, whether with the consent of the landowner or plundered illegally, should definitely be avoided. A list of specialist suppliers of native seeds and plants is available at www.nature-bureau.co.uk/pages/floraloc/resources/sources/suppliers.html
- Try to ensure that the garden is linked by hedges, watercourses, rough grassland or woodland to other wildlife habitats in the vicinity – these 'corridors' enable butterflies and other forms of wildlife to colonise and maintain their populations. In urban and suburban gardens, such links will usually exist in the form of neighbouring gardens; country properties are often more isolated.
- Take advice from Natural England or the local Wildlife Trust before applying fertilisers or weedkillers to a lawn containing a wide variety of native sedges, grasses and herbs, or waxcap fungi. Normal regular mowing regimes are beneficial, provided that the arisings are removed.
- If areas of long grass harbour grass snakes or slow worms, try to move them by walking through the area before mowing.

Vegetation maintenance and management

The current edition of *The Plant Finder* (a regular publication by the Royal Horticultural Society; www.rhs.org.uk/rhsplantfinder) lists over 73,000 plants now available from the many nurseries listed. This remarkable bible provides a valuable source for those who are seeking to replace or extend their collections. But the successful upkeep and maintenance of plants in historic sites may require, where possible and realistic, the use of authentic species or cultivars, which may not be too easy to locate. There is also the challenge of understanding how, and where, to grow them effectively. There is nothing new about this challenge, of course: gardeners centuries ago were experimenting with and usually succeeding in growing many strange and new exotics.

Effective life of plants

All plants have finite lives – at some stage a decision to remove or replace them is inevitable. Life cycles vary enormously (see picture 94). Woody plants often cause the most deliberation and sometimes heartache when it is time for them to go. The effective lives of trees, some shrubs and hedge types can be extended by husbandry and remedial techniques (see page 134).

The following categories are included in this section:

- **Woody plants** Trees, conifers, shrubs (including roses), wall plants and climbers
- **Non-woody plants** Herbaceous perennials, bulbs, corms, tubers, annuals, biennials, grass and turf

93. Opposite: tree ferns at Trebah require a very humid, frost-free micro-climate.
94. Below: each vegetation type (annual, perennial, shrub or tree) has its own cycle of growth: establishment (E), maturity (M) and death (D). The art of the gardener is to keep all these in balance. These cycles can vary from less than one year to many hundreds.

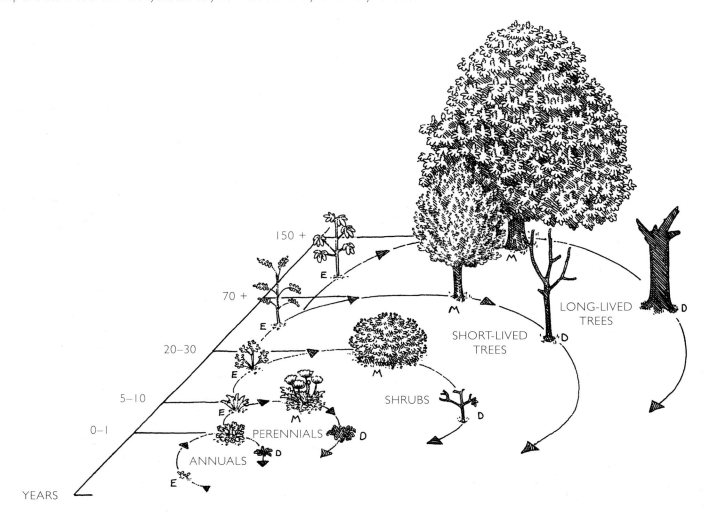

EFFECTIVE LIFE OF TREES

age in years

		50	100	150	200	250	300	350	400	450	500	frequently older

CANOPY TREES

			frequently older
Acer platanoides	Norway Maple		
Acer pseudoplatanus	Sycamore		✔
Aesculus hippocastanum	Horse Chestnut		
Alnus glutinosa	Common Alder		
Betula sp	Birches		
Carpinus betulus	Hornbeam		
Castanea sativa	Sweet Chestnut		✔
Fagus sylvatica	Beech		✔
Fraxinus excelsior	Ash		✔
Juglans sp.	Walnuts		✔
Platanus sp	Planes		
Populus sp.	Poplars		✔
Quercus robur	English Oak		✔
Salix sp	Willows		
Tilia europea and others	Lime		✔
Zelkova sp			

FLOWERING TREES

			frequently older
Crataegus sp and cvs	Thorns		✔
Laburnum sp and cvs	Laburnums		
Malus	Flowering Crab Apples		
Morus nigra	Mulberry		
Prunus	Flowering Cherry group		
Prunus avium	Native Gean/Wild Cherry		✔
Sorbus acuparia	Rowan, Whitebeam		✔
Ulmus sp	Elms		

EVERGREEN TREES, CONIFEROUS

			frequently older
Cedrus atlantica, C. libani	Cedars		✔
Chamaecyparis sp.	Cypresses		✔
Pinus radiata	Pines, W. USA		✔
Pinus sylvestris, P. nigra	Pines, European		
Sequoia, Sequoiadendron	Wellingtonias, Redwoods		✔
Taxodium distichum	Swamp Cypress		✔
Taxus baccata	Yew		✔

EVERGREEN TREES, NON-CONIFEROUS

			frequently older
Buxus sempervirens	Box		
Ilex aqifolium	and other Hollies		✔
Quercus ilex	Holm Oak		✔

TREES

Trees and shrubs, climbers and occasionally sub-shrubs usually comprise the woody plants in most parks and gardens. Trees normally develop a permanent or semi-permanent framework of branches arising from a basal trunk or rootstock, and this trunk can assume massive proportions and be persistent for many centuries. Shorter-lived woody plants, including many garden shrubs such as roses, buddleias and lavateras, are usually multi-stemmed and may need hard cutting back or constant renewal of a branch system to perpetuate a reasonable life-cycle. Sub-shrubs include many Mediterranean examples such as lavenders, sages and santolinas, which generally establish easily but usually have a relatively short effective life.

The essential objectives are to maintain healthy effective growth for as long as possible, which requires good husbandry as well as some regulation of the shape and size of a plant. The required arboricultural practices, pruning, nutrient applications and pest and disease control are examined here.

Trees, as the longest-living woody component in the landscape, have a very special place in historic gardens and parks. They have also been the subject of an abundance of publications that include comprehensive reference works, illustrated guides and the journals of many specialist groups and societies (the bibliography and references include a selection of these). This section focuses on the main stages in the selection and establishment of trees, and the processes and operations in their management from maturity to old age. Appendices Tables 1 and 2 give guidelines on dates of introduction and effective lives which will be useful for those managing historic sites. Trees as single specimens, groups, clumps, roundels and avenues may need different management considerations , and the restoration and perpetuation of larger-scale plantings such as in arboreta, pineta and woodlands conclude this important this section.

Planting Initial planting and early maintenance treatments are critical in ensuring a tree's healthy establishment and longevity.

Specification categories Four principle categories are normally offered by nurseries, the selection of which may be determined by season of planting, type of plant and cost.

1. Bare root or open ground (OG): trees that are lifted from the nursery and planted during the dormant season November–March. Strongly recommended for all deciduous types, including hedging. Evergreen types, including conifers, do not transplant very successfully by this method.

2. Root wrapped or balled (burlapped): stock that is lifted during a more extended period which may be October–April and the root ball wrapped in hessian or plastic. This method gives better protection for more vulnerable root systems, and is recommended for evergreen trees such as holm oak (*Quercus ilex*), hollies (*Ilex*) and conifers.

3. Containerised: stock that is lifted from the open ground (possibly during a longer season than categories 1 and 2) and transferred to rigid or non-rigid containers, which are then available in various sizes, depending upon the size and species of the tree. Roots of trees treated in this way may have to be pruned harder than with categories 1 and 2, but there is less risk of drying out. The cost is generally higher.

4. Container grown: stock that has been grown throughout its nursery life in containers, with progressive re-potting into larger sizes of rigid or non-rigid containers. A well-established practice, favoured by the garden centre industry and garden contractors, its advantage is that stock can be planted out at any time of year. It is much used for conifers, and some evergreen trees, as well as a great range of other woody and non-woody plants.

The disadvantage, applying particularly to trees and shrubs for longer-term planting, is that containers are often too small for a healthy root system, and if the stock has been left in them too long, the resulting spiralled or curly roots may fail to grow out properly when planted out. Container design for larger semi-mature tree transplanting is always under review to reduce this problem, but wherever possible bare root or root-balled systems are recommended. The cost is usually higher than for open ground stock.

The progeny and origins of the tree should be checked wherever possible, especially for long-term planting in parkland, avenues and as specimens, where known clones of good performance and reliability are important. Trueness to name is obviously important.

Young stock is also preferable in the long term. Impetuosity is seldom justified for trees for posterity, the choice of semi-mature or extra heavy standards being justified only in exceptional circumstances.

95. Container-grown plants.

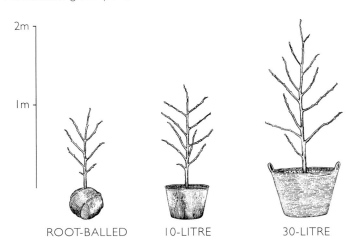

ROOT-BALLED   10-LITRE   30-LITRE

PLANTING SIZES, MAIN USES AND SEASONS

PARKLAND, FARM GARDEN HEDGES, FORESTRY,
NEW PLANTATIONS, COPSES, SHELTER BELTS
Open ground: (bare root) transplants, whips, feathered 60–80cm
(2–2ft 6in)

Deciduous
Plant November–mid March, ideally November–December
Support none or short stakes
Shelters and/or pest protection

Conifers/evergreens
Always root-balled or in containers, best 60–80cm
Plant November–April
Pest protection only

SPECIMENS, GROUPS, CLUMPS, AVENUES, ETC.
Open ground: feathered to half or full standards 200–300m (3–6ft)

Decidous
Plant November–mid-March, ideally November–December
Support short stakes
Pest protection

Conifers/evergreens
Best as smaller sizes

Note: extra-heavy or semi-mature open ground trees are an
alternative for more immediate effects or special cases, but subsequent
establishment may be slower, and after-care more important. Costs are
another factor.

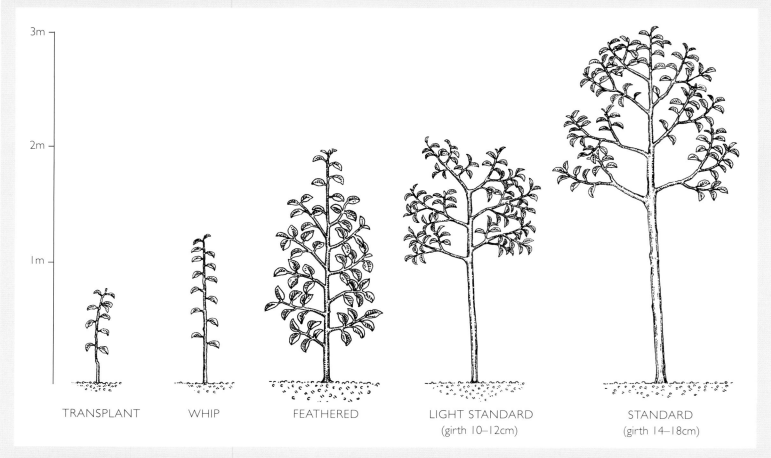

96. Bare root nursery stock sizes available from nursery suppliers. Girth sizes 1m from the ground are also given for the standard trees.

Planting techniques A recommended selection of literature and instruction manuals on methods of planting trees and other woody plants can be found in the bibliography. Failure or poor growth after planting occur too often; the following guidelines may help to deal with possible causes.

Soil and site preparation
Drainage Except for trees that are adapted to naturally wet sites, waterlogged or poorly drained ground can be a serious situation for new planting. Where this is only temporary on heavy clay soil, gravel or pea shingle can be incorporated in the planting pit to improve the drainage. Where the whole planting area is water-logged, a drainage system should be considered before planting is carried out.

Mound planting is used in special cases on clay-based flat sites where drainage is more difficult: the tree is planted on a gentle mound of prepared soil, with good aftercare such as mulching and watering.

Planting pits The aim is to get the young tree to develop a strong root system beyond the original planting pit, so the pit should be regarded as the first stage in this process. It should be wide and deep enough to accommodate the roots. Soil conditioners are rarely beneficial and peat-based products should never be used.

Support Very young trees such as whips and feathered types, if in favoured locations or extensive woodland schemes, may not need any form of support. But they will need some protection against predators, and protection devices can often be combined with support (see below).

For larger trees such as standards or extra heavy standards, a number of different methods of staking or guying can be used.

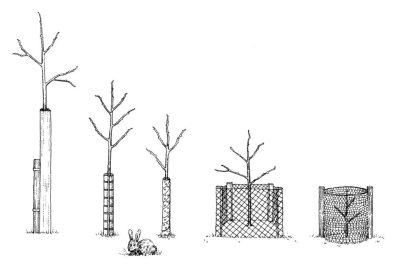

98. Temporary tree protection: large tree guard, small tree guard, spiral rabbit guard, and rabbit-free enclosures using four or two stakes.

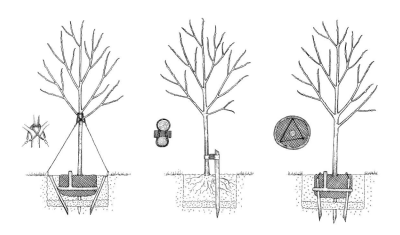

97. Tree supports. Left: overhead staking is suitable for trees in large planted beds; it is, however, prone to vandalism (note the buried irrigation tube). Centre: standard bare-rooted trees are best supported with a short stake; a rubber spacer protects the stem from chafing. Right: underground guying is suitable for trees in urban areas where trip hazards and vandalism are a problem; it is thought better for the development of the tree as it enables movement of the stem.

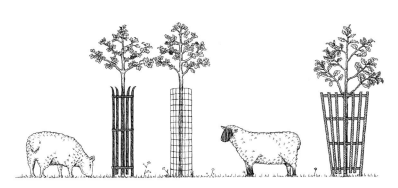

99. Permanent tree protection needs to be of a size and construction to withstand attempts by stock to eat the trees.

Protection Protection against predators such as rabbits and deer (and careless strimmers!) is advisable, and the technology and products available are constantly being updated. The type and degree of protection, its size and durability, will depend upon the size of the trees being planted and also the location (see figs. 98, 99). It can often be an advantage to combine the guard with some support, such as a stake. In parkland or sites where there are cattle, horses or deer, strong protective structures are really important, and must be wide and high enough to prevent browsing.

Aftercare Aftercare is quite as important as planting, and poor maintenance can result in failure or poor stunted growth. The first five years or so can be critical in encouraging good establishment. A planned schedule of maintenance, which need not be arduous or time-consuming, should be included in work programmes (see box, page 121).

Nutrients and fertilisers As a general rule, trees do not require regular fertilisers or feeding, but an occasional boost of suitable nutrients may be beneficial if a tree has had a period of stress as a result of drought or flooding, or if it is showing signs of poor growth due to compaction or other causes, but only if the compaction has first been relieved.

Where young trees have been planted with a watering tube incorporated, this can be used for liquid fertiliser treatment. In the case of mature trees, slow-release fertilisers can be injected in the drip-line area using a bulb-planting tool or similar to make shallow plugs into which the feed is applied. Fertiliser should never be included with the backfill on newly planted trees as it is largely leached out before the roots have grown sufficiently to use it.

Arboriculture or tree surgery Many techniques and operations may be used to ensure the long-term health, shape and structure of

100. A planting tube protects newly planted whips and transplants.

101. A pot-bound shrub, two years after planting.

COMPACTION

Root systems can be affected by often insidious and at times imperceptible damage caused by compaction. In historic garden and parks, this is most likely to come from the pressure of feet from visitors, especially around veteran trees, and animals. Car parking too close to trees is also a problem.

Compaction impairs soil aeration, affecting the uptake of nutrients and water. There may also be localised drought effects, since hard compacted layers cause more run-off during periods of rain.

Surface roots may be physically damaged – for example, if events such as garden shows allow the installation of exhibits that require turf lifting and foundation bases over, or too close to, tree roots.

Relief or prevention In severe cases, some form of barrier protection may be the answer. Where barriers are not favoured, aeration measures such as spiking, or breaking the hard 'pan' under and around the tree using the 'terra-lift' system which injects compressed air into the soil, can be combined with additional slow-release nutrients. Areas treated should be at least Im outside the 'drip-line' or crown spread of the tree, not just close to the trunk.

Consider diverting roads or paths if they are too near particular trees.

102. Compaction from feet can have a severe impact on the health of trees.

103. Inset: treatment of a specimen tree at Kew to relieve compaction at its base.

MAINTENANCE SCHEDULE

- **Weed control** Invading weeds, especially grasses, can compete for moisture and nutrients in the early years. A good mulch after planting and occasional further applications can help to smother weed growth, but some physical hand-pulling or hoeing may be required. Mulch mats can be used but results are variable. Chemical control with approved herbicides can be very effective. A circle approximately 1m in diameter should be kept weed-free for the first four or five years; strimmers and mowers should also keep 1m clear.

- **Irrigation** During very dry periods after planting, especially in spring and summer and if planting has been left rather late, watering is important – a good soak rather than a sprinkle. Young whips and transplants in extensive planting schemes may need only one good watering, using a bowser or similar, so that the roots are encouraged as soon as possible to look for moisture in the mother soil. For larger trees, irrigation tubes can be incorporated in the planting pits.

- **Support adjustment** Check support systems regularly and make any required adjustments, such as loosening ties to allow for tree growth, and re-tying and replacing guards or supports. After a period of time, where possible, remove all supports – but remember that in parkland and the like, trees will continue to need long-term protection from grazing stock.

- **Long-term aftercare** Once established, trees may need only periodic attention, unless affected by exceptional weather conditions such as storms; excessive root compaction and other pressures, or serious pest or disease.

105. A semi-mature tree with a watering point providing access to an irrigation tube placed at the bottom of the planting pit.

104. Tree ties, a good example.

106. Tree ties, a bad example which has been left on too long and is without a spacer separating the tree from the stake.

107. Parkland trees showing browsing lines from grazing stock..

108. A thinned woodland will enable selected trees to develop into mature trees.

109. Formative tree pruning to remove a twin leader.
110. Inset:: detail showing twin leader.

trees, from the nursery stage through maturity to eventual decline and fall. Trees have a remarkable adaptability and tenacity, and may often exist for a lifetime with little or no intervention, especially indigenous trees in their natural habitat which have regenerated from self-sown seed. Their eventual size and shape, however, will be governed by competition with others in a forest or woodland.

Trees intended for specific garden or parkland purposes, as specimens, effective groups or avenues, usually need some formative shaping and control from the nursery stage onwards in order to ensure long-lived, well-shaped individuals.

The nursery stage Broad-leaved deciduous types intended for long-term planting, such as oaks, beeches, limes and planes, should be encouraged to develop a single leader with subordinate lateral or side branches, forming a broadly tapering silhouette. A young tree should already have this form when it leaves the nursery, and it is good practice to inspect trees before they are delivered.

Early establishment and formative pruning With the more vigorous species such as limes, a forked or double leader may develop, or one or more laterals may grow too strongly, affecting the future balance and shape of the tree. Formative pruning is important before a tree becomes large and misshapen. The main aim is to encourage a strong crown development in the early stages, which should determine the treee's shape and balance throughout its life.

111. A twin leader will develop into an inherent weakness in most trees.

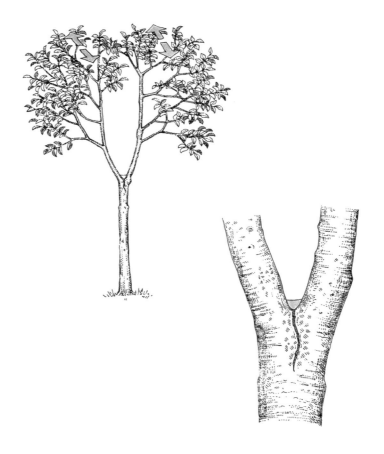

If a leader is damaged or broken off, the only answer is to encourage a new leader by cutting back to the next main side branch.

If, for whatever reason, a tree develops several leaders, it will tend to form a more stunted or round-headed form rather like a pollarded tree, and a decision will have to be made whether to keep it or plant a replacement. This can be important when avenues are being established (see Hampton Court Case Study, 3.5).

Flowering trees This is rather a general term for ornamental trees, such as flowering cherries (*Prunus)* and crab apples (*Malus*), which are normally produced in the nursery by budding or grafting on to selected rootstocks on a single stem or trunk. Various accepted heights and sizes are available.

They are normally compact spreading or round-headed without a leader, along with fastigiate and pendulous forms, and tend to be comparatively short-lived. The only formative pruning in the early years is to maintain a balanced crown, especially if they are damaged in any way, and to remove any suckers that may arise from the rootstock. These generally have a different habit from the desired cultivar, and are usually more vigorous; if not removed, they may eventually dominate the main tree.

Many fruit trees come into this category, and they are covered in 'Walled kitchen gardens' (pages 204–9).

Veteran and ancient trees The very character and age of many historic gardens and parks have bequeathed a legacy of old, veteran and ancient trees. These add to the romantic and timeless charm of the place, but can give rise to some serious and often quite controversial decisions when it comes to major surgery or removal.

In recent years, the health and safety issue has become a major factor in determining whether an old tree is potentially or actually dangerous. But these trees are invariably important for historic, cultural and ecological reasons, so keeping them for as long as

112. Stag-headed tree indicating signs of stress.

possible is important. Old, decaying and even dead trees are vitally important habitats for wildlife (see 'Nature conservation', 2.2).

It is usually possible to prolong or extend the life of veteran trees by careful management and various arboricultural operations. But before considering the need for such work, owners and managers should consider their responsibilities. The storms of 1987 and 1990, a startling reminder of the vulnerability of trees, made owners aware of the need to have a long-term succession of healthy examples, and to carry our regular checks on their condition and wellbeing. When any advice is being sought, check that it is realistic and authoritative – contact the professional bodies involved in tree work (these are listed in the Appendices with contact details).

Owners or agents of gardens and parks open to the public have a legal obligation to ensure that trees on their land are safe. The safest and most sensible management strategy is to have trees inspected on regular basis by a competent arboriculturist, who can assess their condition and make any recommendations for work required. It is advisable to separate the tree inspection and management stages, particularly where public bodies are involved: inspectors should concentrate on the health of the tree and its structural stability, and recognised arboricultural contractors should carry out any work that arises. For important veteran trees, alternatives to surgery or removal, such as fencing off, re-routing of paths, etc., should always be considered.

PRUNING OF ESTABLISHED AND MATURE TREES

Once the structure and form are well developed, the need for pruning should be much reduced. However, depending on the tree, its location and the character and type of garden or park, the following issues may lead to a requirement for pruning:

*   Health and safety

*   The need to remove lower branches which may interfere with access by people and vehicles

*   The removal of diseased or damaged branches.

*   Improving the aesthetic appearance of a tree by sensitive thinning of the crown and the removal of excessive and unwieldy growth of laterals (these can be the result of poor clones being planted)

*   Competition with other trees

*   Undue closeness to buildings

Summary of the most common arboricultural operations

Shigo 'revolution' One of the greatest impacts on traditional tree work came when Dr Alex Shigo of the US Forestry Service published *A New Tree Biology* in 1970, the result of years of detailed observations and experiments. He was able to show that many long-established practices were in fact working against a tree's natural ability to maintain health. Damaged trees, if left to their own devices, often have internal mechanisms for coping with injuries. His work has gradually led to a major revision of arboricultural practices and some of these are embodied here.

Cavities Current treatment is generally now to leave cavities untouched. The former practice of filling them created a constantly damp microclimate which aided decay organisms. Cavities should not be drained: Shigo showed that de-oxygenated water held in a cavity inhibits decay, whereas the damp, airy conditions in drained cavities favour decay. Wound sealants are no longer used, as they were found to be ineffective in preventing decay.

Branch removal In most cases, branches should not be cut back close to the main trunk, but to the front of the 'branch bark collar' that retains the living zone containing most of the tree's natural defences against decay. This also greatly reduces the size of the wound and cut surface.

114. Pruning in three stages. Stage 1. Undercut to prevent tearing.

115. Stage 2. Cut forward from the undercut until the branch falls.

113. Branch removal: the Shigo 'revolution' showed the principles behind the pruning and healing of woody tissue. The figure illustrates the likely healing pattern from different-positioned cuts. Note that the ideal cut should be made between points W and X to ensure complete healing.

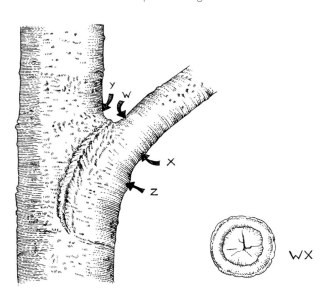

116. Stage 3. Branch removed (small stub remains).

117. Stage 4. Small stub removed in one cut.

118. Crown lifting is undertaken to trees in urban areas in order to provide access for people and vehicles. In many gardens today the latterday browsing line of parkland trees has been replaced by the mower access line.

119. Crown thinning can reduce the density of shade cast by trees.

120. Above: crown reduction is often undertaken on trees that are too large for their location but it spoils their natural appearance. The 'benefits' are short-lived since a healthy tree responds to pruning by making new growth.

Summer branch drop This is an occasional and disturbing phenomenon of fine weather periods, when quite large limbs fall without warning and without apparent cause during calm, hot weather and in the late afternoon. The causes are still not fully understaood and are not easy to detect. Regular inspection is advised, and overhanging branches near paths or public a ccess may need bracing or removing. Stress caused by lack of water is believed to be a strong contributing factor, so drought, soil compaction and root disease should be alleviated where possible.

Removal of deadwood The term deadwood – dead, diseased, dying or broken branches or stubs – generally applies to branches more than 25mm in diameter. Deadwood removal will always be a question of judgement. It may be very important for health and safety reasons where visitors are around, and it can improve the general aesthetic appearance of some trees. But it has a very important wildlife value, especially for bats and birds.

The picturesque gnarled character of veteran trees, such as old oaks and chestnuts with stag-headed crowns and dying limbs, are part of historic parkland and, health and safety permitting, may

often be left untreated (see picture 112). Deadwood of some species, such as oaks, may be quite stable with even large branches not liable to break off. Others, including some poplars, have very brittle wood. A compromise known as 'conservation dead-wooding' involves the removal only of large limbs. Long snags up to 300mm are left, or reduced gradually over several years, giving both maximum deadwood and maximum stability. Cuts can be made part way before removal, to leave a more natural, shattered branch end, or specially adapted 'coronet' cutting may be used.

Crown treatments These include crown lifting, crown thinning and crown reduction.

Pollarding Cutting the entire branch system hard back to the main trunk or main limbs was a common practice for the production of timber, firewood and annual fodder until the nineteenth century. It also used to be routine, if unsightly, for disciplining trees in streets and some urban parks, before a more understanding knowledge and practice ended it. Pollarding is now likely to be carried out only on a tree with serious crown defects or that has suffered substantial damage but needs to be retained.

Removal of epicormic growth These are shoots that often develop from the bases and lower trunks of some trees such as limes and oaks, and the decision whether to leave or remove them is probably largely aesthetic. They may cause some diversion of a tree's resources, but the main downside is that they mask the trunks, blurring the repetitive columnar impact in avenues.

122. Removal of epicormic growth.

Cable bracing This is usually a remedial operation on large mature trees whose branches have developed potentially dangerous forking, or are at an angle and spreading over paths, roads, gardens or buildings. Branches may have become too heavy, needing support against wind damage and falls of snow – often the case with all three species of cedar, especially Cedar of Lebanon.

In most cases, regular inspection can spot the potential for the problem at an early stage. One or more flexible cable braces are inserted, and usually tied in to the main trunk at one or more points. Such bracing may be carried out in conjunction with crown thinning. It is a specialised job only for competent tree surgeons. Bracing systems will need regular inspection and adjustment.

Propping This can be effective with low and often heavy branches that it may not be feasible to cable brace. The downsweeping or near horizontal branches of cedars can be treated in this way. With ancient mulberry trees, which have notoriously sprawling and brittle branches, propping is almost a necessity. Props, which can be wooden or metal, should be in keeping with the character of the tree and site, on a firm base, and the branch prop junction protected with a rubber or similar cushion.

Felling Before felling a particular tree, check that it is not covered by a Tree Preservation Order (TPO) (see 'The legal framework', 1.5). Felling procedure may need some thought. It should only be undertaken by properly trained, experienced staff or contractors. The tree may need bringing down in sections if space is limited or there is risk of damage to other nearby trees, shrubs or buildings. Felling is normally done just above ground level, leaving a stump that will have to be treated (see below, page 127). Where space

121. Pollarding/repollarding of oaks in field margins for the production of wood.

Re-pollarding The cutting back of all branches and growths to a previously pollarded point was traditionally carried out on a regular cycle of between 5 and 50 years, often in woodlands or forests. Much of this management has died out or is in abeyance – in Burnham Beeches pollards have been left for 100 years or more. The Corporation of London, which owns and manages Burnham and Epping Forest, is now undertaking a re-pollarding programme of these neglected trees.

Riverside willows, particularly the crack willow (*Salix fragilis*), are a characteristic feature of many of our lowland river landscapes. They should be regularly pollarded to keep a balanced crown; brittle and fast-growing, these trees if neglected soon fall apart or lose branches.

Great care should be taken when starting to repollard old pollards that have been uncut for many years. Expert advice should be sought and the work should never be undertaken in one go.

allows, another technique is to uproot the entire tree with a powerful digger (see Hampton Court Palace Case Study, page 275). In historic parks and gardens, always take a tree ring count for the archives before it is too late.

Stump treatment There are four options for dealing with stumps.

- **Doing nothing** If the tree was dead before felling, the stump will gradually rot away. The time this takes will depend upon the species, the size and the cause of death – root or butt rot fungi accelerates the decay of the stump. However, a word of warning: a dead stump can frequently be a host of honey or bootlace fungus (*Armillaria*) if that killed the tree in the first place (see 'Pests and diseases', page 231). It is advisable to remove or treat such an infected stump.

   If the tree was alive when felled, the stump may die and eventually decay; this is the case with the majority of conifers. Many broadleaved trees, however, produce new shoots from the stumps which will continue to grow. The extent and persistence of this growth depends upon the species and the age of the tree – for example, beech and very old oaks may shoot briefly in the first year or so, then die away. Lime and sycamore grow strongly and perform like coppice trees, developing into thickets of branch clusters. However, regular removal will gradually stop this sort of growth and the main stump will continue to rot away, even if parts throw up coppice shoots.

- **Treating** Unless it is part of a coppice regime, the stump may need treatment with a chemical to prevent re-growth. Several products are on the market, and their mode of action can be accelerated by drilling holes in the outer circle of living wood, or cross cutting with a chainsaw, and then applying the chemical. An alternative is to allow the stump to re-shoot, and then treat the shoots with a systemic herbicide while in active growth. With very vigorous cases, it may be necessary to repeat this treatment.

- **Digging out** Depending on the size of the stump and its location, this may be done manually or mechanically using a wide range of digging equipment; hand-digging can be labour-intensive and time-consuming. With small to medium sized stumps a winching technique may be practicable. At felling, part of the trunk should be left intact to provide leverage for a cable winch and nylon strops – the stump and quite a proportion of the roots can be extracted in this way.

   Stump removal can be a disruptive operation. If the site forms part of a Scheduled Monument or has historic importance that could involve archaeology, English Heritage should be consulted before any work gets under way.

- **Grinding or chipping** Machines for this range from pedestrian models for small and difficult sites, to large machines that can grind or chip large stumps to considerable depths. The chipped or ground material can be part of a composting regime. Whether to hire or purchase thr equipment will depend on the scale of the enterprise and the amount of continual use it is likely to receive.

123. Cable bracing supporting the branches of a mature pine.
124. Inset: detail.

125. Using a prop to support a large branch over a footpath.

126. Many historic gardens have impressive specimens of *Cedrus libanii*, a few over 250 years old.

CONIFERS

The great majority of coniferous trees now in cultivation, whether for commercial forestry or ornamental and other purposes, are not native to the British Isles. Their natural habitats range from cold temperate to warmer Mediterranean climates and, although most have adapted to suitable sites and locations, there is considerable variation in their cultural preferences, maintenance and effective lives.

Britain has only three indigenous evergreen conifers, Scots pine (*Pinus sylvestris*), yew (*Taxus baccata*) and common juniper (*Juniperus communis*) and one deciduous species, common larch (*Larix decidua*). The pine and larch are used in forestry as well as ornamental planting, and can grow into fine decorative trees. The yew can make a massive spreading tree of limited height, often living to a great age. It has a long history of planting in gardens, parks, churchyards and cemeteries — as groves, specimens and clipped forms. It makes a fine hedge plant. Junipers are usually little more than shrubs of varying shapes, found as a range of garden cultivars.

From the middle of the nineteenth century there was a remarkable introduction of conifers from many temperate parts of the world, notably North America and also the far east. They found a place in arboreta, woodland gardens and public parks, in the UK as well as western Europe. Their evergreen columnar or spear-shaped outlines and statuesque habits created a new experience in

127. Fastigiate yews in Watts Chapel cemetery.

128. Wellingtonias (*Sequoiadendron giganteum*) became almost a status symbol in many large country estates and gardens in the mid nineteenth century; avenues or specimen plantings are often indicators of date.

the softer, rounded contours of deciduous landscapes. In California, specimens of *Sequoia* and *Sequoiadendron* more than 3,000 years old have been recorded. The tallest in the UK are now over 52m (170ft) and are still growing well.

Most conifers were introduced as species as found in their native habitats, but some developed cultivars after being in cultivation for some years, the Lawson cypress (*Chamaecyparis lawsoniana*) being a good example. This native of South West Oregon and North West California, where it grows to 60m, was first introduced to the UK in 1854 when seeds were sent to Lawson's Nursery in Edinburgh. By the turn of the twentieth century it had over 50 cultivars, with a great diversity of foliage colours and forms, heights and growth patterns; over 100 are now listed. A grove of Lawson cultivars planted 70 years ago at the National Pinetum at Bedgebury in Kent is a spectacular sight.

Maintenance and management of coniferous trees

The very wide diversity among conifers in growth habit, longevity and functions make it difficult to prescribe any blueprint operations. They have been divided here into two groups, in terms of habit and function, with summaries of appropriate care and attention.

Longer-term types as specimens or for distinctive groups or avenues This group includes the usually magnificent and stately cedars, redwoods, firs, hemlocks, spruces and pines, and the deciduous species. For the majority of these, the prime object is to encourage or train a leader during the formative period in the nursery, in order to develop the typical coniferous spire or conical outline with spreading or downsweeping branches. Once this stage has been reached, and after the tree has become established in its permanent home, little or no attention should be required as the tree develops its shapely form, with branches clothed to the ground.

Removal of branches Depending on the design and the situation, a decision may be required on the removal of the lowest branches, either for access or, in the case of groups or avenues, to display a procession of trunks and basal architectural buttressing. Many conifers tend to lose their lowest branches naturally as they mature, which sometimes leads to unsightly effects as the branches die back (this is typical of some cypresses).

Lost leaders Another development in some conifers when they become mature or overmature is a marked slowing down of their vigour and growth, leading to the eventual loss of the main leader and the pyramidal outline. This is very typical of cedars and pines, which can gradually develop a spreading umbrella form. Many of the fine old cedars in historic parks and gardens planted two or more centuries ago are now in this picturesque, veteran state, a form that would have been unknown to those who planted them as immature trees with a conical form (such as Lancelot Brown, one of the first to plant Cedars of Lebanon as a landscape feature). Lightning or storm damage can also affect leaders, and generally few mature coniferous trees are capable of regenerating a replacement leader.

Maturity and damage Once a cedar has reached the umbrella stage, which may take two or more centuries (many fine old examples exist, some nearing three centuries in age), there is bound to be a slow but inevitable deteriorating process, and a progressive loss of main branches. These branches may be massive and nearing a horizontal angle, so that heavy snowfall or severe winds can wrench off limbs or leave ugly wounds. Even very heavy rain can bring some branches down with the sheer weight of water.

Remedial action is best taken before serious damage is likely, by a system of bracing or reducing the weightload of the canopy. Parks and gardens open to the public have health and safety issues to consider, and trees that could be a potential danger may need cordoning off until they are treated. The 1987 and 1990 storms mangled many cedars and reduced them to wrecks of their former magnificence, but they have a great tenacity for survival, and some can still be seen as gaunt veterans. Regeneration of a new canopy

129. This mature Cedar of Lebanon retains vitality and a picturesque form despite losing its leader during storm damage.

seldom occurs, however, and a longer-term policy should be to plant new specimens; when these are beginning to make some impact, remove the old ones.

Pines as a rule are faster-growing and shorter-lived than cedars. The Scots pine can develop a picturesque form in its mature stages.

Rejuvenation Most conifers do not respond to hard pruning or the equivalent of stooling or coppicing that can be successful with many deciduous trees and shrubs. Exceptions are Yew and Coast Redwood, which are capable of rejuvenation from hard cutting back to the original trunk or base.

Slower-growing, compact and dwarfer conifers One has to tread warily in the category of what are often summarised as 'dwarf conifers', which comprise almost a miniature jungle of fascinating shapes, textures and colours, in the form of columns, globes, buns, carpets and hummocks, represented by almost every genera of *Coniferae*. Many have proved popular for small gardens and patios, being tough and a fixed type of asset; a smaller range is involved in historic gardens. Excluding conifers for hedges (see page 152) and in rock gardens (see page 193), many of these slower-growing types can really be treated as shrubs, and they are referred to again in that section.

Some slower-growing and more architectural conifers have been used in many larger and historic gardens. Important in this category are the various forms of yew, as shaped topiary or architectural forms. The Irish Yew (*Taxus baccata* 'Fastigiata') has been grown in gardens, parks and churchyards since it was discovered in Ireland in 1780, its formal upright habit lending itself to lining access paths and drives. Its management problems tend to develop in its mature stage, when it is inclined to spreading or billowing which can be accentuated by heavy rain or snowfall. Discreet tying in with wire, or corseting with netting before the trees start to fall apart, is usually successful. If they have really got out of hand, a more drastic remedy is to cut all branches back to the original trunk or to the base. Most healthy yews respond to this treatment, forming a new framework in a few years. In order to reduce stress to the tree, this can be udertaken in stages, for example cutting back to the main stem first to encourage the development of healthy new regrowth before shortening or coppicing.

Some of the columnar juvenile foliage forms of Lawson cypress, such as *Chamaecyparis lawsoniana* 'Ellwoodii' *and C. l.* 'Fletcheri' (usually regarded as slow-growing specimens for rock gardens) are also inclined to billow and spread after 25 years or more. These, however, will not respond to severe cutting back, and the only treatment is tying in, some light clipping or in bad cases, elimination. *Juniperus communis* 'Hibernica' is similar.

The true Italian cypress (*Cupressus sempervirens*), first planted in Britain the late seventeenth century for a fast-growing pillar effect, can be variable; a good form should be selected in the nursery. It is also not fully hardy, and may need occasional clipping to keep a tight shape, especially when producing heavy crops of cones.

ARBORETA, PINETA, HISTORIC FEATURES, WOODLANDS

Arboreta and pineta

- **Arboretum** Usually defined in broad terms as a living collection of trees and shrubs, planted for scientific and educational purposes.

- **Pinetum** May be part of an arboretum, but is more specifically concerned with collections of conifers.

Botanic gardens and private parks started such collections in the seventeenth century, but it was not until the late eighteenth century, when plants from overseas were being grown by collectors and landowners, that arboreta really became a fashion. During the nineteenth century, the discovery and introduction of many apparently suitable trees and shrubs from the Americas, Asia, Australasia, China and Japan stimulated the establishment of a number of important arboreta, such as Westonbirt in Gloucestershire (1829), and the Derby Arboretum (1861).

Many of these introductions also found an important place in the fine woodland gardens created during the late nineteenth and early twentieth centuries, such as Wakehurst Place and Sheffield Park in Sussex (see Case Study, page 291). Many of these were, in effect, arboreta, but it is probably the case that they were primarily designed and planted for their visual and landscape effects, rather than for scientific and botanical reasons. Westonbirt Arboretum and the National Pinetum at Bedgebury in Kent (1924) were planned from the start as visually exciting experiences, with avenues, bold group plantings and, at Bedgebury, water features, but they also carried out trials for timber production and other research. They were recently amalgamated under the title the National Arboreta, and are managed by the Forestry Commission.

The now world-famous Sir Harold Hillier Gardens and Arboretum were started in the 1950s by Sir Harold Hillier near Winchester with the aim of assembling and conserving the most

130. Rejuvenation of mature yews at Brodsworth Hall; note the young shoots sprouting from the trunk.

comprehensive collection of temperate woody plants on one site; many came from the Hillier family nurseries. In 1977 Sir Harold offered the gardens and arboretum to Hampshire County Council in the form of a Trust, in order to conserve them in perpetuity. They now contain some 42,000 plants, including eleven national collections under the National Council for the Conservation of Plants and Gardens (NCCPG).

Management The conservation and management of arboreta and pineta require the same approach as for other woody plants of historic and arboricultural importance, such as the woodland gardens of Sheffield Park in Sussex (see Case Study, page 291).

131. Winkworth Arboretum in Surrey is known for its autumn colour.

Botanical, scientific and educational guidelines Planning and planting should consider the grouping of species according to selection criteria, such as country or countries of origin, use as ornamentals, timber etc. There should be good access to view the specimens and a clear labelling system, backed up by cataloguing with details of provenance, source of stock and country of origin, dates of planting, etc. It is advisable to plant several specimens of each species, if space allows, to select the best at a later date.

Historic features

Clumps and roundels These were often planted as designed features in eighteenth-century landscape parks, dispersed across extensive undulating landscapes according to character, topography, and the whims of the owner and the designer. Brown and Repton favoured these features, and frequently specified planting procedures for them. Clumps and roundels were, for the most part, composed of native deciduous species, and were fenced against grazing animals. Repton favoured the use of faster-growing coniferous species such as pines or firs as nurse or 'filler' trees in the early establishment stages, in a ratio of about one long-term tree to five or ten 'nurses', the latter being removed or thinned as the clump or roundel developed. Primarily intended to enhance visual satisfaction, they would have an effective life of two centuries or more, depending upon the species used and their management.

Where clumps and roundels form a distinctive feature of an important historic park, their perpetuation is really important, and one of two options may be a possibility.

1. Clear fell and replant on the same site, using appropriate long-term species and nurse types (preferably conifers or faster-

> ### OUTLINE COURSES OF ACTION
>
> - Access to any data, notes and plans of the original layout and planting.
>
> - Understanding significance and main objectives.
>
> - Site surveys to detect, if possible, any changes or alterations.
>
> - Replanting and renewal should follow and enhance the essential character and style of the arboretum or pinetum, avoiding ad hoc planting or unsympathetic changes.
>
> - Changes of use, such as visitor facilities, car parking and other recreational or educational needs, may be needed to fulfil aims and help with management costs. By their very nature, these places have rather specialised attraction, and cannot normally be considered money-spinners.

growing deciduous types; see also 'Shelter belts', page 150). Plant 1–2m apart, using young stock. Fencing and protection are essential. The conifers or other nurse trees should be thinned or removed over a period of 10–20 years, depending on how well the main trees establish.

2. Re-site a new clump or clumps as close as possible to the original, if the latter still have some useful life. This is sometimes called 'shadow planting', and it means taking land out of agriculture or other uses if the new features are allowed to establish before the old ones are removed.

To make any impact in a panoramic landscape, a clump or roundel needs to be at least 50m in diameter.

134. A parkland clump of the Stone Pine.

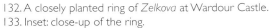

132. A closely planted ring of *Zelkova* at Wardour Castle.
133. Inset: close-up of the ring.

135. Below: there has been a steady decline and loss of clumps and roundels over the years. Where grazed parkland has been converted to more intensive agricultural production, clumps have been removed, especially if they were in decline. Renewal tends to be a low priority.

Avenues Avenues are undoubtedly one of the greatest problems facing landowners and managers today. Mature intact avenues, often planted two centuries or more ago, are unique features whose very character and drama depend on their uniformity and the long cathedral-like perspective of even columnar trunks and arching canopies. Once they become uneven and gappy due to damage, decay or death, their grandeur and impact are lost (see Hampton Court Case Study, page 271). Because many need solutions in the immediate or very near future, a series of potential treatments has been developed by John Workman, former Forestry Adviser to the National Trust (see box). If an avenue has not yet reached the renewal stage, there are remedial techniques (see arboriculture in 2.3).

Woodlands

A number of historic houses with their gardens, parklands and estates may still retain woodlands of varying age and extent; this is the case with at least four of the Case Study sites (Part 3). A recent Forestry Commission inventory found more than 40,000 small woods of less than 10 ha in England alone, which together make up 17 per cent of England's woodlands. They also provide an important component of the landscape character of many country estates.

Woodland management Extensive areas of woodland in most cases involve traditional or new techniques of forestry practice which are beyond the scope of this book. The management of woodlands of intermediate to smaller size, which may have considerable landscape, conservation and possibly historic values, may be a lower priority, especially where resources are limited and economic returns are low (often the case where woodlands are not open to the public).

A wood can be allowed to develop naturally, with little or no management, and still give pleasure to the owner for relaxation and for conservation. However, all woods eventually need some

MANAGEMENT OF AVENUES

1. Clear fell and replant the entire feature – a bold, drastic decision but the visual shock is bound to be sensational. The big problem is usually in timing the felling. Ecological damage may be severe.

2. Clear fell sections of a long avenue, preferably significant lengths of about 30m at a time with adjacent sides, and replace with even-age, well-grown nursery stock, at 10-year intervals. Stump removal and ground preparation will have to be as thorough as possible.

3. Cut out every other tree and replant. This is generally not too successful, since the new trees will face competition for light, water and nutrients, and may be slow to establish and become poor and distorted. Shade-loving species such as beech or oak may stand this treatment, but the long-term results will never be as dramatic as even-aged trees.

4. For double avenues, remove the inner or outer row and replace on a phased basis. However, if the rows are too close, the younger trees will still be overshadowed by the mature row alongside and will tend to grow out at an angle towards the light, and retain this shape in the future.

5. Plant a new avenue on the inside or the outside of the existing line, if space allows. This can be very effective culturally, but will change the design intention and is very demanding of land space. It may not be suitable for important historic sites.

6. Enjoy the old avenue for as long as possible.

7. Replace trees individually as they fall. This is the most common remedy but in the long term the least rewarding. The avenue will always look uneven, without the fine colonnade effect.

8. Accept a heterogeneous or mixed avenue, with flowering trees or evergreens; however, this is not really an avenue. To quote John Workman, 'Avenues ought to be superlative!'

9. If more than one avenue exists on the same property, consider eventually having each one of a different species, to ensure against disease or other casualties.

136. Hampton Court avenues before replanting.

137. Avenue at Clumber Park.

ANCIENT WOODLANDS

These are sites that have been continuously wooded for at least 400 years; many go back even further. They are often associated with historic estates, and usually shown on the earliest reliable county and estate maps. They are usually subdivided into two main groups:

- Ancient Semi-Natural Woodland (ASNW), composed of species native to the locality, represent about 18 per cent of England's woodlands.

- Plantations on Ancient Woodland Sites (PAWS), managed as plantations, often with conifers, represent about 13 per cent of England's woodlands.

Ancient Woodlands usually also have an important conservation and wildlife value, and some may be designated SSSIs (see 'Nature conservation', 2.2).

broadleaved or coniferous, retaining the best trees and also allowing natural regeneration of selected species and, where necessary, some interplanting. The objective is to avoid clear felling and to ensure a continuous canopy cover which reduces the need for weed control. A continuity of trees of different maturity or uneven age is encouraged. There will be a programme of selected felling from within the mixed planting.

Wood pasture Similar to grazed parkland with standard trees, the understorey is grass or herbs; cattle or sheep have access under a controlled regime. Boundary fencing and individual tree protection, as well as stock management, could be limiting factors along with extra labour costs. Wood pasture can be created from coppice with standards by removing all coppice stools and encouraging pasture to develop; the herb layer here will depend on the shade from the canopy trees and also the intensity and frequency of grazing.

138. High forest with standard oaks.

139. Sweet chestnut coppice with ground flora of bluebells.

form of management for a number of reasons – access; avoidance of fire risk, vandalism and fly tipping, and providing a continuity of wildlife habitat.

High Forest with standards Often for more extensive tracts of broad-leaved or coniferous species. Selected main broad-leaved or coniferous species are thinned to allow optimum growth into good quality timber trees. Understorey competition is limited provided the canopy is closed. Ultimately, clear felling and replanting is the normal practice.

Coppice with standards Longer-term trees, typically ash or oak, selected and spaced to allow an understorey crop of coppice stools, usually hazel. This is cut on a rotational cycle of 10–15 years, and the timber used for hurdles or other woodland products.

Coppice on its own, without standard trees, is also a practice in some localities, using sweet chestnut or hazel. The cycle of cutting is also 10–15 years, with a market for chestnut fencing and poles. Ground flora including bluebells can be spectacular in favourable locations, especially in the years after cutting before the developing canopy creates too much shade.

Continuous cover forestry (uneven-age sylviculture) Now coming back into favour, the policy is to work with existing species on site,

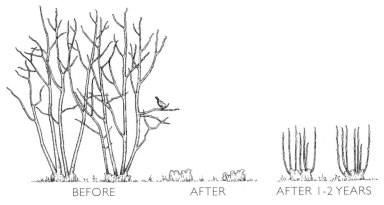

BEFORE   AFTER   AFTER 1-2 YEARS

140. A cycle of coppicing is important to maintain the biodiversity of sweet chestnut woodlands.

Restoration of unmanaged woodland Depending on the state of the woodland and whether it ever had coppice treatment, there may be a dense understorey of scrub and brambles, and overcrowded trees of varying age and condition, often with regenerated thickets of seedling ash, sycamore and birch. A major

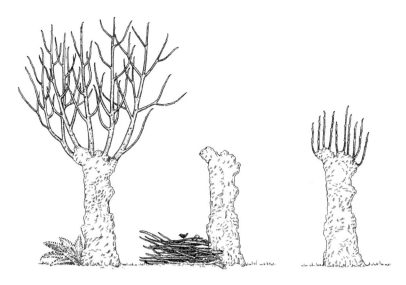

141. Many standard oaks were managed as pollards to produce timber of a particular quality or shape.

ECONOMICS OF MANAGING MIXED WOODLAND
From P. Adlard, Royal Forestry Society *Quarterly Journal*, January 2004

EXPENDITURE
Over 35 per cent of the total expenditure was on thinning done by a contractor
17 per cent on running and maintaining vehicles (tractor, Land Rover, etc.)
14 per cent on deer fencing
10 per cent on marketing

INCOME
Over 50 per cent of the total income was from produce sold, comprising:
    25 per cent timber
    11 per cent bars and poles
    14 per cent firewood
20 per cent grants, including from the Woodland Grant Scheme

thinning operation has to be undertaken, with decisions on what species of tree will remain to dominate the wood. Oak or ash are favourites, beech on calcareous soils; sycamore and birch are not recommended, the first often being damaged by grey squirrels, and the second having a more limited life. If coppicing is to be part of the restored wood, the stools may have to be protected from deer and rabbits which love to browse new coppice shoots.

Thinning and felling will normally require a felling licence from the Forestry Commission, but there are certain exemptions (see 1.5, page 77). Thinning must be timed to avoid the bird nesting season (end of February to July).

Many health and safety regulations need to be recognised in these operations, and in forestry and woodland work generally.

Other management aspects include:
- fencing, where necessary
- woodland ride and track maintenance for timber extraction and access
- ride edge management for visual appearance and habitat maintenance, epecially wild flowers and butterflies
- tree maintenance for health and safety where the public have access
- understorey management such as weeding; control of brambles and vigorous invasive shrubs such as *Rhododendron ponticum*; protection from deer and rabbit damage; grey squirrel control.

SHRUBS

Shrubs are the bushy layer of woody vegetation, usually multi-stemmed and often denser-growing and shorter-lived than trees. Their introduction into gardens goes back to some of the early shrub roses of the fifteenth and sixteenth centuries and thickets of hedges and boskage mainly of native origin. A steady flow of increasing diversity in the later eighteenth century grew into a veritable torrent of introductions in the nineteenth and early twentieth centuries, many from temperate regions of the world. Appendices Table 4 presents a representative range of shrubs in cultivation today, with dates of introduction, and it is clear from this that shrubs and shrubberies became an important feature in Victorian and Edwardian gardens and parks. It may also act as a

guide for those wishing to undertake authentic restoration planting from previous periods in garden history.

Another characteristic and very noteworthy impact came in the late nineteenth and twentieth centuries from the work of enthusiastic individuals. These included the Rothschilds (Exbury), the Aberconways (Wales), the Surrey firms of Knaphill and Waterers, who introduced countless new varieties of rhododendrons and azaleas and other special shrubs from their own selection and breeding programmes, and the Williams family (Cornwall) who produced many fine camellia cultivars.

Similar work was done in this period by individuals and nurseries on the Continent, particularly in France, with many

142. Plantation of hardy hybrid Rhododendrons at Belsay Hall.

143. Ornamental woodland garden at Sandling Park.

144. A diagram illustrating a variety of habits that can be provided by shrubs.

BARE STEM   FACERS   BUSHY   VERTICAL   PROSTRATE

introductions of shrubs and particularly roses, hence the many French names for some of the best-known older varieties.

Maintenance and management

There is a proliferation of published information on shrubs, including maintenance techniques (a selection of recommended references are included in the bibliography). Some particular aspects are highlighted here which apply more especially to shrub management in historic parks and gardens.

Age cycles and effective life

In all parks and gardens, historic and in general, there will be shrubs of different species, age structures and growth cycles. These may cover short-lived examples such as lavenders and *Cistus*, to longer-lived rhododendrons and magnolias, some of these assuming tree-like habits. Consequently, management decisions will be needed to maintain healthy growth cycles for as long as possible and, as with trees, positive and sometimes controversial action will be called for when the end date has been reached. There is no real difficulty with the renewal of fast-growing short-cycle types, but for those with a longer life – and some may have a rarity value – rejuvenation techniques may be possible and these are considered here.

An important reminder: the effective life of a shrub begins with healthy nursery-grown stock, careful planting and proper care and attention during the establishment period, very much as has been described for trees (pages 117-22).

Pruning

The basic principle is that most pruning operations have either immediate or longer-term effects on the life cycle. Pruning stimulates new or more vigorous basal or lateral growths, which in turn have an effect on the proportions of current vegetative wood and older flowering and fruiting wood. Excessive pruning may upset the balance for a time by generating a surge of new growth, whereas little or no pruning may lead to a greater abundance of flowering wood, but also an increasingly dense, crowded and thicket-like habit. For many garden shrubs, the object is to achieve a balance of younger and older wood, while developing a pleasing shape and character.

The aim should be wherever possible to maintain the natural shape of the shrub, leaving aside any topiary or sculptural forms. All too often there is a temptation to clip and manicure shrubs, irrespective of species, into shaven clumps or balls – the 'short

MAIN REASONS FOR PRUNING

- To limit, correct, or enhance the overall habit and size
- To manage and promote flowering and, if applicable, fruiting
- To remove diseased, damaged, dead or dying wood
- To rejuvenate overmature specimens

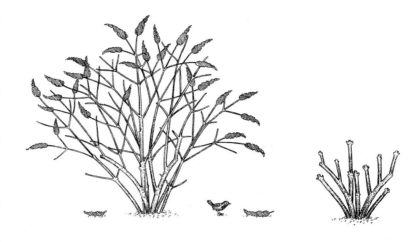

145. Hard pruning a buddleia to produce vigorous growth and larger flowers.

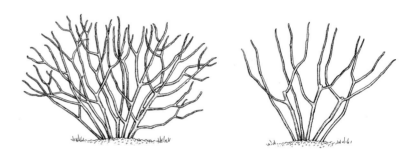

146. Replacement pruning: one-third of the oldest growths are removed to reduce overcrowding, letting in light to encourage the healthy growth of new shoots, as with this shrub rose.

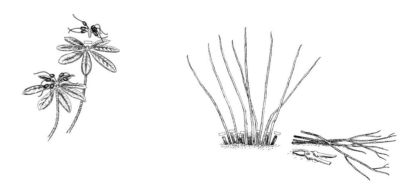

147. Above left: deadheading, as shown with this Rhododendron, prevents the formation of seed, thus promoting vigour and shoot growth.
Above right: cutting back to ground level the older flowered shoots of a Hydrangea, leaving one- and two-year-old growths.

148. A shrub informally pruned, retaining one-year-old wood which will produce flowers the following year. Removal of old flowering wood provides space and light for new growth.

back and sides' treatment, achieved with the array of powered clippers, cutters and pruners now on the market.

For detailed information on shrub pruning schedules and techniques, follow the recommended references in the bibliography. Information on rose pruning can be found in the rose section (page 147), and further information on pruning can be found in Appendices Table 14.

Nutrition

Once established, most shrubs should not require the regular use of fertilisers. It is good practice is to keep a regular mulch around the base, especially where shrubs are on light, free-draining soil, and to apply perhaps every other year a slow-release fertiliser in late winter or early spring. Shrubs in woodland areas where there is usually a natural organic layer may need no extra nutrients. Foliar or liquid feeds may be a helpful boost for shrubs after a stress period such as drought or severe frost, when new growth is underway.

On very alkaline soils with a naturally high pH, members of the *Ericaceae* family may develop pale or anaemic-looking leaves and be stunted, a condition known as lime-induced chlorosis. These shrubs prefer acidic soils, and the condition is a form of plant anaemia due to deficiency of iron or magnesium, which are less available on alkaline soils. Treat the shrubs *in situ*, if not too large, with a liqiuid iron chelate solution such as Sequestrene; or move those affected to a more favourable site if there is one in the garden; or, if manageable, transfer them to lime-free soil in containers.

Rejuvenation

Historic parks and gardens may have a legacy of old or over-mature shrubs, and decisions have to made on removal or rejuvenation. As with trees, a firm policy is best in the long run — to keep

149. Shrubs trimmed to an informal shape to create an effect. Hedge-cutters are ideal for small-leaved shrubs whereas secateurs are preferable for large-leaved shrubs to prevent cut leaves which can be unsightly.

150. Mature shrubs at the late Graham Thomas's former front garden in Surrey.

ailing specimens in a poor declining state is not good practice. If the shrubs are rare or special, it is worth trying to propagate them by any means possible.

However, it may be possible to rejuvenate or at least extend the life cycle of some shrubs. Success is more likely if the species is naturally medium- to long-lived. The rootstock or lower branch system must still be in good condition and free from disease, and be capable of generating new growth after tough remedial treatment.

One technique is stooling or coppicing: cutting back all growths to near ground level. If all goes well, new shoots should arise from the rootstock. Coppicing is an age-old practice still used in some traditional woodland management. Native hazel, for example, may develop into a vigorous shrub or a multi-stem tree; hazel rootstocks are known to live to a great age, and still retain their vitality. Some of the more resilient and longer-lived garden shrubs can respond to the same treatment. Examples are *Cotinus*

coggygria and its cultivars, and shrubs whose coloured stems of new growth are attractive in winter such as *Cornus alba* and *Salix alba* cultivars. Stooling is best done in late winter or early spring.

Some rhododendrons, notably hardy hybrids, and some species including azaleas that have grown straggly and out of scale can be cut hard back to about 0.5–1m from the ground, but advice should be sought, as not all will respond to this treatment. Camellias can also be tamed this way.

Faster-growing shrubs such as sun roses (*Cistus*) and brooms (*Cytisus*), once leggy and overmature, do not respond to such hard pruning. They should be removed and replaced.

Overmature shrubberies

Shrubberies have been a typical feature of large gardens and parklands, and were often planted in pleasure grounds, for shaded walks and informal retreats. Planting was characterised by the more vigorous and tough evergreens such as common laurel

151. *Cornus stolonifera* 'Sibirica' pruned by stooling creates brightly coloured stems for winter colour.

152. Laurel responds vigorously to stooling by developing masses of new growth.

(*Prunus laurocerasus*), Portuguese laurel (*Prunus lusitanica*) and cherry laurel (*Aucuba japonica*); box, hollies, rhododendrons (on suitable soil) and strong-growing deciduous shrubs such as lilacs and *Philadelphus*; also some conifers.

Being relatively robust, shrubberies tend to be lower down in the maintenance schedules and gradually become overmature. If left unmanaged, they may grow into near woodland proportions, but with many shrubs becoming excessively tall, straggling and eventually collapsing as a sprawling jungle.

Restoration and renewal call for tough treatment. Dead or dying shrubs need grubbing out, roots and all, and most of the evergreens cut hard back following stooling or coppicing. Rhododendrons, conifers or possibly more unusual shrubs may not take kindly to hard cutting back and will need less rigorous treatment. It may be necessary to seek expert advice, and planting records may help. Any gaps left by casualties should be planted up with appropriate types. Soils in old shrubberies are inclined to be poor and impoverished, so a good mulch and slow-release fertiliser application will help the rejuvenation process. Winter and early spring are good times to do such work, but if spring bulbs are known to be present, late autumn and winter are preferable.

See also pests and diseases of shrubs (page 229).

WALL PLANTS AND CLIMBERS

It has been a long and much-favoured practice to use walls to grow a great range of plants. This section is primarily concerned with hardy ornamental woody plants for walls and other means of support. 'Walled kitchen gardens' (pages 204–8) covers the equally long tradition of specialised fruit growing in kitchen and walled gardens.

There are many different wall types, as well as other surfaces and means of support, for growing plants in this group. There are also many different methods of attaching and supporting these plants, from traditional to more recent techniques.

Walls will be the most frequently used structures; they may be free-standing, enclosing an area, or be part of the house or associated buildings. Walls are microclimates, so aspect is important. Planting can be adapted to suit the aspect – i.e. north or south, hot or cool (see also 'The plant environment', page 92). Fences, pergolas, arches, trellises and other garden structures, also old trees and stumps, can also be used for climbing and scrambling plants.

Maintenance and management

Woody climbers and wall plants, as traditionally grown, will involve a fair amount of ongoing attention if the desired effect is to be achieved. There are the choice and suitability of plants for a given site and aspect; the space available; the methods of training and support, and the garden staff's time and skills to do a proper job. Unless disciplined, such plants can soon get out of hand (the Italian word for them is *rampicante*).

Planting

Wall and fence sites can often be dry with a 'rain shadow' effect, and soils can be poor and disturbed. Similar problems of dryness and competition might be present when growing climbers up trees or with others on pergolas and arches. A well prepared planting pit is therefore important.

Early support and training

Getting the plant started on its upward climb is a critical phase. The necessary support system must be provided while growth is still young and flexible. This will be determined in part by the plant's nature and habit of growth. The future framework and spread for the longer-lived types such as wistaria and some roses should be started as soon as possible (see box, pages 144-5).

Historic gardens and sites open to the public tend to require more ordered systems of managing these plants. In Vita Sackville-

153. A laburnum tunnel.

154. Self-clinging climbers will attach themselves to walls without the need of trellis or wires.

155. Climbing plants may attach themselves to vertical surfaces by adventitious roots (ivy: left), twining stems (honeysuckle: centre) and tendrills (sweet pea: right).

West's day at Sissinghurst Castle, roses and other climbers were allowed to cascade and sprawl from walls and arbours. Such profusion would be more difficult today, with unimpeded access and health and safety issues to take into account – no scratched faces!

However, if the situation offers opportunities, there is scope for a less fastidious and more relaxed maintenance regime. Many flowering climbers such as clematis, roses or wistaria, can be allowed to run free over a dull shrub or an old or unsightly tree.

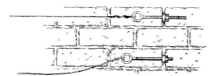

156. Training and attachments.
Top: vine eyes and straining bolt producing straight, tight, wall wires. Bottom: examples of vine eyes that can be either hammered or screwed into wall mortar joints.

GROUP I

SELF-CLINGING ADHESIVE PADS OR AERIAL ROOTS
No additional support normally needed.

Campsis (Bignonia), Trumpet Vine. Full sun. M D
Hedera sp and cvs, ivies. Part sun /deep shade. L E
Hydrangea petiolaris (H. anomala), Climbing Hydrangea.
     Shade/N. wall L E
Schizophragma sp. L D
Parthenocissus henryana. Shade. L D
Parthenocissus quinquifolia, Virginia Creeper. Sun/shade. L D
Parthenocissus tricuspidata, Boston Ivy. Sun/shade. L D
Pileostegia viburnoides. Shade/N. wall. L E
Trachelospermum. Full sun. Fragrant. L E

Training and pruning Trellises and wires not normally needed. Some support in early establishment period. Once the required height and space coverage reached, regular cutting back necessary with shears, secateurs or hedge trimmers. Beware excessive growth behind or over drainage pipes, gutters, tiles, etc. Renewal programme not normally needed for some years, but old or overmature plants can be rejuvenated by cutting down to near ground level and making a fresh start.

M = medium, L = large, E = evergreen, D = deciduous

157. A variety of climbers clothing a house.

MANAGEMENT OF WALL PLANTS AND CLIMBERS

GROUP 2
CLIMBING AND CLINGING BY TENDRILS, LEAF PETIOLES AND TRAILING STEMS
Support needed.

Akebia quinata. Sun/shade. M D
Clematis sp. and hybrids (see below). Sun/part shade. M D
Celastrus. Sun/shade. M D
Jasminum sp. and hybrids. M E
Lonicera sp. and hybrids, Honeysuckle. Part shade. M D/E
Passiflora sp and hybrids. Sun. M semi-E
Fallopia (Polygonum) baldschuanica, Russian Vine. Sun/shade. M D
Roses (see under Group 3)
Vitis sp and hybrids. ornamental vines, esp. *V. coignetiae, V. vinifera purpurea, V. 'Brant'.* Sun/shade. L D
Wistaria sp and hybrids (see below). Sun/part shade. L D

Training and pruning A range of support and training methods depending upon the plant type and situation. On walls, use trellis (less damage to walls), wire netting, wires, masonry nails, vine eyes, etc. Vigorous types for pergolas, arches, and for clothing bare-stemmed trees and shrubs.

Pruning depends upon the plant. Support needed at all times as well as at establishment stages, and then pruning or regulation of growth once allotted space is filled or covered. Progressive renewal and thinning as the plant ages.

Clematis Two main classes for pruning:

1. Those that flower in spring or early summer on previous season's growth, e.g. *C. macropetala, C. Montana.* Generally little pruning for a time, cutting back or tying in new or vigorous extension growths and removing any dead material. After a number of years, a great tangle may develop – good for nesting birds, but flowering too high up or diminishing. After flowering and when birds have flown in early summer, cut really hard back and start again, plus mulch and feed.

2. Those that flower in summer or early autumn mostly on new growths made earlier in the same year – e.g. large-flowered hybrids, *jackmanni* types and *C. viticella* types. These are best cut back hard in the spring to living buds, removing at least one third to one half of last year's growth. Some may even be cut back to near ground level and used for low-growing summer flowering over shrubs such as winter-flowering heathers, or as ground cover under roses, etc.

Wistaria All species and hybrids are vigorous, and once established need strict discipline, especially to promote free flowering. There are up to three stages of pruning:

(a) Summer pruning in July/August of laterals or long trailing shoots, cutting back to about 15mm from the older wood.

(b) Winter pruning: shortening back of these laterals to two to three buds to form flowering spurs.

(c) Training in new growths as required, and cutting out weak, old or dying wood.

GROUP 3
SCRAMBLING AND CLIMBING BY MEANS OF VIGOROUS EXTENSION GROWTHS
All need some support or structure

Actinidia sp., Kiwi Fruit. Sun. L D
Roses (see below).
Schisandra sp. Shade. L D/E
Solanum sp., Climbing Potato. Sun. M D

Training and pruning Similar to Group 2. Can be very vigorous.

Roses Climbing and rambling roses are the main types in this group. Some need rather special pruning (see 'Roses', page 147). A very large and complex range here, but summarised in two main categories:

1. Rambling roses, including many vigorous species and hybrids, e.g. *RR. banksiae, filipes, multiflora, wichuriana,* 'Wedding Day', 'Rambling Rector', 'American Pillar', 'Dorothy Perkins', 'Paul's Hilamalayan Musk'.

These produce vigorous scrambling and scandent-growing new shoots and laterals, often very thorny, which can be encouraged to grow up and through trees, or more systematically trained on walls, arbours and fences.

The aim should be to follow a renewal system of cutting out very old wood and laterals, and encouraging new basal shoots. However, there are cases in historic gardens, where space allows, where ultra-vigorous types such as 'Kiftsgate', 'Bobbie James' and some of those listed above can grow to considerable heights, often over old trees, producing superb cascades of scented flower clusters in early summer. These can often be left to grow freely for many years with minimal attention. Periodic intervention will inevitably be needed and a good clear-out of old or tangled growth or a more severe cutting-back to ground level, to start again with new basal growths.

Where space is more limited, such as on walls and fences, a more frequent regime of renewal and training should promote free flowering, as well as prevent thorny tangles from developing. Few roses in this group are repeat-flowering, but some do produce colourful autumn hips.

2. Climbing roses. Many of these are vigorous sports of Hybrid Teas (HT) and Floribundas, e.g. climbing 'Crimson Glory', 'Peace', 'Iceberg'. They tend to produce rather stiff, vigorous, upright-growing shoots from the base or as laterals, and are generally much less flexible and sinuous than the Ramblers. With their HT origins they also respond to a more regular pruning and training regime. They are therefore best suited to walls and structures in more formal or designed planting schemes; many are repeat-flowering and will provide a much longer seasonal display than the Ramblers.

Like all roses they flower on new season's growth, so once they have covered their allotted space, there can be two stages of pruning:

(a) Summer/late summer: cut back laterals and side growths which have flowered to about 3-4 buds (a dead-heading exercise)

(b) Late winter or early spring: remove old, dead or diseased material and, most important, tie in strong new shoots to fill any gaps or to replace old shoots. Laterals should also be shortened back to about 150mm.

Where roses have become weakened or overmature, but still have some vigour, drastic cutting back to near ground level is worth trying. A new framework of basal shoots should develop, encouraged by feed and mulch. Take care, however, that these new growths are not suckers.

ROSES

Evolution of rose cultivation

There is little doubt that roses were grown in ancient gardens in China, and later by the Greeks and Romans. The Arabs were growing roses in their exotic gardens during Britain's Dark Ages and by the thirteenth and fourteenth centuries a flourishing perfume industry was established near Paris using the Apothecary's Rose or Rose de Provins. Dutch flower paintings of the early seventeenth century depict, among others, damask, cabbage and moss roses, then being grown in many European gardens. After slow development in most of the eighteenth century, the period towards the end and into the nineteenth century saw a transformation in rose breeding and introduction into gardens. Much of this was centred on France, hence the names of so many roses of that remarkable era, some still popular today. The stage was set for the development of modern roses, drawing on old and new genetic blood with hybridists and rose-growers worldwide adding to what is now a countless list of varieties.

The story of their evolution and introduction to gardens throughout the world has been the subject of many eminent specialists; among them the late Graham Stuart Thomas ranks as a major pioneering figure. His books are an invaluable source of first-hand information on roses (see bibliography).

Maintenance and management

There is a proliferation of publications on roses, covering all aspects of cultivation (see bibliography). A summary is included here of their maintenance and the treatment of the different groups.

Pruning and rejuvenation

Roses are, in effect, summer-flowering shrubs with a comparatively limited life. Their health, effectiveness and longevity are determined by cultural techniques, the most important of which are pruning and rejuvenation. Most roses flower from early to midsummer, with either a short period of display, or some repeat-flowering into the autumn. Roses flower on new wood produced in the same season as they flower, and pruning techniques should recognise this fact.

Another characteristic is the production of strong vegetative shoots from or near the base; the laterals or secondary growths from these will carry the flowers. These shoots usually become weaker as they age, and will be replaced by successive growths. Therefore the general principle of rose pruning should be one of progressive renewal – over a varying period of time, cut out old, weak or dying wood and encourage strong new replacement growth, while still maintaining the desired shape and size. Such a regime will depend upon the type of rose and its place in any planting scheme.

Pruning systems also vary with the groups of roses. As misunderstandings constantly occur, summaries of these are given here for the main groups.

Botanical, species, shrub and 'old fashioned' roses Many in this group will be the most important and most frequently grown in historic gardens. Thanks to their promotion by Graham Stuart Thomas and by hybridists and producers such as David Austin and Peter Beales, they are also now of great appeal to gardeners.

It is possible to leave some roses in this category almost entirely unpruned for a number of years – especially the species, once the formative stage after planting has been reached and the general habit of the bush established. However, as they age, some pruning is advisable. Pruning techniques and the amount of attention required depend on the types of roses in this overall group.

The sweet briars (*R. rubiginosa*) and the burnet roses (*R. pimpinellifolia*, *R. rugosa* and cultivars derived from these) form quite dense bushes, and do not regularly produce vigorous basal growths once they reach maturity. Pruning can be minimal for a time, just shortening extension shoots during the summer to keep the size and habit. These roses are not repeat-flowering. They can be used as informal hedges. Some produce colourful hips in the autumn (much beloved by birds), so clipping should allow for this, with a final clip in late winter.

Older roses such as the Provence rose (*R. centifolia*), red rose of Lancaster (*R. gallica*) and white rose of York *(R. alba semiplena)*, are of moderate vigour, although some make quite straggly bushes. They are not repeat-flowering, and apart from deadheading as the flowers go over, pruning should not be too severe. They should certainly not be treated like the more modern hybrid tea and floribundas, where hard cutting back to near ground level is the normal practice.

Another numerous and attractive group includes the Bourbon, hybrid perpetuals and hybrid musk roses, which can be classed as vigorous shrubs, and the more recent David Austin 'English' roses. Many are repeat-flowering. They can throw up vigorous basal shoots that may reach 2–3m in one growing season; if left unpruned, these new shoots will normally produce a profusion of flowering laterals, often in clusters. They need to be suitably trained or restrained, or they will sprawl and upset the balance and size of the bush. These long shoots are important in the renewal process; they should be either reduced by one-third in the winter period, or trained or pegged down.

Hybrid teas and floribundas These include roses for bedding displays, the justifiably popular and traditional mainstay of many public and private rose gardens and favourites with rose enthusiasts and for exhibition showing. There are now a huge number of varieties, and breeding and selection still goes on. There is renewed interest in some of the older hybrid tea varieties of the Edwardian era and the 1920s and 1930s, which can now be regarded as historic, and also in some of the first polyantha roses. They are generally less vigorous in constitution, and need some care and attention. They have a comparatively short life, but may still be found as ageing specimens in the rose gardens of that period.

SUMMARY OF THE MAIN GROUPS OF ROSES IN HISTORICAL SEQUENCE

BC TO LATE EIGHTEENTH CENTURY, 'ANCIENT' ROSES

Rosa gallica var. *officinalis* Red rose of Lancaster, Apothecary's rose, Rose de Provins and various other names. Grown by Greeks and Romans. Used in the fourteenth-century perfume industry at Provins, France, in apothecary's conserve.

Rosa gallica 'Versicolor' (syn. *Rosa* 'Mundi') Sport of above in fifteenth–sixteenth centuries. Pink/white striped flower. Gallicas are hardy and strongly scented.

Rosa x *damascena* Damask rose. Mixed parentage. Summer damask and repeat-flowering autumn damask. Popular in sixteenth century.

Rosa x *damascena* 'Versicolor' York and Lancaster rose. Damasks generally less hardy than gallicas.

Rosa x *alba* White rose of York (*R.* x 'Alba semiplena'). Albas are of hybrid origin. Used for attar of roses. Vigorous and hardy, with good scent.

Rosa x *centifolia* Cabbage rose, Holland rose, Provence rose. Appeared at the end of the sixteeth century. Parents include autumn damask and alba. Large straggly bushes, white, double, very scented flowers. Hardy. The form 'Muscosa', moss rose, appeared in 1720. Many more since, especially 'Cristata', crested moss rose, 1820.

Rosa 'Duchess of Portland' Named after 2nd Duchess of Portland. Hybrid autumn damask and *R. gallica* var. *officinalis*, late flowering forerunner of hybrid perpetuals.

158. Rosa moyesii, red-flowered but also grown for its bottle-shaped hips.

159. Rose cattinery: a stout rope hung between large posts makes an attractive structure on which to train roses, as used in some Edwardian gardens.

LATE EIGHTEENTH CENTURY TO MODERN

China roses, long cultivated in China, introduced to European gardens in the 1790s. Valued for perpetual-flowering character. One of the first cultivars, Parson's pink china (now called Old Blush), introduced in 1793. Original Chinas were dwarf with red or pink flowers. Moderately hardy.

Tea roses (*Rosa* x *odorata*), hybrid of *R. chinensis* and *R. gigantea*, grown for centuries in China. Some introduced in early nineteenth century. Tea-scented, with pink or yellow flowers, not very hardy. Many later hybrids, giving rise to Hybrid Teas. *R.* x *odorata* 'Pseudindica', Fortune's Double Yellow, was introduced by him in 1845, found in an old Chinese garden.

Bourbon roses, the original a chance cross between *R. chinensis* and Autumn Damask in a garden on the Île de Bourbon (now Réunion) in the early 1820s. Good scent and autumn flowering. Later, many hybrids under this heading from 1820; typical examples include Souvenir de la Malmaison and Zephyrine Drouhin.

Noisettes, the originals large-flowered climbers from a hybrid raised in 1802 by Champneys in the USA using *R. moschata*, the vigorous musk, and Parson's pink china. Examples include Maréchal Niel from 1864 and Mme Alfred Carrière from 1879. They prefer a protected site.

160. Rosa rugosa: repeat-flowering, with excellent hips and good autumn colour. It makes a good hedging plant.

Hybrid perpetuals Over a thousand varieties were raised in the mid to late nineteenth century, but less than a hundred survive today. Derived from *R.* Duchess of Portland x *R. Chinensis*. Reine des Violettes from 1867. Loose, vigorous habit; hardy.

Hybrid teas, **polyantha**, **grandiflora** and **floribunda roses** and many **climbing roses** are part of the modern scene, mostly derived from the older and ancient roses summarised here. Two groups from the 1920s–30s are still important today:

161. Rosa spinnosissima 'Hugonis'.

• **Hybrid musks**, raised by Revd Joseph Pemberton of Essex in the 1920s with mainly hybrid tea and some musk origins. Hardy and repeat-flowering, e.g. Penelope and Felicia.

162. Rosa 'Cornelia', a hybrid musk.

• **Earlier hybrid teas** of this period, much used in the rose gardens of the time. Mme Butterfly, 1918; Shot Silk, 1924; Lady Sylvia, 1925.

Species roses, including some native to the UK, are used in less formal sites, wild gardens or for hedging. They include *RR. canina, rubiginosa, rugosa* and *spinosissima*. Some have been used for selection work, such as *R. xanthina* 'Canary Bird'.

163. Rosa 'Constance Spry'.

164. A rose trained to upright canes will make a cylinder of flower.

165. A rose trained and tied down over a structure of hazel will make a sphere of flower.

166. Informal pruning will make an open, well-balanced shrub rose.

Hybrid teas and floribundas flower on the new season's growth, with a succession of flowers from early summer to late autumn. Regular dead-heading is important. These roses respond to regular hard pruning to encourage a succession of strong growths, keep an open-centred vase shape (usually stiff and angular), and to remove rigorously any weak or dying shoots. Very old bushes can be given the rejuvenation treatment.

Organic manuring and regular feeding is a menu they like. Their array of potential pests and diseases, often listed in the literature, depends very much on the situation and the attitude of the grower.

Climbing and rambling roses See box, pages 144–45.

Occasional maintenance problems
Suckering Most roses are propagated commercially by budding or grafting on to selected rootstocks originating from various wild rose species, resulting in a more vigorous and faster-growing bush. However, one problem may be the production of shoots or suckers from the actual rootstock itself; if these are not removed, they may eventually overwhelm or weaken the grafted variety. Such suckers usually have smaller leaflets and more noticeable thorns than the variety. They should be cut out at their point of origin as soon as they are noticed.

Wind rock This refers to the rocking or, in extreme cases, keeling over of newly planted or unstable bushes when the ground is very wet or waterlogged, and the root anchorage not yet developed. Pruning back at planting of taller growths should reduce this, and firming in later where necessary once the ground is accessible.

Rose sickness Also known as 'replant disease', this particularly affects members of the *Rosaceae* family which also includes apples, cherries and plums. When trees and shrubs of this family are planted in sites that have been used for growing such species over a long period, they may have stunted or poor growth and may even die. This is more likely to be found with roses, as rose gardens and display beds are a tradition in many sites. The plants often recover if moved to fresh soil.

The causes are still not fully understood, but seem to be related to a build-up of damaging fungi and nematodes, and insufficient nutrients, organic matter and beneficial mycorrhiza. Not all sites are affected. A remedial practice of changing the soil can be disruptive and expensive at larger sites, and soil sterilisation, effective though it can be, now has legal restrictions.

The recommendation is therefore to improve the fertility and texture of the soil by generous mulches and the incorporation of slow-release fertilisers. These not only help the roses to get established and perpetuate healthy growth, but can also encourage native mycorrhizal fungi whose presence is now regarded as an important factor in dealing with this problem. It is also possible to add a proprietary mycorrhizal product at planting: this may be beneficial, but it is worth checking with professional sources about the reliability of any such product.

SHELTER, HEDGES AND SCREENS

Shelter planting, hedges and screens have been very traditional and historic features of many gardens, parklands and estates from early times. The complexities of intimate hedged enclosures and clipped boundary and ornamental features reached levels of near fantasy in the elaborate Renaissance gardens of Italy and France in the seventeenth century. Many Baroque styles in other European gardens also featured different green architectural forms. Gardens in the Netherlands had an important bearing on the formal Anglo-Dutch designs in a number of English gardens of this period; one of the best examples is at Hampton Court Palace (see Case Study, page 271).

On a much larger scale, the extensive landscape parks created by Lancelot 'Capability' Brown and Humphry Repton in the eighteenth and early nineteenth centuries embodied the visual and physical principles of shelter and enclosure for screening and concealing effects. They also afforded protection from winds – rolling parklands are often windy places – for the comfort and wellbeing of humans and livestock. Pleasure grounds were woodland-style informal places for more intimate and sheltered walking, while denser thickets also created physical barriers against undesirable intruders.

The management of these essentially large-scale features was also on a longer time-scale, and may have been shared with forestry and estate staff. In more recent times, the creation of outdoor rooms using hedges and living screens, in such famous gardens as Sissinghurst and Hidcote, now matches the general popularity of having sanctuaries and private enclosed spaces in the gardens.

167. Hedges provide an important structure to many gardens.

Shelter belts and shelter planting

The emphasis here is on two main aspects: the design and establishment of new shelter belts, windbreak and screening features; and the conservation and/or renewal of historic planting.

New planting When a new or replacement belt or screen is being considered, and before any final plans are made, a number of questions should be raised.

- Reasons for the feature. This may be to screen or protect a historic site from recent intrusions such as roads, or industrial or housing development. It could also be to reinstate a planted feature known to have existed from old plans and records

- Ultimate height and visual appearance – evergreen, deciduous or mixed

- Features and areas to be sheltered or screened

- Soil and site conditions and costs of establishment: plants, protection, weed control, etc.

- Time scale from planting to early maturity, longevity and possible economic returns

- Design and siting

For bold, large-scale planting following the styles of Brown and Repton, the shape, alignment and location of belts or windbreaks need careful consideration, and should always be decided on site. The topography of the land is important. Tree belts need not be straight, or of constant width; often a fairly free shape is more interesting and less disruptive of the natural ground pattern.

Profiles and aerodynamics Where wind protection is also an important objective, an accepted formula shows the relationship between the height of the belt and the area to be sheltered (see picture 168). As a general rule, a marked wind reduction covers a zone approximately ten times the height of the belt. Thus a belt 30m high will protect an area of about 300m on the leeward side, with very little wind close to the belt, but a gradual increase as one moves away from it. The belt should have a degree of permeability to reduce eddying effects; this can also be achieved by designing a plantation with a broadly concave profile. Local knowledge and experience should be a guide to the prevailing wind and the siting of the belt.

Guide for planning To be effective and also to have good visual impact, a belt should be not less than 30m wide and contain a choice of species of different height and character to create a broad aerodynamic profile. Planting should not be too spotty or indiscriminate, and preferably in groups. These should be composed of one or more dominant species, with supporting species kept to the centre of the belt; boundary or fringe species should be along the outer edges. The width might be adjusted to accommodate an informal access path.

The dominant species, such as beech or oak, will become the long-term feature of the belt, and some of the supporting species will act as nurse trees during the establishment period. Conifers, such as larch or pine, are effective for this. Evergreens may also be important to increase the year-round sheltering effect in very exposed sites; these in general should be kept to the spine of the belt.

The list of species for shelter belt and shelter planting (box, page 152) gives a general guide to a recommended range of species for a mixed belt as shown in pictures 169 and 170. However, choice of species will also be governed by regional climate and aspect, such as maritime, inland, upland or flat.

A measured planting grid is usually the simplest method of setting out, with plants 2m apart in staggered rows, but allowing for the grouping of the various species as shown on the plan. Young, open-ground, 2–3-year transplants of the deciduous species usually grow away well, assuming proper attention to planting which will be preferably in November–March. Evergreens such as pines, firs and hollies are normally container-grown or root-balled, and their planting season may be extended into late spring, especially if site conditions are very wet.

In most situations, protection against deer and rabbits will be essential. In grassland sites, weed and grass control around the young tree bases is equally important (see also pages 117-22).

Maintenance and management A plan should be drawn up as a practical document to cover the anticipated effective life of the plantation. For the first four or five years, this will include routine inspection, making good any losses, weed control and protection. A thinning programme then needs to be included, its timing and extent being determined by the composition, rates of growth and any special features to be encouraged. Where conifers have been used as nurse-trees, they may be alien to the character of the area; the plan should leave clear instructions on their phased removal, before competition with the dominant species becomes serious. Some thinning of the dominants and supporting species, to allow more light and space, may also be needed, but it should not be so drastic as to reduce the sheltering effect.

As the shading effect increases, any original pasture grasses will gradually be suppressed, but other more shade-tolerant vegetation may take over and a woodland edge flora develop. This is good for wildlife and, in most situations, the plantation or shelter belt does not need to be too manicured or tidy (see also pages 134-6).

Conservation, renovation and restoration of overmature and neglected plantations and shelter belts A specification and management plan is important here, but it is the case that these more remote features often have to receive a lower priority of management; they therefore tend to get a lower standard of attention. The work involved can really be considered as linear woodland management which may also involve a range of arboricultural practices; reference to these are in the relevant sections below.

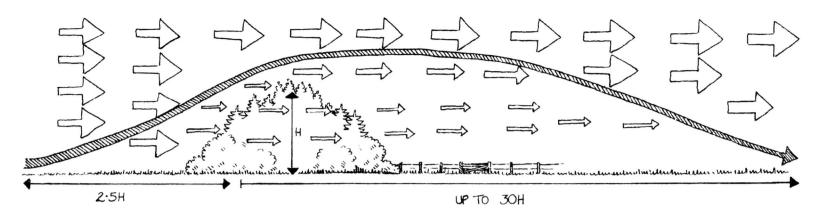

168. By filtering winds, tree belts can reduce wind speeds for a distance up to thirty times the height of the trees in the belt.

169. Elevation of planned tree belt, showing a mix of deciduous and evergreen trees and a shrub layer to provide continuous protection.

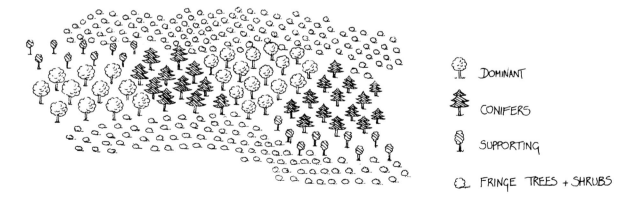

170. Tree belt planting plan.

GUIDE TO SPECIES FOR SHELTER BELT AND SHELTER PLANTING

Soil type	Dominant	Supporting	Conifers/evergreens	Fringe planting
Deep loam	Oak, ash, lime	Sycamore, poplar, ash, Turkey oak	Douglas fir, Austrian pine, larch, *Thuya plicata*, cypresses, ?holly	Wild cherry, field maple, hawthorn, blackthorn, willow, hazel
Sandy loam	Scots pine, birch	Oak, sweet chestnut, Robinia, sycamore	Scots pine, Austrian/ Corsican pine, larch, cypresses, holly	Rowan, hawthorn, goat willow
Chalk and limestone	Holm oak	Ash, hornbeam, Norway maple, sycamore, poplars, Italian alder, holm oak	Austrian pine, holm oak, holly, yew	Hawthorn, field maple, whitebeam, dogwood, blackthorn, wild cherry
Heavy clay	Oaks, ash	Poplars, willows, alder, ash	Larch, Sitka spruce, Norway spruce, holly	Alder, willow, hawthorn, blackthorn, field maple
Maritime north	Sycamore, Scots pine, Austrian pine	Scots pine, beech, alder	Scots pine, Astrian pine, cypresses, holly	Hawthorn, field maple, willows
Maritime south	Beech, Monterey pine, Corsican pine, holm oak	Beech, holm oak, sycamore, Robinia, white poplar	Monterey pine, Corsican pine, holm oak, holly	Hawthorn, field maple, blackthorn

171. A rather solid belt of Cupressocyparis Leylandii is a dense barrier that may result in wind eddies.

Hedges and screens

These may be defined as linear and continuous communities of woody plants which, by reason of their dense busy growth and response to regular pruning and clipping, develop into effective living barriers, screens and enclosures.

Hedges are usually on a smaller scale than shelter belts, and their effect is to create local shelter and microclimates, giving some protection to enclosed spaces in a garden. Taller and more architectural forms created by pleaching and specialised training are also included here. All require regular and close attention to maintenance to be effective.

Siting, planting and early establishment In historic and well-established gardens, existing hedges will probably be part of the original design. If a new hedge is being considered, a number of questions need to be asked and decisions made at the pre-planning stage. As with most shelter belts, a good hedge should be a long-term investment; making the right decisions will have a bearing on the subsequent maintenance and longevity of the hedge.

Planting The importance of the planting stage to the successful establishment and healthy longevity of a hedge has already been highlighted. Space does not allow a detailed specification of hedge-planting practices, but these guidelines are an outline of best practice (see box, opposite, and page 158).

Maintenance: clipping or cutting The objectives should be to encourage a tight, narrow and uniform hedge. In the first year after planting, little or no pruning is normally advised, as the new plants need to make good new growth to form a strong root system. Control begins in the second year, by clipping the side growths and possible light pruning of vigorous leaders; where height is wanted as quickly as possible, the leaders may be left uncut for the next year or more, until the required height is reached. In the following years, regular trimming or clipping becomes a routine operation. The frequency and tightness of cutting and the methods used will vary with the species and the purpose of the hedge. Appendices Table 12 summarises a range of recommended species, rates of growth and clipping frequencies.

A huge array of equipment for hedge cutting is available. Powered tools are now in general use, but there is still a case for a good pair of hand shears. Where time and speed are not the main objectives, shears are quiet, relaxing to use, and also good for beginners. They are also advisable for special topiary features.

Nutrition The constant removal of clippings or pruned material that is an essential part of proper hedge maintenance also results in a steady removal of nutrients that may cause decreased growth and eventual impoverishment. Hedges are not generally high in nutrient demands, but some regular replacement of lost elements is necessary for sustained growth. This can be done by an annual application of a balanced slow-release fertiliser in late winter or early spring, combined with an organic mulch. Older hedges may have competition from ivy and other tough, woody, weed species such as brambles and elder, which can colonise hedge bases. Removing these before they get too established will also benefit the hedge. In less manicured situations, hedge bases can be used to grow a medley of less competitive herbaceous plants such as violets, dwarf ferns, wild strawberries and spring bulbs, which can add charm and less formality to a site.

Rejuvenation and restoration of very old or overmature hedges Provided there is no serious disease or decay, and reasonable vigour still in the hedge trunks or rootstocks, some species can be restored to their original shape, or completely rejuvenated by hard cutting back to the original trunks. This treatment is usually successful with evergreen species such as yew, holly, laurels, privet and box, where the rejuvenation can be reasonably fast; it is also effective but slower with the deciduous types such as beech and hornbeam. Hawthorn and blackthorn respond well to hedge laying. All the cypress species used for hedging, including Leyland cypress, seldom, if ever, respond to this very hard cutting back, and the results are usually ugly and irreversible. Western red cedar (*Thuja plicata*) may stand some harder pruning, and may rejuvenate from the base if conditions are favourable. With species that do not respond to hard pruning, it is advisable to cut back one side at a time, with an interval of a year or more, to reduce the stress on the hedge; after cutting back, apply a mulch and fertiliser dressing.

Hedge laying This ancient craft for farm and countryside hedges became more widespread after the eighteenth-century Enclosure Acts. The object was to create thick, stock-proof barriers by training fast-growing woody types such as thorn, field maples, hazel, blackthorn and dogwood. The method used has local variations. On farms and country estates where there is an interest in demonstrating traditional manual skills and old techniques, there has been quite a revival of this practice. It can be an effective way of bringing back neglected and overgrown farm and roadside hedges, assuming that a hedge layer can be found. A follow-up maintenance programme is needed to develop a good thick hedge.

The high hedge controversy Conflicts – even fatalities – have occurred in situations where hedges between neighbouring properties have been allowed to grow to excessive heights, blocking out light and views. Such disputes are mainly in residential areas, and the hedge culprit is nearly always Leyland cypress – naturally fast-growing, if left unpruned it can reach a height of 35m or more. Legislation was enacted under Part 8 of the Anti-Social Behaviour Act 2003 to give some recourse to home-owners blighted by excessively high hedges (see 1.5, page 75). Such tall hedges are seldom an issue in historic gardens, and there is plenty of evidence to show that well-disciplined Leyland hedges, clipped once or twice annually, can be made very trim and tight.

It is also true, however, that this cypress resents being cut back to very old wood or even the trunks of larger trees, and will rarely regenerate with new basal or adventitious growth. The only answer in this case is to grub out the old hedge or screen and start again.

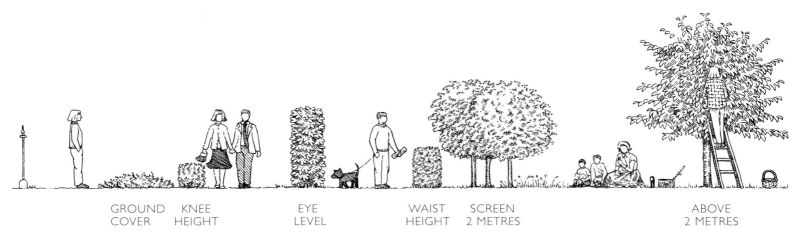

GROUND COVER · KNEE HEIGHT · EYE LEVEL · WAIST HEIGHT · SCREEN 2 METRES · ABOVE 2 METRES

172. The relationship between the height and the purpose of a hedge or planting. The decision on height will be important in determining views within and beyond a enclosure, and it will also affect maintenance requirements.

173. A young hedge and pleached limes during establishment.

HEDGES: POINTS TO CONSIDER

- Harmony or relationship with the style and character of the garden and any other hedges present

- Composition – evergreen, deciduous or mixed ('tapestry')

- Texture, colour and density, barrier effect

- Ultimate height, vigour and maintenance needs – frequency of cutting

- Longevity and reliability

- Root competition, toxicity of leaves, wildlife values

- Costs of preparation, plants, their early establishment and protection

174. Cutting a high hedge with a hedge trimmer extension avoids the need for platforms.

175. A cherry-picker platform with spider-like legs is ideal for cutting the cloud hedge at Walmer Castle and causes minimum disturbance to other planting.

176. Below: a simple wheeled platform is ideal for cutting this formal hedge next to a hard path.

177. Right: a frame used as a template to ensure that the yews in the Hampton Court parterre are clipped accurately.

178. Below: the Head Gardener at Great Dixter in the 1930s, with an instrument for determining batter and for checking the accuracy of clipping. The batter of this hedge is four inches to each foot of hedge. The cross batten at the top is marked with lines, each of which represents an inch of batter to a foot of height. A pin passing through a hole in the guide to holes in the cross-piece keeps this to the required batter. Maintaining the ideal batter enables sufficient light to reach the base of the hedge.

YEW HEDGE REJUVENATION

179a. The hedge has become too wide and lost its batter.

179b. Winter of the first year: cut back one side almost to the main stem.

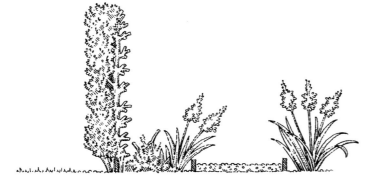

179c. Winter of the second year: cut back the second side.

179d. Regrowth after four years.

180. Before: the original proportions have been lost.

181 Right: a sectional view.

182. After: laterals have been cut back to the main stem and the plant top-dressed, irrigated and mulched to encourage the healthy regrowth shown. Interpretation is important to explain to visitors the aim of this apparently drastic treatment.

183. The hedge re-established to its correct proportions after three to four years.

184. Right: beech hedge rejuvenation after neglect.

Pests and diseases Well-maintained hedges are not usually prone to serious onslaughts from pest and disease problems. Protection from deer and rabbits is important in the early establishment stages; where hedges are alongside areas grazed by horses and cattle, strong fencing is really necessary. Horses can reach up to 2m and can soon chew into a hedge; yew foliage, even cut or dessicated on the ground, is fatal to horses. Mice and voles may also occasionally bark the young shoots. Squirrels may be a problem on beech hedges. Insect pests may include yew scale, and various caterpillars and aphids.

Honey or bootlace fungus (*Armellaria*) is probably the most serious disease that can affect hedges, with privet particularly susceptible. Other diseases include box blight and *Phytopthera* which kills yew (see page 229).

Wildlife conservation Hedges have a very important role in offering habitats for a range of wildlife, particularly birds for nesting sites and foraging. Small mammals and many insects find refuges there (and not only pests!). Any hedge work, especially cutting, should respect birds' nesting periods – avoid March to June if possible.

Windy upland sites Shelter planting is invaluable as a first line of defence as windbreaks, shelter belts and strong hedges. Apply the usual guidleines when selecting stock and planting.

Maritime and coastal areas These conditions present particular and unique problems for plant growth and establishment, which can be limited by:

- **Wind force** Can be up to 30 per cent greater in exposed sites than further inland
- **Salt spray** In severe gales, spray may be carried several miles inland. It can cause scorching and dessication of susceptible foliage, especially in the spring and early summer.

HEDGE PLANTING: BEST PRACTICE

- Start with well-grown, healthy and even stock. Open-ground stock is recommended for deciduous hedging species such as beech, hornbeam and thorn, as 2–3-year transplants, height 80–120mm. Look for good root systems. Evergreens such as holly, yew, laurels, etc., should be root-balled or container-grown to 2–3 litre size. Larger stock is usually available but at greater cost, and does not necessarily make a quicker hedge in the long run.

- Plant open ground deciduous stock during the dormant period November–March. Late planting can lead to losses in drought conditions. Evergreens (not open ground) can be planted over a longer period, October–April as a guide. Plant in well prepared trenches or individual pits.

- Protect from vermin, deer, rabbits etc., if these are known to be a problem.

- Mulch after planting, and water in very dry periods during the first year.

186. A well managed Leyland conifer hedge.

185. A newly re-laid field boundary hedge. Each county will often have its own local style for this type of hedge management.

187. A hipped hedge.

188. Wind-pruned trees at a south coast resort.

- **Soil types** Saline sands, shingles and silts may be tougher on plant growth.

There are considerable regional variations in the UK from the colder east and north-east coasts to the much milder south-west and western locations. Beneficial factors include:

- **Tempering effect** of adjacent seas, which act as a reservoir of more constant temperatures, reducing the incidence of severe frosts. The Gulf Stream effect on the western coasts of the UK is another factor, enabling sub-tropical planting in the Isles of Scilly, western Scotland and western Ireland.

- **Greater humidity**

- **Higher average sunshine**

Plants adapted to coastal habitats include trees and shrubs with thick, waxy, or needle-like leaves, and perennials with grey, felted or fleshy leaves and compact growth (see Appendices, Table 11).

189. A shelter belt of deciduous and evergreen trees protects the garden at Osborne from strong salt-laden winds.

HISTORIC MARITIME SHELTER PLANTING

Several fine historic gardens were created in the nineteenth century by pioneering individuals who saw the essential need to create shelter and windbreaks on very hostile sites.

- **Tresco, Isles of Scilly** In 1834 Augustus Smith took over the lease of the isles from the Duchy of Cornwall, and started gardens of some 12 acres by planting on the seaward side shelter belts of *Pinus radiata* and *Cupressus macrocarpa*, both from the rugged Monterey peninsula of California, and massed hedges of *Quercus ilex*, the holm oak. On the lee side he planted sycamores, elms, oaks and poplars. He created his now world-famous gardens from a bare site of gorse and heathers with no trees; they still flourish today.

- **Inverewe, north-west Scotland** In 1862 Osgood Mackenzie was given a piece of land by his mother on a barren peninsula of black soggy peat and rocky outcrops, exposed to the full fury of the Atlantic ocean. The only growth was of heather, dwarf willows and scrub. Osgood began by constructing a fence across the neck of the peninsula, and in 1864 planted a thick belt of *Pinus nigra* and *Pinus sylvestris* which provided the eventual protection for the great garden that gradually came into being. He had to wait some 15 years before any garden planting could begin.

HERBACEOUS PERENNIALS

This term refers to a very large group of plants which can persist for a number of years by means of a perennial rootstock from which new growth and flowers are produced each year. They are generally shorter-lived than the woody plants, but their various rootstock adaptations, which include bulbs and corms, mean that they are very resilient. On dying down at the end of their growing season, these living organisms are protected from winter frosts and summer droughts.

During the evolution of historic gardens, perennials would have been included with herbs; in monastic and later medieval, Tudor and Elizabethan gardens, they had a range of domestic properties and uses, primarily culinary and medicinal. Many would have been native species. By the seventeenth century, more spectacular flowering perennials were being introduced, especially bulbs such as tulips, narcissi and lilies, depicted in splendid Dutch and French floral paintings.

A steady flow from many countries continued during the eighteenth century, but the real popularity of herbaceous plants started in the mid-Victorian period (see table, appendices). Beautifully illustrated books by John and Jane Loudon were soon followed by the powerful advocacy of Willam Robinson and Gertrude Jekyll. Robinson demonstrated the great potential of herbaceous perennials and bulbs for naturalising in meadows and woodlands; Jekyll held the same views, and also showed the way by her use of colour and texture in the many borders she designed for a wide range of clients. These included some historic gardens, and there must have been very few libraries in country houses great and small that did not include some of her eminently practical and so clearly written books.

The post-1945 period saw a revival of gardens after wartime neglect, and new or revived styles of herbaceous planting. Alan Bloom at his famous Norfolk nurseries promoted 'island beds' that tended to be kidney-shaped, using shorter, sturdier, labour-saving cultivars that did not need staking. Margery Fish of East Lambrook Manor in Somerset developed cottage gardening on a wider scale, also collecting many older varieties of once common plants.

190. Island beds at Logan Botanic Garden.

Christopher Lloyd of Great Dixter in Sussex (see Case Study, page 265) had long been an advocate of the mixed border which combined compact trees and shrubs with herbaceous perennials and annuals to create colour and interest over a long season. He also encouraged the 'meadow gardening' movement.

The last two decades of the twentieth century saw a massive revival of interest in plants of this group. The restoration of gardens of the Jekyll period, as well as a revival of the Robinson wild garden approach, have been ongoing in some historic and larger gardens, although they have brought with them an awareness of the maintenance implications of such styles. The ecological principles in selecting plants suitable for their natural environment are better understood; Beth Chatto has been a leading figure in this, through books and the highly imaginative and successful garden linked to her nursery and prize-winning exhibits at the Chelsea Show in the 1980s.

History is inclined to turn full circle. A century after William Robinson was promoting wild gardens, a new movement begun by Karl Forester at the University of Munich's trial gardens at Weihenstephan has been taken up by other German, Dutch and Belgian garden designers. Now styled as 'new naturalism' or the 'new perennial movement', it is based on careful selection of a

192. East Lambrook Manor, laid out by Margery Fish.

193. Beth Chatto's dry garden, an experiment in gardening without irrigation in one of England's driest counties.

191. An engraved plate from *The Ladies Flower Garden* by Jane Loudon, 1841.

very broad range of herbaceous perennials according to ecological requirements, and their management as semi-natural communties (see page 168).

Management of perennials by growth type

To manage herbaceous plants effectively, it is important to understand their quite diverse growth habit and form. It is possible to divide them broadly into four fairly distinct groups.

Rootstocks or clump-forming

Examples *Aster, Delphinium, Hosta, Miscanthus*

These grow into a dense collection of stems arsing from many fibrous roots, hence a rootstock or clump. As the plant grows it develops a slowly expanding circle of new shoots on the outside of the clump, allowing it spread out and colonise new ground. As this process continues, the original centre of the clump tends to decline and die out, and this may happen about five years after planting. By this time, perennial weeds such as dandelions – or, worse, ground elder or couch grass – may have invaded the rootstocks, so a programme of lifting and dividing is standard practice, in autumn or early spring. New healthy divisions are selected for replanting, and the old clump fragments composted, but look out for the perennial weeds.

194. A strawberry plant with runners.

Runners and stolons

Examples *Ajuga, Fragaria, Lamium, Vinca*

These grow from dense rosettes formed in late summer and autumn, often overwintering in the evergreen state. In spring and early summer, after flowering, they produce vigorous trailing or creeping stems along the surface of the ground (runners) or just below the surface (stolons). These form new rosettes which then root at short intervals along the stems. Strawberry runners are a typical example.

195. An Aster rootstock with stolons.

Plants of this type can make ideal ground cover by their spring growth and rapid spread; those that are shade-tolerant, such as *Vinca*, are very effective as shade ground cover. However, some of the more invasive types in this group may have to be controlled; growth can be restricted by mechanical or chemical means.

Fleshy tap-rooted perennials

Examples *Acanthus, Crambe, Eryngium, Gypsophia, Paeonia, Rheum*

These are some of the longest-lived herbaceous plants. Once established, they develop thick fleshy roots that can go down to some depth, and they resent disturbance. They can become semi-permanent features in a planting scheme. The old cottage garden *Paeonia officinalis* has been known to live for half a century or more – to quote Graham Thomas, 'it loves peace and sunshine – as we all do!' Root clusters are capable of regenerating new plants from buds at their apex; domestic rhubarb is a good example. This can be a means of starting new groups, especially if the old plants are in real decline or overwhelmed by weeds.

Bulbs, corms, tubers and rhizomes

Examples *Anemone, Crocus, Cyclamen, Gladiolus, Iris, Lilium, Narcissus, Tulip*

Members of this very important and colourful group have evolved various storage mechanisms that enable them to remain alive and dormant in the ground during periods of excessive heat, drought and cold. Their main dislike is very poorly drained or wet sites. Bulbs such as onions, narcissi, lilies and tulips consist of a number of closely packed or scale-like swollen leaves arising from a base plate that is really a compressed stem, with roots generated from it also. The bulb may be protected by an outer sheath or tunic, as with tulips. After flowering, the leaves help to produce new bulbils or offsets, before dying down for what may be a long dormant period.

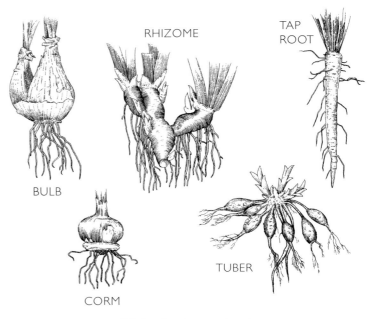

196. Swollen stems and roots.

197. Narcissus can have great effect when naturalised en masse, as can be see at Waddesdon Manor.

198. Narcissus naturalised in short grass at Logan Botanic Gardens.

199. Crocus naturalised at Great Dixter.

- **Corms**, such as cyclamen and gladioli, are swollen rounded stems, from which the leaves, flowers and roots are produced. The period of dormancy varies with the genera and species.

- **Tubers** are somewhat similar, and may be swollen stems or roots as in the potato and the dahlia.

- **Rhizomes**, as with irises and some geraniums, are short horizontal swollen stems, which can root into the soil, so that the plants gradually radiate out from the original centre. As with the clumps, they may need lifting and dividing after a time. Irises tend to have a dormancy period in midsummer after flowering.

Cultivation and management

Recommended references and sources of further information on herbaceous plants can be found in the bibliography. Both traditional and innovative uses of perennials require specialist maintenance attention, and these are highlighted below.

Traditional herbaceous borders and island beds

Renovation cycles Such borders and planting schemes respond best to a 3-5-year renovation cycle, which will also be dependent on soil type, growth of plants and available time. The treatment of plants varies with their growth habit, but for many it will mean lifting and dividing, and re-invigorating the soil by incorporating bulky organic matter. This will also be a good opportunity for clearing out any invasive weeds, and making modifications to the original planting design.

Support During these cycles, and for traditional borders, some form of support is usually essential, especially where there will be medium to tall growing groups that need to be kept upright. For many this is a time-consuming and rather irksome task. A wide range of materials are available for supporting or staking, and the type used will depend on the character of the borders, the plants and their ultimate size. For traditional or historical period borders, natural supports are preferred – such as short hazel or birch twigs, cut during the winter from estate woodlands or other local sources. Forms of support should not be too obvious.

Island or floating -type irregular borders can be massed with denser, lower-growing perennials selected for robustness and stability; these may require little or no support.

Mixed and cottage-style borders

These are usually characterised by a mixture of woody plants in the design, with a semi-permanent or much longer life-cycle – it is the perennial groups that can be given the shorter-term lift and divide treatment in the pockets or areas where they occur. These shrubs can also offer support to neighbouring perennials, so only localised staking or other support may be needed. Mixed border management is therefore less intensive and more relaxed (see Great Dixter Case Study, page 265).

A feeding and mulching programme is important for all borders in these groups. Perennials respond to a good diet, and

200. The pleached hornbeam walk at Sissinghurst provides a formal setting for a 'bulb catalogue display' of informal planted groups of different bulbous plants.

201. *Lilium lancifolium*.

202. *Cardiocrinum giganteum* make a stately group in the quarry woodland garden at Belsay in Northumberland.

203. *Narcissus cyclamineus* is early to flower in the meadow at the RHS garden at Wisley.

204. At the Royal Botanic Gardens Edinburgh, spring birch branches are twisted into supports for the herbaceous border in early spring.

205. The same border in summer: the plants have grown through the birch supports, making them no longer visible. In winter, when the border is cut down, both the dead tops of the herbaceous plants and the birch branches can be shredded and composted, providing a fully recyclable support system.

206. Netting is strung over a herbaceous border to provide support for developing perennial plants.

February

April

May

June

August

October

207. The long mixed border at Great Dixter is planted and managed to give a long season of interest.

208. Bog gardens, such as this one at Gresgarth Hall, unless planted with vigorous perennial plants, require regular weeding as the plentiful supply of moisture is ideal for weed growth.

neglected borders can soon look tired and stunted (see Great Dixter Case Study, page 267).

Bog gardens

Naturally very damp or wet sites, which may be associated with water gardens or be sited in low-lying hollows, can be an ideal habitat for a number of bold and luxuriant perennials, and many of these can flourish for years with no frequent lifting or division. Examples are *Gunnera manicata, Astilbe, Senecio, Rodgersia and Persicaria (Polygonum)*. Most of these, being of the rootstock type of growth, can, if space allows, effectively colonise large areas with the minimum of attention.

209. Planting illustrating the new perennial movement.

The new perennial movement

An application of ideas and practices from the past, this identifies garden habitats – such as woodland, woodland edge, open ground, or dry and sunny – and then groups or masses perennials in selected communities adapted to these sites. Plantings based on such ecological principles are far from maintenance-free; during the establishment period, unwanted and often invasive native weeds will need rigorous removal. Staking and supporting are not necessary, and nutritional levels are kept to a minimum. Some spectacular prairie-like effects can be developed, although these will be rather less attractive in the dark days of late autumn and winter.

Perennials of most growth categories may be included in these schemes, but there should be less frequent lifting and division. It is essential to maintain balance so that one type does not swamp the rest.

Irrigation

Decisions on whether to water or not will depend on the type of soil, the location and range of plants used, and the weather patterns. Ideally, planting should be planned to cope with the amount of natural water available; features such as 'dry' and 'gravel' gardens are based on this surmise. The increasing need to conserve water must be a factor, but certain sites and situations will justify some level of irrigation or watering. Many systems are available, from overhead sprays to soil-based drip and trickle ('weep hoses'). The latter are preferred as they direct the water to the plant roots, there is less evaporation loss and they do not damage foliage or flowers.

ANNUALS AND BIENNIALS

Annuals are short-lived plants which complete their life cycle from seed to flowering in one growing season.

Biennials require two seasons: the first to establish a strong growing plant, and the second to flower and set seed.

Many short-lived herbaceous perennials can be treated as annuals or biennials. These are the most ephemeral but also the most spectacular and colourful of the vegetation groups in this chapter, and there is a constant selection of new hybrids appearing all the time.

The earliest introductions into gardens in England were mainly selections and improvements of annuals found in the wild in various European countries. In the sixteenth and seventeenth centuries, new annuals were introduced to Britain from many parts of the world. These included the French and African marigolds (*Tagetes*) from Mexico in the late sixteenth century, Marvel of Peru (*Mirabilis*) from South America, and introductions from Russia and eastern North America by such adventurous plantsmen as the Tradescants, Elder and Younger. A range of these were planted in the great formal parterres that were laid out in the seventeenth century. The Privy Garden at Hampton Court uses these historic annuals for summer planting displays (see Case Study, page 271).

Appendices Table 9 gives a range of annuals in use today, with notes on their dates of introduction and other characteristics.

Uses in historic gardens and parks

Apart from cases where restoration programmes require, as far as is possible, authentic planting, many sites and planting schemes can use annuals and biennials, depending on the character and appropriateness of the sites, and bearing in mind the plants' ephemeral character. Modern fashions in plant breeding have led to short and even F1 cultivars of bedding plants, but authentic historic planting reproductions will need to source larger, period-correct cultivars or unimproved species. Their use usually means higher maintenance, but they will reward this with varied and colourful displays.

They may be grown in borders on their own, in mixed borders, grown as cut flowers or among rock plants, on sunny banks, in woodland gardens, and the climbing species over walls or supports. Hardy annuals can also be very effective if direct sown as an annual border in a well-prepared seed bed in March.

Naturalising or self-seeding annuals can be very effective in mixed planting. Forget-me-not creates carpets of blue flowers in the spring. If left *in situ* until seeding occurs, seedlings will emerge in late summer, so any weeding regime needs to allow for this. These seedlings overwinter and flower the following spring, so they are in effect semi-biennial.

Biennials such as honesty and foxglove can be allowed to naturalise in woodland clearings or semi-shaded sites; as with

210. The formal parterre at Waddesdon Manor planted with annual and half-hardy bedding plants to provide contrasting colours and textures.

HISTORIC BEDDING SCHEMES

An invasion of new plants in the nineteenth century included a colourful range of half-hardy annuals, which found an important place in great Victorian formal bedding schemes, including Celosia, Dahlia and Pelargonium (treated as annuals), Nicotiana, Petunia, Salvia and Verbena. Those that needed more protection were grown in conservatories and display glasshouses (see page 210).

211. Care should be taken when planting out to minimise compaction. In wet weather it can be advisable to stand on a short board while planting to spread the weight.

212. Plants spaced in their pots prior to planting out at Hampton Court.

forget-me-not, seedlings need to be noted or marked to avoid being weeded out by mistake. Other examples are poppies and verbascum. See Great Dixter Case Study (page 265).

Spring bedding

Typical Victorian or Edwardian spring bedding schemes, now having something of a revival, were usually in formal settings, particularly in public parks. To provide more interest, they often utilised a specimen hardy evergreen shrub, such as *Fatsia*, or a large ivy as a feature in the centre of the bed. The main planting was typically something like forget-me-nots, wallflowers, polyanthus, daisies, etc., with interplanting of tulips or narcissi. These annual plants can be raised from seed if facilities exist, but generally it may be more economic to buy them in.

Displays in pots, vases and other containers

Many of these plants, as well as half-hardy shrubs and short-lived perennials, can provide exuberant displays from early summer onwards. To be really successful, the type of container must be carefully selected, especially in historic settings, as well as the plants. A routine schedule of maintenance – watering, feeding, dead-heading – is vital to maintain a healthy display all spring and summer (see 'Container growing', page 218).

213. Above: the blue of self-seeding *Myosotis* at Great Dixter provides important unity to spring plantings.

214. Right: *Nigella* in early summer at Tintinhull provides a complementary carpet for *Allium christophii*.

215. The contrasting colours of winter-flowering *Viola* cultivars will provide a long season of winter display at Waddesdon Manor.

216. Bedding out with ornamental salad vegetables at Waddesdon Manor.

217. Right: from the mid nineteenth century, Hampton Court has retained the excellent tradition of bedding out for spring and summer colour. It is a useful place to visit for inspiration.

219. At Osborne, planting showing concentric bands.

222. The Old Rose Garden at Great Dixter, now replanted as a sub-tropical garden, provides a long season of interest until the first frosts which it is hoped do not arrive until November.

220. At Osborne, carpet bedding was used to celebrate the centenary of Queen Victoria's death in 1901. This design was planned, then ordered from a specialist nursery which deliverd the plants in modules which were then slotted together. This form of carpet bedding should be trimmed with sheep's shears once a week by a gardener suspended over the planting on boards. The clippings can then removed as shown here.

223. Penstemons at Logan Botanic Garden may be grown as half-hardy annuals propagated from late summer cuttings. However, they will over-winter in mild winters when they are best treated as sub-shrubs and trimmed back in March.

221. Right: municipal carpet bedding such as this floral clock in Edinburgh is now rare, as it is expensive to implement and maintain. However, in high-profile areas it is much enjoyed and photographed by tourists.

224. Right: dahlias, popular in Edwardian gardens, are true tender perennials. They are best planted out in early summer, after the last frosts, from autumn cuttings or from potted over-wintered tubers grown in a protected glasshouse.

218. Opposite: the ultimate Victorian parterre at Osborne, planted with summer bedding.

225. Autumn-sown annuals such as *Schizanthus*, Poor Man's Orchid, will flower in a frost-free glasshouse in early spring from an August sowing. The secret of growing compact large plants such as these is to ensure maximum light and good ventilation to avoid sharp fluctuations in temperature. The plants here were flowering at 1m in a 10-litre pot.

Annuals under glass

These plants have long been grown in glasshouses and conservatories, to provide colourful displays from late winter onwards. Some will be biennials, or perennials with a limited life. Examples include *Begonia, Calceolaria, Cyclamen, Pelargonium, Primula, Salpiglossis and Schizanthus* (see Appendices Table 9). Techniques for raising and maintaining such plants can be found in the recommended bibliography.

226 Right: *Pericallis* x *hybrida* (syn. *Cineraria*), grown as above. As with many half-hardy and tender annuals, it can also be sown in February to provide summer colour on smaller plants.

TURF AND GRASSLAND

The earliest areas of managed turf that were a feature in the intricate pleasure gardens of the Tudor and Elizabethan periods were modest in size and included 'flowery meads' and bowling greens. Beyond the castle and garden walls were, by comparison, vast areas of native grasslands as deer parks and grazed pastures throughout much of the country. The eighteenth-century landscape parks embodied and adapted these 'natural landscapes' in the great creations by Brown and Repton, where only the ha-ha or sunken fence prevented grazing animals from intruding on the smooth-scythed lawns around the mansion.

Dr Budding's mechanical cylinder or roller mower, introduced in the 1830s, revolutionised lawn mowing, in gardens large and small. Scythe mowing was abandoned as a whole array of mechanical mowers were developed in the nineteenth and early twentieth centuries. These were followed in turn by powered mowers, of which today there is a vast range and complexity.

From the maintenance and management point of view, turf and grass areas usually occupy a quite significant percentage of the total area of large gardens and parks, as is very evident in the Case Studies (Part 3). Hourly work figures also show that mowing and other grass maintenance operations often represent the highest proportion of total working hours in the year (see page 276).

Composition of turf and growth forms

Grasses belong to the great botanical family *Graminae*, of which there are about 10,000 species worldwide; about 160 are native to Britain. Six main species have formed the basis for what is now a complex and wide-ranging number of hybrids and strains on which breeding, selection work and trials are ongoing.

Most of these grasses are perennial plants, and they can broadly be divided into two growth forms: tussocks or tufts; and creeping and stoloniferous. It is a combination of these two types that forms a typical sward, and the selection of species and strains in the turf will determine wear and tear, colour, texture and resistance to drought and disease.

227. At Standen (National Trust), a striped lawn contrasts with the meadow beyond the ha-ha.

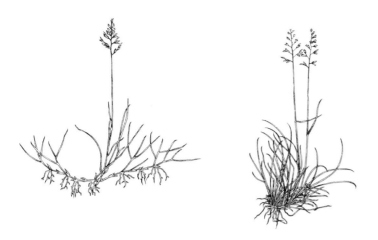

228. Growth habits: *Poa trivialis* (rhizomatous, left) and *Poa annua* (right), which is more tufted.

Growth habit

Most grasses used for lawns and recreational purposes can be regarded as evergreen due to the fact that, when regularly mown, they are constantly producing new shoots and leaves from tussocks or stolons, which are very dependent upon a healthy root system. Growth is very slow or suspended during the dormant season, due to low temperatures and light levels, but becomes very rapid from spring onwards, when regular mowing promotes dense basal leaf growth. If mowing is intentionally withheld, as in meadow garden practice, grasses then run up to flower; if they are not then mown, a period of brown or dead-looking grass can result. Roots tend to be fibrous and shallow, rarely extending down more than 75–100mm, and are sensitive to extremes of drought or poor drainage, and excessive wear and tear.

For the successful management of healthy grass plants, it is valuable to understand the basic principles of photosynthesis. Energy and sugar for growth comes from the raw materials of water and carbon dioxide. Water is provided by the roots, and carbon dioxide absorbed directly by the leaves. For leaves and roots to grow and function properly they need to respire, and respiration requires ready access to oxygen. Leaves very rarely have problems with obtaining sufficient oxygen as it is in all surrounding air and is also a by-product of photosynthesis. In most soils, innumerable air spaces between particles provide sufficient oxygen for roots to respire. In soils where these air spaces are absent or waterlogged, the roots of most plants begin to die.

Maintenance

It cannot be stressed too highly that all the uses of grassland, both current and predicted, must be taken into account when planning a management regime. These can include:

- Formal recreation, e.g. sport
- Informal recreation, e.g. picnicking, walking
- Events, from small open days to large concerts or re-enactments

High quality lawns with little access In a traditional lawn, for looking at rather than walking on, fine grasses dominate. Visual aspects are valued, such as an even colour and the striped effect of box mowing with cylinder mowers. The full sports field maintenance programme is recommended for these areas, with the exception of verti-draining (see pages, 238, 239) which is unlikely to be necessary unless the area is naturally badly drained.

High quality lawns with access These lawns are valued for the same features as those above, but are accessible to visitors, even if only for limited periods. The full sports field maintenance programme is recommended, including verti-draining which might be necessary annually if usage is high, but bi- or tri-annually if not intensive.

Good quality lawns and pleasure grounds (accessible grass areas) Grass areas which are freely accessible at all times, possibly for sports activities or picnicking, require an even and well-maintained appearance but do not usually need the stripes distinctive of high-quality lawns. Again, the full sports field maintenance programme is an ideal. Verti-draining might be necessary annually if usage is high or very intensive for a short period (for example, a season of concerts in one area), or if there are particularly well-used desire lines. Verti draining could be done bi- or tri-annually in other less intensively used areas.

229. The Rose Garden at Hampton Court: a very high-quality lawn with access.

230. The Mercury Vista at Walmer Castle: good-quality grass for accessible areas.

Long grass for wildlife benefit In areas that contain a natural species-rich grass sward, the fauna benefit and management is directed solely towards the maintenance and enhancement of the ecosystem. These sites may be nationally or internationally important SSSIs, locally important County Wildlife Sites or simply visually attractive and good for wildlife.

Much less intensive maintenance should be necessary in these areas; it may be restricted to just cutting and clearing the arisings.

If access pathways are cut through, these may require more intensive care, particularly spiking. Generally, the most diverse swards are found on the poorest soils – they were originally created by the 'nitrogen pump' effect of being grazed only during the day. The animals were taken off at night and folded on pastures closer to human habitation, both for their protection and to allow their dung to fertilise arable fields, so those nutrients were lost from the downs. Maintenance therefore concentrates on keeping fertility low. This is now achieved either by animal grazing alone (stock rarely being removed every day) or by ensuring that arisings are removed after cutting to prevent the nutrients being recycled (and also to prevent damage to the sward by laying the arisings on top after cutting). (See Great Dixter Case Study, page 265).

The use of fertilisers or pesticides, or imported grass seed, should be carefully considered – these can very quickly change the dynamics of a natural population. On an SSSI their use would require approval from Natural England.

Long grass for visitor management Areas which are principally for visitor management may have wildlife benefits, but this is not their main function. Long grass is used as a visitor management tool for several reasons:

- **To guide visitors** Cutting short grass paths through long grass is an established method of guiding visitors along certain routes. Because grass is a living organism these can be changed by simply mowing a new path and letting the existing grow up (this is easier to achieve if planned in advance).

- **To protect sensitive areas** Leaving grass to grow long discourages visitors from walking over certain areas; this may be beneficial, for example, to areas containing sensitive archaeology.

- **To reduce erosion** This is particularly effective on banks, where long grass discourages visitors (particularly children) from running up and down the slopes. It also reduces the stress on the grass – banks are often drier than level areas, and regular

231. *Orchis morio* in abundance in Marden meadow.

232. A mown grass path through grassland managed as meadow.

cutting can lead to water stress, weakening the grass and making it less able to cope with erosion.

- **To protect visitors** Long grass acts as a visual barrier and can be effective as a safety measure to warn visitors of an obstacle, change of slope or similar. This is a less obtrusive measure than fencing, but a careful risk assessment should be undertaken to inform its use.

Again, much less intensive maintenance should be necessary in these areas; it may be restricted to just cutting and clearing the arisings. If access pathways are cut through, these may require more intensive care, particularly aeration.

As with the previous category, the use of fertilisers or pesticides, or imported grass seed, should be carefully considered. Fertilising long grass areas could lead to a preponderance of coarse grasses, which are visually less attractive. If over-fertilised, they grow quickly then tend to flop over, becoming unsightly, particularly in wet weather.

Long grass for visual effect Areas that contain a diverse mixture of flowering species, artificially created for visual effect, may be regularly enhanced with planting to maintain the diversity. Although not natural, these areas can have a very natural appearance and considerable wildlife benefit.

Similar to the above, these should need much less intensive management, although maintaining and improving sward diversity by planting plugs of different species can be expensive and time-consuming.

Mowing Mowing is necessary to maintain a lawn or grass areas in a defined condition – which may vary from pristine lawn to wildflower meadow. Mowing is simply a management tool that stops natural succession, thus preventing a grass area from becoming, ultimately, a woodland.

Before deciding on a mowing regime it is important to know what the management objectives for any particular area will be, and this is something which should be covered in the site management plan. For some areas of grassland, grazing may be more appropriate than mowing (and more economic) and this form of management is considered below. It may also be appropriate in some areas to have a combination, for example cutting grass in late summer and then grazing over autumn and winter.

Frequency of cutting will vary according to the standard required, the season and the type of season. For example, fine lawns will generally require cutting on a 7-day cycle, but during a warm, wet spring this might need to be reduced to 5 days and during a hot, dry summer it might need to be increased to 10 days. Where sites have their own gardeners or estate staff this is usually easy to achieve, with the head gardener/estate manager making a decision. Where sites are managed by contract it is advisable to use a form of agreement either on a 'per cut' basis with the site manager ordering cuts as necessary, or on a 'performance' basis where a standard is set (e.g. grass must be maintained at 25–50 mm long). The 'per cut' option has the disadvantage that costs are less

233. Differential mowing can be used to direct visitors and create interesting visual effects.

234. Removal of a hay crop is important in order to maintain the low fertility of the meadow.

predictable – in a wet year the number of cuts (and hence the cost) will be greater than in a dry year.

An almost infinite variety of mowers are available from literally dozens of different manufacturers; these are considered in 'Machinery' (page 233).

Arisings The final decision to be made when mowing is whether or not to collect the arisings – an operation that increases costs because the collection takes time (even with box mowers) and the cost of disposal is high. If grass clippings are produced it is invaluable to have a compost heap so that they can be recycled back into the garden. In most cases where long grass areas are cut, it is imperative that the arisings are removed – either to prevent nutrient enrichment (for ecological reasons) or more simply because, if left, the cut grass would form an unsightly mass and kill off the grass beneath. On areas of short grass, it is quite common for arisings to be 'let fly' because they are less likely to form unsightly mats and kill the grass beneath – although when the grass is growing rapidly in spring or during wet weather this may not always be the case. However, leaving arisings can increase long-term costs by increasing the build-up of thatch, encouraging worm activity by providing organic matter and spreading weeds by both seed and vegetative means.

A further consideration is how visitor movements over the site are managed. Damp or wet grass will stick to visitors' feet and gradually drop off as it dries or is brushed against a hard surface. It may be inadvertently spread over pathways or into buildings, requiring additional work to clear up.

Grazing In many more extensive landscape situations, grazing can be an effective, appropriate and cost-effective method of maintaining grassland areas. It is particularly beneficial in areas important for nature conservation:

- There is a net nutrient loss from the system which encourages a diverse sward and inhibits rampant growth by coarse grasses

- Annual plants can be given an opportunity to flower and set seed

- Minor scuffing and damage to the sward surface provides opportunities for seeds to germinate

- A 'patchwork' effect can build up because of different grazing preferences, which provides greater opportunities for a variety of flora and fauna

Other benefits of grazing include:

- Historically appropriate: many large parkland areas have been traditionally grazed by a range of animals

- rights are let commercially. It may require a small outlay to persuade graziers to bring animals to sites, but still represent a saving on the cost of cutting and clearing grass

- Added attraction: visitors may enjoy seeing animals on sites, particularly if these are infrequently seen types or rare breeds

- Logistically the best option: areas that are inaccessible or have steep banks may be difficult to cut with machines or even by hand, but may be easily accessible to certain breeds of sheep or goat.

Disadvantages of grazing:

- Areas need to be fenced, at least with a perimeter fence to prevent animals wandering off the property, and internal fences either permanent or temporary as appropriate

- Supplementary feeding needs to be carefully controlled to prevent erosion in particular areas through overuse

- Animals need to have access to water. If this is natural (lakes, ponds or rivers), damage may occur at regular points of use. If there is no natural water, a trough will be needed and this requires a water source (which may need to be installed); it could become another erosion point

- Most grazing animals will deposit dung at random over the whole grazed area and this may be inappropriate if visitors walk through the area or if events are held there. Horses are an

exception, in that they tend to favour particular areas for dunging, though this needs to be watched to prevent erosion and build-up of weeds because of increased fertility. These problems can be overcome by carefully managing the grazing periods and regular use of a harrow

- Dogs need to be controlled in grazed areas

Wear and tear Increasing numbers of visitors will cause a predictable decline in the quality of grass surface, particularly in shady areas and on grass paths. The first indications are yellowing, caused by damage to the leaf blades, followed by brown and patchy areas with some damage to stems and leaf sheaths. This stage is the absolute limit at which recovery of the existing turf is possible, if the source of wear is removed.

If nothing is done the downward spiral continues with large areas becoming bare, indicating complete loss of stems and leaf sheaths. Partial re-colonisation may occur during off-peak periods but generally only by broad-leaved and annual species with no wear tolerance. As visitor pressure continues, areas of wear spread further and further until the loss of vegetation is complete and only bare earth remains.

In addition to problems caused by feet and the resultant compaction, poor drainage causes similar problems to compaction, particularly if areas are waterlogged for long periods. This can be the result of previously installed drainage systems ceasing to function if the pipes or outlets get blocked up. Areas can also have naturally poor drainage, usually if the soil, or layers within it, contain a high proportion of heavy clay.

- **Move paths** Spreading wear and compaction in a controlled fashion over a wider area gives some areas a complete rest from pressure.

- **Use wear-tolerant grass species** Most established grass areas are a mixture of grasses, either those found naturally at the site or a sown mix originally chosen for its appearance. Many of these mixtures are not naturally tolerant of erosion. Many sports field grasses, particularly ryegrasses, have been especially bred for their ability to tolerate heavy erosion. The wear

235. Although a rectangle of compacted gravel has been placed in front of this sign, it is clearly not big enough.

TURF DAMAGE

Thousands or hundreds of thousands of pairs of feet walking over grass can cause damage in four ways:

- By crushing grass blades, damaging their delicate internal structure, disrupting photosynthesis and possibly causing excessive moisture loss by damaging the external surfaces

- By tearing leaves and stems as the foot 'kicks back' as it is lifted, especially with deeply indented soles

- By smearing mud over the leaf surface during wet weather

- By compaction of the soil, destroying its structure and greatly reducing the amount of air spaces between the particles. This inhibits root respiration, makes physical root growth difficult and interferes with the movement and availability of water in the soil.

characteristics of the sward will be improved by replacing the existing grass with these mixtures, regular overseeding and carrying out repairs with ryegrass cultivars recommended for use on areas of heavy wear in sports fields, such as goal mouths.

The ecological value of the site must be considered – obviously, in an SSSI the introduction of sports grass cultivars might be unacceptable.

- **Use sports field style maintenance** The strategies used to keep intensive sports pitches in good repair can be usefully applied to most grass areas, subject to resources:

  - regular cutting to encourage a low, dense sward

  - regular aeration, using a solid tine spiker, to relieve compaction and improve drainage

  - annual or biannual use of a 'deep penetration spiker' or 'verti-drain' with 300–400 mm penetration: the 'kick-back' action gives major drainage and aeration improvements. Such expensive equipment is usually hired in.

  - regular fertilising in spring and summer with high-nitrogen fertilisers, and in autumn with low-nitrogen, high-phosphorus and potassium fertilisers

  - scarifying to remove any thatch layer, followed by spiking, overseeding and topdressing over the whole area in autumn

  - light harrowing when necessary to disperse any worm casts or similar and to prevent mud from being smeared over the leaf surface

  - pest control when necessary and especially removal of any molehills before these become spread out, covering grass and providing seed beds for weeds

  - weedkilling whenever necessary to remove broad-leaved weeds (which have very low wear tolerance). All the preceding activities should serve to maintain a very dense, healthy sward and prevent weed establishment

  - watering, especially in exposed areas with thin soil which is very susceptible to drying out. Grass recovering from a period of wear particularly needs to be watered during dry spells

- repairing any damage or badly worn areas early

- improving drainage in areas where this is a problem by helping soil structure with the addition of sand or organic matter, and maintaining drainage systems, cleaning and unblocking exits and installing new systems

- using grass reinforcement at pinch-points, to increase wear tolerance or simply to provide a sacrificial layer to prevent erosion becoming worse. Many different types of reinforcement are available that aim to protect the root zone and growing point of the grass. When properly installed, they will increase wearing capacity within certain limits, but they should not be considered the answer to all wear problems since each has a breaking point above which levels of wear will still prevent grass from surviving.

236. A temporary plastic reinforcement net has been placed on the surface of the grass. In this case it has been unsuccessful: the ground was too soft and soon became uneven with the weight of vehicles, and the plastic surface became slippery to both pedestrians and vehicles.

237. Egg-box type grass reinforcement shows how protection of the grass meristems just below the top of the form avoids wear and compaction of the grass plant when compared with the unprotected turf area shown in the lower half of the photograph.

GENERAL PRINCIPLES OF GRASS MANAGEMENT

- Always remember the basic requirements for good grass growth: good soil structure, undamaged roots and leaf blades, and leaf blades not covered by mud

- In areas of high wear, spread the wear wherever possible, giving some areas respite before it becomes serious and carrying out repairs if necessary

- In areas of high wear, consider turf reinforcement, even if only as a sacrificial layer

- Where possible, introduce more wear-tolerant species of grass, such as dwarf ryegrasses, and reduce levels of wear-susceptible grass and broad-leaved species

- Carry out as much intensive sports field type maintenance as possible on susceptible areas

- Where funds are limited, choose the most beneficial maintenance that can be afforded. Spiking, which relives compaction and improves aeration and drainage, is by far the most beneficial operation

- Ensure drainage systems are working properly: poor drainage inhibits root growth and puts grasses under stress.

238. At Garden House, Devon, narrow grass are paths liable to very heavy wear; they are protected with Yorkstone paving sunk to the level of the turf.

239. An event car park under construction at Witley Court. Plastic egg box panels are laid on a level and compacted stone base, before being filled with soil and grass sown. The final level of the soil should be just below the top surface to prevent wear from vehicle wheels to the grass growing point.

240. Inset: detail.

Drainage The ability of soil to retain water is vital for healthy plant growth, but water in the soil is a delicate balancing act – too little water and plants cannot sustain life; too much and the roots cannot respire and quickly die. Natural drainage varies widely, depending on a number of factors:

- **Soil texture** Sandy soils drain quickly and freely; heavy clay soils barely drain at all

- **Soil structure** Well-structured soils with plenty of interconnected air spaces and fissures drain freely, while compacted or badly structured soils drain badly

- **Sub-soil conditions** Where topsoil and subsoil are considerably different, a badly drained sandy soil may be caused by an underlying clay subsoil

- **Water table** The level of groundwater may be influenced by rivers, rainfall, type of bedrock, etc., and may vary throughout the year

There are four main advantages of good drainage:

- The soil warms up faster in spring, promoting good growth

- Soil aeration is improved

- Soil structure is improved, hastening the removal of excess water and promoting healthy root growth

- Areas of use can be extended because damage is less likely

Surface drainage is designed to hasten the removal of excess water from the top 300 mm or so of soil, the principle root zone of the turf. It is particularly important on soils with a high clay content where the natural movement of water through the soil is slow. It is also important for high-use areas where compaction is a problem, because all forms of surface drainage also increase aeration and relieve compaction.

- **Sand slitting** Cutting a series of slits approximately 50 mm wide by 250 mm deep at 500 mm intervals, and backfilling them

SIGNS OF POOR DRAINAGE

- Visible standing water

- Growth of plants associated with bog conditions, such as rushes and sedges

- Ground wet underfoot for a long time after rain or even during dry periods

- Dark grey or blue-blackish discoloration in the soil profile, indicating permanent waterlogging at that level (healthy soils show a uniform brown profile)

- Rust-coloured mottling in the soil profile, indicating periodic waterlogging at that level

- Formation of soil 'pans' (impervious layers)

- Poor soil structure, principally a lack of air spaces

- Poor root growth

with medium-grade sand. Where sub-surface drainage exists, the slits should be cut at right angles to the sub-surface drainage.

- **Verti-draining** A larger, more powerful version of the common spiker, the verti-drain pushes solid tine spikes up to 400 mm vertically into the soil which 'kick back' slightly as they are withdrawn. This double action creates a deep vertical hole with peripheral fracturing, improving drainage, aeration and soil structure.

- **Spiking** This is principally used for aeration (see below), but is included here because it has some surface drainage benefit.

Sub-surface drainage is designed to remove water over a much greater depth of soil, or even to lower the water table over an area.

- **Mole drainage** A fast and simple way of creating drainage, but only suitable for soils with a high percentage of clay. A mole plough is drawn through the soil, creating a cylindrical channel at a set depth and a fissuring effect above. Mole drains have a limited life, but in ideal clay soils this may be more than 10 years. If the soil is not uniform, with pockets of sand, silt or gravel, the mole drain will collapse much sooner.

- **Tile drains** Full-blown drainage systems where a trench is excavated, a drainage pipe laid on the bottom and backfilled with coarse, free-draining material such as gravel to within 150–200 mm of the surface, and topped off with topsoil. A geotextile fabric is often used to separate the gravel and topsoil, to prevent the latter being washed into the former. In some instances, the drainage pipe may also be surrounded by geotextile that allows water to pass through but not soil particles. Drainage pipes were originally made with a triangle of flat clay tile (hence the name), but these were replaced by purpose-made clay pipes which have in turn been superseded by continuous flexible plastic drainage tubes.

  Tile drains need to be laid to a fall; every location requires a carefully planned system to ensure that all areas are equally drained. The main systems are herringbone and fan, but individual areas may require hybrids. Installing tile drainage is an expensive option, but should yield good, long-lasting results. It is worth having the system properly designed by an experienced drainage engineer.

Aeration Good soil aeration is vital for healthy root growth. Poor aeration may be caused by a combination of factors including:

- Build up of thatch, a common cultural problem. During the growing season, a healthy sward produces a mat of mostly dead material at the base of the stems. If this is allowed to build up, it can become almost impervious to water and air. A 'spongy' feel to the grass surface is the likeliest way it gets noticed

- Compaction

- Breakdown of soil structure, caused by constant waterlogging or excessive compaction

Aeration can be improved by:

TINES

- Solid tines, the most commonly used, are simply solid metal spikes approximately 3–5mm in diameter. Solid tine spiking can be carried out regularly, especially in areas liable to compaction, and at any time of year, although in dry periods the tine may not penetrate far into the surface.

- Slit tines are triangular-shaped metal blades which are inserted 75–100 mm into the surface. These aerate and cut roots, encouraging fresh growth, but should not be used in dry periods when the grass is under stress. They cause more surface disturbance than solid tines and should be used only in spring or autumn when encouraging root growth is beneficial.

- Hollow tines, about 10 mm in diameter, remove a small core of soil and turf which is deposited on the surface and can be swept up and removed. The resulting holes improve drainage and aeration and may be left open or, if carried out in conjunction with topdressing, filled with suitable material. Hollow tining should not be carried out more than once or, on heavy soils, twice a year and only in the spring or autumn.

- **Scarification**, only beneficial if there is a thatch layer. On small areas it can be done by hand, by vigorously raking the surface with a spring-tined rake, pulling out all the dead material. For larger areas, self-propelled (even tractor-drawn) machines are available (see 'Machinery', page 233). When using powered scarifiers, great care must be taken not to lower the blades too deep or roots can be torn up. Even at the correct depth, a surprising amount of material will be removed and the grass surface will be left looking quite bare, but it should quickly recover. Scarification should not be carried out more than once a year, except in exceptional circumstances. The ideal time is in autumn.

- **Spiking**, which consists of driving metal tines into the ground through the surface of the grass, usually to a depth of 75–100 mm, but on occasion deeper. It relieves compaction as well as improving aeration. Three main types of metal tine are used (see box, above).

Topdressing has a number of purposes, including:

- **Producing a level surface** A high-quality box-mown lawn requires a very level surface so that it can be cut evenly. Other areas may not need to be perfectly level, but any method of cutting is improved by a good surface and a reasonably level surface reduces the risk of trip hazards

- **Increasing organic matter content** Useful on very sandy soils to improve their capacity to retain water and nutrients.

- **Increasing mineral content** Useful on clay soils to improve drainage by using sharp sand as the top dressing

- **Returning nutrients lost to mowing** Fertiliser can be included with topdressing

241. Above: a pedestrian scarifier will loosen thatch made up of weeds, moss and dead grass, combined with aeration of the rooting medium by solid- or hollow-tine aerators. These operations will enable the grass to withstand better both wear and drought.

242. Right: a tractor-mounted slitter improves surface drainage and aeration by loosening surface compaction.

243. Using true lute to incorporate top dressing.

Topdressings are usually made up from bulky organic or inorganic materials and may be a mixture or both. Sand is widely used, as are (sterilised) soil and loam. Composted and shredded bark or leaf mould may be used to increase water holding on sandy soils.

Topdressing is normally carried out as the last part of autumn renovations, after any operations such as scarifying or spiking. It can, however, be done at any time of year in appropriate conditions – the ground needs to be dry during application, ideally followed by rain (or irrigation). On a small scale, topdressing can be spread by hand and worked in using a 'tru-lute'; on a larger scale, application can be by spreader with the material worked in by tractor-mounted tru-lute or brushes.

Overseeding is the addition of new seed into an existing grass sward. The purpose may be to repair damaged areas without digging up the whole site, to introduce new cultivars (for example, to bolster the sward's wear capabilities) or to thicken it. Unlike initial seeding, where seed is sown on a prepared area with ideal conditions for growth, overseeding introduces seed into an area in which pre-established plants are immediately ready to compete. Because of this, it is often carried out after spiking and scarifying, which provide a number of small bare areas in which the seed can establish, and before topdressing which provides an ideal covering and growth medium.

Brushing, matting, switching are carried out only on fine turf areas. Their sole purpose is to break up any worm casts or to disperse morning dew. Worm casts are unsightly and potentially damaging to mowers by making the surface uneven; they provide a seed bed for weeds and can get smeared across the leaf blades. Morning dew can delay mowing but, more importantly, it provides ideal conditions for the spread of fungal spores.

Harrowing, using chain harrows, is basically an agricultural operation but is of use for large areas of grass (though not normally fine turf). Chain harrows are double-sided with small metal pegs protruding from the chains on one side and flat on the other. Using the flat side, the harrow will disperse dew, worm casts and, to some extent, molehills (provided these are very dry). It will also help to spread out any uneven lumps of material such as topdressing or clumps of cut grass which tend to accumulate if cutting is carried out in the wet. The pegged side has a slight scarifying effect, pulling out thatch and breaking any surface pan.

There is no direct equivalent to a harrow for small areas, but a springbok rake or tru-lute or stiff brush will have a similar effect.

244. Germination and subsequent growth of grass seedlings can be enhanced with the protection of horticultural fleece.

Rolling is rarely ever a solution for turf problems and will usually do more harm than good. It should not be done without very specific reasons. Many misconceptions about rolling arise from its use in the preparation of cricket wickets – which for many people is the highest form of the groundsman's art. However, rolling does not make wickets level – they are level to start with! If un-level areas are rolled they remain un-level, just more compacted. Rollers are used to compact cricket wickets and make them very hard for the specific purpose of the game – the very reverse of what is needed for healthy grass growth. Any groundsman will confirm that at the end of each cricket season a large amount of work is needed to relieve the compaction caused by rolling.

Irrigation Whether to irrigate grass during dry periods is an important question, likely to become more so with global warming. The decision can only be taken on a site-by-site basis. It will be influenced by the availability of water, restrictions placed by the water supplier, restrictions due to cost and the example the manager of the site wishes to set.

On the practical side, it is probably not feasible to water very large areas of grass – a suitable area is determined by water pressure and the availability of staff to move sprinklers unless automatic systems are installed. Watering overnight or in the early morning or late evening is more beneficial and less disruptive for visitors.

Alternative measures to reduce stress on the grass include raising the height of cut, and letting arisings fly to act as a mulch; remember that the latter increases the build-up of thatch and the spread needs to be light and even to prevent patches of grass being damaged.

Pests and diseases

- **Moles** can be a spasmodic problem depending on season, locality, the presence of earthworms (the moles' main diet) and other factors. Trapping is still probably the most successful method of control. Other discouragements include smoke cartridges, electronic devices and spiny objects in the runs. There is a plus side: the soil from mole hills makes very good friable loam for potting composts.

- **Earthworms**, which produce casts, can be regarded as beneficial or a nuisance, depending on the type of turf and its uses. Many garden birds, especially song thrushes, depend on them for their diet, and they can play a valuable part in turf and soil improvement and aeration. However, sports turf managers would wish to remove or control them.

- **Badgers** see Appendices Table 13.

- **Turf diseases** are not usually a problem, but can be serious in high-quality sports turf, in which case specialist advice should be sought.

Weed control Intensively managed turf for precision ball games such as golf and bowling need to consist of monocultures of closely mown grasses for accurate play. Routine in sports turf management regimes would be the control of weeds – including moss – by chemical and physical means.

This treatment may also apply to grass paths and other areas in parks and gardens where there is likely to be wear and tear. For most pleasure lawns and extensive areas of grass, whether to control or tolerate – or even welcome – some weed species is largely a question of aesthetics and will depend very much on the views of the owner or manager (see Case Studies, Part 3).

See the bibliography for a range of information on all aspects of turf and grass management.

WATER FEATURES

Water has played an important part in garden creation from its very beginnings. As one of the life-supporting elements, it has always had an essential place in all communities, and later its many forms and uses became part of the designs of an infinite variety of gardens and landscape parks. These can broadly be seen as two main groups: still or slow-moving water found in natural or man-made lakes and pools or as natural rivers and man-made canals; and moving water such as complex hydraulic devices to power theatrical displays, or fountains, cascades and natural or devised flowing streams. All water features, and more especially those that are man-made, require an understanding of hydrology and in many cases, specialist maintenance and management techniques.

Still or slow-moving water

Quiet pools were often an important feature in Chinese and Japanese gardens, intended for contemplation, reflective surfaces, and also as places for special birds and plants. They were inspired by the grandeur of natural landscapes and scenery, but scaled down into more intimate compositions. A derivation of these, many centuries later and on a much grander scale, were the lakes and river-like areas of water in many eighteenth-century landscape gardens and parks. On a smaller scale, garden pools and ponds, often associated with rockwork, became very popular over the last century or so.

Natural lakes, as in upland areas such as Cumbria, Wales and Scotland, have as their main management aims wildlife conservation, pollution control, recreational uses and the maintenance of water sources and levels.

Man-made reservoirs, in effect lakes of varying extent, design and volume, are found in lowland and upland areas, and are managed by a number of water authorities. There may be similar aspects of management, but pollution and water reserves are key issues, with generally lesser uses for recreation.

Ornamental lakes and similar extensive areas of water, as notable features of many historic gardens and landscapes, are almost always man-made or semi-natural, many being created during the eighteenth-century landscape movement by designers such as Lancelot Brown and Humphry Repton. In most cases, this meant working with the local topography of the site, and installing a dam to hold water from various sources such as springs, a reliable stream or small river or by directing surface water into the lake. The water appears to be still or, in most cases, is slow-moving.

The management of all the above features will be more problematical at times, on account of natural ageing processes and gradual deterioration; many existing features are now over two centuries old (see box, page 188).

245. Opposite: the Cascade at Sheffield Park in Sussex.
246. Below: Lancelot Brown's informal lake and landscape planting at Blenheim Palace.

MAIN MANAGEMENT POINTS

- All reservoirs and their dams which are capable of holding more than 25,000 cubic metres of water above natural ground level fall under the safety regimes of the Reservoirs Act 1975. All such reservoirs coming within the ambit of the Act must be inspected and supervised by appropriate engineers appointed under the Act by the Secretary of State for that purpose. A listing of such engineers and more detailed information may be found on the DEFRA website: www.defra.gov.uk/environment/water/rs.

- The condition of a lake, its margins and dam, and state of repair. Leaks may be an increasing problem and not easy to detect.

- Recurrent dredging, depending upon the situation and degree of silting up (see Sheffield Park Garden Case Study 291). Care is required not to damage the original lining – puddle clay, stone, etc. The safe and legal disposal of dredgings which, depending upon the method used, may be solid or slurrified. Fish and other wildlife must be conserved.

- Marginal or lakeside planting – overhanging trees, loss of visual contrasts.

- Submergent planting – lilies, pond weeds, etc. – may become too dominant and block open water (see also page 191).

- Source of water and sustaining levels in situations where there is increasing local extraction.

- Pollution and wildlife management.

- Structure and level of maintenance of outfalls such as cascades, waterfalls, sluices, etc.

- Recreational uses – health and safety aspects; protective barriers and signage; fishing, boating and bathing.

The care and long-term management of these features can be complex and may involve considerable expense. It is strongly advised that appropriate specialists are called in before any repair or restoration work is undertaken.

247. Ascot Park Skating Pool silted up and overgrown with water lilies.

249. The fate of all lakes is to become silted up and turn water to marsh, then scrub and wood. All lakes will eventually need dredging to reverse this process, the requirement obviously depending on their depth. This is an expensive and, in the short term, a destructive process requiring heavy machinery to remove the silt.

248. Ascot Park Skating Pool drained, following the removal of silt and repairs to the edges.

250. At the Serpentine in Hyde Park, London, protective fencing prevents small children from falling into deep water.

251. A formal pool at Osborne on the Isle of Wight.

252. The six-sided cold bath at Rousham in Oxfordshire, designed by William Kent, is fed by a rill that runs along the centre of the path.

253. Open water in early summer is ideal for the growth of algae. Filamentous algae can become a serious problem, choking other plants and wildlife and looking unattractive when it forms floating green islands on the water's surface. In small formal ponds, it is easily removed with a springbok rake as shown here.

Garden Pools In many instances, where relatively small or medium-sized pools are part of an existing design or a new pool is to be installed this can be handled by the owner and/or garden staff. For reference sources see the bibliography. The main points are included here as a guide.

Formal Pools Quite a few materials can be used in pool construction and installation, but unless a very fashionable feature is part of the plan, more traditional and proven forms of construction and repair are advised.

Concrete is still recommended for the most permanent and trouble-free pool, in association with stone or paved surrounds. Details of the preparation and construction process can be found in many practical books on the subject; this section is more concerned with subsequent maintenance.

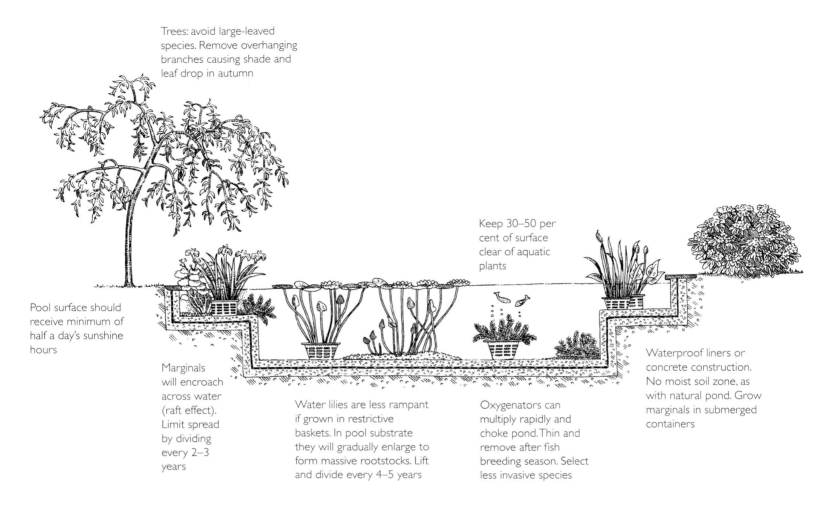

Trees: avoid large-leaved species. Remove overhanging branches causing shade and leaf drop in autumn

Keep 30–50 per cent of surface clear of aquatic plants

Pool surface should receive minimum of half a day's sunshine hours

Marginals will encroach across water (raft effect). Limit spread by dividing every 2–3 years

Water lilies are less rampant if grown in restrictive baskets. In pool substrate they will gradually enlarge to form massive rootstocks. Lift and divide every 4–5 years

Oxygenators can multiply rapidly and choke pond. Thin and remove after fish breeding season. Select less invasive species

Waterproof liners or concrete construction. No moist soil zone, as with natural pond. Grow marginals in submerged containers

254. A formal pool designed to have associated marginal and aquatic planting, with notes indicating maintenance advice. No fountain or sculptural water feature is shown, but if this is to be installed the power supply for a pump (unless the feature is gravity-fed) should be suitably concealed. Remember that water lily flowers are inclined to be spoiled by falling water droplets.

'Natural' Pools Concrete can be used as a longer-term material and laid to create a dished or contoured profile. Gently shelving margins can give a natural effect, but an area of moist soil for marginal planting must be allowed for in the design and construction. Make sure the foundations are sufficient, otherwise remedial work may be necessary later to repair cracks and leaks.

A membrane or liner using heavy-gauge plastic, pvc or butyl rubber is used in many modern pools, and also offers a cost-effective means of repairing leaking concrete constructions. Such liners have a limited life, and can be perforated by accident; use of barrier materials such as 'Terram' can reduce accidental damage and degradation by ultra violet light. PVC tailored membranes can be embedded in a concrete liner to give the advantages of both.

Puddled clay is a traditional water-holding material that was formerly used for pools. It still has possibilities if a supply of the right sort of clay can be found, and the area of the water feature is limited. Dew ponds also had such a clay lining. Problems can occur with clay-lined ponds and lakes when water levels drop – the clay dries out and shrinks, inducing cracking. In some cases the cracks may need to be filled and the dried clay moistened and repuddled in order to reinstate a watertight surface. Care should be taken not to remove the waterproof clay liner when dredging to remove silt.

Pool maintenance guidelines As the drawings and illustrations on these pages show, constructed garden pools have variations in their design and cross-sections, from steeper walls to more shelving margins. General points of management and good pond-keeping, however, apply to all types to keep them in good health and appearance.

- **Shade** As a rough guide, not more than 25 per cent of the pool area should be shaded or overhung by branches. In autumn, leaves in the water can be reduced by stretching a layer of fine netting across the surface to catch the bulk of them.

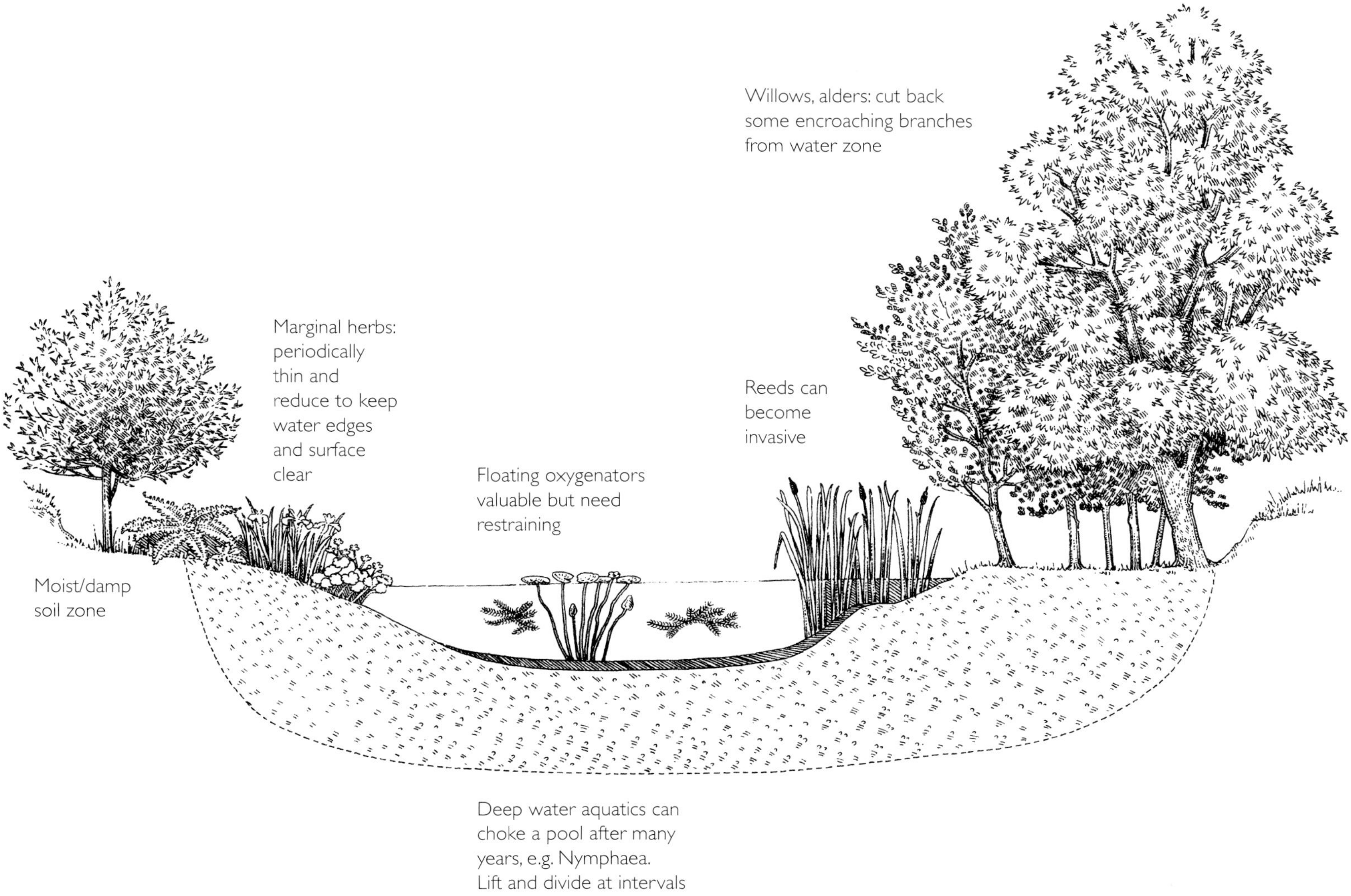

Willows, alders: cut back
some encroaching branches
from water zone

Marginal herbs:
periodically
thin and
reduce to keep
water edges
and surface
clear

Reeds can
become
invasive

Floating oxygenators
valuable but need
restraining

Moist/damp
soil zone

Deep water aquatics can
choke a pool after many
years, e.g. Nymphaea.
Lift and divide at intervals

255. A 'natural' pool, with some maintenance notes.

- **Roots** Trees such as willows and poplars should not be too close, since their invasive roots can damage or displace pool linings.

- **Control of plant growth** A balance should be maintained of clear water areas and marginal or floating plants. Try to keep 30–50 per cent of the water surface clear of plants, to encourage fish (if present) and reflections. Hand-pulling or cutting plants can, for a time, prevent excessive choking from oxygenating and marginal vegetation; depending upon the depth of the pool and how it has been maintained, every three or four years a fairly major clearance is usually necessary.

   The timing of this operation can be critical if wildlife is to be conserved or encouraged: although there may be a case for a clear out in early spring, this is the time when frogs, newts and fish are breeding and dragonfly nymphs and other aquatic creatures are developing. Also the water can be quite cold! So a recommended time is September, when most of the pool inhabitants have completed one stage of their life cycle, water lilies and other flowering aquatics are over, and the water is often warmer for putting in your hands among the plants. The tougher rootstock types such as water lilies, bulrushes and irises will need lifting out, dividing and then, if necessary, replanting with healthy divisions. Clearing operations should not be too zealous – some submerged plants should be left for young fish and other creatures. Vigorous alien aquatic weeds such as *Crassula helmsii* and *Myriophyllum aquaticum* are now becoming widespread and must be controlled.

   Avoid the use of aquatic herbicides if possible. Even those in present use may be withdrawn for health and safety reasons in the future.

- **Clarity** Cloudiness and murky green conditions in water are frequently a problem, and may be due to a number of complex

256. The fountains designed by Paxton for his Crystal Palace Park brought the glories of royal formal gardens to the ordinary people of south London.

causes. Green, opaque water is due to masses of single-celled algae that thrive on mineral salts. This may be a temporary problem, since the right balance of plants and animal life, including snails, absorb the algae. Such a balance usually happens in pools of a fair size, but very small ponds can remain obstinately murky. Chemical clearing agents are available from specialist aquatic suppliers, and some of these are acceptable to organic gardeners.

Moving water

The animation, sparkle and sound of moving water have appealed to garden-makers since ancient times, especially in Middle Eastern and Mediterranean climates. Some 2,000 years ago, Roman villa gardens featured a range of water devices; Pliny the Younger's Tuscan garden had a multitude of fountains and water works. The Renaissance gardens of Italy and the Moorish gardens of Spain combined moving water with formal canals and tanks. In the seventeenth and eighteenth centuries, the great Baroque gardens of Europe, notably Le Nôtre's creations at Vaux Le Vicomte and Versailles, had a fantastic array of hydraulic devices to please and entertain, such as fountains, cascades, waterfalls, jets ('aqua giocchi'), rills and artificial streams. Owners of great historic

places in England were inspired to create similar features. Many have long vanished, abandoned because of the high costs of installation and repair, the need for constant maintenance and problems of water supply. But some survive, such as the cascade and fountains at Chatsworth and The Long Water at Hampton Court Palace (see Case Studies 3.2 and 3.5). Maintaining the water supply, however, is becoming an increasing problem with some of the famous features in Italian gardens, and at these and places such as Versailles the water displays may be restricted to certain days. Water in both contemporary and traditional designs continues to be a popular attraction in many gardens and parks today.

Restoration, reconstruction and maintenance guidelines

- Archive research, site surveys and archaeological investigations can be revealing and successful where few traces of water features remain on the ground.

- Canals suffer from deterioration or collapse of the walls, and tend to silt up. The original water supply may have been intercepted or no longer exist, and leaks are common.

- Fountains and basins, in particular, may be listed if they are in important historic sites; if in poor condition, they will require specialists to undertake repairs. These can be costly, and grants may be available (see 'Grant aid & funding bodies', page 358).

- Reliable water supply is essential, whether as a running source from a continuous stream or header reservoir, or for topping up where water is recycled by pumps in fountains and cascades.

- Original sources of water may be reduced or severely restricted with the increasing use of water for industrial and domestic purposes. This is a growing problem with some famous water features in Italian gardens, while at Versailles the water supply for the fountains (always problematic) is now restricted to Sundays only for the full display.

- Health and safety issues cause concern for many managers and owners of sites open to the public (see 'Occupiers' liability', page 74). Assessment should be undertaken to gauge the potential risk of harm to visitors from infected or polluted water in fountains and basins. Appropriate guidance and warning of potential hazards are essential to prevent accidents.

- Water conservation is an increasing matter for all those involved in land management; there is likely to be increasing control of water use and abstraction. Questions may eventually be raised on the ethics of irrigation in gardens.

ROCK GARDENS

Rocks in one form or another have a long tradition in the evolution of historic gardens, although the fashion for constructing larger 'rock gardens' really dates from the mid-nineteenth century. The emphasis in this section is on the management and maintenance of these. Many were introduced during the era of great garden expansion and development in the late nineteenth and early twentieth centuries (see Graham Stuart Thomas, *The Rock Garden and its Plants*, 2006).

Structural rock work

The use of natural stone, often in fantastic and symbolic forms, can be traced back to the great dynastic gardens of China in the second century BC. In the later Imperial gardens of Japan, selected rocks and stones were carefully sited along with a strictly limited repertoire of plants. Grottoes also had a long history in the more classical European gardens; they were largely of stone construction, with fantasy and allegory playing an important part.

257. Over a number of generations during the Victorian and Edwardian period, Pulham and Co. designed and built impressive rock features. When natural stone of the right size or quantity was not available, they developed an artificial stone called Pulhamite which enabled them to create dramatic structures such as this one at Bristol Botanic Gardens.

258. The Grotto Island at Painshill Park can be approached by boat or by foot over the Chinese Bridge.

259. The dramatic scale of the rock garden at Cragside in Northumberland, although artificial, looks completely natural. It is now planted with low-maintenance ground-covering ericaceous plants.

The 'picturesque 'and 'sublime' movements of eighteenth- and early nineteenth-century landscape gardens aimed at improving on 'awesome nature' with great outcrops of local stone for spectacular and scenic effects, with plants usually playing a subordinate role. Such creations were also introduced in some of the great country house gardens, and in public urban parks. Joseph Paxton introduced massive rock outcrops at Chatsworth (see Case Study, page 253), Birkenhead Park and the Crystal Palace. Many other examples survive today, since they were solidly and durably constructed.

The rock garden movement

This section concentrates on features, often very large-scale, which aimed to recreate 'natural' alpine or rocky landscapes by the skilful combination of selected stone and the bold planting of alpine and rock plants. The rock garden movement was given a stimulating boost by the lively writings of Reginald Farrer (*The English Rock Garden*, 1948). He had a good first-hand knowledge of the newly fashionable alpine plants as a collector, and experimented with building such gardens in the limestone hills of his native Lancashire.

Some botanic gardens also led the way. The rock garden at Kew, using Cheddar limestone, was begun in 1882 with a gift of over 2,500 alpine plants; it has been remodelled several times since. The rock garden at the Cambridge University Botanic Garden was built between 1911 and 1920 using Oxfordshire sandstone.

Many leading landscape companies built prodigious extravaganzas for private individuals, especially between 1900 and 1939. One pioneering firm, James Backhouse of York, was very early on the scene. In the early 1880s they built an alpine garden on a grand scale for Ellen Willmott at Warley Place in Essex, some of which survives today. In 1892 they put up a rock garden of 250 tons of millstone grit at the Birmingham Botanic Gardens. In one of their most ambitious efforts, for Sir Frank Crisp at Friar Park, Henley-on-Thames, they used 7,000 tons of Yorkshire limestone with an imitation Matterhorn of shining quartz.

Another pioneering firm was founded by James Pulham, who began building rock work and rock gardens in the 1820s, specialising at first in 'ferneries' (see page 198). The firm invented a synthetic stone, made to a secret formula – named Pulhamite, it had a remarkably natural appearance with fissures and crevices. It was used in rock work in many parts of the country, including the

260. The quarrying of stone for the new house at Belsay created a canyon leading to the old castle, creating the ideal environment for the exotic plants being collected from the Himalayas in the latter half of the nineteenth and early part of the twentieth centuries.

first main phase of the rock garden at the RHS Garden at Wisley, and at Sheffield Park (see Case Study, page 291). It proved durable and quite resistant to water and weather. The firm finally closed in 1939.

Rockeries, scree gardens and dry stone walls

These and other stone and rock features are often used in gardens, composed of stone of various sources and sizes together with suitable (or sometime unsuitable) planting. They tended to become features in the smaller-scale garden designs of the last century. If sited and constructed well, they can be very attractive and offer much scope for many plants in the alpine and rock plant group. They are often on a smaller and more intimate and domestic scale than rock gardens, and their construction and maintenance is well documented in gardening literature (especially Farrer, *The English Rock Garden*).

Restoration, conservation and maintenance

Graham Thomas observes that rock gardens could be considered the newest art form in the long history of gardening. To be successful they combine an understanding of science (geology, soils and special plants) with the visual effects and artistry of siting, construction and design. Rock gardens contain few historic layers, many being additions to large and historic gardens as a response to fashion.

In the early part of the last century there was a 'Japanese' craze, and so-called Japanese gardens got curiously mixed up with Farrer's style of natural rock gardening. This resulted in some vast but hybrid creations in a kind of Anglo-Japanese style, with the more obvious elements of Japanese gardens – lanterns, stepping-stone paths, streams, bridges, possibly a tea house, clipped or trained evergreens – blended or mixed incongruously with English-style rock and alpine gardens. Many owners caught up in this movement had to find a suitable location, which was not always easy. Even with no real limit on space or site, to fit a very different art form into the more accepted and understood features of a garden or park presented difficulties. Some rock gardens were given remote and 'secret' sites in the wilder parts of the grounds, containing an element of surprise and exploration; others were added as extensions to existing 'picturesque' features, such as grottoes, cascades and alien rock outcrops. Most were high-maintenance as regards planting and weed control, and owners who were really keen alpine plant enthusiasts trained garden staff to spend many hours among great collections of specialist plants.

The decline and neglect of so many fine rock gardens has been sad and perhaps inevitable, and the reasons are not far to trace. Rock gardens were not usually on the priority list of maintenance schedules; many, out of sight and out of mind, simply became abandoned. They needed specialist attention, knowledge and plant skills to remain effective. In many cases, bold rock formations are all that can be rediscovered, the original alpine plants of a century or more ago having long disappeared or been engulfed by scrub and brambles; slow-growing shrubs and conifers are often the only survivors. Such neglect is deplored by G. S. Thomas (*The Rock Garden*), who makes a strong case for salvation and restoration:

261. A raised bed offering dry-stone wall habitats as well as a free-draining surface for many different plants.

262. Old glazed or stone sinks are frequently used to grow compact alpine or rock garden plants.

263. A small rock garden showing restrained use of stones. Siting and careful choice of plants will also determine the success or failure of a rock garden.

264. The great craze for rock gardens in the 1920s and '30s was fuelled by the writing of Reginald Farrer and the great rock bank exhibits at the Chelsea Flower Show. Although they are presently unfashionable, specialist companies keep up the tradition at the show.

'There is no doubt that we have watched the flowering and the fading of this unique, English, garden art without raising a finger to arrest its downward progress. And not only are we losing the great naturally inspired creations of beautiful rock, but also those incredible masterpieces by Messrs Pulham. Together they are as much period pieces as any other art form. Like buildings, they have to be tended and restored on the spot: one cannot take a rock garden to an expert to be restored in a workshop . . . and yet I suggest that only the application of normal expertise is needed to save these garden masterpieces . . . but what it all rests upon, of course, is the amount of work (and the cost) involved in restoration and maintenance.'

Restoration of a large rock garden

- **Site survey and archive research** Check for evidence of any important builder such as Pulham or Backhouse, or more recent creations by Gavin Jones and others (rock gardens were once regular features at the Chelsea Flower Show).

- **Reasons for and feasibility of restoration** Important decisions may involve possible repair and rebuilding costs and subsequent aftercare.

- **Site works** This may be a major exercise, especially if the period of neglect has been long enough to allow scrub and seedling trees to take over. In most cases, real alpines and rock plants will have gone long ago, and weeds such as ground elder, bindweed, couch grass and horsetail may have become dominant. Some survivors may be worth retaining, such as unusual or veteran dwarf trees, shrubs and conifers. Such plants need to be protected or marked and, where possible, a means of propagation should be sought.

The stumps and roots of unwanted trees should be dug or winched out, which may cause some disturbance. All other scrub and weed growth should be cut back when convenient with hand tools or a brush cutter. Where there is a serious weed population, particularly of deep-rooted and matted perennial types such as ground elder, the whole area may need to be kept fallow for up to a year and persistent weeds treated with a translocated weed killer as soon as growth is under way, which may be spring or early summer. It will often be necessary to repeat this when any re-growth appears. Pay particular attention to directing weedkiller among rocks and stone steps or paths, where the perennials will be lurking.

PLANTS FOR ROCK GARDENS

- **Alpine plants** are usually described as coming from the true high alpine or mountainous regions of the world, many adapted to the extreme conditions in these places. Their exposed habitats, with naturally stony and free-draining soils, and dislike of waterlogged conditions around the roots are a guide to the rather specialised care they require in a constructed rock garden. Pockets of well-drained gravel or a scree-type feature can be successful.

- **Rock plants** cover a more general group of plants that also favour dry stony places at varying altitudes, and they are usually more adaptable and maintenance-free in cultivation. There are also a number of delightful small bulbous species, usually in scale and at home in rock garden conditions.

- **Dwarf shrubs and conifers** may not necessarily be alpine in origin, but their slow-growing and often spreading habit make many of them suitable for rock garden planting. Many are relatively maintenance-free. They can give scale and structure to match the rockwork, but it is wise to check their true habits. The terms 'dwarf' and 'slow-growing' are not always reliable or predictable – some 'dwarf' conifers can exceed 3-4 metres in height in a matter of a few years.

- **Rocks, stone and water features** After spraying and weed elimination, the site should be free of unwanted vegetation and the rock features revealed. Some reconstruction and repairs may be needed: repositioning dislodged rocks, repairs to steps and paths and, if there is a legacy of cascades, to pools and water courses. Decisions will be required on whether to restore such systems in part or entirely, or whether to keep them as dry features. Much depends here on cost, future upkeep, use and a reliable water supply. Don't forget the health and safety factor if a rock garden is to be accessible to the public.

- **Planting** Whatever the range and character of the planting, the rocks should be the dominant feature, not buried or hiding behind luxuriant vegetation. Future maintenance will be a critical factor. Historical guidelines may be followed from that trio of alpine enthusiasts Farrer, Robinson and Jekyll, whose advice is still fresh and applicable over a century on.

    Before any planting, and if time allows, it is wise to leave the site fallow for one growing season to ensure that perennial weeds have been eradicated – partially killed weeds, whose roots were well established among rocks and stones, will soon take over again.

    The next stage is to fork over all the pockets and areas between the rocks that are to be planted, removing dead roots, debris and any persistent weeds. Follow this by adding a 75mm (3in) layer of gritty compost, more if much of the original soil has been lost. If the site is very impoverished, include a slow-release fertiliser in the compost.

    Bearing future upkeep in mind, plant boldly, realistically and compatibly with the situation and the site. A more natural effect from cushions, hummocks and sheets of low shrubs, conifers and alpine and rock plants can be achieved by being fairly restrained at the selection stage, and planting in groups and patches. Specialised pockets can always be used if the collecting bug becomes irresistible (there is a huge and fascinating range of plants to choose from), but this depends on the scale and extent of the rock garden, and its essential aftercare.

General maintenance of alpines and rock plants

Since these groups may include dwarf shrubs, conifers, evergreen or deciduous perennials, cushion-forming plants and bulbs, no real blueprint can be formulated for their maintenance. The real answers lie in the site, the habitat, the construction and the plant selection being right in the first place. Regular hand-weeding, frequent in the first years, with the prompt removal of any perennial weeds is important. A mulch or top dressing of grit or chippings will help drainage and reduce weed invasions. The more invasive, spreading types must have their growth curbed; others must be routinely clipped after flowering. Casualties or ageing specimens should be removed. Slugs and snails may be a nuisance, but the grit and gravel should deter them. Any heavy leaf fall in the autumn should be removed.

265. Although many rock and alpine plants will effectively cover the ground, they are high-maintenance garden features needing very regular and 'informed' weeding. Unwanted plants must be removed at the seedling stage before they can affect the growth of the alpine plants which are unable to compete with more vigorous species.

266. The fernery rock garden at Brodsworth is an early, rather unnatural, form of rock garden where rocks are placed to make terraced planting pockets for plants (see Case Study, page 249).

FERNERIES

Popular in the nineteenth century, these were usually sited in naturally moist and shaded places, sometimes as part of the main rock garden or more often as a cool, quiet place for meditation. They usually featured various assemblages of rocks, and a natural style of planting of ferns and associated shade-loving plants.

Restoration procedures will depend upon the location, the feature itself and the extent of the neglect. It may be necessary to let in more light, if overhanging branches and encroaching shrub growth are dominating the site, and there may be a similar problem with weeds and scrub as for rock gardens.

After clearance, any new soil or compost to be added should be more leafy or contain a peat-substitute material. Ferns are becoming very popular again, and most prefer a cool, leafy, growing medium. They could be blended with woodland planting, including bulbs. Future maintenance can be reasonably low, provided the original preparation and weed control is thoroughly done.

267. Formal topiary in a reconstructed knot garden at Hatfield House.

PARTERRES, KNOT GARDENS, MAZES AND LABYRINTHS, TOPIARY

In the late sixteenth and early seventeenth centuries there were two main types of formal ornamental gardens: the parterre, extensive beds and squares in a geometric layout; and the knot garden, usually smaller and comprising a more intimate interwoven pattern of evergreens and herbs.

Parterres

The parterre has been attributed to the French royal gardener Claude Mollet, who devised what he called a 'Parterre de Broderie', with box popular as the evergreen division between the formal designs. Flowers, herbs, sands and gravels became typical components of these French parterres.

The word parterre literally means 'on' or 'along' the ground, and it came to mean a formal section of the garden which was best appreciated from a more elevated position, in particular from the house, which was often a royal palace (see Hampton Court Case Study, page 271). The main view was from a central grand room on the first floor, from which there would be a commanding and spectacular outlook over the parterre. Parterres were highly formal, geometric in plan, and essentially part of a unified design of house and garden. Classic examples are André Le Nôtre's great design at Vaux Le Vicomte near Paris, Schönbrunn Palace in Vienna, and Hampton Court Palace Privy Garden in London. They were often on a grand scale to match the size of the house or palace, and their success and impact depended on this fact. The house was the symbol of authority, and the associated parterre was seen as the mastery of man over nature. They were by definition labour-intensive and demanded high levels of maintenance.

In England, where close-mown lawns and turf were a feature of seventeenth- and early eighteenth-century gardens, the use of grass as the main feature, shaped and cut to various patterns ('gazon coupé'), became a very specific characteristic. Other features were clipped and shaped evergreens – box, yew and holly – and borders for flowers, 'plates-bandes'. Access paths and walks were of raked gravel. Statuary, urns and vases provided structural ornamentation, and formal water features such as fountains were popular. Raised walks around the parterre gave prospects across the garden, and also views out into the surrounding park or landscape; shaded arbours and walks added to comfort.

Restoration and management Parterres call for the highest standards of upkeep. Being sited front of stage, so to speak, they will be constantly observed and criticised. The input and skills a parterre will require depend greatly on its design, style and intricacy. Techniques can be developed for keeping topiary, clipped shrubs and hedges to the right shape and size (see Hampton Court Case Study, page 271); and complex cut grass scrolls and the like can be given a permanent edging strip. The routine raking of sand or gravel, and the general care of planting, however, are all hand work and cannot be neglected.

269. Wartime neglect and damage from heavy snow led to the formal double yew hedge framing the herbaceous border at Walmer Castle, Kent, evolving into the present 'cloud' hedge.

268. Oposite: planting in 'plates bandes' forms part of the reconstruction of the large 'parterre de broderie' created originally for King William and Queen Mary at Hampton Court (see Case Study, page 271).

Before a start is made, a schedule of operations should be drawn up in consultation with garden staff. Annual applications of slow-release fertilisers, combined with a mulching programme, should maintain nutrient levels. An automatic irrigation system, although expensive to install, will save time and labour costs when compared with hand-watering.

On completion, a detailed maintenance plan should be prepared covering an agreed period of time, linked to the CMP for the whole site.

Pests and diseases These are not normally a problem, but the recent incidence of box blight has been serious in some places. Where alternatives to box are required as replacements, *Lonicera nitida* and *Ilex crenata* have been used with varying degrees of success. (See also under Pests and Diseases.)

Knot gardens

Knot gardens became popular in Tudor and Elizabethan gardens, but their origins go back much earlier to Celtic and Roman designs. The true 'knot' is a figure of continuous interlacing patterns, expressing an unchanging or endless state, infinity. They were often planted with herbs and flowers, along with coloured sands and gravels. They are similar in many respects to parterres, but on a smaller and more intimate scale. Patterns and designs can be authentic and historic to match the period and style of the garden or house in question, or more contemporary if there are no historic constraints (there is an abundance of reference literature). Dwarf box is usually chosen for the structural planting of hedges and topiary features; the patterns and spaces can be infilled with low planting, or coloured sands, gravels and other inert materials. Maintenance needs to be impeccable.

270. Topiary fox hunt at Knightshayes Court, Devon.

271. Topiary fighting cocks created by Nathaniel Lloyd at Great Dixter, East Sussex.

272. Below: the intricate box knot garden in the garden of the Tradescant Trust in Lambeth, London.

273. The maze or labyrinth at Glendurgan, Cornwall, planted on one side of a narrow valley, can be enjoyed for its architectural form from the other side of the valley.

Mazes and labyrinths

Like knots, these are currently being revived to an almost obsessive degree, from the hedged mazes in historic gardens to ephemeral and often ingenious designs in agricultural maize fields. Their origin goes back thousands of years to the labyrinths of Egypt and Crete. Hedged mazes became common in the elaborate formal gardens of Europe in the sixteenth and seventeenth centuries – the first still survives at Hampton Court. For the management of hedges in historic mazes, see pages 152-8).

Topiary

Topiary may be defined as the art of shaping trees and shrubs by clipping and training. Most of these are woody evergreens.

It is an ancient art that has responded to many changing fashions in garden evolution and design. In the Roman period, the word *toparius* was used to describe some ornamental gardens in which *toparii*, gardeners skilled in this art, were employed. Pliny the Younger (AD 61–113) describes all manner of works in topiary at his Tuscan villa, using box clipped into innumerable shapes.

In the Tudor and Elizabethan periods, topiary was often associated with knots on a more intimate scale as favoured by the Dutch, but the art became more complex and grander in scale in Italian and French parterre gardens of the seventeenth century. Many royal and aristocratic seats also had elaborate parterres,

using box, yew and holly for topiary forms in the latest fashion. The Privy Garden at Hampton Court is a fine example (see Case Study, page 271). Then came the inevitable movement away from what came to be seen as artificiality – 'the marks of the scissors upon every plant and bush,' as Joseph Addison commented in the *Spectator* – towards the more natural styles of eighteenth-century English landscape gardens. Levens Hall was one of the few examples where such change was resisted (see Case Study, page 279). Topiary came back into fashion in the nineteenth century, with the Victorians' love of highly furnished gardens. The art has been a feature of many English gardens to the present day.

The maintenance of topiary features is similar to that of hedges (see pages 152-8). Regular careful trimming and clipping, usually with hand shears, should be matched by a regular slow-release fertiliser application often best mixed with a mulch in late winter or early spring.

Slower- and denser-growing evergreens make the best and crispest topiary, such as box, yew and holly. Shaping and training are an art, best carried out with patience and perhaps the help of wire or cane structures as templates. Old or over-mature specimens can often be revitalised and re-shaped by hard cutting back and a good feed.

Box Blight disease is probably the most serious problem, more likely in damper, shaded situations.

WALLED KITCHEN GARDENS

The walled garden in its Victorian heyday was very much the territory of the head gardener and his staff: not only the family but the whole household depended upon their skills to keep the kitchens supplied with fresh fruit and vegetables. When the family was in London, it was not uncommon for daily supplies from the country estate to be sent up to the kitchen of the town house. The scale of the productive garden was in keeping with the size and wealth of the household. A gentleman farmer may have had an acre of walled garden and employed one full-time gardener; a member of the gentry may have had five acres, with frame yards, hot beds, hot walls and glasshouses capable of producing a wide range of produce, some exotic. The extent of a walled garden could be eight acres for minor aristocrats, and over fourteen acres for great aristocrats and magnates.

From the late eighteenth century, productive walled gardens were usually laid to a fairly standard plan – rectangular, with the longest wall running from east to west to provide maximum space for the warmest north wall which was used for apricots, peaches and nectarines. The wealthy installed glasshouses to force these fruit, as well as to cultivate exotics such as pineapples and vines (see page 210).

Walls were rarely less than 12ft high and often 17ft. The inside was frequently brick, as this was thought to retain heat best and provide better opportunities for training fruit. Branches were secured to nails in the wall with pieces of rag or knotted willow stems; by the mid-nineteenth century, nails had been replaced with horizontal tensioned wires placed 6in or 12in apart. The coping usually protruded from the wall to protect the fruit from rain, which can blemish it and introduce fungal diseases. Hooks or angle irons at the top of the wall enabled the attachment of glazed frames for forcing, matting to protect from frost and netting to keep birds away from the fruit. The east and west walls were used for the less precocious fruits, such as apples, pears, plums, cherries, damsons and greengages. The coldest and shadiest southern wall was used for Morello cherries, filberts and currants.

The garden was divided into four equal blocks by two main hoggin or gravel paths. The formal path, often through the south wall, was lined with a narrow border planted with blocks of flowers for cutting, backed by espalier-grown fruit trees on a framework and, at the end of the vista, a small pavilion, covered seating place or glasshouse. In some gardens, where the two main paths crossed a focal point was provided in the form of a dipping pool, ornamental well or arbour. A narrow bed, usually equal in width to the height of the wall, was managed for the wall-trained fruit. In front of permanent crops such as artichokes, sea kale, asparagus, rhubarb, strawberries and raspberries, blocks of herbs

274. Crops grown in rows make for easier hoeing.

WALLED KITCHEN GARDENS: ARE THEY WORTH IT?

It is easy to get carried away with the romantic notion of a restored, productive, walled kitchen garden. However, this is an expensive undertaking and should not be considered lightly.

- Can it be financed from existing income, and are the attractions of a productive garden and fresh produce worth the cost? What will be done with any spare produce?

- What is the existing cost of maintaining the garden in an unproductive state?

- If a garden is open to the paying public, estimate the value, in increased visitors, that a restored productive garden will add.

- Factor in the costs of harvesting, which is time-consuming but may be undertaken with the aid of volunteers.

- Produce a cropping plan, remembering that it will take a number of years for fruit to reach full cropping and two years to gain full organic status from the Soil Association so it is best to calculate this over three to five years. Calculate the full costs: salaries for gardeners (and pickers if required); equipment (tractor and trailer, irrigation, tools, their replacement and repair); fuel for heating if there is a glasshouse; composts, fertilisers, pesticides etc. Work out how much produce will be available each year and calculate the income it will bring from sales to restaurants, visitors or wholesalers.

or small batches of salad catch crops such as lettuces, carrots or radishes were raised. The four main beds were managed to provide a continuous supply of staple vegetables on a three- or four-year rotation plan (see box, page 206).

A further enclosure was often created behind the north wall, to enclose back sheds against the wall and a frame yard which may also have had hot beds and glasshouses (called 'pit houses') sunk into the ground. In large establishments the back sheds could be quite extensive, providing accommodation for tool, potting and store sheds as well as a boiler room, forcing house, head gardener's office – and the apprentices' living quarters, conveniently next to the boiler room for late-night stoking.

Fruit and vegetables

Cultivating fruit and vegetables in a historic walled garden is unlikely to be cost-effective for the produce alone, but a well maintained kitchen garden can be a considerable attraction for a historic site open to the public, and fresh fruit and vegetables can be sold directly to visitors, through a restaurant or, less profitably, to a wholesaler. It is worth growing historic varieties both to aid their conservation and to provide an interesting range. It is best to grow crops that are difficult or expensive to buy in shops, as these will have a premium. For example, 20 sq m of Pink Fir Apple potatoes will be worth much more than a common variety such as Desirée or King Edward. Many gardens now produce organic vegetables, which appeal to an increasing market and can bring in higher prices, although the advantage is lessening due to supermarket imports from countries with cheaper labour.

A conflict can sometimes arise when a walled kitchen garden is required both to be attractive for visitors and to produce a maximum amount of crops for sale. As soon as the rows or blocks of vegetables have reached maturity and look their best ornamentally, they are harvested. Different gardens manage this in different ways. The Model Vegetable Garden at Wisley grows its vegetables purely for show: crops are harvested when they are past their best, then composted. At Audley End, each crop is harvested for sale when it reaches maturity, but a wide range of fruit and vegetables and cultivars maturing at different rates mean there is always plenty for visitors to see.

Microclimate The walled garden, designed to accentuate the effects of microclimate, is discussed in 2.1 (page 92). North-facing walls will generally be much cooler than those facing south. East-facing walls, receiving less sun in the afternoon, cool rapidly overnight but warm quickly in the morning, producing big temperature gradients and consequent frost damage. West-facing walls, receiving sun in the afternoon, cool slowly overnight and do not exhibit the same extremes of temperature as east-facing walls. The main factors to consider are dry soils against south-facing walls, and the probable need for more irrigation there. Species and cultivars with frost susceptibility are likely to be less successful against east-facing walls.

Soil The original nature of the soil is likely to have been considerably altered in an established walled garden. Organic matter content will generally be raised by years of crop production, improving both fertility and water-holding capacity. However, even crop rotation will not necessarily lead to the perfect soil conditions for each crop. Particularly when setting up a new project, soil analysis should be carried out, sampling areas that are obviously distinct. Carefully dig trial pits adjacent to the walls to establish soil depth and nature. Sample separately there, particularly if high soil pH is suspected due to the washing-down effects of lime mortar.

Site facilities Manures and mulches can reduce the need for irrigation, but all crops are likely to need irrigation at certain periods. At an early stage of the project, establish an adequate mains supply and storage facilities which do not compromise the integrity of a historic site. Access points and path widths should be considered in relation to the use of modern machinery and the movement of irrigation equipment. Can machinery get through gates and move along paths? What are the options for providing service roads to gates, or for modifying gate widths and paths?

Crop rotation The main idea is to rotate the crops around the walled garden, to provide optimum nutrition for each group and reduce pest and disease problems, by breaking the life cycle of damaging organisms. Vegetable crops fit into three main groups:

- **Legumes** (peas and beans) have nitrogen-fixing nodules in the soil that enrich it at the end of the season when the roots are left in situ

FOUR-PLOT, FOUR-YEAR CROP ROTATION
used at Audley End by Mike Thurlow HDRA

	Year 1	Year 2	Year 3	Year 4
Plot 1	Root crops	Potatoes	Legumes	Brassicas
Plot 2	Brassicas	Root crops	Potatoes	Legumes
Plot 3	Legumes	Brassicas	Root crops	Potatoes
Plot 4	Potatoes	Legumes	Brassicas	Root crops

The potatoes are useful in improving soil structure. Other rotation permutations can be considered: three plots could be used for crops, for example, and the fourth sown with rye grasses to improve soil structure or clover to improve fertility.

- **Brassicas** (cabbages, cauliflowers) are hungry feeders and follow legumes
- **Root crops** (beetroot, carrots and parsnips) are generally moderate feeders and follow brassicas

Salad crops do not consitute a main group, but are fitted into the rotation depending on their season of use. Trained fruit trees will fit into the rotation if grown on wires near to the path margins. Raspberries and currants grown as row-trained and free-standing plants will have a life of six years or more and are best located with perennial vegetables such as artichokes and asparagus. Strawberries with up to three years of cropping should also be located in this rotation, adjacent to the warm south walls of glasshouses, or in pots and beds under glass.

Harvesting and storage The planned use of the produce must be considered at the outset to determine the cropping pattern. Many crops, such as lettuce, have a short window of harvesting. In hot weather, soft leafy crops and soft fruits should be harvested as early in the day as possible and the produce moved to a cool place, ideally cool storage or cabinets. Natural storage of apples and pears is possible, usually in a dry sunken pit building with shelving. Storing root crops in clamps is a traditional technique, needing few resources.

Fruit

- **Long-lived**
  Top fruits (tree fruits with pips), such as apples, pears, quinces and medlars.
  Stone fruits, such as plums, apricots, peaches, nectarines, cherries and almonds.
  Figs and grape vines. These can live well beyond fifty years in established gardens. Grapes planted for quality dessert fruit in the eighteenth and nineteenth centuries under south-facing vineries still survive.
  These crops are planted either against walls, free-standing in separate areas from vegetables and flowers, or adjacent to paths.
- **Shorter-term** Cane fruits, such as raspberries, blackberries and loganberries; currants and strawberries.

Selection of stock A number of nurseries specialise in producing a wide range of historic varieties, with a great variety of shape, colour, cropping dates and yields. Stock should be purchased from known reputable nurserymen and be certified as of true type and free from pests and diseases; visiting the propagation source is a good option. Generally top and stone fruit should be selected as maiden feathered trees with a minimum of six to eight branches. Older tree forms trained as fans and espaliers can sometimes be purchased, but their quality should be checked before purchase. Remember that the existing placement of the branch arms of espalier trees will determine the positioning of training wires.

Cane fruit is normally purchased in bundles of ten plants, although container plants of blackberries and other hybrid berries can be purchased. Bush fruits, including blackcurrants and redcurrants, are best planted as one-year-old stooled bushes; gooseberries on a leg as one- or two-year-old bushes. Bare-root plants from strawberry runner beds have been partly replaced by container plants, often with a larger crown size. It is unwise to replant strawberries from runners produced from fruiting beds – virus infection from aphids and eelworms can be a particular problem, reducing growth and yield.

Planting The normal period to plant bare-rooted trees, cane fruit and bush fruit is after leaf fall, from November until March. It is crucial for establishment not to allow roots to dry out – make sure stock is received with damp roots in bags. Heel in and lift to bags before planting. Container-raised stock must be moist, then watered in after planting.

ROOTSTOCKS FOR FRUIT TREES

Crop	Rootstock & tree height when freestanding	Use
Apples	M27: 2m	Trained trees
	M9: 2.75–3m	Trained & bush trees
	M26: 3m	Trained & bush trees
	MM106: 3.5–4m	Trained & half-standard trees
	MM111 & M25: 4m+	Standard trees
Pears, Quinces	Quince C: 3m	Trained & bush trees
	Quince A: 3.5–4m	Trained & bush trees
	Pyrus rootstocks: 4m+	Standard trees
Plums	Pixy: 3m	Trained & bush trees
	St Julien A: 3.5–4m+	Trained, bush and standard trees
Cherries	Tabel: 2–2.5m	Trained & bush trees
	Gisela 5: 2.5–3m	Trained & bush trees
	Colt: 3.5m+	Trained & standard trees
Medlars	Quince A: 3.5m	Trained & bush trees
	Crataegus: 3.5m	Bush & half-standard trees

275. If walls are not available, apples, pears and other bush fruit can be trained to horizontal wires supported on wooden or metal posts.

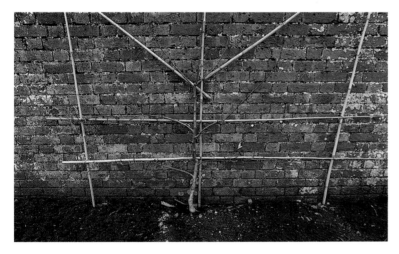

276. Trained fruit forms are best established from maiden stock which can then be trained to a variety of forms.

277. Trained fruit such as this pear makes efficient use of wall space as well as being an attractive architectural form in its own right.

Strawberries provide a number of options for cropping, and should ideally be planted in early August as runners lifted from the field or in pots if they are to produce a crop next season. Plants with two to three crowns are likely to produce the heaviest maiden crop. Autumn-planted summer-fruiting strawberries should be cropped for no more than three years, to reduce disease problems.

Rootstocks Dwarfing stocks have been used for several centuries to grow apples and pears as trained trees on walls, with the aim of controlling tree size and cropping. Virus-free rootstocks should be used for apples, with budding height at about 30cm.

Tree form, training and pruning

- **Fan** Lends itself to the growth of stone fruits, which are too vigorous for espaliers.
- **Espalier** Relies on less vigorous regrowth from the spur system formed on the permanent horizontal arms, suitable for apples and pears
- **Cordon** Grown vertically or obliquely as one stem with spurs, or as a series of vertical stems in candelabra form, particularly suited to the weaker growth of apples and pears.

All these forms and variations were used on walls and arches in the eighteenth and nineteenth centuries. There was great enthusiasm for a wide range of dwarf tree forms on the Continent.

Formative pruning is essentially a winter job, with some summer work on stone fruits to reduce the incidence of bacterial canker and silver leaf disease. Training work is carried out in summer and winter; detailed pruning to form spur systems in July and August. It is important to know where the fruit is produced on the tree to train and prune it for optimum cropping. Apples, pears, plums, apricots and sweet cherries will fruit on short spurs, normally on two-year or older wood; branches must be retained to fruit for a number of years. Peaches, nectarines and sour cherries fruit on one-year-old wood, therefore annual renewal pruning must be done to establish smaller one-year fruiting shoots. Figs normally produce only one crop a year in a temperate climate. Embryonic figs formed on the tip of the current year's shoots by the end of the season will crop the following year. It is therefore necessary to build up smaller shoots on the main laterals by summer pruning.

There are distinct differences in the fruiting habits of blackcurrants and redcurrants. The former will only crop on one-year wood, which must be renewed by growing in a stooling system. Redcurrants and gooseberries will crop on spurs on a branch framework that will last a number of years; both are suitable for wall-trained cordons.

The initial establishment of fans and espaliers from maiden trees with few or no branches can sometimes cause problems if the nursery trees were weak. Allowing trees to grow for a year without pruning and then cutting back in the second winter can produce stronger growth of the initial branch arms. The aim with all wall forms is to produce a thin plane of growth for maximum light interception.

278. Above: redcurrants can be both productive and attractive when grown as cordons against a north wall.

Free-standing apple and pear trees can be trained as goblets, or in any other form that allows the tree to produce sufficient growth for branch formation. A range of these forms can be seen at the gardens at West Dean in Sussex and at Hatton Garden Horticultural Research International at East Malling in Kent. Apples grown on rootstock MM106 will make small standard trees suitable for larger walled gardens.

Pollination Essential for cropping, pollinators should have overlapping flowering periods and not exhibit incompatibility with each other. Consider the wall aspect: early-flowering crops and cultivars should be planted adjacent to the warmest walls to increase the chance of fertilisation. Peaches and nectarines, for example, which are self-fertile, can be provided with shelters and can be hand pollinated. Older strawberries, forwarded with cloches, can produce malformed fruit from flowers that open in cooler weather.

Insect pollination is important. Bee pollinators should be as close as possible to aid pollen transfer. Experiments have shown that the red mason bee is a good pollinator: it has no real sting and commercial tube nests are available. Encourage other pollinators by using wildflower insect banks; these will also be useful for fruiting vegetables.

Thinning Over set of apples, pears and plums can lead to small fruit, less flower in the following year and, with free-standing plums in particular, branch breakage. In an over set situation, thin apples by hand when 10–15mm in diameter to a single fruit on each cluster. Pears can be similarly thinned, but not until the fruits have bent over. Smaller trees of plums can have the fruit thinned by hand when it is about half full size.

Fruit under glass The warmer conditions of a protected environment lend themselves to quality dessert grape production. However, vine powdery mildew is a common problem, best managed by avoiding crowded growth, giving adequate ventilation with additional supplementary heat when needed, and fungicides. Peaches and nectarines are particularly useful under glass, with better fruit set than without protection; they also suffer far less peach leaf curl disease in the drier conditions of a glasshouse. Pests such as mealy bug and red spider mite can be a considerable nuisance.

Vegetables

Intercropping Consider the groupings of particular combination of vegetables. Do they fit into the crop rotation in relation to soil fertility and carry over of pests and diseases? Quick-growing crops that are harvested before they compete with the longer-term crop, such as radishes between rows of parsnips, provide useful combinations. Growth habit is an important factor here. Combine crops with an upright habit with those that spread – sweetcorn and marrows, for example. Whatever the combinations, access must be provided for cultivation throughout the growing period.

Cultivation The traditional four-plot rotation system is useful for growing vegetables in single rows, with sufficient space for weed hoeing. This is particularly important if organic growing practices are adopted and no herbicides are used. Bed systems, closing the spacing between rows but increasing it within the row, can produce higher yields of better quality, particularly with smaller

279. Trained fruit forms: espalier, single cordon and fan.

280. The vinery at Chatsworth has been designed purely for the production of glasshouse dessert grapes.

281. The maintainance of such glasshouse fruit is a labour-intensive task requiring regular attention, such as tying in the vines.

282. The Cherry House at Ascot enables early crops to be grown.

vegetable crops (carrots, for example). 1.5m-wide beds with narrow walking paths of around 0.3m wide can be very effective on heavier soils which become compacted with much treading in single-row systems, particularly when physical weed control methods are used. Newly germinated annual weeds in prepared beds, or soil prepared for single-row spacing, can be treated with a contact herbicide prior to sowing. Subsequent weed control can be either with a residual herbicide directly after sowing, or hand weeding and hoeing from the bed paths.

It is also important to consider ease of movement between areas. It may be possible to position short-term leafy salad crops that need regular harvesting close to packing or storage areas, to reduce movement in the field and retain crop freshness. Soft leafy vegetables must be moved into cool storage as soon as possible. Root vegetables such as carrots, turnips and parsnips, with longer storage potential, can be held in the ground when ready rather than being lifted immediately.

283. Speciality crops such as herbs, asparagus and artichokes were grown in narrow beds lining the walls as they were required in smaller amounts and could be given better attention.

CONSERVATORIES, GREENHOUSES, GLASSHOUSES, ETC.

Conservatory and greenhouse were originally different terms for the same structure, a place to conserve or house greens (variegated hollies, citrus, myrtles and oleanders). Modern usage has allowed these terms to evolve so that today a greenhouse describes a glass structure in which plants are raised, and a conservatory, often attached to a dwelling, is a glazed living space where plants may or may not be significantly important. The term glasshouse refers to a glazed structure used to raise plants; it is most frequently used today to describe large structures such as those used in commercial production or to display ornamental plants at botanic gardens. Garden frames are wooden or brick boxes with removable glazed lights on top, used to protect small batches of plants. Cloches consist of small panes of glass joined to make a glazed tent to protect a single plant or a row in the vegetable garden.

Although some evidence shows that the Romans used frame-like structures to protect tender plants from the cold, it was not until the seventeenth century that large structures were built to protect the 'greens' that were so fashionable in wealthy households. The cultivation of oranges and lemons was so popular that special orangeries were built for winter protection, heavy structures of stone and wood with large windows. Early orangeries — such as the one at the Oxford University Botanic Garden dating, from 1620–50 — were heated by portable braziers on wheels. Such

284. A frame yard fitted with large English lights, which are heavier than Dutch lights and require two people to lift them safely.

285. Frames fitted with the single paned Dutch lights are be easily handled by one person.

286. A range of cloches are used for protecting young tender plants such as courgettes directly after planting.

287. Free-standing glasshouses provided a very flexible growing environment and were better for taller-growing crops.

heating was as bad for the oranges as it was for the gardener; improved designs heated the orangery by warm air flues in the floor or walls. In 1818, heating by piped hot water was introduced: large-bore pipes were placed under glasshouse benching and below grilles in the path, producing uniform, smoke-free heat. This meant that ideal conditions could be maintained under glass for the great influx of tropical plants being introduced at the time. As engineering technology developed and plants' needs were better understood, improved structures were built with a large surface area of glass supported by iron or wooden glazing bars. However, it was not until the repeal of the glass tax in 1845 that the great glasshouse boom took off. Conservatories were built adjacent to houses, to show off the owners' exotic plant collections; walled gardens were lined with greenhouses for the raising of exotic plants and out-of-season fruit and vegetables.

Sir Joseph Paxton, head gardener to the Duke of Devonshire, created the Great Conservatory at Chatsworth in 1836–40, a huge glasshouse with mechanics based on the structure of the giant water-lily *Victoria amazonica*. He later went on to design the Crystal Palace, the largest glass structure of its time, which housed the Great Exhibition of 1851. Undoubtedly the most famous and influential glasshouse is the Palm House at Kew, a beautiful curvilinear structure designed by Decimus Burton and Richard Turner and built in 1845–48. Many of these large Victorian glasshouses

288. Old large-bore glasshouse heating pipes.

declined and were lost after the Second World War, due to a shortage of funds for their maintenance and the cost of fuel to heat them. The recent restoration of walled garden glasshouses, such as the one at Heligan, is linked with more prosperous times and the potential of Heritage Lottery Funding. This has led to a greater interest in conservatories and functional glasshouse structures, and a number of important restorations.

289. Pit houses were sunk into the ground, providing better economy of heat and a more humid environment.

290. Aluminium became widely available after 1945 for commercial and amateur structures. It is now available in powder-coated form for high-quality structures to replace their Victorian or Edwardian predecessors.

291. Glazing bars are part of the glasshouse structure that hold the glass in place. Older glasshouses with timber glazing bars hold the glass in place with pins and putty (a). However, some Dutch light structures in timber or aluminium may use a dry glazing system (b), in which the glass is slid into place and secured with an end plate. Cheaper aluminium glasshouses may use a sprung clip to hold the glass in place at the four corners (c). Modern glasshouses with both wooden and aluminium glazing bars use a bar cap system (d), which aids better heat conservation and the replacement of glass.

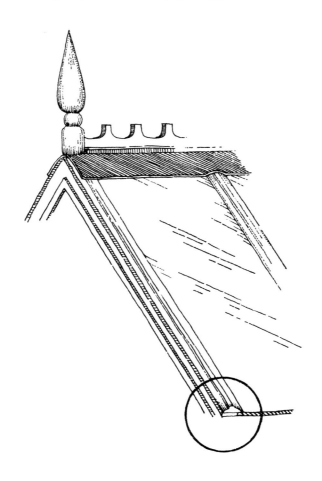

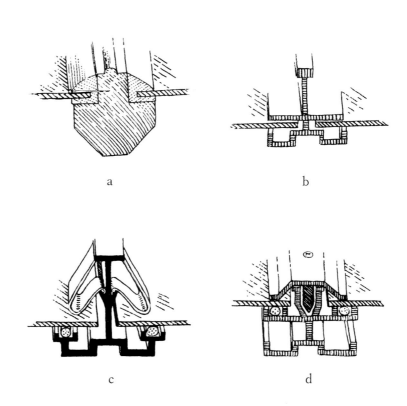

Restoration When considering the restoration of a glasshouse or conservatory, it is important to keep in mind its functional use and future maintenance requirements. Most structures have declined after years of little maintenance: unpainted glazing bars, unreplaced broken glass and uncleared gutters will have resulted in serious water ingress to both wooden and metal elements, resulting in rot and rust. A good conservation architect will be able to advise on the best course of action to repair the structure, while retaining most of the original wood or metal. Once restored, it is vital to recoat both wood (except for teak and red cedar) and metal every 4–6 years with appropriate paint if they are not to deteriorate again. In the damp atmosphere of the glasshouse, all moving parts on ventilators and doors will need greasing and oiling to keep them functional. When re-equipping a glasshouse or conservatory for growing or displaying plants, remember that any services need to be designed for a wet and humid atmosphere, therefore all electrical fittings need to be fully water resistant.

Managing the environment The success of a glasshouse environment depends on the efficient management of temperature, light and humidity to suit the plants being grown. Temperature is managed by heating when cold and ventilating, shading and damping down when hot. Light levels are optimised by keeping the glass clean, which is especially important in winter. The alignment of the glasshouse east to west or on a south-facing wall will provide a maximum amount of direct sunlight and reduce the effect of shading from the glazing bars. Glasshouses constructed against north walls were often used for the cultivation of shade-loving tender ferns. Shading can be used to reduce light levels.

See 'Container growing' to find guidance on the management of pot grown plants (page 218).

Temperature In the UK, where the average temperature over the summer rarely exceeds 25°C, artificial cooling is rarely considered – natural cooling by shading, ventilation and damping down will reduce summer temperatures to a level suitable for most plants. In winter, many temperate and tropical plants will require the glasshouse to be heated if they are to be maintained in a healthy state. If temperate and tropical plants are grown a range of temperatures will need to be maintained, either in separate structures or separate sections of the same structure. Such demands need to be planned from the outset as they will affect the heating engineer's design and the arrangement of pipes and heating controls. Coal was the Victorian fuel of choice for heating but is now regarded as dirty and expensive; oil and gas (natural or bottled) are the most popular options today.

Before buying a glasshouse heating system, the heating requirement, expressed as kilowatts per hour (kw/hr), needs to be calculated. Heaters and boilers should have the kw output printed on them or supplied with them. The calculation is made from the following measurements:

1. Inside surface area of glazed area.

2. Inside surface area of dwarf brick walls.

292. Above: regular maintenance of this iron glasshouse has prevented moisture ingress and the formation of rust.

293. Right: regularly clearing gutters and painting will prevent structural decay such as this.

3. Temperature lift: the maximum normal temperature difference required between inside and outside. The outside temperature should be the average lowest temperature over twenty years, taken from local meteorological records.

$$\text{Heat loss (kw)} = \frac{8 \times \text{'equivalent' surface area (m}^2) \times \text{temperature lift (C}°)}{1000}$$

The 'equivalent' surface area is the glazed area (glass plus glazing bars) plus half the brickwork area.

It is normally a good idea to add an additional 25 per cent to the calculated heat requirement, so that the chosen heating system can cope with any sudden demands and make up any shortfall between the stated and the actual heater output.

This calculation is for a traditional single-glazed glass structure. If the glasshouse is double-glazed the heat loss can be halved. Where other glazing materials are used, the supplier should be able to give accurate heat loss figures.

It is useful to understand a little about the movement of heat energy, so that it can be conserved when the glasshouse needs to be heated, and removed when the glasshouse is too hot.

Glasshouse pipes are heated by warm water and release electromagnetic energy to the air in the form of long-wave radiation.

COST OF HEATING A GLASSHOUSE TO DIFFERENT TEMPERATURES

Minimum winter temperature	Conditions	Cost
4°C	Frost-free	a
7°C	Cool	a x 1.5
10°C	Cool temperate	a x 2
13°C	Warm temperate	a x 4
18°C	Tropical	a x 5

a = minimum cost of providing frost-free conditions; the cost of maintaining higher temperatures is calculated approximately in multiples of this minimum.

Convection currents of warm air rise while cool air falls, creating a constant movement of air within the glasshouse. If there are any gaps or openings in the structure, this warm air is rapidly lost, especially in windy conditions when warm air is sucked out of any opening. For example, a new commercial glasshouse can lose half its warm air from seepage; a small glasshouse in poor condition can receive two to four air changes per hour due to convection currents. As warm air rises it heats the structure. The heat passes through the glass and glazing bars to the outside by conduction, where it is carried away by convection currents. One way to prevent heat loss is to clad the inside of the glasshouse with materials that are poor conductors, thus reducing heat loss through the structure. Sealing any gaps or holes will reduce air movement out of the glasshouse by convection; a secondary layer of insulation will assist this aim, although these solutions may not be suitable for all historic structures.

Heat conservation Having worked out how much heat is lost from a basic glasshouse structure, you should look at practical measures to reduce costs by altering plant management and limiting heat loss. The more of the following points that can be carried, out the greater the savings, but even if only a few can be put into practice it will be worth while.

1. The glasshouse should ideally be sited away from cold winds, which put a heavy burden on any heating system. In many parts of Britain, the coldest winds in winter come from the north and east, where air has been cooled by passing over frozen continents. The correct siting of the glasshouse, in the shelter of a windbreak, will overcome this problem. Trees and hedges provide the best natural windbreaks, but permeable barriers can be erected though they require firm anchorage to prevent them blowing away. To provide maximum protection, the minimum length of a windbreak should be twelve times its height and the average distance from the glasshouse should be four times the windbreak height. However, on the sunless side, windbreaks can be placed nearer to the glasshouse without risk of casting shadow.

2. Avoid having to heat glasshouses in frost hollows, where cold air collects and is unable to drain away. Such areas can be quite a few degrees colder than where there is good air drainage.

3. Seal up any holes or cracks in the structure with an appropriate sealant. A clear silicone lap sealant may be used for gaps between panes of glass. These measures will prevent any needless heat loss.

4. If exterior roller shading is fitted, this can be lowered at night to reduce heat loss by acting as a thermal blanket.

5. Where glasshouses are used mainly to overwinter tender plants and raise summer bedding plants, a large heated propagator will allow the early sowing of bedding plants while the glasshouse is kept just frost-free. In late winter when the days are longer, the minimum temperature can be increased from 4°C to 7°C, as plants will be starting to grow and better able to make use of warmer conditions.

6. Economy night-tariff electricity is available in some countries. In glasshouses the maximum energy demand is at night, so these meters provide good savings.

7. Warm air will gather below the glasshouse ridge. By fitting a recirculation fan with ducting, this can be recycled down to plant level where it is required.

294. Glasshouse benching at waist height for the easy maintenance of the potted plants. The higher benching maximises use of space but can be awkward to manage as steps are needed to reach the plants.

295. In a display glasshouse or conservatory plants can be grown in beds which cuts down on the daily maintenance required. However with plenty of rooting space many exotic trees and shrubs soon outgrow the glasshouse and will need a regular pruning and replacement programme.

balance between solar gain and heat loss frequently means that artificial heat is needed to maintain required temperatures. However, in summer, solar gain is many times greater than heat loss, so measures have to be taken to allow this excess hot air to escape.

Hot air can be removed in two ways – natural ventilation, where an opening is made in the roof to allow warm air to escape and cooler air to enter; and forced ventilation, where motorised fans suck warm air out of the glasshouse, pulling cool air in. As well as halting a rapid rise in temperature, ventilation is used to replace stale air and reduce relative humidity. But to prevent humidity getting too low in summer, glasshouse floors and benches should be damped down – as the water evaporates it helps to cool the glasshouse (a process called evaporative cooling).

296. Natural ventilation with side and roof openings.

8. Heat loss can be halved by insulation. Insulating materials are rarely aesthetically pleasing, so often a compromise is necessary if heat loss is an important consideration. The cheapest method involves attaching an internal skin of polythene to the inside of the glasshouse, which can give a heat saving of 30 per cent. Bubble polythene incorporating two layers gives a saving of 40–47 per cent. But each layer of polythene will reduce light in the glasshouse by 10–14 per cent, so a compromise has to be found between the benefits of reduced heating bills and the decrease in plant quality due to reduced light. If light-demanding winter crops are grown, insulation could be left off the sunny side, to make the most of the winter sun. Polythene intended for glasshouses should incorporate UV inhibitors to keep it in a good condition for up to three years; untreated polythene exposed to the sun will become yellow and brittle within a year. Many catalogues offer netting materials that can be used inside to provide shading in summer and some insulation in winter. They are generally not as good as polythene and will cast too much shade for winter use.

Ventilation Whereas heat loss in winter is a problem, extremely high temperatures in summer can be harmful to plants: sufficient and working ventilation is absolutely necessary. In winter, the

Natural ventilation If cooling by natural ventilation, it is important to have enough ventilators to achieve adequate cooling. As a rule of thumb, a ventilator area of between one-fifth and one-sixth of the floor space should be provided as a minimum. To obtain the maximum number of air changes on hot days, the ventilators should be able to open up to an angle of 50°. It is best to have both ridge and side ventilators, as this provides a more rapid movement of air. Cool air is drawn in from the side vents; as it heats up, it rises until it is drawn out of the top vents. Where only top ventilation is fitted, care should be taken not to open ventilators too rapidly – on cold days, rising warm air will be replaced by a block of cold air that can prove a shock to plants.

A wide range of ventilation types may be found in historic glasshouses and conservatories. Early structures had sash ventilation; later lean-to structures had both ridge and wall ventilation openings (the fruit house at Audley End lacks any ridge ventilation, but has large side panels that can be either opened or completely removed in summer). It is ideal if ventilation is provided on all sides, so that the windward side can be closed to prevent draughts on windy days, while ventilation remains open on the leeward side.

Control of ventilators The ventilation of Victorian structures was manually controlled. During fluctuating spring and autumn

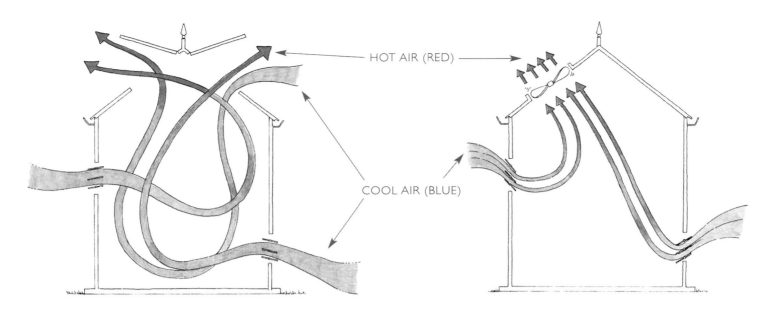

HOT AIR (RED)

COOL AIR (BLUE)

297. Natural ventilation. Glasshouses should have as much roof ventilation as possible to enable hot air to escape and be replaced by cool air from lower openings.

298. Forced air ventilation. This works by a fan extracting hot air, which is replaced with cool.

temperatures it took up a considerable amount of the gardener's time. Modern gardens rarely have enough staff to manage manual ventilation, so many Victorian systems have been adapted for automatic operation.

For a single large ventilator, a small electrically operated hydraulic ram connected to a thermostat gives good automatic control. In order to lift the heavy weight of continuous ridge ventilators, a rack-and-pinion system may be found in many structures, which can be operated manually by chains or automatically by motor. Dutch light structures have ventilators operated by a wire-and-pulley system which can be controlled manually or automated.

Forced air ventilation works by pulling warm air out of the glasshouse on one side and replacing it with cool from the other. This system is frequently used where natural ventilation is insufficient or where the structure will not take the weight of conventional ventilator mechanisms. The fans should be able to move large volumes of air at slow speeds, to avoid creating draughts which can adversely affect plant growth. Fans are usually placed high up in the glasshouse, frequently at gable ends; they should be shuttered to prevent cool air blowing through when the fan is inoperative. When selecting fans, it is important to seek advice from the supplier so that the type and size will be sufficient to provide the required ventilation. With natural ventilation, a glasshouse temperature can never be cooler than the outside, which is a disadvantage in warm climates. This can be overcome with fan ventilation by attaching water-soaked pads over the air inlet – the air sucked in is cooled by the water, raising humidity as well as lowering temperature.

The major disadvantage of a forced air system is that it is noisy and totally reliant on electricity with no emergency manual override. On hot days, the fan will have to run continuously; in a power cut, the glasshouse would overheat. It is more expensive to run than an automated natural ventilation system and, except where extra cooling is required, no better.

Ceiling or paddle fans are sold for glasshouse use – they increase air circulation but have no effect on temperature.

Automatic Ventilation Control Automatic electric ventilator systems should be controlled by an accurate thermostat. Ordinary rod or household thermostats will give incorrect readings if placed in direct sunlight: to record air temperature accurately they should be placed in an aspirated screen. This is an insulated box, fitted with a fan at one end which draws air over the thermostats so they record the temperature of the air rather than the warmth of the sun.

Many glasshouses are fully automated, with computers controlling heating, shading, ventilation, watering and feeding. These systems can be expensive, but are widely used by commercial nurseries which can justify the cost by a reduction in labour costs and better environmental control, improving the quality of the plants. In recent years, computerised environmental controls have fallen in price; they are now available in cut-down versions suitable for smaller set-ups. They are therefore worth considering, as they will provide accurate environmental control as well as reducing heating costs.

Shading The primary reason for shading a glasshouse is to reduce the internal temperature by cutting back the amount of sun that reaches it. Where light-demanding plants such as cacti, tomatoes or chrysanthemums are grown, only light shade should be used and temperature reduced by ventilation. Shade-loving plants, such as begonias, gloxinias and orchids, require up to 70 per cent shade to prevent them overheating. If grown in too much light, many large-leaved foliage plants will produce smaller, thicker leaves, frequently with less coloration. Seedlings and newly rooted cuttings require shading, since even with good ventilation the heat of the sun can dessicate sensitive leaves, making them bleached and marked.

Exterior Shading The most effective form of shading should be able to reduce the sun's intensity before it can warm the glasshouse structure. This is best achieved by placing the shading material on a support 30cm above the glasshouse roof, to allow good air circulation. On older structures, cedar lath blinds were often used, formed by slats joined by copper links; they could be rolled down to protect plants in bright conditions, and rolled up in dull weather. Wooden slatted blinds are still available: they are expensive, but last a long time. Other types of exterior roller blinds are available, such as synthetic shade cloth or plastic reeds, linked by nylon thread. Although not as attractive as wooden slats, they achieve the same result, at a lower cost but with a shorter life.

Where blinds are too expensive or difficult to fit, shading paints will give good sun protection if applied from early spring; traditionally, a mixture of flour and water was used. Modern glasshouse shade paints, sold as 'Coolglass' or 'Varishade', are supplied in concentrated form and need diluting before being applied. By varying the dilution rate, a heavier or lighter shade is produced. Once diluted, the paint is either lightly sprayed or painted with a long-handled brush on the glass; if spraying, it is advisable to select a calm day. The paint requires a few hours to dry and harden, so should be applied on days when there is little risk of rain. After hardening, the paint is rain-fast but will become more translucent when wet, letting in more light on rainy days. In autumn, when the sun has lost its intensity, the shade paint should be removed. This can be done in stages, starting with the shady side in early autumn and finishing off with the sunny side two weeks later. Removal is easy, since the paint can be rubbed off with dry cloths or with a brush and water. This operation can be combined with a general autumn clean-up of the structure, such as removing any moss lodged on the glasshouse roof.

Interior shading Interior shading will reduce glare on the plants, but is not as effective as exterior shading at reducing temperature. A wide range of materials is available, from simple green shade cloth to Venetian or cane blinds. Materials suitable for house extensions are not the right choice for the damp, humid atmosphere of a working glasshouse, as they will soon become mouldy and rot. Remember that bright colours will rapidly fade in the conditions of a glasshouse or conservatory.

In commercial glasshouses, thermal screens are used to reduce heat loss during winter nights and provide shade during the summer. The fabric is hung from horizontal wires stretched between the glasshouse eves. At some nurseries the system is automated, with light sensors operating motors that draw shade cloth across the glasshouse when the light intensity reaches a pre-determined level.

299. Traditional exterior roller blinds made of cedar slats joined by copper links are an attractive solution to cooling and shading a glasshouse. They can be rolled up on cool or cloudy days or lowered on cold nights. They will also aid heat retention.

300. Glasshouse shading paints are a cost-effective solution that should be put on in March and removed in September.

CONTAINER GROWING

Container growing has been an integral part of plant cultivation for many thousands of years. It allows maximum control over the growth of the plant, and enables it to be portable and placed in any environment. Early engravings demonstrate how gardeners were growing plants in pots to expand the season and timing of cultivation and harvest, particularly herbs, fruit and vegetables. Pot culture also enables the gardener to experiment with new plants, protect vulnerable plants from predation, place plants in a controlled environment for propagation, and put them in temporary artistic arrangements. Here we are reminded that gardening is both an art and a science – container growing allows for the convenient scientific study of plants as well as their aesthetic appreciation.

Many historic garden layouts show ornamental containers as an integral part of a garden design. These can be of considerable size: a venerable grapefruit tree in one Italian garden is housed in a pot 5ft high. These ornamental, rather than functional, containers are often placed outside with seasonal planting, or semi-permanently planted with a specimen such as a yucca or topiary box. In warm climates, containers were part of the garden design throughout the year, planted to ensure a succession of interest. However, in colder climates, containers and their plants were removed to a frost-free environment in winter, to protect tender specimens and the expensive ornamental containers themselves from the ravages of damp and frost.

Clay: terracotta, china

Clay pots are traditionally hand-thrown by local potters. The introduction of mass-produced pots pressed from moulds came after the Industrial Revolution and led to a reduction of local styles. However, there are a number of specialist British potters who still produce pots in the traditional manner and will make copies to order of lost designs. Their beauty and better ability to withstand frost compensate for their high cost. It is advisable to ensure that even frost-resistant pots are insulated from the ground in winter by being raised on clay 'pot feet' or small blocks of wood. Unglazed china and clay pots are permeable to both air and water; this encourages a healthy root system, but does mean that they dry out much more than non-permeable pots. For this reason many gardeners achieve more success with clay pots by using compost containing a proportion of loam – purely organic composts dry out quickly and can be difficult to rewet.

Care should be exercised when bringing pot plants into the house and placing them on polished surfaces – even glazed saucers will enable moisture to penetrate through if they have the slightest imperfection. Avoid damage to expensive or much-loved furniture by placing the saucer on a glazed tile or piece of cut glass. Ornamental porcelain pots are best used as attractive outer containers for pot plants – replacement plants can be easily swapped over and vigorous pot-bound plants will not crack the porcelain. Some containers are not suitable for permanent plants – they may not

301. Left: summer visitors to the restored Privy Garden at Hampton Court see a host of container-grown exotics, from large citrus and evergreens in Versailles tubs to smaller specimens grown and displayed in hand-thrown clay pots. In winter this area is bare: the large plants are removed to an orangery to be kept in a cool, dry, frost-free and fairly dark environment, almost in suspended animation, until they can be placed outside again in late spring. The smaller plants are protected in garden frames or pit houses – glasshouses partially sunk into the ground to provide additional insulation from winter cold. (See Case Study, page 371.)

302. Opposite: the Orangery Garden at Versailles. All the plants placed out in the garden are grown in Versailles tubs; they are packed into the Orangery in winter for frost protection.

303. Left: spring bulbs grown in pots can provide useful concentrated colour at a sparse time of year.

have holes at the base, or a constricted rim may not allow removal of the rootball.

Wood: seasoned oak, cedar or sweet chestnut Wood has been widely used to construct shallow boxes for plant propagation as well as large containers for specimens. They are less used now as they are expensive, difficult to store and more easily harbour pests and diseases than their plastic replacements. The wooden barrels used in the whisky and wine industry have traditionally found a second life as water butts or, cut in half, as containers.

Versailles tubs are named after the square wooden containers used at Versailles for the large specimen plants displayed on the orangery terrace in summer and housed in the orangery in winter. True Versailles tubs are specially designed for plants such as citrus and palm trees. Their wooden sides are attached to a frame that can be unbolted and removed to enable root pruning to take place in spring. Old compost is teased away from the rootball and replaced with new to ensure the vigour of these venerable specimens.

Paper and peat These cheap pots were used by growers from the mid twentieth century for modular propagation and growing on quick crops such as bedding plants, but have now largely replaced by plastic modular trays and pots. They are available in a variety of forms, including paper combined with thin polythene or impregnated with bitumen, and compressed peat. Large bitumen-impregnated pots were used for growing glasshouse crops such as tomatoes, melons and cucumbers, but this practice has now been replaced by hydroculture.

Lead Ornamental lead containers may be part of a formal garden layout, designed to hold plants or to act as rainwater cisterns. Care should be taken when moving lead containers: they are very heavy, even without plants and soil, and can represent a considerable health and safety risk. Lead is a soft metal which is easily scratched or dented if poorly handled, and can be expensive to repair. Lead containers have been subject to theft, so care should be given to their placing and security.

Stone The most basic stone containers are old agricultural water troughs, made from a hollowed block of stone or, in some areas, joined slabs of stone. They are now widely used for the cultivation of alpine or rock plants, or as rustic containers for bedding plants. Depending on the conditions and the type of stone, protection from winter damp and frost may be required to prevent flaking or cracking. A specialist conservator will be able to give advice on the best repair strategy.

Reconstituted stone was widely used in the Victorian era as a cheap and mass-produced alternative to natural stone, and many copies of antique pieces were made at this time. Some of the most attractive copies were made of Coade Stone (an early artificial stone), and these are now extremely valuable in themselves. Reconstituted stone is now widely used for replica pots and ornaments.

304. Below: a summer display of potted plants used to proviide focus in a paved area.

305. Pot displays need a back-up area for plants to be grown on, as shown here in the frame yard at Great Dixter.

306. Far left: a Coade Stone urn at Chiswick moved into the conservatory for protection from the elements.

OLD POT SIZES

From W. E. Shewell-Cooper, *The ABC of the Greenhouse*, 1955

Clay pot sizes *	Diameter at top		Depth	
Thimbles	2in	(5.1cm)	2in	(5.1cm)
Thumbs	2¹/₂in	(6.3cm)	2¹/₂in	(6.3cm)
Sixties (60s)	3in	(7.6cm)	3¹/₂in	(8.9cm)
Forty-eights (48s)	4¹/₂in	(11.4cm)	5in	(12.7cm)
Thirty-twos (32s)	6in	(15.2cm)	6in	(15.2cm)
Twenty-fours (24s)	8¹/₂in	(21.6cm)	8in	(20.3cm)
Sixteens (16s)	9¹/₂in	(24.1cm)	9in	(22.9cm)
Twelves (12s)	11¹/₂in	(29.2cm)	10in	(25.4cm)
Eights (8s)	12in	(30.5cm)	11in	(27.9cm)
Sixes (6s)	13in	(33cm)	12in	(30.5cm)
Fours (4s)	15in	(38.1cm)	13in	(33cm)
Twos (2s)	18in	(45.7cm)	4in	(35.6cm)

* Historically, clay pots were named according to the number that could be made from a measured 'cast' of clay

Other sizes Bushel boxes etc. 1 bushel (bsh. or bu.) = 36.37 litres

SOME MODERN POT SIZES

Litres	Diameter at top	Use
—	9cm	Herbs, young bedding plants
2	15cm	Young shrubs, perennials
3	18cm	Roses
4	—	Long pot
10	24cm	Specimen plants
50	50cm	Semi-mature shrub. small tree
120	65cm	Fully grown shrub, tree
500	100cm	Specimen tree

307. Garden sculpture under repair.

Principles of replacing original materials When restoring a historic garden layout, or replacing missing or broken containers in an existing layout, replacements should ideally be of the original construction and material and made to the same quality. But truly authentic replacements are rarely affordable either in materials or staff time, even if purists insist that only hand-made clay pots are used, that gardeners give up watering with hosepipes and use only watering cans, and that they assess the dryness of a pot by hitting it with a 'watering' stick! One compromise is to propagate plants in plastic pots but use clay pots for display. If restoring a historic formal garden, original or good copies should be used so that the quality of the artefacts matches the quality of the landscape.

308. The reconstruction of Burlington's Exedra at Chiswick used good-quality copies of the original sculptures.

Concrete was widely introduced from the 1950s as an exciting and flexible alternative to natural materials. It was cheap and easy to produce in a wide range of designs and finishes. Concrete garden ornaments and containers made with added asbestos fibres for strength were particularly popular in the 1960s and 1970s. These are no longer available due to concern over asbestos, and specialist contractors should be employed to remove and dispose of them.

Artificial materials: plastics, recycled plastics, polythene and polystyrene The relatively cheap cost of oil in the late twentieth century resulted in plastic propagation pots and trays becoming the nurseryman's choice. They are cheap to buy, easy to store, hygienic, and can be mass-produced in virtually any shape or form. Excellent 'facsimiles' of almost any material are available in plastic: some of the best copies of large terracotta pots or lead containers can be very convincing from a distance, but they lack the qualities of the genuine materials when handled and seen close to. In general, plastic pots are not permeable to air or water and therefore need sufficient holes at the bottom to provide drainage. Plants grown in plastic pots will require less watering than their counterparts in clay. Although modern plastics are more stable, some plastics may become brittle after many years of exposure to ultraviolet light. The dies in most plastics fade in time, giving them a shorter life-span than natural materials.

Security Theft of garden ornaments is a growing problem, with a number of high-profile cases widely reported in the press. If a garden has valuable pieces, it is worth obtaining advice from the police and specialist security consultants. In some cases, insurance companies require certain precautions as a condition of cover. Things to consider include:

- ease of access: how secure is the boundary?
- secure fixings for all items
- provision of alarms: radio-controlled alarms can be placed under the fixings and primed to go off if the item is moved
- keeping a good replica outside and moving the original to a more secure position

Growing plants in containers Plants in containers, unlike those growing in the ground, are totally dependent on the gardener for their wellbeing. They therefore require a consistently high level of maintenance.

Compost A wide range of container composts is available. They can be broadly divided into loam-based (those with a high constituent of soil) and organic-based (those with a high proportion of organic contents). A range of inorganic constituents may be found in commercial composts, such as rockwool, vermiculite and perlite – all are light and have good water- and nutrient-retaining properties. Composts with no or very little peat are recommended, as they are less likely to have caused damage to the ecological and archaeological environment of precious peat bogs. Loam-based composts are ideal for permanent pot-grown plants: loam is heavy, providing good stability for the container, and it holds on to nutrients and water better than purely organic composts.

309. Cameras are being increasingly used to aid security but do need careful siting as they can be an eyesore in historic gardens.

310. An in-line diluter is a useful tool when many plants need liquid feeding.

Rejuvenating root-bound plants in containers Plants that are too large their pots eventually lose vigour when they can no longer take up sufficient water and feed. If plants are only slightly pot-bound, the top few centimetres of soil can be removed and replaced with fresh compost and watered in. Plants that have been in their pots for some time should be carefully removed, and the compost prized away from the outside of the rootball using an old label or cane. Using a knife or secateurs, cut away up to one-third of the outer roots, especially any that were badly twined around the pot. Put the plant back into its original pot, making sure that all voids are filled with fresh compost. This treatment can cause a shock to some established plants, causing them to drop their leaves – minimise the risk by undertaking the procedure in late winter before any new growth takes place.

Watering Plants dry out more quickly in warm, dry and draughty conditions, as these increase water loss from the leaves. Plants that are actively growing require extra water to expand their cells – a pot-bound plant has less space to hold moisture, and will therefore dry out more quickly, sometimes needing watering twice a day. In the depth of winter, when days are short and conditions cool and humid, little growth takes place and plants may stay moist for many weeks.

Organic-based composts should always feel slightly moist – if allowed to dry out too much, they will crack away from the pot, making rewetting difficult. Loam-based composts, such as John Innes, should be allowed to become almost dry at the surface between waterings, as the small particles of soil can hold a large reservoir of water.

During summer, check plants for watering at least twice a day. Supply sufficient water to permeate through all the compost in the pot: small doses of water only wet the top few centimeters and the bottom of the pot remains dry, discouraging root development.

Feeding Except where complete slow-release feeds are incorporated into the compost, regular liquid feeds are needed to top up nutrient deficiencies. Liquid feeds are best bought as balanced mixtures that are diluted and watered into the pot. As a general rule, it is best to feed a plant after every third watering. During the summer this can work out as much as once or twice a week, but during the winter as little as once or twice a month, depending on the plant and the prevailing weather conditions. Foliar feeds are absorbed through the leaves as well as the roots.

If only a few plants need feeding, liquid feeds can be made up as recommended by the manufacturer in a watering can and watered in or sprayed over the foliage with a fine rose. If many plants require feeding it can be a labour-intensive job to use a watering can; the feed can be administered instead via a proportional diluter fitted to a garden hose. This injects feed at the required concentration into the water as it flows through the hose; if properly set up, it will give accurate rates of feeding. When using a garden hose – on its own or with a diluter – it is now a legal requirement in the UK to fit a non-return valve to the tap to prevent contaminated water siphoning back into the mains system.

WEED CONTROL

Weeds are often defined as 'plants in the wrong place', in that they do not normally belong in a planting scheme or design. Despite the fact that some are quite attractive and decorative (most are British native plants), their invasive or competitive tendencies can impair the visual qualities of planned garden areas, as well as competing for growth and living space. Ideally, weed control should be a regular job throughout the growing season, but the critical months have been shown by experiment and experience to be May and June, when a serious check on the growth of cultivated plants may occur if weeding is neglected.

However, weed control should really only be practised when there are definite or specific reasons and justifications, such as the management of planned plant associations and the maintenance of high-quality lawns. There may also be other reasons, for example the controlling of invasive species such as bracken or Japanese Knotweed, or the protection of the public from poisonous or injurious plants such as Giant Hogweed (*Heracleum*) which can inflict painful skin rashes.

The concept of weediness is really not always easy to define, since it is a subjective thing in the eye of the beholder. With increasing trends towards wildlife conservation and wildlife gardening, and the inclusion of British native 'weeds' in some planting schemes and designs, there may follow a consequent change of attitude in agreeing standards of maintenance.

In determining control measures, an important factor will be the nature of the weeds to be controlled. These will be annuals with a short growth cycle, some biennials, and the more persistent perennials such as ground elder and couch grass.

Control measures broadly fall into three categories:

* Physical control using hand tools and/or mechanisation.

* Mulches

* Chemicals

Physical control

Hand removal Using a fork, spade, trowel or the hand, this is simple but effective, and very flexible even when using unskilled labour. However, it is time-consuming and labour costs often make it prohibitively expensive. It is useful for individual perennial weeds, small areas or high-profile garden areas.

Hoeing Again done by hand, this is useful in beds and borders, but requires some skill to prevent damage to retained plants. Weeds may be left to die if conditions are dry but may re-root if wet, especially if they have been dragged out of the soil rather than sliced off. Hoeing is only fully effective against annuals; perennial weeds generally regrow. The best results are obtained when weeds are small and shrivel up quickly; larger weeds may require removal after hoeing in high-profile areas.

Cutting May be used as a last resort to help reduce spread and future problems caused by seeding, or as a planned method of permanent control. Neither will improve the immediate appearance of the area in the short term. Weeds can be cut to prevent flowering or seed dispersal by hand or, in sufficiently large areas, by pedestrian- or tractor-drawn equipment. Arisings should be removed for two reasons: first, because they look untidy and may present a fire hazard; secondly, because many weed species are capable of producing viable seed before dying, even if cut down quite soon after flowering. Cutting may also encourage the spread of some weeds by vegetative means.

312. Hoeing in dry weather is an effective way to kill weeds.

311. Opposite: hosepipes should be neatly stored to prevent risk of tripping.

313. An acid mulch of pine needles under rhododendrons helps to retain moisture and smother weeds.

Using cutting as a planned method for permanent control works on the basis that, unlike grasses, most broadleaved plants cannot survive being regularly cut to ground level. Generally, this method requires cutting on three or four occasions during the growing season; for some weeds this process may need to be repeated for two or three years to ensure eradication.

Pulling Unlike cutting, pulling removes a substantial part of the weed from ground and below ground levels. This has the advantage of greatly reducing vigour and in some cases may eradicate the plant entirely after one operation. Pulling is only suitable, however, for plants with tall stems and/or flowering shoots with a reasonably strong connection to the lower parts of the plant, so that these will be pulled up with the stem or at least seriously damaged. Candidates include thistles, ragwort and bracken, but not Japanese knotweed. If pulling by hand, take suitable precautions to protect the hands from thistles and from sap (especially ragwort sap). Pulling can be done on a large scale using specially developed machinery.

Burning Flame guns are designed to sear the surface of plants, which then shrivel up, achieving good weed control on paths and gravel areas. This operation may need to be repeated on a number of occasions throughout the year as fresh seeds germinate and perennial plants regrow, although regular treatment will eradicate these.

Foaming A new method of control, really a variation of burning, which involves spraying a hot organic foam over target areas or weeds. The foam cools and breaks down naturally leaving no harmful residue, but has the advantage of no naked flame and increased contact time. It can be used on walls or other vertical surfaces where naked flames are not suitable, for reasons or safety or risk of damage. Improved control may also be possible on troublesome perennial weeds by direct injection of the foam into rootstocks or rhizomes; this method is currently being trialled.

Rolling This is used successfully to control bracken on large, reasonably level areas. Rolling is preferred to cutting because it flattens and damages the fronds along their whole length, causing fluid loss through numerous tears which further sap energy from the plant. Rolling needs to be carried out on a number of occasions and, on well-established stands, over several years to provide effective control.

Mulching

Very effective against annual weeds if put down in early spring before weeds growth starts. Perennial weeds push through most mulches, but are generally isolated and can be dealt with quickly. Added advantages are that mulches reduce water loss from the soil, benefiting plants in the bed, and that most gradually become mixed into and improve the soil; some can improve its appearance.

Biological control

Unlike with pest control, biological control of weeds is little used in the UK – the last occasion was in 1969–70 when the beetle *Haltica arvensis* was used in an unsuccessful attempt to control creeping thistle. Biological methods for controlling Japanese knotweed, including beetles, rusts and leaf spot fungi, are currently under examination.

Chemical control

It is good management to have a presumption against the use of chemicals unless there is strong justification. If necessary, the least environmentally damaging chemical should be used. Use of chemicals involves a number of legal restrictions (see 1.5).

Herbicides come in several hundred different formulations, but most fit into two main categories, selective and non-selective, each of which can be further subdivided into residual or non-residual, and contact or translocated.

314. Tree growing in wall.

ADVANTAGES AND DISADVANTAGES OF MULCHING

MULCH	ADVANTAGES	DISADVANTAGES
Chipped bark	• Good weed suppressant • Retains moisture • Readily available • Many different grades available to suit situation • Improves soil structure by encouraging earthworm activity	• If home-produced, must be weathered before use (commercial material is ready to use) • Rots down over time and needs renewal • Rotting process may extract nitrogen from the soil • Often proves attractive to birds for dust-bathing in dry weather and may be dispersed over paths • Possibility of spreading disease ??
Shredded timber	• Good weed suppressant • Retains moisture	• If home-produced, must be weathered before use (commercial material is ready to use) • Rots down over time and needs renewal • Rotting process may extract nitrogen from the soil • Coarse appearance may be considered unattractive
Polythene	• Very good weed suppressant • Retains moisture well • If used under chipped bark or similar it slows the decomposition of the bark. • Black polythene will help soil warm up quickly in spring	• Unattractive in amenity situations, although can be covered by chipped bark, gravel or similar • Can be easily torn by humans or animals • Liable to be blown loose if torn or not securely fixed • Sheds all moisture elsewhere – so run-off needs to be considered • Difficult to use on areas with established plants – best if laid on clear soil and planted through • Colours other than black may allow weed growth beneath
Geotextile fabric	• Quite good weed suppressant • Retains moisture • Allows rainfall through to the surface • If used under chipped bark or similar it slows the decomposition of the bark	• Potentially unattractive in amenity situations, although can be covered by chipped bark, gravel or similar • Most types allow some light through so weed growth can occur, but this can be prevented by covering with chipped bark or similar • Difficult to use on areas with established plants – best if laid on clear soil and planted through
Gravel	• Suppresses some weeds • Retains moisture • Allows rainfall through to the surface	• Can quickly become colonised by ephemeral weeds rooted in the gravel itself
Grass clippings	• Good weed suppression	• Very unsightly • Rot quite quickly, extracting nitrogen from soil • Heat up rapidly while rotting and may damage shallow roots • Thick layers may degenerate to slimy black ooze beneath surface • Thick layers may impede soil/air gaseous exchange • May form crust and shed rainwater away • Potential for herbicide damage if grass previously treated
Straw	• Some weed suppression • Moisture retention • Soil conditioner due to increased earthworm activity	• Rots quite quickly, extracting nitrogen from soil, therefore need to add nitrogen • Mostly used to keep fruit clean (e.g. strawberries) • Potential for herbicide damage if growing wheat or barley previously treated. • Unsightly until well rotted
Manure	• Helps moisture retention • Improves soil nutrient levels • Improves soil structure by encouraging earthworm activity	• No weed suppression unless sterilised • Even when sterilised, surface can be easily colonised by wind-blown seed • Care needed to avoid scorching if chicken manure used
Compost	• Helps moisture retention • Improves soil nutrient levels • Improves soil structure by encouraging earthworm activity	• No weed suppression unless sterilised • Even when sterilised, surface can be easily colonised by wind-blown seed • Potential to spread disease if not sterilised • pH can be quite variable
Old carpet	• Good weed suppression • Good moisture retention	• Visually unattractive • Use of foam- or rubber-backed carpet could cause toxicity problems • Dense weave may reduce soil/air gaseous exchange
Newspaper, cardboard	• Good weed suppression • Fairly good moisture retention	• Visually unattractive • Dense layer may reduce soil/air gaseous exchange

Peat is not included in the above table partially because it has limitations as a mulch – lowering the pH, being liable to blow away when dry and being difficult to re-wet once dry – but primarily because its use for horticultural operations should be avoided wherever possible due to the serious ecological and archaeological implications of peat extraction.

The list of approved chemicals and codes of practice for their application regularly change – see the Defra publication, *Pesticides – Codes of practice for using plant protection products* (available from www.defra.gov.uk). It is advisable to get suitably qualified expert advice before using chemical control.

Selective or non-selective Unfortunately, these terms imply rather more control than is achieved in practice. Non-selective herbicides, as the name implies, will kill any plant material; selective herbicides control either dicotyledons (broadleaved plants) or monocotyledons (grasses). No herbicide has been developed (yet!) which is so selective that it will control, for example, valerian without harming anything else.

Residual or non-residual Residual herbicides remain active and in the soil for prolonged periods and may affect plants in the area sprayed for a year, occasionally longer. Approved chemicals of this type are used to control the germination of annual weeds, more widely on gravel paths than planted areas, since a build-up of residual herbicide in the soil may reduce the vigour of some permanent planting. Non-residual herbicides are broken down into harmless substances on contact with the soil and become inactive almost immediately.

Contact or translocated Contact herbicides kill only the plant tissue they are sprayed on or come into contact with, so are ideal for clearing annual weeds from a non-crop area. Translocated herbicides are absorbed into the plant and move with the sap system before becoming fully active, so spraying a few leaves could result in the death of the whole plant; this makes them more suitable for controlling perennial weeds, such as nettles or ground elder. This is particularly important to consider when there is any chance of drift on to non-targeted plants.

Methods

Weed wiping Consists of wiping the leaves of undesirable plants with a special glove or cloth soaked with a translocated herbicide, which is transferred to the leaves and stems and absorbed to move through the plant. Weed wiping can be carried out very successfully on a large scale using tractor-mounted weed wipers, provided there is a distinct difference between the height of the target species and the surrounding non-target vegetation – for example, the treatment of thistles or ragwort in areas of pasture.

Painting Similar to weed wiping, except that the herbicide is painted directly on the leaves or cut stumps using a brush. Chemicals are usually in a gel form for ease of use and to prevent run-off.

Both the above methods can be quite labour-intensive, although with a translocated herbicide it is not necessary to achieve 100 per cent coverage of every leaf surface: so long as a reasonable proportion of the plant is treated, the chemical moves within it. However, both have the advantage of being highly accurate, with minimal chance of non-target plants being affected.

315. A weed wiper in detail.

316. A weed wiper can be used when it is necessary to spot treat weed with a translocated herbicide.

Spraying Can be carried out by sprayers with hand-held lances, pedestrian- or tractor-mounted boom sprayers or even aerial sprayers. Sprayers with hand-held lances work by carrying a pressurised container in a knapsack. For large operations, the containers are transported by vehicles with several lances attached; pressure within the tank forces liquid chemical through piping to the lance and out in the form of a spray with varying (adjustable) droplet size. This spray can be directed over entire areas (blanket spraying) or particular plants (spot treatment) by using the on/off switch on the lance. Blanket spraying of herbicide should be avoided except in areas where large, dense tracts of weed exist without other plants. Spot treatment is preferable. Spraying is not as accurate as weed wiping or painting, because however carefully it is carried out there is always some fall-out on to plants lower than the target and invariably some drift.

Boom sprayers are used only for reasonably large, open areas of turf (or crops in agriculture) and cannot spot treat. Aerial spraying, from planes or helicopters, is mostly confined to agriculture and forestry, and is likely to be considered viable outside these areas only for the control of very large-scale weed infestation such as that caused by *Rhododendron ponticum*, Japanese knotweed or bracken.

Guidelines

- Consider carefully what target needs to be achieved
- Choose the most specific and least damaging method
- Consider the environmental impact of the proposals
- Comply with all relevant legislation

PESTS AND DISEASES

In historic gardens and parks, incidences of serious pest infestations and disease outbreaks are much less likely than may be the case in the agricultural and horticultural industries, where large-scale mono-cropping may lead to a build-up of such problems. The great diversity of potential host plants and their age range discourage such epidemics and, in the case of many pests, there are usually many predators to effect natural control.

However, exceptions can occur, as with the devastating Dutch Elm disease in the 1970s which wiped out huge populations of elms in the UK and much of western Europe.

The once widespread use of chemicals has seen a dramatic change in the last two decades or so, in favour of natural predators in biological control regimes and Integrated Pest Management (IPM) programmes, the latter usually for more intensive commercial production. This trend away from chemicals has also been prompted by health and safety issues, and wildlife conservation.

The move towards Integrated Pest Management (IPM), has been partially driven by technical advances, but mainly by legislation to reduce the quantity of toxic chemicals used in the industry. The IPM approach now works through the horticultural sector at all scales, including historic parks and gardens. IPM practices have numerous benefits, including:

- Reduced health and safety risks compared to chemical-only control measures
- Reduced costs for pesticides, application equipment, personal protection equipment (PPE) and storage
- Reduced garden closure time due to pesticide application
- Clear environmental benefits from reduced chemical use
- Reduced likelihood of insect pests becoming resistant to chemical treatment
- Improved public awareness and perception of horticulture's role in environmental issues

One of the key factors in any pest and disease control programme is monitoring. Early identification of outbreaks provides a better chance of cheap and efficient control, as opposed to fighting an expensive battle later on when the damage is often done. Usual monitoring methods are as simple as checking plants visually on a regular basis and using 'sticky traps' in glasshouses to trap samples of pests. Be especially vigilant at times of the year when specific pests and diseases are expected, and when weather patterns become favourable for their development.

Basic hygiene and cultural control are important. Often pests and diseases have alternate host plants where they live, hide or feed. By removing these, which are often weeds or plant debris, the risk to the plants you wish to protect is reduced.

Plants can also be put at risk by normal horticultural activities carried out badly – for example, bad pruning cuts, damage to root systems during soil cultivation, 'soil splash' during irrigation, and lack of air circulation caused by over-dense planting.

For detailed lists of the pests, diseases and disorders affecting both outdoor and indoor plants, see Appendices Table 13.

Pests

Pests are animals that damage cultivated plants and plant products. The range of pests that may occur in parks and gardens is potentially very extensive and the severity of the problem will depend upon the style and character of each site, and the complexity of its components. Glasshouses, productive walled gardens and specialised planting areas will have a much greater range of potential pests than shrubberies and parkland, for example.

The pest groups that need to be considered are divided into vertebrates and invertebrates.

Vertebrate pests

- **Deer** Increasing and widespread in woodlands, plantations, gardens, shrubs, roses, etc.

317. In gardens that cannot be kept free of rabbits, it is important to protect plants with netting.

- **Grey squirrels** Widespread, barking young trees, etc. Increasing problem.

- **Rabbits** A serious problem to woody and non-woody plants, especially new plantations. Major epidemics in some areas.

- **Birds** Mainly small birds stripping fruit and flower buds. Others relish cherries and soft fruit. Pheasants like tulip bulbs.

- **Mice/voles** Occasional damage to small bulbs, etc.

- **Moles** Seasonal disruptive tunnelling in lawns and borders.

Invertebrate pests

- **Eelworms (nematodes)** Parasitic species are up to a few millimetres long; most are slender and worm-like, and many move through the soil in water. They can affect all parts of a plant. An example is *Ditylenchus dipsaci* (stem and bulb eelworm), which is a damaging pest of narcissus. Beneficial parasitic species can be used for biological control of some insects and slugs.

- **Flatworms** Two introduced species, *Arthurdendyus tringulatus* (New Zealand flatworm) and *Australoplana sanguinea* (Australian flatworm), feed exclusively on earthworms and have no natural enemies in Britain. The former occurs mainly

in the north, and the latter in south-west England. They have been responsible for a considerable lowering of earthworm populations in some areas, affecting soil quality and threatening animals that feed on earthworms. Spread can be limited only by reducing soil movement, and inspection of nursery stock from infested gardens and nurseries.

- **Slugs and snails** Of the several species, slugs are the most damaging although *Helix aspera* (garden snail) can be a pest – their rasping mouth-parts make ragged holes in leaves, and they create glistening slime trails.

- **Insects with piercing and sucking mouthparts** Aphids, leaf hoppers, mealy bugs, scale insects, whiteflies and thrips can all be damaging on a wide range of ornamental plants. There are some biological control agents for certain species, and systemic insecticides control many.

- **Insects with biting and chewing mouthparts** These include butterflies (mainly cabbage white caterpillars, moth and sawfly caterpillars), earwigs and various beetles and weevils. Many butterfly and moth adults are useful pollinators and certain groups of beetle are pest predators. Earwigs are also predatory.

- **Spiders and mites** Spiders are useful predators, but several mites (most of which are 1mm or less in size) feed by sucking the sap of a range of ornamental plants. *Tetranychus urticae* (two-spotted spider mite) can be particularly troublesome under glass. However, a number of fast-moving native and

NATURALLY OCCURRING BENEFICIAL INVERTEBRATES

Beneficial invertebrates	Pests consumed
Anthocorid bugs	Aphids, spider mites, scale insects, small caterpillars, thrips, various eggs
Nabid bugs and other capsids	Caterpillars, capsids, aphids
Lacewings	Aphids, spider mites
Ladybirds	Aphids, spider mites, thrips, small caterpillars, scale insects
Ground beetles (Carabids)	Wide range of soil pests
Rove beetles (Staphylinids)	Wide range of soil pests
Parasitic wasps	Specific prey type and species
Solitary and social wasps and bees	Mostly caterpillars and aphids
Hoverflies	Mainly aphids
Other predatory flies and midges	Aphids and spider mites
Parasitic flies (Tachinids)	Caterpillars, beetles and snails
Mites (Phytoseiids)	Plant-feeding mites
Other mites (Anystids, Trombids, etc.)	Plant-feeding mites, aphids, insect mites
Spiders, centipedes, earwigs	Wide range of foliage and soil pests

introduced predatory mites exert at least some control over pest species.

- **Millipedes** These can damage bulbs, corms, rhizomes, tubers and seedlings. They should not be confused with fast-moving centipedes (often uncovered when cultivating the soil), which are beneficial predators.

Diseases

These are living organisms, other than plants or animals, called pathogens, which interfere with the normal structure, function or value of plants. The main groups include:

- **Fungi** These consist of branching threads (hyphae) that move through and feed in the soil or plant, and fruiting bodies such as toadstools and bracket fungi. There are species that damage all types of higher plant, from large trees to annuals. Two diseases of recent concern are *Phytophthora ramorum* (sudden oak death), seen on an increasing range of woody species including some native trees (the website www.defra.gov.uk/planth/oak.htm gives useful information) and box blight, caused by species of *Cylindrocladium* and *Pseudonectria rousseliana* and spread from infected nursery stock and at pruning. All infected material, prunings and whole plants, should be removed as soon as possible.

- **Bacteria** These minute single-celled organisms cause blights, cankers, galls and soft rots in a range of plants. *Pseudomonas mors-prunorum* bacterial cankers infect a range of *Prunus* species. There are some canker-resistant rootstocks for tree species. Pruning time can be critical with this disease, and copper sprays are possible for some species. There are no permitted antibiotic treatments for bacterial disease of plants.

- **Viruses** Complex, minute biochemicals – the many plant viruses cause stunting, foliage mottling, flower colour breaking and death. Spread is by many means, particularly by sucking insects such as aphids; also by eelworms and sap transmission on contact.

Disorders

Of the wide range of disorders in plants many are primary, but others are more complex (for example, chlorosis or stunting in plants is associated with insects feeding on root systems that then function poorly).

- **Nutritional disorders** Nitrogen, phosphorus, potassium, magnesium and trace elements are associated with growth processes within the plant. Deficiency, excess or imbalance can cause a whole range of growth disorders. Soil structure, texture, pH, and attack by pests and diseases can affect the plant's ability to absorb nutrients as well as the amount of

319. The yellowing of Camellia leaves indicates lime-induced chlorosis.

ARMILLARIA MELLEA (HONEY FUNGUS)

This can be a troublesome disease at historic sites, infecting many woody species. Effective chemical treatments are not available and physical treatments are difficult, other than removal of as much infected root material as possible and replanting of susceptible species away from infection sites to give isolation. Species resistant to honey fungus may be the answer in some cases: these include *Acer negundo, Juglans nigra, Taxus baccata, Abies procera, Phyllostachys* spp., *Carpinus betulus, Fagus sylvatica, Fraxinus* spp., *Hedera helix, Juniperus* spp., *Prunus laurocerasus* and *Quercus* spp.

318. *Armillaria mellea* is present in most mature gardens. Its rhyzomorphs, commonly called bootlaces, enable it to spread through the ground to a new host. Clusters of fruiting bodies are produced in the autumn.

soluble nutrient within the soil. Physical examination of the soil in dug pits and soil analysis can be important in determining the nature of the problem.

- **Climate** Important factors include high and low temperature, high and low light intensities, dry or waterlogged soils, humidity levels, exposure to strong wind and hail damage to leaves, flowers and fruits.
- **Mechanical damage** This can be caused by mowing machines at the base of trees (use grass-free tree circles or guards in some situations). Ties that are not loosened or removed can strangle a tree. Root growth can be restricted in container plants.
- **Chemicals** This includes exposure to salt-laden winds, industrial and traffic pollution (select tolerant species) and herbicide damage. Secondary pest or disease attacks can be associated with these problems.

Control

Risk assessment will determine the most appropriate method of control to be effective, and to protect people and the environment. Using a system of scoring levels, this process can identify the safest controls for eliminating a hazard when it presents a clear risk. Regulations include Management of Health and Safety at Work 1992 and Control of Substances Hazardous to Health 1988 (COSHH).

Chemical Select the product with the shortest persistence and with a narrow spectrum of target species (ideally, only the target organism). Only products approved for use under the Control of Pesticides Regulations 1986 (COPR) and the Control of Pesticides (Amended) Regulations 1997 (COPAR) may be used; information on these is given in *The UK Pesticide Guide* (the 'Green Book'). Remember that growth regulators and wood preservatives are classed as pesticides. As the list of approved products changes, it is important to check regularly (go to the websites for the Plant Safety Directorate or the Health and Safety Executives). All those using pesticides should be adequately trained in their use; there is a statutory requirement for most users to obtain certificates of competence (administered by the National Proficiency Test Council and the Scottish Skills Testing Service). Contact details for these organisations are given in the Green Book.

Labels on pesticide containers show a 'statutory box', stating the 'approved field of use' (for example, agriculture and horticulture) and all the conditions that the user should follow to apply the material. Guidelines are available on the safe storage of pesticides (Health and Safety Executives Agricultural information sheet No. 16; available on their website). Storage facilities will provide space for PPE and washing requirements when carrying out chemical pesticide operations.

Although some chemicals used to control pests and fungal diseases are systemic in their action, it is still important to get good cover of plant surfaces. For this reason, hollow-cone nozzles with higher pressure and fine to medium droplet sizes are used.

In some cases, continued use of particular products will lead to pest or disease resistance. For example, Benlate (benomyl) was widely used for the control of *Botrytis cinerea*, but became less effective over time. Ring the changes: select chemicals from different groups and apply them in rotation. There are no effective chemical treatments for the direct control of plant viruses; treatments are generally applied against the virus-carrying agents (vectors), such as aphids.

Biological Research continues worldwide to increase the range of invertebrates that can be used to control pests and diseases of plants. The bacterial agent *Bacillus thuringiensis* has been used to control caterpillars, and the fungus *Verticillium lecanii* to control aphids (this has specific temperature and humidity requirements). If the trend to warmer climatic conditions continues, a wider range of biological agents should become available. Any new agent must be cleared for use in this country, and it is important to consider its effect on the natural environment. Make a point of identifying the main groups of natural predators on a site (see box); they can give an idea of local biodiversity.

Physical Basic hygiene may reduce the incidence of disease outbreaks; clean all tools and equipment after use, especially if working on ground where a known transferable disease infection is occurring. Take care in the disposal and siting of infected or infested material; it may have to be burnt on site. Do not accept nursery stock clearly affected by a known pest or disease organism. In some cases, for example with sudden oak death, brought-in nursery stock may need to be held for a period in a quarantine area to determine its health status.

Some weed species are hosts for specific pests and diseases, such as aphids. Hoeing these out from planted beds could be the easiest control option.

Pruning of trees and shrubs must be carried out skilfully, to remove any diseased material. Some species must be cut to a node to avoid die-back. Timing of pruning can also be critical; *Prunus* species susceptible to *Chondrostereum purpureum* (silver leaf disease) are less likely to be infected if pruned when actively growing.

In the walled kitchen garden, rotation can reduce the inoculum levels of some harmful organisms. 'Ground keepers', which may act as source of infection, must be removed from the vegetable garden. Careful roguing (the removal of infected plants) is important in the flower garden – for example, tulips infected with *Botrytis tulipae* (tulip fire) should be removed and destroyed.

The movement of visitors on to, within and out of historic garden sites can present problems, with access to infected areas out of bounds if transferable diseases are confirmed. Infestations of shrubby species with irritant caterpillars may also require restrictions on access until these are dealt with. Although it is impossible to avoid all problems, plant sales should be carefully managed to reduce the chance of transferring pests and diseases off site – visitors will be less than happy to receive plants infested with vine weevil grubs! These problems could be greater at on-site plant fairs, when the plant health status of visiting nurseries may be unknown.

Plant resistance

The resistance to pests and diseases found in many plants has been introduced by deliberate breeding or by chance. Historic parks and gardens with significant plant collections offer the opportunity to record any obvious differences in susceptibility. Some roses exhibit resistance to *Diplocarpon rosae* (rose black spot), but may be susceptible instead to powdery mildew and rusts. Mutation in disease organisms can overcome resistance in some cases.

The control of larger animal pests

Compared to insects, the control of larger animal pests with fur or feathers is often an emotive issue, especially in parks and gardens open to the public who may see them not as pests but as popular local wildlife. Control may best be carried out in areas away from public activity or during periods when visitor numbers are low. Whatever options are chosen, it is easier to communicate with the public on pest control issues when they are made aware of the conservation or ecological problems the pest species may bring. Interpretation and educational programmes can play an important role.

Not only can a pest species be protected by law, but the control itself can be heavily licensed and controlled. All control measures must comply with regulations where relevant and be as humane as possible. Often, to be effective, control is best carried out by skilled and experienced staff or contractors.

If trapping forms part of the control programme, traps must be inspected on a regular basis and be of a type and in a location where other animals and humans are not put at risk. If poisoning is carried out, an animal may die in a public location, so regular checks and disposal will be necessary.

Details of the major animal pests and their control methods are given in the Appendices Table 13.

Guidelines

- Prevention is better than cure
- Monitor regularly
- Have a broad strategy for pest and disease control
- Avoid the use of chemical pesticides wherever possible to protect your own health, that of others and the wider environment.

MACHINERY

The purpose here is to take an overview of the range of machinery available for landscape and horticultural work, not to describe in detail the vast array of models offered by different manufacturers, which are regularly changed and improved. Readers contemplating the purchase of machinery are advised to consider exactly what purpose it is needed for and then to look carefully at the different models available. Most manufacturers have websites listing their equipment and many produce brochures with full details. Professional or trade journals, such as *Horticulture Week* (available by subscription), produce regular supplements that look in some detail at current models. The annual IoG-SALTEX exhibition (usually in early September at Windsor racecourse) provides an opportunity to see a huge range of machinery from different suppliers.

Owners and managers should be aware of the importance of health and safety with regard to machinery. A machine itself is not inherently dangerous, but it can be – to both user and bystanders – if used inappropriately. It is extremely important for operators to be properly trained and to be fully aware of all safety features as well as capabilities and limitations. It is also advisable for managers to keep up-to-date records detailing staff training on machines, and logs detailing the use, maintenance and repair history of machines. *The Control of Vibration at Work Regulations*, produced by the Health and Safety Executive in 2005, relate to the use of

powered tools and equipment such as mowers and hedge cutters. Detailed information is available from www.hse.gov.uk/pubns/indg175.pdf.

There are four main ways of obtaining machinery: outright purchase, leasing, hiring and machinery rings. Leasing may not be an option on all types of machine. Machinery 'rings' started as an agricultural self-help operation but now often include non-agricultural equipment; in some places, 'green rings' have started which concentrate on machinery for nature conservation work.

Mowers

Mowers come in a wide range of shapes and sizes, with an equally wide range of operating modes. These can be grouped into four basic size ranges and five different modes of operation.

Size It is clearly important to choose the right-sized equipment for any job. If it is too small, the work will take much longer than necessary and may cause unnecessary strain to the operator and excessive wear and tear to the machine. If it is too big, there is a strong likelihood of causing unnecessary damage.

- **Pedestrian-operated** These machines are relatively small and in most cases can be lifted by one or two people. The engine may drive both the cutting mechanism and the forward/reverse motion or, with smaller models, it may drive only the

320. Pedestrian cylinder mower.

321. High-quality ride-on cylinder mower.

322. Ride-on rotary mover with grass collection.

323. Rotary hover mower, useful for cutting slopes.

324. Set of gang mowers, made up of cylinder units, suitable for cutting large expanses of grass.

325. Heavy duty tractor-mounted flail, suitable for clearing areas of scrub.

cutting mechanism with the operator being required to propel the machine. These mowers are generally wheeled, or occasionally fitted with tracks or a roller, and the operators walk behind. The Flymo works by creating a cushion of air on which it floats. The strimmer (or 'clearing saw', when fitted with a circular blade rather than cords) is carried by the operator on a specially adapted harness, although versions on wheels are also now available.

- **Ride-on** Designed to carry both the cutting mechanism and the operator, these generally resemble small tractors, with a central seat above four wheels. The cutting equipment is mounted centrally at the front beneath the operator's seat, at the sides, or a combination of both. They require less physical strength to operate than pedestrial mowers.

- **Tractor-mounted** This type of equipment is fixed to the three-point linkage at the back of a tractor (more rarely at the front) and carried by it. It cannot operate in isolation without a tractor. The tractor provides the motion and also powers the cutting mechanism independently through the power take-off (PTO) shaft. The height of the machinery above ground is controlled by the tractor. Tractor-mounted equipment also includes hydraulic arms which can be fitted with various attachments and can reach into otherwise inaccessible places.

- **Tractor-towed** Similar to the above, but not generally fitted to and operated through the three-point linkage, although some may be connected to it for safety and stability. The equipment is fitted with independent wheels which support its weight. Some equipment is simply pulled by the tractor, with the forward motion driving the cutting mechanism, e.g. gang mowers. In other cases, the cutting mechanism may be powered independently by the PTO shaft.

Modes of operation

- **Cylinder mowers** A spinning cylinder with up to twelve blades laps against a fixed horizontal blade, cutting any grass between the two in a scissor-like action. The more blades to the cylinder, the finer the cut. Often fitted with rollers front and rear, these machines produce the highest-quality cut and the traditional striped pattern on lawns. A disadvantage is that the height of cut can only be raised to about 75mm and these cannot therefore cope with long grass over about 100mm. Cylinder mowers are quieter than other types, but vulnerable to careless use, objects, etc.

- **Rotary mowers** A disc with one or more blades, or a single flat blade, spins horizontally at high speed cutting any grass it comes into contact with. Rotary mowers are generally fitted with wheels, although some are fitted with rollers and give a reasonable quality of cut. One advantage of rotary mowers is that the cut can be set quite high – as much as 200mm or even more on some machines – so they are much more able to cope with long grass than cylinder mowers. They can be used very effectively to reduce the height over several cuts. Hover mowers are a form of rotary mower which ride on a cushion of air created by the spinning blade; they are well known for their use in cutting grass banks. Properly set rotary mowers can produce a surprisingly high quality of cut; they are more rubust but noisier than cylinder mowers. Flymos are a specialised form of rotary mower.

- **Flail mowers** A central horizontal shaft or drum spins round at high speed and the attached flails – flat blades or chains – spin vertically, pulverising anything in their path. Flail mowers will cut grass, coarse vegetation, and woody growth such as hedges and sapling trees, up to 1m or higher if mounted on a telescopic arm.

- **Reciprocating knife mowers** These consist of a forward-mounted horizontal bar with fixed teeth through which a sharpened blade moves from side to side. As the machine advances, the fixed blades guide the vegetation towards the moving blade which slices it off. Often termed Allen Scythes after the original make, they are very effective on upright, soft (grass and herb) vegetation. They are particularly useful for conservation areas where seed is required – unlike flail mowers, they cut vegetation neatly and leave it otherwise undamaged. They are less effective where vegetation is matted or has been flattened. Although the blade will cut through thin woody growth, they are not recommended for areas with scrub within the vegetation. Reciprocating knife mowers effectively imitate the action of a scythe: they produce a much cleaner finish than flails, and are favoured for meadow areas where the herbage is required to be in good condition for animals, seed collection or use as green hay.

326. Pedestrian reciprocating knife mower, ideal for cutting small to medium-sized meadow gardens.

- **Strimmers** These unique machines have an engine mounted at one end of a long pole, driving a high-speed spinning disc at the other. The disc is fitted with up to four nylon cords which cut through any grass and coarse herbage they come into contact with. Strimmers are very versatile and can be used for

327. Strimmers are useful for trimming grass and non-woody weeds, but care must be taken around trees to avoid damaging stems and removing bark.

trimming edges, around obstacles and cutting areas where other mowers cannot operate. Their disadvantage is that they are easy to use badly, producing scalped areas and uneven cuts. They are also capable of stripping the bark from young trees. On some strimmers the spinning disc can be replaced with a metal blade enabling much thicker material, including scrub and small trees, to be cut – in this format they are generally referred to as 'clearing saws'.

Availability

- **Cylinder mowers** Used to be common as hand-operated machines, although these are now rare. Most pedestrian and ride-on machines collect the arisings with boxes mounted in front of or behind the cylinder; tractor-mounted or towed machines invariably let arisings fly. Available in all sizes:
  Pedestrian 40–75cm/16–30in width of cut
  Ride-on Up to 2m/6ft 8in width of cut, with three or five sets of blades
  Tractor-mounted Up to 2.5m/8ft width of cut, with five or seven sets of blades
  Tractor-towed Up to 3.5m/12ft width of cut, with up to twelve sets of blades

- **Rotary Mowers** Never available hand-operated because an engine is needed to spin the blade at a sufficiently high speed. Available in all sizes, with fitted bags or boxes to collect arisings:
  Pedestrian 30–75cm/12–30in width of cut
  Ride-on Up to 2m/6ft 8in width of cut
  Tractor-mounted Up to 2.5m/8ft width of cut, with up to five sets of blades, also attachments for hydraulic arm
  Tractor-towed Up to 3.5m/12ft width of cut, with up to five sets of blades

- **Flail mowers** Available only as pedestrian or tractor-mounted machines; the latter may be large machines fitted to the three-point linkage or smaller, highly versatile versions, fitted on to telescopic arms. Most flails are not fitted with collection devices. Available in some sizes:

  Pedestrian 75–90cm/30–36in width of cut
  Ride-on Not available
  Tractor-mounted 1.8–2.5m/6–8ft width of cut, also as a smaller drum on a hydraulic arm
  Tractor-towed Not available

- **Reciprocating knife mowers** Generally available only as pedestrian machines, although rarely may be seen as tractor-mounted on a telescopic arm. They cannot be fitted with collection devices. Available in some sizes:
  Pedestrian 60–90cm/24–36in width of cut
  Ride-on Not available
  Tractor-mounted Hydraulic arm
  Tractor-towed Not available

- **Strimmers** Available only as pedestrian machines, either hand-held or wheeled.

Hedge cutters

Hand-held electric, battery- or petrol-driven hedge trimmers are widely used and can give very high-quality results; they are much faster and easier to use than traditional hand shears. Electric and battery-powered trimmers are lighter and quieter than petrol-engined types. Care needs to be taken with the electric flex on electric types, and these generally require a separate generator to provide power, unless used conveniently close to buildings. Battery-operated machines used to be primarily for domestic use, but are increasingly seen as viable in professional situations because of their light weight, their lack of flex and no need for a generator. The machine selected must be robust and additional batteries (at least one and possibly two or more) should be purchased to ensure that work can continue uninterrupted. Petrol-engine machines are still used and available, but heavy to use for prolonged periods.

Different lengths of cutter bar are usually available, and the most appropriate for the main use should be selected. For long runs of straight hedging, use a longer bar; for intricate topiary, a shorter bar is preferable. Specialist types with extra long reach for high hedges can also be obtained, but can be tiring to use for prolonged periods.

328. Petrol-powered hedge cutters, heavier than electric machines, are more powerful and flexible.

329. A knapsack sprayer can be used to apply most pesticides; however, it is important to have a separate marked sprayer for herbicides only.

For field hedges, particularly long runs, flail mowers on hydraulic arms which can cut both top and sides of a hedge are frequently used. Flails are invaluable for trimming hedges, but are not suitable for renovating overgrown hedges. If carefully used, flails can produce a reasonable finish, but they are often used too quickly by inexperienced operators and the results look appalling.

Circular saws on hydraulic arms can give a good finish, but again can produce bad results if not used with care. With field (or farm) and informal hedges, the preferred height and density will affect cutting frequency. If intended to be stock-proof, unmanaged hedges may need a traditional hedge-laying treatment. If only a taller boundary feature, cutting may be less frequent for aesthetic and ecological reasons

Sprayers

Sprayers are available in every size from hand-held to agricultural boom sprayers and aeroplane- or helicopter-mounted sprayers. Although obviously the larger end of the market is mainly concerned with agricultural crop spraying, knapsack-style sprayers carrying around 15 litres of fluid are frequently used in landscape management. Pedestrian-operated sprayers are commonly used on turf areas; larger tractor-mounted units may be required if very large areas, such as sports fields, need treating.

Controlled Droplet Application (CDA) sprayers are widely used. These produce a closely defined range of droplet sizes from a spinning disc; they use much less liquid than conventional sprayers and are consequently lighter to use, and as the disc is electrically powered the operator is not required to pump. CDA sprayers require specially formulated chemical mixtures and these are not available for every pesticide, so their use is not possible in all situations.

Sprayers excluding CDA can be used for the application of both pesticides and liquid fertilisers.

See the Health and Safety, COSHH and FEBA regulations (pages 75–6).

Weed control (other than spraying)

Where spraying is inappropriate, chemical treatment can be by using weed-wipers or weed pullers. Tractor-mounted equipment is available. A distinct differential in height between the weeds to be controlled and the non-target vegetation is required. Weed pullers need to be used with weed species that do not easily break off

OPTIONS FOR OBTAINING MACHINERY

OUTRIGHT PURCHASE

Advantages
- Machine is owned
- Machine is always available
- Machine is exactly the size and model required
- Staff become familiar with machine

Disadvantages
- Capital cost
- All maintenance costs
- Risk of breakdown (inconvenience and repair cost)
- Care needed at outset to ensure machine is exactly the size and model required and likely to be in regular use
- Reduced flexibility if conditions change or better models become available
- Questionable resale value
- Need to store equipment

LEASING

Advantages
- No capital outlay
- Machine is (effectively) owned
- Machine is always available
- Flexibility to change models (depending on lease agreement)
- Regular payments cover maintenance and breakdown repair (no unexpected costs)
- No resale problems (returned at end of agreement)
- Staff become familiar with machine

Disadvantages
- Lease payments may be expensive
- Not necessarily available for all equipment
- Need to store equipment

HIRING

Advantages
- No capital outlay
- Good flexibility over size of machine (and sometimes model)
- No maintenance or breakdown costs
- No need to store equipment
- No resale problems

Disadvantages
- Can be expensive
- Required machine not always available when required (although good planning should alleviate this problem)
- Staff may initially be unfamiliar with machine

MACHINERY RINGS

Advantages
- No capital outlay
- Promotes local networking
- Reciprocal: owned machines can be put up for hire, thus reducing cost of owning them
- Hire cost may include experienced operator

Disadvantages
- Choice of available machines may be limited
- Machine not always available when required (particularly with very specialised machinery, which the owner will clearly want to use at the optimum time of year)
- Staff may initially be unfamiliar with machine

---

leaving viable roots to re-grow, and in conditions that assist in the removal of the whole plant.

Tractor-towed 'bracken bruisers' can be used to control bracken; they work by causing damage to the stems, causing the plant to 'bleed' and thus, over time, weakening it. These are basically modified rollers, often with a ribbed surface to cause maximum damage.

Weed burners are available as pedestrian-operated machines; their use is mainly confined to hard surface. They work by producing a stream of very hot air, a brief exposure to which causes plant cells to burst and then wither. Most operate using a propane burner. Older types which directly expose the plant to a flame are less effective and no longer much used.

Fertiliser application

Unlike liquid fertilisers, which can be sprayed on to soil or plants, 'dry' fertilisers come as granules or powder and need to be evenly spread over the ground surface. Similar to sprayers, fertiliser applicators are available in a wide range of sizes. In landscape management their used is principally on grass. Hoppers with a spinning disc or a revolving belt are most frequently used. Spinning-disc applicators are available in hand-held, pedestrian and tractor-mounted sizes, while the less popular belt types are available as pedestrian and tractor-mounted machines only.

Turf aeration

- **Scarifiers** These consist of a central shaft spinning at high speed with a series of closely spaced vertical metal blades attached. The spinning metal blades are lowered into the top few millimetres of the grass surface and moved forward. Scarifiers are available as pedestrian-operated or tractor-mounted machines, both usually fitted with detachable collection boxes similar to those found on cylinder mowers. Small hand-powered machines, similar to a rake on wheels, are also available but are viable only for small areas.

- **Spikers** Basic models consist of metal spikes mounted vertically on a horizontal bar, which dig into the ground and pull out as the machine moves forward. These are normally found as tractor-towed machines (although some pedestrian versions are available) and are fitted with solid or slit tines. One disadvantage of these machines is that if ground conditions are too dry they do not penetrate fully, and if too wet they can tear the grass surface because entry and exit are not fully vertical. More advanced versions consist of rows of hydraulically operated spikes which are punched vertically into the ground and out again. These are available as pedestrian or tractor-mounted machines and can usually be fitted with solid, slit or hollow tines. Small hand-powered machines, usually with four or five tines, are also available but are only viable for small areas.

- **Verti-drain** Also known as deep penetration spikers, these have a similar mechanism to advanced spikers, with hydraulically driven vertical penetration into the ground, but they are fitted with a slight backward kick on withdrawal designed to

330. A pedestrian spiker is used to aerate lawns in spring and autumn.

331. A tractor-mounted Vertidrain may be hired to aerate very compacted lawn areas. It is important to make sure that there are no services (electricity, gas, water) under the lawn likely to be punctured.

cause soil fissuring, which greatly enhances drainage and aeration. These machines are capable of penetrating up to 400mm into the soil. They are available with a wide range of solid and hollow tines.

Overseeding by contravator

Contravators consist of a series of paired discs mounted below a hopper, which cut and open a slit in the turf and drop grass seed from the hopper directly into the slit. A roller follows, sealing the slit with the seed inside. Contravators are available only as tractor-mounted machines.

Excavation

Manual excavation in still common in parks and gardens, and remains a sensible option for small amounts and difficult locations. The range of powered excavators is now very large; although these machines are expensive to buy, they are relatively easy and inexpensive to hire. Tracked excavators range in size from under 1,200mm-wide units which will fit into almost any domestic garden up to full-sized JCB and HyMac excavators which can move hundreds of tons of earth in a day. Large amounts of time and effort can be saved by hiring appropriate equipment.

Specialised trenching equipment is also available, which can cut trenches of precise depth and width. These are very useful for the installation of cabling or drainage with minimum disturbance.

Soil cultivation

Ploughing can obviously be done on large areas and ploughs are available in a wide range of sizes. However, the more commonly used equipment in landscape management is the rotovator, available as both pedestrian and larger tractor-mounted equipment. Ploughing and rotovating should not be regularly carried out at the same depth, since both can produce a 'pan' in the soil that acts as a barrier to water, nutrient and root movement. Variation of cultivation depth, occasional deep ploughing or 'pan busting' (where appropriate) can alleviate this problem.

Spading machines are sometimes used in the commercial stock industry. Pulled behind a caterpillar tractor, they consist of either a horizontal bar with rows of curved, pointed spades, or a double row of hydraulically operated spades. As the machine moves, the spades are pushed into the soil and then flicked forward, imitating a digging action. They can operate down to approximately 1m and do not cause pan problems because the spades create an uneven bottom finish. Although not generally used in gardens, they may be helpful for particular jobs, such as long borders, particularly if they can be hired.

Stone buriers or pickers

Tractor-mounted equipment is available which, if used after cultivation, will either bury or pick off all the stones from the soil surface, leaving a stone-free, fine tilth finish.

Tractor mounted 'rotoburiers', a heavy-duty version of stone buriers, are used on uncultivated surfaces and can bury surface

332. The handles of many rotavators can be swivelled to one side, to avoid walking on the cultivated soil.

333. A leaf blowers is used here to clear a path of sawdust following tree work.

vegetation 150–200cm deep. They are used for the creation of bare ground in certain ecological niches.

Leaf clearance

In addition to the trusty hand rake, a number of machines are available to assist in leaf collection. Leaf sweepers are available as pedestrian and tractor-mounted or towed machines. Most work on the principle of a stiff brush, driven by the forward motion of the wheels (or sometimes the tractor power take-off or PTO shaft), which flicks leaves up and backwards into a collector. In ideal conditions, when leaves are not too wet, these collectors can work very well, although they rarely give the perfect final finish of hand-raking. They certainly enable more frequent leaf collection during autumn, particularly on large areas. They can help managers keep on top of the leaf problem, with perhaps only a final hand-rake necessary on prestige areas. For best results, the ground needs to be fairly level, particularly with larger machines which tend to miss low-lying areas.

Wheeled or knapsack-style leaf blowers are also very useful for blowing leaves into lines or other collection areas, or into shrubberies and borders where appropriate eventually to become a mulch. Blowers produce an excellent finish in dry conditions, but become progressively less effective as ground and leaves become wetter. They also have the disadvantage of being very noisy.

Leaf suckers are available as machines to mount on to trailers, with a hand-directed tube that sucks leaves directly from the ground into the trailer. Suckers are used only for picking up already raked piles or lines of leaves. Like blowers they can be noisy, but they save a lot of time by avoiding hand-loading of trailers. Also, like blowers, they are most effective in reasonably dry conditions when leaves are fresh; they become progressively less effective if leaves are wet or have started to mulch down.

All leaf clearance machinery works best on areas of short grass or hard landscape. None works well, if at all, in long grass.

Stump removal

Five types of machinery are available for removing stumps:

- **Stump grinders** Consist of a circular plate on a vertical axis with a number of specially hardened metal teeth around the outer edge. The plate, spinning at high speed, is applied to the surface of the stump and moved backwards and forwards, getter deeper with each pass. Stump grinders are available as pedestrian or tractor-mounted machines. Larger grinders are capable of grinding stumps to c. 300mm below ground level

- **Stump chippers** Attachments that fit on to the hydraulic arm of a JCB or similar, they effectively consists of a single large metal claw, which is forced into the stump and then ripped back, pulling a large section of stump and root with it.

334. Chainsaws are invaluable for branch and timber removal; however, specialist staff training is required to ensure their safe use.

335. Below: a chipper being used to chip branches and leaves after coppicing.

- **Diggers** (see above) Can be used to dig stumps out of the ground

- **Root-cutting chainsaws** A relatively new introduction, these are chainsaws with specially designed features, including a modified guide bar and chain with carbide-capped teeth that can be used to cut through roots below ground level.

- **Winches** (e.g. 'Turfor') Designed to be connected to a tree trunk and an anchor, a hand-operated mechanism tightens the cable, levering the stump out of the ground. It is important to observe all operational and health and safety advice – cables breaking under stress are *extremely dangerous*. Cables and winches require regular inspection and certification by qualified professionals. The anchor point must be properly protected, especially if it is a living tree, and should be more firmly established than the stump.

Vegetation waste disposal

Two types of equipment are of particular interest here.

- **Chippers** The basic design consists of a series of blades, usually on a revolving drum, which chop (or chip) up into

small pieces any material that is fed into them. Chippers vary in size from small electric domestic machines, through small machines with their own engine, to tractor-mounted machines driven by the PTO shaft and large trailer-mounted machines with their own large, powerful engines. The size of vegetation which can be chipped depends on the size and power of the machine – the small domestic type can cope with some woody material up to pencil thickness, whereas the largest self-powered machines are capable of chipping logs up to 200mm diameter.

- **Tub grinders** Much larger versions of the chipper, consisting of a very large tub (hopper) into which material is fed, usually by a JCB. Tub grinders cost tens of thousands of pounds, and are rarely viable for a single park or estate. However, they are readily available for hire, and if space exists for storing waste material it can be economic to bring one in for a few days once or twice a year.

Chippers and tub grinders are valuable for a number of reasons. First they reduce the volume of waste by a huge margin and the resulting chips are easier to deal with than masses of branches. It is usually possible to chip at the site of production and direct the outflow directly into trailers, bins or waste bags, thus avoiding double handling. Additionally, chipped waste is much easier and quicker to compost than woody material. If it is mostly wood chips, it may be usable as mulch or path surfacing and may

thus be useful on site rather than needing to be disposed of as green waste.

Watering and irrigation

Irrigation ranges from very high-tech computerised sprinkler systems down to simple water bowsers. An experienced irrigation engineer should be consulted before embarking on any high-tech or fixed system to ensure that requirements are not likely to change substantially during its lifetime. It is important to consider the balance between the cost of installing and running the system and the amount of staff time (moving hosepipes, spinklers, etc.) that will be saved. High-tech maintenance is likely to be expensive and will require specially trained staff.

A problem frequently encountered is low water pressure, which makes any watering system difficult. If this cannot be rectified by the water provider, a pumped system may be advisable, with a central reservoir and outlets at suitable locations. Again, consult an engineer, since the calculation of flow rate and size of reservoir is critical to the success of any system.

As a rule of thumb, low-tech solutions are much less expensive and more flexible. 'Leaky hoses' or drip irrigation systems which can be covered from view are more effective and less wasteful than old-style sprinklers. An independent brown water supply is likely to become important for drier counties in drought years, when restrictions are likely to be placed on the irrigation of gardens using mains tapwater.

336. An irrigation system with pop-up sprinklers can be expensive to install and maintain but is efficient and convienient.

337. One main advantage is that the sprinklers are not visible when the irrigation is off.

339. A low-level portable sprinkler.

338. Drip irrigation is a very useful system for watering containers.

340. A leaky hose is a low-tech irrigation system made from recycled tyres which will seep droplets of water when under pressure.

341 A high-level portable sprinkler.

HAND TOOL CHECKLIST

- **Trowels, handforks** For planting and weeding.

- **Digging spade** Should have small horizontal footplates at top of blade for ease of use and to prevent damage to footwear when digging. 'D'- or 'T'-shaped handles available according to personal preference.

- **Digging fork** Bar along top of prongs is thicker than a spade so no footplates are required. Handles as for spade.

- **Border ('lady's') spade, fork** Smaller versions of above, useful for working on beds or borders or for planting containerised stock.

- **Manure fork** Light fork with widely spaced, long, thin, slightly curved prongs, specially designed for picking up bulky organic material.

- **Potato fork** Specialist, rather rare fork with wide, flattened prongs designed to prevent damage to root vegetables when digging up.

- **Mattock** Correct tool for digging out stumps or cutting roots – its use will save a lot of damage to spades!

- **Hoe** Various types available. The principle two are Dutch hoes which are pushed, and draw hoes which are pulled. Modifications of these include two-, three- or four-pronged cultivators and rotating, spiked wheels. Onion hoes are used for close work between plants.

- **Garden rake** Metal-headed rake used principally for producing a fine tilth on a cultivated area.

- **Springbok rake** Wire rake used for raking gravel paths, leaves from lawns and for small-scale scarification work on grass.

- **Landscape rake** May be entirely wood or with an aluminium head. Used for levelling and initial raking of cultivated areas and for rough raking of leaves from grass areas.

- **Secateurs** Two principle types. Anvil has a top blade that cuts down on to a flat bottom blade; cross-cut (also 'parrot-bill' or 'bypass') has blades that slice past one another like scissors. Cross-cut are the most popular, but personal preference is usually the deciding factor.

- **Loppers** Large versions of secateurs, usually cross-cut (but some are anvil), they come in a range of sizes and are used to cut thicker branches.

- **Long-arm pruners** Lopper/secateur-like action on the end of an extendable pole, operated by a string or arm. Useful for pruning awkard high branches from the ground, but tiring to use for long.

- **Saws** Wide range of handsaws available. Modern small folding saws with replaceable blades are very effective and convenient. Bow-saws, also useful, come in a range of sizes; the bigger ones are quite clumsy to use and cutting anything that requires these might be better achieved with a chainsaw.

- **Pole saws** Saws fixed on the end of a long (often extendable) pole for sawing high branches. Useful, but tiring to use for long.

- **Grass shears** Used for trimming small areas of grass, particularly around trees or plants where strimmers are inappropriate

- **Hedge shears** Used for hedge cutting. Easy to distinguish from grass shears because they have a notch near the point where the blades cross which can be used for cutting through slightly thicker wood.

- **Edging shears** Long-handled shears used for trimming grass edges.

- **Half-moon** Edging tool used for cutting (or re-cutting) grass edges.

342. A well-organised potting shed aids an efficient operation.

Tractors

The smallest are at home in a garden situation, while the largest are capable of hauling whole trees from the forest or twelve-bladed ploughs through the soil. The first and most important consideration is what the tractor will be required to do.

- **Size** Larger tractors are more powerful and can support larger attachments. Choose an appropriate size for the planned work.

- **Access** Consider the areas the tractor will be used in – an 8ft-wide tractor cannot get access along 6-ft wide paths.

- **Storage** Do you have a safe place to keep the tractor when not in use? Tractors are expensive and secure storage is essential, ideally under cover. Bear in mind the access limitations, both width and height, of any existing sheds or barns.

- **Fuel** Most tractors run on diesel. How much will it use during a working day, and how much needs to be stored for a week or a month's use? Are there appropriate facilities for storing this amount of fuel in a safe and legal manner?

- **Attachments** What will be used with the tractor and how is it to be attached? Most tractors come with a tow hitch, but not all have three-point linkage as standard. If any attachments need power, make sure the tractor is fitted with a PTO shaft. The tractor must be suitable for the attachment, regarding both size and power requirements. Some equipment is very heavy and requires counterbalancing weights at the front of the tractor, so ensure there is a suitable bar for these to be attached to. Some attachments are designed to fit on to the front of a tractor, so ensure that it has appropriate couplings at the front end.

- **Safety and comfort** All tractors should have minimum safety features as standard (roll bar, PTO cover and guard, etc.) but extra features may be needed for particular uses. Air conditioning may be needed for constant use in open areas in summer, or for sealed and pressurised cabs if very dusty work or spraying is being carried out.

- **Licensing, etc.** If the tractor is to be used on a public highway, ensure that it is properly licensed and has appropriate MOT, insurance, etc. Drivers must be fully trained in the use of the tractor. The minimum for an operator on the public highway is a full licence for an agricultural vehicle, although a full driving licence is preferable.

Two-wheeled tractors

These are not really tractors, but two-wheeled power units on to the front of which a wide range of attachments can be fitted. The operator walks behind and controls the equipment in the fashion of a pedestrian mower. They provide a high level of power, a light footprint and remarkable versatility. One obvious disadvantage is that if the power unit is not working, neither are the attachments. It is also advisable to check how universal the couplings are across models, in case these are changed or cease to be available.

The increasing range of attachments includes mowers, balers, wood chippers, sweepers, cultivators, stone buriers, snow ploughs, sprayers, saw benches, harrows and water pumps.

Trailers

Trailers can be almost as varied as tractors but the main points to consider are:

- **Size (1)** What and where are the main uses going to be? There is no point buying a huge trailer when its only use is for moving small amounts of material or if access to where it is needed is restricted. Some trailers can have extra side boards fitted for times when bulky but light materials (e.g. leaves in autumn) are being carried.

- **Size (2)** Make sure the trailer is a suitable size for the tractor it will be attached to!

- **Tipping** Not all trailers are made to tip, so check for this function if it is needed. Tipping trailers are usually hydraulically operated, and must be compatible with the tractor

- **Hitching** Obviously the hitch arrangements must suit the tractor, but also consider ease of hitching (trailers that are difficult to hitch are a potential health and safety problem). Also consider how the trailer sits when it is unhitched, especially if it is to be left at a location to be filled while the tractor is elsewhere. The hitching point must be stable and supported at a level where the tractor can pick it up without difficulty – hand manoeuvring an empty trailer is difficult, when it is full it is simply dangerous.

- **On-road use** If the trailer is to be used on the public highway it will require a number plate to match the tractor towing it and a full set of working lights.

Barrows

Wheelbarrows come in a surprising variety of forms, although there are only two basic designs – front-wheel barrows which need to be lifted at the back and pushed forward, and mid-wheel barrows (often called 'trolley barrows' or 'trucks') which can be lifted or pushed down at either end and pushed or pulled. Front-wheel barrows can be the traditional single-wheel or (usually larger) double-wheeled versions. Trolleys are usually double- and sometimes quadruple-wheeled. Barrows can be wood or metal or a mixture of both. Choosing a type depends on:

- **Main use** Single-wheeled barrows are good for light loads, but become harder to use with heavier loads

- **Type of materials to be transported** Trucks are often better for heavier and bulkier loads because they generally have a larger capacity

- **Access** Trolleys, generally larger, may not be easily usable in a small or intricate garden.

Wheels are generally pneumatic (air-filled). The solid wheels found on small domestic wheelbarrows are not suitable for continuous use or larger capacity, and present difficulties on anything but a solid surface. Powered barrows are excellent for moving large amounts of heavy material. They are not usually viable as a permanent addition to the equipment list, but can be readily hired for particular projects. Always check surfacing and access, especially with regard to turning requirements, before hiring.

Part Three

Ten case studies

No two maintenance and management systems are ever quite alike, whether in historic gardens or indeed any gardens of appreciable size and merit. The ten historic sites chosen for study here have been selected in order to show, in a very practical presentation, the different approaches to management determined by many factors. These include historic evolution and character, size, present ownership and direction, and also techniques and strategies for adapting to the situation facing historic gardens and parks in the twenty-first century.

These case studies are a record of the status quo in the year 2004 when most of the facts and figures were compiled, and our thanks go to the owners, agents and managing gardeners and staff for their help and cooperation. Details that are liable to change — opening times and periods, staff and personnel, and possibly certain management decisions — should be checked in current literature or on the internet.

3.1   Brodsworth Hall, South Yorkshire   249

3.2   Chatsworth, Derbyshire   253

3.3   Down House, Kent   259

3.4   Great Dixter, East Sussex   265

3.5   Hampton Court Palace, Surrey   271

3.6   Levens Hall, Cumbria   279

3.7   Sheffield Botanic Garden, South Yorkshire   285

3.8   Sheffield Park Garden, East Sussex   291

3.9   Squerryes Court, Kent   297

3.10 Stonehenge, Wiltshire   303

343. Brodsworth Hall: view from the classical summerhouse over the evergreen shrubberies and formal flower garden towards the hall.

Brodsworth Hall, South Yorkshire

BRODSWORTH HALL
Doncaster, South Yorkshire DN5 7XJ
www.english-heritage.org.uk
Ordnance Survey map reference SE506070
English Heritage Register Grade II*
Ownership: English Heritage

SUMMARY OF OPENING ARRANGEMENTS
House 1 April–29 September 1–5 p.m. Tuesday–Sunday and Bank
Holiday Mondays
30 September–29 October: 12 noon–4 p.m. Saturday and Sunday
30 October–30 March: closed
Gardens 1 April– 29 October 10 a.m.–5.30 p.m. every day
30 October–31 March: 10 a.m.–4 p.m. Saturday and Sunday, except
24–26, 30–31 December: closed
Last admission half an hour before closing time

Plant sales Small-scale plant displays (four trolleys) outside ticket
office

Visitor numbers Have increased by c. 2 per cent over the last five
years. 2003–4: 52,000 (26,000 garden and house, 26,000 garden only)

HISTORY

Brodsworth estate was bought by Peter Thellusson in 1791, six
years before his death. His will was eventually settled in 1859 and
the estate inherited by Charles Sabine Augustus Thellusson. The
new hall was built 1861–3 and Samuel Taylor was employed as
head gardener in 1861. Extensive works were then carried out to
the grounds, which included laying out a formal and a flower
garden. A quarry garden with a fern dell was created (Joseph
Barron may have worked here: records from 1865 show an estimate for work on a 'Rockery') and improvements to the parkland
were undertaken.

Charles Thellusson died in 1885 and the estate eventually
passed down through marriage in 1931 to Charles Grant-Dalton.
Much of the house was not used and garden staff was reduced.
After Grant-Dalton's death in 1952, his widow Sylvia continued to
occupy the house until her death in 1987 and during this period the
garden was much neglected.

344. Aerial view.

345. Spring bedding in the formal flower garden.

Brodsworth Hall became an English Heritage property in 1989. The garden is a rare survival of a high Victorian garden with few changes after the early 1870s.

In the last five years the garden has undergone intensive restoration to re-present the garden as it was in its heyday, with the help of a £233,000 grant from the Heritage Lottery Fund.

MANAGEMENT

The main part of the garden is formal in character and high-maintenance in its requirements. It includes formal flower gardens (0.25 ha) and formal shrubberies (0.5 ha); the rest is made up of grassland (1–2 ha) and woodland (4–5 ha).

STAFF

Full time: head gardener Dan Booth, garden supervisor, senior gardener and three gardeners, with support from an extensive volunteer programme.

POLICIES

Policies and techniques for the main areas and features to include where applicable:

Grass areas

Currently under two mowing regimes: Most grass is cut weekly with high-quality cylinder or rotary mowers. All edges are cut weekly using mechanical lawn-edger or edging shears. All grass path edges are tidied fortnightly using adjustable strimmer. A large zone (0.25–0.5 ha) is managed as a meadow and is cut at the end of

August or start of September. No herbicides or fertilisers used. Autumn and spring maintenance include spiking and scarification. Currently all arisings are removed.

Ornamental gardens, borders

During the growing season, the flower garden is maintained weekly, including dead-heading, weeding, watering and feeding. During autumn and winter, leaves and worm casts are removed. Biannual top-dressing of beds is undertaken, using leaf mould or imported, screened, peat-free compost. Flower bed edges are re-cut every three years, using a board and edging iron. The formal bedding is changed twice a year: the spring display is planted in autumn, taking five staff around seven working days; the summer display is planted in late spring, taking five staff five working days. Bed preparation, including the removal of the old plants, takes five staff three working days. The regular management of pests, including rabbits, pheasants, squirrels and moles, is necessary on a regular basis.

Pleasure grounds and shrubberies

Maintenance includes: weekly weeding, monthly dead-wooding and leaf removal, and shrub pruning and shaping two or three times a year (using mainly hand-shears for a better finish). Large-scale regeneration work is undertaken throughout late autumn, winter and early spring.

346. Italian white marble statues by Chevalier Casentini dating from 1866 stand out from the garden's evergreen shrubberies.

Hedges and topiary

Hedges are cut annually, using a hedge-trimmer and hand-shears. Topiary is cut up to three times a year, with hand-shears. Dead-wooding and remedial pruning undertaken in autumn and winter.

Support glasshouses

These were built as part of the restoration project for the production of garden plants by a team of volunteers.

Rock gardens

Fern Dell has a weekly programme of weeding, watering and deadheading, taking two staff one day a week. Inter-planting is done throughout the growing season for a succession of interest in the Fern Dell. The beds are top-dressed annually, using peat-free compost, sharp sand and chick grit. In late autumn tender ferns are tied up and given winter protection. Paths are swept, scrubbed and/or gritted monthly; when required in winter.

Rose garden

During the growing season the roses require weekly weeding and watering, taking two staff four hours. A weekly feeding regime from mid-spring until the first blooms also takes four hours. Pruning and dead-wooding are undertaken in autumn.

Woodlands

Shrubs receive remedial pruning in winter. All major formal shrubs and/or topiary are clipped, which normally takes three staff five weeks a year. During the growing season the grass in all woodland areas is cut weekly with a rough rotary mower, or every three weeks with strimmers, taking two staff two to three days. Weeding is undertaken bi-weekly in the more formal woodlands, taking four staff three days.

Paths

Paths are swept weekly during the opening season and as required during the closed season, taking two staff four hours.

Recent repair and restoration works

Summer house re-built, major re-planting schemes throughout the woodland garden (800 Viburnum, 2,000 box, 1,000 Portuguese laurel, 160 holly, 100 Chameacyparis, 100,000 snowdrops). New gardeners' yard developed, including a glasshouse and potting shed. Other works include a bridge reconstruction, planting of 2,000 ferns and creation of 1,000 sq. m of wildflower meadows.

FUTURE POLICY

Mary of the garden areas declined into secondary woodland after the first and second world wars, the restoration has focused on re-presenting the these areas prior to their decline. Following this intensive period of garden restoration a new set of priorities for next five years will focus on sustaining the restored garden, developing plant collections and changing the focus of garden work from restoration and plant establishment to maintenance.

347. Above: the restored rock garden and fern collection in the former quarry. Paths on the quarry tops are delineated with posts and chains with trained ivy.

348. Above: tall planting of *Sequoiadendron* and beech trees in the spine banks accentuate the drama of the grove.

349. Above: the rose garden at the northern end of the grove has over 100 rose cultivars, many Portland roses.

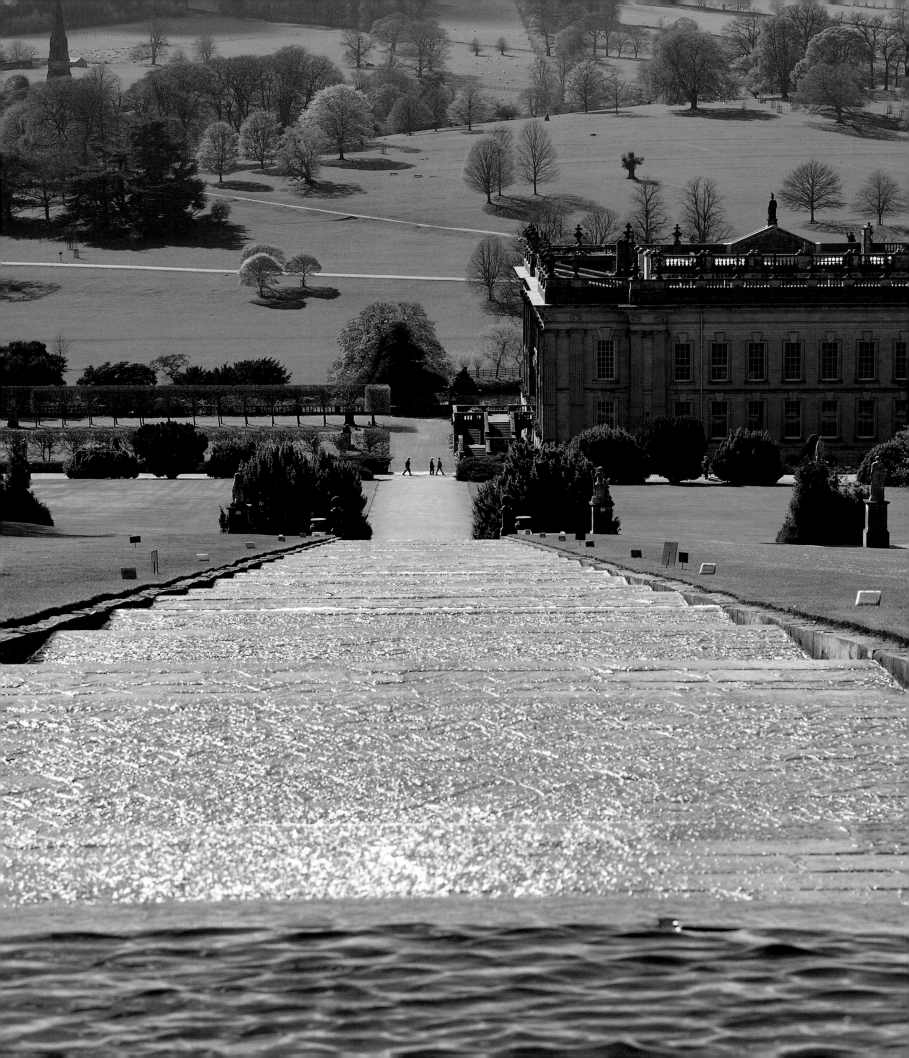

3.2

Chatsworth, Derbyshire

CHATSWORTH
Bakewell, Derbyshire DE45 IPP
www.chatsworth.org/
Ordnance Survey map reference SK2670, Peak District National Park
English Heritage Register Grade I
Ownership: Trustees of the Chatsworth Settlement on behalf of the
Duke and the Duchess of Devonshire, leased to the Chatsworth House
Trust, Registered Charity no. 511149. All admission income goes to the
charity; no external funding sought or accepted for management or
upkeep of garden

SUMMARY OF OPENING ARRANGEMENTS
House and garden mid March–mid December, with a range of
admission prices including rates for adults, senior citizens, students,
children and families. Separate price for garden only
Extensive parkland open all year (no charge)
Excellent facilities, including shops, restaurant, a working farmyard and
woodland adventure playground.

Events In 2004: international horse trials, angling fair, country fair and
open-air concerts. House and garden specially decorated and floodlit
for pre-Christmas openings

Visitor numbers Have increased substantially over last ten years.
2004: over 470,000 to the house and garden

HISTORY

Chatsworth House and its gardens have a rich and well-docu-
mented history over four hundred years, well presented in an
excellent guide book which is strongly recommended as a reference source. As with many other historic houses, several periods of
distinctive styles were matched in the gardens and parklands.

Elizabethan
Earliest mention of the garden is in 1560 by Bess of Hardwick,
who wanted a 'letell garden' around the new house that she and
her husband Sir William Cavendish had built on the location of the
present house. It was primarily for food production with orchards
and fish ponds, but also had gazebos and pavilions.

Baroque
In 1690s the Ist Duke of Devonshire rebuilt the house in a grand
style much of which still exists today. He employed London and
Wise to lay out formal gardens and parterres.

351. Aerial view.

Landscape movement

In 1760s the 4th Duke made sweeping changes to the setting of the house, building a bridge over the River Derwent and bringing in Lancelot 'Capability' Brown to remodel some features of the gardens and park. He removed parterres, but left the seventeenth-century Cascade, Canal Pond and Sea Horse Fountain.

Victorian

Dramatic changes established much of today's features. The young 6th Duke engaged the equally young (23-year-old) Joseph Paxton as head gardener in 1826. He transformed the gardens over the next twenty years with the great Emperor Fountain, the vast and theatrical rock garden, restored formal parterres and a unique range of glass structures – the Conservative Wall or The Case – for camellias and other exotics. The Great Stove or Conservatory, opened in 1840, was at that time the largest glass structure of its type in the world. Neglect and the impossibility of heating it during World War One led to decision to demolish it in 1920. Its stone walls remain, but its once great interior site has been replaced with a maze. Paxton died in 1865 aged sixty-two, and is buried at Edensor, the village he helped to build close to Chatsworth.

Twentieth and twenty-first centuries

High standards and traditions are being perpetuated, with innovations and effective visitor facilities and presentation. The 11th Duke and Duchess worked tirelessly to conserve, develop and promote Chatsworth from the time the Duke inherited it in 1950, with the Duchess playing a major part in direction and the addition of new features.

MANAGEMENT

Gardens cover 260 ha, under jurisdiction and responsibility of garden staff. Park and woodlands cover some 2,470 ha, managed by estate staff.

STAFF

Head gardener Andrew Webster, 19 full-time, one part-time, one student as part of Professional Gardeners' Guild training scheme, some students for short-term summer work, no volunteers. Number of staff consistent for last few years. In 2004 the line of communication was from the Dowager Duchess, who acts as director of the gardens, to agent to head gardener. Two-way radios used for communication between estate staff. Head gardener and outside foreman designate jobs on a daily basis; inside foreman organises work in glasshouses.

Staff responsibilities Four in glasshouses, including foreman; three in fruit, vegetable and cut flower gardens; twelve in pleasure grounds, borders, etc. Staff normally work in groups of two or four, with one group mainly responsible for mowing in growing season.

Three or four have arboricultural/tree climbing qualifications; six have chain-saw certificates for work on the ground.

Working hours generally 8 a.m.–4.30 p.m., five days a week. Duty rota of four staff cover for evenings and weekends, mainly in glasshouse. Overtime paid at a set rate.

Contractors used only for special work such as major tree operations.

Construction work, structural repairs and maintenance done by estate staff, who have a range of skills such as masonry, carpentry, etc. They liaise with the head gardener.

The farm is a separate enterprise. There is also a garden centre in the park, run by a concessionaire.

Fine-mown lawns

50 ha, normally mown weekly throughout the season from mid-March to end September. One man responsible, using a John Deere ride-on mower.

Salisbury Lawn is of great historical and ecological interest, with a unique flora. Once part of the formal parterre, it has remained largely unchanged and unimproved (other than for mowing) for over two centuries.

Rough grass

Some 84 ha, cut from about second week of July (after daffodils have died down) to mid-October, a labour-intensive operation done by two staff. On banks and under low branches, a wide range of machinery used, including Modus grass collection system, tractor-mounted flails, Ferris dual-drive pedestrian mower, Grillo climber rough-terrain mower, power scythe and strimmers.

Ornamental gardens, borders, pleasure grounds, shrubberies, etc.

Usually maintained by four staff, mostly in early spring and autumn. Not continuous work.

Hedges and topiary

About 8 km of clipped hedges, equal to 2.2 ha cut surface area. Hedge-cutting done by four staff using hand-held electric and petrol hedge-trimmers, mid-July to end September.

Kitchen garden

Covers 1.2 ha, maintained by three full-time staff. A wide range of vegetables and fruit grown, winter vegetables forced, and propagation of tomatoes, melons, cucumbers and bedding display plants. 696 sq m of cut flowers, early and late, such as dahlias, chrysanthemums and sweet peas. Orchids also grown.

Conservatories and glasshouses

1,644 sq m, consisting of vinery, peach house, the 11th Duke's Conservatory, and the Conservative wall houses. Maintained by four full-time staff. Propagation in ornamental plant glasshouses.

352. Opposite: the maze, with a Perspex diagram of Paxton's great conservatory to help visitors visualise the structure.

JOSEPH PAXTON'S GREAT CONSERVATORY COMPLETED 1840 AND DEMOLISHED 1920

Please adjust your stance and posture to see the Great Conservatory back in situ. The Conservatory was 227ft/84m long, 123ft/37.5m wide and 67ft/20.4m high; it was the biggest greenhouse in the world at the time it was built in 1840. It was also tropical.

353. Rock outcrop.

Rock garden

Extensive and dramatic series of rock 'outcrops' created by Paxton in the 1840s, with emphasis on massive creations 'to copy the most picturesque assemblages of natural rocks'. One section extensively restored in 2003–4. Maintenance as and when necessary, controlling invasive vegetation, notably ivy.

Cottage garden

Feature inspired by Cheshire Women's Institute exhibit at 1988 Chelsea Flower Show; mainly responsibility of a student as a year-long project.

Woodland

Includes Pinetum and Arboretum created by 6th Duke and Paxton. Work mainly in winter months, cutting back invading *Rhododendron ponticum*, laurels, etc. Trees checked for dead or hanging branches. Four staff, trained in tree-climbing and use of chainsaws.

Water areas

Use of ornamental water one of the great attractions at Chatsworth. Some 1.52 ha, including Canal Pond, Cascade, Grotto Pond and fountains. Series of three collecting lakes in the moors above the garden were original source of 1st Duke's formal features such as the Cascade, Canal Pond, Willow Tree and Great Fountains. Paxton made major changes to gravity-powered water system, creating a new Emperor Lake of about 3.24 ha with one of its main objects being to boost the Emperor Fountain by a massive pipe system that drops 122m: the force enables a superb jet of over 100m when valve fully opened. Most of Paxton's pipework is still operating, but there have been periodic restorations and renewals of the Willow Tree Fountain. Otherwise, maintenance is to ensure inlets and outlets remain clear, especially during heavy rainstorms. Aquatic weeds cleared manually.

Paths, drives, terraces, etc.

Extensive system involves re-surfacing when necessary before public opening in spring, and making good potholes and ruts. There are over 4km of 'green road' round the garden.

RECENT DEVELOPMENTS

Rock Garden renovation To mark the bicentenary of Paxton's birth, in 2003 an area was restored where a monumental rock 'tower' had collapsed. This enabled installation of a new viewing platform, with wheelchair access, as well as clearance of invading scrub.

Great Conservatory heating system 300 tons of coal were needed every winter to feed the eight furnaces of this great structure. Recent work has revealed the large coal hole where fuel was unloaded from carts after a two-mile journey from the nearest railway station, and opened up the tunnel Paxton created to take it to the Conservatory.

Sensory Garden Opened in 2004 and has proved popular with visitors.

General renovation Over the last fifteen years, Chatsworth House Trust has spent large sums on conservation of stone buildings, terraces, pipework and waterworks. If estate staff cannot complete a project without outside assistance, local materials and expertise are used whenever possible.

INTERPRETATION

Conducted tours of the gardens; groups can book guided tours of garden and greenhouse; short talks (free of charge) on certain days by garden staff; comprehensive 64-page guidebook.

FUTURE PLANS

The 11th Duke was succeeded by his son in 2005. The Estate has plans to extend the range of educational opportunities in the garden, in conjunction with the farmyard's well-established education programme.

354. Paxton's Conservative wall houses.

3.3
Down House, Kent

DOWN HOUSE
Luxted Road, Downe, near Orpington, Kent BR6 7JT
www.english-heritage.org.uk
Ordnance Survey map reference TQ4361, between A21 and A233
(brown tourist signs) on top of North Kent Downs, five miles south-
east of Bromley
English Heritage Register Grade II
Ownership: English Heritage
SUMMARY OF OPENING ARRANGEMENTS
1 April–16 July, 1–30 September and bank holidays: 10 a.m.– 6 p.m.
Wednesday–Sunday
17 July–31 August: 10 a.m.– 6 p.m. (house 11 a.m.–5 p.m.) every day
1–31 October: 10 a.m.–5 p.m. Wednesday–Sunday
1 November–18 December: 10 a.m. – 4 p.m. Wednesday–Sunday
18 December–6 February: closed
Last admission half an hour before closing time
Inclusive audio tours of house, gift shop, tea room, disabled access to
first floor by lift
One-hour garden guided tours Wednesday and Sunday; group bookings
by prior arrangement
Fungi guided tours every Sunday in November
Visitor numbers 25,050, limited due to access and parking limitations

HISTORY

Down House was the home of Charles Darwin from 1842 until his death in 1882, then of his family until his widow Emma died in 1896. Subsequently it was leased to various tenants until 1907, when Down House School for Girls was established. This successful school outgrew the site by 1922, and moved to Newbury; it was followed by a less successful school. In 1927 Sir George Buckston Browne bought the site to open it as a museum dedicated to Darwin, entrusting it to the British Association for the Advancement of Science; it opened as a museum in June 1929. In 1952 ownership transferred to the Royal College of Surgeons and from 1993 to 1996 it was managed by the Natural History Museum. English Heritage purchased the property in 1996 with support from the Wellcome Trust and the Heritage Lottery Fund.

Charles and Emma Darwin moved from central London to Downe in September 1842 with their two young children, and went on to have eight more (three died in childhood). As the family grew, so did the house, with additions of an extended bow window for the dining room (1843), a new drawing room (1858), a verandah for the drawing room (1872) and a new study (1877). The garden evolved to suit the family's needs. The earliest developments were the provision of windbreaks by planting trees and shrubberies, and the creation of banks following the excavation of

the road. In 1846 an adjacent strip of land was rented from a neighbour and planted as a copse with a circuitous walk known as the Sandwalk, used by Darwin for his daily constitutional when he mulled over his theories. One small section of the greenhouses grew to five sections as Darwin's botanical work became more detailed. The final part of the garden was bought in 1881 for a tennis court.

Darwin wrote the majority of his books at Down House including *The Origin of Species*, published in 1859. Darwin then turned his attention to the many botanical questions that his theories had raised. By 1860 he had become a practical botanical scientist, using his garden, meadows and neighbouring countryside in his research. Through the plants he observed on his walks and those he grew in his garden he discovered evolutionary plant adaptations such as heterostyly (differing flower structures on the same species of plant), how orchids are pollinated, various methods employed by climbing plants, how carnivorous plants gain their nutrients and the benefits of cross-pollination as opposed to self-pollination.

MANAGEMENT

The overriding policy is to depict the gardens as Darwin would have seen them; they are domestic in scale and English Heritage

356. Aerial view.

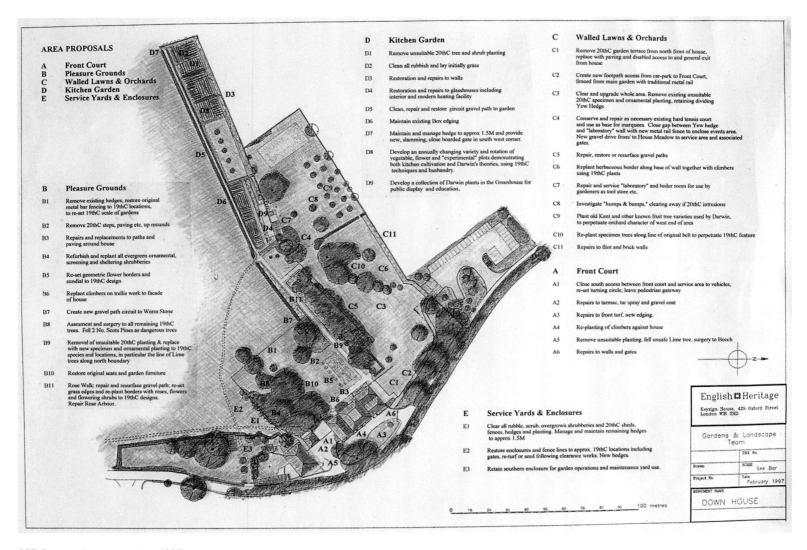

AREA PROPOSALS

A   **Front Court**
B   **Pleasure Grounds**
C   **Walled Lawns & Orchards**
D   **Kitchen Garden**
E   **Service Yards & Enclosures**

B   **Pleasure Grounds**

B1   Remove existing hedges, restore original metal bar fencing to 19thC locations, to re-set 19thC scale of gardens

B2   Remove 20thC steps, paving etc. up mounds

B3   Repairs and replacements to paths and paving around house

B4   Refurbish and replant all evergreen ornamental, screening and sheltering shrubberies

B5   Re-set geometric flower borders and sundial to 19thC design

B6   Replant climbers on trellis work to facade of house

B7   Create new gravel path circuit to Worm Stone

B8   Assessment and surgery to all remaining 19thC trees. Fell 2 No. Scots Pines as dangerous trees

B9   Removal of unsuitable 20thC planting & replace with new specimen and ornamental planting to 19thC species and locations, in particular the line of Lime trees along north boundary

B10   Restore original seats and garden furniture

B11   Rose Walk: repair and resurface gravel path; re-set grass edges and re-plant borders with roses, flowers and flowering shrubs to 19thC designs. Repair Rose Arbour.

D   **Kitchen Garden**

D1   Remove unsuitable 20thC tree and shrub planting

D2   Clean all rubbish and lay initially grass

D3   Restoration and repairs to walls

D4   Restoration and repairs to glasshouses including interior and modern heating facility

D5   Clean, repair and restore circuit gravel path to garden

D6   Maintain existing Box edging

D7   Maintain and manage hedge to approx 1.5M and provide new, slamming, close boarded gate in south west corner.

D8   Develop an annually changing variety and rotation of vegetable, flower and "experimental" plots demonstrating both kitchen cultivation and Darwin's theories, using 19thC techniques and husbandry.

D9   Develop a collection of Darwin plants in the Greenhouse for public display and education.

C   **Walled Lawns & Orchards**

C1   Remove 20thC garden terrace from north front of house, replace with paving and disabled access to and general exit from house

C2   Create new footpath access from car-park to Front Court, fenced from main garden with traditional metal rail

C3   Clear and upgrade whole area. Remove existing unsuitable 20thC specimen and ornamental planting, retaining dividing Yew Hedge

C4   Conserve and repair as necessary existing hard tennis court and use as base for marquees. Close gap between Yew hedge and "laboratory" wall with new metal rail fence to enclose events area. New gravel drive from/ to House Meadow to service area and associated gates.

C5   Repair, restore or resurface gravel paths

C6   Replant herbaceous border along base of wall together with climbers using 19thC plants

C7   Repair and service "laboratory" and boiler room for use by gardeners as tool store etc.

C8   Investigate "humps & bumps," clearing away if 20thC intrusions

C9   Plant old Kent and other known fruit tree varieties used by Darwin, to perpetuate orchard character of west end of area

C10   Re-plant specimen trees along line of original belt to perpetuate 19thC feature

C11   Repairs to flint and brick walls

A   **Front Court**

A1   Close south access between front court and service area to vehicles, re-set turning circle, leave pedestrian gateway

A2   Repairs to tarmac, tar spray and gravel coat

A3   Repairs to front turf, new edging

A4   Re-planting of climbers against house

A5   Remove unsuitable planting, fell unsafe Lime tree, surgery to Beech

A6   Repairs to walls and gates

E   **Service Yards & Enclosures**

E1   Clear all rubble, scrub, overgrown shrubberies and 20thC sheds, fences, hedges and planting. Manage and maintain remaining hedges to approx 1.5M

E2   Restore enclosures and fence lines to approx. 19thC locations including gates, re-turf or seed following clearance works. New hedges.

E3   Retain southern enclosure for garden operations and maintenance yard use.

English ✦ Heritage
Keysign House, 429 Oxford Street
London W1R 2HD

Gardens & Landscape Team

Drawn | SCALE See Bar
Project No. | Date February 1997

MONUMENT NAME
DOWN HOUSE

0   10   20   30   40   50   60   70   80   90   100 metres

357. Restoration master plan, 1997.

aims to maintain the feel of a family home. They are used to depict experiments that Darwin would have carried out during his research.

The layout of the paths, beds and borders has been restored and the garden is being planted with species that the Darwins list in their correspondence and other writings. The wealth of archival information enables a historically accurate selection of plants; a Darwin reference is intended for each of the plants in the garden. Where authentic plants are unavailable, plants of the right period will be used instead.

STAFF

Head gardener Toby Beasley, trainee gardener, volunteers and contractors.

Daily meetings to issue work carried out by English Heritage staff and volunteers. Formal monthly meetings are held between the head gardener and contractor to discuss programme and other site issues. Garden contractors currently undertake all grass cutting, hedge cutting, shrub pruning and path weeding. Their work is specified in a five-year grounds maintenance contract, monitored by the head gardener.

Volunteers, directed by the head gardener or trainee gardener, maintain flower beds and borders, shrubberies, kitchen garden and greenhouse, and undertake some tasks in woodland. As enthusiasts of Darwin they prove very effective as garden interpreters, and a small group has been trained to take guided tours. Twenty-seven volunteers do a minimum of half a day per fortnight from, organised on a rota system.

A trainee gardener – a sandwich-course student or recent graduate on a fixed one-year contract – gains experience in all aspects of gardening. He or she helps manage and develop the volunteer workforce, and also develops an understanding of the Darwins at Down in order to take guided tours.

The head gardener carries out direction of maintenance, development of the grounds and research, in a varied job which can entail weeding one day and writing management plans the next.

Lawns

Two small lawns of c. 1,950 sq m, cut to a height of 25mm. No maintenance apart from cutting, so they are full of moss and other grassland weeds, providing an appropriate rustic appearance and an ideal environment for over 200 different varieties of grassland fungi. Some are rare, and maintenance has to take their management into account.

Extended orchard and tennis court areas of c. 7,750 sq m, with grass cut to a height of 35mm for a deeper sward which maintains its colour during summer. In the orchard (1,280 sq m), grass is left to grow and cut only at the end of summer in order to replicate the Darwins' management.

All lawn areas cut by garden contractors, using a pedestrian rotary mower with a roller for closer-cut lawns, a small ride-on mower on the orchard and tennis court area and strimmers in the long grass of the orchard. All arisings collected and composted.

Meadows

7.28 ha of Darwin's hay meadow and a further 4.45 ha bought by Buckstone Browne come under head gardener's remit. Hay is cut towards end of summer and animals graze meadows through winter, both activities contracted out to local farmers. The aim is to lower the nutrient status of the soil to allow for a greater diversity of plants in the sward. This is a long-term restoration which will be measured by five-yearly surveys from a base-line survey in 2003.

358. View from the Sandwalk over the meadow towards the house and kitchen garden.

Beds, borders and shrubberies

Numerous small flowerbeds and borders planted with bedding, herbaceous plants, bulbs, annuals and shrubs, maintained by English Heritage staff and volunteers. The policy is to recreate the Darwins' planting in terms of the plants and their arrangement. Historic photographs taken by the family, correspondence and annotations in books have been used to determine the restoration. Where evidence is not forthcoming, borders are being maintained

359. Historical family photographs and garden archaeology were essential for the accurate restoration of the flower beds.

unchanged until evidence comes to light or an agreeable policy is determined.

- Flower beds: 66 sq m
- Herbaceous and mixed borders: 720 sq m
- Shrubberies: 1,020 sq m

Hedges

Two regimes of hedge cutting both undertaken by contractors. 1,380 sq m of garden hedges cut twice a year in June and October, by hand using mechanical hedge trimmers to a formal shape. 700 sq m of hedges surrounding the meadows cut once a year in December or January, with a rotary disc-cutter mounted on the back of a tractor. No flails used.

Kitchen garden and orchards

1,510 sq m of kitchen garden used to grow and display fruit, vegetables, herbs, cut flowers and Darwin's experiments. Much less archive information available, so policy is to treat it as a typical Victorian kitchen garden. The borders are planted with herbs and cut flowers. The vegetable plot is divided into six sub plots, one to produce roses for cut flowers, one for permanently planted crops such as asparagus and rhubarb, and the remaining four used to rotate different types of vegetable. As it is difficult to obtain vegetables introduced prior to 1882 (the date of Darwin's death), if a contemporary variety is not available a later cut-off date of 1900 is used.

Greenhouse

A small wooden lean-to range of three sections, described by Darwin as his greenhouse. Each frost-free section has a different temperature, a minimum of 10°C and the last section a minimum of 15°C, enabling a broad range of the plants that Darwin studied and experimented on to be grown and shown. There are four

360. The glasshouse exhibits examples of plants used by Darwin in his experiments, such as carnivorous plants and orchids.

361. Darwin's weed experiment reconstructed.

themed collections: climbing plants, orchids, insectivorous plants and mini-experiments. Each display is interpreted with a folder containing a brief text outlining Darwin's discovery; volunteers are also stationed in the greenhouse to help answer questions. The overriding aim is to display the plants that Darwin used for research to write his books and papers.

Experiments

Other parts of the grounds are also used to re-create Darwin's experiments, to give the impression that his work is still being carried out. A section of the kitchen garden (310 sq m) has been set aside for nursery-style experiments. Here, many examples of one type of plant are grown – 522 cowslips, for example, to help demonstrate heterostyly as Darwin did. Two different forms of the flowers are marked with sticks and different-coloured wool, as his experiment reports. The weed experiments carried out while Darwin wrote The Origin of Species are re-created in the lawns and data collected through the growing period..

Sandwalk Wood

This was originally a wooded bank that the Darwins extended to create a copse of approximately 1 ha. Made up of native species, it was originally planted on a grid-style matrix and has a circuitous path. The aim is to present this wood as a wild garden, reflecting its historic use as a place for contemplation and observation. Sandwalk Wood also has varied wildlife, ranging from fungi and woodland bulbs to bats, deer and birds. A compromise has to be achieved between visitor access and maintaining the plantings in an acceptable manner with no detriment to the wildlife. Trees are inspected every year, necessary health and safety work is carried out, and invasive or dense shade-creating species such as brambles, sycamore and holly are weeded out.

Paths

Archaeological excavations suggested the materials the Darwins used and these are followed: paths are constructed on a hoggin base with large 25mm shingle rolled into the surface to create a hard, cobble-like path. Maintenance consists of using flame-guns to burn off emerging weeds and rolling the paths annually to ensure the surface remains solid. Local repairs will be carried out yearly to make good scuffed surfaces and control water puddling. Total area of all paths: 2,225 sq m.

Weed control

It is policy not to use chemicals anywhere, even on paths: good plant husbandry and biological pest control should eliminate any need for them, and they might threaten the valuable fungi collection in the lawns.

RECENT DEVELOPMENTS

The main restoration of the garden has been completed after a five-year plan, the original layout re-established as far as practically possible. Modern plants are being removed from the kitchen garden border and replaced with correct Darwinian species. The removal of a blown-over tree has allowed one area to be replanted with shrubs. Restorative shrub pruning (coppicing) is used to try to re-establish the correct proportions and shapes of the evergreen shrubberies.

INTERPRETATION

Interpretation is used sparingly in the garden in order to maintain the period feel, but it is used to help explain the experiments. The greenhouse displays are accompanied by brief descriptions of Darwin's research, incorporating facsimiles of his original work. An interactive leaflet for one of the experiments in *The Origin of Species* is being worked on. Volunteers working in the garden act as interpreters.

INCOME

Guided tours

These have been offered since 2003, with charges of £50 for pre-booked parties irrespective of size; £2 per adult and £1 per child for individuals. Total income from guided tours in 2003 was £600.

Plant and vegetable sales

Plant sales from April to October; vegetable sales from midsummer to early autumn, subject to availability. Vegetables on the EU-approved list were sold to the public for the first time in 2003. In order to make the operation less time-consuming for staff and to eliminate the need for weights and measures, sales were restricted to vegetables that could be sold individually or in bunches (e.g. carrots, lettuce). Peas, potatoes and other produce that needs to be sold by weight were offered to volunteers as a reward. Total income from vegetable sales in 2003 was £700: when set against harvesting costs, there is little profit.

Expenditure

Grounds maintenance budget for 2003–4 was £30,000 (excluding salaries for the head gardener and student). Of this, £17,500 goes to the contractor, and the remainder is used for the purchase of new plants, seeds and sundries, wildlife surveys, machinery and garden renovation projects.

Grants and funding

The restoration project was funded by the Wellcome Trust, Heritage Lottery Fund and English Heritage. Funding for maintenance may be sought under the Woodlands Grants Scheme for the Sandwalk and under the Stewardship Scheme for the meadows. Funding may also be sought to support further outreach activities.

FUTURE POLICY

Policy will remain to depict the garden as Darwin would have known it. Style and standard of maintenance will continue to show the domestic status of the garden, by cutting grass areas slightly longer and planting borders in a sympathetic style. Use of historic growing techniques will enhance visual accuracy. High standards of horticulture are required.

An ongoing programme of border evaluation and replanting will aim to continue the development of a correct collection of plants. This principle will extend to greenhouse plant collections and vegetable varieties.

362. The enclosed old rose garden made the national news when Christopher Lloyd replaced the roses, which were suffering from sickness, with dramatic sub-tropical planting.

GREAT DIXTER
Northiam, Rye, East Sussex TN31 6PH
www.greatdixter.co.uk
Ordnance Survey map reference TQ8125, c. 0.5km west of the A28
from Tenterden to Hastings, on the western edge of the village of
Northiam
English Heritage Register Grade I
Ownership: Great Dixter Charitable Trust, Olivia Eller

SUMMARY OF OPENING ARRANGEMENTS
House and gardens I April–31 October, 2–5 p.m. Tuesday–Sunday,
additional opening on bank holidays

Visitor numbers 2000: 35,281; 2001: 39,597; 2002: 38,620;
2003 38,490; 2004: 41,000; 2005: 43,838; 2006: 37,000

HISTORY

The earliest part of the present house dates from the mid fifteenth
century. The property passed through various families until the
house, immediate grounds and farm buildings were purchased by
Nathaniel Lloyd in 1910. He commissioned Sir Edwin Lutyens in
1911 to restore and enlarge the house and lay out the gardens; the
slope of the site, from east to west, plays a significant part in the
garden layout. On Nathaniel Lloyd's death in 1933, the house and
estate (c.182 ha including Little Dixter) was run by his widow; and
since her death in 1972 by their son Christopher. The gardens have
had modifications, additions and continuous development, and are
well known for Christopher Lloyd's elaborate and innovative
planting, the philosophy and details of which may be found in his
regular column in *Country Life* and his books, such as *The Year at
Great Dixter* (1987), *The Well-Tempered Garden* (1970), *The Mixed
Border* (1957; 1985) and *Meadows* (2004).

Christopher Lloyd died on 27 January 2006, aged 84. Two
years earlier, he had set up the Great Dixter Charitable Trust to
provide a future for the Estate after his death. The following text,
prepared in 2004, has not been updated since it provides a unique
view of the garden's management during the thirty years that he
had responsibility for it.

MANAGEMENT

2.22 ha gardens, approximately half of which is meadow.

- Water areas: 572.26 sq m
- Lawn areas: 935.97 sq m
- Meadows: 16,077.9 sq m

- Ornamental borders, including bedding, vegetables and the
  normal mixed borders: 3,367.08 sq m
- Woodlands: 16.17 ha, maintained by a woodsman but managed
  by the garden staff who bring up firewood and cut it, deal with
  pea sticks, apply for grants, etc.

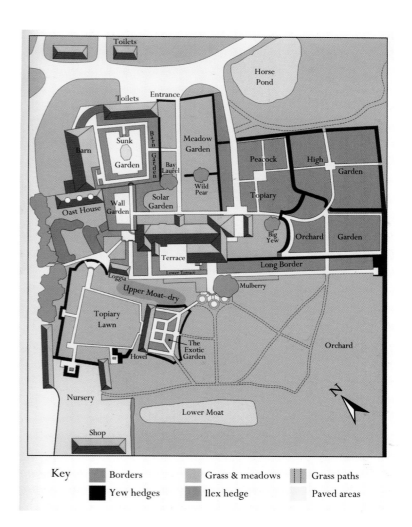

363. Right: Garden plan.

364. The orchard meadow was planted with narcissus, fashionable in 1912, and subsequently with a range of crocus, Snake's Head Fritillary (*Fritillaria meleagris*) and Early Purple and Green-winged Orchids (*Orchis morio* and *Orchis mascula*), which produce a rich display from February to June.

STAFF

One head gardener, three full-time gardeners (one full-time on vegetables), two nursery staff (plus two of the gardeners at weekends during the open season, with time taken off in lieu during week), one part-timer selling during the week, two staff on building repairs, grass and hedge cutting.

Volunteers: one to two full-time, March–November; one part-time four hours per week, sometimes more; annual volunteer weekend in March with approximately twenty students from Kew and Wisley.

Owner and head gardener

Much of the success of Great Dixter in recent years was due to the unique partnership between head gardener Fergus Garrett and the late Christopher Lloyd. They sat on various RHS committees, travelled and lectured together, and Mr Garrett acted as Mr Lloyd's personal assistant. Mr Lloyd made the final decisions on the garden – he was extremely creative but allowed the head gardener considerable input. They met every morning to discuss the day's work. Mr Garrett consulted and monitored other staff on a regular basis, working alongside the gardening team for much of the day. Mr Lloyd came to see the gardening team before lunch and again before the end of the day. Mr Garrett and Mr Lloyd met again at end of the day to discuss anything of interest, work on a current book, attend to the nursery catalogue, order seeds and bulbs, and do other administration.

Business manager/owner relationship

The business manager was responsible for the maintenance of the property and all visitor and commercial operations. He met the owner every morning to discuss relevant business and also consulted the head gardener. The business manager had his own secretary, guides and a shopkeeper to deal with on a daily basis. The head gardener and business manager worked very closely and oversaw the whole business with the owner.

PROMOTION AND ADVERTISING

Advertising budget is several thousand pounds a year. Free advertising comes from Mr Lloyd's books, articles and television appearances; the head gardener also writes occasionally, lectures widely and appears on television. The quality of garden and the overall visit is important to encourage repeat visits; the house also

365. The prairie garden.

has a friendly, slightly quirky, atmosphere and the feeling of a home. Articles by other horticultural writers are encouraged, as are visits by television and radio companies. Restricting advertising to spring and autumn is being considered, to encourage visitors in April and October when numbers are relatively low (entry in these two months is half-price for horticultural groups, free for horticultural students).

MAINTENANCE AND MANAGEMENT

Meadows

Cut two times a year, sometimes three, depending on vigour of sward, with reciprocal mower first and then rotary mower. First cut starts second week in August; final cut in October or November. Prairie area cut once only in October or November depending on state of sward. One very vigorous area cut as early as July, again in August, and then October or November (*Inula magnifica* in this area is mown round). All cuttings collected and composted. Planting of 1,000–2,000 crocus takes place in the autumn. *Erythronium dens-canis* split and planted in April after flowering. Total area 0.8 ha.

Lawns

Cut once a week during April and October with rotary mower. Edged every two weeks. No fertilising; no scarifying; occasional annual control of broadleaf weeds with selective weedkiller. Household dog fouling cleared daily from front lawn. Total area 0.2 ha.

Grass car parks

Cut every five weeks during May and October using ride-on rotary mower. Clippings picked up. The garden team is experimenting by enclosing areas of the car park and using sheep as 'organic mowers'. Total area 0.6 ha.

Mixed borders

Very intensive, especially with integrated use of bedding. Some areas may be bedded out three times a year. Trees, shrubs, perennials, annuals, biennials and climbers used. All plants raised in the nursery, but bulbs bought in.

Hedges and topiary

Rough hedges cut once a year in November with petrol hedge cutter. Topiary cut once a year, starting in August, with electric hedge cutter. Holm Oak Hedge cut once a year in December or January. 40–45 eight-hour days to complete cutting. London Zoo collects clippings for giraffes.

- Yew hedge and topiary: 580 m
- Box hedging: 39 m
- Rough hedging: 203

Kitchen garden

One person full-time to sow, grow, weed, pick, blanch and freeze vegetables. Salad crops (lettuce, chicory, herbs, rocket, chervil, pak choi, megacress, radicchio, some sown in succession as owner needed a little at a time), tomatoes, beetroot, turnip, carrot, parsnip, potatoes, artichokes (globe and Jerusalem), leeks, Brussel sprouts, Calabrese, cauliflower, Romanesco, celeriac. Wall fruit trained and orchard fruit picked. Fruit cage containing a range of soft fruit pruned and manured. The kitchen gardener consulted with the owner on menu, walked his dogs four times a day, carried in his logs and started fires. Fruit and vegetables not consumed are sold to visitors. Total area 0.4 ha.

Glasshouses and frames

For propagation and growing on of display material, four small glasshouses (6 sq m each) kept at different temperatures. The coldest is frost-free and the hottest at a minimum of 10°C. Single and double (unheated) frames. Mist unit under glass.

Pot displays

Very important part of the garden display from April to end of October. Several clusters around the garden as well as in the house. They stay in the nursery until ready and are then taken up to the house.

366. The high garden, enclosed by yew hedges and divided by a network of paths, is used as a kitchen garden and nursery growing-on area.

367. The sunken garden with its octagonal pond was designed by Lutyens as a formal feature. Christopher Lloyd's exuberant intensive planting softens this hard layout: self-seeding *Aceana* grows in the paving cracks, producing a green carpet that reddens in late summer when the spiky seed-heads mature.

Water areas

One formal pond (sunken garden) is cleaned as and when necessary. One large semi-natural pond (horse pond) needs cleaning twice a year (three people, two days each time), once to thin out water lilies and again to restore balance within the pond. One boggy area (lower moat) has troublesome weeds removed once or twice a year, sometimes by hand and at other times with systemic weedkiller.

Paths

Weed killed twice a year. Rocking paving slabs regularly relaid. Gravel paths topped up with fresh gravel twice a year.

Terrace

Informal, with a considerable amount of self-seeding. Hand-weeded twice a year (three people, one day), systemic weedkiller used twice a year.

Water

Pumped up from a well. Silt deposition a problem: pipes blown clean three times a year (two gardeners for a day each time).

Firewood

Brought up from coppiced woods on the estate (about 15 tractor trailer loads) and then sawn. Kept under cover and brought into the house on a daily basis.

House and outbuilding maintenance

This employs one person almost all year round, but saves on builders' bills.

Nursery

An important part of the business, employing two people full-time. Potting compost is loam-based, made from own loam harvested from adjacent field and sterilised on site before mixing.

368. Early summer planting bordering the paths in the high garden.

FUTURE POLICY

It was Christopher Lloyd's wish that the Great Dixter Charitable Trust would own the Estate when he died. The Trustees, together with the highly committed team of staff led by Fergus Garrett, are determined to ensure that the spirit of Dixter continues to thrive into the future. Their aim is to secure continued public access to the house and gardens and to build a new educational dimension to stimulate the interest of people of all ages in horticulture.

On Mr Lloyd's death, his 40 per cent share of the Estate passed to the Trust, which is now launching an appeal to raise approximately £5 million. This is needed to help fulfil the Trust's charitable objectives of maintaining, conserving and enhancing the house and gardens. It is also the Trustees' intention to acquire the remainder of the Estate and thereby secure it in perpetuity for the benefit of the visiting public and garden enthusiasts.

369. Opposite: the great vista from the Palace roof looking across the Fountain Garden to the Long Water and Home Park. Note the new double lime avenue replanted in early spring 2004.

Hampton Court Palace, Surrey

HAMPTON COURT PALACE
Historic Royal Palaces, East Molesey, Surrey KT8 9AU
www.historicroyalpalaces.org/webcode/hampton_home.asp
Ordnance Survey map reference TQ1568, close to Kingston and Hampton Wick, some 16km from the centre of London
English Heritage Register Grade I
Owner: gardens, estate and landscape owned by the sovereign on behalf of the nation
Cared for by Historic Royal Palaces (HRP; charitable status), which

manages the Tower of London, Kensington Palace, Kew Palace and the Banqueting House in Whitehall on behalf of the Secretary of State for Culture, Media and Sport

SUMMARY OF OPENING ARRANGEMENTS
Palace, gardens and maze Summer, daily 10 a.m.–5 p.m.
Winter, daily 10 a.m.–3.30 p.m.
Palace and grounds closed 24–26 December
There is a charge for entry to the formal gardens in summer
Always check for current information before visiting

370. Leonard Knyff (1650–1722), *A View of Hampton Court.*

HISTORY

An abundance of literature and other sources of information on this world-famous palace are noted in the reference section. In essence, Hampton Court contains the finest baroque layout in Britain – elegant parterres, walks with superb vistas, fine statuary and ironwork, walled enclosures, and a park bisected by canals and avenues, framed on one side by the River Thames. The park covers 303.5 ha, the gardens over 24.3 ha. The palace buildings alone cover 2.43 ha.

Early history and Tudor

In the fifteenth century, the open heathland site in a wide river setting was owned by the Knights Templars. In 1514 it was acquired by Cardinal Wolsey who built his first palace with an intimate garden: 'my garden sweet with walles strong . . . the knots so enknotted it cannot be expres't, with arbors and alyes so pleasant and dulce'. In 1526 it was given to Henry VIII , who enlarged the palace and gardens, and enclosed the Home Park and adjacent Bushy Park as two hunting reserves. Henry's new features included a tilt yard, ornamental orchards, a privy garden and a pond yard, creating the largest gardens in the country. Remarkably, the fundamental layout and divisions of these features still survive today .

Seventeenth century

Charles I added another important feature a century later, by creating a man-made river to bring running water to Hampton Court. In less than one year in 1638–9, a 20 km (13 mile) channel, the Longford River, was dug from the River Colne to the north-west. It still runs today, and remains the source of most of the water for the fountains and the Long Water, passing through three London boroughs and under Heathrow airport.

Charles II had great visions for Hampton Court after his restoration in 1660. One of his most spectacular projects was to divert the course of his father's Longford River when it reached Home Park, to create a canal some 1.206m long. Known as the Long Water Canal, it was embellished with a double row of lime trees, a fine feature admired by John Evelyn in his diary of 1662. A bold decision to replace this over-mature avenue totally was completed very successfully in spring 2004.

The reign of William and Mary was in many ways the Palace's greatest time, with much building and garden work done in a comparatively short time (1689–1702). Sir Christopher Wren, Surveyor of Works, was asked to rebuild the palace totally in baroque style, but only the State apartments were completed. The monarchs had already created fine gardens at Het Loo in the Netherlands, where Mary Stuart, a keen plantswoman, had built up a great collection of greenhouse exotics. An impressive Royal Gardens team was assembled to remodel the grounds, concentrating on the Privy Garden and Fountain Garden on the east front. George London, Deputy Superintendent of the Royal Gardens, was an important and active member, later joined by his business partner Henry Wise. The Privy Garden was constructed

371. View from the palace roof printed in *The Thames Illustrated*, c. 1897.

in 1690–1702, although King William halted work for a time at Queen Mary's death from smallpox in 1694. He himself died after a fall from his horse in Hampton Court Park in 1702, so neither monarch was really able to enjoy the great gardens they had created.

Eighteenth and nineteenth centuries

For the next century or so, monarchs continued to live at Hampton Court but with no real drive to change the gardens dramatically. Queen Anne, concerned at the cost of upkeep, simplified the Great Fountain Garden. Lancelot 'Capability' Brown was appointed Royal Gardener from 1764 until his death in 1783, and was responsible in 1768 for planting the famous vine that still flourishes today, but he made few changes to the garden. He recognised its historical importance and felt it should be preserved 'out of respect for my profession'.

After 1737, the royal families ceased to reside permanently at the palace, and there followed a lengthy period of inertia. With the court absent, all incentive to modernise ceased, and successive Royal Gardeners did little more than maintain existing structures and layout. A slow decline set in, and the place became inhabited by selected residents who lived rent-free by the grace and favour of the sovereign.

In 1829 the gardens were further diminished by the removal of all the statuary by George IV for his new East Terrace Garden at Windsor.

In 1838 Queen Victoria authorised the opening of Hampton Court and its grounds to the general public. At the same time, there was a Treasury enquiry into the management, superintendence and expenditure of the Royal Gardens. Edward Jesse, deputy director of the Office of Woods and Forests, initiated a number of very successful improvements to the gardens. Visitor numbers rapidly increased when the South-Western Railway extended the line from London to Hampton Court in 1849. A golf club was established in Home Park in 1895. Carpet and display bedding schemes, very much the fashion, were introduced into the

Fountain Garden from the 1870s, and the Wilderness was converted to a 'wild garden' in the William Robinson style in the early 1900s.

Twentieth-century revival

Ernest Law, a great Superintendent, pioneered one of the longest flower borders in the country along the Broad Walk – nearly half a mile in length, it included a herbaceous border that became renowned for its impact and planting. His *Flower-Lover's Guide to the Gardens of Hampton Court* (1923), illustrated with plans and photographs, gives a detailed account of the gardens at that time. An historian, he revived the old names for some areas, such as the Pond Garden, the Tiltyard and the Wilderness.

The many fine trees in the park and gardens suffered two disasters still remembered today. In the 1970s, Dutch Elm disease killed all the elms on the estate – in the Wilderness, along the river Thames Barge Walk, and in the 'tunnel'-like bower or arbour in the Privy Garden. In October 1987, the great storm felled about 500 trees, many being over-mature, especially in the avenues.

Renaissance

A strong awareness of Hampton Court's unique history, with the need to have a better match between the palace and its gardens, was a reflection of increasing national interest in historic garden research and conservation in the late twentieth century. Two important and highly successful restoration projects, part of a longer-term strategy that covers the complete gardens and parkland, are summarised below.

THE PRIVY GARDEN

This undertaking is considered to be the greatest and most authentic restoration of a baroque garden in the UK to date, with the whole project completed in less than five years (the full and fascinating story can be found in the references). The main stages only are summarised here.

- **1986** A serious fire in the King's Apartments in March focused attention on the overgrown Privy Garden, dating from the same period.

- **1990** The Historic Royal Palaces agency was established, one of its objectives being to treat the palace and its gardens as one entity.

- **1992** Exhibition showing various options for the Privy Garden, based on a wide range of archive material. The restored King's Apartments offered a fine prospect over the gardens and how they might look if restored.

- **1992–3** Tree and vegetation survey of the garden confirmed that a high percentage of the original or near-contemporary yews and variegated hollies (most still intact) were very over-mature and unlikely to respond to hard cutting back, which had been one of the proposals. A decision made for a wholesale restoration, followed by total clearance of the site during the winter of 1993.

- **1994–5** Major archaeological survey in the spring and summer 1994 revealed the outlines of the garden much as it was laid out in 1701–2, confirming archive material and old plans. Autumn 1994 to late spring 1995 saw the planting of all features, based on major historic research. Statuary also in place.

- **1995** The Garden opened by the Prince of Wales in July.

- **2004** Internal review of the planting and management of the Privy Garden.

The planting was the result of widespread and careful research into European gardens of the same period, including close reference to those at Het Loo in the Netherlands. Valuable archive sources in the palace, including plans and original orders for plants, provided further evidence.

The essential elements are woody trees or shrubs as clipped structural elements such as edging box (*Buxus*), grass or raked sand, and two seasonal displays mainly of bulbs in the spring and annuals in the summer. Wherever possible, authentic planting has been attempted.

The main structural features are pyramid yews (*Taxus baccata*), a total of 170 with heights of 2m or 2.5m depending on location, and hollies (*Ilex aquifolium* 'Argentea Marginata'), 80 round-headed or mushroom-shaped standards on short stems, and also 2.5m pyramids. Regularly spaced shrubs are clipped into balls in the borders (plates-bandes), which include *Rosa centifolia*, *Rosa rubiginosa*, junipers and lavenders. Short standard honeysuckles are featured in allotted places.

There are over 20,000 box plants in the edging. The first planting, of *Buxus sempervirens* 'Suffruticosa', proved unsatisfactory and it was replaced by *Buxus microphylla* 'Faulkner', which is very successful if not truly authentic.

372. The Privy Garden in the mid twentieth century.

373. The reconstructed Privy Garden of William and Mary.

374. The Privy Garden uncovered, prior to reconstruction.

For spring display, there are some 20,700 spring-flowering bulbs – mainly tulips, narcissi, crocus and hyacinths of historic varieties (where possible) – and 4,600 spring-flowering plants, including violas and red and white daisies (*Bellis perennis* varieties), also authentic as far as possible.

Summer planting, using annuals based on historic research, has been less successful. Reasons include the difficulty of locating authentic types, of keeping them compact and controlled, and of finding adequate spaces between the shrubs, which tend to increase gradually in size as they age, despite clipping. Some 2,200 plants are used in the central beds alone.

The turf areas were seeded, as far as possible, with a mix of grass species based on the local river gravel swards that existed along the Thames in the early eighteenth century.

The other main feature is the Bower, an oak-framed tunnel planted with hornbeam which is establishing well (previously it had been elm).

Exotics were known to have been an important feature of the gardens at Hampton Court. They were a passion of Queen Mary, whose collections from many overseas sources were grown in what was then the Upper Orangery (now a gallery for the Mantegna pictures). The Gardens Department has formed a good collection of these historic exotics, which are now stood out in the Privy Garden, well labelled, in a variety of pots, vases and tubs. They are housed under glass in winter.

MANAGEMENT

About 45 garden staff, responsible for the total maintenance of the gardens today, work under Gardens Manager Terry Gough (down from a staff of 72 some fifteen years ago). Five to six are responsible for the Privy Garden under a supervisor, requiring some 7,000 staff hours a year.

The table on page 276 shows the range of operations needed to keep up the high standards required, and the percentage of time spent on each. Not included is the regular watering of the exotics in containers stood out in the garden: this is the responsibility of the nursery staff, and is done weekly on average with a small tractor and bowser.

The high figure for edging is being partly modified by the introduction of metal edging in some areas, particularly for the complex scrollwork where the precise interface pattern between grass and sand is soon lost.

The health and shape of the clipped shrubs is a constantly monitored; some (such as the roses) need more hours of clipping than expected to maintain a ball shape. *Juniperus sabina* is also not very happy to be treated as a globe.

Avenues

A progressive programme of restoring the historic avenues began with the Fountain Garden Avenue in 1987, the first and very controversial planting. This was followed by 1,247 trees in the great Cross Avenue in Home Park in 1996, and the very focal Long Water Avenue, completed in March 2004.

This Long Water Avenue, planted in 1661 by Charles II after he had completed the Long Water Canal, was a double row of lime trees on each side totalling 544 trees. It is known that they were imported from Holland and were of the cultivar *Tilia × europaea* 'Koningslinde', listed as 'Pallida' in Hillier's manual. The life expectancy of these limes is 200–250 years, and surveys showed that progressive decay and loss had occurred:

376. The hornbeam tunnel or bower.

- 1661, at planting: 544
- 1981, survey: 479
- 1988, survey: 329 (post-1987 storm)
- 2002, survey: 300.

This represented a 45 per cent loss since the original planting. Although the visual effect from the Fountain Garden remained quite impressive, aerial photographs showed what a gap-toothed feature it had become. Seven options were considered for its future management:

1 Do nothing and allow the trees to decline still further.
2 Continue to interplant trees when replacements were necessary.
3 Replace trees by groups.
4 Remove one line of the double row.
5 Plant up a new double row outside the existing rows.
6 Pollard all trees to produce uniformity and height.
7 Clear, fell and replant the entire double avenue.

A decision was taken to go for option 7, and it was followed by a major public relations exercise with a two-tier approach — opinion-formers first, then the local community. Planning permission also had to be sought. A Dutch nursery was alerted to confirm a supply of 550 of the same clone as the original *Tilia* 'Koningslinde', on their own roots, as heavy standards at 16–18cm in girth.

375. Replanted avenue trees.

ALLOCATION OF STAFF HOURS FOR THE MAIN OPERATIONS IN THE PRIVY GARDEN, 2001
Based on information supplied by Gardens Office and Staff

Operation	% of total based on 700 hours or 5–6 staff	Frequency	Time period
GRASS CUTTING			
Parterre: cylinder cut	2.7	Regular	March–November
Parterre: rotary cut	3.0	Regular	March–November
Terrace banks	5.3	Regular	March–November
Triangle Garden	1.1	Regular	March–October
[Total grass cutting	12.1]		
GRASS HUSBANDRY			
Weed control, fertilising, scarifying, etc.	3.5	3–4 times	April, August, October
GRASS AND GRAVEL			
Sweeping	0.5	Regular	March–October
Trimming fences, etc.	0.9	Regular	March–October
EDGING			
Whole garden	31.0	Regular	February–November
Cutwork only	4.1	Regular	February–November
Sand alleys only	4.1	Regular	February–November
Path surfaces raking, etc.	0.6	Regular	February–November
PLANTING			
Plates-bandes weed/tidy	3.5	Regular	February–November
Plates-bandes plant/clear spring display	7.2	2 times	October, May
SHAPED TREES			
Yew pyramids	4.5	1 clip	August
Holly standards	1.8	2 clips	May, September
Holly pyramids	1.0	2 clips	May, September
Phillyrea pyramids	1.0	1 clip	September
SHRUBS			
Roses	6.6	3 + clip/prune	May, July, September
Lonicera	0.3	Occasional	July, September
Savins	0.4	Occasional	July, September
Lavenders	0.2	Approx. 2 clips	July, September
Box edging	11.7	1 clip	July, August
Bower cutting hornbeam	4.0	1 prune	September/October
Miscellaneous machinery on site etc.	1.0	Regular	n/a
Total	**100%**		

An ecological survey of the avenue was commissioned, as bats in particular were known to be present.

Felling the old trees began in November 2003 and all planting was completed by the end of March 2004. Most of the 280 trees that remained were felled using a revolutionary (but very basic!) technique of pushing the trees over with a large JCB machine. This process had the added advantage of removing the trees complete with their root plates, which proved to be time-efficient. Field ecologists were employed to oversee the Ecological Mitigation Strategy prepared during the survey stages. After felling clearance, garden archaeologists were able to identify all 544 original historic planting positions for the new trees. Planting was carried out by the palace's gardens and estates team, who also undertook some reconfiguring of the banks of the Long Water Canal.

Protection from browsing deer followed the original seventeenth-century style of tree crate, constructed of three oak panels in a triangular structure. Each tree was secured by a cross-member into which a watering tube was introduced to provide water and nutrients to the root zone.

The whole restoration project was completed within six months, and there were no tree failures in the season that followed in 2004.

An extra feature (for which there is no apparent historical evidence) is a terminal fountain at the Kingston end of the Canal, donated by a sponsor and installed in November 2003. Its main tall jet is operated as a timed performance.

FUTURE POLICY

The future policy for the gardens and estate team will be to follow the guidelines set out in the Palace Gardens and Estate Landscape CMP produced in 2004; the intention is to revise this in 2009. A Views Management Plan was also prepared in 2004 to safeguard the strategic views and vistas that are an essential and unique part of the Palace's gardens and parks.

It is also intended to continue and possibly extend training programmes for employed staff and trainees, to maintain standards of horticultural excellence and to safeguard essential skills into the future.

377. Detail of the planting of the plates-bandes in the Privy Garden.

3.6
Levens Hall, Cumbria

LEVENS HALL
Kendal, Cumbria LA8 0PD
www.levenshall.co.uk
Ordnance Survey map reference SD4985, five miles south of Kendal on
the A6 (exit M6 at Junction 36)
English Heritage Register Grade I
Ownership: Mr C. H. Bagot

SUMMARY OF OPENING ARRANGEMENTS
House and garden Early April–mid-October, Sunday–Thursday,
10 a.m.–5 p.m.
Deer park With network of public footpaths, open all year
Tea rooms, gift shop, plant centre
Plant sales A small area is stocked on a sale-or-return basis from a
local wholesale nursery
Events At present no income-raising main events, no corporate
entertainment. Wear and tear can be a problem on grass paths during
wet weather
Visitor numbers Now over 40,000 paying visitors to the gardens
annually, a steady increase over recent years. Newly implemented
visitor flow allows people to visit the tea room and shop without
investing in a full ticket

HISTORY

The excellent guide book is very informative and well presented.
The special character of Levens lies in the fact that the garden and
park were laid out in the late seventeenth century in the formal
architectural style then popular and, remarkably, the original
design has remained virtually intact since that time, with very few
changes. Landscape and garden fashions have come and gone
through the intervening centuries, but Levens has never been the
subject of any major replanning, renewal or restoration.

The gardens contain many features of horticultural interest,
notably an extensive collection of topiary, set within a formal box-
edged parterre; very large, old, beech hedges, and one of the
oldest ha-has in the country looking out towards eighteenth-
century parkland.

The oldest part of the hall embodies a thirteenth-century pele
tower and hall, subsequently converted into a more comfortable
Elizabethan house, which in 1688 was acquired by Colonel James

379. Aerial view.

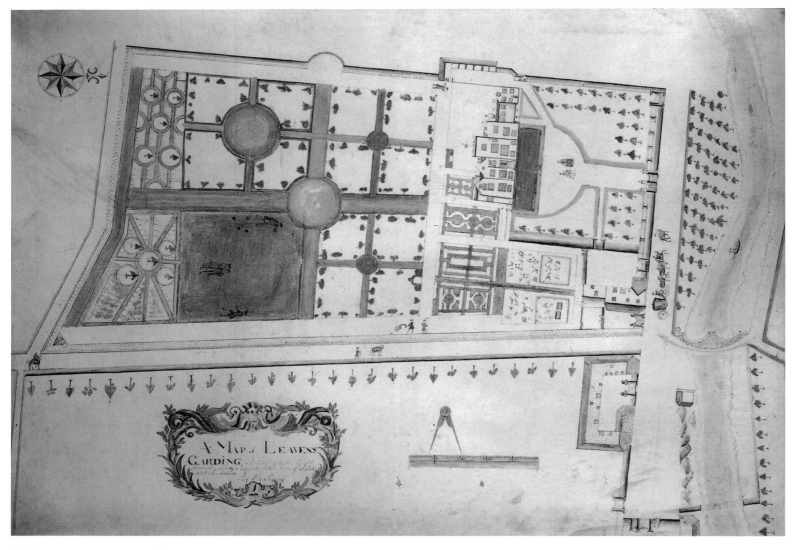

380. Beaumont garden plan, 1730.

Grahme. His improvement of the house and estate included designing a formal garden in the Dutch style of the William and Mary period, done by Guillaume Beaumont, one-time gardener to James II. His design still survives (above), and the garden as it is today is essentially his plan. Later descendants were mainly in the female line – they liked and respected the romantic formal garden, and no dramatic 'masculine' changes were made. Mrs Mary Howard, the last direct descendant of Colonel Grahme, died childless and left Levens to a distant relation, Josceline Bagot, in the late nineteenth century; the Bagot family have lived there since that time.

MANAGEMENT

The aerial view shows the essential features of the main gardens. These cover about 4 ha, and are mostly high-maintenance display. Associated parkland extends to about 90 ha, and is home to famous residential herds of Bagot goats and black fallow deer. Woodlands comprise mostly hardwoods which are planted for landscape effect as well as commercial timber.

Levens is low-lying, adjacent to the upper tidal reaches of the River Kent estuary; during winter much of the garden and parkland is liable to flooding. Being close to Morecambe Bay and the sea, snow is rare, although strong winds and occasional severe frosts do occur. The underlying rock is limestone, and the soil a neutral loam. Average rainfall is around 1,100mm.

STAFF

Full-time staff of four, including head gardener Chris Crowder. Six to ten volunteers, and recently two Modern Apprenticeship Scheme students.

Regular meetings between Mr Bagot and the head gardener to agree schedules of work and any new projects.

Parkland and woodland are maintained in part by estate staff, but increasingly through contractors.

Grass areas

All lawns mown once a week during the growing season, using pedestrian and ride-on rotary and cylinder mowers; clippings are boxed off and removed. The historic Bowling Green, shown in a plan of c. 1730, was dug up for vegetable growing in the Second World War, but is now restored as a lawn feature.

Topiary garden and parterre

In this unique feature there are over 100 topiary specimens, each clipped to an unusual and individual design. Many are nameless; others have fanciful names such as 'The Judge's Wig', 'Queen Elizabeth and her Maids of Honour', and 'A Jug of Moroccan Ale', named after a particularly strong brew once produced here. They are of varying age and occasionally very old specimens need renewing. Topiary is clipped once a year from mid-August to December, usually using electric and petrol clippers although some pieces are still done with hand shears. Some specimens, such

as 'The Giant Umbrella Tree' are of considerable height, requiring lightweight scaffold towers and a hired hydraulic lift.

The topiary is mostly of yew, Taxus baccata, and its golden form Taxus baccata 'Aurea', with various forms of box. Many are part of a close-knit parterre design following Beaumont's original design, with grass areas and display beds edged with Buxus sempervirens 'Suffruticosa'.

Display beds

Planted out for two seasonal displays. Spring shows pansies, violas, forget-me-nots, polyanthus, double daisies and tulips. Summer varieties include Verbena venosa, Helichrysum petiolare 'Limelight', Artemisia 'Powis Castle' and Argyranthemum foeniculaceum. Some 15,000 plants are used each year, most produced at Levens in a modern glasshouse unit. Each bed is dug and manured in the autumn.

381. Topiary garden.

382. Above: great beech hedge.

383. Above: inside hedge.

Shrub and wall borders

Given a thick mulch of decayed leaves in spring to help suppress weeds and give uniformity of finish. Herbaceous borders mulched at this time with spent mushroom compost for a similar effect.

Rose garden

Laid out in the 1950s and now planted with David Austin's English roses which do well here.

Great beech hedges

Thought to be an original feature from the 1690s layout, a massive central rondel which in effect quarters the garden. Despite being over-mature and decaying in some places, they are a remarkable survival. Annual winter clipping is a major task, taking two staff about six weeks. Sides are done from scaffolding, top using a hydraulic lift. A cumbersome previous system used a planking walkway laid on poles to reach the top – remnants of this can still be seen.

Orchard, herb garden and vegetable borders

Vegetable borders used for decorative as well as culinary use. They include a collection of different runner beans, and a spectacular assemblage of gourds, squashes, pumpkins, marrows and courgettes.

Seventeenth-century garden

Laid out near the house in 1990 and designed to reflect the Bagots' concept of a garden of their time.

Fountain garden

Partial reinstatement of Beaumont's original design on a site that had become a hard tennis court and vegetable and flower garden. A new feature, not in Beaumont's plan, is a central circular pool and fountain. This is highly successful, and the sound of splashing water helps divert attention from what the guidebook calls the gardens' greatest twenty-first-century pest – traffic noise.

The Wilderness

Now being considered for a renovation programme.

Ha-ha

Also originally planned by Beaumont. Ha-ha considered to be the first recorded use of such a feature in Britain. It also fulfils a drainage function, taking excess water from the garden to the river.

384. Orchard.

Park

Originally a medieval deer park, landscaped by Beaumont at about the same time as the gardens. He anticipated the trend towards the landscape movement of the next century, by planting trees in natural groupings and woodlands following the winding curves of the river Kent. Management policy is to maintain the integrity of Beaumont's design wherever possible, planting replacement trees as near as possible to the site of those that have died. Black fallow deer and a herd of Bagot goats roam the park in a landscape little changed over centuries.

FUTURE POLICY

It has been necessary in recent years to adopt a more commercial approach to all aspects of house and garden opening. No grant aid or outside funding is received for the garden. It is hoped that the garden heritage will continue to develop in sympathy with its past and give pleasure for generations to come.

385. Main entrance arch and Victorian garden.

Sheffield Botanical Gardens, South Yorkshire

SHEFFIELD BOTANICAL GARDENS
Clarkehouse Road, Sheffield, South Yorkshire S10 2LN
www.sbg.org.uk
Ordnance Survey map reference: SK33 7862
2 miles south-west of Sheffield city centre
English Heritage Register Grade II
Ownership: Sheffield Town Trust, managed by Sheffield City Council on behalf of the Town Trust on a 125-year lease, due to expire in 2050

SUMMARY OF OPENING ARRANGEMENTS
Summer
Gardens: weekdays 8 a.m.–dusk/7.45 p.m.; weekends and Bank Holidays 10 a.m.–dusk/7.45 p.m.
Glass pavilions: 11 a.m.–5 p.m.
Winter
Gardens: weekdays 8 a.m.–4 p.m.; weekends and Bank Holidays 10 a.m.–4 p.m.
Glass pavilions: 11 a.m.–3.30 p.m.
The gardens, gatehouse gift shop, tea rooms and restaurant are closed on Christmas Day, Boxing Day and New Year's Day. Visitors should telephone when big events are taking place to confirm opening and closing times
Visitor numbers c. 100,000 visitors per year

HISTORY

Sheffield Botanical Gardens were created in 1833 by the Sheffield Botanical and Horticultural Society, whose aims were to promote healthy recreation and self-education. The gardens were set up on 18 acres of south-facing farmland purchased for £7,500 with money raised through shares. A series of financial crises eventually resulted in their sale in 1898 to the Sheffield Town Trust, which still owns them today. In 1951 the management of the gardens passed to the Sheffield Corporation on a long-term lease.

The gardens were designed by Robert Marnock, one of the outstanding horticulturalists and garden designers of the nineteenth century, who was considered by his contemporaries to be the best exponent of the highly fashionable 'Gardenesque' school of landscaping. The main characteristic of this style is that all trees, shrubs and plants are positioned in scattered plantings so that each plant can be displayed to its full potential.

Marnock was appointed in 1834 to design and lay out the Botanical Gardens for an annual salary of £100; he became their first curator in 1836. His Gardenesque design involved the creation of small-scale landscapes to promote beauty, variety and mystery. Many of the style's distinguishing features can still be seen, such as winding paths, dotted island beds, expanses of grass and tree-planted mounds.

Typical of municipal urban parks, the gardens suffered from decreasing maintenance budgets in the 1980s and 1990s, and gradually fell into decline. The pavilions became unsafe and were closed, while the landscape became overgrown. The advent of the Heritage Lottery Fund (HLF) Urban Parks Programme in 1996 halted this decline. In 1997 the gardens were awarded £5.06 million towards a major restoration worth £6.79 million.

The restoration has retained the spirit of the original design, while adapting it for contemporary needs. It incorporates thirteen distinct garden areas, each based on a different botanical or geographical theme. A unique 90m range of curvilinear and ridge-and-furrow glasshouses was fully restored and opened in 2003, housing a collection of temperate plants.

KEY PHILOSOPHIES

- To celebrate in all future design development and management decisions the three functions of the place as a botanical garden, listed historical landscape and a public park.

386. Aerial view showing the Botanical Gardens in their urban setting.

387. Fountain at the end of the Broadwalk.

- To nurture the key philosophy of the restoration project to restore the gardens on the basis of their late nineteenth-century condition, capturing the spirit of the layout of this period with its design intentions, while at the same time addressing contemporary requirements.

- To reflect the original historic aims of the gardens by restoring and enhancing them to become a 'flagship' of horticultural excellence at local, regional and national level.

- To develop and promote the role of the gardens as a centre of excellence for horticultural and botanical education and interpretation in the city and the region.

- To improve, develop and promote facilities for free access and enjoyment for all.

VISION FOR THE GARDENS 2006

Reviewed at the end of the major restoration project: 'To provide a rich and enjoyable experience for *all* visitors to the gardens through their heritage, amenity, educational and horticultural excellence.'

Aims to achieve the vision

- To promote public access and provide a safe, attractive and welcoming environment for *all* visitors.

- To conserve and enhance the gardens, recognising their international importance as a registered (Grade II) historic designed landscape containing a number of listed buildings and structures.

- To raise the profile of the gardens to become a 'flagship' of botanical and horticultural excellence at local, regional and national levels.

- To provide a high-quality education and training service in horticulture and biology at all levels.

SITE DESCRIPTION

- Total area of site: 7.7 ha
- Fine and medium grass: 7,000 sq m
- Trial prairie meadow: 900 sq m
- Hedge (Ilex) behind herbaceous borders: 100 m

- Bound gravel paths: 11,000 sq m
- Flower borders: 13,000 sq m
- Managed trees: c. 650
- Woodland: c. 3,000 sq m
- Lakes: pond in water garden

Features of the historic designed landscape

- Glass pavilions (listed Grade II*)
- Gatehouse (listed Grade II)
- South Lodge (listed Grade II)
- Bear pit (listed Grade II)
- Fountain
- Pan statue
- Gates, railings, turnstile (listed Grade II)
- Paths, steps, walls, urns

Specific garden areas

The gardens comprise eighteen different areas, each representing a particular botanical or geographical theme:

Four Seasons garden Provides a continually changing display all year round.

Birch hill A wide variety of different types of birches have been added to the existing collection and underplanted with masses of spring bulbs.

Main lawns This landscape has been restored to the original Gardenesque style, which featured curving bed shapes cut out of lawns and semi-natural planting arrangements.

Mediterranean climate garden This area has mounds of low-growing plants with gravel paths winding between them. Plants include lavender, sunflowers, rosemary and verbascums.

Rose garden The original layout has been reinstated and planted with a wide range of traditional, modern and climbing roses.

Asian garden A showcase for trees and shrubs from China and the Himalayas, including rhododendrons, fuschias and callicarpas.

Evolution garden Shows how plants have developed from primitive life forms, and includes ferns and mosses, a monkey puzzle tree and a 'fossil tree'.

Osborn's Field New tender plants and modern cultivars are able to be grown in this sheltered, sunny location.

Marnock Garden Using the theme 'ideas to take home', this area demonstrates new gardening ideas including planting styles, garden features and garden management approaches.

Rock and water garden New planting has enhanced existing trees, plants and ponds, with particular emphasis on local plants native to the Pennines.

Award of Garden Merit (AGM) border Features plants that have been awarded this RHS accolade for excellence.

388. Pan statue in the restored rose garden.

Woodland garden This area has been transformed from a dark and gloomy place into a woodland garden with dappled shade and year-round interest.

Prairie area Swathes of annual and perennial meadow plants and grasses giving a naturalistic prairie effect, providing a changing display from spring through to autumn.

Pavilion The restored glasshouse now displays a collection of plants from temperate regions of the world.

Victorian garden A formal garden with authentic historic Victorian planting.

Long border Collections of shrubs and perennials native to the Americas.

Lower lawns Sloping lawns framed by mature trees.

Thompson Road Walk Rich planting including autumn and winter colours.

New-built features Select pieces of art installed as part of a riddle trail for children.

MANAGEMENT

Finance

Capital 1996–2005 Over the life of the restoration project, £6.7 million capital was invested in the gardens, of which £1.2m was raised by the fundraising trust. Works include restoration of buildings and structures, improvements to infrastructure and development of landscape, including the plant collections.

Expenditure 2005–6 Total annual expenditure: £287,983
- Total staffing costs: £209,800
- Non-staff maintenance costs (e.g. machinery, sundries, services, etc.): £78,683

Income 2005–6 Total annual income: £288,483
- Sheffield City Council grant: £252,483
- Income earned (shop and restaurant franchise, weddings and events) and donations: £36,000

The Heritage Lottery Fund required a ten-year management plan to be produced as part of the project and it included a business plan and a detailed review of the gardens' future management.

STAFF, TECHNICAL AND VOLUNTEER SUPPORT

Garden staff
- Curator Joe Rowntree (Dip. Hort. Kew)
- Garden supervisor (C & G Hort. L2)
- Five full-time gardening staff (RHS Gen. Hort.)
- Two part-time gardening staff (RHS Gen. Hort.)

389. Volunteers seed sowing prairie garden.

- Part-time administration assistant
- Lodge tenant for security duties

Staff in café and shop
Employed directly by the franchises; they also monitor the CCTV and condition of the toilets.

Technical support
Provided in kind when required from within Sheffield City Council, Parks Countryside Service:
- One operational parks manager, with thirty years' experience (landscape manager)
- One district parks officer (landscape manager)
- One project development officer (landscape architect)
- One project assistant (landscape architect)
- One buildings manager (Quantity Surveyor)
- Other professional services: solicitors, accountants, engineers, public relations

External support
- About thirty volunteers from Friends of the Botanical Gardens Sheffield (with 500 members) do regular practical maintenance and garden tours. They have diverse backgrounds, including some from horticulture, botany or parks management.
- Ten members of Sheffield Botanical Gardens Trust (fundraising charitable trust), with diverse backgrounds, including some from horticulture, botany or parks management.
- Other support is given by members of the Florilegium Society, Rose Society, Disabled Garden Society, and University of Sheffield Landscape and Plant Sciences Departments.

MACHINERY AND EQUIPMENT

Four transport vehicles (one with bucket); shredder/clipper; top dreeser; tractor-mounted scarifier; cylinder mower; tractor-mounted transport box; two mini-trailers; ride-on cylinder mower; pedestrian cyclinder mower; soil shredder; winch; strimmer; chainsaw; hedge cutter, rotary mower; leaf blower; rotary grass cutter and a range of horticultural hand tools.

In addition, the gardens have access to other machinery, equipment and staff, which are part of the Sheffield City Council Parks and Countryside Service portfolio.

PARTNERSHIP

One of the strengths of the restoration project was the robust partnership formed to submit the bid to the Heritage Lottery Fund in 1996, which developed to become the project steering group and has now evolved to support the long-term management of the botanic garden. It comprises:
- Sheffield Town Trust, owners

390. West view of glasshouse pavilions.

- Sheffield City Council, Parks and Countryside Service, managers
- Friends of the Botanical Gardens (FOBS)
- Sheffield Botanical Gardens Trust, a charitable body established to raise the matched funding required to complete the project (£1.2 million raised by November 2005).
- Sheffield University Department of Landscape, which provides expert horticultural and botanical advice.

ADDITIONAL INFORMATION

- The Friends group has been an active volunteer group since 1984; their need for improved facilities for educational work was a catalyst for pulling the bid together for HLF.

- A key principle of the restoration was public involvement, promoted through regular guided tours, newsletters, project open days, and talks and lectures by all partners to a variety of interested groups.
- As part of the HLF grant application process, a ten-year Management and Maintenance Plan was completed in January 2006 which now guides the maintenance and management of the site.
- Many diverse groups already use the gardens for their activities, including the Florilegium Botanical Illustration Society, Disabled Gardening Society, University of the Third Age, RSPB, local schools, etc.
- The completed gardens have huge potential in terms of education and interpretation at all levels, and the Botanic Garden is looking at ways to harness this in the future via a further stage of development.

391. View over Sheffield Park Garden lake in autumn.

Sheffield Park Garden, East Sussex

SHEFFIELD PARK GARDEN
Uckfield, East Sussex TN22 3XQ
www.nationaltrust.org.uk/sheffieldpark/
Ordnance Survey map reference TQ4124
English Heritage Register Grade I
Ownership: The National Trust

SUMMARY OF OPENING ARRANGEMENTS
January–February weekends only, 10.30 a.m.–4 p.m.
March–22 December daily, except Mondays, 10.30 a.m.–6 p.m.

Visitor numbers Marked increase in 2003 to over 199,000, the average for the previous four years being nearer 150,000. The target is 160,000, on which projections for income and budgets are based

HISTORY

National Trust booklet Sheffield Park Garden gives a very good illustrated summary; many other sources of information, some listed in references. Evolution of the present garden covers several layers or historic overlays going back over 1,000 years.

Original site and early landscape

On the southern edge of the ancient and now much-reduced Ashdown Forest, 'Sheffield' appears in the Domesday Book to indicate a sheep clearing, suggesting that forest clearances may go back to Saxon times. The first known estate map in 1745 was drawn for the Ist Earl de la Warr, whose family had owned what was known as Sheffield Place at various times since 1292. The map shows that Lord de la Warr had developed the landscape around the house, planting avenues in what had been a deer park (the sheep pasture), and using a local stream to create a lake overlooked by formal gardens south of the house.

Eighteenth-century 'improvements'

In 1769 the Sheffield Estate was sold to John Baker Holroyd, who became Baron Sheffield in 1781, and Earl of Sheffield in 1816. He began a long programme of transforming the estate, which set the scene for the essential elements present today; the first of these changes can be seen in Scale's ornate ovoid map of 1774. In 1774–5 Holroyd called in Lancelot 'Capability' Brown, but there is no detailed evidence of work that he carried out. Informal paths in

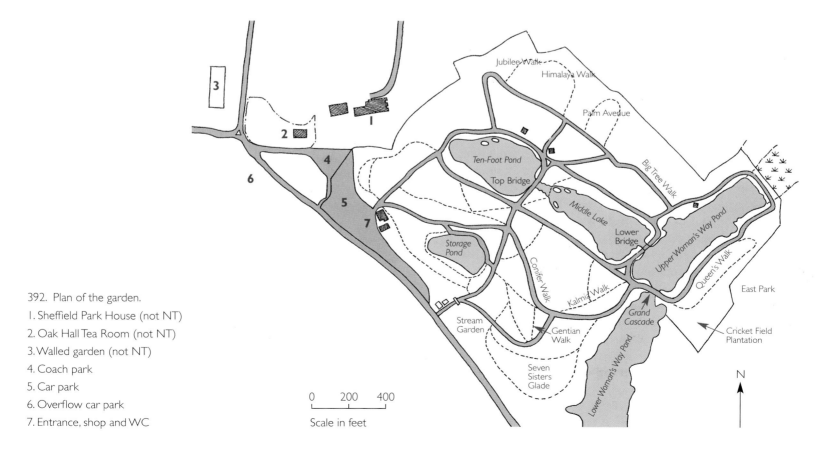

392. Plan of the garden.

1. Sheffield Park House (not NT)
2. Oak Hall Tea Room (not NT)
3. Walled garden (not NT)
4. Coach park
5. Car park
6. Overflow car park
7. Entrance, shop and WC

0   200   400

Scale in feet

the local Sheffield Wood were opened out, creating belts, clumps and groves in parkland areas. Holroyd's major and dramatic move was to ask James Wyatt to remodel the house in Gothick style in 1776–7 and again in 1780–90, and the mansion acts as an imposing eye-catcher from the gardens today.

Humphry Repton also worked at Sheffield Park, visiting several times in 1789 and 1790, but no 'Red Book' has been found, and exact details of his input are therefore a matter of conjecture. He seems to have created four small lakes on the site of the present First Lake (now Ten-Foot Pond) and added more planting around them; he also divided the lower lake by a bridge into Upper and Lower Woman's Way Ponds, which take their name from the ghost of a headless woman who allegedly walks this part of the garden. Many new plantations were added at this time.

Nineteenth-century planting and embellishments

Henry Holroyd, the future 3rd Earl, was responsible for a great impact after inheriting the estate in 1876; he also had the job of reviving it from the somewhat neglected condition it was left in by the 2nd Earl, who had succeeded his father in 1821. He enlarged the Ten-Foot Pond, created the Second or Middle Lake from two of Repton's ponds, and used the natural land form and lake dams to build two rocky waterfalls, the work of James Pulham and Sons. They also supplied the stonework for the Top Bridge between 1882 and 1885. The Grand Cascade between the Upper and Lower Woman's Way Ponds was also built then, but not by Pulham.

Cricket

The 3rd Earl was a cricket enthusiast, and one of his priorities was to build a cricket pitch on the estate. He levelled a raised site southeast of the park above the Upper Woman's Way Pond, with pavilions for ladies and gentlemen. Between 1884 and 1896 the Australian Team always opened their England tours with a match against Lord Sheffield's XI. The final match in 1896 was attended by the Prince of Wales and over 25,000 spectators, all admitted free. W. G. Grace was Captain and the prize was the Sheffield Shield Trophy.

The 3rd Earl also started a major long-term planting programme with the aid of his gardener, William Thomas Moore, which laid out the skeleton of much of the now mature tree planting to be seen today. The dramatic long axis seen from the main lawn (or roof of the house) over a series of 'water terraces' to the distant cricket pitch was the setting for much of his planting. By 1885 he had begun an arboretum of exotic and native trees, including newly introduced American conifers such as Wellingtonias and maritime pines, massed rhododendrons, azaleas and Japanese maples. He was particularly keen on spring colour to coincide with the opening of the cricket season, making an interesting contrast to the next chapter of planting at Sheffield Park.

Twentieth-century flowering of garden and landscape

The 3rd Earl died in 1909, unmarried and heavily in debt. In 1910 the estate was purchased by one of his principle creditors, Arthur Gilstrap Soames, also a keen gardener. Soames immediately began planting on a grand scale, including a fine collection of hardy hybrid rhododendrons for late spring effect (the magnificent rhododendron 'Angelo' hybrids are his own raising) and also one of Sheffield Park's greatest attractions, the spectacular autumn colour from Scarlet American oaks, Tupelo Trees (*Nyssa sylvatica*), more Japanese maples and deciduous swamp cypresses (*Taxodium distichum*). He fully exploited the reflection effects of such planting seen from across the lakes and continued the tradition of opening the garden to the public.

In 1919 he married Agnes Peel, granddaughter of the Victorian prime minister; there were no children. On his death in 1934, Agnes Peel remained as a tenant for life, keeping an eye on the garden during the Second World War, when Sheffield Park became the HQ for the Canadian Armoured Division. In 1949 she passed the estate to her nephew, Captain Granville Soames, who carried out a restoration programme with the valued help of Mr T. H. Setford, head gardener for over forty years.

Break-up of the estate

Captain Soames was obliged to sell the mansion and estate in 1953, and regrettably it was split into a number of different lots. Thanks to a bequest from Dr F. B. Penfold, support from the Royal Horticultural Society, local grants and an appeal, the National Trust was able to acquire the main garden with its lakes and some woodland, now known as Sheffield Park Garden. The mansion and its associated buildings, the main parkland to the north and south, some woodlands, the farm, the fine walled garden and its conservatory range all went to different owners, a situation that still exists today.

Input of the National Trust

From 1954 the Trust implemented an active programme of new and replacement planting, lake dredging and clearances, as well as planning for the reception and access of an ever-increasing

393. Bridge.

394. Spectacular autumn colour from the Tupelo trees (*Nyssa sylvatica*).

number of visitors. For many years, this work was overseen by the Trust's main garden adviser, Graham Stuart Thomas, working with Archie Skinner, the head gardener: they must both take great credit for their outstanding part in restoring and perpetuating this fine garden. Archie Skinner had to handle the trauma and devastation of the great storm of 1987, which felled or damaged thousands of trees. A vigorous and ongoing re-planting campaign includes renewing the important shelter belts protecting the garden.

MANAGEMENT

The 'historic interest' curtilage, designated by English Heritage in 1988, lies on the southern edge of Ashdown Forest.

Peak time is October for renowned autumn colour. Unlike the other case studies in this volume, there is not the additional attraction of a house and formal gardens.

There is local wear and tear, and a tendency for paths (which have no formal edges) to get wider and grass worn in main viewing places. Some erosion of hoggin paths in heavy rain. Major path renewal programme planned.

National Trust garden and associated land (mostly woodland) covers 74 ha; land in private ownership extends to 104 ha, much of this including Home Park. The River Ouse forms the southern boundary of the estate, and to the east beyond the cricket ground and East Park lies the village of Fletching, whose church spire appears in early views from the house.

The garden is 80–100m above sea level, mostly in a shallow valley setting but exposed to the south and east. Average rainfall is 892mm. Soil averages 5.5 pH, and is acidic woodland type of Wealden clay overlying Tunbridge Wells sandstone. Drainage is poor in some areas, with consequent water-logging. Land drainage schemes are in progress, and mound planting is practised in very wet sites.

STAFF

Five full-time garden staff under head gardener Andy Gasson and an assistant head gardener. Head gardener reports to property manager, who in turn consults the Trust's Area Director. Regional parks and gardens curator and gardens adviser also have input, with occasional visits. Assistant head gardener holds weekly meetings and draws up working plans for the week.

Staff level has remained stable at five or six for some years. Group of 12–15 volunteers support the horticultural team with practical gardening work; known as the Monday Group, they work every other Monday throughout the year. All volunteers carry out tasks set by the head gardener, and are given assistance and instruction as required. Other regular groups work on selected weekends, occasionally camping and working over longer periods such as bank holidays. Work experience students are also taken on.

Range of training courses and exchange programmes, such as National Trust national courses on 'managing people', skills and specialist craft training, e.g. fruit pruning, organised by National Trust head gardeners in the region. Secondments to other National Trust gardens to perpetuate techniques not in use at Sheffield Park, e.g. rose pruning, fine turf work, etc. The National Trust's Gardens section at Swindon also arranges tree and turf days, plantsmen's days and RHS links with Wisley.

MANAGEMENT POLICIES AND TECHNIQUES

In contrast to the other case studies, Sheffield Park Garden comprises only the informal pleasure grounds of a once diverse estate. Despite being disembodied from its historic nerve centre (the house), the present garden, defined as a wooded landscape park, is of international importance and holds the NCCPG collection of Ghent Azaleas.

The garden plan shows the essential characteristics that largely determine the management systems used. These include a wide range of trees (exotic, native and conifers), massed and specimen shrubs, extensive zones of grassland as glades and fringes, and four extensive lakes that act as the main axis, all linked by paths and walkways. Eighteen different character zones have been identified, determined by planting and location, and these form the basis of the Garden Conservation Plan now completed.

The only National Trust buildings used by the public are the comparatively modest reception centre and shop, and toilets. Catering facilities are under separate ownership and management in former estate buildings. The car park was not purpose-built, but adapted among mature trees at the main garden entrance; overflow parking is on adjacent land, part owned by the Trust and part leased from the tenant farmer.

Machinery

The gardens are well equipped with machinery including a tractor with back hoe and front loader, flail attachment, tractor-mounted sweeper, two ride-on deck mowers, two Flymos, two leaf blowers, two strimmers, chain-saws, woodchipper and a full range of hand tools. For work on the lakes there is a boat and outboard motor. A Land Rover is available for getting round the gardens and for local transport.

Grass cutting

Some 1,344 staff hours are spent on mowing and cutting grass, with different regimes depending on the area and nature of the grass. These include more natural glades, where a succession of spring bulbs such as narcissi, anemones and bluebells are followed by native orchids. These receive a later meadow-type cut in July. More accessible places have regular mowing from March onwards.

Mulching and feeding

Newly planted special trees and shrubs and any showing signs of stress or malnutrition are given a generous mulch and slow-release fertiliser application. Home-produced leaf mould and compost is augmented with Local Authority 'Greenway' compost, made from recycled waste. More recently, a Scots pine bark and compost mix from a Suffolk source with a pH of 5.5 is being used on special groups such as the Ghent Azaleas. No watering is done except in the nursery.

Chemicals

The National Trust has a general policy of minimal use of chemicals for control of weeds, pests and diseases. Where weed control is needed, the Nomix-Chipman Touche and Hilite system is used; it is Glyphosate-based and available pre-mixed for application from a special knapsack/lance sprayer. Disposal is safe and easy.

Lakes

The five lakes are registered reservoirs – they and their catchment areas require annual inspection and any work identified must be carried out. Programme of dredging and de-silting: Middle Lake in 1998, Upper Woman's Way Pond (capacity 29,100 cu m) in 2003 after a breach in the cascade and dam between the Woman's Way ponds caused it to drain away; major repair was completed in autumn 2003.

Water is circulated from the storage pond. Recent leaks in the top lake have been dealt with, so that the upper cascade has a better flow. The waterfalls require regular maintenance by one member of the team for up to 200 hours a year.

At intervals, water lilies are cut out mechanically using the boat or wading, to about one-third lily pads to two-thirds clear water, with flow around the lake edges. The lakes act as great mirrors, and emergent vegetation has to be controlled.

Recent projects

- 'Planting for the Future', 2002–8, some 9,000 trees and shrubs.

- Shelter belt planting in the Seven Sisters Glade and north-east corner of the garden where 1987 storm losses were particularly severe.

- Intention to renew and regenerate native and exotic trees and shrubs which give Sheffield Park its special woodland garden character. A holding nursery is part of this programme, with special trees being propagated such as the fine Montezume Pine. Tree and shrub bank being built up.

- Climate change project being monitored in conjunction with the RHS.

FUTURE POLICY

- Continue to work on repair projects, i.e. lake system, phased path restoration, improvements to car parking

- Find a balance between visitors' increasing demands for more facilities – lavatories, bigger shop, catering etc. – and peace and tranquility and the proper conservation of the garden and its character.

- Ongoing programme of working with residents and occupants of those sites not under National Trust ownership to restore, as far as is feasible, planted elements of the Repton and early nineteenth-century landscape.

395. Opposite: water edge.

Squerryes Court, Kent

SQUERRYES COURT
Westerham, Kent TN16 1SJ
www.squerryes.co.uk
Ordnance Survey map reference: TQ4453
English Heritage Register Grade II
Ownership: Mrs and Mrs J. St A. Warde

SUMMARY OF OPENING ARRANGEMENTS
Normally open 1 April–31 September: Wednesdays, Thursdays, Sundays
and Bank Holidays
Garden open 12–5.30 p.m.; House 1 p.m.–5.30 p.m.
Groups welcome by appointment

Visitor numbers Increase in recent years of visitors paying at the
gate, now steady at about 8,500. It is noticeable that the development
of the gardens is becoming more important for visitor satisfaction. This
is helped by a leaflet that explains the history and main features of the
garden, given free to all visitors on arrival. Special events in the park
and weddings in the garden account for a further 5,000 visitors.

HISTORY

Squerryes was a lesser manor of the manor of Westerham, and
was recorded in the Domesday Book. The present owner of
Squerryes retains the title of Lord of the Manor of Westerham. It
is known from old documents that a family called de Squerrie were
living here in the reign of Henry III (1216–72). The last member of
that family died in 1463, leaving his two sisters as co-heiresses. For
the next two centuries or so, the house changed hands many times.
In 1658 the diarist John Evelyn visited Squerryes and described it
as 'a pretty, finely wooded, well watered seate, the stables good, the
house old but convenient'.

In 1680, Sir Nicholas Crisp purchased the estate, pulled down
the old house and built the present handsome building. The new
house is shown on an estate map dated 1686 which bears his arms.
He died in 1698, and in 1700 his son sold Squerryes to Edward
Villiers, 1st Earl of Jersey, who at that time was Master of the

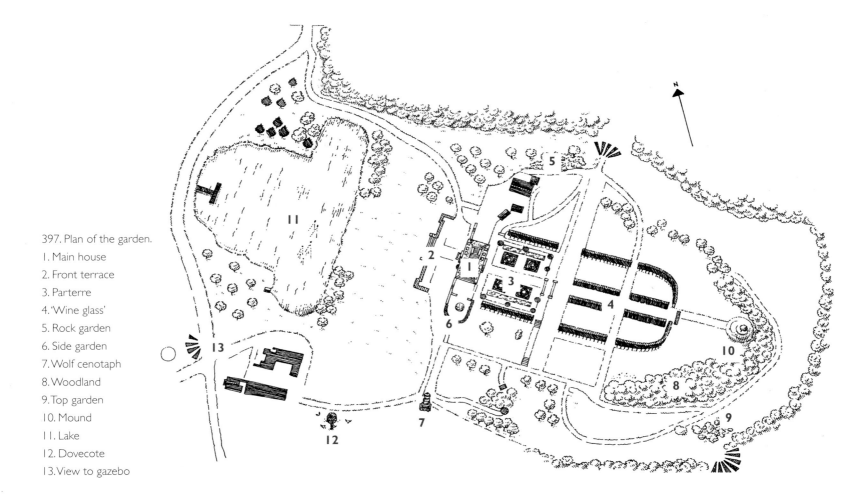

397. Plan of the garden.

1. Main house
2. Front terrace
3. Parterre
4. 'Wine glass'
5. Rock garden
6. Side garden
7. Wolf cenotaph
8. Woodland
9. Top garden
10. Mound
11. Lake
12. Dovecote
13. View to gazebo

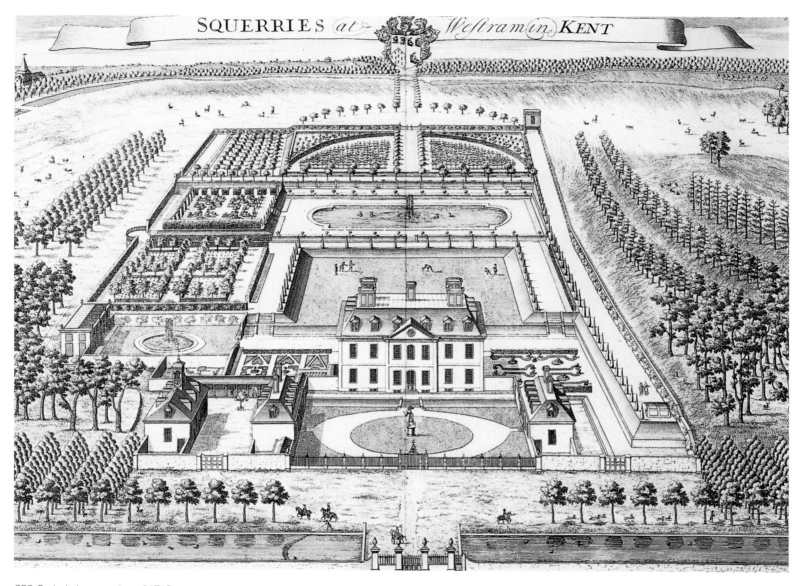

398. Badeslade engraving of 1719.

Horse to Queen Mary II and Lord Chamberlain to the Royal Household. King William III honoured him with a visit to Squerryes. It seems very likely that this Earl of Jersey laid out the extensive formal gardens in an Anglo-Dutch style, depicted on Badeslade's bird's eye view engraving of 1719.

The estate remained in the ownership of the Villiers family until 1731, when it was bought from the 3rd Earl of Jersey by his friend John Warde, whose family have lived here ever since. During their three centuries of ownership, the Wardes have seen inevitable changes to the house and landscape. Early in the nineteenth century, the three service wings – which provided domestic facilities such as kitchens, larders, staff accomodation and brew house – were pulled down; the house was not fully restored to its original form until after the Second World War. Although not recorded, the formal gardens and water features were also changed in the nineteenth and early twentieth centuries to a less ordered and more naturalistic character. Recent projects to restore some of the original Anglo-Dutch style of gardens are summarised here.

MANAGEMENT

The house and gardens are surrounded by 121.4 ha of farm and parkland, and a further 101.17 ha of woodland. There are also adjoining commons of about 141.64 ha. An estate plan of 1689 shows the surrounding fields; the boundaries are virtually unchanged today. The whole garden covers approximately 10.11 ha, including some 5.26 ha of shrubberies and woodland and a lake of 1.13 ha.

The original estate was smaller than at present. The parkland is all grazed by beef animals, and some is let for horses. Most of the eighteenth- and nineteenth-century park trees have disappeared, and there has been no planting since 1912 when the present owner's grandfather died. Some of the woodland is managed commercially, but forestry staff are no longer employed. Some areas are given over to natural regeneration.

The storm of 1987 caused widespread devastation: almost one-third of the trees were lost, and the garden and parkland also

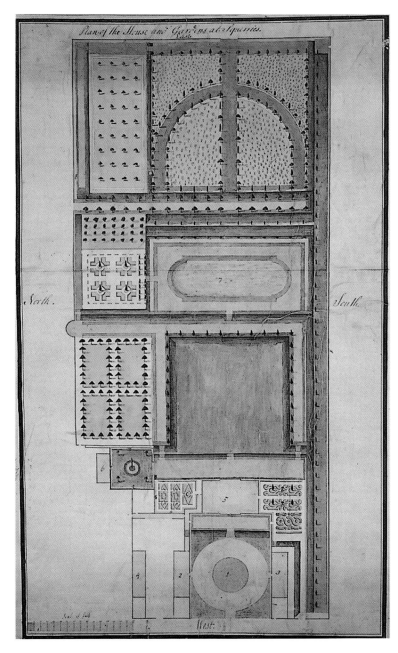

399. Coloured plan showing a formal Baroque-style layout.

a number of changes, particularly in the early twentieth century. One important feature was the rectangular level terrace, shown as a bowling green in the engraving. This had become an ornamental garden with mixed borders on two sides, four circular rose beds, and peripheral Irish yews and specimen rhododendrons. It did not match the superb quality and symmetry of the house that overlooked it.

The decision was taken to remove the rose beds and create a formal parterre with two pairs of square box-edged beds, based on designs in the Badeslade plan. These were planted in 1989, using box to depict the patterns and infilling with grey cotton lavender (*Santolina*) and purple sage (*Salvia*) with central yew topiary features. The rhododendrons were removed, but the Irish yews were retained after some re-shaping and clipping and incorporated into an enclosing hedge of yews planted in 1990. The two mixed flower borders were retained, but replanted with older roses and perennials.

The success of this scheme prompted a decision to proceed with the restoration of the semi-circular 'wine glass' planting. In 1992 the long central axis was framed with hornbeam hedges, terminating in a donated wrought iron gate. Beyond the gate, this axis leads up to a possibly man-made mound with enclosing woodland and rhododendrons. The flanks of this mound were planted with mixed laurels, hollies and other evergreens in 2000. The arcs of the plan were planted with limes in 1992, to be pleached to an agreed shape and height. Storm-damaged trees were re-shaped in 1988–9 and there was some replanting in the garden and park.

A document was discovered in a tin chest in the old orangery some three or four years ago. It is a unique inventory, or 'Impris', of the house and garden, drawn up in September 1718 on behalf of the 2nd Earl of Jersey for one Abel Alleyne who was proposing to lease Squerryes. It details most of the features of the formal garden shown in the Badeslade engraving, right down to the exact number of trees, shrubs and other items to be seen on the view – and it therefore means that the garden must have been in existence at that time.

400. Following the 1987 storm.

affected. A series of four fish ponds (shown on a seventtenth-century plan) have been restored. Two follies in the park – a ruined tower and a gazebo, built in the mid-eighteenth century – are not accessible to the public.

Recent projects

The 1987 storm and its impact provided Mr and Mrs Warde with the opportunity to reconsider some features of the main garden to the south of the house, which featured in the 1719 Badeslade engraving. This coincided with the discovery of a coloured plan of the very similar, formal Baroque-style layout, showing, in some detail, plans of the planting and main features. Although the broad structure of this layout could still be traced in part, there had been

MAINTENANCE AND MANAGEMENT POLICIES AND TECHNIQUES

Staff

A necessary constraint on all restoration and planting schemes has been the employment of just one full-time gardener, Terry Darnton, with some part-time help, at present consisting of three staff working a total of about 40 hours per week. There are no volunteers, but the family give a hand. Mrs Warde is mainly responsible for the gardens, and has a regular daily meeting with the gardener to agree jobs and work programmes. These are allocated on a daily basis according to weather and priorities. Some jobs are not possible during public visiting hours.

Grass

- Parterre lawn is close-mown in the growing season, normally weekly, using a cylinder mower; cuttings are boxed off and composted.

- Semi-formal lawns are mown with a Hayter rotary mower about every ten days, and the mowings collected and composted.

- Paddock-length grass is mown about every two weeks, depending upon growth, with a Ford 12.20 tractor and Wessex rotary mower. Mowings not collected.

- Meadow grass is cut in the last week of July with a rotary mower; grass brushed off with a Wessex rotary brush, removed for stacking and composting.

These grass areas take up about 40 per cent of the gardener's time in summer, with part-time help in tasks such as edging off.

Hedges and topiary

- Box hedges in parterres cut twice annually, in May and early September, using a powered hedge trimmer.

- Yew topiary features in parterres cut with hand shears every six weeks; others once a year in September.

- Hornbeam hedges and pleached limes cut once in winter.

- For off-the-ground work a Henchman ladder/platform has proved very safe and effective.

Ornamental gardens, borders, etc.

- Winter–spring: pruning, herbaceous plants split and replanted, mulching.

- Spring–autumn: weeding, staking, dead-heading, edging off.

Combined efforts, with two part-time gardeners concentrating on the border work.

Rock garden

Added in the early twentieth century, this is really a rock bank, backed by a shrubbery and woodland on the east side of the garden. A number of fanciful topiary sculptures were created by the previous head gardener. The sandstone rocks were remodelled in the early 1990s and lower-maintenance planting introduced. There are no pernicious weeds and this feature is not now a problem to maintain.

Pleasure grounds, shrubberies

These include ornamental woodland areas with rhododendron groups and fine carpets of spring bulbs, especially bluebells, and a recently created Top Garden following the contours of an earlier 'Japanese-style' garden, now almost lost.

Mainly the responsibility of the second gardener, who assists with routine work such as strimming, also winter work, pruning, clearing, planting and chain-saw jobs.

Woodlands in the main garden (not estate woodlands)

Mainly the responsibility of the second gardener. Clearance work of old neglected areas still in progress. New plantings of trees and shrubs need rabbit protection, weeding and mulching. Naturalised bulbs are a very fine spectacle in spring, extensive drifts of snow-drops being followed by a range of narcissi that include some of the older cultivars. The grass areas are therefore cut or strimmed selectively from the middle of June, with the aim of keeping these areas fairly wild to encourage wild flowers and wild life.

Paths

Mainly gravel. Sprayed in early spring with glyphosate. Some spot weeding during the season when necessary. Leaves are removed in autumn and composted.

Water areas

Reeds are cut after wild fowl have nested. The small stream and pools are cleaned after the winter.

Walled kitchen garden

This is at some distance from the main house, and not open to the public. It was built in the mid-eighteenth century and extended to approximately 1.21 ha in the nineteenth century. Until 1947 it was run as a kitchen garden, employing three gardeners. It was subsequently run, not too successfully, as a commercial market garden until 1958. It is now rented out as a livery yard.

ECONOMIC ASPECTS

The income from visitors is almost static, but more than covers the cost of opening. Special events have brought considerable additional income to help maintain the house and gardens. When combined, these make a significant contribution to the running costs of the garden. The Wardes have not had any grants during the last five years; the balance of running costs and any improvements have been funded by other income.

401. View from the house roof showing the long axis with the restored parterre and 'Wine Glass'. Compare this with the Badeslade engraving of 1719 (picture 398).

FUTURE POLICY

The recent improvement of toilet facilities and the addition of a conservatory for catering have greatly helped with the management of visitors. Further gradual development of garden and woodland areas should increase visitor numbers.

402. Detail of the parterre.

403. Aerial view, 1986.

STONEHENGE
Near Amesbury, Wiltshire
www.english-heritage.org.uk/stonehenge
Ordnance Survey map reference: SSU 122422 (OS Map 184)
Scheduled Ancient Monument, World Heritage Site
Ownership: English Heritage

SUMMARY OF OPENING ARRANGEMENTS
All year (times vary)
Visitor numbers Over 750,000

HISTORY

Stonehenge is the substantial remnant of the last sequence of an ancient stone circle, erected c. 3000–1600 BC. It sits in an ancient landscape full of burial mounds and other ancient earthworks, on Salisbury Plain in Wiltshire, just north of the city of Salisbury.

Stonehenge is arguably the best-known ancient monument in the UK, possibly in the world, and has long been the subject of tourist visits. Gilbert White, visiting in 1768, described it as 'that amazing work of antiquity', and early photographic records from c. 1870 show top-hatted visitors admiring the stones. In recent times the visitor numbers have risen dramatically; by 1999 the annual figure had reached a peak of 870,000 visitors.

- Total area of site: 11.5 ha
- Fine grass: 1 ha
- Medium grass: 3.8 ha
- Meadow: 6.7 ha

FINANCE

Expenditure on contractors: £20,000.

MANAGEMENT

So many visitors to what is a remarkably small monument – the diameter of the centre circle is only 30m and that of the surrounding ditch and bank only about 120m – cause enormous turfwear problems. After access to the centre circle was stopped in 1978, all visitors were directed around the monument, initially on a tarmac path that leads from the tunnel exit and cuts across part of the site. At the end of this path they were directed around the outside of the encircling ditch and bank, on the grass, to the fence by the heel stone, and then back again, because of the sensitive archaeology of the avenue which runs next to the heel stone, thus doubling the wear on an area of turf only about 4,000 sq m. Access over this area was unrestricted and by 1986 it was markedly eroded. Two years later the situation had become so bad that there were increasing calls for the tarmac path to be extended.

For both archaeological and aesthetic reasons these calls were resisted, and a decision was taken to re-turf the damaged area using more wear-tolerant grass species, implement a programme of high-intensity sportsfield maintenance and strictly manage the flow of visitors. The success of this management regime was immediate and it has remained successful to the present day.

There are three key elements in the successful prevention of erosion at Stonehenge.

Use of wear-tolerant grass species

The whole area regularly used by visitors was re-turfed using 100 per cent ryegrass; it is regularly overseeded to maintain this homogeneous cover.

404. The stones provide a valuable habitat to some significant lichen species.

405. Condition of the ground surrounding the stones prior to 1988.

406. Condition of the ground following re-turfing and the introduction of a sportsfield-type maintenance regime.

Continuous maintenance

The area is subject to a sportsfield style maintenance regime consisting of:

- regular cutting to encourage a low, dense sward;

- regular aeration using a solid-tine spiker to relieve compaction and improve aeration and drainage;

- regular fertilising, with high-nitrogen fertilisers in spring and summer to encourage strong leaf growth and with low-nitrogen, high-phosphorus and potassium fertilisers in autumn to encourage root growth and slower, hardier leaf growth for the winter;

- light harrowing when necessary to disperse any worm casts or similar and prevent mud being smeared over the leaf surface;

- autumn restoration: scarifying to remove any thatch, followed by spiking, overseeding and topdressing, carried out over the whole area;

- pest control when necessary and especially removal of any molehills before these become spread out, covering grass and providing seed beds for weeds;

- weedkilling whenever necessary to remove broad-leaved weeds (which have very low wear tolerance). It is interesting to note that all the preceding measures have served to maintain a very dense, healthy grass sward which has prevented weed establishment: no weedkilling has been necessary for six years.

- watering: the very thin soil at Stonehenge and the open, exposed nature of the site make it highly susceptible to drying out. Grass recovering from a period of wear is watered during dry spells. This is something of a problem on a site with very low water pressure: ordinary sprinklers are ineffective and soaker hoses are employed.

- early repair of any wear as quickly as possible to prevent it spreading.

Management of visitor flow

Individual walkways are marked out using unobtrusive low-level ropes, and visitors are encouraged to keep within the designated walkway. There is room for approximately ten individual walkways on the maintained area, and these are alternated regularly at the first sign of wear. This may be daily during peak periods, or every two to three days off-peak.

GENERAL PRINCIPLES

Taken individually, all the measures above help to reduce wear on turf and delay the onset of erosion to some degree. Success at Stonehenge, with its high visitor numbers, is due to a combination of all three measures: on this site any one taken in isolation would not be sufficient.

The principles applied at Stonehenge might well be followed in other parks and gardens where wear and tear are a problem:

- Always remember basic requirements for good grass growth: good soil structure, undamaged roots and leaf blades, and leaf blades not covered by mud.

- In areas of high wear, spread the wear wherever possible, giving some areas respite before wear becomes serious, carrying out repairs if necessary.

- Where possible, introduce more wear-tolerant species of grass such as ryegrass, and reduce levels of wear where possible. (The ecological value of the site must be considered: obviously in an SSSI, the introduction of sportsgrass cultivars might be unacceptable.)

- Carry out as much sportsfield maintenance as possible on susceptible areas.

- Where funds are limited, choose the most beneficial maintenance that can be afforded. As a guide, spiking – which relives compaction and improves aeration and drainage – is by far the most beneficial operation.

407. Opposite: grass cutting at Stonehenge, using a tractor-mounted mower with a grass collection system.

Appendices

Plant tables

Introduction   308

PLANT GROUPS

1   A range of trees (excluding conifers) in general cultivation   309

2   A range of conifers in general cultivation   312

3   A short guide to some Rhododendron species and hardy
    hybrids, including Azaleas   314

4   Shrubs   316

5   Herbaceous plants   322

6   Ornamental grasses, rushes and sedges   326

7   Ferns   326

8   Aquatic plants   327

9   Annual and biennial plants for garden and cool
    glasshouse display   328

10 Historic and widely grown fruit and vegetable cultivars   331

11 Plants for maritime conditions   340

PLANT MANAGEMENT

12 Hedge maintenance   342

13 Pest, diseases and disorders   344

14 Guide to shrub pruning related to age and size   354

Useful contacts   355

Grant aid & funding bodies   358

References   359

Bibliography   361

Index   364

Plant tables

These tables are intended as a reference guide only. The woody plant tables alone could be far more comprehensive, and these along with others such as the herbaceous perennials and annuals represent a selection only of the genera and species (with some cultivars) that are more widely found in cultivation. The dates of introduction and the countries of origin, where known, have been included, since these could be of special interest for those conserving and managing historic gardens.

Many cultivars (cvs) in genera such as *Rosa*, *Rhododendron* and many others have arisen by chance or by hybridising, and these are shown by the symbol GO indicating Garden Origin. However, this is a very complex subject, as a reference to *The RHS Plant-finder* makes evident.

In the case of the woody plants, some indication of approximate heights and effective lives is shown.

Nomenclature is always changing, and in compiling these tables references have come from a number of sources to be found in the Bibliography. Particular plant management is summarised in the last three tables.

TABLE 1: A RANGE OF TREES (EXCLUDING CONIFERS) IN GENERAL CULTIVATION

BOTANICAL NAME	COUNTRY OF ORIGIN	INTRODUCTION DATE	EFFECTIVE LIFESPAN	DESCRIPTION	D or E
xLaburnocytisus 'Adamii'	GO, nursery of M. Adam near Paris	1825	S	Small	D
Acer campestre + cvs	Europe	Native	M	Medium	D
Acer cappodocicum	W Asia	1838	M	Medium/large	D
Acer griseum	C China	1901	SM	Small	D
Acer grosseri	China	1923	SM	Medium	D
Acer negundo + cvs	North America, Mexico, Guatemala	Cult. 1688	SM	Medium/large	D
Acer pensylvanicum	E North America	1755	SM	Small	D
Acer platanoides + cvs	Europe, Caucasus	Long cult.	M	Large	D
Acer pseudoplatanus + cvs	Europe, W. Asia	Long cult.	L	Large	D
Acer rubrum	E North America	Cult. 1656	ML	Large	D
Acer saccharinum	E North America	1725	ML	Large	D
Aesculus flava	SE USA	1764	M	Medium/large	D
Aesculus hippocastanum + cvs	Greece to Albania	W Europe 1576, UK c. 1616	M	Large	D
Aesculus indica	NW Himalaya	1851	ML	Large	D
Aesculus turbinata	Japan	pre 1880	SM	Large	D
Aesculus x carnea		Cult. 1820	SM	Large	D
Ailianthus altissima	N China	1751	M	Large	D
Albizia julibrissin	Iran to China, Taiwan	1745	M	Small	D
Albizia julibrissin 'Rosea'	Korea	1918	ML	Small	D
Alnus cordata	Corsica to S Italy	1820	M	Large	D
Alnus glutinosa	Europe, W Asia, N Africa	Native	ML	Small/medium	D
Arbutus unedo	Mediterranean Region, SW Ireland	Native	ML	Small	E
Azara microphylla	Chile, Argentina	1861	S	Small	E
Betula albosinensis + cvs	W China	1901	M	Medium	D
Betula ermanii + cvs	NE Asia		M	Medium	D
Betula papyrifera	North America	1750	M	Large	D
Betula pendula + cvs	Europe, N Asia	Native	M	Medium	D
Betula pubescens	Europe, N Asia	Native	M	Medium	D
Betula utilis + cvs	SW China to Nepal	1849	M	Medium	D
Betula utilis var. jacquemontii	N India, C & W Nepal	Cult. 1880	M	Medium	D
Carpinus betulus	Europe, Asia Minor	Native	ML	Medium/large	D
Carya cordiformis	E USA	1766	M	Medium/large	D
Castanea sativa	S Europe, N Africa, Asia Minor	By the Romans	ML	Large	D
Catalpa bignonioides	E USA	1726	M	Medium	D
Catalpa bungei	N China	1905	M	Small	D
Celtis australis	S Europe	Since 16th cent.	M	Medium/large	D
Celtis occidentalis	N USA	1656	M	Medium	D
Cercidiphyllum japonicum	Japan, China	1881	SM	Small/medium	D
Cercis canadensis	SE Canada, E USA, NE Mexico	1730	SM	Small	D
Cercis siliquastrum	E Mediterranean Region	16th cent.	SM	Small	D
Cladrastis kentukea	SE USA	1812	M	Medium	D
Cladrastis sinensis	China	1901	M	Medium	D
Cordyline australis	New Zealand	1823	M	Small	E
Cornus controversa	China/Taiwan	1880	M	Small	D
Cornus nuttallii	W North America	1835	M	Medium	D
Corylus colurna	SE Europe, W Asia	1582	ML	Large	D
Crataegus laevigata (C. oxycantha) + cvs	NW & C Europe	Native	M	Small	D
Crataegus monogyna + cvs	Europe, W Asia, N Africa	Native	M	Small	D
Crataegus mollis	C USA	GO	M	Small	D
Crataegus persimilis 'Prunifolia'	E USA	GO	M	Small	D
Cydonia oblonga	N Iran & Turkestan		SM	Small	D
Davidia involucrata	C & W China	1904	M	Medium	D
Embothrium coccineum	Chile	1846	SM	Medium	E
Eucalyptus gunnii	Tasmania	Cult. 1853	M	Large	E
Eucalyptus johnstonii	Tasmania	Cult. 1886	M	Large	E
Fagus sylvatica + cvs	Europe	Native	L	Large	D
Fraxinus angustifolia + cvs	S Europe	1890 + GO	M	Medium	D
Fraxinus excelsior + cvs	Europe	Native	ML	Large	D
Fraxinus ornus	S Europe, SW Asia	pre 1700	M	Medium	D

S Short-lived: 30–50 yrs; SM Short/Medium: 50–75 yrs; M Medium: 75–150 yrs; ML Medium/Long: 150–200 yrs; L Long-lived: 200 + yrs
D Deciduous; E Evergreen. GO Garden Origin

(Continued . . .)

TABLE 1: A RANGE OF TREES (EXCLUDING CONIFERS) IN GENERAL CULTIVATION (CONTINUED)

BOTANICAL NAME	COUNTRY OF ORIGIN	INTRODUCTION DATE	EFFECTIVE LIFESPAN	DESCRIPTION	D or E
Fraxinus pennsylvanica	E North America	1783	M	Medium	D
Gleditsia japonica	Japan	1894	M	Medium	D
Gleditsia triacanthos	C & E USA	1700	M	Large	D
Halesia carolina	SE USA	1756	S/M	Small	
Ilex x altaclarensis + cvs	GO		M	Medium	E
Ilex aquifolium	W & S Europe, N Africa & W Asia	Native	L	Medium	DE
Juglans nigra	E & C USA	Cult. 1686	L	Large	D
Juglans regia	SE Europe, Himalaya, China	Many cent.	ML	Medium/large	D
Koelreuteria paniculata	China	1763	M	Small/medium	D
Laburnum alpinum	C & S Europe	Cult. 1596	SM	Small	D
Laburnum anagyroides + cvs	C & S Europe	Cult. 1560	SM	Small	D
Laurus nobilis	Mediterranean Region	Cult. 1562	ML	Small	E
Liquidambar styraciflua + cvs	E USA	17th cent.	ML	Large	D
Liriodendron tulipifera	E North America	Cult. 1688	L	Large	D
Magnolia acuminata	E USA	1736	M/L	Large	D
Magnolia campbellii	E Nepal, Sikkim, Bhutan, SW China	1865	M	Large	D
Magnolia campbellii subsp. Mollicomata	SE Tibet, N Burma, Yunnan	1924	M	Large	D
Malus baccata	Asia	1784	SM	Small/medium	D
Malus coronaria	E USA	1724	SM	Small/medium	D
Malus floribunda	Japan	1862	SM	Small medium	D
Malus hupehensis	China, Japan	1900	SM	Small	D
Malus hybrids (see refs)	GO		SM	Small	D
Malus transitoria	China	1911	SM	Small	D
Mespilus germanica	SE Europe to C Asia	Long cult.	SM	Small	D
Morus alba	C to E Asia	1596?	L	Small/medium	D
Morus nigra	W Asia	Early 16th cent.?	M	Small	D
Nothofagus antarctica	Chile	1830	M	Medium	D
Nothofagus betuloides	Chile, Argentina	1830	M	Medium/large	E
Nothofagus moorei	New South Wales, Queensland	1892	M	Small/medium	E
Nothofagus obliqua	Chile, Argentina	1902	M	Large	D
Nothofagus solandri	New Zealand	Cult. 1917	ML	Medium	E
Nyssa sylvatica	S Canada, E USA, C & S Mexico	1750	M	Medium/large	D
Ostrya carpinifolia	S Europe, W Asia	1724	M	Medium	D
Paulownia fargesii	W China	1896	SM	Medium	D
Paulownia tomentosa	China	1834	SM	Small/medium	D
Phellodendron amurense	NE Asia	1885	SM	Small	D
Photinia beauverdiana	W China	1900	M	Small	D
Platanus orientalis	SE Europe	Cult. early 16th cent.	L	Large	D
Platanus x hispanica		Cult. 1663	L	Large	D
Populus x canescens	W, C & S Europe	Native?	ML	Medium/large	D
Populus alba	C & SE Europe to C Asia	Long cult.	M	Large	D
Populus balsamifera	North America	pre 1689	SM	Large	D
Populus koreana	Korea	1918	SM	Medium	D
Populus lasiocarpa	C China	1900	SM	Medium	D
Populus nigra 'Italica'	Europe	1758	M	Large	D
Populus nigra subsp. Betufolia	E & C England	Native	ML	Large	D
Populus tremula	Europe, Asia to N Africa	Native	M	Large	D
Prunus armeniaca	S Europe	Long cult.	SM	Small/medium	D
Prunus avium	W Asia	Native	M	Medium/large	D
Prunus cerasifera + cvs	Unknown in the wild	Cult. 16th cent.	SM	Small	D
Prunus dulcis + cvs	N Africa to W Asia	Cult. 16th cent. or earlier	SM	Small	D
Prunus mume+ cvs	China, Korea, Japan (cultivation)	1844	SM	Small	D
Prunus padus + cvs	Europe, N Asia to Japan	Native	M	Small/medium	D
Prunus sargentii	Japan, Korea	1890	SM	Small/medium	D
Prunus serrula	W China	1908	SM	Small	D
Prunus subhirtella + cvs	GO	1894	S	Small	D
Prunus Japanese cherries of uncertain origin (see refs)	GO		S	Small/medium	D

S Short-lived: 30–50 yrs; SM Short/Medium: 50–75 yrs; M Medium: 75–150 yrs; ML Medium/Long: 150–200 yrs; L Long-lived: 200 + yrs
D Deciduous; E Evergreen. GO Garden Origin

TABLE I 311

TABLE I: A RANGE OF TREES (EXCLUDING CONIFERS) IN GENERAL CULTIVATION (CONTINUED)					
BOTANICAL NAME	COUNTRY OF ORIGIN	INTRODUCTION DATE	EFFECTIVE LIFESPAN	DESCRIPTION	D or E
Ptelea trifoliata	E USA, Mexico	1704	S	Small/medium	D
Pterocarya fraxinifolia	Caucasus, N Iran	1782	L	Large	D
Pterocarya x rehderiana	USA (Arnold Arboretum)	1874	ML	Large	D
Pyrus betulifolia	N China	1882	M	Small	D
Pyrus calleryana	China	1908	M	Medium	D
Pyrus communis		Long cult.	M	Medium	D
Pyrus nivalis	S Europe	1800	SM	Small	D
Pyrus salicifolia	Caucasus	1780	SM	Small	D
Quercus castaneifolia	Caucasus, Iran	1846	ML	Large	D
Quercus cerris	S Europe, SW Asia	1735	L	Large	D
Quercus coccinea	SE Canada, E USA	1691	ML	Large	D
Quercus frainetto	SE Europe	1838	L	Large	D
Quercus ilex	Mediterranean Region, SW Europe	Cult. 16th cent.	L	Large	E
Quercus macrocarpa	NE & NC North America	1811	ML	Medium	D
Quercus palustris	SE Canada, E USA	1800	ML	Large	D
Quercus petraea	W, C & SE Europe, SW Asia	Native	L	Large	D
Quercus phellos	E USA	1723	ML	Large	D
Quercus robur	Europe, Caucasus, SW Asia, N Africa	Native	L	Large	D
Quercus rubra	E North America	1724	ML	Large	D
Quercus suber	S Europe, N Africa	Cult. 1699	ML	Medium	E
Quercus x hispanica 'Lucombeana'	Garden origin, raised by Mr Lucombe, Exeter	circa 1762	ML	Large	D
Quercus x turneri	Garden origin, raised by Mr Turner, Essex	late 18th cent.	ML	Medium/large	D/E
Rhus potaninii	CW China	1902	SM	Small	D
Rhus verniciflua	Japan, China, Himalaya	Cult. pre 1862	SM	Medium	D
Robinia pseudoacacia + cvs	E USA	circa 1630	M	Large	D
Salix alba + cvs	Europe, W Asia	Native	SM	Large	D
Salix babylonica + cvs	China	circa 1730	SM	Medium	D
Salix caprea	Native		S	Small	D
Salix fragilis	Europe, N Asia	Native	SM	Large	D
Salix pentandra	Europe, N Asia	Native	SM	Small/medium	D
Salix triandra	Europe	Long cult.	S	Small	D
Sassafras albidum	E USA	1633	SM	Medium	D
Sophora japonica	China, Japan (cultivation)	1753	M	Medium/large	D
Sorbus aria	Europe	Native	M	Small/medium	D
Sorbus aucuparia	Europe	Native	ML	Small/medium	D
Sorbus domestica	S & E Europe	Native	SM	Medium	D
Sorbus intermedia	NW Europe		M	Small/medium	D
Sorbus sargentiana	W China	1908	SM	Small/medium	D
Sorbus torminalis	Europe, Asia Minor, N Africa	Native	M	Medium	D
Stewartia pseudocamellia	Japan	Cult. pre 1878	SM	Small/medium	D
Stewartia serrata	Japan	Cult. pre 1915	SM	Small	D
Tetradium daniellii	China, Korea	1905	M	Small/medium	D
Tilia cordata	Europe	Native	ML	Medium/large	D
Tilia oliveri	C China	1900	ML	Medium/large	D
Tilia platyphyllos + cvs	C & S Europe to N France and SW Sweden	Native	ML	Large	D
Tilia x euchlora		1860 GO	ML	Large	D
Tilia tomentosa + cvs	SE & EC Europe	1767	ML	Large	D
Tilia x europaea + cvs			L	Large	D
Tilia mongolicca	E Russia, Mongolia	1880	ML	Medium/large	D
Toona sinensis	N & W China	1862	SM	Medium	D
Ulmus glabra	Europe, N & W Asia	Native	L*	Large	D
Ulmus minor	Europe, N Africa, SW Asia	Bronze Age	L*	Large	D
Ulmus minor subsp. *Angustifolia*	Dorset, Devon and Cornwall & Brittany	Anglo-Saxon times	L*	Large	D
Ulmus procera	SW Europe	Native	L*	Large	D
Umbelluaria californica	California & Oregon	1829	SM	Small	E
Zelkova carpinifolia	Caucasus, N Iran	1760	M	Large	D
Zelkova serrata	Japan, Korea, Taiwan, China	1861	M	Medium	D

S Short-lived: 30–50 yrs; SM Short/Medium: 50–75 yrs; M Medium: 75–150 yrs; ML Medium/Long: 150–200 yrs; L Long-lived: 200 + yrs
D Deciduous; E Evergreen. GO Garden Origin

TABLE 2: A RANGE OF CONIFERS IN GENERAL CULTIVATION			
BOTANICAL NAME (COMMON NAME)	COUNTRY INTRODUCTION DATE	EFFECTIVE LIFESPAN	SIZE/HEIGHT ETC.
Abies alba (Silver Fir)	Europe circa 1603	ML	Tall
Abies grandis (Giant Fir)	N USA 1830	ML	Tall
Abies pinsapo (Spanish Fir)	S Spain 1839	ML	Medium/tall
Abies procera (Noble Fir)	W USA 1830	ML	Tall
Araucaria araucana (Monkey Puzzle)	S America 1795/1844	ML	Tall
Calocedrus decurrens (Incense Cedar)	W USA 1853	M	Medium/tall
Cedrus atlantica (Atlas Cedar)	N Africa 1840	L	Tall
Cedrus deodara (Deodar)	W Himalaya 1831	L	Tall
Cedrrus libanii (Lebanon Cedar)	SW Asia/Syria 1645	L+	Tall
Cephalotaxus fortunei (Chinese Plum Yew)	China 1849	M	Medium/small
Chamarcyparis lawsoniana (Lawson Cypress) many cvs	W USA 1854	ML	Medium
Chamycaparis nootkatensis (Nootka Cypress)	N USA 1793	ML	Medium/tall
Chamaecyparis obtusa (Hinoki Cypress) + cvs	Japan 1861	M	Small/medium
Chamaecyparis pisifera (Sawara Cypress) + cvs	Japan 1861	M	Small/medium
Cryptomeria japonica (Japanese Cedar) + cvs esp. C. j. 'Elegans'	Japan 1842	M	Medium/tall
xCupressocyparis leylandii (Leyland Cypress)	UK early 1900s? GO	M	Medium/tall
Cupressus arizonica (Arizona Cypress)	Arizona 1907	M	Small/medium
Cupressus macrocarpa (Monterey Cypress)	California 1838	M	Medium/tall
Cupressus sempervirens (Italian Cypress)	Mediterranean cult. since 17th cent.?	M	Medium
Ginko biloba (Maiidenhair Tree)	China 1754	ML	Medium/tall Deciduous
Juniperus chinensis (Chinese Juniper) + cvs	China 1804	M	Small/medium
Juniperus communis (Common Juniper) = cvs	Europe/native in UK	SM	Small
Juniperus horizontalis many cvs	N USA 1830	SM	Small
Juniperus x pfitzeriana many cvs	NE Asia 20th cent. GO	SM	Small
Juniperus sabina (Savin)	Europe/Asia 1548	SM	Small
Juniperus squamata many cvs	Asia 1824	SM	Small/medium
Juniperus virginiana (Pencil Cedar)	Central USA 1664	M	Medium
Larix decidua (Common Larch)	Europe circa 1620	ML	Medium /tall Deciduous
Larix kaempferi (Japanese Larch)	Japan 1861	ML	Medium/tall Deciduous
Metasequoia glyptostroboides (Dawn Redwood)	China circa 1948	ML	Medium Deciduous
Picea abies (Norway Spruce) + cvs	Europe circa 1500	ML	Medium/tall

Life span: S Short 25–50 yrs. SM Short/Medium 50–100yrs. M Medium 100–150 yrs. ML Medium/Long 150–200 yrs +. L Long-lived 200–300 yrs + approx.
Size/height: Small 1.5–2m. Small/Medium 2.5–4m Medium 5–7m. Medium/Tall 8–10m. Tall 15m +

TABLE 2 313

TABLE 2: A RANGE OF CONIFERS IN GENERAL CULTIVATION (CONTINUED)			
BOTANICAL NAME (COMMON NAME)	COUNTRY INTRODUCTION DATE	EFFECTIVE LIFESPAN	SIZE/HEIGHT ETC.
Picea breweriana (Brewer's Weeping Spruce)	NW California 1897	ML	Medium
Picea mariana (Black Spruce)	N USA no date	M	Small/medium
Picea omorika (Serbian Spruce)	Serbia 1889	M	Medium
Picea pungens + cvs (Colorado Spruce)	Colorado USA 1862	M	Medium
Pinus cembra (Arolla Pine)	Europe 1746	M	Small/mediuym
Pinus contorta (Beach Pine)	W USA 1831	M	Medium/tall
Pinus montezeumae (Montezeume Pine)	Mexico 1839	ML	Medium
Pinus mugo + cvs (Mountain Pine)	Europe no date long cult.	M	Small/medium
Pinus muricata (Bishop Pine)	California 1848	M	Medium
Pinus nigra (Austrian Pine)	N Europe 1835	ML	Medium/tall
Pinus nigra maritima (Corsican Pine)	S Italy/Corsica 1759	ML	Medium/tall
Pinus parviflora (Japanese White Pine)	Japan 1861	M	Small/medium
Pinus pinaster (Maritime Pine)	Mediterranean Long cult.	ML	Medium/tall
Pinus radiata (Monterey Pine)	California 1833	ML	Medium/tall
Pinus strobus (Weymouth Pine)	USA early 1700s	M	Medium/tall
Pinus sylvestris (Scots Pine) + cvs	Europe/native	ML	Medium/tall
Pinus wallichiana (Bhutan Pine)	Himalayas 1823	ML	Medium/tall
Pseudolarix amabilis (Golden Larch)	China 1852	M	Medium Deciduous
Pseudotsuga meziesii (Douglas Fir)	W USA 1827	ML	Tall
Sciadopitys verticillata (Japanese Umbrella Pine)	Japan 1853/1861	M	Medium
Sequoia sempervirens (Californian Redwood)	California 1843	L	Tall
Sequoiadendron giganteum (Wellingtonia, Calif. Big Tree)	California 1853	L	Tall
Taxodium distichum (Swamp Cypress)	S USA/Florida 1640	L	Medium/tall Deciduous
Taxus baccata (Common Yew) + cvs	Europe/native	L	Medium
Taxus baccata 'Fastigiata' (Irish Yew)	Ireland 1780	L	Small/medium
Thuya occidentalis + cvs (American Arbor-vitae)	E USA 1534	M	Small/medium
Thuya orientalis + cvs (now Platycladus) (Chinese Arbor-vitae)	China 1690	L	Small/medium
Thuya plicata + cvs (Western Red Cedar)	W USA 1853	M	Medium/tall
Tsuga canadensis (Eastern Hemlock)	E USA 1736	M	Medium/tall
Tsuga heterophylla (Western Hemlock)	W USA 1851	M	Medium/tall

Life span: S Short 25–50 yrs. SM Short/Medium 50–100yrs. M Medium 100–150 yrs. ML Medium/Long 150–200 yrs +. L Long-lived 200–300 yrs + approx.
Size/height: Small 1.5–2m. Small/medium 2.5–4m Medium 5–7m. Medium/tall 8–10m. Tall 15m +

TABLE 3: A SHORT GUIDE TO SOME RHODODENDRON SPECIES AND HARDY HYBRIDS, INCLUDING AZALEAS

SPECIES	ORIGIN	INTRODUCTION DATE	APPROX. SIZE	DECIDUOUS/ EVERGREEN
Rh. arboreum	Himalaya	1810	Large, tree-like	E
Rh. augustinii	China	1899	Medium	E
Rh. calophytum	China	1904	Large	E
Rh. campylocarpum	E Nepal, Sikkim	1849	Medium	E
Rh. catawbiense	SE USA	1809	Medium/large	E
Rh.decorum	China	1901	Medium	E
Rh. fortunei	China	1900	Medium	E
Rh. griffithianum	E Nepal, N India	1850	Medium	E
Rh. griersonianum	Yunnan, N Burma	1917	Small/medium	E
Rh. luteum (Azalea pontica)	E Europe	1793	Medium	D
Rh. molle (Azalea mollis)	China	1823	Medium	D
Rh. occidentale (Azalea occidentalis)	W North America	1851	Medium	D
Rh. ponticum	N Turkey, Caucasus	1763	Medium/large	E
Rh. thomsonii	E Nepal, India	1850	Medium	E
Rh. vaseyi (Azalea vaseyi)	N Carolina, USA	1880	Medium	D
Rh. wardii	Yunnan, Tibet	1913	Medium	E
Rh. williamsianum	China	1908	Small	E
Rh. yakushimanum	Japan	1934	Small	E
Rh. viscosum (Azalea viscosa)	E North America	1734	Medium	D
Rh. indicum (Azalea indica)	S Japan	1877	Small	E
Rh. kurume hybrids (Azalea kurume)	Japan and GO	Early 20th cent.	Small	E

A SELECTION OF HARDY HYBRID RHODODENDRONS

	ORIGIN	INTRODUCTION DATE	APPROX. SIZE	DECIDUOUS/ EVERGREEN
	All grouped here as of GO		Generally medium/large	All E
'Bagshot Ruby'		1916		
'Beauty of Littleworth'		1900		
'Britannia'		1921		
'Christmas Cheer'		1908		
'Countess of Athlone'		1923		
'Cunningham's White'		19th cent.		
'Cynthia'		1870		
'Doncaster'		Early 20th cent.		
'Fastuosum flore pleno'		1846		
'Goldsworth Yellow'		1925		
'Gomer Waterer'		Early 1900	Medium	
'Marchioness of Landsdowne'		1879		
'Mother of Pearl'		1914	Medium	
'Mrs A. T. De La Mare'				
'Nobleanum'		1832	Medium	
'Pink Pearl'		1897	Medium	
'Polar Bear'		1926	Medium/large	
'Purple Splendour'		Pre 1900	Medium	
'Sappho'		Pre 1867	Medium	
'Souvenir of Anthony Waterer'		Pre 1924	Medium	

Rhododendrons constitute a huge genus of over 800 species and countless hybrids and cultivars. Many of these are described in the references. For the purposes of this book concerned primarily with historic gardens, a short selection is given here of some of the main species introduced during the nineteenth century which have given rise to many important hybrids. This is followed by another short summary of those known as the Hardy Hybrid Rhododendrons, which formed an important basis for some of the first grown in large gardens and parks; they are still valued for their toughness and reliability.

TABLE 3 315

TABLE 3: A SHORT GUIDE TO SOME RHODODENDRON SPECIES AND HARDY HYBRIDS, INCLUDING AZALEAS (CONT.)				
SPECIES	ORIGIN	INTRODUCTION DATE	APPROX. SIZE	DECIDUOUS/ EVERGREEN
EARLY AZALEA INTRODUCTIONS				
Ghent Hybrids	All Belgium, UK	1830–1850	All medium	All D
'Coccineum Speciosum'		Pre 1846		
'Daviesii'		circa 1840		
'Gloria Mundi'		1846		
'Nancy Waterer'		Pre 1876		
'Narcissiflorum'		Pre 1871		
'Raphael de Smet'		Pre 1889		
'Unique'		Pre 1875D		
Knap Hill Hybrids	UK	20th cent.	Medium	D
Mollis Azaleas	All Belgium	From 1870s	All medium	All D
'Altaclarence'		1862		
'Comte de Gomer'		1872		
'Floradora'		1910		
'Kosters Brilliant Red'		1918		
'Sunbeam'		1895		
Occidentale and Rustica Hybrids		Mainly since 1900	Medium	D
EVERGREEN AZALEAS				
Kaempferi Hybrids	Holland	1920s	Medium	E
Kurume Azaleas	All Japan	19th cent. Introduced by Ernest Wilson in the 1920s as 'Wilson's fifty' and developed from then	All compact	All E
'Hinomayo'		1910		
'Kirin'		1922, Wilson		
'Hinode-giri'		Wilson		
and others				
Obtusum Azaleas	All China, Japan	Long cult.	All compact	All E
'Amoenum'		1844		
'Amoenum Coccineum'		1850s		

TABLE 4: SHRUBS				
BOTANICAL NAME	COUNTRY OF ORIGIN	INTRODUCTION DATE	DESCRIPTION	D OR E
Abelia chinensis	C & E China	Cult. 1844	Small	D
Abelia floribunda	Mexico	1841	Medium	D/E
Abutilon megapotamicum	Brazil	1804	Small/medium	D
Abutilon vitifolium	Chile	1836	Large	D
Acer palmatum + cvs (see mainly Table 1)	Japan, China	1820	Large	D
Aesculus paviflora	SE USA	1851	Medium/tall	E
Aloysia triphylla (Lippia)	Argentina, Chile	1784	Medium/large	D *
Amelanchier lamarckii	C & S Europe, N Africa, W Asia	1596	Medium/large	D
Arctostaphylos uva-ursi	Cool–temperate N Hemisphere	Native	Creeping	E
Aucuba japonica + cvs	Japan	1783	Medium	E
Aucuba japonica 'Variegata'	Japan	1783	Medium	E
Azaleas (see Table 3)			Medium	D
Berberis darwinii	Argentina, Chile	1849	Medium	E
Berberis thunbergii + cvs	Japan	circa 1864	Small	D
Berberis wilsonii	Argentina, Chile	1927	Medium	E
Berberis x stenophylla + cvs	GO	Cult. 1860	Medium	E
Buddleja auriculata	S Africa, Zimbabwe to Cape Province		Medium	E *
Buddleja davidii + cvs	C & W China, Japan	Cult. 1890	Medium	D
Buddleja globosa	Andes of Chile, Peru, Argentina	1774	Medium	D
Buddleja salviifolia	South Africa	Cult. 1783	Medium	D
Buxus microphylla + cvs	Japan + GO	1860	Dwarf/small	E
Buxus sempervirens + cvs	Native GO		Small/medium	E
Callicarpa bodinieri	C & W China	circa 1845	Medium	D
Callicarpa bodinieri var. giraldii	E to W China	Cult. 1900	Medium/large	D
Callistemon citrinus + cvs	E Australia	1788	Medium	E
Calluna vulgaris + cvs	Europe, Asia Minor	Native	Dwarf/small	E
Calycanthus floridus	SE USA	1726	Medium	D
Camellia japonica + cvs	Japan, China	1739	Large	E
Camellia xwiilliamsii cvs	GO	1925	Medium/large	E
Camellia reticulata + cvs	Yunnan, China	1820	Large	E
Camellia reticulata (wild form)	W China	1924	Large	E
Camellia saluenensis	W China	1924	Medium	E
Camellia sasanqua	Japan	1896	Medium	E
Carpenteria californica	California	circa 1880	Medium	E *
Caryopteris x clandonensis + cvs	Japan, Korea, China, Taiwan	1844 + GO	Small	D
Ceanothus arboreus 'Trewithen Blue'	GO	20th cent.	Large	E
Ceanothus dentatus (x lobbianus)	California	1853	Spreading	E
Ceanothus x delileanus + cvs	GO	1870s GO	Small/medium	D
Ceanothus x lobbianus	California	circa 1853	Large	E
Ceanothus thyrsiflorus + cvs	GO	1837	Medium	E
Ceanothus x veitchianus	California	circa 1853	Large	E
Ceratostigma willmottianum	W China	1908	Small	D
Chaenomeles cathayensis	C China	circa 1800	Large	D
Chaenomeles japonica	Japan	circa 1869	Small	D
Chaenomeles speciosa + cvs	China	1869	Medium	D
Chamaecytisus albus (Cytisus albus)	C & SE Europe	1806	Dwarf	D
Chamaecytisus austriacus	C & SE Europe to C Russia	1741	Dwarf	D
Chamaecytisus purpureus	C & SE Europe	1792	Small	D
Chimonanthus praecox + cvs	China	1766	Medium	D
Choisya 'Aztec Pearl'	GO	1982	Medium	E
Choisya ternata	SW Mexico	1825	Medium	E
Cistus x argenteus 'Silver Pink'	GO	1910	Small	E
Cistus ladanifer	SW Europe/N.Africa	1629	Medium/large	E
Cistus laurifolius	SW Europe to Turkey, N Africa	1731	Medium	E
Cistus populifolius	SW Europe	1634	Medium/large	E
Clerodendrum bungei	China	1844	Medium	D
Clerodendrum trichotomum	China, Japan	circa 1880	Large	D
Clerodendrum trichotomum var. fargesii	W China	1898	Large	D
Clianthus puniceus	New Zealand (North Island)	1831	Medium	D/E *
Cllethra alnifolia + cvs	E USA	1731	Medium	D/E
Colletia hystrix (C. armata)	Chile, N Argentina	circa 1882	Medium	D
Cornus alba	Siberia to Manchuria, N Korea	1741	Medium/large	D
Cornus alba 'Sibirica'	GO	Cult. 1838	Medium	D
Cornus florida + cvs	E USA	1730	Large	D
Cornus kousa	Japan, Korea	1875	Large	D
Cornus mas	CS Europe	Long cult.	Large	D

Size: Dwarf 0.5m. Small 0.5–1.0m. Small/medium 1.0–1.5m. Medium 1.5–2.0m. Medium/large 2.0–3.0m. Large 3.0m +.
D Deciduous; E Evergreen. GO Garden Origin. * Frost-tender.

TABLE 4 317

TABLE 4: SHRUBS (CONTINUED)				
BOTANICAL NAME	COUNTRY OF ORIGIN	INTRODUCTION DATE	DESCRIPTION	D OR E
Cornus kousa var. chinensis	China	1907	Large	D
Cornus sanguinea	Europe	Native		D
Corokia cotoneaster	New Zealand	1875	Medium	E
Corylopsis glabrescens	Japan	1905	Medium/large	D
Corylopsis pauciflora	Japan, Taiwan	circa 1860	Medium	D
Corylopsis spicata	Japan	circa 1860	Medium	D
Cotinus coggygria	C & S Europe to Himalaya & China	Cult. 1656	Medium/large	D
Cotoneaster bullatus	W China	1898	Large	D
Cotoneaster conspicuous	SE Tibet	1925	Medium	E
Cotoneaster franchetii	China	1895	Medium	D/E
Cotoneaster horizontalis	W China	1870	Spreading	D
Cotoneaster lacteus	China	1813	Medium	E
Cotoneaster rotundifolius	Himalaya	1825	Small	E
Cotonester 'Rothschildianus'	GO		Medium/large	E
Cotoneaster salicifolius + cvs	China	1908	Medium/large	E
Cotoneaster simonsii	Himalaya	1865	Medium	D/E
Cotoneaster xwatereri + cvs	GO		Large	E
Crinodendron hookerianum	Chile	1848	Large	E
Cytisus battandieri	Morocco	1922	Large	D/E
Cytisus nigricans	C and SE Europe/Russia	1730	Small	D
Cytisus multiflorus (C. albus)	Iberia/N Africa	1752	Large	E
Cytisus scoparius (Sarothamnus) + cvs	Europe	Native	Medium	D
Cytisus x praecox + cvs	GO	1867	Small	D
Daboecia cantabrica + cvs	W Europe	Cult. 1800	Dwarf	E
Danäe racemosa	SW Asia to N Iran	1713	Small	E
Daphne bholua	Himalaya	Cult. 1938	Medium	D/E
Daphne genkwa	China, Taiwan	1843	Small	D
Daphne laureola	Native SW Europe	Long Cult	Small	E
Daphne odora	China, Japan	1771	Small	D
Daphne pontica	SE Bulgaria, N Iran, N Turkey	1752	Small	E
Dendromecon rigida	California	1854	Large	E *
Desfontainia spinosa	Costa Rica to Cape Horn	1843	Medium	E
Deutzia discolor + cvs	China	1901	Medium	D
Deutzia gracilis	Japan	1840	Medium	D
Deutzia purpurascens	Yunnan	1915	Medium	D
Deutzia scabra	Japan, China	1822	Tall	D
Diervilla lonicera	North America	1720	Small	D
Drimys lanceolata	Tasmania, SE Australia	1843	Medium/large	E
Drimys winteri	Chile	1827	Medium	E
Edgeworthia chrysantha	Himalaya & china	1845	Small	D
Elaeagnus angustifolia	S Europe/W Asia	Long cult.	Large	D
Elaeagnus commutata	N USA	1813	Medium	D
Elaeagnus umbellata	Japan, China	1830	Medium	D
Elaeagnus pungens + cvs	Japan	1830	Large	E
Elaeagnus x ebbingei	Garden origin	1929	Large	E
Enkianthus campanulatus	Japan	1880	Large	D
Erica arborea + cvs	S Europe, SW Asia, N & E Africa	1658	Medium/large	E
Erica australis	Spain, Portugal	1769	Medium	E *
Erica carnea + cvs	Alps of C Europe		Dwarf	E
Erica ciliaris + cvs	SW Europe	Native	Dwarf	E
Erica cinerea + cvs	W Europe	Native	Dwarf	E
Erica lusitanica	Portugal		Medium/large	E
Erica terminalis	W Mediterranean Region	1765	Medium	E
Erica tetralix + cvs	N & W Europe	Native	Dwarf	E
Erica vagans + cvs	SW Europe	Native	Dwarf	E
Erica x darleyensis 'Darley Dale'	GO, Darley Dale Nurseries, Derbyshire	circa 1890	Dwarf	E
Escallonia 'Edinensis'	GO, Royal Botanic Garden, Edinburgh	pre 1914	Medium	E
Escallonia 'Langleyensis'	GO	1893	Medium	E
Escallonia illinita	Chile	1830	Large	E
Escallonia 'Iveyi'	GO		Medium	E
Escallonia rubra + cvs	Chile	1827	Medium	E
Escallonia rubra var. macrantha	Chiloe	1848	Large	E
Escallonia virgata	Chile	1866	Small	D
Escallonia x exoniensis	GO		Large	
Eucryphia cordifolia	Chile	1851	Large	E
Eucryphia glutinosa	Chile	1859	Medium/large	D
Eucryphia x Nymansensis	GO		Large	E

SIze: Dwarf 0.5m. Small 0.5–1.0m. Small/medium 1.0–1.5m. Medium 1.5–2.0m. Medium/large 2.0–3.0m. Large 3.0m +.
D Deciduous; E Evergreen. GO Garden Origin. * Frost-tender.

(Continued . . .)

TABLE 4: SHRUBS (CONTINUED)				
BOTANICAL NAME	COUNTRY OF ORIGIN	INTRODUCTION DATE	DESCRIPTION	D OR E
Euonymus alatus	China/Japan	1860	Medium	D
Euonymus europaeus	Native		Medium/Large	D
Euonymus fortunei + vvs	China	1907	Sprawling	E
Euonymus japonicus + cvs	China, Japan		Large	E
Euonymus planipes	NE Asia	1892	Large	D
Euryops pectinatus	South Africa	1731	Small	E
Euryops virgineus	South Africa	1821	Small	E
Fatsia japonica	Japan	1838	Medium/large	E
xFatshedera lizei	GO		Small/medium	E
Ficus carica + cvs	W Asia	Cult. early 16th cent.	Large	D
Forsythia ovata	Korea	1918	Small	D
Forsythia suspense + cvs	China	1833	Large	D
Forsythia x intermedia + cvs		Cult. before 1880	Medium/large	D
Fothergilla gardenii	SE USA	1765	Small	D
Fothergilla major	Alleghany Mts, USA	1780	Medium/large	D
Fremontodendron californicum	California, Arizona	1851	Large	D/E *
Fuchsia magellanica + cvs	Chile, Argentina	1788	Medium	D
Garrya elliptica	California, Oregon	1828	Large	E
Gaultheria mucronata + cvs	Chile to Magellan region	1828	Dwarf	E
Gaultheria procumbens	E North America	before 1762	Creeping	E
Gaultheria shallon	W North America	1826	Dwarf	E
Genista aetnensis	Sardinia/Sicily		Medium/large	E
Genista hispanica	SW Europe	1759	Small	E
Genista lydia	E Balkans	1926	Dwarf	D
Genista monspessulanus	S Europe, SW Asia, N Africa	Cult. 1735	Medium	D/E
Genista tenera	Madeira	1777	Large	D/E
Genista tinctoria	Europe, Turkey	Native	Medium	D
Griselinia littorailis + cvs	New Zealand	circa 1850	Large	E
Halimium lasianthum + cvs	S Portugal, S Spain, N Africa	1780?	Small	E
Halimium ocymoides	Portugal, Spain	Cult. 1800	Small	E
Hamamelis japonica	Japan	1862	Large	D
Hamamelis mollis + cvs	China	1879	Large	D
Hamamelis x intermedia + cvs	GO		Large	D
Hebe brachysiphon	South Island, New Zealand	1868	Medium	E
Hebe cupressoides	Mts of South Island, New Zealand	1880	Small/medium	E
Hebe albicans	GO	1880	Small/medium	E
Hebe hulkeana	South Island, New Zealand	circa 1860	Medium	E
Hebe rakaiensis	GO		Small	E
Hebe speciosa + cvs	North and South Islands, New Zealand		Small	E
Helianthemum nummularium	Europe	Native	Dwarf	E
Helianthemum hybrids	GO		Dwarf	E
Helichrysum italicum	SW Europe	Long cult.	Small	E
Hibiscus syriacus + cvs	E Asia	Cult. 16th cent.	Medium/large	D
Hoheria populnea	New Zealand	1912	Large	D/E
Hydrangea arborescens	E USA	1736	Small shrub	D
Hydrangea Hortensia Group	GO	18th cent. onwards	Medium/Large	D
Hydrangea paniculata + cvs	Japan, China, Taiwan	1861	Medium/large	D
Hydrangea Lace Caps Group	GO		Medium /large	D
Hydrangea quercifolia	SE USA	1803	Medium	D
Hydrangea serrata + cvs	Japan, Korea	1843	Dwarf	D
Hypericum calycinum	SE Bulgaria, N Turkey	1676	Dwarf	E
Hypericum 'Hidcote'	GO Hidcote garden		Medium	D/E
Hypericum forrestii	China/Burma	1906	Small/medium	D/E
Hypericum x moserianum	GO	circa 1887	Dwarf	D
Jasminum humile + cvs	Afghanistan to Yunnan & Sichuan, China	Cult. 1656	Small/medium	D/E
Jasminum nudiflorum	W China	1844	Medium/large/sprawling	D/E
Kalmia angustifolia + cvs	E North America	1736	Small	E
Kalmia latifolia + cvs	E North America	1734	Medium	E
Kerria japonica	China	1834	Medium	D
Kolkwitzia amabilis	W China	1901	Medium	D
Lavandula angustifolia + cvs	SW & SC Europe to Greece		Dwarf	E
Lavandula stoechas + cvs	Mediterranean Region, N Africa	Cult. mid 16th cent.	Dwarf	E
Lavateraxclementii + cvs	GO		Large	D
Leptospermum scoparium + cvs	Australia, Tasmania, New Zealand	1771	Large	E *
Lespedesia thunbergii	China/Japan	1837	Small/medium	D
Leycesteria Formosa	Himalaya	1824	Medium	D
Ligustrum japonicum + cvs	China, Korea, Taiwan, Japan	1845	Medium/large	E

Size: Dwarf 0.5m. Small 0.5–1.0m. Small/medium 1.0–1.5m. Medium 1.5–2.0m. Medium/large 2.0–3.0m. Large 3.0m +.
D Deciduous; E Evergreen. GO Garden Origin. * Frost-tender.

TABLE 4 319

TABLE 4: SHRUBS (CONTINUED)				
BOTANICAL NAME	COUNTRY OF ORIGIN	INTRODUCTION DATE	DESCRIPTION	D OR E
Ligustrum ovalifolium	Japan	Cult. 1885	Large	E
Ligustrum ovalifolium 'Aureum'	GO	Cult. 1862	Large	E
Ligustrum quihoui	China	circa 1862	Medium	D
Ligustrum sempervirens	W China	1913	Medium	E
Ligustrum sinense	China, Vietnam	circa 1852	Large	D
Ligustrum vulgare	Europe, N Africa, SW Asia	Native	Large	D/E
Lonicera fragrantissima	China	1845	Medium	D/E
Lonicera nitida + cvs	W China	1908	Medium	E
Lonicera syringantha	China, Tibet	circa 1890	Small/medium	D
Lonicera tartarica + cvs	C Asia to Russia	1752	Medium	D
Lupinus arboreus	California	Cult. 1793	Medium	E
Magnolia grandiflora + cvs	SE USA	1734 + GO	Large	E
Magnolia liliiflora	C China	1790	Medium/large	D
Magnolia sieboldii	Japan, Korea	1865	Large	D
Magnolia sieboldii subsp. *Sinensis*	NW Sichuan (W China)	1908	Large	D
Magnolia x soulangeana + cvs	GO		Large	D
Magnolia stellata + cvs	Tokai District, Japan	1862	Medium/large	D
Magnolia wilsonii	China	1908	Medium/large	D
Mahonia aquifolium + cvs	W North America	1893	Small	E
Mahonia bealei	China	circa 1849	Medium/large	E
Mahonia japonica	Long cult. in Japan	Uncertain	Medium/large	E
Mahonia x media cvs	GO		Medium/large	E
Myrica gale	Native		Small	D
Myrtus communis + cvs	Mediterranean, SW Europe, W Asia	Cult. 16th cent.	Large	E
Nandina domestica	China, Japan	1804	Medium	E
Olearia avicenniifolia + cvs	New Zealand	1910	Medium/large	E
Olearia macrodonta	New Zealand	1886	Medium	E
Olearia phlogopappa + cvs	Tasmania, SE Australia	1848	Medium	E
Olearia x haastii	New Zealand	1858	Medium	E
OsmanthusxBurkwoodi	GO		Medium/large	E
Osmanthus decorus	W Asia	1866	Medium/large	E
Osmanthus delavayi	China (Yunnan, Sichuan)	1890	Medium	E
Osmanthus heterophyllus +cvs	Japan/Taiwan	1856	Medium	E
Pachysandra terminalis	Japan	1882	Dwarf	E
Paeonia delavayi	W China	1908	Medium	D
Paeonia delavayi Lutea Group	Yunnan	1886	Medium	D
Paeonia rockii	China		Medium	D
Paeonia suffruticosa + cvs	China (SW Shanxi & Shaanxi)		Medium	D
Paeonia x lemoinei + cvs	GO	circa 1909	Medium	D
Parahebe perfoliata	Australia	1834	Dwarf	D
Pernettya mucronata + cvs (now *Gaultheria*)	Chile	1828	Small	E
Philadelphus 'Lemoinei' Group	GO		Medium	D
Philadelphus 'Purpureomaculatus' Group	GO		Medium	D
Philadelphus coronarius	Europe	Long cult.	Large	D
Philadelphus virginalis Group	GO		Medium	D
Philadelphus purpurascens	China	1911	Medium	D
Philadelphus microphyllus	SW USA	1883	Small	D
Phillyrea latifolia	S Europe	1597	Medium	E
Phillyrea angustifolia	N Africa, S Europe	Cult. pre 1597	Medium	E
Photinia x Fraseri + cvs	GO	GO	Medium/large	E
Phormium tenax + cvs	New Zealand	1789	Large	E
Phygelius capensis	South Africa	Cult. 1855	Small	D/E
Pieris floribunda	SE USA	1800	Small/medium	E
Pieris Formosa + cvs	E Himalaya, Upper Burma, SW & C China	Cult. 1858	Large	E
Pieris formosa Forrestii Group	SW China, NE Upper Burma	1905	Medium	E
Pieris japonica	Japan, E China, Taiwan	Cult. 1870	Medium	E
Pieris japonica Taiwanensis Group	Taiwan	1918	Medium	E
Physocarpus opulifolius + cvs	E USA	1687 + GO	Medium/large	D
Piptanthus nepalensis	Himalaya	1821	Large	E
Pittosporum tenuifolium + cvs	New Zealand & GO		Large	E *
Poncirus trifoliata	N China	1850	Medium	D
Potentilla fruticosa + cvs	Throughout N Hemisphere	Native	Small	D
Prunus laurocerasus	E Europe, SW Asia	1576	Large	E
Prunus laurocerasus 'Otto Luyken'	GO	1940	Small	E
Prunus pumila	NE USA	1756	Medium	D
Prunus triloba	China	1884	Medium/large	D
Pyracantha angustifolia	W China	1899	Medium/large	E

Size: Dwarf 0.5m. Small 0.5–1.0m. Small/medium 1.0–1.5m. Medium 1.5–2.0m. Medium/large 2.0–3.0m. Large 3.0m +.
D Deciduous; E Evergreen. GO Garden Origin. * Frost-tender.

(Continued . . .)

TABLE 4: SHRUBS (CONTINUED)				
BOTANICAL NAME	COUNTRY OF ORIGIN	INTRODUCTION DATE	DESCRIPTION	D OR E
Pyracantha coccinea + cvs	S Europe, SW Asia	1629	Large	E
Pyracantha rogersiana	W China	1911	Large	E
Quercus coccifera	Mediterranean	Since 17th cent.	Small	E
Rhododendron Early species introductions (See Table 3)				
Rhododendron arboreum + cvs etc.	Himalaya	1810	Large	E
Rhododendron augustinii	E Sichuan	1899	Small/medium	E
Rhododendron auriculatum	Sichuan	1901	Large	E
Rhododendron barbatum	N India, Tibet	1829	Large	E
Rhododendron catawbiense	SE USA (Allegheny Mts)	1809	Medium/large	E
Rhododendron caucasium	Caucasus, NE Turkey	1803	Medium	
Rhododendron ciliatum	E Nepal, Sikkim, SE Tibet, Bhutan	1850	Small shrub	E
Rhododendron cinnabarinum + cvs	E Nepal, Sikkim, SE Tibet, Bhutan	1849	Medium/large	E
Rhododendron falconeri	E Nepal, Sikkiim, Bhutan	1850	Large/medium	
Rhododendron luteum (Azalea pontica)	Caucasus, N Turkey, E Europe	1793	Medium	D
Rhododendron molle (Azalea mollis) + cvs	E & C China	1823	Small/medium	
Rhododendron occidentale (Azalea occidentalis) + cvs	W North America (S Oregon to S California)	circa 1851	Medium	D
Rhododendron ponticum	Bulgaria, N Turkey, Caucasus, Lebanon, SW Spain, S Portugal	1763	Large	D
Rhododendron veitchianum	Burma, Laos, Thiland	1850	Medium	
Rhododendron schlippenbachii (Azalea)	Korea, E.Russia	1854	Medium	D
Rhododendron viscosum	E North America	1734	Medium	D
Rhododendron wardii	NW Yunnan, SW Sichuan, SE Tibet	1913	Medium/large	E
Rhododendron yakushimanum + cvs	Japan	1934	small	E
Rhus aromatica	E USA	1759	Small	D
Rhus copallina	E North America	1688	Small/medium	D
Rhus glabra	E North America	Cult. 1620	Medium	D
Rhus typhina	E USA	1629	Medium/large	D
Ribes sanguineum	W North America	1817	Medium	D
Ribes sanguineum 'Splendens'		Cult. 1900	Medium	D
Ribes speciosum	California	1828	Medium	D/E
Ribes x gordonianum	GO	1837	Medium	D
Robinia hispida	SE USA	1743	Medium	D
Rosa Limited species selection only				
Rosa canina	Native		Medium	D
Rosa glauca	Mts C and S Europe	Pre 1830	Medium/large	D
Rosa moyesii	W China	1894	Medium/large	D
Rosa multiflora	Japan, Korea	1804	Large shrub/rambler	D
Rosa pimpinellifolia	Native		Small/medium	D
Rosa villosa	Europe, N Asia	Native	Small	D
Rosa rugosa	NE Asia	1796	Medium	D
Rosa wichurana	E Asia	1891	Large, trailing	D/E
Rosmarinus officinalis	S Europe, Asia Minor	circa 1340	Medium	E
Rubus 'Benenden'	GO		Medium	D
Rubus biflorus	Himalaya	1818	Medium	D
Rubus deliciosus	Rocky Mountains, Colorado	1870	Medium	D
Rubus odoratus	E North America	1770	Medium	D
Rubus parviflorus	W North America	1827	Medium	D
Rubus phoenicolasius	Japan, China, Korea	circa 1876	Medium	D
Rubus spectabilis	W North America	1827	Medium	D
Rubus tricolor	W china	1908	Creeping	E
Ruscus aculeatus	S Europe	Native	Small shrub	E
Salix (see Table 1)				
Salix cinerea	Native		Medium/large	D
Salix fargesi	China	1911	Medium	D
Salix gracistylis	Japan, Korea, China	1895	Medium	D
Salix purpurea	Europe, C Asia	Native	Medium/large	D
Salix irrorata	SW USA	1895	Medium	D
Salix rosmarinifolia	GO		Small/medium	
Salvia involucrata	Mexico	1824	Small	D
Salvia microphylla + cvs	Mexico, GO	1829	Small	D
Salvia officinalis + cvs	S Europe	Cult. pre 1597	Dwarf/small	D/E
Sambucus canadensis	SE Canada, E USA	1761	Medium/large	D
Sambucus nigra + cvs	Native		Large	D
Sambucus racemosa + cvs	Europe, W Asia	Cult. 16th cent.	Medium/large	D
Santolina chamaecyparissus	S France, Pyrenees	Cult. 16th cent.	Dwarf	E

Size: Dwarf 0.5m. Small 0.5–1.0m. Small/medium 1.0–1.5m. Medium 1.5–2.0m. Medium/large 2.0–3.0m. Large 3.0m +.
D Deciduous; E Evergreen. GO Garden Origin. * Frost-tender.

TABLE 4 321

BOTANICAL NAME	COUNTRY OF ORIGIN	INTRODUCTION DATE	DESCRIPTION	D OR E
		TABLE 4: SHRUBS (CONTINUED)		
Sarcococca confusa	Unknown in the wild, probably China	Cult. 1916	Small	E
Sarcococca hookeriana + cvs	Himalaya		Small	E
Sarcococca ruscifolia	China	Cult. 1901	Small	E
Senecio greyii (Brachyglottis 'Sunshine')	GO		Small	E
Skimmia japonica + cvs	China, Japan	Cult. 1838	Small	E
Skimmia × confusa (S. laureola)	GO		Smalll	E
Spartium junceum	Mediterranean region, SW Europe	circa 1548	Large	D
Spiraea canescens	Himalaya	1837	Medium	D
Spiraea douglasii	W North America	1838	Medium	D
Spiraea douglasii subsp. menziesii	W North America	1838		
Spiraea japonica + cvs	Japan, Korea, China to the Himalayas	Cult. 1870	Small	D
Spiraea thunbergi + cvs	China, Japan (cult.)	circa 1863	Small/medium	D
Spiraea × vanhouttei	GO	pre 1866	Medium	D/E
Stachyurus praecox + cvs	Japan	1864	Medium/large	D
Staphylea colchica	S Caucasus	1850	Medium/large	D
Stephanandra incisa	Japan, Korea	1872	Small	D
Stephanadra tanakae	Japan	1893	Small	D
Stewartia malacodendron	SE USA	Cult. 1742	Large	D
Stewartia ovata	SE USA	pre 1785	Large	D
Stewartia pseudocamellia	Japan	1878	Large	D
Stranvaesia davidiana + cvs *(Photinia)*	W China	1917	Large	E
Symphoricarpos albus var. laevigatus	W North America	1817	Medium	D
Symphoricarpos orbiculatus	E USA	1730	Medium	D
Symphoricarpos × chenaultii	GO		Small/medium	D
Syringa emodi	W Himalaya	1838	Large	D
Syringa josikaea + cvs	C & E Europe	1830	Large	D
Syringa ×prestoniae hybrids (see refs)	Canada + GO	1920s	Large	D
Syringa vulgaris hybrids (see refs)	Europe + GO		Large	D
Tamarix anglica	native		Medium	D/E
Tamarix pentandra	WC Asia	1885	Medium	D/E
Tamarix tetrandra	SW Europe, W Asia	1821	Large	D
Ulex europaeus + cvs	W Europe to Italy	Native	Medium	E
Ulex galli	native		Small	E
Vaccinium corymbosum	E USA	1765	Medium	D/E
Vaccinium myrtillus	native		Small	E
Vaccinium ovatum	W USA	1826	Medium	E
Viburnum betulifolium	WC China	1901	Large	D
Viburnum × burkwoodii	GO	1924	Medium/large	E
Viburnum carlesii + cvs	Korea + GO	1902	Small/medium	D
Viburnum davidii	W China	1904	Small	E
Viburnum lantana	native		Medium	D
Viburnum macrocephalum 'Sterile'	GO, China	1844	Medium	D/E
Viburnum opulus + cvs	Europe, N & W Asia, N Africa (Algeria)	Native	Large	D
Viburnum plicatum + cvs	China, Japan, Taiwan	circa 1865	Medium/large	D
Viburnum rhytidophllyum	C & W China	1900	Large	E
Viburnum tinus + cvs	Mediterranean, SE Europe	Cult. late 16th cent.	Medium/large	E
Viburnum × bodnantense	GO Royal Botanic Garden, Edinburgh	1933	Medium/large	D
Vitex agnus-castus	S Europe	1570	Medium/large	D
Weigela florida + cvs	Japan, Korea, N China, Manchuria + GO	1845	Medium	D
Xanthorhiza simplicissima	E USA	1776	Small	D
Yucca flaccida	SE USA	1816	Small	E
Yucca gloriosa	SE USA	1550	Medium	E
Yucca recurvifolia	SE USA	1794	Medium	E
Xanthoceras sorbifolium	N China	1866	Medium	D
Zenobia pulverulenta	E USA	1801	Small/medium	D/E

Size: Dwarf 0.5m. Small 0.5–1.0m. Small/medium 1.0–1.5m. Medium 1.5–2.0m. Medium/large 2.0–3.0m. Large 3.0m +.
D Deciduous; E Evergreen. GO Garden Origin. * Frost-tender.

TABLE 5: HERBACEOUS PLANTS				
MAINLY SPECIES BOTANICAL NAME	COUNTRY OF ORIGIN	INTRODUCTION DATE	APPROX. HEIGHT IN METRES	FLOWERING PERIOD
Acanthus mollis (Tp)	Italy	1548	1.5	Late Summer
Achillea 'Coronation Gold' (Ro)	hybrid	1950	0.9	Summer
Achillea filipendula (Ro)	Caucasus	1803	1.2	Summer
Aconitum napellus (Ro)	Europe	1596	1.5	Late Summer
Agapanthus africanus (B)	Cape Province	1679	0.9	Late Summer
Agave Americana (Tp)	Mexico		1.8	Summer
Alchemilla mollis (Ro)	Asia Minor	1874	0.5	Early Summer
Allium christophii (B)	Turkestan	1901	0.5	Summer
Allium sphaerocephalum (B)	Europe	1594	0.5	Summer
Alstromeria ligtu (Rh)	Chile	1838	1.2	Early Summer
Althaea rosea (Tp)	Orient	1573	2.7	Late Summer/Autumn
Amaryllis belladonna (B)	South Africa	1712	0.6	Late Summer/early Autumn
Anchusa azurea (Ro)	Caucasus	1597	0.9	Early Summer
Anemone japonica (of gardens) (Ro)	China	1848	1.5	Early Autumn
Anemone nemorosa (C)	Europe	Native	0.15	Spring
Anthericum liliago (B)	S Europe	1596	0.6	Early Summer
Aquilegia vulgaris (Ro)	Europe	Native	0.9	Early Summer
Arisaema candidissimum (T)	W China	1924	0.3	Summer
Arisaema triphyllum (T)	E North America	1664	0.3	Early Summer
Armeria plantaginea (cushion)	Europe	1740	0.46	Early Summer
Artemisia abrotanum (subshrub)	S Europe	1548	0.9	Summer
Artemisia absinthium (subshrub)	Europe, temperate Asia	Native	0.9	Summer
Artemisia arborescens (subshrub)	S Europe	1640	0.9	Summer/Autumn
Arum italicum (Ro)	SE Europe, Canary Isles	1683	0.46	Spring
Aruncus dioicus (Ro)	N Hemisphere	1633	1.8	Summer
Asclepias tuberosa (Tp)	E North America	1690	0.46	Early Autumn
Asphodeline lutea (Ro)	Sicily	1596	0.9	Early Summer
Asphodelus albus (Ro)	S Europe	1596	0.9	Early Summer
Aspidistra lurida (Ro)	China	1822	0.46	Early Summer
Astelia nervosa (Ro)	New Zealand	1853	0.6	Summer
Aster amellus (Ro)	Europe, Asia Minor	1659	0.3	Late Summer/early Autumn
Aster novae-anglae (Ro)	North America	1710	1.5	Late Summer/early Autumn
Aster novae-belgii (Ro)	E United States	1710	0.9	Early Autumn
Aster tradescantii (Ro)	North America	1633	1.2	Autumn
Astilbe rivularis (Ro)	Nepal, W China	1825	1.8	Summer
Astrantia major (Ro)	Austria	1597	0.6	Summer/Autumn
Begonia grandis (RoB)	Malay, China, Japan	1804	0.3	Summer/Autumn
Bergenia xschmidtii (Rh)	Hybrid	1878	0.3	Early Spring
Bletilla striata (Rh)	China	1802	0.38	Early Summer
Bomarea hirtella (T)	South America	1801		Summer
Brunnera macrophylla (RoRh)	W Caucasus	1713	0.46	Spring
Bulbinella hookeri (Ro)	New Zealand	1850	0.6	Summer
Buphthalmum salicifolia (Ro)	Austria	1759	0.6	Summer
Calanthe discolor (B/T)	Japan	1837	0.3	Early Summer
Caltha palustris (Ro)	N temperate regions	Native	0.3	Spring
Camassia quamash (B)	W North America	1837	0.9	Early Summer
Campanula lactiflora (Tp)	Caucasus	1814	1.2	Early Summer/late Autumn
Campanula pyramidalis (Ro)	Europe	1596	1.5	Summer
Canna indica (Ro)	South America	1570	1.2	Late Summer
Canna irridiflora (Ro)	Peru	1816	1.5	Late Summer/Autumn
Cardiocrinum giganteum (B)	W China	1841	1.8	Summer
Cautleya gracilis (T)	Himalaya	1887	0.46	Summer
Centauria montana (Ro)	Europe	1596	0.46	Early Summer
Ceratostigma plumbaginoides (R/S)	China	1846	0.3	Autumn
Cestrum parqui (subshrub)	Chile	1787	1.5	Late Summer
Chelone obliqua (Ro)	North America	1752	0.9	Autumn
Chrysanthemum coccineum (Ro)	Middle East	1804	0.6	Early Summer
Chrysanthemum frutescens (subshrub)	Canary Islands	1699	0.9	Summer
Cimicifuga racemosa (Ro)	E North America	1732	0.9	Summer
Clematis recta 'Purpurea' (Tp)	Europe	1772	1.2	Summer
Colchicum agrippinum (B)	S Europe	1600	0.3	Autumn
Convallaria majalis (Rh)	N temperate regions	Native	0.23	Late Spring
Coreopsis verticillata (Ro)	E North America	1759	0.6	Summer/Autumn
Cosmos atrosanguineus (T)	Mexico	1835	0.75	Late Summer
Crambe cordifolia (Tp)	Caucasus	1822	1.8	Early Summer
Crinum bulbispermum (B)	South Africa	1752	1.2	Summer
Crocosmia pottsii (C)	South Africa	1877	0.9	Late Summer
Crocus biflorus (B)	SE Europe, Central Asia	1629	0.05	Spring
Crocus sativus (B)	S Europe to Kasmir	<1753	0.07	Autumn
Cyclamen coum (C)	SE Europe to Caucasus	1596	0.8	Winter
Cynara cardunculus (Tp)	Europe	1658	1.8	Summer
Dahlia coccinea (T)	Mexico	1798	1.2	Summer/early Autumn
Delphinium elatum (Tp)	W Europe to E Asia	1578	1.8	Summer
Dianthus 'Musgrave's Pink' (cushion)	Garden Origin	1730		Summer
Dianthus 'Old Crimson Clove' (cushion)	Europe	16th cent.		Summer
Diascia rigescens (Ro)	S Africa, E Cape	1836 & 1978	0.46	Early–late Summer

Ro rootstock/clump. R/S runners/stolins. Tp tap-rooted. Rh rhizomatous. B bulb. C corm. T tuber.

TABLE 5 323

TABLE 5: HERBACEOUS PLANTS (CONTINUED)

MAINLY SPECIES BOTANICAL NAME	COUNTRY OF ORIGIN	INTRODUCTION DATE	APPROX. HEIGHT IN METRES	FLOWERING PERIOD
Dicentra spectabilis (Tp)	Siberia, Japan	1810	0.6	Late Spring/early Summer
Dictamnus albus (Tp)	Europe, Asia	1596	0.9	Early Summer
Digitalis grandiflora (seed)	Greece	1596	0.6	Summer
Dodecatheon meadia (Ro?)	N America	1744	0.3	Spring
Doronicum plantagineum (Ro)	Europe, Britain	1570	0.75	Spring
Dracunculus vulgaris (T)	Mediterranean	1300	0.9	Summer
Eccremocarpus scaber (seed)	Chile	1824		Summer
Echinacea purpurea (Tp)	North America	1699	1.2	Summer
Echinops ritro (Ro)	Europe, W Asia	1570	1.2	Late Summer
Epimedium grandiflorum (Ro)	Japan, Manchuria	1830	0.3	Early Spring
Eranthus hyemalis (C)	Italy	1596	0.07	Winter
Eremurus robustus (Tp)	Turkestan	1874	2.4	Summer
Erigeron glaucus (Ro)	W North America	1812	0.3	Early–late Summer
Eryngium alpinum (Tp)	Europe	1597	0.75	Summer
Erythrina crista-galli (subshrub)	Brazil	1771	1.2	Summer/Autumn
Erythronium dens-canis (C)	Europe	1596	0.09	Spring
Eucomis autumnalis subsp. *autumnalis* (B)	South Africa	1760	0.3	Late Summer
Eupatorium purpureum (Ro)	North America	1640	2.4	Early Summer
Euphorbia griffithii (Tp/Ro)	W Asia	1949	0.9	Early Summer
Euphorbia palustris (Tp/Ro)	Europe	1570	0.9	Late Spring
Euphorbia polychroma (Tp/Ro)	Europe	1805	0.46	Spring
Fascicularia bicolour (Ro/seed)	Chile	1851	0.46	Summer/Autumn
Filipendula purpurea (Ro)	Japan	1765	1.2	Summer
Filipendula ulmaria (Ro)	Europe, Asia	Native	0.9	Summer
Foeniculum vulgare (seed)	Europe		1.8	Summer
Francoa sonchifolia (Tp)	Chile	1830	0.9	Summer
Fritillaria imperialis (B)	W Himalaya	>1590	1.2	Spring
Fuchsia magellanica (subshrub)	South America	1788	1.2	Summer/Autumn
Galtonia candicans (B)	South Africa	1860	1.2	Late Summer
Gaura lindheimeri (seed)	SE North America	1850	1.2	Summer/Autumn
Gentiana asclepiadea (Ro)	Europe	1629	0.9	Early Autumn
Geranium clarkei (R/Ro)	Kashmir	1968	0.3	Early Summer
Geranium endressii (R/Ro)	Pyrenees	1812	0.46	Summer/Autumn
Geranium macrorrhizum (R/Ro)	S Europe	1576	0.3	Late Spring
Gillenia trifoliata (Ro)	North America	1826	0.6	Early Summer
Gladiolus byzantinus (C)	Europe	1629	0.9	Early Summer
Glycyrrhiza glabra (Tp)	Mediterranean	1562	1.2	Late Summer
Gunnera manicata (Ro)	S Brazil	1867	1.8	Early Summer
Gypsophila paniculata (Tp)	E Europe, Siberia	1759	1.2	Summer
Hedychium coccineum (T)	India, Burma	1815	1.5	Late Summer
Helenium autumnale (Ro)	E North America	1729	1.5	Early Autumn
Helianthus 'Soleil d'Or' (Ro)	North America	1889	1.5	Late Summer
Heliopsis helianthoides (Ro)	North America	1714	1.5	Autumn
Helleborus foetidus (Tp)	S Europe, British Isles	Native	0.46	Winter/Spring
Helleborus niger (Tp)	Europe, W Asia		0.3	Winter
Helleborus orientalis (Tp)	Bithynian Olympus, Asia Minor	1839	0.46	Winter/Spring
Hemerocallis 'Kwanso Flore Pleno' (Ro)	Japan	1860	0.9	Summer
Hemerocallis lilio-asphodelus (Ro)	E Asia, SE Europe	1596	0.75	Spring
Hermadoctylus tuberosus (T)	S Europe	1597	0.3	Late Spring
Hesperis matronalis (seed)	S Europe, Siberia	1350	1.2	Summer
Heuchera sanguinea (Ro)	SW North America	1882	0.46	Early Summer
Hibiscus moschatus (seed)	E North America	1574	0.9	Summer
Hieracium villosum (R/S)	C Europe	1739	0.3	Summer
Hippeastrum pratense (B)	Chile	1840	0.38	Early Summer
Hosta lancifolia (Ro)	Japan	1829	0.6	Late Summer
Hosta plantaginea (Ro)	China	1780	0.6	Late Summer
Hosta ventricosa (Ro)	E Asia	1790	1.2	Late Summer
Houttuynia cordata (R/S)	Far East	1820	0.46	Summer
Humulus lupulus 'Aureus' (climber)	GO	1889	Climber	Late Summer
Hyacinthus orientalis (B)	W Asia	1596	0.2	Late Winter/Spring
Hycinthoides hispanica (B)	Spain	1683	0.6	Late Spring
Incarvillea delavayi (Tp)	W China, Tibet	1893	0.6	Early Summer
Inula ensiflora (Ro)	Caucasus	1791	0.3	Late Summer
Iris kaempferi (Rh)	Japan, E Asia	1839	0.9	Summer
Iris sibirica (Rh)	Europe, N Asia	circa 1700	0.9	Early Summer
Iris spuria (Rh)	Algeria to W Asia	1573	1.5	Early Summer
Kirengeshoma palmata (Ro)	Japan	1891	0.9	Early Autumn
Kniphofia uvaria (Ro)	Cape Peninsula	1705	1.5	Summer
Lamium orvala (R/S)	Europe	1596	0.3	Spring
Lathyrus latifolius (Tp)	Europe	1596	Climber	Summer/Autumn
Lathyrus vernus (Tp)	Europe	1629	0.38	Spring
Lavatera olbia (subshrub)	S France	1570	1.8	Summer/Autumn
Lavatera thuringiaca (subshrub)	SE Europe	1731	1.5	Summer
Leucojum aestivum (B)	Europe, E to Turkey & Caucasus	Native	0.6	Spring
Liatris spicata (Ro)	North America	1732	0.6	Summer
Libertia Formosa (Ro)	Chile	1837	0.9	Early Summer

Ro rootstock/clump. R/S runners/stolins. Tp tap-rooted. Rh rhizomatous. B bulb. C corm. T tuber.

(Continued . . .)

TABLE 5: HERBACEOUS PLANTS (CONTINUED)				
MAINLY SPECIES BOTANICAL NAME	COUNTRY OF ORIGIN	INTRODUCTION DATE	APPROX. HEIGHT IN METRES	FLOWERING PERIOD
Ligularia przewalskii (Ro)	N China	1866	1.8	Summer
Lilium bulbiferium croceum 'Flore Pleno' (B)	S Europe	1596	1.5	Summer
Lilium regale (B)	W China	1910	2	Summer
Lilium superbum (B)	E North America	1727	3	Summer
Limonium latifolium (Tp)	Bulgaria, S Rusia	1791	0.3	Late Summer
Linaria purpurea (seed)	E Europe	1648	0.9	Summer
Linum narbonense (seed)	S Europe	1759	0.46	Summer
Liriope muscari (Ro)	E Asia		0.3	Autumn
Lobelia cardinalis (Ro)	N America	1626	0.9	Late Summer
Lunaria rediviva (seed)	Europe	1596	0.6	Spring
Lupinus arboreus (seed)	California	1793	1.5	Summer
Lupinus polyphyllus (seed)	W North America	1826	1.2	Early Summer
Lychnis chalcedonica (Ro)	E Russia	1593	0.9	Summer
Lychnis coronaria (seed)	S Europe	1596	0.9	Summer
Lysichitum americanum (Ro)	W North America	1901	1.2	Early Spring
Lysichitum camtschatcense (Ro)	Kamchatka	1886	0.9	Early Spring
Lysimachia ephemerum (Ro)	SW Europe	1730	0.9	Summer
Lythrum salicaria (Tp)	Europe, temperate Asia	Native	1.2	Summer
Macleaya cordata (Ro)	China, Japan	1795	2.1	Summer
Malva alcea (seed)	Europe	1707	1.2	Summer
Meconopsis grandis (seed)	Nepal to China	1895	0.9	Early Summer
Melianthus major (Tp/subshrub?)	South Africa	1688	2.4	Late Summer
Melissa officinalis (Ro)	S Europe	Non-native	0.6	Summer
Mertensia virginica (Ro)	North America	1799	0.46	Spring
Meum athamanticum (seed)	Europe	1774	0.46	Summer
Mimulus guttatus (R/S)	North America	1826	0.6	Summer
Mimulus ringens (Ro/R/S)	E North America	1759	0.9	Summer
Mirabilis jalapa (T)	Tropical America	1596	0.6	Summer
Monarda fistulosa (Ro)	Virginia	1637	1.2	Summer
Morea iridoides (Rh)	South Africa	1758	0.6	Early Summer
Morina longifolia (seed)	Nepal to China	1839	0.9	Summer
Muscari comosum (B)	Europe	1596	0.15	Spring
Musa basjoo (Tp/Ro)	Japan	1890	1.8	Late Summer
Myosotis scorpiodes (R/S)	Europe, Asia, N America	Native	0.23	Summer
Myrrhis odorata (seed)	S Europe	Non-native	0.6	Early Summer
Narcissus poeticus radiiflorus (B)	S & C Europe, Balkans	1570	0.2	Spring
Mysotidium hortensia (Ro)	Chatham Islands	1859	0.46	Early Summer
Nepeta x *faassenii* (Ro)	Garden Origin	1784	0.46	Early/late Summer
Nerine bowdenii (B)	South Africa	1889	0.6	Autumn
Nerine sarniensis (B)	South Africa	1659	0.6	Autumn
Oenothera tetragonal (seed)	E North America	1737	0.46	Summer
Omphalodes verna (Ro)	Europe	1659		Late Winter/Spring
Origanum vulgare (Ro)	Europe	Native	0.46	Summer
Ornithogalum pyramidale (B)	Mediterranean	1752	0.6	Summer
Paeonia anomala (Tp)	E Russia, Central Asia	1788	0.6	Late Spring
Paeonia officinalis (Tp)	S Europe	circa 900	0.6	Late Spring/early Summer
Paeonia tenuifolia (Tp)	Caucasus	1594	0.46	Early Summer
Pancratium illyricum (B)	S Europe	1592	1.2	Early Summer
Papaver orientale 'Mrs Perry' (Tp)	GO	1906	1.2	Early Summer
Paradisea liliastrum (Ro/B)	S Europe	1629	0.6	Early Summer
Paris polyphylla (Ro)	Himalaya	1826	0.9	Summer
Peltiphyllum peltatum (Ro)	California	1873	0.9	Spring
Penstemon barbatus (Ro)	Colorado	1784	0.9	Summer
Petasites tuberosa (Ro)	E Europe to Siberia	1759	1.2	Summer
Phlox paniculata (Ro)	E North America	1730	1.2	Late Summer
Phormium tenax (Ro)	New Zealand	1789	3	Summer
Phuopsos stylosa (R/S)	Caucasus	1836	0.3	Summer
Phygelius capensis (subshrub)	South Africa	1855	1.2	Summer/Autumn
Physalis alkekengi (R/S)	Caucasus to China	1549	0.46	Autumn
Physostegia virginiana (Ro)	E North America	1683	0.9	Late Summer
Phyteuma spicatum (Ro)	Europe, S Norway, Estonia to N Spain	Native listed from 1597	0.6	Summer
Phytolacca americana (Tp/seed)	Florida	1615	1.2	Late Summer
Plantago major 'Rosularis' (Ro)		cv non-native	0.3	Summer
Platycodon grandiflorus (Ro)	Far East	1782	0.46	Late Summer
Podophyllum peltatum (Ro)	North America	1664	0.46	Spring
Polemonium caeruleum (seed)	N & C Europe, N Asia, W North America	Native	0.6	Early Summer
Polianthes tuberosa (B)	Mexico	1594	1	Late Summer
Polygonatum x *hybridum* (Ro)	GO		0.9	Late Spring
Polygonium campanulatum (Ro)	Himalaya	1909	0.9	Summer/Autumn
Potentilla recta sulphurea (Ro)	Europe to Asia	1648	0.6	Summer
Primula auriculata (Ro)	S Caucasus, Turkey	1596	0.25	Spring
Primula denticulata (seed)	Himalaya West China	1842	0.3	Spring
Pulmonaria officinalis (Ro)	Europe	>1597	0.25	Spring
Pulsatilla vulgaris (seed)	UK, W France to Ukraine	Native	0.3	Spring
Puya alpestris (seed?)	Chile	1869	0.9	Early Summer

Ro rootstock/clump. R/S runners/stolins. Tp tap-rooted. Rh rhizomatous. B bulb. C corm. T tuber.

TABLE 5 325

TABLE 5: HERBACEOUS PLANTS (CONTINUED)				
MAINLY SPECIES BOTANICAL NAME	COUNTRY OF ORIGIN	INTRODUCTION DATE	APPROX. HEIGHT IN METRES	FLOWERING PERIOD
Ranunculus aconitifolius 'Flore Pleno' (Ro)	Native selection	circa 1500	0.6	Late Spring
Ranunculus acris 'Flore Pleno' (Ro)	Native selection	1480	0.9	Late Spring
Rehmannia angulata (Ro?)	China	1890	0.6	Early Summer
Rheum palmatum (Tp)	China	1763	1.8	Early Summer
Rodgersia podophylla (Ro)	Japan	1880	0.9	Summer
Romneya coulteri (Tp R/S)	SW California	1875	2.1	Summer/Autumn
Roscoea purpurea (Ro)	India, Nepal	1804	0.3	Late Summer
Rudbeckia laciniata (Ro)	N America	1640	1.8	Summer
Salvia argentea (seed)	E Mediterranean	1594	0.9	Summer
Salvia verticillata (seed)	Europe, Caucasus	1594	1.2	Late Summer
Sanguisorba canadensis (Ro)	E North America	1633	1.8	Late Summer
Saponaria officinalis 'Albo Plena' (Ro)	Europe, naturalised	circa 1500	0.75	Summer
Sarracenia purpurea (Ro)	E North America	1640	0.3	Early Summer
Saxifraga fortunei (R/S)	China, Japan	1863	0.46	Autumn
Scabiosa graminifolia (Ro)	S Europe	1683	0.46	Summer/Autumn
Scabiosa ochroleuca (Ro)	SE Europe	1517	0.9	Late Summer
Schizostylis coccinea (Ro)	S Africa	1864	0.6	Early Autumn
Scilla peruviana (B)	Mediterranean	1608	0.46	Early Summer
Scopolia carniolica (Ro)	C & SE Europe	1780	0.6	Early Spring
Sedum aizoon (R/S)	Far East	1757	0.46	Summer
Senecio cineraria (subshrub)	S Europe	1633	0.6	Summer/Autumn
Sidalcea malviflora (Ro)	California	1838	1.2	Summer
Silene dioica 'Flore Pleno' (Ro/seed)	Europe	1730	0.6	Early Summer
Sisyrinchium striatum (Ro)	Chile	1788	0.6	Summer
Smilacina racemosa (Ro)	N America	1640	0.75	Spring
Solidago canadensis (Ro)	N America	1648	1.5	Summer
Spigelia marilandica (?)	SE North America	1694	0.6	Summer
Stachys alpina (Ro)	S Europe	1597	1.5	Summer
Stachys byzantina (Ro)	Caucasus to Iran	1782	0.46	Summer
Stokesia laevis (Ro)	North America	1766	0.46	Summer
Symphytum officinale (Ro)	EC Europe	1350	1.2	Late Summer
Teucrium hyrcanicum (seed)	Persia	1763	0.6	Late Summer
Thalictrum aquiligiifolium (Tp)	Europe, N Asia	<1710	0.9	Early Summer
Thermopsis montana (Ro)	W North America	1818	0.9	Early Summer
Tigridia pavonia (B)	Mexico	1796	0.46	Summer
Tovaria virginiana (Ro)	N America, Japan	1640	0.6	Summer
Trachystemon orientale (Ro)	Asia Minor, Caucasus	1752	0.47	Spring
Tradescantia virginiana (Ro)	E North America	1629	0.46	Summer/Autumn
Tricyrtis hirta (Ro)	Japan	1863	0.9	Early Autumn
Trilium grandiflorum (Ro)	E North America	1799	0.38	Spring
Tritonia squalida (C)	South Africa	1774	0.9	Late Summer
Trollius europaeus (Ro)	Europe, Caucasus, N America	Native	0.6	Spring
Tropaeolum speciosum (seed)	Chile	1847	0.6	Summer/Autumn
Tulbaghia violacea (Ro)	South Africa	1838	0.6	Spring/Autumn
Tulipa gesneriana (B)	E Europe and Asia	1577	0.23	Spring
Uvularia grandiflora (Ro)	E North America	1802	0.6	Spring
Valeriana officinalis (seed)	Europe, Asia	1561	1.2	Summer
Vallota speciosa (B)	South Africa	1774	0.46	Early Autumn
Veltheimia bracteata (B)	South Africa	1768	0.46	Spring
Veratrum album (Ro)	Europe, Siberia	1548	1.8	Late Summer
Verbascum phoeniceum (seed)	S Europe, N Asia	1796	1.2	Early Summer
Verbena bonariensis (seed)	South America	1737	1.5	Summer/Autumn
Verbena rigida (seed)	Brazil to Arrgentina	1830	0.46	Summer/Autumn
Veronica teucrium (Ro)	Europe, N Asia	1596	0.46	Summer
Veronicastrum virginicum (Ro)	E North America	1714	1.2	Late Summer
Viola cornuta (Ro)	Pyrenees	1776	0.3	Early/late Summer
Yucca filamentosa (Tp/Ro)	SE North America	1675	1.5	Late Summer
Yucca gloriosa (Tp/Ro)	SE North America	1596	1.8	Autumn
Zantedeschia aethopica (Ro)	South Africa	1731	1.2	Summer
Zephyranthes atamasco (B)	N America	1629	0.15	Late Spring/Summer

Ro rootstock/clump. R/S runners/stolins. Tp tap-rooted. Rh rhizomatous. B bulb. C corm. T tuber.

TABLE 6: ORNAMENTAL GRASSES, RUSHES AND SEDGES

The majority are clump-forming, or creeping and stoloniferous, and respond to regular division once overmature. Some, however, such as pampas grass and the *Miscanthus* groups, can be massive and long-lived. New cultivars of these (and others not listed) are continually being introduced.

BOTANICAL NAME	ORIGIN/INTRODUCTION	GROWTH TYPE
Arundo donax	S Europe, 1305	St/Rh
Calamagrostis x acutiflora + cvs	Europe, Russia	Cl
Carex pendula	Native	Cl
Cortaderia selloana + cvs	S America, 1848	Cl
Cyperus longus	Native	Cl
Deschampsia caespitosa	Native	Cl
Elymus arenarius	Native	St. I
Eragrostis trichodes	USA	Cl
Festuca glauca + cvs	Europe	Cl
Hakonechloa macra	Japan	Rh
Helictotrichon sempervirens	SW Europe, 1820	Cl
Miscanthus saccharifolius	E Asia, 1862	Cl/Rh
Miscanthus sinensis + cvs	China/Japan 1875	Cl
Molinia caerulea + cvs	Native	Cl
Pennisetum alopecuroides	Asia/Australia 1820	Cl
Pennisetem villosum (syn. P. longistylum)	NE Africa, 1891	Cl
Phalaris arundinacea	N Hemisphere, 1596	St. I
Spartina pectinata	N America	St. I
Stipa arundinacea	New Zealand, 1882	Cl
Stipa calamagrostis	S Europe	Cl
Stipa gigantea	Spain	Cl

Cl clump. Rh rhizomatous. St stoloniferous. I invasive.

TABLE 7: FERNS

A selection of more widely grown ferns, classed as herbaceous perennials, persisting as woody rootstocks which can be divided when the plants become overmature, or invasive in some cases. Many prefer cool, semi-shaded or shaded sites. Their popularity began in the Victorian period when they were allocated shaded, rocky retreats or 'ferneries'. Those marked * need protection.

BOTANICAL/COMMON NAME	ORIGIN/INTRODUCTION	HERBACEOUS H EVERGREEN E
Adiantum pedatum	Europe, 1656	H
Asplenium scolopendrium (Hart's Tongue)	Native	E
Asplenium adiantum-nigrum (Spleenwort)	Native	D
Athyrium filix-femina (Lady Fern)	Native	H
Blechnum chilense (B. tabulare)	Chile	E
Blechnum spicant (Hard Fern)	Native	E
Cystopteris fragilis (Bladder Fern)	Native	E
Dicksonia antarctica (Tree Fern)	Australia/New Zealand	E *
Dryopteris aemula (Buckler Fern)	Native	E
Dryopteris filix-mas (Male Fern)	Native	H
Matteuccia struthiopteris (Ostrich Plume Fern)	N Hemisphere, 1766	H
Onoclea sensibilis (Sensitive Fern)	N United States, E Asia	H
Osmunda regalis (Royal Fern)	Native	H
Polypodium vulgare (Polypody)	Native	E
Polystichum setiferum + cvs (Shield Fern)	Native	E
Woodwardia radicans	S Europe/Asia	E *

TABLE 8 327

TABLE 8: AQUATIC PLANTS

The plants listed are those that will tolerate or need varying depths of water in which to grow – the true aquatics. Not included are those often classed as 'marginals' which prefer damp or occasionally submerged conditions, but not normally underwater. Most of these prefer still or slow-moving water. N native.

FOR DEEPER WATER 0.5–1.0M APPROX.

For planting and growing in pond or lake bed (or occasionally submerged containers).

Nymphaea species and hybrids (Water Lily); *Nymphaea alba* N

Nuphar lutea (Yellow Water Lily) N. Can be invasive

FOR SHALLOWER WATER 0.3–0.5M APPROX.

Mostly rooted in pond substrate.

Acorus calamus (Sweet Flag) N

Alisma plantago-aquatica (Water Plantain) N

Butomus umbellatus (Flowering Rush) N

Carex pseudocyperus N

Carex riparia (Great Pond Sedge) N

Iris laevigata (Japanese water Iris)

Iris pseudacorus (Yellow Flag) N

Menyanthes trifoliata (Bogbean) N

Phragmites australis (Common Reed) N

Ranunculus lingua (Great Spearwort) N

Rumex hydrolapathum (Great Water Dock) N

Sagittaria sagittifolia (Arrowhead) N

Scirpus lacustris (Bulrush) N

Sparganium erectum (Bur-reed) N

Typha latifolia (Reedmace) N

FREE-FLOATING AT VARYING WATER DEPTHS WITH FLOATING AND/OR SUBMERGED LEAVES

Those marked O are important as oxygenating, fish-refuge and fish-breeding plants. Some may also root into shallow pond substrate.

Azolla caroliniana (Floating Fern) Invasive

Ceratophyllum demersum (Hornwort) O

Hydrocharis morsus-ranae (Frogbit) N

Lemna gibba (Duckweed) N

Myriophyllum spicatum (Milfoil) ON

Potamogeton natans. (Pondweed) N

Polygonum amphibium (Amphibious Bistort) N

Ranunculus aquatilis (Water Buttercup) ON Prefers running water

WARNING The three following plants are non-native introductions, mainly by the aquarist trade, which are becoming prolific in ponds and wet places. They are very invasive, can outcompete native aquatics, and can soon choke up a pond or pool.

Elodaea canadensis (Canadian Pond Weed)

Crassula helmsii (New Zealand Pygmy Weed)

Myriophyllum aquaticum (Parrot's Feather)

TABLE 9: ANNUAL AND BIENNIAL PLANTS FOR GARDEN AND COOL GLASSHOUSE DISPLAY

BOTANICAL NAME	COMMON NAME	COUNTRY OF ORIGIN	INTRO. DATE	LIFE SPAN (GROWN AS)	TIME TO SOW	DUE TO FLOWER	APPROXIMATE LENGTH OF FLOWERING PERIOD	HEIGHT	SUITABILITY FOR GLASSHOUSE POT DISPLAY
Ageratum houstonianum	Floss Flower	Mexico	1822	HHA	Jan–Feb (CG)	May–June	10–12 weeks	30–60 cm	✓
Alonsoa warscewiczii	Mask Flower	Peru	1858	P (HHA)	Jan–Feb (CG)	April–May	8–10 weeks	30–40 cm	✓
Amberboa moschata	Sweet Sultan	Turkey, Caucasus	1630	HA	Sept–Oct (CG)	May	10–12 weeks	45–60 cm	✓
Anchusa capensis		S Africa	1800	B (FHA)	Feb–March (CG)	June–July	10–12 weeks	45–60 cm	
Antirrhinum majus	Common Snapdragon	SW Europe	Pre 1600	P (HHA)	Jan–Feb (CG)	April–May	8–10 weeks	45 cm	✓
					Aug–Sept (CG)	May	8–10 weeks	30–90 cm	
					Jan–Feb (CG)	June (end)	8–10 weeks	(according to variety)	
Arctotis fastuosa	Monarch of the Veldt	S Africa	Circa 1774	P (TA)	February (CG)	May	12 weeks	45–75 cm	✓
Bassia scoparia f. trichophylla	Burning Bush	Asia, N America	1629	HHA	March–April (CG)	Foliage plant	Colours in autumn	90 cm	✓
Begonia (fibrous-rooted)	Semperflorens Begonia		1829	P (TA)	Feb–March (CG)	August	12 weeks	30 cm	✓
Begonia × tuberhybrida	Tuberous Begonia		Circa 1860	P (TA)	February (CG)	August	12 weeks	30 cm	✓
Brachyscome iberidifolia	Swan River daisy	W & S Australia	1843	HHA	Feb–March (CG)	May–June	10–12 weeks	30–40 cm	✓
Browallia speciosa	Bush Violet	Colombia	1846	P (TA)	March (CG)	Sept–November	12 weeks	60 cm	✓
Calceolaria integrifolia	Slipperwort	Mexico	1822	P (HHA)	May–June (CG)	April–May	6 weeks	45–75 cm	✓
Calendula officinalis	Common Marigold	unknown	Roman/circa 1100	HA	February (CG)	May–June	8–10 weeks	30–45 cm	✓
					And at intervals to flower more or less throughout the year (CG)				
Callistephus chinensis	China Aster	China	1731	HHA	April–May	June–October	8–10 weeks	15–90 cm	
Campanula isophylla	Star of Bethlehem	N Italy	1868	P (HHA)	March–April (CG)	June (12 months)	10–12 weeks	Trailing	✓
Campanula medium	Canterbury Bell	S Europe	1597	HB	May–June (CG)	May (12 months)	6 weeks	60–75 cm	✓
Campanula pyramidalis	Chimney Bellflower	N Italy, NW Balkans	Pre 1597	P (FHB)	March–April (CG)	August (12 months)	10–12 weeks	120–150 cm	✓
Celosia argentea	Cockscomb	Equatorial tropical regions	1570	P (HHA)	Feb–March (CG)	July–Oct	10–12 weeks	30–60 cm	✓
Centaurea cyanthus	Cornflower	Northern temperate regions	Roman	HA	Aug–October (CG)	March–April	6–8 weeks	90–120 cm	✓
					March–April (DS)	June–July	6–8 weeks	90–120 cm	
Chrysanthemum carinatum	Painted Daisy	Morocco	1796	HHA	Feb–March (DS)	June	6 weeks	30–40 cm	
Chrysanthemum, 'Perennial Cascade', 'Charm'		GO	Circa 1950s	T–HA	Feb–March (CG)	October (end)	8–10 weeks	Cascade: 150–210 cm; Charm: 45–60 cm	✓
Clarkia amoena	Satin Flower	California	1814	HA	March–April (DS)	June–August	6–8 weeks	40–90 cm	
Clarkia unguiculata		California	1832	HA	September (CG)	May	6 weeks	90–120 cm	✓
Consolida ajacis	Larkspur	Mediterranean	1573	HA	February (CG)	June (end)	8–10 weeks	60 cm	
					September (CG)	June	8–10 weeks	120–150 cm	
Cyclamen persicum	Persian Cyclamen	SE Mediterranean, N Africa	Circa 1600 & 1731	P (TA)	Aug–Oct (CG)	November (12 months)	12 weeks	30–40 cm	✓
Datura metel	Horn of Plenty	Pan tropical distribution	1596	HHA	March (CG)	August	8–10 weeks	60–90 cm	
Delphinium grandiflorum	Siberian Larkspur	Siberia, Mongolia, China, Japan	1741	P (A)	July–Aug (CG)	June	8–10 weeks	40–45 cm	✓
Dianthus chinensis	Indian Pink	China	1705	P (HA)	Feb–March (CG)	July	6 weeks	40–45 cm	✓
					September (CG)	June	6–8 weeks	30 cm	
Digitalis purpurea	Common Foxglove	Europe (W particularly)	Native	HB–P	May (DS, CG)	May	4 weeks	60–180 cm	✓
Dimorphotheca pluvialis	Rain Daisy	Namibia, S Africa	1752	HHA	July (CG)	April	10–12 weeks	45–60 cm	✓
Dimorphotheca sinuata	Star of the Veldt	S Africa	1780	HHA	March (CG)	July	10–12 weeks	45–60 cm	
Erysimum cheiri	Wallflower	S Europe	Circa 1066	P (HB)	January (CG)	May	10–12 weeks	30–40 cm	✓
Eschscholzia californica	Californian Poppy	USA (Oregon to coastal California)	1825	HA	June (CG)	December onwards	8–10 weeks	45–60 cm	✓
					March–April (DS)	May–October	26 weeks	40 cm	
Exacum affine	Persian Violet	Yemen (Socotra)	1884	P (TA)	March (CG)	August	10–12 weeks	40 cm	✓

T Tender. HH Half-hardy. FH Frost-hardy. H Hardy. A Annual. B Biennial. P Perennial. CG Cool glasshouse. WG Warm glasshouse. DS Direct sow.

TABLE 9 329

TABLE 9: ANNUAL AND BIENNIAL PLANTS FOR GARDEN AND COOL GLASSHOUSE DISPLAY (CONTINUED)

BOTANICAL NAME	COMMON NAME	COUNTRY OF ORIGIN	INTRO. DATE	LIFE SPAN (GROWN AS)	TIME TO SOW	DUE TO FLOWER	APPROXIMATE LENGTH OF FLOWERING PERIOD	HEIGHT	SUITABILITY FOR GLASSHOUSE POT DISPLAY
Felicia amoena		S Africa	Circa 1780	P (TA)	May–June (CG)	Jan–Feb	10–12 weeks	40–45 cm	✓
Francoa ramosa	Wand Flower	Chile	1831	FHP	May–June (CG)	July (12 months)	6–8 weeks	60–90 cm	✓
Helianthus annuus	Sunflower	USA to C America	1596	HA					
Hunnemannia fumariifolia	Mexican Tulip Poppy	Mexico	1827	P (HHA)	March (CG)	July–Sept	10–12 weeks	40–45 cm	✓
					August (CG)	May onwards	12–14 weeks	40–45 cm	
Impatiens balsamina	Balsam	India, China, Malaysia	1596	TA	March (CG)	July–Aug	6–8 weeks	30–45 cm	✓
Impatiens walleriana	Busy Lizzie	E Africa	1896	P (TA)	March (CG)	August	10–12 weeks	20–40 cm	✓
Ipomopsis rubra		USA (Texas to Florida & S Carolina)	Circa 1691	HB–P	September (CG)	July (12 months)	8–10 weeks	90–120 cm	✓
Lathyrus odoratus	Sweet Pea	Italy (inc. Sicily)	1699	HA	October (CG)	May	10–12 weeks	180 cm	
Limonium sinuatum	Statice	Mediterranean	1629	P (FHA)	February (CG)	July	8–10 weeks	45 cm	✓
Lobelia erinus	Edging Lobelia	S Africa	1752	P (HHA)	February (CG)	June	10–12 weeks	15 cm	✓
Matthiola East Lothian Series	East Lothian stock	GO	Early 20th cent.	P (HA–B)	July (CG)	April–May	10–12 weeks	15 cm	✓
Matthiola incana	stock	Coastal S and W Europe to Egypt	1715	P (HA–B)	March (CG)	Aug–Sept	8–10 weeks	40–45 cm	✓
Matthiola Mammoth/Beauty Series	Mammoth stock	GO	Circa 1950	P (HA–B)	July–August (CG)	April–May	6–8 weeks	45–60 cm	✓
Matthiola Ten-Week Series	Ten-week stock	GO	1730	P (HA–B)	June–August (CG)	Dec–Feb	8–10 weeks	45–60 cm	✓
Mimulus x hybridus cultivars	Monkey Flower, Musk	GO	Late 19th/early 20th cent.	P (HA)	March–April (CG)	July–august	6–8 weeks	40–45 cm	✓
Myosotis sylvatica	Garden Forget-Me-Not	Europe	Pre 15th cent.	B–P (HB)	June–July (CG)	November onwards	8–10 weeks	30 cm	✓
Nemesia strumosa		S Africa	1892	HHA	January (CG)	May	8–10 weeks	30–40 cm	✓
					March (CG)	June–July	8–10 weeks	30–40 cm	
					June–July (CG)	Sept–Oct	8–10 weeks	30–40 cm	
					July–Aug (CG)	Nov–Dec	8–10 weeks	30–40 cm	
Nicotiana alata	Flowering Tobacco	S Brazil, N Argentina	Mid 19th cent.	P (HHA)	Feb–March (CG)	May (end)	10–12 weeks	45–75 cm	✓
					September (CG)	April–May	10–12 weeks	60–120 cm	
Osteospermum ecklonis		S Africa (Eastern Cape)	1897	P (FHA)	March (CG)	Aug–Sept	8–10 weeks	60–90 cm	✓
Papaver rhoeas	Corn Poppy, Field Poppy	Eurasia, N Africa	Native	HA	September (CG)	May	4–5 weeks	40–60 cm	
					March–April (DS)	June	4–5 weeks	40–60 cm	
Petunia x hybrida	Petunia	GO	Post 1823	A–P (HHA)	February (CG)	June	12–14 weeks	30–45 cm	✓
Phlox drummondii	Annual Phlox	USA (E Texas)	1835	FHA	February (CG)	June	12–14 weeks	30–45 cm	✓
					September (CG)	May	12–14 weeks	30–45 cm	
Primula malacoides	Fairy Primrose	China	1908	P (HHA)	June–July (CG)	January	3 months	30–40 cm	✓
Primula obconica		China	1880	P (FHA)	January (end) (CG)	October (end)	5 months	30 cm	✓
Primula sinensis		Poss. N China	1825	P (HHA)	March–June (CG)	Dec–Jan	8–10 weeks	30–45 cm	✓
Psylliostachys suworowii	Statice	Iran, W Turkmenistan, N Afganistan, C Asia	1883	HHA	March (CG)	June–August	8–10 weeks	45 cm	✓
Rehmannia elata	Chinese Foxglove	China	1850	P (HB)	August (end) (CG)	May	8–10 weeks	120–150 cm	✓
Reseda odorata	Common Mignonette	N Africa	1752	HA	Jan–March (CG)	June	10–12 weeks	30 cm	✓
					June (CG)	Autumn and winter	10–12 weeks	30 cm	
					Aug–Sept (CG)	Spring	10–12 weeks	30 cm	
Rhodanthe chlorocephala subsp. rosea	Strawflower	SW Australia	Circa 1842	HHA	February (CG)	May (end)	6–8 weeks	30–40 cm	✓
					Sept–Oct (CG)	April–May	6–8 weeks	30–40 cm	
Rhodanthe manglesii	Strawflower	W Australia	Circa 1830	HHA	February (CG)	May (end)	6–8 weeks	30–40 cm	✓
					Sept–Oct (CG)	April–May	6–8 weeks	30–40 cm	

T Tender. HH Half-hardy. FH Frost-hardy. H Hardy. A Annual. B Biennial. P Perennial. CG Cool glasshouse. WG Warm glasshouse. DS Direct sow.

(Continued ...)

TABLE 9: ANNUAL AND BIENNIAL PLANTS FOR GARDEN AND COOL GLASSHOUSE DISPLAY (CONTINUED)

BOTANICAL NAME	COMMON NAME	COUNTRY OF ORIGIN	INTRO. DATE	LIFE SPAN (GROWN AS)	TIME TO SOW	DUE TO FLOWER	APPROXIMATE LENGTH OF FLOWERING PERIOD	HEIGHT	SUITABILITY FOR GLASSHOUSE POT DISPLAY
Salpiglossis sinuata		Peru, Argentina	1652	HHA	Jan–Feb (CG)	June	6–8 weeks	60–90 cm	✓
Scabiosa atropurpurea	Pincushion Flower, Sweet Scabious	S Europe	1620	HB–P	September (CG)	April–May	6–8 weeks	90–120 cm	
					October (CG)	June–October	20 weeks	90–120 cm	
Schizanthus pinnatus	Poor Man's Orchid	Chile	1822	TA	Aug–Sept (CG)	April–May	8–10 weeks	45–75 cm	✓
					February (CG)	August	4–6 weeks	45–60 cm	
Senecio cineraria	Dusty Miller	W & C Mediterranean	Pre 1600	P (FHA)	April–June (CG)	Jan–April (according to time of sowing and treatment)	6 weeks	40 cm to 90 cm (according to variety)	✓
Silene coeli-rosa	Rose of Heaven	Mediterranean	1713	HA	October (CG)	April–May	6–8 weeks	30–40 cm	✓
					March (CG)	June–July	6–8 weeks	30–40 cm	
Tagetes erecta	African Marigold	Mexico and C America	1535	HHA	March–April (CG)	June–October	20 weeks	40–60 cm	
Tagetes patula	French Marigold	Mexico to Guatemala	1572	HHA	March–April (CG)	June–October	20 weeks	40–60 cm	
Torenia fournieri	Wishbone Flower	Tropical Asia	Circa 1880	TA	Feb–March (CG)	July	8–10 weeks	30–40 cm	✓
Trachelium caeruleum	Blue Throatwort	W & C Mediterranean	1640	P (HHA)	Feb–March (CG)	July	10 weeks	45–60 cm	✓
					July–Aug (CG)	June	10 weeks	45–60 cm	
Trachymene coerulea	Blue Lace Flower	W Australia	1827	HHA–B	February (CG)	July	8–10 weeks	30–45 cm	✓
					Aug–Sept (CG)	May–June	8–10 weeks	30–45 cm	
Tropaeolum majus	Garden Nasturtium	Bolivia to Colombia	1686	TA	Feb–March (CG)	May (middle)	8–10 weeks	40–150 cm	
					July (CG)	October	8–10 weeks	40–150 cm	✓
					October (CG)	March	8–10 weeks	40–150 cm	✓
Ursinia anethoides		S Africa	1928	P (HHA)	Feb–March (CG)	May	8–10 weeks	30–40 cm	✓
Verbascum arcturus		Greece (Crete)	1780	P (FHA–B)	March–April (CG)	June	10–12 weeks	45–60 cm	✓
Verbascum creticum	Cretan Mullein	W Mediterranean	Circa 1803	H–P	March (CG)	July	8–10 weeks	150–180 cm	✓
					August (CG)	January onwards	8–10 weeks	30–60 cm	
Verbena bonariensis		S America	1726	P (HH–P)	February (WG)	June–October	20 weeks	90–120 cm	✓
Verbena x hybrida		GO	Circa 1837	P (HHA)	February (WG)	June–October	20 weeks	30–40 cm	✓
Verbena rigida		S America	1830	P (FHA)	February (WG)	June–October	20 weeks	30 cm	✓
Verbena tenuisecta	Moss Verbena	S South America	1837	P (HA–P)	February (WG)	June–October	20 weeks	15–20 cm	✓
Xanthophthalmum coronarium	Crown Daisy	Mediterranean	1629	HA	Feb–March (CG, DS)	June	6 weeks	45 cm	✓
Xanthophthalmum segetum	Corn Marigold	Mediterranean	Roman	HA	Feb–March (CG, DS)	June	6 weeks	45 cm	
Zinnia elegans		Mexico	1796	TA	Feb–March (CG)	July	6–8 weeks	60–75 cm	✓
					June–July (CG)	September	6–8 weeks	60–75 cm	

T Tender. HH Half-hardy. FH Frost-hardy. H Hardy. A Annual. B Biennial. P Perennial. CG Cool glasshouse. WG Warm glasshouse. DS Direct sow.

Hardy annuals (HA) may be sown in spring in the open ground where they are to flower, either in September–October or March–April. If sown in early autumn and grown in cool or cold glasshouses, they will make large plants flowering in spring/early summer.
Half-hardy annuals (HHA) require to be sown under glass and planted out when danger of frost is over.
Tender annuals (TA) are grown and flower in pots under glass or, with careful hardening off, may be planted outside in sheltered positions in late May or early June.

TABLE 10 331

TABLE 10: HISTORIC AND WIDELY GROWN FRUIT CULTIVARS				
CULTIVAR NAME	INTRODUCTION DATE	HARVESTING	SEASON	COMMENTS/ POLLINATION GROUPS
Apples, Dessert				
'Adam's Pearmain'	circa 1826	Early/mid October	November–March	Orange/red flush, nutty 2
'Ashmead's Kernel'	mid 19th cent.	Early/mid October	December–February	Green/yellow, russet/ sweet/sharp 5
'Claygate Pearmain'	1821	Early/mid October	December–February	Flushed orange/red rich/nutty 4
'Court Pendu Plat'	described circa 1613	Mid/late October	January–April	Flushed red pineapple/ sweet/striped 5
'Cox's Orange Pippin'	circa 1850	Late September	October–January	Flushed orange red/striped, sweet/aromatic; difficult 3
'Discovery'	raised circa 1949	Mid/late August	Late August–mid September	Bright red flush, crisp/juicy; disease resistant 3
'Egremont Russet'	1883	Late September/ early October	October–November	Russet, aromatic 2
Paradise Apple	recorded 1398	Widely used as dwarfing rootstock by late 17th cent.		
'Red Devil'	raised 1975	Mid–late September	October–December	Scarlet flush, crisp/juicy; pink in flesh; disease resistant 3
'Ribston Pippin'	listed 1769	Late September– early October	October–January	Brown/orange flush, aromatic 2T
'St Edmund's Pippin'	RHS 1875	Mid September	Late September–October	Russet, sweet 2
'Sunset'	raised circa 1918	Late September	October–December	Orange/red flush stripes/gold; intense flavour 3
'Worcester Pearmain'	1876	Early–mid September	September–October	Bright red over green, strawberry flavour; slow to crop 1
Apples, Culinary				
'Annie Elizabeth'	circa 1868	Early–mid October	November–April	Good for stewing 4
'Blenheim Orange'	1822	Late September	From late September	Cooks to stiff purée; sweet, dual purpose 3T
'Bramley's Seedling'	1865	Late August– early October	November–June	Strong acidity, cooks to purée, excellent flavour and wide range of uses 3T
'Dumelow's Seedling'	raised late 1700s	Early–mid October	November–April	Sharp flavour; bake/purée 3
'Golden Noble'	circa 1769	Early October	October–March	Good for pies 4
'Howgate Wonder'	1932	Early–mid October	November–March	Exhibition, but weak flavour; keeps shape 3
'Lane's Prince Albert'	circa 1850	Mid October	November–March	Lemon-colour purée; weaker flavour 4
'Lord Suffield'	circa 1836	Mid August	August–September	Cooks to froth 2
'Peasgood Nonsuch'	1872	Mid September	September–December	Purée or bake; good in vegetable salads 3
Pears				
'Beurre Hardy'	circa 1840	Mid September	October	Round/conical, medium, light green/russet, rose-water flavour 4
'Catillac'	recorded 1665	Mid October	January–April	Round conical, large; excellent cooking pear 4T
'Concorde'	selected 1977	Late September	October–November	Pyriform, medium; pale green to yellow/ some russet; sweet 4
'Conference'	circa 1885	Late September	October–November	Pyriform, medium; yellow/green/russet; sweet 3
'Doyenne du Comice'	1858	Early October	Mid October– mid November	Pyriform/conical, medium/ large; pale green/yellow/ flush red/some russet; excellent flavour 4
'Josephine de Malines'	raised circa 1830	Late October	January–February	Small, often short conical; pale green/yellowish/variable russet; sweet 4
'William's Bon Chretien'	circa 1814	Early September	Mid–late September	Medium, pyriform golden yellow when ripe/little russet; sweet/musky 3

Pollination groups are given in terms of flowering, with 1 the earliest and 5 the latest. Pollinators should be selected from the same period or the number either side of that. Those marked with a T are triploid and will therefore be no use as pollinators for other cultivars. In these cases, two pollinators will be needed, one to pollinate the other pollinator cultivar.

(Continued . . .)

TABLE 10: HISTORIC AND WIDELY GROWN FRUIT CULTIVARS (CONTINUED)				
CULTIVAR NAME	INTRODUCTION DATE	HARVESTING	SEASON	COMMENTS/ POLLINATION GROUPS
Plums and Gages				
'Czar'	1875	Early August	Early	Blue-black, medium/small, culinary; self fertile
'Denniston's Superb'	circa 1790	Late August	Mid season	Yellow, medium size oval fruit, dessert; self fertile
'Marjorie's Seedling'	1928	Late September– early October	Late	Blue-black large oval fruit, culinary; self fertile; growth upright
'Oullin's Golden Gage'	Received by Rivers nurseries pre 1856	Mid August	Early–mid season	Yellow medium/large, round, dessert/culinary; self fertile
'Victoria'	Introduced circa 1840 by a Brixton nurseryman	August–early September	Mid season	Red, medium to large oval fruit; dual purpose; self fertile and reliable
Peaches and Nectarines				
Peach 'Peregrine'	1906	Late August	Late	White flesh; self fertile
Peach 'Rochester'	1900	Mid August	Mid season	Yellow flesh; self fertile
Nectarine 'Lord Napier'	1860	Early August	Early	White flesh; self fertile
Nectarine 'Pineapple'	1872	Early September	Late	Yellow flesh; self fertile
Apricots				
'Alfred'	1965	Late July– early August	Early–mid season	Small/medium; skin & flesh orange; self fertile
'Moor Park'	1760	August	Mid season	Deep orange brownish, red flesh; self fertile
'New Early Large'	raised 1873	Mid - July	Early	Pale with orange flesh; self fertile
Cherries				
'Stella'	1968	Early–mid July	Mid season	Large black fruit; susceptible to bacterial canker; self fertile
'Sunburst'	1983	Mid July	Mid season	Large black fruit; resists splitting; self fertile
'Morello'	pre 1629	Mid July–September	Late	Blackish-red culinary fruit; self fertile; good for north walls
Medlars				
'Dutch'	pre 1760	October	Autumn	Large rich russet brown fruit; fair flavour; self fertile
'Nottingham'	pre 1597	October	Autumn	Small russet brown fruit of good flavour; self fertile
Quinces				
'Meech's Prolific'	1885	October	Autumn	Medium to large pear shaped bright golden yellow smooth fruit; self fertile
'Portugal'	1611	October	Autumn (early cultivar)	Large oval/oblong bright orange fruit; self fertile
'Vranja'	very old	October	Autumn	Large pear shaped golden yellow fragrant fruit; fruit; self fertile
Figs and Black Mulberries				
'Brown Turkey'	1880	August/September	Mid season	Medium dark chocolate fruit with red flesh; forces well
'White Marseilles'	pre 1669	August into September	Early	Large pale yellowish green fruits of good flavour ;outside or under glass
'Chelsea' ('King James 1' mulberry)	17th cent.	August	Summer	Ornamental tree; fresh fruit
Hazel Nuts				
'Cosford'	1816	August & early October	Late summer–winter	Short husk; good flavour; pollinates Kentish Cob
'Kentish Cob' (Longue d'Espagne)	raised about 1830	August & early October	Late summer–winter	Long husk (filbert); heavy cropper; pollinates Cosford

TABLE 10 333

TABLE 10: HISTORIC AND WIDELY GROWN FRUIT CULTIVARS (CONTINUED)				
CULTIVAR NAME	INTRODUCTION DATE	HARVESTING	SEASON	COMMENTS/ POLLINATION GROUPS
Raspberries				
'Glen Ample'	reported 1994	July	Mid/late	High yield of large fruit with good shelf life; canes spine free, vigorous & upright
'Glen Moy'	released 1980	July	Early	Firm large fruit on spine free erect canes
'Malling Jewel'	1949	July	Mid season	Fruit tends to darken; shorter canes
'Autumn Bliss'	1983	August & September	Autumn	Large easily plugged fruits
Blackberries and Hybrid Berries				
'Ashton Cross'	selected in the 1920s	August & September	Summer/autumn	Heavy yields of small round fruits; vigorous thorny canes
'Tayberry'	released 1977	Early June–mid August	Summer	Large purple/red fruits; fresh or frozen; long very spiny canes
Strawberries				
'Cambridge Favourite'	named in 1953	Mid June–mid July	Mid season	Medium size round/conical pale orange fruits; moderate firmness & yield; grows well in many soils
'Cambridge Late Pine'	named in 1953	July	Mid/late season	Medium/small dark red fruits of good flavour; moderate yield
'Elsanta'	1982	June–October with manipulation	Summer autumn	Large to medium attractive fruit; very good shelf life; susceptible to Verticillium Wilt
'Everest'	1998	July–October	Autumn fruiting	Heavy yield of darker red firm fruit with good shelf life
Currants				
'Baldwin' (Black currant)	19th cent.	August	Mid/late season	Good for juice & other culinary uses; frost sensitive at flowering
'Ben Lomond' (Black currant)	1975	August	Mid season	Reliable heavy yielding; frost resistance at flowering; good juice & other culinary uses
'Stanza' (Red currant)	1967	July/August	Mid/late	Heavy yields of good flavoured well presented berries; fresh or culinary
'Redstart' (Red currant)	1982	July–mid August	Late	Long strigs; fresh or culinary
'White Versailles' (White currant)	pre 1883	July	Early/mid season	Long strigs with large pale yellow fruit; summer puddings, sauces or fresh
Gooseberries				
'Careless'	1855	May (thinnings) & mid June–mid July	Early/mid season	Heavy yielding from compact bushes; culinary & fresh fruit
'Invicta'	1981	Mid June–mid July	Early/mid season	Very heavy crops on large mildew resistant bushes; culinary & fresh fruit
'Leveller'	1851	Mid June–mid July	Mid season	Yellow/green large berries for fresh fruit; bushes rather spreading
'Whinham's Industry'	pre 1850	Mid June–mid July	Mid season	Red hairy fruits; performs well on a range of soils; vigorous
Grapes under glass				
'Black Hamburgh'	Planted at Hampton Court around 1768	September	Late summer/autumn	Well known glasshouse grape; black, sweet dessert

(Continued ...)

TABLE 10: HISTORIC AND WIDELY GROWN VEGETABLE CULTIVARS

CULTIVAR NAME	INTRODUCTION DATE	HARVESTING	SEASON	COMMENTS/ POLLINATION GROUPS
Cabbages				
'Brunswick'	1800	August–October	Summer/autumn	Very large tight heads; keeps & stands well in the field
'Christmas Drumhead'	1881	October–December	Late autumn/winter	Small round, blue/ green heads
'Durham Early'	circa 1890	February–May August–September	Spring or late summer/autumn	For spring greens or hearts; conical heads
'Greyhound'	1898	Late June–September	Summer/autumn	Quick grower, pointed hearts
'January King'	1867	November–January	Winter	Very hardy, blue/green/ purple veins
'Mammoth Red Rock'	1889	October–February/March	Autumn/spring	Large, late-maturing red heads; stores & good for pickling
'Ormskirk'	1899	December–March	Winter	Savoy: wrinkled dark green leaves; very hardy
'Vertus'	1859	December–January	Winter	Ormskirk type; hardy
'Wheeler's Imperial'	1849	April/May & autumn	Spring & autumn	Dark green compact pointed heads
Brussels Sprouts				
'Bedfordshire Fillibasket'	Pre 1925	Late October–Christmas	Maincrop	90–120 cm; dark green even sprouts
'Noisette''	Old French variety	October–December	Maincrop	Small to medium sprouts: nutty flavour
'Peer Gynt'	20th cent.	September–Christmas	Early	Nutty flavour; loose sprouts if picking irregular
'Red Bull'	1930s	October–December	Maincrop	Red sprouts of good quality
'Rubine'	1930s	December–February	Late, 3–4 weeks	Purple red sprouts, loose; plus tops
'Seven Hills'	1890	Christmas–late January	Late	Plants mature at different times
Kale				
'Dwarf Green Curled'	1779	November–April	Late autumn–mid spring	Very hardy; good on light soils; tightly curled & deep green
'Hungry Gap'	1923	February–April	Late winter/spring	Blue leaves with a red/ purple hue
'Nero di Toscano'	1885	Late summer–early spring	Long season	Hardy; dark green blistered leaves
Oriental Brassicas				
'One Kilo SB'	20th cent.	August & September	Late summer & early autumn	Large barrel-shaped heads; creamy white inside & slow to bolt; stir fry or salads
Cauliflowers				
'All the Year Round'	Pre 1933	June–September	Summer/autumn	Compact and firm
'Purple Cape'	1808	March–May	Early–late spring	Purple heads; eat raw or cooked
'Snowball'	1890s (maybe earlier)	June/July	Summer	Reliable; freezes well
Broccoli and Calabrese				
'Early Purple Sprouting'	1834	February/March	Late winter	Large purple spears; green when cooked
'White Purple Sprouting'	1862	March/April	Spring	Cream white spears become lighter green when cooked
'Italian Sprouting' (Calabrese)	1859	June–October	Summer/autumn	Large cauliflower-like head; can also use side branches
Kohl Rabi				
'Purple Vienna'	1859	May–October	Summer /autumn	Swollen purplish stems; sweet turnip like flavour
'White Vienna'	1859	May–October	Summer/autumn	Pale green skin
Radishes				
'Black Spanish' (Round)	1548	October into winter	Autumn/winter	Black skin & cream/white flesh
'China Rose'	1845	November–late winter	Autumn/winter	Carmine skin & white flesh; medium length
'French Breakfast'	1865	One month from sowing	Spring–autumn	Oblong to 5 cm; red with white tip

TABLE 10   335

CULTIVAR NAME	INTRODUCTION DATE	HARVESTING	SEASON	COMMENTS/ POLLINATION GROUPS
Turnips and Swedes				
'Acme Purple Top' (Swede)	1852	October–April	Autumn/winter	Medium sized & globe shaped; of fine texture
'Golden Ball'	1857	July–mid October & winter storage	Summer, autumn & winter	Round yellow skinned & fleshed turnips
'Manchester Market' ('Green Stone Top')	1857	July–mid October & winter storage	Summer, autumn & winter	Green top & white flesh; very hardy
'Milan Red'	1885	July–mid October & winter storage	Summer, autumn & winter	Round/flattened roots; white with a purple top
'Veitch's Red Globe'	1871	July–mid October & winter storage	Summer, autumn & winter	Round to slightly flattened; white with a reddish-purple top
Beetroot				
'Burpee's Golden Beet'	1828	Early June–October	Early & maincrop	Orange roots, golden-yellow when cooked & of good flavour; tops for greens; stores & bolt resistant
'Boltardy'	1960s	June–November	Early crop & maincrop, resists bolting	Medium size globe shaped roots of good flavour & texture
'Bull's Blood'	1840	June–November	Early & maincrop (best young)	Medium sized spherical roots & crimson leaves; tops for greens
'Cheltenham Green Top'	1883	June–November	Early & maincrop	Long deep red roots; texture can be rough; stores well
'Detroit Dark Red'	1897	July–November	Maincrop	Medium size; for storage or canning
'Dobies Purple'	Early 1900s	July–November	Maincrop	Long large & tender tapered roots
'Egyptian Turnip Rooted'	1849	June–November	Early crop, resists bolting	Large heart shaped roots of good flavour; can be eaten raw
Carrots				
'Autumn King'	1932	Early summer–October, & then for winter storage	Late maincrop (can be used early)	Large with blunt tips; overwinters & stores
'Chantenay Red Cored'	1820	May–September	Early maincrop	Large short wedge-shaped carrots; orange/red; grows quickly, warm soils
'James's Intermediate'	1858	May–October	Early maincrop	Long tapering roots; pull young or later for store
'Long Red Surrey'	1821	May–September	Early maincrop	Long slender carrots with a yellow core; drought resistant
'Nantes'	1867	Crops June–October	Maincrop	Blunt tipped cylindrical carrots
'Oxheart'	1884	May–October	Early	Good for heavy soils; carrots large, short pointed & thick, storing well
Parsnips				
'Hollow Crown'	1825	September–April	Autumn–spring	Long tapering white-fleshed roots; best on deeper soils
'The Student'	1861	September–April	Autumn–spring	Long slender mild-flavoured roots
'Tender and True'	1897	September–April	Autumn–spring	Long/broad roots of good flavour; canker resistant
Potatoes (later cultivars store)				
'Concorde'	20th cent.	June–mid July	Very early	Large oval potatoes with pale yellow flesh
'Edzell Blue'	1915	August & September	Second early	Blue/purple skin & white floury flesh
'Epicure'	1897	June–mid July	Early - recovers from frost damage	High yields of white floury good flavoured potatoes
'Estima'	1973	August & September	Second Early	High yields of yellowish potatoes
'Majestic'	1911	September & October	Maincrop	Big white tubers & heavy yields on a wide range of soils; keeps well
'Pink Fir Apple'	1850	September & October	Maincrop/late	Long knobbly tubers with yellow flesh; good for salads

TABLE 10: HISTORIC AND WIDELY GROWN VEGETABLE CULTIVARS (CONTINUED)

(Continued ...)

TABLE 10: HISTORIC AND WIDELY GROWN VEGETABLE CULTIVARS (CONTINUED)				
CULTIVAR NAME	INTRODUCTION DATE	HARVESTING	SEASON	COMMENTS/ POLLINATION GROUPS
'Sante'	1983	August–October	Early maincrop, widely grown for organic cropping	Oval/round tubers with creamy yellow flesh; eelworm & blight resistant
'Wilja'	1967	August & September	Second early	High yields of pale yellow potatoes
Onions (many store well)				
'Ailsa Craig'	1887	August–October	Summer/winter	Large straw-coloured globe shaped onions
'Bedfordshire Champion'	1869	August–October	Summer/winter	Large, pale mild-flavoured onion
'Giant Zittau'	1876	August–October	Summer/winter	Large semi globular onions with yellow skin; good keeper
'Long Red Florence'	1885	August–October	Summer/winter	Torpedo-shaped deep purple/red onions; mild flavour & good for slicing
'Southport Red Globe'	circa 1873	August–October	Summer/winter	Large dark red onions with a mild flavour, for salads; good keeper
'White Lisbon'	1787	From late August	Long season	White spring onion
Leeks				
'The Lyon'	1883	September–November	Late summer/autumn	Thick white stems with a mild flavour
'Monstruso de Carentan'	1879	October–early January	Autumn/winter	Short thick stems; blue green foliage
'Musselburgh'	1834	December–April	Winter/spring	Broad-leaved and tall
Garlic and Shallots				
'Cristo' (Garlic)	20th cent.	July/August	Keeps until spring	Heavy yields; white skin & pink cloves (up to 15 a bulb)
'Hative de Niort' (Shallot)	1885	July/August	Store for many months	Pear-shaped bulbs, with dark brown skin & white flesh
Celery				
'Celebrity'	20th cent.	July–September	Early maturing Summer/autumn	Self-blanching, with short stringless petioles; matures quickly & resists bolting
'Golden Self Blanching'	1867	August & September	Summer/autumn	Yellow foliage & cream stalks; good flavour
'Solid White'	1787	November–February	Autumn/winter	Crisp
Celeriac				
'Giant Prague'	1871	Late September–November	Autumn & winter	Round & smooth-skinned; fresh or store
Florence Fennel				
Romanesco'	1786	July–October	Summer & autumn	Big white bulbs with an aniseed flavour
Broad Beans				
'Aquadulce Claudia'	1850	Late May/July	Late spring/summer	White-seeded
'Green Windsor'	1777	July/August	Summer	Large beans of good flavour
'The Sutton'	1923	Late May/July	Late spring/summer	Good garden cultivar, only 30 cm tall
Runner Beans				
'Enorma'	After 'Prizewinner' of which it is said to be a selection	July–October	Long season Summer/autumn	Heavy yields of long stringless beans
'Kelvedon Marvel'	20th cent.	July–October	Early Summer/autumn	Heavy crops of medium length beans
'Painted Lady'	Possibly as early as 1633	July–October	Summer/autumn	Bi-coloured red/white flowers; medium length good flavoured beans
'Prizewinner'	1892	July–October	Long season Summer/autumn	Long straight good-flavoured and textured beans
'Scarlet Emperor' (selected from 'Scarlet Runner')	Probably 1633	July–October	Early	Beans to 30 cm long; can be grown as bush beans

TABLE 10 337

TABLE 10: HISTORIC AND WIDELY GROWN VEGETABLE CULTIVARS (CONTINUED)				
CULTIVAR NAME	INTRODUCTION DATE	HARVESTING	SEASON	COMMENTS/ POLLINATION GROUPS
French and Haricot Beans				
'Blue Lake' (Climbing French Bean)	1885	July–October	Early maturing summer/autumn	White-seeded dark green beans; multi-purpose
'Canadian Wonder' (Dwarf French Bean)	1873	July–October	Summer/autumn	Vigorous bushy plant, with a heavy crop of bright green flat beans
'Chevrier Vert'	1878	July–October	Summer/autumn	Green flageolet bean
'Purple Queen' ('St Marthe', Dwarf French Bean)	19th cent.	July–October	Summer/autumn	Heavy crops of purple, waxy, stringless beans that turn green when cooked
'Beurre de Roquencourt' (Snap Bush Bean)	1850	July–October	Summer/autumn	Yellow pods & black seeds
'The Prince' (Dwarf French Bean)	1927	July–October	Summer/autumn	Long slim bi-coloured beans; these need picking early for tenderness
Peas and Mangetout				
'Alderman'	1891	July–September	Maincrop	Tall, needs support; long pods; wrinkle seeded with good flavour
'Hurst's Kelvedon Wonder'	1925	July–September	Good for successional sowings	Dwarf marrowfat pea; not drought tolerant
'Little Marvel'	1900	Late May/June & autumn	Early & autumn	Dwarf, for shelling
'Ne Plus Ultra'	1847	Until September	Late season	Hardy, tall, wrinkle-seed, good flavour
'Pilot'	1904	Late May–autumn	Early & long season	Hardy; round seeded
'Tall White Sugar' (Mangetout)	1859	July–September	Summer & autumn	Large broad flat pods
Courgettes and Marrows				
'Custard White'	1590	July–October	Summer/autumn	Compact plants; flat cream/white fruits
'Green Bush'	1860s	July–September	Summer/autumn	Mid green courgettes; medium size green/pale green striped marrows
'Long Green Trailing'	1879	July–September	Summer/autumn	Large trailing plants; dark green/pale striped marrows
'Long White Bush'	1849	July–September	Summer/autumn	Yellow/white fruits; courgettes or marrows
Pumpkins, Squash and Melons				
'Buttercup' (Turban Squash)	1925	August–October	Summer/autumn	Goblet-shaped with dark green skin & orange flesh; 1–2 kg; keeps well; for pies or roasted
'Butternut' (Squash)	Known in North America since the 16th cent.	August–October	Summer/autumn	Elongated to 25 cm orange flushed fruits; makes a creamy soup
'Connecticut Field' (Pumpkin)	1700	August–October	Summer/autumn	Large; for Halloween
'Golden Hubbard' (Squash)	1895	August–October	Summer/autumn	Up to 3 kg lemon-shaped ridged fruits, with orange/yellow flesh; stores; trailing plants
'Green Nutmeg' (Cantaloupe Melon)	Pre 1863	August–October	Summer/autumn	Heavy yields, 1–1.5 kg fruit; sweet green flesh
'Sweetheart' F1 (Cantaloupe Melon)	20th cent.	August–October	Summer/autumn	Medium size fruits with firm salmon pink flesh; good flavour; can be grown outside
'Turk's Turban'	1817	August–October	Summer/autumn	Flattish (turban shaped) orange/striped fruit; eat or ornamental; stores
Cucumbers				
Butcher's Disease Resisting	1903	July–September	Glasshouse	Medium smooth fruit; tolerates low temperatures & leaf spot resistant
'Burpless Tasty Green'	20th cent.	Mid July–October	Summer/autumn	Long slender dark green fruits; for slicing; outside or under glass
'Telegraph Improved'	1880	July–September	Summer/autumn	Straight dark green fruits; good flavour/crispness; glasshouse

(Continued ...)

TABLE 10: HISTORIC AND WIDELY GROWN VEGETABLE CULTIVARS (CONTINUED)

CULTIVAR NAME	INTRODUCTION DATE	HARVESTING	SEASON	COMMENTS/ POLLINATION GROUPS
Tomatoes				
'Ailsa Craig'	1910	July–September	Summer/autumn	Medium sized red tough-skinned fruits with green back; glass or outside on a south wall
'Gardener's Delight' ('Red Cherry', 1795, is a similar fruiting type)	1870	July–September	Summer/autumn	Long trusses of cherry-sized fruits; good for salads; outside or glass
'Golden Sunrise'	1896	July–September	Summer/autumn	Bush type with golden yellow fruit for outside; early & heavy yields
Aubergines, Peppers and Chillies				
'Bell Boy' (sweet pepper)	20th cent.	July (cold glass), August–October outside	Summer/autumn	Deep green thick-walled fruits
'Long Red Cayenne' (hot pepper)	1542	August & September	Autumn	Fruits red or green; to 10 cm long; pickled red
'Black Beauty' (aubergine)	1902	August & September outside	Early, summer/autumn	Deep purple oval to round fruit (about 10 cm); moderate yields; stores well
'Long Purple' (aubergine)	1905	August & September outside	Summer/autumn	Long deep purple fruits of good flavour; slice & fry
Lettuce				
'All the Year Round'	1868 (possibly earlier)	May–October	Spring–late autumn	Medium size butterhead lettuce
'Little Gem'	1880	May–October	Spring–late autumn	Semi-cos type; quick-maturing, crisp & sweet
'Lolla Rossa'	20th cent. selections of this type	May–October	Spring–late autumn	Non-hearting red-tinged serrated-edged leaves
'Tom Thumb'	1868	April–October	Spring–late autumn	Dwarf butterhead lettuce; hearts quickly & slow to bolt
'Webb's Wonderful'	1890	May–October	Spring–late autumn	Crisphead lettuce; solid & large size; mature heads last well in the field
Chicory and Endive				
'Variegata di Castelfranco' (chicory)	1700s	Lift October	Use in winter	Red chicory (radicchio); leaves green & heavily blotched red; for forcing
'Whitloof' (chicory)	1876	Lift October	Use in winter	For forcing
'Ruffec Green Curled' (endive)	1863	Lift October blanch, or use earlier for leaves	Summer/winter	Curled deep green crisp leaves for garnish; needs little tying to blanch; very hardy
Chard and Leaf Beet				
'Rhubarb Chard'	1857	June/July into the autumn	Summer/autumn	Dark green leaves with bright red midribs; can use all parts of the leaves
'Swiss Chard'	Pre 1750	June/July into the autumn	Summer/autumn	Dark green leaves with white midribs; use as 'Rhubarb Chard'
Spinach				
'Bloomsdale Long Standing'	1920s	July–autumn & winter–June	Most of the year	Vigorous with dark glossy green crumpled leaves; tender & of good flavour; slow to bolt
Asparagus				
'Connover's Colossal'	1870	May–July	Early cropper Spring/summer	Mid-green spears; heavy yields
Cardoons and Globe Artichokes				
'Artichoke Leaved' (cardoon, for stem/leaves)	1845	Autumn	Lift & blanch for autumn/winter use	Strong grower; good quality
'Green Globe' (artichoke)	1828	July/August	Summer	Flower heads deep green with purple tints
'Plein Blanc Inerme' (cardoon, for stem/leaves)	1750	Autumn	Lift & blanch for autumn/winter use	Rather tough when cooked

TABLE 10 339

TABLE 10: HISTORIC AND WIDELY GROWN VEGETABLE CULTIVARS (CONTINUED)				
CULTIVAR NAME	INTRODUCTION DATE	HARVESTING	SEASON	COMMENTS/ POLLINATION GROUPS
Herbs				
Chives	1500s	Summer/autumn	Summer/autumn	Re-sow every 2–3 years
Parsley 'Moss Curled'	1865	Autumn sown: April onwards Spring sown: June onwards	Long season	Bright green crinkled leaves
Jerusalem Artichoke				
'Fusea'	A selection of the type grown in North America for centuries	Lift tubers November–January	Winter	High yields of large tubers; boil & use with a white sauce
Rhubarb				
'Champagne'	Pre 1908	May/June; earlier if forced	Spring/early summer	Early cropper; can be forced
'Timperley Early'	1947	May/June; earlier if forced	Spring/early summer	Early & vigorous; excellent for forcing
'Victoria'	1849	May/June	Spring/early summer	Reliable cropper
Sweetcorn (many recent F1 hybrids available)				
'Golden Bantam'	1902	August–October	Summer/autumn	Sweet slender smaller cobs; early & resists lodging

TABLE 11: PLANTS FOR MARITIME CONDITIONS

A: TREES FOR SHELTER / WINDBREAKS

A1: Evergreen species. Foliage must be wind and salt tolerant.

HARDINESS	BOTANICAL NAME	COMMON NAME	GROWTH RATE
Hardy species	xCupressocyparis leylandii	Leyland Cypress	Fast
	Ilex aquifolium	Holly	Slow
	Pinus contorta var. latifolia	Lodgepole Pine	Moderate
	Pinus nigra	Australian Pine	Moderate
	Pinus sylvestris	Scots Pine	Moderate
	Quercus ilex	Holm Oak	Slow to establish then fast
Less hardy sp.	Cupressus arizonica var. glabra	Smooth Arizona Cypress	Fast
(W and SW Coast)	Cupressus macrocarpa	Monterey Cypress	Fast
	Eucalyptus sp.		Fast

A2: Deciduous species

Hardy species	Acer campestre	Field Maple	Slow
	Acer pseudoplatanus	Sycamore	Fast
	Crataegus monogyna	Hawthorn	Moderate
	Populus alba	White Poplar	Fast, suckers freely in sand dunes and shallow soil
	Populus x canescens	Grey Poplar	Fast
	Salix caprea	Goat Willow	Fast in shallow soils
	Sorbus aria	Whitebeam	Moderate

B: SHRUBS
Once shelter has been established, a wide range of shrubs may be planted. The list covers only those that are normally tolerant of the conditions imposed by this environment.

B1: Hedging and screening shrubs, 2–3m high, planted 0.3–0.5m apart.

BOTANICAL NAME	COMMON NAME	DECIDUOUS (D) OR EVERGREEN (E)
Eleagnus angustifolia	Oleaster	D
Eleagnus x ebbingii		E
Escallonia rubra var. macrantha		E
Euonymus japonicus		E
Griselinia littoralis	New Zealand Broadleaf	E
Olearia macrodonta	New Zealand Holly	E
Pittosporum tenuifolium		E
Tamarix sp.	Tamarisks	D & E

B2: Shrubs grown for sturdy habit and attractive foliage and flowers

Atriplex halimus	Tree Purslane	DE
Berberis wilsoniae		E
Brachyglottis greyi		D
Bupleurum fruticosum	Shrubby Hare's Ear	E
Cordyline australis + cvs	Cabbage Palm	E
Cotoneaster Dwarf species		D & E
Cytisus scoparius + cvs	Common Broom	E
Escallonia cultivars		E
Fuchsia magellanica + cvs	Lady's Eardrops	D
Genista hispanica	Spanish Gorse	E
Heathers, where soil is favourable		E
Hebes		E
Hardy dwarf species:		
H. colensoi 'Glauca'		E
H. cupressiodes		E
H. 'Edinensis'		E
H. odora		E
H. pagei		E
Less hardy taller species/cultivars		
H. x andersonii		E
H. 'Autumn Glory'		E
H. 'Great Orme'		E
H. salicifolia		E
H. speciosa 'La Séduisante'		E

TABLE II 341

TABLE II: PLANTS FOR MARITIME CONDITIONS (CONTINUED)		
BOTANICAL NAME	COMMON NAME	DECIDUOUS (D) OR EVERGREEN (E)
Lavandula sp. + cvs	Lavenders	E
Lavatera maritima		D
Lupinus arboreus	Yellow Tree Lupin	D & E
Olearia x *haastii*		E
Olearia phlogopappa	Tasmanian Daisy Bush	E
Phlomis fruticosa	Jerusalem Sage	E
Phormium sp.	New Zealand Flax	E
Rosa sp.	Rose	D
Rosmarinus officinalis	Rosemary	E
Salix repens var. *argentea* (establishes well on sand dunes)	Creeping Willow	D
Spartium junceum	Spanish Broom	E
Ulex minor	Dwarf Gorse	E
Yucca sp.		E
B3: NATIVE SHRUBS		
Calluna vulgaris	Heather	E
Erica especially *E. vagans*	Cornish Heath	E
Hippophae rhamnoides	Sea Buckthorn	D
Ilex aquifolium	Holly	E
Prunus spinosa	Blackthorn	D
Rosa arvensis	Field Rose	D
Rosa pimpinellifolia	Scotch Rose, Burnet Rose	D
Salix repens	Creeping Willow	D
Tamarix gallica	Common Tamarisk	D
Ulex europaeus	Common Gorse	E

C1: PERENNIALS

Many grey-leaved and fleshy-leaved perennials thrive in coastal sites on sandy soils and in dry, sunny environments. Establish well on sloping sites. Ground cover. This list is only a short selection.

BOTANICAL NAME	COMMON NAME
Anaphalis sp.	Pearl Everlasting
Artemisia lactiflora + other sp. + cvs	White Mugwort
Ballota pseudodictamnus	
Carpobrotus edulis	Hottenton Fig
Delosperma sp.	
Gazania cvs	
Lampranthus sp.	
Limonium latifolium	Sea Lavender
Mesembryanthemum (see under *Delosperma* and *Lampranthus*)	
Stachys byzantina	Woolly Woundwort, Lamb's Ear
Ornamental grasses, bamboos, etc.	

C2: NOTEWORTHY NATIVE PERENNIAL SPECIES

BOTANICAL NAME	COMMON NAME
Armeria maritima	Thrift
Calystegia soldanella	Sea Bindweed
Crambe autumnalis	Sea-Kale
Eryngium maritimum	Sea-Holly
Geranium sanguineum	Bloody Crane's-Bill
Glaucium flavum	Yellow Horned-Poppy
Limonium vulgare	Common Sea Lavender
Scilla verna	Spring Squill
Scilla autumnalis	Autumn Squill
Silene uniflora	Sea Campion

TABLE 12: HEDGE MAINTENANCE				
HEDGE SPECIES	USUAL NO. OF CUTS PER YEAR	SEASONS OF CUTTING	AVERAGE RANGE OF HEIGHT IN METRES	RATE OF GROWTH & FLOWER COLOUR
1. Deciduous foliage hedges				
Acer campestre (Field Maple)	One	Sept–Mar	1.5–3	Moderate
Carpinus betulus (Hornbeam)	One	Sept–Mar	1.5–3	Moderate
Crataegus sp. (Hawthorn)	Two	July Nov–Mar	1.5–3	Moderate to fast
Fagus sylvatica (Beech, also purple- or copper-leaved cultivars)	One	Sept–Mar	1.5–3	Moderate to slow
Prunus cerasifera (Myrobalan Plum and purple-leaved forms)	Two	June–July Nov–Dec	1.5–3	Fast
Rosa rubiginosa (Sweet Briar)	Two	July Nov–Mar	0.75–1.5	Fast
Rosa rugosa (Ramanas Rose)	Two	July Nov–Mar	0.75–1	Moderate
Viburnum lantana (Wayfaring Tree)	One	Nov–Mar	1–2	Moderate
2. Flowering deciduous hedges				
Chaenomeles sp. (Japonica)	Two	May Dec–Mar	1–1.5	Relatively fast. Discerning pruning to avoid cutting out all flowering wood. Varied flower colours
Cornus mas (Cornelian Cherry)	Two	June Dec–Mar	1–2	Relatively fast. Discerning pruning to avoid cutting out all flowering wood Yellow flowers
Cotoneaster simonsii	Two	June Dec–Mar	1–1.5	Relatively fast. Discerning pruning to avoid cutting out all flowering wood. Pink-tinged white flowers
Forsythia x *intermedia* 'Spectabilis'	Two	May Dec–Mar	1–1.5	Relatively fast. Discerning pruning to avoid cutting out all flowering wood. Produces yellow flowers
Ribes uva-crispa (Gooseberry)	Two	June Dec–Mar	0.75–1	Moderate. Produce fruit but picking is tricky within the hedge
Ribes rubrum (Redcurrant)	One	Nov–Mar	0.75–1	Moderate. Produce fruit but picking is tricky within the hedge
3. Evergreen hedges				
Buxus sempervirens (Common Box)	Two/three	June–Sept	0.15–1	Slow
Chamaecyparis lawsoniana (Lawson's Cypress + cvs)	One	Feb–Mar	1.5–3	Moderate. Avoid excess hard cutting into old wood
x*Cupressocyparis leylandii* (Leyland Cypress)	One/two	July–Apr	2–10	Very fast. One cut in March may be adequate for tall hedges
Elaeagnus sp.	One	Aug	2–3	Moderate informal hedge
Euonymus japonicus	Two	June–Sept	1.5–2	Moderate
Ilex acquifolium (Common Holly + cvs)	One	July–Aug	2.5	Slow
Ligustrum ovalifolium (Privet)	Four	May–Sept	1–3	Fast. Frequent clipping to keep in shape
Lonicera nitida	Four/five	May–Sept	0.5–1.5	Fast. Needs regular clipping
Pittsporum tenuifolium	One	Aug–Sept	1.5–3	Moderate to fast. Suitable for milder and S, SW areas. Cut foliage value
Phillyrea angustifolia	One	May–June	2–4	Slow. Careful hand pruning with secateurs. Shears can disfigure
Prunus laurocerasus (Common Laurel)	One	May–June	2–5	Slow. Careful hand pruning with secateurs. Shears can disfigure

TABLE 12 343

TABLE 12: HEDGE MAINTENANCE (CONTINUED)				
HEDGE SPECIES	USUAL NO. OF CUTS PER YEAR	SEASONS OF CUTTING	AVERAGE RANGE OF HEIGHT IN METRES	RATE OF GROWTH & FLOWER COLOUR
Prunus lusitanica (Portuguese Laurel)	One	May–June	2–5	Slow. Careful hand pruning with secateurs. Shears can disfigure. Not in cold areas
Quercus ilex (Holm Oak)	One/two	Apr–Aug	1.5–5	Slow. Not to be planted in very cold areas
Taxus baccata (Yew)	One	Aug–Sept	1.5–4	Moderate. The best architectural hedge
Thuja plicata (Western Red Cedar)	One	Mar	2–5	Moderate. Excellent hedge
4. Flowering evergreen hedges				
Berberis darwinii	One	May–June	0.75–1.5	Slow. Lacks density. Orange-yellow flowers
Berberis julianae	One	June–July	1–2	Moderate. Spiny barrier. Red-tinged flowers
Cotoneaster lacteus	One	June–July	1–1.5	Moderate. Produces white flowers and red berries
Escallonia rubra var. *macrantha* and others	One/two	Apr–Aug	1–2	Fast. Seaside hedge Red flowers
Fuchsia 'Riccartonii'	One	Mar	1–2	Fast. Suitable for milder SW areas. Flowers have scarlet tubes and sepals and dark purple corollas
Olearia macrodonta (New Zealand Holly)	One	Mar	1.5–2	Fast. Seaside berries. White flowers
Osmanthus x burkwoodii	One/two	May–Aug	1–2	Slow. Scented white flowers
Osmanthus delavayi	One/two	May–Aug	0.5–1.5	Slow. Scented white flowers.
Rhododendron ponticum	One	July–Aug	2–4	Moderate. Acid soils. Purple flowers
Viburnum tinus (Laurustinus)	One	Apr–May	1.5–3	Moderate. Winter flowering. Pollution resistant

TABLE 13: PESTS, DISEASES AND DISORDERS OF OUTDOOR PLANTS

PEST	SYMPTOMS	TREATMENT
Root-eating/Soil-inhabiting		
Cabbage Root Fly *Delia radicum*	Cultivated brassicas: plants collapse and die, particularly in dry weather after planting. White maggots feed on roots.	Winter cultivation and good hygiene, to reduce overwintering pupae. On a small scale, 10–15 cm disks around plants to stop females laying eggs, and encourage predatory ground beetles. Approved insecticides on established plants.
Earthworms on lawns Main pest species in lawns are *Allolobophora longa* and *Allolobophora nocturna*	*Allobophora species* produce casts on the surface of lawns, damaging mowing blades and smearing the surface. Sites for weed development.	Disperse casts by sweeping with a birch broom on smaller sports areas, before mowing. Compost dressings with organic matter and heavy liming will encourage worms.
Leatherjackets Commonest are *Tipula paludosa*, *Tipula oleracea* and *Nephrotoma maculata* Grey-brown larvae, up to 5 cm long; immature stage of the crane fly	Feed on roots at any time of the year, but much damage can be done during the spring. A wide range of plants are attacked including grasses in lawns.	Firstly establish by sampling that Leatherjackets are present. Neglected lawns are the main problem areas. Smaller ones can be watered and covered overnight. The larvae will work their way to the surface and can be removed the following morning. The eelworm *Steinernema carpocapsae* can be used to control Leatherjackets (minimum soil temperature of 14°C).
Nematodes (Eelworms) *Ditylenchus dipsaci* (Stem Eelworm) *Ditylenchus destructor* (Potato Tuber Eelworm) *Aphelenchoises ritzemabosi* (Chrysanthemum Eelworm) *Aphelenchoides blastophthorus* (Scabious Bud Eelworm) *Meloidogyne* spp. (Root-Knotb Eelworms) These are microscopic worms, normally 1–2 mm long in plant-feeding species. They may be free-living in the soil water, or feed within the plant tissue. Some species are useful parasites of other pests.	A wide range of symptoms, depending on the tissue fed on. Growth is checked with root-feeding species. Distortion of leaves and stems with those that feed on these tissues. Some eelworms are important vectors of viruses that cause stunting and other symptoms.	This is a very large group and control depends on species. Hygiene, control of weed hosts, use of healthy stock, resistant cultivars, heat treatment, approved nematicides and soil sterilants are all methods used, depending on host and eelworm species.
Vine Weevil *Otiorhynchus sulcatus* Curved, creamy white, plump larvae with brown heads, up to 1 cm long, feed on roots of many plants. Beetle-like adults found on foliage.	Plants wilt when the roots are chewed. Leaf margins eaten by adults.	Use of approved insecticides, particularly in the compost of nursery stock plants, to prevent the spread from site to site. Biological control outside can be attempted when soil temperatures are above 12°C, using the nematodes *Heterorhabditis megidis* and *Steinernema carpocapsae*.
Foliage-eating		
Aphids *Homoptera aphididae*, 45 spp. described Pear-shaped sap-feeding insects, usually 1–5 mm long. Winged and wingless forms. A wide range of species, often with alternative hosts.	Usually host specific; colonies of green to pink to black insects feeding on the younger growth. Plants become stunted and distorted. Honeydew and sooty moulds may form.	Determine species present; it may be possible to eliminate some alternative weed hosts. Encourage and plant predator banks where feasible. Check forecasting programmes to predict periods of attack. Use approved systemic insecticides from different chemical groups, to avoid resistance.
Brown-Tail Moths *Euproctis chrysorrhoea* Dark brown caterpillars up to 30 mm long with tufts of brown hairs feed in colonies on hawthorns, sloes, roses and some other plants. Most feeding activity is in the spring and early summer.	Colonies spin silk forming obvious protective canopies. The main problem is one of health, as the caterpillars shed hairs, causing skin irritation and allergies. Although not common, this moth could cause problems at sites where visitors are present.	Remove and destroy the colonies in protective canopies, in the winter when these can be seen. Where appropriate protective clothing. Apply approved contact insecticides as soon as the young caterpillars are seen.
Cabbage White Butterflies *Pieris rapae* The Large and Small White Butterflies are common species, laying eggs on different species of brassica. Caterpillars feed on exposed parts of plants, although the Small White will feed on the hearts of cabbages.	Leaves chewed and in cases of severs damage, only the leaf veins remaining. Often on older plants.	Inspect plants for attack regularly. Apply approved contact insecticides. An approved formula of the bacterial insecticide *Bacillus thuringiensis* could also be used.
Fruit Tortrix *Pammene rhediella* (Fruitlet Mining Tortrix) *Adoxophyes orana* (Summer Fruit Tortrix) *Archips podana* (Fruit Tree Tortrix) **Codling Moths** *Cydia pomonella* Moths small and inconspicuous, flying in the summer.	Tortrix caterpillars produce superficial feeding areas on apples, often attaching to the fruit surface with silken webs. Codling moth caterpillars into the fruit core of apples; this often then rots.	Pheromone traps sited to catch male moths and predict peak egg laying, will enable chemical sprays to be timed to reduce caterpillar numbers.
Common Gooseberry Sawfly *Nematus ribesii* Adults are small, black and orange-yellow. There can be three generations in a year; the larvae, green with black heads, feed on the leaves.	Leaves can be reduced to a skeleton of veins. Feeding can be rapid, from the centre of the bush, and may be overlooked until massive damage is done.	Bushes should be inspected weekly from May onwards, to check for caterpillar activity. Outbreaks will usually start in the centre of bushes. Where necessary, apply high-volume approved contact insecticides.

TABLE 13   345

TABLE 13: PESTS, DISEASES AND DISORDERS OF OUTDOOR PLANTS (CONTINUED)

PEST	SYMPTOMS	TREATMENT
Common Green Capsid *Lygocoris pabulinus* **and Tarnished Plant Bug** *Lygus rugulipennis* Somewhat flattened active insects with piercing and sucking mouthparts. Saliva is injected; this kills plant tissues, causing distortion.	Ragged holes in young leaves; general distortion and tattering of foliage and flowers. Lumps on the surfaces of fruit. A wide range of plants is attacked.	Fruits and ornamental plants are attacked. The Tarnished Plant Bug shelters overwinter in leaf debris and coarse herbage. Clean this out where attacks have occurred and this is practical. Use approved systemic insecticides, in spring and summer if attacks warrant these, but avoid the flowering periods, when pollinating insects may be active.
Gladiolus Thrips *Thrips simplex* Elongate cylindrical insects, 3–4 mm long. Many species; the adults are often noticeable in large numbers in humid thundery weather.	A severe pest on gladioli, causing flecking on foliage and flowers. In severe attacks, these may wilt and die. Damage to corms can occur in store.	Approved chemical treatment of corms should break the life cycle.
Leaf Miners Number of species, e.g. *Phytomyza ilicis* (Holly Leaf Miner) and *Cerodontha iridis* (Iris leaf miner) The larvae of certain flies and moths tunnel in the leaf laminas of several species of woody plants.	Serpentine or blotch miners are visible on the leaf surfaces.	These are generally not a major problem requiring control. However Chrysanthemum Leaf Miner, which attacks this and some other cultivated plants outdoors in the summer, can cause unacceptable damage. Remove and destroy mined leaves and host weeds around attacked plants. Use approved systemic insecticides. The parasitic wasps *Dacnusa sibirica* or *Diglyphus isaea* could be introduced, but are more effective under glass.
Scale Insects Many species of *Hemiptera: Coccoidea*, e.g. *Coccus hesperidum* (soft scale) and *Parthenolecanium corni* (brown scale) Sap feeding insects; several species feed outdoors on the leaves or woody parts of plants. Mature females are up to 5 mm long and are limpet-like in appearance.	Honeydew is excreted and unsightly sooty moulds may form. Severe attacks can weaken some species of plants.	The Horse Chestnut Scale occurring on this tree, limes, elms, maples, magnolias, cornus and Bay Laurel, is becoming more widespread, and forms dense colonies on the branches and trunks. Currently no control measures are recommended. It would be difficult to apply pesticides to large trees in streets, parks and gardens. Careful checks need to be made on nursery stock to reduce spread.
Slugs and Snails Many species of *Mollusca: Gastropoda*, e.g. *Arion hortensis* (garden slug) and *Helix aspersa* (garden snail).	Chewed foliage, stems and flowers (margins are ragged). Silvery trails over plant surfaces.	Approved slug pellets should be applied precisely to product instructions to reduce risk to the environment. Drenching infested areas with a suspension of the nematode *Phasmarrhabditis* can reduce populations, but soil temperatures should be above 5°C. Control methods should aim at reducing populations before planting susceptible species.

FUNGAL DISEASE	SYMPTOMS	TREATMENT
Apple Scab *Venturia inaequalis*	Dark green/black rounded corky patches on the surfaces of apple and pear fruit. Necrotic lesions on one year old wood; particularly noticeable on pears.	Fungicides should be applied to predictive monitoring methods, generally from bud burst, and possibly until near harvest. Where there are few trees, collect and burn fallen leaves to break the life cycle. Also cut out and destroy wood scab at winter pruning.
Beech Heart Rots *Ganoderma applanatum* and *Pleurotus ostreatus* *Ganoderma applanatum* and *Pleurotus applanatum* are the main causal organisms.	Soft white rots. *Ganoderma* produces bracket-like fruiting bodies, and *Pleurotus* fan-shaped fructifications (edible Oyster Mushroom).	Qualified tree surgeons should inspect trees with suspected Heart Rot. Careful pruning to retain the branch collar will aid the healing of healthy wounds.
Black Spot on Roses *Diplocarpon rosae*	Leaves with dark brown/black blotches. They often turn yellow and drop prematurely.	Overwinter survival is on the shoots, and harder spring pruning may reduce initial infection. Use cultivars with some resistance where possible and maintain good drainage. Apply approved systemic fungicides.
Box Blight *Cylindrocladium buxicola* and *Volutella buxi* Affecting *Buxus sempervirens* and its cultivars.	Leaves to turn brown and fall. Whole branches may die with severe damage to box topiary. Spore-bearing patches occur on the leaves; pinkish in *P. rousseliana* and greyish in *Cylindrocladium*. It is thought that infection spreads in the spring from infected fallen leaves that have remained over winter.	There are no chemicals approved for the control of box blights. All infected leaves and branches should be removed and burnt as soon as the disease is confirmed. Severely infected plants should be grubbed. Inspect new plants coming on site carefully or propagate from existing healthy material on site.
Coral Spot *Nectria cinnabarina* The fungus is generally saprophytic but can be parasitic on a wide range of woody plants.	Small pinkish cushion-like pustules occur on dead and dying branches. Larger branches may wilt and die during the summer.	Remove piles of dead branches from around small trees, particularly fruit trees and bushes. Destroy severely infected plants. Otherwise prune out infected branches into healthy wood. Do not leave dead branch stubs.

(Continued ...)

TABLE 13: PESTS, DISEASES AND DISORDERS OF OUTDOOR PLANTS (CONTINUED)		
FUNGAL DISEASE	SYMPTOMS	TREATMENT
Club Root *Plasmodiophora brassicae* This disease affects a wide range of brassicas, including vegetables and wallflowers.	Roots are swollen and distorted, but there are no obvious organisms on or within them. Aerial parts of the plant may wilt and show mineral deficiency symptoms.	Control is difficult, as the disease is persistent in the soil and many races exist. If at all possible plant only stock from known uninfected sources into land known to be free of the disease.
Damping Off Soil borne fungi, mainly species of *Pythium* and *Rhizoctonia solani*, are the responsible fungi.	Seedlings die out, often in patches, and there may be lesions near soil level.	See tables of pest and diseases of protected crops.
Dutch Elm Disease *Ophiostoma novo-ulmi* and *Ophiostoma ulmi* The current epidemic is caused by the fungus *Ophiostoma novo-ulmi* and is spread by elm bark beetles, particularly *Scolytus scolytus*.	Leaves turn yellow and die. At first only part of the tree may be affected, but soon the whole tree dies. Beetle feeding galleries under the bark.	In public parks and gardens, recently dead trees should be removed and the bark stripped and burnt to reduce further infection. Severing root systems between healthy and infected trees may reduce spread. The introduction of resistant species has begun, and there may be resistance within native elms.
Greymould *Botrytis*	Soft watery rots of stems, leaves and flowers, particularly in the bud stage. Spotting on flowers. Also in softer fruits and on woody plant parts, such as raspberry stems. Masses of greyish spores are often present. Affects annuals, herbaceous perennials and smaller woody species.	See table of pest and diseases of protected crops.
Honey Fungus *Armillaria mellea* and other *Armillaria* sp. The basal parts of tree trunks, shrub stems and roots are infected by mycelium that kills the tissues.	White mycelium between the dead bark and wood, also black aggregates of mycelium 'bootlaces' in the soil, which spread the disease from plant to plant. Yellowish-brown toadstools on tree stumps. Dieback occurs, and may take a year or two to be complete.	Removal and destruction of as much infected material as possible (including tree stumps). Do not plant susceptible species in soil known to carry infection.
Potato Blight *Phytophthora infestans* A serious disease of potatoes, but also on tomatoes.	Black soft patches bearing white mould growth, on leaves. Tomato fruits show dryish rot patches.	Select healthy potato tubers and resistant cultivars. Spray potato plants with protectant sprays if needed.
Powdery (many sp. *Erysiphaceae*) **and Downy Mildews** (many sp. *Peronosporaceae*) Unrelated groups of fungi. Powdery Mildews are generally more prevalent in dry conditions, Downy Mildews in wet ones. Lettuce and Grapevine Downy Mildews can be important diseases.	In Powdery Mildews (on apples and roses, for example), powdery spore masses are clearly seen. Plants show debilitation. Surface spore masses of Downy Mildews are often not well defined, but underlying affected tissue is yellow.	This is covered in the table of pests and diseases of protected crops. Primary powdery mildew infections on some species should be cut out in the spring and destroyed.
Rusts *Basidiomycete* fungi of the order *Uredinales* Fungi with complex life cycles, affecting a wide range of ornamental plants, fruits and vegetables. Species are often specific in the plants that they attack, and have alternative plant hosts.	Depending on species attacked, pustules of various colours are produced on the underside of the leaves and also on stems. Plants may be disfigured and premature leaf fall occur.	In some species, resistant cultivars can be selected. Eliminating alternative hosts my be possible. Treat with approved fungicides where appropriate.
Fairy Rings in Turf *Marasmius oreades* is the commonest A toadstool-producing fungus.	Extending rings of bright green grass, with poor grass growth inside the ring. Fungal mycelium within the ring exhausts nutrients, dies and then forms a barrier impervious to water.	Improve aeration by spiking within the impervious barrier. Apply fertilisers to improve nutrition.
Red-Thread in Turf *Laetisaria fuciformis*	Particularly after long periods of heavy rain, or other conditions depleting soil nitrogen. Red fescues are particularly susceptible. Reddish patches of dying grass, with pinkish strands among the leaves.	Nitrogen-rich fertilisers in the spring. Approved fungicides.
Sudden Oak Death/Ramorum Dieback *Phytophthora ramorum* is causal organism Spread of fungal spores likely to be by water- or moisture-borne methods. The range of known susceptible species in Britain is increasing: mainly rhododendrons and viburnums, but other shrubby species have been affected. Some outbreaks on exotic oaks, beech, horse- and sweet-chestnut.	Symptoms in shrubs include stem dieback and leaf blight. Susceptible trees show stem and leaf dieback, trunk lesions and bleeding canker. Some species generally survive infection, others die rapidly.	Long-distance spread has been mainly by the movement of infected plants in trade. The disease is notifiable and the local Plant Health and Seeds Inspectorate (PHSI) should be informed if infection is suspected. Control is by inspection, destruction of infected material and quarantine. A Plant Passporting Scheme is in place for certain susceptible species. PHSI can advise on the species covered by this scheme.
Verticillium Wilt *Verticillium* sp. Several species attack a wide range of fruit, vegetables, ornamentals.	Brown to black discoloration is seen in the conducting tissues of the stem, well above soil level. Plants may wilt suddenly, are debilitated and may die.	The disease is persistent in the soil. Plant resistant species and cultivars; some strawberries are resistant. Where possible, remove and destroy affected plants and some surrounding contaminated soil.

TABLE 13 347

TABLE 13: PESTS, DISEASES AND DISORDERS OF OUTDOOR PLANTS (CONTINUED)

BACTERIAL DISEASE	SYMPTOMS	TREATMENT
Bacterial Canker in Stone Fruit *Neonectria galligena* Apple and pear canker Affects ornamental and fruiting *Prunus* species.	Branches and buds ooze gum and die back occurs. Holes in the leaves during summer.	Pruning carried out during active growth from May (to reduce Silver Leaf Disease) should reduce infection. Cut out and destroy infected branches. Approved copper sprays around leaf fall to protect wounds; particularly useful in nursery stock. Select resistant cultivars where possible.
Fireblight *Erwinia amylovora* A serious disease of pears, apples, hawthorns, pyracantha and other related pome-like fruits.	Slime exuded from shoots that die back to give burnt appearance. Flowers and leaves shrivel. Cultivars that flower late are most susceptible.	Report infections to DEFRA if outbreak is in an exclusion zone. Cut out infected branches into healthy wood and destroy. Sterilise tools between cuts. Reduce planting of susceptible species, particularly in hedges around apple and pear orchards.

VIRUS DISEASE	SYMPTOMS	TREATMENT
Apple Mosaic Virus Spread is slow, probably in sap during propagation.	Irregular yellowish mottles and patterns on leaves.	Certificated virus-free stock.
Arabis Mosaic Virus In strawberry, raspberry, cherry and some ornamental plants. Spread by free-living nematodes.	Symptoms vary by species affected, but slowly spreading patches of stunted plants are seen.	Certificated stock. Do not replant on known eelworm infected sites. Approved chemical soil sterilisation treatments to control eelworms.
Dahlia Mosaic Virus Aphid transmitted virus.	Vein banding on leaves and in some cases overall plant stunting.	Approved systemic insecticides during the propagation stage. Rogue obviously infected stock.
Plum Pox Virus (Sharka) Serious in plums, some other fruiting and ornamental prunus. Primary spread is by aphids.	Leaf symptoms vary, but pale green diffuse spots are common. Fruiting plums show various skin colour patterns and necrosis. In particularly sensitive cultivars, affected fruit is useless.	Plant virus-tested and -free stock. Grub and destroy infected trees. Systemic aphicides in the nursery. These may also help reduce spread in the orchard.
Tulip Breaking Virus Particularly on the petals of pink, purple and red flowered cultivars. Aphid-transmitted virus.	White and yellow striping in the flowers, which can look unsightly if a percentage of plants are infected.	Remove affected plants.
Tobacco Necrosis Virus in Tulips Transmitted by the soil-inhabiting fungus, *Olpidium brassicae*.	Necrotic areas in all parts of the plant, which may be killed.	Remove affected plants as soon as possible.

OTHER PROBLEMS	SYMPTOMS	TREATMENT
Specific Replant Effects A wide range of species can be affected. Commonly seen in apples, roses and pansies. It is suspected that a number of organisms are involved, attacking newly established plants, which established plants can tolerate.	Replanting the same or closely related species on the same site results in poor growth over a number of years.	Treatment depends on the species grown. Avoid replanting with the same or closely related species. Replant with container plants in sterilised compost, keeping the root ball intact (useful for pansies). Use fresh planting compost in the planting pits. Approved chemical soil sterilisation (with some fruit crops) and use partially resistant rootstocks.
Algae	Green algae can be a problem growing on the surface of some plants, in ponds and on paths (causing slippery conditions).	Physical removal and use of grit on paths. Algicides may also be applied to label recommendations on paths. Pond water quality will influence the growth of algae; check nutrient levels and site factors that would affect algae proliferation.
Ivy *Hedera* sp.	On walls and in trees. There are varying opinions on its effect on these. It can provide useful habitats for wildlife and protect surfaces, although in some cases it can smother trees and damage walls.	Each case should be looked at separately. Severing ivy from its root source will not necessarily stop its growth on walls. If the decision is taken to control it on walls, all growth should be removed.
Mistletoe *Viscum album* is the species encountered in Britain.	Semi-parasitic on trees, but not usually causing weakening of growth.	Leave the mistletoe in situ.
Mineral Nutrient Disorders	There are many symptoms of nutrient disorder, caused either by direct excess or deficiency in the soil, by physical soil conditions, pH or attack by pests or pathogens to the plant.	Investigate the cause of the disorder; it may be that a pest or disease organism is damaging the roots. In some cases, soil and/or leaf analysis should be carried out to determine nutrient levels in the soil and plant.
Drought This may be due to such factors as inadequate irrigation, exposure to wind and high temperatures, and soil texture.	Symptoms of wilting can be rapid in newly planted soft material. Trees can suffer less obvious but serious effects over a longer period.	Irrigation of plants prior to and immediately after planting. Organic matter in the soil and soil mulches. Adequate weed control and shelter from wind.

(Continued . . .)

TABLE 13: PESTS, DISEASES AND DISORDERS OF OUTDOOR PLANTS (CONTINUED)

OTHER PROBLEMS	SYMPTOMS	TREATMENT
Waterlogging Caused by poor soil structure, inadequate drainage, spring lines and over watering.	Growth will cease, and the leaves will show various nutrient deficiency symptoms, and may die. Roots will die and trees will become poorly anchored.	Grow plants adapted to wet ground. Improve drainage prior to planting and if possible within the planted site. Do not use excessive irrigation, and insure that irrigation systems are functioning correctly.
Frost	Early-flowering plants such as camellias can show obvious flower-browning and fruit crops may fail to set fruit. Trunks of trees exposed to low night temperatures can split, if subsequent temperature rise is rapid on their eastern sides. Frost-heave of newly planted material can be a problem. Tender plants can blacken and die.	Careful selection of species in relation to local climatic conditions. Timing of planting and provision of temporary frost screens. Increase drainage of cold air through the site.
Wind Water loss through excess transpiration can lead to tissue damage to stems and leaves. Excessive movement in young trees can damage root systems (but some movement improves anchorage).	Wilting, scorching and death of foliage and branches of trees on the windward side. Large branches fall from trees and trees may topple. Wind-rocking of trees and shrubs, which then grow poorly. New plantings of soft leafy species wilt and leaves tatter.	Select wind-tolerant species. Plant shelter hedges, preferably well in advance of other major plantings. Artificial windbreaks can be used as temporary screens, while establishing living shelter breaks.
Pollution This may be caused by a wide range of gaseous materials in the atmosphere (industrial, home pollutants, vehicles) or acid rain. Salt applied to road surfaces, or salt-laden winds. Herbicides applied deliberately to plants, or from nearby drift, can cause problems.	Directional pollution may show clear symptoms on one side of plants, such as leaf scorch. Other less obvious reduction in growth may be difficult to relate to pollutants. Leaves covered in dust or soot in city areas will function less efficiently. If herbicides have been sprayed on plants or nearby, then chlorosis, necrosis or leaf/stem distortion may be seen.	Select pollution-tolerant species. These may also screen less tolerant ones. Plant away from surfaces likely to receive roadside pollutants. Avoid herbicide drift, using low-drift nozzles and controlled droplet application techniques where possible.

TABLE 13: PESTS, DISEASES AND DISORDERS OF GLASSHOUSE PLANTS

PEST	SYMPTOM	TREATMENT
Root-eating/Soil-inhabiting		
Root Aphids Varied aphid species attack plant roots. Live on young roots near soil surface and on edge of pots. Covered with white wool or meal.	Plant droops. Shoots die back.	Suitable insecticidal contact drench to compost. Wash pest and compost off roots and repot in sterilised compost, or take cuttings and dispose of plant.
Root Mealy Bugs *Falcifer* is the most widespread and troublesome. Similar to root aphids, covered in wax.	As for root aphids.	As for root aphids.
Sciarid Flies and larvae Tiny grey-black flies. Larvae approx 3mm/⅛in long thrive in moist compost where they appear as small white maggots with black heads.	Root damage. Slowed growth. Death of seedlings and soft cuttings.	Water less frequently. Remove dead leaves from soil surface. † Parasitic nematode (microscopic round worm) as a soil drench up to 4 times during growing season or suitable insecticidal contact drench.
Slugs and Snails Many species of *Mollusca: Gastropoda*, e.g. *Arion hortensis* (garden slug) and *Helix aspersa* (garden snail).	Chewed foliage/stems/flowers. Silvery trails.	Slug bait and contact sprays.
Vine Weevils *Otiorhynchus sulcatus* Curved, creamy white, plump larvae with brown heads, over 1cm/½in long, found feeding among roots. Beetle-like adults found on foliage.	Wilting. Chewed roots. Leaf margins eaten by adults.	Squash the adults which are seen only at night † Parasitic nematode (microscopic round worm), applied as above.
Foliage-eating		
Aphids *Homoptera: Aphididae* Green- or Blackfly – (?) May also be yellow or pink.	Honeydew and sooty mould. Stunted, distorted growth.	Remove small infestations with moist cotton wool. Horticultural soap. † *Chrysoperla carnea* (lacewing); *Aphidoletes aphidimyza; Aphidius matricariae*, or suitable contact insecticide.
Caterpillars Many sp. *Lepidoptera*, e.g. *Cydia nigricana* (pea moth) or *Lacanobia oleracea* (tomato moth)	Uneven cuts on leaves. Excreta on foliage. Leaves tightly webbed together with silk.	Destroy caterpillars by hand. † Spray with *Bacillus thuringiensis* or suitable contact insecticide.

† Biological Control

TABLE 13 349

TABLE 13: PESTS, DISEASES AND DISORDERS OF GLASSHOUSE PLANTS (CONTINUED)

PEST	SYMPTOM	TREATMENT
Glasshouse Leafhoppers *Hauptidia maroccana* Approx. 3mm/⅛in long with slender, tapering body. Found on underside of leaves. Jump and fly from leaf to leaf when disturbed.	Coarse white mottling on upper surface of leaves. Underside of leaves covered with moulted skins.	Remove leaves covered in eggs, although difficult to see. Suitable contact insecticide.
Leaf Miners Number of species, e.g. *Phytomyza ilicis* (Holly Leaf Miner) and *Cerodontha iridis* (Iris Leaf Miner) Larvae of fly, moth and beetle species. Visible in leaf mines as small grubs approx. 3mm/⅛in long.	Irregular blotches on leaves. Wiggly brown or white lines on foliage.	Remove and destroy mined leaves † *Dacnusa sibirica*; *Diglyphus isaea* or suitable systemic insecticide.
Mealy Bugs Many species *Hemiptera: Pseudococcidae*, e.g. *Pseudococcus viburni* (Glasshouse Mealybug) and *Trionymus diminutus* (Phormium Mealybug) Small insects covered in white waxy secretion found on growing points and leaf joints.	Similar to aphid infestation (see above).	Horticultural soap † *Cryptolaemus montrouzieri* (Black Ladybird) if temperatures over 21°C or suitable contact or systemic insecticide.
Scale Insects Many species *Hemiptera: Coccoidea*, e.g. *Coccus hesperidum* (soft scale) or *Parthenolecanium corni* (brown scale) Tiny whitish, yellowish, or brown scale-like insects on stems/leaves	Similar to aphid infestation (see above). Honeydew, yellowing and defoliation.	Remove adult scales with moist cotton wool. Adult scales resistant to most chemicals. Kill young scales with horticultural soap. Suitable systemic insecticide.
Two-Spotted or Red Spider Mites *Tetranychus urticae* (Glasshouse Red Spider Mite) Yellowish-green with two distinct spots on the front of the body during the summer. Turn orange-red prior to hibernation.	Fine yellow speckles on foliage. Shrivelled and dead leaves. Silken threads over plant in severe cases.	Keep humidity high. Dampen undersides of foliage † *Phytoseiulus persimilis* or suitable systemic insecticide.
Western Flower Thrips *Frankliniella occidentalis* Adults are approx. 1mm/¹⁄₁₆in long and grey/yellow-brown in colour Can seriously affect flowering pot plants such as *Streptocarpus*, and crops such as cucumbers.	Silvering and mottling of foliage and flowers. Stunted growth in severe cases. Distortion of fruit.	Remove and destroy faded flowers containing thrips. Resistant to most chemicals. † *Amblyseius cucumeris*; *Amblyseius barkeri*; anthocorid bugs when above 20°C.
Whiteflies Many species, *Hemiptera: Aleyrodidae*, e.g. *Trialeurodes vaporariorum* (Glasshouse Whitefly) or *Aleurotrachelus jelinekii* (Viburnum Whitefly) Egg-laying adults are tiny, white, moth-like insects, found on youngest foliage. Immature, scale-like stages found on older foliage. Serious pest for most glasshouse plants.	Honeydew and sooty mould. Yellowing and defoliation in severe cases.	Resistant to most insecticides. Horticultural soap † *Encarsia formosa* (parasitic wasp) once daytime temperatures are over 15°C.

DISEASE	SYMPTOM	TREATMENT
Black Leg *Pythium* species, Pelargonium Black Leg Soil-borne fungi. Frequent problem with Pelargoniums	Blackening on the stem of a cutting, causing it to shrivel and die.	Use pots free of fungal spores (see under Damping Off). Use only sterilised compost. Use clean water. Suitable fungicide.
Damping Off Caused by soil- and water-borne fungi.	Young seedlings collapse and die at soil level.	Ensure good hygiene. Use sterilised compost for seed sowing. Wash all containers before use in a proprietary disinfectant to kill off any fungal spores, and rinse well afterwards. Water in seed with a suitable fungicide. Do not sow seed too thickly and prick out when seed leaves are fully expanded.
Downy Mildew Many species *Peronosporaceae* Caused by a variety of fungal parasites. Favours humid conditions.	Yellowish patches on leave.s Whitish mould on underside.	Remove infected foliage. Improve air circulation around plant. Avoid splashing leaves with water. Suitable fungicide.
Grey Mould *Botrytis* Thrives in damp conditions.	Fluffy grey fungal growth. Water-soaked foliage. Pale spotting on flowers.	Remove infected plant material and debris. Improve air circulation around plant. Avoid splashing foliage in humid conditions. Suitable fungicide.

† Biological Control

(Continued . . .)

TABLE 13: PESTS, DISEASES AND DISORDERS OF GLASSHOUSE PLANTS (CONTINUED)		
DISEASE	SYMPTOM	TREATMENT
Oedema Caused by the plant taking up more water from its roots than it can lose through its leaves by transpiration.	Warty growths on the stem and underside of leaves.	Reduce watering. Increase spacing. Improve ventilation. Do *not* remove leaves as this will slow down water loss.
Powdery Mildew . Many species *Erysiphaceae* Spread by spores in leaf debris and in the air.	Powdery white coating on leaves and stems Yellowing and defoliation.	Remove infected leaves and stems. Keep roots more moist. Improve air circulation around plant. Suitable fungicide.
Rust *Basidiomycete* fungi of the order *Uredinales* Variable disease which can affect many different plants.	Pale yellow spots on leaves. Orange or brown spots on the underside of leaves. Stunted and distorted growth.	Remove infected leaves. Improve air circulation around plant. Suitable fungicide.
Sooty Mould Various non pathogenic fungi, especially species of *Cladosporium,* grow on contaminated surfaces and produce sooty deposits. Grows on honeydew excreted by sap-sucking insects such as aphids, whitefly, scale insects and mealy bugs.	Black sooty deposits on leaves. Reduction in plant vigour in severe cases.	Control the insect pest, and then remove mould with a moistened sponge.
Tobacco Mosaic Virus Affects a wide range of plants in many plant families. Spread by pests such as aphids.	Leaf mottling and distortion. Weak, stunted growth.	Destroy infected plants. Control virus-spreading pests.
Tomato Mosaic Virus	As for tobacco mosaic virus.	As for tobacco mosaic virus.

† Biological Control

TABLE 13 351

TABLE 13: ANIMAL PEST CONTROL

Compared to insect pests, the control of animal pests is often an emotive issue. This is especially common when controlling animal pests in parks and gardens open to the public. Careful consideration must be taken where the general public may not see these animals as pests, but as popular local wildlife. Control measures may be best carried out in areas away from public activity or during periods when visitor numbers are low.

Whatever options are chosen, it is easier to communicate with the public on pest control issues when they are made aware of the conservation or ecological problems the pest species may brings. Interpretation and education programmes can play an important role in this. Not only can the pest species be protected by law, but the control itself can be heavily licensed and controlled.

All control measures must comply with licensing regulations where relevant and be as humane as possible. Often, to be effective, it is a job best carried out by skilled and experienced staff or contractors. If traps form part of the control programme, these must be inspected on a regular basis and be of a type and located where other animals and humans are not put at risk.

If poisoning is carried out there is a chance that the animal may die in a public location, so regular checks and disposal will be necessary.

CANADA GEESE
Branta canadensis
Introduced from North America in 1665

Prefered habitat Lakes, ponds and grassland

Food source Geese are largely herbivorous, grazing on grassland or in water. Often fed by humans.

Life cycle Can live up to 30 years, breeding from 2–3 years. Females lay up to nine eggs in March/April, nesting singly or in small groups near water bodies with islands or similar secure sites. Adults moult after breeding for 35–40 days in June/July and are flightless, staying in water to avoid predators. Autumn–winter spent on grazing sites.

Types of damage
Vegetation damage Grazing damage around lawns and lakes and oxygenating plants in water bodies.
Droppings Unsightly and slippery on lawns, grassland and paths with possible health risks if ingested. Can upset nutrient levels in water bodies, especially where water circulation is poor.
Physical damage Large numbers can cause soil erosion on banks.
Aggression Towards humans, animals and other waterfowl during breeding season.

Extent of damage Dependent on numbers, nature and size of site. High on smaller formal sites, low on larger informal sites.

Management options Population monitoring needed first and coordination with neighbouring landowners, as control techniques used in isolation are unlikely to be effective. Control methods are aimed at reducing the numbers, rather than complete exclusion of geese from a site, as this is usually impossible to achieve. Control methods may be less effective the smaller the population.

Site-based management This will be restricted by the need to preserve historic features, planting layouts, etc.
• Exclusion from islands using fencing and increased vegetation cover to stop flight access.
• Reduce access and visibility of grazing sites to water bodies using fencing.
• Reduce public feeding of geese by controlling access to public areas and through interpretation on nature conservation and aquatic ecology.
• Scaring of geese is widely used in agriculture, but can be disturbing to visitors and local residents.

Population-based management
• Translocation to another site. Used in the past, but no longer encouraged. Other geese may then colonise the site. Requires a licence.
• Egg-pricking, oiling or boiling, killing the embryos before the eggs can hatch. Very effective in the long term. Requires a licence.
• Culling. Shooting difficult on most sites. Can be rounded up for humane culling during the moult when they are unable to fly. Requires a licence during the close season, Feb–Aug.

Licensing of control operations Protected as wild birds under the Wildlife & Countryside Act, 1981. Licences for culling in the close season, egg-pricking or translocation of Canada Geese are issued by Defra for agricultural sites and by the Office of the Deputy Prime Minister (ODPM) for other sites.

Additional effects of control measures
• Can increase numbers and diversity of other waterfowl.
• Can help improve water quality.

GREY SQUIRREL
Sciurus carolinensis
Introduced from North America in the 19th century as 'an aesthetic addition to the fauna of the British countryside'.

Preferred habitat Mature and semi-mature broadleaved and mixed woodlands and copses. Can survive in any location with trees and shrub cover, even in suburban areas. Occurs throughout mainland Britain in the South, Midlands and Wales, and moving north. In Scotland ranges between Glasgow and Edinburgh.

Food source Grey squirrels are omnivorous. Their main diet is nuts and berries but they will eat a variety of things, including birds' eggs.

Life cycle Living in grass-lined 'dreys' high up in trees, females have an average of three young twice a year. Disease and predators do not control population numbers, but the supply of winter foods does.

Types of damage
Plant damage Bark stripping, shoot damage and unearthing and damage to bulbs and corms.
Wildlife damage Grey squirrels are omnivorous and will eat birds' eggs. They can kill rats, rabbits, leverets, stoats, nesting birds, hatchlings, grey and red squirrels, but this is very occasional.
Aggression If they feel threatened or trapped they will bite or scratch.
Buildings Nesting in buildings, particularly attics, chewing woodwork and cables. A fire hazard and source of flea/tick infestation.

Extent of damage Bark stripping rarely kills trees but disfigures growth. It is linked to social behaviour and occurs May–September. Shoot damage occurs in the spring, is linked to feeding, and may disfigure young trees. Bulb and corm damage occurs but not on a large scale. Wildlife damage and aggression is difficult to quantify and is only likely to occur if populations are high or food is scarce. Damage to buildings is relative to any lack rodent protection.

Management options Control measures will be more effective if they are continuous throughout the year, or at least throughout the damage danger period (April–July) and are repeated annually. One-off measures are unlikely to have much impact. Control measures over a wider area will be more effective. Collaborating with neighbours with yield better results.
• Cage trapping using bait. A very effective form of control. Trapped animals cannot be released by law so must be humanely killed.
• Tunnel trapping. An instant kill method. A tunnel is used to prevent other animals entering it.
• Poisoning, using bait treated with Warfarin dispensed from hoppers accessible by grey squirrels only. Most squirrels die in their drey after a week.
• Shooting. Most effective during winter months when leaf cover is reduced. Safety issues and disturbance to public and local residents limit its applications.
• Drey-poking with long, lightweight poles to disrupt or destroy the drey.
• Repellents. These have had limited success in the past, but there are currently no approved chemicals available.
• Physical barriers do not provide plants any protection from grey squirrels.

Licensing of control operations
Grey squirrels are classified as vermin so no special licensing is required to carry out control and management operations. Red squirrels are protected by the Wildlife & Countryside Act 1981 and any form of control is both illegal and unnecessary.

Additional effects of control measures
Squirrels have mobile populations and can repopulate cleared areas in a matter of weeks in summer months.

(Continued ...)

TABLE 13: ANIMAL PEST CONTROL (CONTINUED)

RABBITS

Oryctolagus cuniculus
Introduced by the Normans in the 12th century; originally from the western Mediterranean.

Preferred habitat Anywhere where they can burrow, usually close to a food supply. They are unlikely to be found above the tree-line, in damp or coniferous woodland.

Food source Rabbits are herbivorous. They eat a wide range of plant material including grass, cereals, root vegetables, bark and soft growing shoots.

Life cycle The breeding season is from January to August. Healthy females can produce one litter of 3–7 young per month during the season. The young appear at the burrow entrance at 18 days and are weaned at 21–25 days. Bucks are able to mate at 4 months, does at 3.5 months. Lifespan is not often more than 3 years. Over 90 per cent die in their first year of life.

Types of damage
Warrens The underground system of burrows which rabbits excavate to live and breed in.
Scrapes Shallow areas of dug soil, usually no more than a few centimetres across and 4cm or so deep.
Ring-barking The nibbling of bark around the base of trees and shrubs.
Crop destruction The consumption of vegetation – crops, grass, vegetables, flowers, etc.

Extent of damage Warrens can be deep and extensive. They are disfiguring to landscapes and can be damaging to areas with sensitive archaeology. In bad cases the tunnels can lead to a general collapse at the surface.
Scrapes are less of a problem, but if populations are high these can be disfiguring, especially on fine grass and lawns.
Ring-barking is a major problem. Rabbits nibble through the bark and feed on the vascular area. Trees and shrubs are often completely ring-barked and die. Destruction of agricultural and horticultural crops is a major concern. Plants are uprooted and shoots and roots are chewed.

Management options
• Trapping using lethal and non-lethal traps. Rabbits can be released elsewhere with the landowner's consent.
• Gassing. Phostoxin tablets are introduced into burrows which are then sealed up. Phosphine gas moves along the tunnel killing any rabbits in its path. Follow-up treatments need to be carried out on any new burrows.
• Shooting. Effective for keeping populations low if carried out regularly, whether day or night lamp shooting. Safety issues and disturbance to public and local residents limit its applications.
• Ferreting. Drives rabbits out of warrens for capture and culling. Will keep populations low if carried out regularly.
• Repellents. A number are available, including Renardine, and discourage rabbits by smell. They are painted on woody plants, are temporary and less effective after heavy rainfall.
• Fencing. Highly successful in long-term protection of areas. The fencing needs to be continuous, sufficiently tall and continue outwards underground slightly to prevent rabbits burrowing under.
• Individual guards can be fixed around newly planted trees and shrubs where fencing whole areas is not practicable.

Licensing of control operations
Rabbits are classified both as ground game (Ground Game Act 1880) and vermin (Pests Act 1954). No special licensing is required to carry out control and management operations and there is no close season or restriction on selling rabbits. Phostoxin is controlled by the Poisons Act 1972.

Additional effects of control measures
Despite their problems, rabbits are efficient grazers, often producing ecologically interesting grassland. In areas where having grassland is essential for landscape or archaeological reasons, some form of vegetation management will have to be introduced.

DEER

There are five species of deer commonly found over much of the UK:
Red Deer (*Cervus elaphus*) Native to the British Isles.
Fallow Deer (*Dama dama*) Possibly introduced by the Romans; certainly by the Normans.
Roe Deer (*Capreolus capreolus*) Native to the British Isles.
Three species are less common and (presently) more restricted in distribution:
Sika Deer (*Cervus Nippon*) Introduced in several locations mainly between 1860 and 1920.
Muntjac (*Muntiacus reevesii*) Introduced originally to Woburn Park in the early 20th century.

Chinese Water Deer (*Hydropotes inermis*) First kept at London Zoo in 1873, but introduced into Woburn Park in early 1900s and then several other parks up to the mid 1950s.

Preferred habitat Woodland and woodland edge where they can easily hide, but all species will venture into the open to feed and in some areas will enter accessible gardens. Chinese Water Deer, as the name suggests, can be found in reed beds as well as broadleaved woodland.

Food source All deer are herbivorous. They eat a wide range of plant material including grass, cereals, leaves, shoots, flowers and occasionally bark of many plants including trees and shrubs. Seeds and fungi may also be eaten.

Life cycle Life cycles vary with species but generally the breeding (rutting) seasons range from mid July to December. Females (does or hinds) produce one (very occasionally two) young (fawns) mostly between May and June, but occasionally as late as November. Muntjac breed throughout the year and young can be produced in any month. The young can walk almost immediately and are usually weaned by late autumn/winter. Males (stags or bucks) are able to mate after first year (but may not get opportunity until older), females at between 1 year 3 months and 3 years (depending on environment). Lifespan may be up to 20 years. During the mating season dominant males fight to maintain a harem of females; only dominant males breed.

Types of damage
Crop destruction Consumption of vegetation: crops, grass, leaves, flowers, etc.
Ring-barking Nibbling of bark around trunks of trees and shrubs. This may be at low level or higher, sometimes only affecting individual branches.
Fraying Deer grow new antlers every year and when these are fully formed they rub them up and down on the trunks of trees to remove the (now redundant) layer of skin ('velvet') which supplied nutrient to the growing antlers. This can do considerable damage to trees.

Extent of damage In gardens deer will often selectively eat whole beds of flowers (roses are often particularly favoured), leaving the rest of the shrub plant undamaged, or completely eat particular plants, leaving those surrounding untouched. Ring-barking can be a major problem particularly to young trees, although less so to mature trees. It can be quite extensive in woodlands/forest plantations and where there are high concentrations of deer. Destruction of agricultural and horticultural crops is a major concern in some areas.

Management options Deer management is a highly specialised subject and because they may move quite considerable distances often requires the co-operation of several adjacent landowners. It is highly recommended that expert advice be sought before embarking on management, but options include:
• Shooting. The shooting of deer is tightly regulated and should only be undertaken by trained professionals.
• Repellents. A number are commercially available, and discourage deer by smell. They are painted on woody plants or plant supports, are temporary and less effective after heavy rainfall. A number of different materials have also been suggested, but availability and success rates seem to differ substantially. These include hair (human and dog), lion dung, mothballs, scented soap and human urine.
• Fencing. Highly successful for the long-term protection of areas. However, deer fencing may be visually obtrusive and can be expensive as it needs to be continuous, sufficiently robust and tall – deer are remarkable jumpers and 2m high is recommended for Red Deer. Fencing needs to be maintained in good condition to remain effective.
• Individual guards can be fixed around newly planted trees, especially in parkland. These can be individually expensive but are very effective, long-lasting (and can be combined with rabbit guards) and can be ornamental. Smaller-scale individual guards may also be useful to protect particularly susceptible plants in gardens where fencing whole areas is not practical.

Licensing of control operations Deer are covered by the Game Licences Act 1860 and the Deer Act 1991. Statutory close seasons exist for all species which differ between species and between males and females. Night shooting is not permitted and the type of weapon that can be used is also regulated. Trapping, snares, nets and poisoning are all prohibited.

Additional effects of control measures
Deer are often an important element in the management of large landscapes and parklands and herds are managed rather than controlled. They are also a highly popular visitor attraction in many locations. Although they can be a major pest is agriculture they are generally just a nuisance in gardens and deterrent; protection rather than control are sufficient.

TABLE 13 353

TABLE 13: ANIMAL PEST CONTROL (CONTINUED)

MOLES
Talpa europaea
British native species

Preferred habitat Moles can be found where there is sufficient depth of soil for tunnel construction. They are believed to be originally inhabitants of deciduous woodland, but thrive in arable and pastoral landscapes. They are uncommon in coniferous forests, moorland and sand-dune systems.

Food source Earthworms, insects larvae and mollusca.

Life cycle Males and females are solitary for most of the year. In the breeding season males tunnel over large areas in search of females. Litters of 3–4 are born in the spring. The young leave their mother's range at 5–6 weeks. Dispersal takes place above ground. The young become sexually mature in the following spring. Most moles live to more than 3 years, some up to 6 years.

Types of Damage
Mole hills Conical piles of soil, usually with no openings, pushed up from underground tunnels up to 1m deep.
Surface tunnels Slightly raised ridges with a tunnel immediately below.
Reduction of worm population Moles feed on insect larvae and mollusca but their principle prey are earthworms.

Extent of damage Moles excavate extensive tunnel systems to trap soil invertebrates. The spoil is brought to the surface as molehills. These can be extensive and disfiguring, especially in lawn areas. Surface tunnels, found when moles are colonising areas or feeding in newly cultivated fields, can also disfigure lawns. Worms are important in nutrient recycling, aeration and drainage in soil; severe reductions will be detrimental to soil health. However, there is very little evidence to show how moles affect worm populations. 'Casting' worms are sometimes controlled in lawns and sportsfields any way.

Management options
Trapping. All mole traps are lethal. The successful positioning and setting of traps requires considerable expertise.
Gassing. Phostoxin tablets are introduced into regularly used tunnels which are then sealed up. Phosphine gas moves along the tunnel killing any mole in its path. Follow-up treatments need to be carried out on any new molehills.
Poisoning. Strychnine-injected worms cause instant death when eaten.
Removal of food source. Extremely difficult. Control of earthworms can lead to problems with soil drainage and aeration.

Licensing of control operations
No special licensing is required to carry out control and management operations on moles. Phostoxin and Strychnine are controlled under the Poisons Act 1972. Strychnine can only be used in areas approved by Defra.

Additional effects of control measures
Control of moles has no detrimental effects; however, control of their food source can lead to soil structure problem. Removal of a mole from its territory is only likely to provide temporary relief before another moves in. Generally there are no ecological problems with mole control, but it is believed that old molehills may be the nucleus for anthills.

BADGERS
Meles meles
British native species. The inclusion of badgers here does not indicate that the authors consider them to be a pest species generally, but acknowledges the fact that they can, in certain instances, be a damaging nuisance. Evidence of their activities are more obvious and can cause significant problems in the historic environment. They also have a history of persecution, and it is this, rather than their rarity on a national scale, that has led to their extensive legal protection.

Preferred habitat Badgers are widespread and common in suitable habitats in Britain, but scarce in some upland and wetland areas. Badgers live in social groups, sometimes called clans. These are territorial.

Food source Badgers are omnivorous, feeding on earthworms, insects, fruits and roots, also carrion and crops.

Life cycle Badgers live in social groups of 4–12 adults. 1–2 female badgers per group breeds. Litters of 2–3 cubs are usually born in February. Around one-fifth of adults die each year, especially in road traffic accidents. Occasionally they can live to 14 years old.

Types of damage
• Setts. These are the tunnel systems badgers dig to live and breed in. There can be up to four diferent types of sett depending on the group.
• Feeding damage. Earthworms are particularly favoured. Insects, fruits and roots, also carrion and crops.

• Latrines. These can be unsightly, and in public access areas may be perceived as a health risk.
• Bovine tuberculosis. In some parts of the country, badgers are widely blamed for the infection of cattle with bovine tuberculosis. Much research has been done on the subject, but the relationship is still poorly understood, and research is continuing. Badgers do carry the disease, but are not seriously affected by it.

Extent of damage Setts can be large and very damaging to the landscape in certain locations, especially to sensitive archaeological sites. Setts are distinguished from tunnels of foxes or rabbits by their size and shape. There are large spoil heaps, often with bedding material, outside active entrances. Feeding damage is usually caused when badgers forage and dig for worms, grubs or nutritious roots and tubers. This may cause considerable damage. Because of their omnivorous appetite other wildlife may suffer. Latrines are unsightly and the smell can be unpleasant. Droppings can carry the parasitic worm *Toxocara* which can cause blindness in children. There is also a theoretical risk of TB, albeit very slight.

Management options If a sett poses a threat to the site, advice from the appropriate licensing authority should be sought as soon as possible. Most management options will require a licence.
• Exclusion. Where the presence of a badger sett is causing damage to a site, or threatening to do so, the main management option may be closure of the sett. This excludes badgers from the problem sett, or parts of it, while allowing them to remain in their territory. Badgers will usually have another sett. Long-established setts may be harder to take mitigating action against. In addition, the damage to the site may already be done. Setts should be monitored routinely.
• Fencing out. Where damage is caused and no sett is present, it may be possible to fence badgers out of susceptible areas. The fence needs to be substantial and sunk into the ground to prevent it being dug under. This may be unacceptable if it deprives the clan of foraging territory.
• Food source removal. If the badgers' food source is another pest species, such as Leatherjackets, control of these may reduce foraging damage. A licence might not be appropriate.
• Latrine removal/covering. If there is concern about a health risk, or latrines are considered intolerable, dung can be removed or covered with soil. A licence is unlikely to be necessary.

Licensing of control operations Badgers are protected under the Protection of Badgers Act 1992. This makes it an offence to kill, injure, capture or cruelly ill-treat a badger, or to interfere with a badger sett. Interference with a sett includes damaging, destroying or obstructing access to a sett, causing a dog to enter a sett, or disturbing a badger when it is occupying a sett. Under Section 10 of the Protection of Badgers Act, licences can be issued to allow otherwise prohibited actions for a number of specific purposes, in particular:
• Defra can issue licences for the purpose of preventing serious damage to land, crops, etc., or any other form of property. This means that if a badger sett is causing damage to property, including scheduled or non-scheduled monuments, listed buildings or historic gardens, a licence application must be made to Defra's National Wildlife Management Team.
• Natural England can issue licences to interfere with badger setts for the purpose of the preservation or archaeological investigation of a monument scheduled under the Ancient Monuments and Archaeological Areas Act 1979. This means that where an operation to preserve or investigate a scheduled monument is likely to result in interference or disturbance to a badger sett, a licence application must be made to Natural England's Licensing Section.
If it is unclear whether a proposed operation requires a licence or not, which licensing authority is responsible, or if the operation appears unlicensable, advice should be sought directly from Natural England or Defra's Wildlife Management Team. The point at which work close to a sett constitutes disturbance to the sett or badgers occupying it is not legally defined. In practice the acceptable distance is likely to depend on the work being carried out. Natural England has provided the following guidelines for developers:
• Light work such as hand digging or scrub clearance within 10m of a sett entrance usually requires a licence.
• Between 10m and 20m from the nearest sett entrance use of hand tools such as chainsaws and brush cutters does not require a licence, provided no digging is involved. Use of machinery would require a licence.
• Use of heavy machinery such as tracked vehicles would require a licence for operations within 30m of a sett entrance.
Conditions attached to the licence will determine what can be done, taking due regard for the animals' welfare, and the breeding season. With all licensed operations there is a presumption in favour of avoiding the breeding season (November to June) if at all possible.

Additional effects of control operations There should be no detrimental side effects from properly licensed control measures.

TABLE 14: GUIDE TO SHRUB PRUNING RELATED TO AGE AND SIZE

Group 1
Shrubs often tree-like or large, 5m
Long-lived 50 years +
Pruning regimes:
R occasional or periodic stooling back or hard pruning
U limited or no normal pruning
Typical examples of genera as a guide only

Arbutus U E
Aronia R D
Buxus R E
Camellia U E
Corylus R D
Cotinus R D
Cotoneaster R D/E
Eucalyptus R E
Fatsia U E
Hippophoe U D
Ilex U E
Ligustrum R E
Magnolia U D/E
Osmanthus R E
Osmaria R E
Prunus (Laurels) R E
Rhododendron U D/E*
Rhus R E
Rosa see separate section
Salix R D
Sambucus R D
Sorbaria R D
Syringa U D
Tamarix U E
Viburnum R D/E

* See also Rhododendrons under overgrown shrubberies and some others in the above genera.

Group 2
Shrubs usually short- to medium-lived,
15–25 years
Often bushy and medium height, 2–3m.
Examples here require different pruning regimes:
R regular pruning/cutting back
O some occasional or periodic thinning and shaping
Cl regular clipping back
This could be a huge list so only the more familiar genera are selected.

Abelia O E
Buddleia R D
Calluna/Erica R Cl E
Chaenomeles R D
Chimonanthus O D
Cytisus R Cl E
Deutzia R D
Escallonia O E
Forsythia R D
Hebe O Cl E
Hibiscus O D
Hypericum R D/E
Hydrangea R D
Indigofera R D
Kolkwitzia O D
Ligustrum O E
Lonicera R D
Olearia O Cl E
Philadelphus R D
Potentilla R Cl D
Ribes R D
Rosa see separate section
Salix (shrubby) R D
Spiraea R D
Weigela R D

Group 3
Short-lived and subshrubs, 5–10 years
Usually dwarf and fast-growing.
Best pruned back in early spring to maintain vigour and compact form. Extent of pruning or clipping depends upon the species and over-wintering factor.

Ballota E
Calluna/Erica E
Caryopteris D
Ceratostigma D
Fuchsia D Also in Group 2
Helichrysum E
Lavandula E
Phlomis E
Rosmarinus E
Santolina E
Brachyglottis (Senecio) E
Teucrium E

D Deciduous. E Evergreen.

Useful contacts

Government departments and agencies

British Standards
389 Chiswick High Road
London W4 4AL
Tel.: 020 8996 9001
Fax: 020 8996 7001
Email: cservices@bsi-global.com
Website: www.bsi-global.com

CABE – Commission for Architecture and the Built Environment and CABE Space
1 Kemble Street
London WC2B 4AN
Tel.: 020 7070 6700
Fax: 020 7070 6777
Email: enquiries@cabe.org.uk
Websites: www.cabe.org.uk and www.cabespace.org.uk

Cadw – Welsh Historic Monuments
Cathays Park
Cardiff CF10 3NQ
Tel.: 029 2050 0200
Fax: 029 2082 6375
Email: cadw@Wales.gsi.gov.uk
Website: www.cadw.wales.gov.uk

Cyngor Cefn Gwlad Cymru-Countryside Council for Wales
Maes y Ffynnon, Ffordd Penrhos
Bangor, Gwynedd LL57 2DN
Tel.: 01248 385 500
Fax 01248 355782
Email: enquiries@ccw.gov.uk
Website: www.ccw.gov.uk

Department of Communities and Local Government (DCLG)
Eland House, Bressenden Place
London SW1E 5DU
Tel.: 020 7944 4400
Fax: 020 7944 4101
Email: contactus@communities.gsi.gov.uk
Website: www.communities.gov.uk

Department for Culture Media and Sport (DCMS)
2–4 Cockspur Street
London SW1Y 5DH
Tel.: 020 7211 6200
Email: enquiries@culture.gov.uk
Website: www.culture.gov.uk

Department for Environment Food and Rural Affairs (Defra)
Nobel House, 17 Smith Square
London SW1P 3JR
Tel.: 020 7238 6000
Email: helpline@defra.gsi.gov.uk
Website: www.defra.gov.uk

English Heritage

North East Region
Bessie Surtees House, 41–44 Sandhill
Newcastle upon Tyne NE1 3JF
Tel.: 0191 261 1585

London Region
1 Waterhouse Square, 138–142 Holborn
London EC1 2ST
Tel.: 020 7973 3000

North West Region
Canada House, 3 Chepstow Street
Manchester M1 5FW
Tel.: 0161 242 1400

East of England Region
Brooklands, 24 Brooklands Avenue
Cambridge CB2 8BU
Tel.: 01223 582700

Yorkshire and the Humber Region
37 Tanner Row
York YO1 6WP
Tel.: 01904 601901

South West Region
29 Queen Square
Bristol BS1 4ND
Tel.: 0117 975 0700

East Midlands Region
44 Derngate
Northampton NN1 1UH
Tel.: 01604 735400

South East Region
Eastgate Court, 195–205 High Street
Guildford GU1 3EH
Tel.: 01483 252000

West Midlands Region
112 Colmore Row
Birmingham B3 3AG
Tel.: 0121 625 6820
Website: www.english-heritage.org.uk

English Heritage – National Monuments Record Centre (NMRC)
NMR Services
Great Western Village, Kemble Drive
Swindon SN2 2GZ
Tel.: 01793 414600
Fax: 01793 414606
Email: info@rchme.co.uk
To find out whether a building or monument is listed, or a cemetery landscape design is registered; free copies provided of the 'listing description' of up to three buildings within five working days (or next day, for a fee)

Environment Agency Head Offices
Rio House, Waterside Drive
Aztec West, Almondsbury
Bristol BS32 4UD
Tel.: 08708 506506
Email: enquiries@environment-agency.gov.uk
Website: www.environment-agency.gov.uk

Health and Safety Executive (HSE)
Wren House, Hedgerows Business Park
Colchester CM2 5FS
Tel.: 01245 706 211
Website: www.hse.gov.uk

HSE Infoline
Tel.: Infoline 08701 545500
Fax: Infoline 02920 859260
Email: hseinformationservices@natbrit.com

Historic Scotland
Longmore House, Salisbury Place
Edinburgh EH9 1SH
Tel.: 0131 668 8600
Website: www.historic-scotland.gov.uk
For conservation publications and free leaflets tel.: 0131 668 8638

Lantra
Lantra House, Stoneleigh Park
Near Coventry CV8 2LG
Tel.: 024 7669 6996
Fax: 024 7669 6732
Email: connect@lantra.co.uk
Website: www.lantra.co.uk

Met Office
FitzRoy Road
Exeter EX1 3PB
Website: www.met-office.gov.uk/corporate/location/exeter.html

Natural England
Northminster House
Peterborough PE1 1UA
Tel.: 0845 600 3078
Fax: 01733 455103
Email: enquiries@naturalengland.org.uk
Website: www.naturalengland.org.uk

Natural England publications
Website: www.naturalengland.org.uk/publications/default.htm

Scottish Natural Heritage (SNH)
12 Hope Terrace
Edinburgh EH9 2AS
Tel.: 0131 4474784
Fax: 0131 446 2277
Website: www.snh.org.uk

UK Climate Impacts Programme
Oxford University Centre for the Environment
Dyson Perrins Building
South Parks Road
Oxford OX1 3QY
Tel.: +44 (0)1865 285717
Fax: +44 (0)1865 285710
Email: enquiries@ukcip.org.uk
Website: www.ukcip.org.uk/

Other Government climate change websites
www.defra.govuk/environment/climatechange
www.climatechange.gov.uk

Visit Britain
Thames Tower, Black's Road
Hammersmith, London W6 9EL
Tel.: 020 8846 9000
Website: www.tourismtrade.org.uk

Visit Northern Ireland
5 Ardgreenan Place
Belfast BT4 3FY
Tel.: 07868734813
Email: info@visitnorthernireland.com
Website: www.visitnorthernireland.com

Garden, landscape and historic environment organisations

Alpine Garden Society
AGS Centre, Avon Bank
Pershore WR10 3JP
Tel.: +44 (0)1386 554 790
Fax: +44 (0)1386 554 801
Email: ags@alpinegardensociety.net
Website: www.alpinegardensociety.net

Architectural Heritage Fund
Clareville House, 26–27 Oxenden St
London SW1Y 4EL
Tel.: 020 7925 0199
Email: ahf@ahfund.org.uk
Website: www.ahfund.org.uk

Association of Gardens Trusts
70 Cowcross Street
London EC1M 6BP
Tel.: 020 7251 2610
Website: www.gardenstrusts.co.uk

Botanic Gardens Conservation International (BGCI)
Descanso House, 199 Kew Road
Richmond TW9 3BW
Tel.: 020 8332 5953
Fax: 020 8332 5956
Website: www.bgci.org/worldwide/contact

Country Land and Business Association (CLA)
16 Belgrave Square
London SW1X 8PQ
Tel.: 020 7235 0511
Fax: 020 7235 4696
Email: mail@cla.org.uk
Website: www.cla.org.uk

Federation of City Farms and Community Gardens
The Green House, Hereford Street
Bristol BS3 4NA
Tel.: 0117 923 1800
Fax: 0117 923 1900
Website: www.farmgarden.org.uk

National Federation of Cemetery Friends
Ms Gwyneth (Secretary)
Stokes, 42 Chestnut Grove
South Croydon CR2 7 LH
Email: Gwyneth1@btinternet.com
Website: www.cemeteryfriends.org.uk

British Trust for Conservation Volunteers (BTCV)
Sedum House, Mallard Way
Potteric Carr
Doncaster DN4 8DB
Tel.: 01302 388888
Email: information@btcv.org.uk
Website: www2.btcv.org.uk

Garden History Society
70 Cowcross Street
London EC1M 6BP
Tel.: 020 7608 2409
Fax: 020 7490 2974
Website: www.gardenhistorysociety.org.uk

Garden Organic (formerly Henry Doubleday Research Association)
Ryton Organic Gardens
Coventry CV8 3LG
Tel.: 024 7630 3517
Fax: 024 7663 9229
Email: enquiry@hdra.org.uk
Website: www.gardenorganic.org.uk

Hardy Plant Society
Mrs Pam Adams
Little Orchard, Great Comberton
Pershore WR10 3DP
Tel.: 01386 710317
Fax: 01386 710117
E-mail: admin@hardy-plant.org.uk
Website: www.hardy-plant.org.uk

Historic Gardens Foundation
34 River Court, Upper Ground
London SE1 9PE
Tel: 020 7633 9165
Fax: 020 7401 7072
Email: office@historicgardens.org

Historic Houses Association
2 Chester Street
London SW1X 7BB
Tel.: 020 7259 5688
Fax: 020 7259 5590
Email: info@hha.org.uk
Website: www.hha.org.uk

National Gardens Scheme
Hatchlands Park, East Clandon
Guildford GU4 7RT
Tel.: 01483 211535
Fax: 01483 211537
Email: ngs@ngs.org.uk
Website: www.ngs.org.uk

National Council for the Conservation of Parks and Gardens
The Stable Courtyard, RHS Wisley
Wisley GU23 6QP
Tel.: 01483 211465
Fax 01483 212404
Email: info@nccpg.org.uk
Website: www.nccpg.com

Landscape Design Trust
Bank Chambers, 1 London Road
Redhill RH1 1LY
Tel.: 01737 779257
Fax: 01737 778987
Email: info@landscape.co.uk
Website: www.landscape.co.uk

Museum of Garden History
Lambeth Palace Road
London SE1 7LB
Tel.: 020 7401 8865
Fax: 020 7401 8869
Email: info@museumgardenhistory.org
Website: www.museumgardenhistory.org

National Trust
PO Box 39
Warrington WA5 7WD
Tel.: 0870 458 4000
Fax: 020 8466 6824
Email: enquiries@thenationaltrust.org.uk
Website: www.nationaltrust.org.uk

National Trust for Scotland
Wemyss House, 28 Charlotte Square
Edinburgh EH2 4ET
Tel.: 0131 243 9300
Fax: 0131 243 9301
Email: information@nts.org.uk
Website: www.nts.org.uk

Plant Network
Judith Cheney
PlantNetwork Administrator
c/o University Computing Service
New Museums Site, Pembroke Street
Cambridge CB2 3QH
Tel.: 01223 763901
Email: jc151 at cam.ac.uk
Website: www.plantnetwork.org

The Royal Horticultural Society
80 Vincent Square
London SW1P 2PE
Tel.: 0845 260 5000
Email: info@rhs.org.uk
Website: www.rhs.org.uk

The Tree Council
71 Newcomen Street
London SE1 1YT
Tel.: 020 7407 9992
Website: www.treecouncil.org.uk

Tree Advice Trust
Alice Holt Lodge, Wrecclesham
Farnham GU10 4LH
Tel.: 09065 161147
Fax: 01420 22000
Email: admin@treehelp.info
Website: www.treehelp.info

The Royal Forestry Society
102 High Street
Tring HP23 4AF
Tel.: 01442 822029
Fax: 01442 890395
Email: rfshq@rfs.org.uk

The Victorian Society
1 Priory Gardens
London W4 0LT
Tel.: 0208 994 1019
Fax: 020 8995 4895
Email: info@victorian-society.org.uk
Website: www.victorian-society.org.uk

Walled Kitchen Garden Network
Website: admin@walledgardens.net

The Georgian Group
6 Fitzroy Square
London W1T 5DX
Tel.: 087 1750 2936
Email: info@georgiangroup.org.uk
Website: www.georgiangroup.org.uk/docs/home/index.php

20th Century Society
70 Cowcross Street
London EC1M 6EJ
Website: www.c20society.org.uk

SAVE Britain's Heritage
70 Cowcross Street
London EC1M 6EJ
Tel.: 020 7253 3500
Fax: 020 7253 3400
Email: save@btinternet.com
Website: www.savebritainsheritage.org

The Fountain Society
Weathertop, Tower Hill
Dorking RH4 2AP
Email: chairman@fountainsoc.org.uk
Website: www.fountainsoc.org.uk

The Folly Fellowship
Email: outings@follies.org.uk
Website: www.follies.org.uk

Mausolea and Monuments Trust
70 Cowcross Street
London EC1M 6EJ
Tel.: 020 7608 1441
Email: mausolea@btconnect.com
Website: www.mausoleamonuments.org.uk

ICOMOS-UK (International Council on Monuments & Sites UK)
70 Cowcross Street
London EC1M 6EJ
Tel.: 020 7566 0031
Fax: 020 7566 0045
Email: admin@ icomos-uk.org
Website: icomos-uk.org

International Centre for the Study of the Preservation and Conservation of Cultural Property (CCROM)
Via di San Michele 13
00153 Rome, Italy
Tel.: (+39) 06 585 531
Fax: (+39) 06 585 53349
Email: iccrom@iccrom.org
Website: www.iccrom.org

Wildlife organisations

The Ancient Tree Forum
c/o The Woodland Trust
Autumn Park, Dysart Road
Grantham NG31 6LL
Website: www.woodland-trust.org.uk/ancient-tree-forum/

The Bat Conservation Trust
15 Cloisters House
8 Battersea Park Road
London SW8 4BG
Tel.: 020 7627 2629
Website: www.bats.org.uk

The British Lichen Society
c/o Department of Botany
Natural History Museum
Cromwell Road
London SW7 5BD
Email: bls@nhm.ac.uk
Website: www.argonet.co.uk/users/
jmgray

Butterfly Conservation
Manor Yard, East Lulworth
Wareham BU20 5QP
Tel.: 0870 774 4309
Fax: 0870 770 6150
Email: info@butterflyconservation.org

The Royal Society for the Protection of Birds (RSPB)
The Lodge
Sandy SG19 2DL
Tel.: 01767 680551
Website: www.rspb.org.uk

The Woodland Trust
Autumn Park, Dysart Road
Grantham NG31 6LL
Tel.: 01476 581111
Website: www.woodland-trust.org.uk

The Wildlife Trusts
The Kiln, Waterside, Mather Road
Newark NG24 1WT
Tel.: 0870 036 7711
Fax: 0870 036 0101
Email: info@wildlife-trusts.cix.co.uk
Website: www.wildlifetrusts.org

Professional and crafts organisations

Arboricultural Association
Ampfield House, Ampfield
Near Romsey SO51 9PA
Tel.: 01794 368717
Website: www.trees.org.uk

The Building Conservation Directory
Website: www.buildingconservation.com
The online information centre for the conservation and restoration of historic buildings, churches and garden landscapes

GreenSpace
Caversham Court, Church Road
Caversham RG4 7AD
Tel.: 0118 901 5200/5270
Email: institute@green-space.org.uk
Website: www.green-space.org.uk
A not-for-profit organisation set up to help those committed to the planning, design, management and use of public parks and open spaces

The Institute of Groundsmanship
28 Stratford Office Village
Walker Avenue, Wolverton Mill East
Milton Keynes MK12 5TW
Tel.: 01908 312511
Website: www.iog.org.uk

Institute of Horticulture
14–15 Belgrave Square
London SW1X 8PS
Tel. & fax: 020 7245 6943
Email: ioh@horticulture.org.uk
Website: www.horticulture.org.uk
The authoritative organisation representing all those professionally engaged in Horticulture in the UK and Ireland

Institute of Leisure and Amenity Managers (ILAM)
ILAM House, Lower Basildon
Reading RG8 9NE
Tel.: 01491 874800
Fax: 01491 874801
Email: info@ilam.co.uk
Website: www.ilam.co.uk
The professional body for leisure professionals

Institute of Parks and Green Space (IPGS)
Caversham Court, Church Road
Reading RG4 7AD
Tel.: 0118 946 9069
Email: institute@green-space.org.uk
Website: www.green-space.org.uk
The UK's only institute solely dedicated to parks and green spaces and related issues

Society for the Environment
The Old School House, Long Street
Atherstone CV9 1AH
Tel.: 0845 337 2951
Fax: 01827 717064
Email: enquiries@socenv.org.uk
Website: www.socenv.org.uk

Royal Institution of Chartered Surveyors
12 Great George Street
London SW1P 3AD
Tel.: 0207 222 7000
Fax: 0207 222 9430
Email: info@rics.org.uk
Website: www.rics.org/building_conservation/constitution
A global professional body that represents, regulates and promotes chartered surveyors and technical surveyors

Landscape Institute
33 Great Portland Street
London W1W 8QG
Tel.: 020 7299 4500
Website: www.l-i.org.uk
The Chartered Institute in the UK for landscape architects, incorporating designers, managers and scientists, concerned with enhancing and conserving the environment

Professional Gardeners Guild
Secretary, Osborne House
East Cowes, Isle of Wight PO32 6JY
Tel.: 01983 280431
Website: www.ppg.org.uk
A society for Head Gardeners, Garden Managers and others engaged in horticulture (such as Assistant Gardeners, Students, Botanists, consultants, etc.) employed in private gardens and establishments

Soil Association
South Plaza, Marlborough Street,
Bristol BS1 3NX
Tel.: 0117 314 5000
Fax: 0117 314 5001
Email: info@soilassociation.org
Website: www.soilassociation.org

Soil Association Scotland
18 Liberton Brae, Tower Mains,
Edinburgh EH16 6AE
Tel.: 0131 666 2474
Fax: 0131 666 1684
Email: contact@sascotland.org
Website: www.soilassociation.org

Sports Turf Research Institute (STRI) Head Office
St Ives Estate
Bingley BD16 1AU
Tel.: 01274 565131
Fax: 01274 561891
Website: www.stri.co.uk

CIWEM (Chartered Institution of Water and Environmental Management)
15 John Street
London WC1N 2EB
Tel.: 020 7831 3110
Fax: 020 7405 4967
Email: admin@ciwem.org
Website: www.ciwem.org

Grant aid & funding bodies

Aggregates Levy Sustainability Fund (ASLF)
Countryside Agency, Bridge House
Sion Place, Bristol BS8 4AS
Tel.: 0117 970 7924
Email: clare.stevens@countryside.gov.uk
Extracting benefits for landscapes and communities

Architectural Heritage Fund
Clareville House, 26–27 Oxenden St
London SW1Y 4EL
Tel.: 020 7925 0199
Email: ahf@ahfund.org.uk
Website: www.ahfund.org.uk
Helps to repair and regenerate historic buildings by helping voluntary and community groups, with grants, low-interest loans, and advice

The Big Lottery
1 Plough Place
London EC4A 1DE
Tel.: 0207 211 1800
Fax: 0207 211 1750
Text tel.: 0845 039 0204
Website: www.nof.org.uk
A Lottery Distributor created to award grants to education, health and environment projects, and communities throughout the UK

Cadw –Welsh Historic Monuments
Cathays Park
Cardiff CF10 3NQ
Tel.: 029 2050 0200
Fax: 029 2082 6375
Email: Cadw@Wales.gsi.gov.uk
Website: www.cadw.wales.gov.uk

Cyngor Cefn Gwlad Cymru – Countryside Council for Wales
Maes y Ffynnon, Ffordd Penrhos
Bangor LL57 2DN
Tel.: 01248 385 500
Fax 01248 355782
Email: enquiries@ccw.gov.uk
Website: www.ccw.gov.uk

Defra and England Rural Development Plan schemes
Website: www.defra.gov.uk/erdp

Land based schemes

Land-based schemes provide financial incentives for land managers (particularly farmers and foresters) to adopt environmentally beneficial land management practices:

Environmental Stewardship
Farm Woodland Premium Scheme
Hill Farm Allowance
Organic Farming Scheme
Woodland Grant Scheme

The new generation of agri-environment incentives from Defra are designed to contribute to sustainable development through:
- *Maintaining, restoring and recreating environmental resources and valuable landscapes and habitats*
- *Underpinning tourism and leisure and thereby contributing to rural quality of life and social well-being and the prosperity of the rural economy*
- *Boosting rural employment and preserving traditional skills*
- *Contributing to farm viability*
- *Restoring the public's perception of farmers and their contribution to local communities*

The five main objectives of the Environmental Stewardship scheme are:
- *Wildlife conservation*
- *Protection of the historic environment*
- *Maintenance and enhancement of landscape quality and character*
- *Promotion of public access and understanding*
- *Resource protection*

The two secondary objectives are:
- *Flood management*
- *Genetic conservation*

Project-based schemes

Project-based schemes are focused on individual developments and projects, and aim to promote imaginative and varied schemes within rural areas:
- *Energy Crops Scheme (Short-rotation Coppice Producer Groups) Processing and Marketing Grant*
- *Rural Enterprise Scheme*
- *Vocational Training Scheme*
Schemes are administered by the Defra regional offices. Grant scheme information, forms and regional office contacts are available on the web

English Heritage
Head Office
1 Waterhouse Square
138–142 Holborn
London EC1 2ST
Tel.: 020 7973 3000
www.english-heritage.org.uk >
conserving historic places >
a guide to grants

European Commission
Jean Monnet House, 8 Storey's Gate,
London SW1P 3AT
Tel.: 020 7973 1992
Fax: 020 7973 1900
Website: www.europe.org.uk/culture/funding/

Forestry Commission
(National Office for England)
Great Eastern House, Tenison Road
Cambridge CB1 2DU
Tel.: 01223 314546
Fax: 01223 460699
E-mail: fc.nat.off.eng@forestry.gsi.gov.uk
Website: www.forestry.gov.uk

Government Funding Information
Website: www.governmentfunding.org.uk

Heritage Lottery Fund
7 Holbein Place
London SW1W 8NR
Tel.: 020 7591 6000
Fax: 020 7591 6271
Website: www.hlf.org.uk
Email: enquire@hlf.org.uk
The Heritage Lottery Fund distributes money raised by the national Lottery to support all aspects of heritage in the UK, from historic buildings and museums to archives, nature conservation and oral history

Historic and Botanic Gardens Bursary Scheme (HBGBS)
Fiona Dennis, Scheme Coordinator
c/o The Pines, RHS Garden Wisley,
Woking GU23 6QB
Email: fiona.dennis@english-heritage.org.uk
Website: www.hbgbs.org.uk

Historic Scotland
Longmore House, Salisbury Place
Edinburgh EH9 1SH
Tel.: 0131 668 8600
Website: www.historic-scotland.gov.uk
For conservation publications and free leaflets, tel.: 0131 668 8638

Inland Revenue Capital Taxes Office – Capital Taxes Relief for Heritage Assets
Capital Taxes Office
Heritage Property Section
Ferrers House, PO Box 38
Castle Meadow Road
Nottingham NG2 1BB
Tel.: 0115 974 2490
www.inlandrevenue.gov.uk/cto/heritage.htm

Landfill Tax Credit Scheme (LTCS)
Website: www.ltcs.org.uk
Encourages and enables landfill operators (LOs) to support a wide range of environmental projects by giving them a 90 per cent tax credit against their contributions to Environmental Bodies (EBs). See website for directory of distributive environmental bodies

Natural England
Northminster House
Peterborough PE1 1UA
Tel.: 0845 600 3078
Fax: 01733 455103
E-mail: enquiries@naturalengland.org.uk
Website: www.naturalengland.org.uk

Scottish Natural Heritage (SNH)
12 Hope Terrace
Edinburgh EH9 2AS
Tel.: 0131 4474784
Fax: 0131 446 2277
Website: www.snh.org.uk

Northern Ireland Environment and Heritage Service (EHS)
Natural Heritage Grants Programme
Commonwealth House, 35 Castle St
Belfast BT1 1GU
Tel: 028 9054 6442
Fax: 028 9054 6660
E-mail: nhgrants@doeni.gov.uk

References

1.2 Historic perspective

Amherst, Alicia (1895) *A History of Gardening in England.* London: Bernard Quaritch

Bacon, Francis (1601) *On Gardens*

Blake, Stephen (1664) *Compleat gardeners practice.* London: Thomas Pierrepoint

Blomfield, Reginald (1891) *The Formal Garden in England.* London: T. Bensley & Son

Crowe, Sylvia (1958) *Garden Design.* London: Country Life

Gerard, John (1597) *The Herball or Generall Histoire of Plantes.* London: J. Norton

Hill, Thomas ('Didymus Mountain') (1586) *The Gardener's Labyrinth.* London: John Wolfe

Jekyll, Gertrude (1908) *Colour Schemes for the Flower Garden*

Knight, Richard Payne (1794) *An Analytical Enquiry into the Principles of Taste.* London

Langley, Batty (1726) *New Principles of Gardening.* London

Lawson, William (1618) *A New Orchard and Garden.* London: Bar. Alsop

Loudon, John Claudius (1826–43) *The Gardener's Magazine.* London

Price, Uvedale (1794) *Essays on the Picturesque.* London: J. Robson

Repton, Humphry (1806) *An Enquiry into the Changes of Taste in Landscape Gardening.* London

——— (1816) *Fragments on the Theory and Practice of Landscape Gardening.* London

Robinson, William (1870) *Wild Garden.* London: Murray

Stroud, Dorothy (1950) *Capability Brown.* London: Country Life

Tunnard, Christopher (1938) *Gardens in the Modern Landscape.* London: Architectural Press

1.3. The Conservation Management Plan (CMP) process

Australia ICOMOS Inc. (1999) *The Burra Charter – The Australia ICOMOS Charter for Places of Cultural Significance*

Bisgrove, Richard and Hadley, Paul (2002) *Gardening in the Global Greenhouse: The impacts of climate change on gardens in the UK.* Oxford: UKCIP (www.ukcip.org.uk)

Brereton, Christopher (1995) *The Repair of Historic Buildings: Advice on principles and methods.* London: English Heritage

CABE Space, London (www.cabespace.org.uk)

(2004) *A Guide to Producing Parks and Green Space Management Plans*

(2004) *Green Space Strategies: A good practice guide*

Cadw (2003) *Guide to Good Practice on Using the Register of Landscapes of Historic Interest in Wales in the Planning and Development Process.* Cardiff: Cadw

CAG Consultants and Land Use Consultants (2001) *Quality of Life Capital: Managing environmental, social and economic benefits.* A joint Countryside Agency, English Heritage, English Nature, Environment Agency publication (see *Application Guide: Managing change on individual sites*). Cheltenham: Countryside Agency

Clark, Kate (1999) *Conservation Plans in Action: Proceedings of the Oxford Conference.* London: English Heritage

——— (2001) *Informed Conservation: Understanding historic buildings and their landscapes for conservation.* London: English Heritage

Clarke, D. L. (ed.) (1988) *Bean's Trees and Shrubs Hardy in the British Isles.* London: John Murray

Countryside Agency, Cheltenham

(2002) *Landscape Character Assessment: Guidance for England and Scotland.* (www.naturalengland.org.uk/Living Landscapes/countryside_character)

(2004) *Conditional Exemption and Heritage Management Plans: An introduction for owners and their advisers*

(2004) *Preparing a Heritage Management Plan*

Countryside Commission, Cheltenham

(1991) *Environmental Assessment: The treatment of landscape and countryside recreation issues* (www.naturalengland.org.uk)

(1998) *Guidelines for Countryside Recreation Project Appraisal. Working Paper*

(1998) *Site Management Planning: A guide*

(1999) *Countryside Character* (www.naturalengland.org.uk/Living Landscapes/countryside_character) and Countryside Council for Wales (1997) *National Park Management Plans Guidance. CCP 525*

DCMS and DTLR (2001) *The Historic Environment: A force for our future.* London: DCMS (www.culture.gov.uk)

Defra and ODPM-funded multi-agency web-based interactive map on environmental schemes and designations (www.magic.gov.uk)

Dingwall, Christopher and Lambert, David (1997) *Historic Parks and Gardens in the Planning System: A handbook.* Reigate: The Landscape Design Trust

English Heritage, London

(1997) *After the Storms: The achievements of the English Heritage grant schemes for storm damage repair in historic parks and gardens*

(1998) *The Care of Historic Buildings and Ancient Monuments: Guidelines for government departments and agencies*

(1998) *The Register of Parks and Gardens. An introduction* (www.english-heritage.org.uk/parksandgardens)

(2001) *Enabling Development and the Conservation of Heritage Assets*

(2003) *Ripping up History: Archaeology under the plough*

(2005) *Caring for Heritage on Your Farm: The Entry Level Scheme and historic features*

English Heritage Contemporary Heritage Garden Scheme (www.english-heritage.org.uk/parksandgardens)

English Heritage, DCMS and ODPM (2003) *Managing Local Authority Heritage Assets: Some guiding principles for decision-makers.* London: English Heritage

English Nature (1998) *UK Biodiversity Group Tranche 2 Action Plans. Volume II: Tterrestrial and freshwater habitats* (includes lowland wood-pasture and parkland habitat action plan). Peterborough: English Nature (on behalf of the UK Biodiversity Group)

Fieldfare Trust (1997) *BT Countryside For All. Standards and Guidelines. A good practice guide to disabled people's access in the countryside.* Sheffield: Fieldfare Trust

Forestry Commission (1995) *Forestry Advice, Note 3: Woodlands in designed landscapes.* Edinburgh: Forestry Commission

Garden History Society research register (www.gardenhistorysociety.org)

Goulty, Sheena Mackellar (1993) *Heritage Gardens: Care, conservation and management.* London: Routledge

Hall, Jeanette (2000) *Veteran Trees: A guide to grants* (A Veteran Trees Initiative publication). Peterborough: English Nature

Harvey, John (1972) *Early Gardening Catalogues.* London: Phillimore

——— (1972) *Early Horticultural Catalogues: A checklist of trade catalogues issued by firms of nurserymen and seedsmen in Great Britain and Ireland down to the year 1850.* Bath: University of Bath Library

——— (1975) *Early Nurserymen.* London: Phillimore

——— (1984) 'Vegetables in the Middle Ages', *Garden History*, Vol. 12, pp. 89–99

——— (1986) 'The Georgian garden: nurseries and plants (evidence of the nursery catalogues)', *The Georgian Group Journal* [1986], pp. 45–54

——— (1988) 'Early nurseries at Exeter', *Garden History Society News* 24 (Autumn), pp. 17–19

——— (1990) *The Nursery Garden.* London: Museum of London

Heritage Lottery Fund, London

(1998) *Preparing Your Business Plan for a Capital Project*

(2002) Access *Plans: Helping your application*

(2002) *Audience Development Plans: Helping your application*

(2004) *Conservation Management Plans*

HMSO (2000) *Countryside and Rights of Way Act 2000*. London: The Stationery Office Limited (www.hmso.govuk/acts and www.defra.gov.uk/wildlife-countryside)

ICOMOS-UK (1999) *Guidelines on Archaeology in the Management of Gardens, Parks and Estates*. London: ICOMOS-UK

Jacques, David (1995) 'The treatment of historic parks and gardens', *Journal of Architectural Conservation* No. 2

JNCC UK Biodiversity Action Plan (www.ukbap.org.uk)

Kerr, James S. (1996) *The Conservation Plan: A guide to the preparation of Conservation Plans for places of European cultural significance* (4th edn.). Sydney: The National Trust of Australia (NSW)

Lambert, David, Goodchild, Peter and Roberts, Judith (1995) *Researching a Garden's History: A guide to documentary and published sources*. Reigate: Landscape Design Trust

MAFF (now Defra) (1998) *Code of Good Agricultural Practice of Air, Water, and Soil* (revised edn.). London: MAFF

ODPM (2002) *Planning Policy Guidance PPG 17: Planning for open space, sport and recreation*. London: ODPM (www.communities.gov.uk > planning)

Read, Helen J. (1999) *Veteran Trees – A guide to good management* (A Veteran Trees Initiative prepared by English Nature, English Heritage and the Countryside Agency). Peterborough: English Nature

Sales, John (2003) 'Landscape, History, Nature and Aesthetics', *Views*, Vol. 38, pp. 16–17. Cirencester: The National Trust

Spon (2004 and annual updates) *Landscape and External Works price book*. SMM7. London: Spon Ltd

Thomas, Graham Stuart (1985) *Recreating the Period Garden*. London

Woudstra, Jan and Fieldhouse, Ken (eds.) (2000) *The Regeneration of Public Parks*. Reigate: Landscape Design Trust

1.5 The legal framework

Cadw, Cardiff

(1998) *Register of Landscapes of Outstanding Historic Interest in Wales*

(2003) *Guide to Good Practice on Using the Register of Landscapes of Historic Interest in Wales in the Planning and Development Process*

Defra, London

(2004) *Code of Practice on How to Prevent the Spread of Ragwort*

[n.d.] *The Weeds Act 1959 – Guidance note on the methods that can be used to control harmful weeds*

DETR (2000) *Tree Preservation Orders: A guide to the law and good practice* (www.odpm.gov.uk > Urban Policy > Cleaner, safer, greener communities > Trees and hedges)

Dingwall, Christopher and Lambert, David (1997) *Historic Parks and Gardens in the Planning System: A handbook*. Reigate: The Landscape Design Trust

DoE, London: ODPM (www.odpm.gov.uk > planning)

(1994) *Planning Policy Guidance 15: Planning and the historic environment*.

(1994) *Planning Policy Guidance 16: Archaeology and planning*

DTLR (1995) *Outdoor advertisements and signs: a guide for advertisers*. London: ODPM

English Heritage, London

(1998) *The Register of Parks and Gardens. An introduction* (www.english-heritage.org.uk/parksandgardens)

(2001) *Enabling Development and the Conservation of Heritage Assets*

HMSO, London

(1949) *National Parks and Access to the Countryside Act 1949*

(1959) *The Weeds Act 1959*

(1981) *Wildlife and Countryside Act 1981*

(1987) *The Town and Country Planning (Use Classes) Order 1987 Statutory Instrument 1987 No. 764* (www.legislation.hmso.gov.uk/si)

(1990) *Environmental Protection Act 1990*

(1990) *Planning (Listed Buildings and Conservation Areas) Act 1990* (www.hmso.gov.uk/acts)

(1990) *Town and Country Planning Act 1990* (www.hmso.gov.uk/acts)

(1992) *The Town and Country Planning (Control of Advertisements) Regulations 1992. Statutory Instrument 1992 No. 666* (www.legislation.hmso.gov.uk/si)

(1995) *The Town and Country Planning (General Permitted Development) Order 1995. Statutory Instrument 1995 No. 418* (www.legislation.hmso.gov.uk/si)

(2000) *Countryside and Rights of Way Act 2000*

(2003) *Ragwort Control Act 2003*

Jupp, Belinda (1992) *Northern Ireland Heritage Gardens Inventory*. Belfast: Northern Ireland Environment and Heritage Service (www.ehsni.gov.uk/pubs/publications)

Mynors, Charles (1999) *Listed Buildings, Conservation Areas & Monuments*. London: Sweet & Maxwell

—— (2002) *The Law of Trees, Forests and Hedgerows*. London: Sweet & Maxwell

ODPM (2002) *Planning Policy Guidance PPG 17: Planning for open space, sport and recreation*. London: ODPM (www.odpm.gov.uk > planning)

Planning Inspectorate, *The Planning Portal* offers a wide range of services and guidance on the planning system, planning permissions and development plans (www.planningportal.gov.uk).

2.1 Maintenance and management in practice

Chandler, T. J. and Gregory, S. (1976), *The Climate of the British Isles*. London: Longman

Evelyn, John (1664) *Kalendarium Hortense*. London

MAFF (1976) *The Agricultural Climate of England and Wales. Technical Bulletin No. 35*. London: HMSO

British Standards Institute (1994) *BS 3882:1994 – Specification for Topsoil*. Bristol: British Standards Institute

Lindley, John (1855) *Theory and Practice of Horticulture*. London

Robinson, William (from 1879) *Gardening Illustrated*.

Watkins, John (1993) *The Glasshouse Garden*. London: Conran Octopus

2.2 Nature conservation

Bellamy, David (1984) *The Queen's Hidden Garden*. London: David & Charles

Boertmann, D. (1995) *The Genus Hygrocybe (Fungi of Northern Europe – 1)*. Danish Mycological Society

Gilbert, O. (2000) *Lichens: A Field Guide*. Richmond: Kingprint

Harding, P. and Rose (1986) *Pasture-woodlands in Lowland Britain: A Review of Their Importance for Wildlife Conservation. Swindon*: Natural Environment Research Council, Institute of Terrestrial Ecology

Owen, J. (1991) *The Ecology of a garden*. Cambridge: Cambridge University Press

Read, Helen J. (2000) *Veteran Trees: A guide to good management*. Peterborough: English Nature

Tolhurst, S. and Oates, M. (2001) *The Breed Profiles Handbook*. Peterborough: English Nature

2.3 Vegetation maintenance and management

Farrer, Reginald (1911) *My Rock Garden* (4th imp.). London: Edward Arnold

Lord, Tony (2004) *RHS Plant Finder (2004–2005) Bicentenary Edition*. London: Dorling Kindersley

Shigo, Alex L. (1986) *A New Tree Biology*. Durham, NH: Shigo and Trees Associates

Thomas, Graham Stuart (1989) *The Rock Garden and its Plants*. London: Dent

Bibliography

1.2 Historic perspective

Amherst, Alicia (1895) *A History of gardening in England*. London: Bernard Quaritch

Batey, Mavis (1996) *Jane Austen and the English Landscape*. London: Barn Elms

Bacon, Francis (1601) *Of Gardens*

Blomfield, Reginald and Thomas, F. Inigo (1892) *The Formal Garden in England*. London: Macmillan

Bradley-Hole, Kathryn (2004) *Lost Gardens of England*. London: Aurum

Brown, Jane (1986) *The English Garden in Our Time*. Woodbridge: Antique Collectors Club

Bushnell, Rebecca (2003) *Green Desire: Imagining early modern English gardens*. Ithaca: Cornell University Press

Chadwick, G. F. (1966) *The Park and the Town*. London: Architectural Press

Crowe, Sylvia (2007) *Garden Design*. Woodbridge: Antique Collectors Club

Currie, Christopher K. (1990) 'Fishponds as garden features c. 1550–1700', *Garden History* 18:1, pp. 22–46

Daniels, Stephen (2000) *Humphry Repton*. New Haven and London: Yale University Press

de Caus, Isaac (1640) *Wilton House*. London: Thomas Rowlett

Desmond, Ray (1988) *A Bibliography of British Gardens*. Winchester: St Paul's Bibliographies

Duthie, Ruth (1990) 'The planting plans of some seventeenth-century gardens', *Garden History* 18:2, pp. 77–102

Elliott, Brent (1986) *Victorian Gardens*. London: Batsford

—— (1995) *The Country House Garden*. London: Mitchell Beazley

—— (2000) 'Historical revivalism in the twentieth century', *Garden History* 28:1, pp. 17–31

Fleming, Lawrence and Gore, Alan (1979) *The English Garden*. Croom Helm

Garden History Society Research Register (www.gardenhistory society.org)

Gerard, John (1597) *Herball, Generall Historie of Plants*. London

Girouard, Mark (1978) *Life in the English Country House*. New Haven and London: Yale University Press

Harvey, John (1981) *Medieval Gardens*. London: Batsford

—— (1988) *The Availability of Hardy Plants of the Late Eighteenth Century*. Garden History Society

Henry John Elwes and Augustine, Henry (1906), *The Trees of Great Britain and Ireland*, 7 vols. Edinburgh

Hill, Thomas (1577) The *Gardeners Labyrinth*. London: H. Ballard

Hussey, Christopher (1967) *English Gardens and Landscape 1700–1750*. London: Country Life

Jacques, David (1983) *Georgian Gardens*. London: Batsford

—— and van der Horst, Arend (1988) *The Gardens of William and Mary*. London: Croom Helm

Lacey, Stephen (1996) *Gardens of the National Trust*. London: National Trust

Laird, Mark (1992) *The Formal Garden*. London: Thames and Hudson

—— (1999) *The Flowering of the Landscape Garden*. Philadelphia: University of Pennsylvania Press

Landsberg, Sylvia (1995) The Medieval Garden. London: British Museum Press

Langley, Batty (1726) *New Principles of Gardening*. London

Longstaffe-Gowan, Tod (2001) *The London Town Garden 1700–1840*. New Haven and London: Yale University Press

Loudon, John Claudius (1822) *An Encyclopedia of Gardening*. London: Longman, Hurst, Rees, Orme & Brown

—— (1987) *In Search of English Gardens: the travels of John Claudius Loudon and his wife Jane*, ed. Priscilla Boniface. Wheathampstead: Lennard

National Trust (2001) *Rooted in History: Studies in garden conservation*. London: National Trust

Jekyll, Gertrude (1908) *Colour in the Flower Garden*. London: Country Life

Jellicoe, Geoffrey (2007) *Geoffrey Jellicoe: Vol. I: Studies of a Landscape Designer over 80 Years*. Woodbridge: Antique Collectors Club

——, Jellicoe, Susan, Goode, Patrick and Lancaster, Michael (eds.) (1986) *The Oxford Companion to the Gardens*. Oxford: Oxford University Press

Phibbs, John (1991) 'Groves and belts', *Garden History*. 1991, pp. 175–86

Quest-Ritson, Charles (2003) *The English Garden: A social history*. Penguin

Strong, Roy (1979) *The Renaissance Garden in England*. London: Thames & Hudson

Thacker, Christopher (1979) *The History of Gardens*. London: Croom Helm

Thomas, Graham Stuart (1979) *Gardens of the National Trust*. London: Book Club Associates

—— (2003) *Recollections of Great Gardeners*. London: Frances Lincoln

Tunnard Christopher (1938) *Gardens in the modern landscape*. Architectural Press

Weaver, Lawrence (1913) *Houses and Gardens by E. Lutyens*. London: Country Life

Williamson, Tom (1995) *Polite Landscapes*. Stroud: Alan Sutton

Woudstra, Jan and Fieldhouse, Ken (2000) *The Regeneration of Public Parks*. Reigate: Landscape Design Trust

2.1 Maintenance and management in practice

Barry, R. G. and Chorley, R. J. (1992) *Atmosphere, Weather and Climate*. London: Routledge

Bisgrove, Richard and Hadley, Paul (2002) *Gardening in the Global Greenhouse: The impacts of climate change on gardening in the UK*. Oxford: UKCIP (www.ukcip.org.uk)

Cassar, May (2005) *Climate Change and the Historic Environment*. London: University College London (www.ucl.ac.uk/sustainableheritage/climatechange)

Kendle, Tony and Sherman, Bob (2004) *Amelioration of Underperforming Soils. Plant User Handbook*. Oxford: Blackwell

Lamb, H. H. (1982) *Climate, History and the Modern World*. London: Methuen

Manley, Gordon (1952) *Climate and the British Scene*. London: Collins

Spoor, Gordon (2004) *Soil Drainage. Plant User Handbook*. Oxford: Blackwell

Stirling, Robin (1997) *The Weather of Britain*. London: Giles de la Mare

Wright, T. W. J., (1982) *Large Gardens and Parks: maintenance, management and design*. London: Granada

2.2 Nature conservation

Ash, H. J., Bennett, R. and Scott, R. (1992) *Flowers in the Grass: Creating and managing grasslands with wild flowers*. Peterborough: English Nature

Chinery, M. (1977) *The Natural History of the Garden*. London: Collins

Emery, M. (1986) *Promoting Nature in Towns and Cities*. London: Croom Helm

Fry, R. (1991) *Habitat conservation for insects – A neglected green issue*. Feltham: Amateur Entomologists' Society

Gibbons, B. and Gibbons, L. (1988) *Creating a Wildlife Garden*. London. Hamlyn

Gilbert, O. (1992) *Rooted in Stone – The natural flora of urban walls*. Peterborough: English Nature

Gilbert, O. L. and Anderson, P. (1998) *Habitat Creation and Repair*. Oxford: Oxford University Press

Harding, P. T. and Wall, T. (eds.) (1999) *Moccas: An English deer park*. Peterborough: English Nature

Jones, R. and Munn, P. (1998) *Habitat Management for Wild bees and Wasps*. Cardiff: International Bee Research Association

Joy, J. (1998) *Bracken for Butterflies*. Butterfly Conservation

Kirby, P. (1992) *Habitat Management for Invertebrates*. Sandy: Royal Society for the Protection of Birds

Page, R. (1984) *The Wildlife of the Royal Estates*. London: Hodder and Stoughton

Sutherland, W. J. and Hill, D. A. (eds.) (1995) *Managing Habitats for Conservation*. Cambridge: Cambridge University Press

English Nature (2003) *Gardening with Wildlife in Mind* (CD-ROM). Lewes: The Plant Press

2.3 Vegetation maintenance and management

Woody plants

Bradshaw, A., Hunt, B. and Walmsley, T. (1995) *Trees in the Urban Landscape: Principles and practice*. London: Spon

Brown, G. E. and Kirkham, J. (2004) *Pruning of Trees, Shrubs and Conifers* (2nd edn.). Portland and Cambridge: Timber Press

Clarke, D. L. (ed.) (1988) *Bean's Trees and Shrubs Hardy in the British Isles*. London: John Murray

Dallimore, W. and Jackson, A. Bruce (1923) *A Handbook of Coniferae*. London: Edward Arnold

Den Ouden, P. and Boom, B. K. (1965) *Manual of Cultivated Conifers*. The Hague: Martinus Nijhof

Elwes, Henry John and Henry, Augustine (1906) *The Trees of Great Britain and Ireland* (7 vols.). Edinburgh

Fieldhouse, Ken and Hitchmough, James (eds.) (2003) *Plant User Handbook: A guide to effective specifying*. Oxford: Blackwell

Hillier, J. and Coombes, Allen (2002) *The Hillier Manual of Trees and Shrubs* (7th edn.). Newton Abbot: David and Charles

Johnson, Owen (2003) *Champion Trees of Britain and Ireland*. Stowmarket: Whittet Books

Jones, Nerys (2004) *Creating Urban Woodlands. Plant User Handbook*. Oxford: Blackwell

Krussman, G. and Epp, M. E. (trans.) (1986) *Manual of Cultivated Broad-leaved Trees and Shrubs* (3 vols.). London: Batsford

More, D. and White, J. (2003) *Cassell's Trees of Britain and Northern Europe*. London: Cassell

Patch, Derek (ed.) (1987) *Advances in Practical Arboriculture: Forestry Commission Bulletin 65*. London: HMSO

Peace, T. R. (1962) *Pathology of Trees and Shrubs*. Oxford: Oxford University Press

Rackham, Oliver (1976) *Trees and Woodland in the British Countryside*. London: J. M. Dent

—— (1994) *The Illustrated History of the Countryside*. London: Phoenix Illustrated

Read, Helen J. (1991, 1996) *Pollard and Veteran Tree Management* (2 vols.). London: Corporation of London

Thomas, Graham Stuart (1983) *Trees in the Landscape*. London: Cape

Tree Register (founded 1988) – www.tree-register.org

Wilkinson, Gerald (1981) *A History of Britain's Trees*. London: Hutchinson

Shrubs, wall plants and roses

Austin, D. (1988) *Heritage of the Rose*. Antique Collectors Club

Beales, P. (1992) *Roses*. London: Harvill

Cairns, T. (2000) *Modern Roses XI. The World Encyclopaedia of Roses*. London: Academic Press

Dunnett, Nigel (2004) *Shrub Mosaic and Woodland Edge. Plant User Handbook*. Oxford: Blackwell

Evison, Raymond (2005) *The Gardener's Guide to Growing Clematis*. Newton Abbot: David & Charles

Gardiner, J. (2000) *Magnolias: A gardener's guide*. Portland: Timber Press

La Dell, Tom (2004) *Climbing Plants. Plant User Handbook*. Oxford: Blackwell

—— (2004) *Pruning Shrubs. Plant User Handbook*. Oxford: Blackwell

Lawson-Hall, T. and Rothera, Brian, R. (2005) *Hydrangeas: A gardener's guide*. Oregon: Timber Press

Leslie, A. C. (1980) *The Rhododendron Handbook*. London: Royal Horticultural Society

Newsholme, C. (1992) *Willows. The Genus Salix*. London: Batsford

Phillips, R. and Rix, Martin (1988) *Roses*. London: Pan

Phillips, R. and Rix, Martin (1989) *Shrubs*. London: Pan

Quest-Ritson, C. (2003) *Climbing Roses of the World*. Portland: Timber Press

—— and Quest-Ritson, B. (2003) *The RHS Encyclopaedia of Roses*. London: Dorling Kinderlsey

Thomas, Graham Stuart (1978) *Climbing Roses Old and New*. London. J. M. Dent

—— (1979) *The Old Shrub Roses*. London: J. M. Dent

—— (1991) *An English Rose Garden*. London: Michael Joseph in association with the National Trust

—— (1992) *Ornamental Shrubs, Climbers and Bamboos*. London: John Murray

—— (1995) *The Graham Stuart Thomas Rose Book*. London: John Murray

Toomey, M. and Leeds, E. (2001) *An Illustrated Encyclopaedia of Clematis*. Portland and Cambridge: Timber Press

Whittaker, P. (2005) *Hardy Bamboos*. Portland: Timber Press

Shelter, hedges and screens

Anti-social Behaviour Act 2003. Part 8: High Hedges (www.opsi.gov.uk/acts/acts2003/30038—i.htm)

RHS, *Practical Guides: Hedges* (2002) London: Dorling Kindersley

Wright, T., Henry, Terence and Bultitude, J. (eds.) (2004) *Hedges and Their Management. Plant User Handbook*. Oxford: Blackwell

Herbaceous perennials

Beckett, K. A .(1981) *Growing Hardy Perennials*. London: Croom Helm

Cooke, I. (1998) *The Plantfinder's Guide to Tender Perennials*. Newton Abbot: David & Charles

Darke, R. (1999) *The Colour Encyclopedia of Ornamental Grasses: Sedges, rushes, restios, cat-tails and selected bamboos*. London: Weidenfeld & Nicolson

—— (2004) *Timber Press Pocket Guide to Ornamental Grasses*. Portland, Oregon: Timber Press

Grounds, R. (1998) *The Plantfinder's Guide to Ornamental Grasses*. Newton Abbot: David & Charles

Hanson, R. and Stahl, F. (1993) *Perennials and Their Garden Habitats*. Cambridge: Cambridge University Press

Hitchmough, James (2004) *Herbaceous Perennials. Plant User Handbook*. Oxford: Blackwell

Hoshizaki, B. J. and Moran, R. (2001) *Fern Growers Manual*. Portland: Timber Press

Jelitto, L. and Schacht, W. (1990) *Hardy Herbaceous Perennials* (2 vols.). London: Batsford

Lloyd, Christopher (2004) *Meadows*. London: Cassell

Loudon, Jane (1843) *Ladies' Flower Garden of Ornamental Perennials* (2 vols.). London: William Smith

Phillips, R. and Rix, Martin (1993) *Perennials* (2 vols.). London: Pan

Schmid, W. S. (2004) *Timber Press Pocket Guide to Shade Perennials*. Portland: Timber Press

Thomas, Graham Stuart (1990) *Perennial Garden Plants or the Modern Florilegium*. London: J. M. Dent and RHS

Annuals and biennials

Armitage, Allan M. (2001) *Armitage's Manual of Annuals, Biennials and Half Hardy Perennials*. Portland and Cambridge: Timber Press

Dunnett, N. (2004) *Bedding Plants. Plant User Handbook*. Oxford: Blackwell

Miller, D. (1996) *Pelargoniums: A gardener's guide to the species, cultivars and hybrids*. London: B. T. Batsford

Phillips, R. and Rix, M. (2002) *Annuals and Biennials*. London: Pan

Turf and grassland

Adam, W. A. and Gibbs, R. J. (1994) *Natural Turf for Sport and Amenity: Science and practice*. Wallingford: CAB International

Boorman, Andy (2004) *Management of Amenity Grasslands. Plant User Handbook*. Oxford: Blackwell

Hacker, John (2004) *Amenity and Sports Turf Seed. Plant User Handbook*. Oxford: Blackwell

Hope, Frank (1978) *Turf Culture – A complete manual for the groundsman*. Poole: Blandford Press

Sports Turf Research Institute (STRI), Bingley, West Yorkshire (for research and publications www.stri.co.uk)

Water features

Jekyll, Gertrude (1900) *Wall and Water Gardening*. London: Country Life/ G. Newnes

Patrick, Kevin (2004) *Aquatic Planting. Plant User Handbook*. Oxford: Blackwell

Robinson, Peter (2003) *Water Gardening*. RHS. London: Dorling Kindersley

Slocum, P. (2005) *Water Lilies, and Lotuses: Species, cultivars, and hybrids*. Portland, Oregon: Timber Press

Stapeley Water Gardens (2000) *The Water Gardening Handbook*. Stapeley Water Gardens (www.stapeleywg.com)

Speichert, G. and Speichert, S. (2004) *Encyclopaedia of Water Garden Plants*. Portland and Cambridge: Timber Press

English Nature (2001/2003) *Wetlands Restoration Manual, Parts One and Two*. Peterborough: English Nature, Environment Agency, Defra, LIFE and NERC

Rock gardens

Clay, S. (1937) *The Present Day Rock Garden*. London and Edinburgh: T. C. and E. C. Jack

Farrer, Reginald (1928) *The English Rock Garden* (4th imp., 2 vols.). London and Edinburgh: T. C. and E. C. Jack

Griffith, A. N. (1964) *Collins Guide to Alpines*. London: Collins

Jermyn, J. (2005) *Alpine Plants of Europe*. Cambridge: Timber Press

Ferneries

See under Herbaceous perennials

Parterres, knot gardens, mazes and labyrinths, topiary

Crowder, Christopher (2006) *Topiary: Design and technique*. Ramsbury: Crowood

Harvey, John (1988) *Restoring Period Gardens*. Aylesbury: Shire

Joyce, David (1999) *Topiary and the Art of Training Plants*. London: Frances Lincoln

See also under 1.2 Historic Perspective

Walled kitchen gardens

Arbury, Jim and Pinhey, Sally (1997) *Pears*. Maidstone: Wells & Winter

Campbell, Susan (1996) *Charleston Kedding: A History of Kitchen Gardening*. London: Ebury Press

Campbell, Susan (2005) *History of Kitchen Gardening*. London: Frances Lincoln

Morgan, Joan and Richards, Alison (2002) *The New Book of Apples*. London: Ebury Press

Pavord, Anna (1996) *The New Kitchen Garden*. London: Dorling Kindersley

Petherick, Tom and Eclare, Melanie (2006) *The Kitchen Garden at Heligan*. London: Weidenfeld Nicolson

Pollock, Mike (2002) *RHS Fruit and Vegetable Gardening*. London: Penguin

Roach, F. A. (1985) *Cultivated Fruits of Britain: Their origin and history*. Oxford: Blackwell

Smit, Tim and Browse, Philip McMillan (2002) *The Heligan Vegetable Bible*. London: Cassell

Conservatories, greenhouses, glasshouses, etc.

Phillips, R. and Rix, M. (1997) *Conservatory and Indoor Plants* (2 vols.). London: Macmillan

Kohlmaier, Georg and Von Sartory, Barna; Harvey, John C. (trans.) (1991) *Houses of Glass: A nineteenth-century building type*. Cambridge, MA: MIT Press

Woods, May and Swartz, Arete Warren (1990) *Glass Houses: A history of greenhouses, orangeries and conservatories*. New York: Rizzoli

Nelson, Paul V. (2002) *Greenhouse Operation and Management*. London: Prentice Hall

Watkins, John (1998) *The Glasshouse Garden*. London: Conran Octopus

Container growing

Spielberg, Sue (2001) *Pots and Containers*. London: The National Trust

2.4 Technical maintenance
Weed control

Child, Lois, and Wade, Max (2000) *The Japanese Knotweed Manual*. Chichester: Packard Publishing

Day, J., Symes, N. and Robertson, P. (2003). *The scrub management handbook. Guidance on the management of scrub on nature conservation sites*. The Forum for the Application of Conservation Techniques (FACT) / English Nature, Wetherby (downloadable from www.naturalengland.org.uk)

Froud-Williams, Bob (2004) *Weed Control in Amenity Plantings. Plant User Handbook*. Oxford: Blackwell

NAAC/BAA (1998) *Code of Practice for the Use of Approved Pesticides in Amenity and Industrial Areas*. National Association of Agricultural Contractors/British Agrochemicals Association

Penrose, Lee, Taylor, Bob and Rotherham, Ian (2003) *Bracken and its Management*. Bingley: STRI

Pests and diseases

Allan, John (1999) *The Management of Problems Caused by Canada Geese – A guide to best practice*. London: DETR

Buczacki, Stefan and Harris, Keith (1981) *Pests, Diseases and Disorders of Garden Plants*. London: Collins (3rd edn., 2005)

Coles, Charles (1997) *Gardens and Deer – A Guide to Damage Limitation*. Shrewsbury: Swan Hill Press

Drakeford, Jackie (1986) *Rabbit Control*. Shrewsbury: Swan Hill Press

Forestry Commission publications, London: HMSO (www.tso.co.uk). Relevant titles include:

Innes, J. L. (1990) *Assessment of Tree Condition*

Greig, J. W. Gregory, S. C. and Strouts, R. G. (1991) *Honey Fungus. FC Bulletin 100*

Gregory, S. C. (1997) *Diseases and Disorders of Forest Trees. FC Field Book 16*

Grissell, Eric (2006) *Insects and Gardens: In pursuit of garden ecology*. Portland: Timber Press

Hogg, George (1986) *Practical Pest Control in the Countryside*. Woodbrige: Boydell

Laidler, Keith (1980) *Squirrels in Britain*. Newton Abbot: David & Charles

Peace, T. R. (1962) *Pathology of Trees and Shrubs*. Oxford: Clarendon Press

Prior, Richard (1994) *Trees and Deer*. Shrewsbury: Swan Hill Press

Roland, Fox (2000) *Armillaria Root Rot Biology and Control*. Andover: Intercept

Machinery

Bacon, J. et al. (2001) *Practical Solutions Handbook* (2nd edn.). London: English Nature (www.naturalengland.org.uk)

Index

Page numbers in *italic* refer to the illustration captions. Major entries are indicated in **bold** print and include illustrations within the page range. (T) after an entry indicates a Table in the Appendices.

A

access audits 60, 75
access roads 62, 205
acid soils 97
administration costs 41
advertisements
    planning consent 71
    see also marketing and promotion
aeration of turf 182, *183*, 238–9, *239*, 305
air pollution 92, *93*
Alexandra Park 20
algae 189, 192
alien species 80
alkaline soils 97, 140
Alnwick Castle Gardens 57
alpine plants 194, 196, 197, *197*, 220
altitude 88
amphibians 79–80, 104, 108, 191
analysis for CMPs 33, 35
ancient woodlands 135
animals 90, 104, 108, 110
    grazing 179, 261, 282
    pests 136, 150, 158, 229–30, 233
    protection 78–80, 250, 277
annuals and biennials **169–74**, 328–30(T)
apprentices 21, 47, 48–9, 280
aquatic plants 188, *190*, 191, *191*, 327(T)
arboreta 131–2, *132*, 256, 292
arboriculture 119, **122–7**
archaeological investigation *24*, *27*, 32, *34*, 192
    Hampton Court 273, *274*, 277
archaeological remains 73
    see also Stonehenge
archives 31, 36, 192
Areas of Outstanding Natural Beauty (AONB) 70, 83
Armillaria mellea (honey fungus) 231
Ascot Park *188*
audio-tours *67*
audio-visual presentations 66
Audley End 18, *24*, *36*, *65*, 205
Austin, David 146
avenues 14, *34*, 123, 134, *134*
    Hampton Court *134*, 272, 275, 277
azaleas *see* rhododendrons

B

back sheds 205
Backhouse nursery, York 19, 194, 196
Bacon, Francis 13
bacterial disease 231
badgers 79
bare root plants 117, *118*

baroque gardens
    Chatsworth 253
    see also Hampton Court, Privy Garden
barrows 245
Barry, Sir Charles 17
bats 79, 104, 106, 109, 110, 111
bedding plants 19, *169*, *171*, *173*, 220
    historic schemes 169, 170, *170*, 274
    Levens Hall 281
    roses 146
Bedgebury, National Pinetum 129, 131
Belsay Hall 64, *137*, *165*, *195*
Biddulph Grange 18
biennials *see* annuals and biennials
biodiversity conservation 81–2, 83, 103
biological control
    pests 101, 230, 232
    weeds 226, 228
birds 78–9, 104–5, 109, 110, 111, 230
    grasslands 106, 108
Birkenhead Park 20, 194
Birmingham Botanic Gardens 194
Blenheim Park 15, 30, *187*
Bloom, Alan 161
bog gardens 168, *168*
borders 19, 161, 164, *166–7*, 168
    Down House 261
    Great Dixter *167*, 267, *269*
    Hampton Court 273
    Squerryes Court 300
botanic gardens 13, 194
    Sheffield Botanical Gardens 285–9
Bowles, E.A. 19
box blight 201, 203, 231
box edging
    Hampton Court *87*, 273
    Squerryes Court 299, 300
bracken 110, 225, 226, 229, 238
branch removal 124, *124*, 130
Brereton, Christopher 25
Bridgeman, Charles 14
bridleways 82
Bristol Botanic Garden *193*
British Association of Landscape Industries (BALI) 54
Broadview Gardens, Hadlow College 57
Brodsworth Hall *19*, *25*, *195*, **248–51**
Brookes, John 22
Brown, Lancelot (Capability) 15, 17, 132, 149, 175, 187, 273
brown tourist signs 59
Buckingham Palace gardens 103
bulbs and corms 161, 162–3, *163*, *164*, 266
Burnham Beeches 126
burning weeds 226, 238
Burra Charter for Places of Cultural Significance 25, 27
business plans 35, 37
    opening to visitors 56, 61
butterflies and moths 108, *108*, 110
byways 82

C

cable bracing 126, *127*
calcicoles 97
calcifuges 97, 140
Cambridge University Botanic Garden 194
camellias 137, 141
canals 192
Cane, Percy 21, *23*
capital allowances 43
Capital Gains Tax 44
car parking 60, *61*, 62, *62*, *181*
carpet bedding 19, *173*
    see also bedding plants
cascades 192, 197
    Chatsworth *253*, 256
    Sheffield Park Garden *187*, *291*, 292
Castle Howard 14
catering facilities 63, *63*
caves 110
cavities in trees 124
cedars *128*, *129*, 130
cemeteries 21
chainsaws
    health and safety at work *241*
    root-cutting *241*
change of use 69, 70
charitable status 42
charitable trusts 42
Chatsworth *33*, 194, 209, 211, **252–7**
    water features 13, 14, 192, *253*, 254, 256
Chatto, Beth 162, *162*
Chelsea Physic Garden *64*, *93*
chemicals
    National Trust policy 294
    pest control 76, 113, 229, 232
    plant disorders 232
    weed control 113, 226, 228–9, *228*, 237
children's facilities 57
Chilham Castle *16*
chippers 240, 241–2, *241*
Chiswick 15, *221*
CITES 81–2
city microclimates 91–3, *93*
Claremont 14, 18
clay pots 218, 220
clay soils 95
climate **87–94**, 159, 232
climbers 143–5, *144*
clipping hedges 153, *155*, 282
cloches 210, *210*
Clumber Park *134*
clumps and roundels 132, *133*
CMP *see* Conservation Management Plans (CMP)
co-operative marketing 58
coach parties 62
Coade Stone 220, *221*
coastal conditions 159, 340–1(T)
Collyweston *34*

colour, herbaceous borders and bedding 19
Colvin, Brenda 21
Commonwealth Institute *22*
compaction 120, *120*, 179, 180, 185
    see also wear and tear
compost 101, *101*, 178, 227
    for containers 223
concrete 222
conifers 18, 116, **129–31**, *151*, 312–13(T)
    nurse trees 132, 150
    pineta 129, 131–2, 256
    planting 117, 118
    for rock gardens 196, *197*
conservation
    historic environment **25–8**
    natural environment 77–82, 83, 101, **103–113**
conservation areas 70, 73, 74
Conservation Management Plans (CMP) 11
    historic parks and gardens **25–8**, 71, 201
    landscapes **30–39**
    opening to visitors 56, 60, 61
    and tax exemption 44
conservation plans 30–35
conservatories *see* glasshouses
consultants 31, 48
container grown plants 117, *117*, *120*
containers 170, **218–23**, *243*
    Great Dixter 268
    Hampton Court Privy Garden 274
    sinks *195*
contract labour 53–4, 178
    Chatsworth 254
    costs 42
    Down House 260, 261
contracts 54–5
contravators 239
Control of Pesticides Regulations 1986 76
Control of Substances Hazardous to Health (COSHH) Regulations 2002 76–7, 232
Convention on International Trade in Endangered Species of Wild Flora and fauna (CITES) 81–2
coppice 135, *135*, 136
    shrubs 141, 142, *142*
COSHH Regulations 76–7, 232
costs *see* economics
cottage gardens 19–20, *20*
Countryside Commission 30
Countryside and Rights of Way (CROW) Act 2000 30, 74, **82–3**
Countryside Stewardship 30
Cragside 18, *194*
cricket pitches 292
crop rotation 100, 205–6

Crowe, Dame Sylvia 21, *22*
crown treatments *125*
Crystal Palace 211
Crystal Palace Park 20, *20*, *192*, 194
cultivation of the soil 96–7, 239
cutting weeds 113, 225–6

D
damage to plants 232
deadwood removal 125
deep bed system 97
deer 136, 150, 158, 229, 277
deer parks 13, 103, 105, 175
    Levens Hall 282
design implications
    for maintenance 37, *39*
    for visitor numbers 61, 62
designations affecting planning 71–4, 111
development control 69–71
digging 96
    spading machines 239
Disability Discrimination Acts 60, 75
Disability Equality Duty 60
disabled access 58, *58*, 60, *60*, 65
diseases *see* pests and diseases
disorders in plants 231–2, *231*, 344–54(T)
donations 44
Down House 49, 66, *107*, **259–63**
drainage
    grass areas 62, 179, 180, 181–2
    soils 95–6, 118
dredging 188, *188*
dwell time 63

E
earthworms 185, 230
East Lambrook Manor 161, *162*
economics **41–5**
    Down House 263
    heating a glasshouse 214
    sale of crops and plants 63–4
    Sheffield Botanical Gardens 288
    Squerryes Court 300
    walled kitchen gardens 205
    weed control 225
    woodland management 136
Edinburgh, Royal Botanic Gardens *166*
education *49*, 57, 63
eelworms 230
Elizabethan style gardens *12*, 253
Eltham Palace, volunteers 49
Elvaston Castle 17
Emmets Garden, Sevenoaks, Kent *30*
employees
    disability 75
    health and safety at work 75–7
English Heritage 18, 69, 73
    conservation principles 28
    Contemporary Heritage Garden
        Scheme 27, *29*, 66
    marketing and promotion 58

plant labelling 66
Register of Parks and Gardens of
    Special Historic Interest in England
    22, 30, 71–2
English landscape gardens 15, 17, 254
    imitations 18
English Nature 73
    Habitats regulations 80
environmental impact assessments 70
Environmental Stewardship 30
epicormic growth 126, *126*
ethnic groups 58
excavators 239
exotic planting *see* plant introductions

F
facilities for visitors 62–3
    children 57
falconry displays 78–9
Farrer, Reginald 19, 194, 195, *196*
felling licences 77, 136
ferneries 194, 198, *198*
    Brodsworth Hall 251, *251*
ferns 326(T)
fertilisers 97, 99
    applicators 237, 238
    for containers 223, *223*
    for grass 177, 178, 180, 184, 305
    for hedges 153
    for shrubs 140
    for trees 119
fertility 97
financial planning 35
Fish, Margery 161, *162*
fishponds 13
flail mowers *234*, 235, 236, 237
flatworms 230
flowering trees 123
flowers for cutting 204
foaming weeds 226
footpaths 82–3
    see also paths
Forester, Karl 162
Forestry Commission 77
    felling licences 77, 136
    National Arboreta 131
forestry management plans 30
formal gardens
    nineteenth century 17
    pools 189, *189*, *190*
    public parks 20
    seventeenth and eighteenth century
        14–15, 192
    see also parterres
fountains 192, *192*, 201
    Chatsworth 13, 254, 256
    frost protection 90
    Levens Hall 282
    Sheffield Botanical Gardens *286*
frames 205, 210, *210*, *218*, *221*
French style gardens 14, 17

Friar Park 17, 194
frost *88*, 89
    protection from 89–90, 218
frost pockets 89
fruit 204, **206–8**, *207*, *208*, *209*
    cultivars 331–33(T)
    frost protection 90
funding *see* grants
fungi 106, *107*, 109, 231, 260

G
garden buildings
    listed 72, 287
    wildlife habitats 104, 110
    see also back sheds; glasshouses
garden designers 48
garden history, study of 17–18
Garden History Society 31, 69
Garden House, Devon *181*
garden managers *see* head gardeners
garden ornaments *221*, *222*, *222*, 223
    see also sculpture
garden staff **45–50**, *46*, 57
    Brodsworth Hall 250
    Chatsworth 254
    costs 41, 42
    Down House 260
    Great Dixter 266
    Hampton Court 275, 276
    Levens Hall 280
    plant sales 63, 64
    Sheffield Botanical Gardens 288
    Sheffield Park 293
    Squerryes Court 300
    staffing levels 50–53
    use of pesticides 232
    see also health and safety
garden visitors 57–8, 59
Gardenesque style 285
General Permitted Development Orders
    (GPDO) 70
geophysical surveys *34*
geotextile membranes 100
Gerard, John 13
Gibberd, Sir Frederick 22
glasshouses 19, 63, 87, **210–217**, 220
    annuals 174, *174*
    Brodsworth Hall 251
    Chatsworth 211, 254, 256, *257*
    costs 41, 42, 53
    Down House 261, *262*
    fruit production 208, *209*
    Great Dixter 268
Glendurgan *203*
Good Gardens Guide 57
gradients, soil erosion 100
grants 37, 43, 44–5
    Down House 263
grass areas 105–8, 112–13, **175–85**
    Brodsworth Hall 250
    Chatsworth 254

Down House 260–61
Great Dixter 267
Levens Hall 280
reinforcement 62, 180, *180*, 181
Sheffield Park 294
Squerryes Court 300
Stonehenge 303, 305
grass species 175, *176*, 179–80, 303,
    326(T)
grass terraces 14
grazing 179, 261, 282
Great Dixter *164*, *170*, *173*, *221*, **264–9**
    borders *167*, 267, *269*
    ponds *105*, 268, *268*
    topiary *202*, 267–8
green manures 97
greenhouses *see* glasshouses
Gresgarth Hall *168*
grey squirrels 136, 158, 230
grottoes 193, *194*
growing days 88
growth cycles *115*
growth regulators 232
guidebooks 66

H
ha-has 15, *16*, 175, *175*
    Levens Hall 279, 282
habitats 136, *138*, 159
    protection 77–8, *79*, 80–81
    see also new perennial movement
Habitats Regulations 80–81
hail 91
Hamilton, Charles *14*
Hampton Court 14, 17, *218*, **270–77**
    avenues *134*, 272, 275, 277
    bedding 169, *170*, *171*
    box edging 273
    Privy Garden 37, *62*, 66, 169, *200*, 272,
        273–4, 276, *277*
    Rose Garden *176*
    topiary *155*, 273
    water features 192, 272
hand tools 244
Harlow New Town 22
harrowing 184–5, 305
Hascome Court, Surrey *23*
Hatfield House *27*, *199*
hazards 74, 76–7
    warnings 65, 74
    see also health and safety
head gardeners 21, 45, 46, 47, 48
health and safety 123, 130, 136, 233
    at work **75–7**, 136, 220, 232
        machinery 233, *241*, 245
    public 74, 178, 188, 192, 197
    signs 65, *65*
heating glasshouses 213–14, 256
hedge cutters 236–7, *237*
hedgerows, regulations 77

hedges 149, *149*, **153–8**, *154–7*, *158*, 342–43(T)
  Brodsworth Hall 251
  Chatsworth 254
  Down House 261
  Great Dixter 267–8
  high evergreen 75, 153, 158
  Levens Hall 282, *282*
  snow damage 91, *201*
  Squerryes Court 300
Heligan 211
Henry Doubleday Research Association (HDRA) 100
herbaceous perennials **161–4**, 168, 322–25(T)
  see also borders
herbicides 113, 226, 228–9, *228*, 237
Heritage Lottery Fund 211, 250
  Public Parks Initiative 30
  Sheffield Botanical Gardens 285, 288, 289
Hestercombe 18, *19*
Hidcote 17, 61, 149
high hedges 75, 153, 158
Highways Authorities 62
Hill, Thomas, *The Gardener's Labyrinth* *12*, 13
hiring machinery 238
The Historic Environment: A Force for our Future 30
historic layers 25
  see also archaeological investigation
historic varieties and cultivars 63, *170*, 205, 206, 308
hoeing *204*, 225, 232, 242
honey fungus 231
hot beds 205
Hutcheson, Francis 14–15
hygiene 232

I

income *see* economics
income tax 42–3
information for visitors 60, **64–7**
inheritance tax 44
injurious weeds 80
inorganic fertilisers 95, 97, 100
insects 230
  grasslands 106, 107
  lakes and ponds 104, 105
  pollination 208
  trees and scrub 109, 110
insurance, volunteers 50
Integrated Pest Management (IPM) 229
interactive computers 66
interpretation 64, 65–6, *65*
  Chatsworth *255*, 256
  Down House 263
invasive species 18, 80, 110, *110*, 113, 225, 226
Inverewe 160

invertebrates 230–31, 232
  see also insects
irrigation 242, *242–3*
  grass areas 185, 305
  herbaceous perennials 168
  trees 121, *121*
  walled gardens 205
island beds 161, *161*, 164, 285
Italian style gardens 17

J

James Pulham and Sons *see* Pulham and Co.
Jekyll, Gertrude 19, *19*, 161, 162
Jellicoe, Geoffrey 21, *23*
job descriptions 45, 48
Jones, Gavin 196

K

Kenilworth Castle *34*
Kensington, RHS Garden 17, *17*
Kent, William 15, *189*
Kenwood 49, *63*, 66
Kew, Royal Botanic Gardens 17, 194, 211
kitchen gardens
  Great Dixter 268, *268*
  see also fruit; glasshouses; vegetables; walled kitchen gardens
Knight, Richard Payne 17
Knightshayes Court *201*
knot gardens 13, *199*, 201, *202*, 203

L

labour *see* contract labour; garden staff; volunteers
laburnum tunnels *143*
lakes 187–8, *187*
  Sheffield Park 292, 294, *295*
  wildlife 104–5, 113
landscape architects 21–2, 48
Langley, Batty 14
latitude 88
lavatory facilities 62–3
lawn mowers 21, *175*
lawns 101, 176
  wildlife 106, 107
  see also grass areas
Lawson cypress 129, 131
laying hedges 153, *158*, 237
Le Nôtre, André 14, *16*, 192, 199
lead containers 220
leaf clearance 240, *240*
leaflets 58, *58*, 60, 65
leasing machinery 238
Levens Hall *16*, 37, 203, **279–83**
lichens 109, *303*
Lincoln Medieval Bishops' Palace *29*, 66
liquid feeds 223, *223*
listed buildings 72–3
  permitted development 70, 71
Lloyd, Christopher 162

loams 95
Local Development Frameworks 70–71, 73
Logan Botanic Garden *161*, *164*, *173*
London, George 253, 272
long grass 177–8
Loudon, Jane 19, 161
Loudon, John Claudius 17, 18, 19, 20, 161
Lutyens, Sir Edwin 265, *268*

M

machinery **233–45**
  costs 41, 42, 43
  Sheffield Botanical Gardens 288
  Sheffield Park 294
McKenzie, Alexander 20
maintenance
  contract labour 53–5
  costs 41–2
  design implications and priorities 37, *39*
  grass 175–85
  pools 190–92
  programmes 49, 50
  rock gardens 195, 197, *197*
  staffing levels 50–53
  trees 121
  for wildlife 112–13
  see also garden staff
management costs 41
Management of Health and Safety at Work Regulations 1992 76
management plans 30
  within the CMP process 30, 35, 37
Marine Park, South Shields 20
maritime conditions 159, 340–41(T)
marketing and promotion 58–9, 60–61
  Great Dixter 266–7
Marnock, Robert 285
mazes 13, 14, 203, *203*
  Chatsworth 254, *255*
meadows 108, *108*
media management 58–9
mice 158, 230
microclimate 87, 91–3, 205
millipedes 231
mixed borders 164, *167*
Modern Apprenticeships 47, 280
Modernism 21–2, *22–3*
mole drainage 182
moles 185, 230
Mollet, Claude 199
mounts 13
mowers 233, *234*, 235–6, *235*
mowing 178–9
mulches 100, 226, *226*, 227, 242
  Levens Hall 281
  Sheffield Park 294
municipal parks 20
mycorrhiza 95, 148

N

National Gardens Scheme Yellow Book 57
National Listing 81
National Nature Reserves 103
National Parks 70
National Trust 18, 58, 59, 61, 65
  Sheffield Park 292–3
native species 101
Natura 2000 80, 81
Natural England 77, 78
  licences 79
neglected landscapes 11
negligence 74
  see also health and safety
Nesfield, William Andrews 17
new perennial movement 162–3, 168, *168*
Newby Hall 57
newspapers 58
newts 79, 104, 108, 111, 191
no digging system 97
non-native species 78, 80
Northern Ireland, designation of historic parks and gardens 72
Nuneham Courtenay 15
nurseries 15
  Great Dixter 268
  Sheffield Park 294
nutrients 97, 98, 119, 231
  see also fertilisers

O

occasional use of open land 70
Occupiers' Liability Acts (OLA) 74, 82
opening to visitors **56–67**, 205
  Hampton Court 272–3
  pests and diseases 232–3
  taxation 43, 44
  see also visitor management
orangeries 210–211, 220
organic fertilisers 97
organic matter 96–7, 100
  compost 101, *101*, 178, 227
organic methods 96–7, 100–101
organic produce 63, 205
orientation plans 65, *65*
ornamental gardens
  Brodsworth Hall 250, *250*
  Chatsworth 254
  Squerryes Court 300
ornamental grasses, rushes and sedges 326(T)
Osborne 17, *27*, 58, *65*, *160*
  bedding plants *173*
  formal pool *189*
overseeding 184, 239
Oxford University Botanic Garden 210

P

Packwood 17
Painshill Park *14*, 57, *57*, 66, *194*
parterres 14, *17*, *24*, 169, **199–201**, 203
  Chatsworth 254
  Levens Hall 279, 281
  Osborne *27*
  Squerryes Court 299, 300, *301*
  see also Hampton Court, Privy
    Garden
partnerships, Sheffield Botanical Gardens
  288–9
paths
  Brodsworth Hall 251
  Chatsworth 256
  Down House 263
  grass 177, *177*, 178, 179, *181*
  Great Dixter 268
  Sheffield Park 293
  Squerryes Court 300
  wood chips 242
Paxton, Sir Joseph 18, 20, 21, *192*
  Chatsworth 194, 211, 254, 256
peak times, visitor capacity 60–61, 62
pergolas 13
period planting
  research 36, 38, 137
  see also historic varieties and cultivars
periodicals 18, 21, *21*
Personal Protective Equipment at Work
  Regulations 1992 76
pesticides 76, 100, 113, 229, 232
pests and diseases **229–33**, 344–54(T)
  animals 136, 150, 158, 229–30, 233,
    277
  box blight 201, 203
  fruit 207, 208
  grass areas 185
  hedges 158
  organic methods 100–101
  regulations 81–2
  rose sickness 148
  vegetables 205
pH scale 97, 205
photographers 58
Picturesque movement 17
pineta 129, 131–2, 256
pit houses 205, 206, *212*, *218*
planning permission **69–74**, 79
Planning Policy Guidance (PPG) 30, 71,
  73
Planning Policy Statements (PPS) 71
Plant Breeders' Rights (PBR) 81
plant collections 13, 66, 131–2, 274
plant health regulations 81–2
plant introductions 13, 15, 18, 87, 137–8,
  169
  conifers 129, *129*
  protection for 87, 211
  see also arboreta

plant labelling 66, *66*, 67, 132
plant passports 81
plant sales 63–4, *64*, 232–3, 263
planting
  containers 223
  fruit trees and bushes 206–7
  hedges 158
  rock gardens 197
  trees 117–19, 150
  wall plants and climbers 143
plastics 222
pleaching *154*, 165
ploughs 239
poisonous plants 57, 80, *110*, 225
policies in the CMP 35
pollarding 125–6, *126*, *136*
pollination 208
ponds 13, 104–5, 113
  Great Dixter *105*, 268, *268*
pools 187, 189–92, *189*, *190*, *191*, *268*
Pope, Alexander 15
pots and vases 170, 218, 220, *220*, 221, 222
  frost protection 90, 218
potting sheds *244*
PPG 9 Nature Conservation 73
PPG 15 Planning and the Historic
  Environment 73
PPG 17 Open Space, Sport and
  Recreation 30
press releases 58
Price, Sir Uvedale 17
professional gardeners 21, 45–8
project teams 31
promotion *see* marketing and promotion
propping branches 126, *127*
protected species *see* wildlife, legal
  aspects
pruning
  fruit trees and bushes 207–8
  hedges 153
  roses 145, 146, 148, *148*
  shrubs 139–40, *139*, *140*, 354(T)
  to reduce disease 232
  trees 122–3, *122*
  wall plants and climbers 144–5
public consultation 31
public opening *see* opening to visitors
public rights of way 82–3
publicity *see* marketing and promotion
Pulham and Co. 18, *18*, *193*, 194–5, 196,
  292
pulling weeds 113, 226, 237–8
purchasing machinery 238

Q

qualifications, garden staff 47
quotations 54–5

R

rabbits 150, 158, 230, *230*
rainfall *88*, 90
raised beds *195*
raised walks 13
Ramsar sites 81
reconstituted stone 220, *221*
  see also Pulham and Co.
reconstruction 27, *27*, 28
reinforced grass areas 62, 180, *180*, 181
rejuvenation
  hedges 153, *156*, *157*
  plants in containers 223
  roses 146, 148
  shrubs 140–41
repair 25, *25*, 28
reptiles 79–80, 104, 108
Repton, Humphry *16*, 17, 18, 132, 149,
  175, 187, 292
research 31–3
  period planting 36
  water features 192
reservoirs 187, 188
Reservoirs Act 1975 188
resistant species 233
restoration 25, 27
  CMP process 25, 28
  glasshouses 213
  hedges 153
  parterres 201
  rock gardens 195–7, 198
  shrubberies 141–2
  unmanaged woodland 135–6
  water features 192, 197
  see also case studies
reviews, CMP 37
rhododendrons 18, 137, *137*, 141, 292,
  314–15(T)
  plant health regulations 81
right to roam 82
risk assessments 50, 62, 76, 232
roads and highways 74
  access roads 62, 205
Robinson, William 18, 161, 162
rock, exposed 110
rock gardens 18, **193–7**, *198*, 220
  Brodsworth Hall 251, *251*
  Chatsworth 194, 254, 256, *256*
  Squerryes Court 300
rock plants 196, 197, *197*
rolling 185, 238
root stocks for fruit trees 206, 207
root-balled plants 117
rose gardens 146, 148
  Brodsworth Hall 251, *251*
  Levens Hall 281
rose sickness 148
roses 139, 145, **146–8**
rotoburiers 239–40
rotovators 239, *240*
roundels 132, *133*

Rousham *189*
Royal Horticultural Society (RHS)
  Award of Garden Merit (AGM) 287
  garden at Kensington 17
rushes 326(T)

S

St Paul's Walden Bury 17
sand slitting 181–2, *183*
Sandling Park 138
sandy soils 95
scarification 182, *183*, 238
Scheduled Monuments (SM) 73
Scotland, designation of historic parks
  and gardens 72
scrub 110, 112
sculptures 222, *222*
  Brodsworth Hall *250*
seasonal work patterns 41
security 223, *223*
sedges 326(T)
Seed Certification 81
semi-mature tree planting 117
Serpentine, Hyde Park *94*, 188
shading glasshouses 216–17, *217*
Sheffield Botanical Gardens **285–9**
Sheffield Park Garden 37, 131, 195,
  290–95
  cascade *187*, *291*, 292
shelter planting **149–52**, 152, *152*,
  159–60, *160*
  see also hedges
Sherringham *16*
Shigo, Alex 124
shops 64
shrubberies 141–2, 250
  Squerryes Court 300
shrubs 117, **137–42**, 316–21(T), 354(T)
  for rock gardens 196, 197
  for wildlife 110, 112
signs 64–5, *65*, 71
silty soils 95
Sir Harold Hillier Gardens and
  Arboretum 131
Sissinghurst 17, 61, *61*, 144, 149, *165*
Sites of Special Scientific Interest (SSSI)
  103, 109, 111, 177
  legal framework 73, **77–8**, 81, 82, 83
skills
  garden staff 47
  volunteers 49
slugs and snails 230
Smith, Augustus 160
Smitt, Tim 59
snow 90–91
Soil Association 100, 205
soil erosion 97, 100
soils **94–7**, 100, 159, 231–2
  compaction 120, *120*, 179, 180, 185
  walled gardens 205

sources for research 31, 36
spading machines 239
Special Areas for Conservation (SAC) 81
Special Protection Areas (SPA) 81
specifications 55
spiders and mites 230–31
spiking 182, 238, 305
sports field maintenance programmes
    176, 180–81
    Stonehenge 303, 305
spraying 229, 237, *237*
sprinkler systems 242, *242*, *243*
Squerryes Court **297–301**
SSSIs *see* Sites of Special Scientific
    Interest (SSSI)
Standen *175*
statements of significance 33, 35
stone buriers/pickers 239–40
stone containers 220
Stonehenge **303–5**
stooling 141, 142, *142*
storage
    fruit and vegetables 206
    pesticides 232
    tractors 244
storm damage 1987 30, *30*, 273, *290*, 293,
    298–9
Stourhead *14*, *15*, 18
Stowe 14, 15, 18
strimmers 235–6, *236*
students 47, 48–9, 266
Studley Royal 14
stump chippers 240
stump grinders 240
stump treatment 127, 196, 240–41
sub-shrubs 117
suckering 148
summer branch drop 125
support
    herbaceous perennials 164, *166*
    wall plants and climbers 143–4
    for young trees 119, *119*, 121, *121*
surveys and maps 32–3, *34*, 192
Sutton Place *23*

T
tall hedges 75, 153, 158
taxes 42–4
television 58–9
temperature 88, 91–2, *93*
    glasshouses 213–17
tender plants *174*
thinning 135–6, 150
Thomas, Graham Stuart *141*, 146, 195–6,
    293
tile drains 182
Tintinhull *170*
tools 244
topdressing 182, 184, *184*
topiary 13, 17, *199*, *201*, 203

Brodsworth Hall 251
Chatsworth 254
Great Dixter *202*, 267–8
Hampton Court *155*, 273
Levens Hall *279*, 281, *281*
Squerryes Court 299, 300
trimming *155*, 203, 236
topsoil 96
    see also soils
tour guides 66
Tourist Information Centres 58
tourist market 56–7
trace elements 97, 98
tractors *234*, 235, **245**
Tradescant Trust *202*
trailers 245
trainees 47, 48–9
training
    climbing plants 143–5
    fruit trees 206, 207–8, *207*, *208*
    roses *147*, *148*
training courses 293
Transfer of Undertakings (Protection of
    Employment) Regulations (TUPE)
    1981 75–6
Trebah *11*, *115*
tree guards 119, *119*
Tree Preservation Orders (TPO) 73–4
tree surgery 119, 122
trees 36, 116, **117–27**, 309–11(T)
    ameliorating urban microclimates 93,
        93
    felling 77, 126–7, 277
    Hampton Court 273
    management as historic features 132,
        134
    near pools 190–91, *190*, *191*
    veteran 103, *104*, 109, *109*, 123, *123*
    for wildlife 108–9, 112
    see also avenues; conifers; windbreaks
trelliswork 13
trenching equipment 239
Tresco 160
tub grinders 242
Tunnard, Christopher 21
two-wheeled tractors 245

V
Value Added Tax (VAT) 42, 43–4
vegetables 204–5, 208–9, *209*, 334–39(T)
    crop rotation 205–6
    Down House 263
    Great Dixter 268
    Levens Hall 282
ventilation of glasshouses 215–16, *216*
Versailles 14, 192, *218*, 220
verti-draining 176, 180, 182, 238–9, *239*
veteran trees 103, *104*, 109, *109*, 123, *123*
Victorian planting 18–19, *19*
vine eyes *144*

viral disease 231, 232
visitor capacity 60–61
visitor centres *67*
visitor management, grass areas 177–8,
    179, 303, 305
visitors *see* opening to visitors
volunteers **49–50**, 57, 63, 66
    Brodsworth Hall 250
    Down House 260, 261
    Great Dixter 266
    Levens Hall 280
    Sheffield Botanical Gardens 288, 289
    Sheffield Park 293

W
Waddesdon Manor 18, *18*, *164*, *169*, *171*
Wakehurst Place 131
Wales, designation of historic parks and
    gardens 72
Walker, Mark Anthony *29*
wall plants 143–5
walled kitchen gardens 63, **204–5**
    Chatsworth 254
    Down House 261
    Squerryes Court 300
    see also fruit; glasshouses; vegetables
walls
    habitats 104, *104*, 110
    microclimates 92, 205
    planting 143–5
    see also walled kitchen gardens
Walmer Castle *155*, *177*, *201*
Wardour Castle *133*
Warley Place 194
waste disposal, vegetation 241–2
water birds 104–5, *111*
water features **187–92**, 197
    Chatsworth 13, 14, 192, *253*, 254, 256
    Great Dixter *105*, 268, *268*
    Hampton Court 192, 272
    Squerryes Court 300
    see also fountains
water supply 192, 205, 242
    Great Dixter 268
    Hampton Court 272
water table 95, 181
waterfalls *see* cascades
watering
    containers 223
    see also irrigation
Watts Chapel cemetery *129*
wear and tear 60, 61–2, *61*, 100, **179–80**
    Sheffield Park 293
    Stonehenge 303, 305
    see also compaction
weather 87, 88–90, *88*
websites 59
weed control 101, 110, *110*, 113, **225–9**,
    232
    Down House 263

grass areas 185, 305
invasive species 80, 110, *110*, 113, 225,
    226
machinery 237–8
rock gardens 196, 197, *197*
tree planting 121
vegetable gardens 209
Weeds Act 1959 80
Welsh Historic Gardens Trust, Gateway
    Project 57–8
Westonbirt Arboretum 131
wetlands, wildlife 104–5, 113
wheel chairs *see* disabled access
wild plants 80, 105, 110, 113
    grasslands 106–8
    walls 104
wildlife 83, **103–110**, 118, 191
    Down House 262
    Hampton Court 277
    legal aspects **77–82**, 83, 111
    management for 110–111, 112–13,
        150, 177, 179
Wildlife and Countryside Act 1981 77–8,
    79–80
Willmott, Ellen 194
Wilton House 13
winches 241
wind 88–9, 97, 148, *159*
windbreaks 150, *151*, 159, *160*
Winkworth Arboretum, Surrey *41*, *132*
Wise, Henry 253, 272
Wisley, RHS garden *90*, *165*, 195, 205
Witley Court 17, *181*
wood containers 220
wood preservatives 232
woodland **134–6**
    Brodsworth Hall 251
    Chatsworth 256
    Down House 262–3
    Squerryes Court 300
    thinning *121*
woodland gardens 18, *138*
    see also Sheffield Park
work experience 49, 50
work study 51, 53
Workman, John 134
worm casts 184

Y
yew 129, *129*, 130–31, *131*, 158
    hedges and topiary *155*, *156*, 273, 299,
        300